Mike Snell
Lars Powers

Microsoft® Visual Studio® 2012

UNLEASHED

D1377420

 | 800 East 96th Street, Indianapolis, Indiana 46240 USA

Microsoft® Visual Studio® 2012 Unleashed

ISBN-13: 978-0-672-33625-6
ISBN-10: 0-672-33625-1

Library of Congress Cataloging-in-Publication Data:

Snell, Mike.
  Microsoft Visual Studio 2012 unleashed / Mike Snell, Lars Powers. – 1 [edition].
     pages cm
  ISBN 978-0-672-33625-6
  1. Microsoft Visual studio. 2. Web site development. 3. Application software–
Development. I. Title.
  TK5105.8885.M57S655 2013
  006.7'882–dc23
                              2012041554

Printed in the United States of America
First Printing November 2012

Trademarks

Warning and Disclaimer

Bulk Sales

Sams Publishing offers excellent discounts on this book when ordered in quantity for bulk purchases or special sales. For more information, please contact

  U.S. Corporate and Government Sales
  1-800-382-3419
  corpsales@pearsontechgroup.com

For sales outside of the U.S., please contact

  International Sales
  international@pearsoned.com

Editor-in-Chief
Greg Wiegand

Acquisitions Editor
Neil Rowe

Development Editor
Mark Renfrow

Managing Editor
Kristy Hart

Project Editor
Anne Goebel

Copy Editor
Keith Cline

Indexer
Brad Herriman

Proofreader
Sarah Kearns

Technical Editor
J. Boyd Nolan

Editorial Assistant
Cindy Teeters

Cover Designer
Anne Jones

Compositor
Nonie Ratcliff

Contents at a Glance

Table of Contents

About the Authors

Mike Snell spends his work life helping teams build great software that exceeds the expectations of end users. Mike runs the Solutions division at CEI (www.ceiamerica.com). Mike and his team deliver architecture, consulting, and mentoring to clients looking for help with enterprise projects, commercial software, mobile applications, or cloud-based solutions. Mike is also a Microsoft Regional director.

Lars Powers is a Software Development Manager with 3M's Health Information Systems Division. Prior to joining 3M, Lars spent many years with Microsoft as a platform evangelist focused on emerging technologies.

Dedications

To my wife, Carrie Snell, who continues to inspire and support.

—Mike Snell

To Mom and Dad, who got me started on my addiction to programming by buying me a Commodore 64 all those years ago. It had no disk drive, so I was forced to re-type my programs every time I powered back up. And the keyboard had a wonky layout. But for a 12-year-old kid, it was pure platinum.

—Lars Powers

Acknowledgments

Mike Snell:

I would like to thank all the fine people involved with the making of this book. This includes the team at Pearson/Sams: Neil Rowe, J. Boyd Nolan, Keith Cline, Mark Renfrow, and Anne Goebel. Of course, I would also like to thank my co-author, Lars Powers, for collaborating with me on yet another work.

Lars Powers:

I would like to acknowledge all of the hard work put into this title by the stellar folks at Pearson and Sams Publishing. Neil Rowe has supported this series from the beginning, and has been a constant north star for us. J. Boyd Nolan kept us honest on the technical front, and Keith Cline, Mark Renfrow, and Anne Goebel shouldered the burden of getting this into your hands with a fit and finish that readers have come to both expect and respect. Thank you!

And lastly, Mike: Yet again, the hard work was fun, and now behind us. Looking forward to the next one!

We Want to Hear from You!

As the reader of this book, *you* are our most important critic and commentator. We value your opinion and want to know what we're doing right, what we could do better, what areas you'd like to see us publish in, and any other words of wisdom you're willing to pass our way.

We welcome your comments. You can email or write to let us know what you did or didn't like about this book—as well as what we can do to make our books better.

Please note that we cannot help you with technical problems related to the topic of this book.

When you write, please be sure to include this book's title and author as well as your name and email address. We will carefully review your comments and share them with the author and editors who worked on the book.

Email: consumer@samspublishing.com

Mail: Sams Publishing
         ATTN: Reader Feedback
         800 East 96th Street
         Indianapolis, IN 46240 USA

Reader Services

Visit our website and register this book at www.informit.com/title/9780672336256 for convenient access to any updates, downloads, or errata that might be available for this book.

Introduction

The release of Visual Studio 2005 and Visual Studio Team System marked a major revision to the .NET development experience. It brought us code snippets, custom project templates, refactoring, data binding wizards, smart tags, modeling tools, automated testing tools, and project and task management—to name just a few features.

Visual Studio 2010 built on these tools, providing additional core changes and additions to the Visual Studio integrated development environment (IDE), and furthering Microsoft's investment in full spectrum application life-cycle management.

And now, Visual Studio 2012 has made the next set of improvements—some radical, some evolutionary—to further the development experience, providing first-class support for Windows Phone development, Windows Store applications, and Windows Azure cloud applications. Visual Studio 2012 is sporting a radically different user interface which, at the very least, will represent a requirement for re-learning some of the old and new tools. A new version of the .NET Framework, version 4.5, makes its appearance alongside Visual Studio 2012, providing tweaks and additions to all the major foundational application programming interfaces (APIs), including Windows Presentation Foundation (WPF), Windows Communication Foundation (WCF), and Windows Workflow Foundation (WF). In addition, the languages themselves have many new improvements. All of these tools are meant to work in concert to increase your productivity and success rate. And this book is meant to help you unlock the many tools built into Visual Studio so that you can realize these gains.

Who Should Read This Book?

Developers who rely on Visual Studio to get work done will want to read this book. It provides great detail on the many features inside the latest version of the IDE. The book covers all of the following key topics:

- ▶ Understanding the basics of solutions, projects, editors, and designers

- ▶ Writing add-ins, and using wizards

- ▶ Using the new Managed Extensions Framework (MEF) to write compelling extensions to the Visual Studio editor

- ▶ Debugging with the IDE

- ▶ Refactoring code

- ▶ Sharing code with team members and other .NET developers all over the world

- ▶ Writing ASP.NET applications

- ▶ Writing Silverlight web applications

- ▶ Implementing Service Oriented Architecture (SOA)-based applications, and consuming services, using the Windows Communication Foundation (WCF)

- ▶ Coding with Windows forms and with Windows Presentation Foundation (WPF)

- ▶ Working with data and databases and leveraging LINQ and Entity Framework to build data-centric applications

- ▶ Creating Windows Azure applications that live in the cloud

- ▶ Creating and hosting workflow-based applications using Windows Workflow Foundation (WF)

This book is not a language book; it is a tools book. If you are trying to understand Visual Basic or C#, you will want a companion book that focuses on those subjects. If you can write C# or Visual Basic code, this book will radically help you to optimize your productivity with Visual Studio. Again, this book is not a primer on the .NET languages. However, we do cover the new language features (such as LINQ) in both C# and Visual Basic. We also try to provide simple examples that can be read by developers of both languages. By and large, however, this book has one primary focus: detailing and explaining the intricacies of the Visual Studio 2012 IDE to enable developers to be work faster and, ultimately, work smarter.

This book also represents a departure for us from earlier versions. We no longer attempt to cover the advanced Visual Studio SKUs that make up the Visual Studio Team Application Lifecycle Management ecosystem. This was a difficult decision to make, but ultimately one that frees us to go even deeper into the core Visual Studio 2012 Professional product used by the vast majority of .NET developers all over the world.

How Is This Book Organized?

You can read this book cover to cover, or you can pick the chapters that apply most to your current need. We sometimes reference content across chapters, but for the most part, each chapter can stand by itself. This organization allows you to jump around and read as time (and interest) permits. There are four parts to the book; each part is described next.

Part I: An Introduction to Visual Studio 2012

The chapters in this part provide an overview of what to expect from Visual Studio 2012. Readers who are familiar only with prior versions of Visual Studio will want to review these chapters. In addition, we cover the new language enhancement for the 2012, .NET 4.5 versions of VB and C#.

Part II: An In-Depth Look at the IDE

This part covers the core development experience relative to Visual Studio. It provides developers with a base understanding of the rich features of their primary tool. The chapters walk through the many menus and windows that define each tool. We cover the base concepts of projects and solutions, and we explore in detail the explorers, editors, and designers.

Part III: Writing and Working with Code

Part III builds on the topics discussed in Part II by digging into the powerful productivity features of Visual Studio 2012. These chapters investigate the developer productivity aids that are present in the IDE, and discuss how to best use Visual Studio for refactoring and debugging your code.

Part IV: Extending Visual Studio

For those developers interested in customizing, automating, or extending the Visual Studio IDE, these chapters are for you. We explain the automation model and then document how to use that API to automate the IDE through macros. We also cover how you can extend the IDE's capabilities by writing your own add-ins.

Part V: Creating Enterprise Applications

Part V focuses on how to work with the IDE tools to write your applications. Each chapter provides an in-depth overview of how to use Visual Studio to help you design and develop an application. We cover writing applications using ASP.NET, web services and WCF, Windows forms, WPF, WF, Windows Azure, Windows 8, and working with data and databases.

Conventions Used in This Book

The following typographic conventions are used in this book:

Code lines, commands, statements, variables, and text you see onscreen appears in a `monospace` typeface.

Placeholders in syntax descriptions appear in an italic monospace typeface. You replace the placeholder with the actual filename, parameter, or whatever element it represents.

Italics highlight technical terms when they're being defined.

A code-continuation icon is used before a line of code that is really a continuation of the preceding line. Sometimes a line of code is too long to fit as a single line on the page. If you see ➡ before a line of code, remember that it's part of the line immediately above it.

The book also contains Notes, Tips, and Cautions to help you spot important or useful information more quickly.

CHAPTER 1

A Quick Tour of Visual Studio 2012

Visual Studio 2012 and the .NET Framework 4.5 introduce many new features to an already full-feature toolset. This latest version is about increasing developer productivity while providing developers with choices and flexibility when building their solutions. If you've been developing for a long time, you've come to expect that a new release of the IDE comes with advanced programming models, more acronyms, a few fresh project types, and improved ways to view and organize code. The 2012 product is no exception. Some highlights for this release include the following:

▶ An improved code editor built on Windows Presentation Foundation (WPF)

▶ Windows 8 development support

▶ A brand-new Metro-style user interface

▶ Improved support for Microsoft Office programming including SharePoint development

▶ A better experience on multiple monitors

▶ Support for simplified, parallel programming against multicore devices

▶ Support for the latest revisions of ASP.NET MVC

▶ Support for building web applications using the latest versions of Silverlight

▶ One-click web deployments

▶ Building for the cloud with Windows Azure

▶ Major additions and improvements to Windows Workflow and Windows Communication Foundation

▶ Increased support for database development on SQL Server, including some advanced tooling for working with SQL Server 2012

▶ Expanded team development with the new architecture explorer, support for Unified Modeling Language (UML), and automated testing improvements built in to the Premium and Ultimate editions

This chapter covers the core makeup and capabilities of Visual Studio 2012. We first help you sort through the product choices available to .NET developers. We then provide a comparison of the .NET programming languages. The remaining sections of the chapter cover the many possibilities open to .NET programmers, including building web, Windows, cloud, data, and service applications. Our hope is to give you enough information in this chapter to get the full picture of what is available to you when you build solutions using Visual Studio.

NOTE

Part I, "An Introduction to Visual Studio 2012," is broken into three chapters. This chapter provides a snapshot of all things Visual Studio. Chapter 2, "The Visual Studio IDE," is an introduction to getting the tool installed, running it, and creating that first project. It also serves to familiarize you with the basics of the IDE. Chapter 3, "The .NET Languages," is a quick primer on coding constructs in VB and C#. It also covers general programming against the .NET Framework.

The Visual Studio Product Line

There are three primary editions of the tool: Professional, Premium, and Ultimate. This should make it easier to understand which tool you need for your development and price point. At a high level, these tools are differentiated as follows; each addition assumes an MSDN subscription, too:

▶ **Professional**—Includes the basic features of the IDE to build applications of all types on all .NET languages. Includes support for writing, debugging, and testing code.

▶ **Premium**—Builds on top of Professional to include many features targeted toward the enterprise developer for testing and verifying code. Also includes database development tools.

▶ **Ultimate**—Includes every tool in the Visual Studio product line as well as surrounding products. It builds on Premium to add additional debugging and testing support, architecture tools, lab management, and more.

NOTE

You can see a detailed product comparison at http://www.microsoft.com/visualstudio/en-us/products.

Of course, there are some peripheral versions and products that surround Visual Studio. These include the Express editions, Test Professional, and Microsoft Expression. You will learn more about all these products in the coming sections.

Express Editions

Microsoft offers the Visual Studio Express editions on a per-platform basis for web, desktop, Windows 8, and Windows Phone development (VB, C#, C++, Web, Windows Phone, and SQL Server 2008 R2). These editions are free, downloadable, low-barrier-to-entry versions targeted directly at the novice, hobbyist, student, or anyone else looking to write some code without breaking the bank. In conjunction with the Express editions, Microsoft has made a few development kits available for things such as Facebook and Windows Live. There are also tutorials, videos, support sites, and fun projects to review. To get started, check out http://www.microsoft.com/express/Resources/.

The Express editions can be seen as Microsoft's answer to all the "freeware" tools available to today's developers. After all, if you are a college student looking to put up a buddy's website, you are more likely to look for a low-cost solution. Of course, five years down the road when you're making decisions for your company, Microsoft wants to be sure you've had a chance to work with its products. The Expression editions fit this niche nicely.

In addition to the standard download locations, the Express Web Edition can also be installed with Microsoft's Web Platform Installer. Along with several Express flavors of the IDE, this installer is also capable of downloading a huge array of base web applications, tools, and templates for building anything from e-commerce sites to content management web apps to blogs (see Figure 1.1).

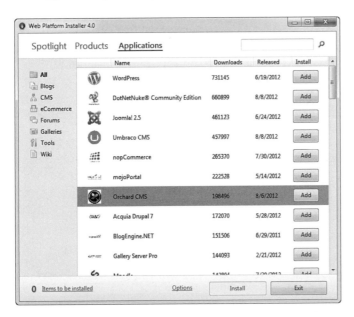

FIGURE 1.1   The Web Platform Installer plus Visual Studio 2012 Express Web Edition enables you to install many application templates to kick-start your projects.

The Express editions purposely do not have all the power of their professional patriarch (a class designer, test-driven development with unit testing, enterprise templates, EXtensible Stylesheet Language (XSLT) support, source code control, and so on). However, they do have full language support (such as LINQ) and access to the .NET Framework libraries such as Windows Presentation Foundation (WPF).

The Express editions also have a more streamlined user experience that does not expose the full complexity (or power) of the Professional editions. However, developers are to create client/server form-based applications, websites, data-driven solutions, and even web services using these tools.

> **NOTE**
>
> For more information about the Visual Studio Express editions or to download one of these editions, you can visit Microsoft's site at http://www.microsoft.com/express.

Professional Edition

Visual Studio Professional is the base entry for most developers who make a living writing code. Visual Studio Professional gives you all the language support (including VB, C#, F#, C++); the capability to write all types of applications, including console, Windows, Windows Services, class libraries, web, cloud, WPF, Silverlight, database, Office, SharePoint; and more.

Visual Studio Professional also gives you access to many additional tools that are key to building professional applications. The following features ship only with Visual Studio Professional (and higher):

- ▶ Unit testing and test-driven development
- ▶ Access to Team Foundation Server (TFS) for source control, continuous integration, and work item tracking
- ▶ Office development, including SharePoint
- ▶ Multicore, parallel development
- ▶ Class designer
- ▶ Server Explorer
- ▶ Refactoring
- ▶ Static code analysis
- ▶ And much more

> **NOTE**
>
> This book targets Visual Studio Professional only. A quick perusal of the book will allow you to see the depth and breadth of what you can do with this powerful tool.

Premium

Visual Studio 2012 Premium is targeted toward professional developers who build both corporate and commercial applications. It provides additional tools that help developers verify, test, and check their code against common issues. It also includes all the features inside Professional plus the following:

- ▶ Code metrics
- ▶ Advanced code profiling
- ▶ Test case management
- ▶ Performance profiling
- ▶ Coded user interface (UI) tests
- ▶ Lab management
- ▶ Database change management, unit testing, data generation, schema and data comparison

Ultimate

Visual Studio 2012 Ultimate is for developers who really need it all. It includes additional testing tools targeted toward both the technical and manual tester. It also provides architecture tools for creating UML models and exploring code visually. This version of the product is the everything-but-the-kitchen-sink option in a single package. The following list highlights the Ultimate features:

- ▶ Historical debugging with IntelliTrace
- ▶ UML modeling support for use case, class, sequence, component, and activity diagrams (including generating sequence diagrams from code)
- ▶ Architecture Explorer, for coming up to speed on a code base
- ▶ Layer diagrams
- ▶ Web, load, and stress testing
- ▶ Test Professional, including test case management, manual testing, and test record and playback
- ▶ Test lab management

MSDN

All editions of Visual Studio (higher than Express) now come with some form of a Microsoft Developer Network (MSDN) subscription. Depending on your edition, you get a little more of MSDN with each version up the product line. The following list provides an overview of your MSDN benefit by product:

▶ **2012 Professional**—Includes a license for TFS, a client access license for TFS; 50 hours per month of Azure hosting; development editions of Windows 7, Windows Server 2008 R2, and SQL Server 2008; access to earlier versions of Windows and SQL; two technical support incidents; priority forums; e-learning access; and MSDN magazine.

▶ **2012 Premium**—Includes everything in Professional with MSDN plus the following: 100 hours per month of Azure hosting; Expression Studio; Office 2010 Plus, Visio, and Project; development editions of Office, Dynamics, SharePoint, Windows embedded, and other Microsoft platform and server products; and four technical support incidents.

▶ **2012 Ultimate**—Includes all the preceding in Premium with the following extras: 250 hours per month of Azure hosting and access to Team Explorer Everywhere.

> **NOTE**
>
> Microsoft also sells a version of 2012 Professional with MSDN essentials. This is a limited MSDN version and does not include things like TFS access, SQL Server, Office, technical support, and MSDN magazine.

Related Tools

A number of additional tools outside Visual Studio surround the Windows development experience. This includes tools targeted toward the development team (Team Foundation Server and Team Explorer), those targeted toward designers (Microsoft Expression), and those targeted toward the tester (Test Professional). It's important to be aware of how these tools can help you build your next solution. This section provides a brief overview of each of these products.

Team Foundation Server

Application Lifecycle Management (ALM) is a broad term applied to the concept of continuous delivery of software through a set of integrated tools and processes. Microsoft refers to all of their collective ALM tools as Visual Studio ALM. Within Visual Studio ALM, Team Foundation Server (TFS) is the central hub that provides that integrated ALM experience around the various development tools and their associated disciplines (see Figure 1.2).

The first version of TFS was delivered with the release of 2005. This included source control, a centralized project management system, build automation, and reporting. By all accounts, these tools have been a great success. Microsoft has built upon this with the release of TFS 2012. In addition to the traditional TFS on-premises product, Microsoft has delivered a hosted version in the cloud called Team Foundation Services. This is a compelling offering for smaller development shops or for those without the necessary infrastructure or expertise to deploy, configure, and monitor their own TFS instances. With Team Foundation Services, Microsoft handles all the IT operations, allowing the ALM users to just focus on the job at hand.

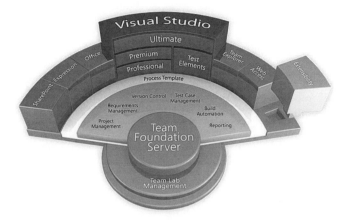

FIGURE 1.2   Team Foundation Server acts as the hub that provides ALM services to the many development products available from Microsoft.

As you can see from the figure, TFS is at the center of development and ALM coordination. The following list highlights the many services provided by TFS:

▶ **Process guidance/template**—TFS includes three process templates out of the box: Microsoft Solutions Framework (MSF) for CMMI 6.0, MSF for Agile 6.0, and Visual Studio Scrum 2.0. All provide a set of work items, workflows, and reports that are uniquely crafted with regard to their specific methodology. They also provide guidance to the team for executing key activities on the project (such as requirements management or build automation).

▶ **Project management**—TFS enables project managers to define their projects in terms of iterations and functional areas. It provides work items that are used to define, assign, and track work on the project. A work item can be a task on the project, a requirement, a bug, a test scenario, and so on. In general, a work item represents a generic unit of work on the project. Of course, work items are customizable and can have states, new fields, and business rules associated with them. Work items play a central part in ensuring project team communication and reporting. Project managers can use the Excel and Project add-ins to Office to manage the work items on a project.

▶ **Requirements management**—TFS provides specific work items for managing requirements. Work items are hierarchical. This means you can create work item children. For example, you might create a requirement work item and then define the tasks required to build that requirement. You might also define the test cases that will be used to verify the requirement. In this way, TFS enables rich reporting through the aggregation of the child work item data (such as tests passing for a requirement or work remaining at the requirement level).

▶ **Test case management**—TFS and Test Professional enable work items specific to test planning and test case management. You can define a set of test cases for a given requirement. Each test case can define the steps required to execute the test case along with the expected results.

▶ **Version control**—The source control features in TFS include enterprise-class features such as change sets, shelving, automatic build rules, the capability to associate work items to changed source, parallel development, a source control policy engine, branching, checkpoints, and more. There are powerful tools included for visualizing branch and changeset relationships.

▶ **Build automation**—The TFS build tools allow for automatic, scheduled, and on-demand builds. Builds are reported against, documented, automatically tested, and analyzed for code coverage and churn (as an example). The build engine is written using Windows Workflow (WF).

▶ **Reporting**—TFS provides a rich set of reports for tracking statistics and the overall health of your project. Reports include those built on SQL Reporting Services (that are accessible from the IDE, the Web, and SharePoint) as well as a new set of Excel reports for working directly with the data.

▶ **Collaboration and dashboards**—TFS includes a SharePoint site for each project. This site provides full access to manage and create work items outside Visual Studio and Office. In addition, it provides a set of dashboard reports for quick analysis of what is happening on the project as well as items specific to the logged-in user. Of course, the SharePoint sites also provide rich collaboration around documents and through a team wiki.

▶ **Web access**—TFS provides a web access version for working with work items over the web (outside SharePoint). This version also includes source control access through a web browser.

▶ **Integration with other IDEs**—TFS is accessible from Visual Studio, Office, SharePoint, and the Web. In addition, there is Team Explorer Everywhere for accessing the TFS features using other IDEs running on operating systems outside Windows. This includes the Eclipse IDE and the Mac OS.

Team Explorer

Some team members will not have a development tool such as Visual Studio, Test Professional, or Expression that provides access to TFS. In this case, they can get full access through Team Explorer. Team Explorer is targeted at project managers, business analysts, directors, and others on the team who need to access TFS but do not do direct development. This tool is purchased as a client access license (CAL). It includes a basic explorer, the Excel and Project add-ins, and full access to the SharePoint site, web access, and reporting.

Test Professional

Visual Studio Test Professional 2012 provides test planning, test case management, and manual testing for those people dedicated to the testing role. This is a separate tool that should seem comfortable and familiar to testers. Test plans are created based on application requirements (to provide traceability). Test cases are created and tracked as work items.

When testers run a test plan, they work through each test case and each step in the test case. They indicate the success or failure of the given test. For failures, they can log bugs (also work items). The bugs can automatically include things such as diagnostic trace information, event log data, network information, and even video recording of the steps the tester was executing when the bug was found.

Test Professional also enables testers to create action recordings of their steps. These recordings can be played back to execute the same steps again. This helps automate many portions of manual tests.

Finally, Test Professional includes lab management, which is a suite of tools for provisioning test environments from a template. These environments are virtual machines that are meant to be set up and torn down as needed for testing. You also can create checkpoint environments for various builds.

Visual Studio Agents 2012 and Load Test Virtual User Packs

Visual Studio Ultimate is used to create web, load, and stress tests; however, when executing these tests, it is limited to simulating up to 250 simultaneous users. Sometimes you need to generate much more load for your tests. In this case, you need to purchase Visual Studio Load Test Virtual User Pack 2012.

This tool is a separate product that works with Visual Studio Agents 2012 (included with Ultimate) to generate massive loads for various load-testing scenarios. You use the VS Agents software to set up a central test controller. You can then put agents on different machines. You add virtual user packs to each agent (depending on how many users you want to simulate per machine). Each user pack you purchase enables you to simulate an additional 1,000 users. The controller then kicks off the agents. The agents report their data back to the controller, where things are centralized and aggregated for reporting.

The Expression Tools

A sister product line to Visual Studio is Microsoft Expression tools. These tools are targeted toward designers who build applications on the Microsoft platform. Microsoft Expression tools offer rich design experiences for building web, Windows, and Silverlight applications.

The Expression tools are also built to enable workflow between designers and developers; that is, a designer can open a solution and work on the design without affecting the code a developer might be working on (and vice versa). These tools can also integrate into TFS for source control and work item tracking.

It is important that you are aware of these tools so that you know where you might use them, and also because they work with Visual Studio projects and project files by offering some similar capabilities (but in different ways). The following list provides a high-level overview of these tools:

▶ **Expression Web**—A design tool for creating ASP.NET web forms and websites that comply with Cascading Style Sheets (CSS) standards.

▶ **Expression Blend**—A tool for designing user interfaces based on Extensible Application Markup Language (XAML) and Silverlight. A version of Blend called Blend for Visual Studio is included with all the Visual Studio SKUs; it specifically targets design and development for Windows 8 (a topic we will tackle in Chapter 25, "Writing Windows Store Applications Using the Windows Runtime Library").

▶ **Expression Design**—A tool that enables a designer to create vector-based illustrations that include drawing, text, and more.

▶ **SketchFlow**—A tool for creating fast prototypes before moving forward with a solution.

▶ **Expression Encoder**—A tool for encoding video and audio and publishing it to Silverlight applications.

▶ **Expression Media**—A tool for organizing and managing design assets (files) into visual catalogs.

▶ **Expression Studio**—The full set of Expression tools for designers who need it all.

NOTE

For more information on the Expression products (which are not covered further in this book), see http://www.microsoft.com/expression/default.aspx.

Languages, Frameworks, and Application Templates

Programming in Visual Studio and the .NET Framework means you have a variety of languages from which to choose. .NET was built to be somewhat language agnostic. The common type system (CTS), the common language specification (CLS), the common language runtime (CLR), and the Framework all work to abstract language from .NET and provide developers with choice. Once deployed and compiled, applications written on .NET are very similar in runtime execution.

Programming Language Choices

What should be important to developers is selecting a language that enables you to be productive and has a high degree of support inside the IDE. Productivity is about developing with syntax that is familiar and logical to you. IDE support means the tools can generate code, help you write code, and provide features and artifacts that accelerate your coding. This is where many third-party (non-Microsoft-supported) languages often fall short. It takes a lot to provide IDE support to build the many application types Visual Studio enables.

The following list provides an overview of the Microsoft-supported languages for .NET development with Visual Studio:

▶ **Visual Basic**—The VB implementation in Visual Studio is about productivity. Developers can rapidly build type-safe, object-oriented applications. Although VB developers have full access to all code constructs in .NET, they tend to use VB because of the productivity features inside the IDE and they are already familiar with it from past experience with VB (or a similar language built on basic).

▶ **Visual C#**—Visual C# is a programming language designed for those who are familiar and comfortable programming in C-style languages (such as C, C++, and Java). C# is type-safe, object-oriented, and targeted for rapid application development. C# developers tend to spend more of their time inside the Visual Studio code editor and less time with the designers.

▶ **Visual C++**—With C++, developers can build .NET managed applications. However, they can also create Windows-based applications that do not rely on .NET. Most C++ developers have a C++ background and are therefore more comfortable inside the C++ world than they are with other languages. A C++ developer also has access to build against Active Template Library (ATL), the Microsoft Foundation Class (MFC) libraries, and the C Runtime Library (CRT).

▶ **Visual F#**—The F# language is said to be multiparadigm because it allows for functional, object-oriented, and imperative programming. It brings .NET developers a solution to many difficult programming problems. There are many features of F# including lightweight function types, functions as values, function composition and pipelining, recursive functions, and lambda expressions, to name a few. F# makes for simpler programming of math, scientific, engineering, and symbolic analysis (such as machine learning) problems.

▶ **JScript 8.0**—A scripting language for .NET. This language is Microsoft's implementation of the ECMA standard for compliance. You can use this language to write a variety of applications including Windows and web applications. On the Web, you can target both server-side as well as client-side processing. JScript 8.0 adds compilation and full object-oriented supports (typed variables, early and late binding, inheritance, overloading, and more) to JScript. It also now allows access to the .NET Framework.

> **NOTE**
>
> The basics of programming the languages of .NET are covered in Chapter 3.

> **NOTE**
>
> If you are familiar with one language but need to program in another (or translate), search for "Keywords Compared in Various Languages" on MSDN (http://msdn.microsoft.com).

The .NET Framework(s)

The .NET Framework represents the base classes, libraries, and useful functions that make programming in .NET so productive. The classes and functions found in the .NET Framework provide the majority of common features you need as a developer. Thanks to the CTS, each language can take advantage of this single Framework of functionality. Framework features include file I/O, web, workflow, collections, Windows, communication, and much, much more.

Of course, as the .NET languages evolve, so does the Framework. However, to maintain backward compatibility, each version of the Framework remains as a separate entity. There are now at least seven versions of the .NET Framework: 4.5, 4.0, 3.5, 3.0, 2.0, 1.1, 1.0. There are also various versions of the .NET Compact Framework (used for mobile devices). There is even a Micro Framework for very small, resource-constrained devices (http://www.microsoft.com/netmf).

Versions 3.0/3.5 of the .NET Framework brought WPF, WCF, and WF support along with modifications for Windows Vista. The latest version (4.5) ships with Visual Studio 2012 and provides language-level support for asynchronous programming patterns, revised WPF, WCF, and WF frameworks, and support for building Metro-style applications. Chapter 3 discusses many of these Framework elements in greater detail.

> **NOTE**
>
> See Chapter 2 for details on how you can target a specific version of the .NET Framework inside of Visual Studio 2012.

The Many Faces of a .NET Application

.NET has become the standard when building applications targeting the Microsoft Windows client or server products. It took only a few years, but it is now fair to say that .NET is everywhere; Windows programming and .NET programming are now synonymous. Many of the user applications we interact with have some if not all of their code base in .NET. This includes rich clients built on Windows, solutions built on Office (including parts of Office itself), smart clients that work across the Web, web applications that run in a browser and execute on a Windows server, and mobile applications that run on devices such as phones. The good news is that the .NET developer is in high demand, and you can leverage your skills to target a wide audience across an array of user experiences.

Figure 1.3 shows the New Project dialog in Visual Studio; it serves as an example of the myriad user solutions that are possible with .NET. This graphic cannot fit all of the possibilities available to you, but it does illustrate that Windows, web, Silverlight, Office, SharePoint, and many other project types are within the reach of .NET developers working with Visual Studio.

FIGURE 1.3   The many application faces made possible by Visual Studio 2012.

As discussed, you have many project templates available for your next solution. What is needed, however, is some sort of road map with respect to user experience. Choosing the right project template is an important part of making the delivery of your solution successful. The following list provides an overview of the core presentation technologies available to the .NET developer:

▶ **Windows Forms application (WinForm)**—Windows form applications are used to deliver business applications and tools built on the Windows platform. You typically select a WinForm application template when you need to build a solution that leverages the resources on the user's machine. This means the application is installed and users expect it to run more responsively than the typical web application. WinForm applications can be standalone or data-driven (often client-server). WinForm applications might connect to web services and work in both connected an unconnected scenarios. Note that WinForm applications are being deemphasized in the current versions of Visual Studio. If you're building a new application, you should consider WPF instead of WinForm.

▶ **WPF application**—Windows Presentation Foundation (WPF) combines features of WinForms with XAML and 3D capabilities to allow you to create the richest, most full-feature client solutions that run on Windows. WPF applications are delivered similar to a WinForm application. You choose WPF when you need to deliver a unique visual experience for your Windows application by taking advantage of vector-based scaling and 3D. In addition, WPF solutions can be browser-hosted in a security sandbox on Windows machines.

▶ **ASP.NET web application (WebForm)**—ASP.NET applications allow you to build solutions that run inside a user's browser but communicate with a web server for application processing. These solutions use HTML, CSS, and AJAX on the client but communicate across HTTP to a server for centralized processing of code and data storage and retrieval. Choose ASP.NET if you need to target a wide client base with low (or no) installation and wish to centralize updates to the application (as you need only update the server).

▶ **Silverlight application**—A Silverlight application is similar to WPF; you can develop highly interactive user experiences that combine video, animation, 3D, and vector-based scaling. However, Silverlight applications are delivered across the Web and run using a browser plug-in. Therefore, unlike WPF, they are not constrained to just Windows machines. They also work on a Mac.

▶ **Office**—Visual Studio enables you to build solutions based on the Office productivity tools, including Excel, Word, Project, Visio, Outlook, PowerPoint, and InfoPath. Choose an Office project when you want to write a business-productivity application centered on, and running within, one of the Office applications or documents (such as an Excel template or spreadsheet).

▶ **SharePoint**—SharePoint applications are for delivering functionality through the collaboration portal. You might write a Web Part to deliver information, work with a document type, or allow users to enter data. You might also define business process workflow centered on a document.

▶ **NetCF**—The .NET Compact Framework 3.5 runs on small devices (phone and PDAs), which enables you to build applications that target mobile devices and mobile users. The .NET CF and mobile software development kit (SDK) is available as a separate download to Visual Studio.

▶ **XNA**—XNA Game Studio 4.0 enables you to build games for Windows, Xbox, and Zune. This, too, is a separate download to Visual Studio.

Each of these UI delivery technologies is supported by Visual Studio. With them, you have many options for creating great user experiences on .NET. The sections that follow highlight a number of these technologies for building both Windows and web solutions.

NOTE

Visual Studio provides many UI platform options. Many are highlighted here; for in-depth coverage, see their specific chapters in this book: Chapter 16, "Creating ASP.NET Form-Based Applications," covers ASP.NET Web Forms and related technologies such as Silverlight; Chapter 17, "Building Websites with Razor and ASP.NET," discusses MVC-based web applications; Chapter 18, "Building Windows Forms Applications," is about standard Windows forms; Chapter 19, "Creating Richer, Smarter User Interfaces," focuses squarely on WPF; and Chapter 23, "Developing Office Business Applications," covers creating solutions based on Microsoft Office.

Developing Rich(er) Clients

Today's users demand a rich, interactive experience when they work with software. The line between what a web-based client can do versus one that runs on Windows has blurred thanks to many UI advancements, technologies, and tools, which can make it difficult to choose the right UI delivery for your next application. It also means that if you do decide to write a Windows-based client, you need to be sure you take full advantage of having the desktop resources at your disposal. Your application should perform well, look great, provide a high degree of interactivity, be able to work with larger data sets at any given time, and more. Here we look at the Windows-based client options for Visual Studio and creating smart, rich applications using WinForms, WPF, and Microsoft Office.

Windows (WinForms)

Visual Studio provides a mature, feature-rich set of tools for the rapid development of Windows applications that includes a drag-and-drop form designer and many controls inside the form toolbox. With these tools, developers can quickly lay out a Windows application that includes menus, toolbars, data access, tabs, resizing support, common controls for working with and printing files, and much more.

You create a Windows application by selecting the Windows Form Application project template in the New Project dialog. This type of application is also called a WinForm application because it is based on the WinForm technology in Visual Studio and the .NET Framework.

The first step in a WinForm application is determining the layout of your form. You might decide to create a document-centric application (such as Word or Excel), or a single utility application (such as Calculator or Disk Defragmenter), or some other type of application. Whatever your choice, layout is typically controlled through the docking of controls to the form (through the Properties dialog) and the use of Panel controls.

For example, Figure 1.4 shows a possible line-of-business application. A MenuStrip control is docked to the top of a WinForm, a StatusStrip docked to the bottom of the form, and a treeview and a tab control occupy the center.

Containing both the treeview and the tab control is a SplitContainer control, which allows two panels to size relative to one another using a splitter bar. Together, these controls define the layout of the main, interactive section of the form. In this case, a user can select records to view in the treeview control, and have a datagrid within the tab control automatically populate with the required information. Each control is added to the appropriate area of the form and then configured via the Properties window.

You can start to see that the initial layout and definition of a WinForm application is a rapid experience. You first need to decide your form layout. The tools make it easy from that point forward.

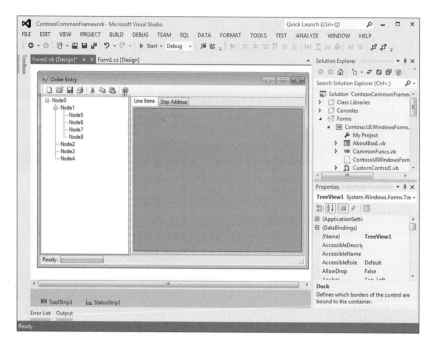

FIGURE 1.4   Building a WinForm application inside Visual Studio 2012.

As with all .NET programming, you first create the visual design and layout of your user interface, and then write code to respond to events. The WinForm application has a standard model that includes such events as Load, Closing, and Closed. You also respond to the events triggered by the controls on the form. For more detailed information about building WinForm applications, see Chapter 18.

Windows Presentation Foundation

Windows Presentation Foundation (WPF) is a set of classes, tools, and controls with which developers can create even richer, more dynamic client solutions for Windows. This includes developing user experiences that combine traditional data view and entry with video, 3D graphics, shading, and vector-based scaling. The results are truly unique, visually appealing, rich applications.

WPF uses markup code to define the UI. This should be very familiar to web developers. The markup is based on XAML. The XAML is created for you using the Visual Studio WPF designer (or a similar tool from Microsoft called Expression Blend). The XAML is then processed by the .NET CLR. The CLR process this XAML on the client, outside the browser. Therefore, it is not bound by the limits of HTML and the browser. Instead, it can create vector-based, hardware-accelerated user experiences.

Visual Studio provides a familiar experience for creating WPF solutions. You first define a WPF project and add WPF forms to the project. When creating your solution, you select a project type based on whether the application runs as a browser add-in or as an installed desktop client. Figure 1.5 shows the WPF project templates. Selecting WPF Application creates a basic WPF application that is pushed to or installed on a client. It might have access to local resources on the client.

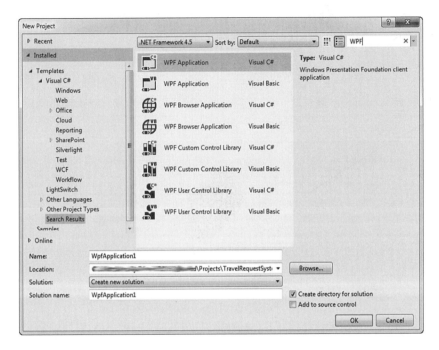

FIGURE 1.5   Creating a new WPF project.

The WPF Browser Application, in contrast, is meant to be deployed through a URL and run as a browser extension. The application, called an XBAP (XAML browser application), runs inside a sandbox. It does not have rights to the client machine and is cleaned up as part of the browser's cache. The application does not require a download provided that users have the right version of the .NET Framework on their machine. It can work with the browser's cookies and is supported by both IE and Firefox.

Making the wrong choice here is not too problematic. You can move the WPF forms between application types. Note that the other two application types highlighted in Figure 1.5 are WPF User Controls and WPF Custom Control Library. Both are for creating reusable controls for WPF applications.

The next step in building your WPF form is to simply open it and drag and drop UI controls onto a design surface. One big difference for developers used to building WinForm applications, however, is that you now have control over the form layout code (or XAML), which is more akin to designing a web form with Visual Studio. Figure 1.6 shows the XAML designer in action.

FIGURE 1.6   Designing a WPF form.

Notice that the XAML controls are listed in the Toolbox on the left. Although they are similar to Windows and web controls, they are their own set of controls just for WPF. Also, notice how the designer has a split view between the design surface and the XAML. These views stay in sync as you develop your code. Finally, the properties window shown on the right provides a familiar experience for WinForm developers when editing the many properties of a selected control. We cover the WPF Form Designer in greater detail in Chapter 19.

Office-Based Solutions

Developers have been able to customize Office for a long time now; some of us still remember writing Excel macros on Windows 3.1 or automating Word with Word Basic. Thankfully, these days the tools used to write Office solutions are built in to Visual Studio. With them, you can create Office-based projects and solutions that leverage Word, Excel, Project, Visio, PowerPoint, Outlook, and InfoPath. Figure 1.7 shows the New Project dialog for Office solutions. The templates shown in the figure are for C#, but the same exist for Visual Basic.

There are a few scenarios that might lead developers to create an application based on Office. The most common is when you need to extend a line-of-business (LOB) application to provide functionality inside the common, information-worker productivity tools of Office. This type of solution typically combines structured, corporate data with a business process workflow that's centered on a document (such as an invoice or a purchase request).

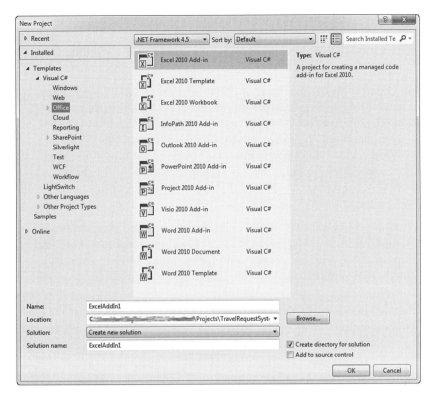

FIGURE 1.7   The many Office project templates inside Visual Studio.

For example, suppose you work with a financial, manufacturing, or payroll application. Each of these fills a specific need. However, users might need to work with the data that is housed inside the application and make key decisions that feed back into these systems. This work is often done through cut and paste and is not captured by the systems. Users lose productivity switching back and forth between the Office tools and the LOB application. This is precisely where you should consider creating an Office Business Application (OBA) to help bridge this gap.

Develop Documents, Templates, and Add-Ins

Notice the many templates in Figure 1.7. There are three separate templates for Excel, for example. Each of these templates provides a specific purpose. Office application templates allow you to create solutions built on a single document, a document template, or as an add-in to the given Office application. The following list provides a brief overview of these three project subtypes:

▶ **Document (Workbook in Excel)**—Document projects allow you to build a solution based on a specific document. There are typically not multiple instances of the document. As an example, suppose you have an Excel workbook that needs to read and write project resource billing information from and to an enterprise resource planning (ERP) system. This document might be updated weekly as part of a resource meeting. The data should be up-to-date and changes should feed the billing system. In this instance, you would create a solution based on this single document.

▶ **Template**—An Office Template project is one that is based on an Office template file (an Excel .xltx, for example). Creating a solution based on an Office template file gives you the flexibility to provide users with assistance when creating a new instance of a given template. You might push common document templates out to your users. When a user creates a new instance, the template might reach into data housed in other systems to help the user fill out the details of the document. You might then, in turn, capture the results in a database after routing the template through a basic SharePoint workflow.

▶ **Add-in**—An Add-in project allows you to extend the features and functionality of a given Office application. You create add-ins to offer additional productivity and solutions inside a given application. You might, for example, write an Outlook add-in that allows users to more easily file and categorize their email.

Whichever template you choose, Visual Studio provides a rich, design-time experience for building your Office solution. For example, Figure 1.8 shows the Visual Studio design experience building a solution for a Word 2010 template. In this example, a user is creating a quote for training. The fields in the document pull from a LOB database that includes customer information, resource data, and common pricing.

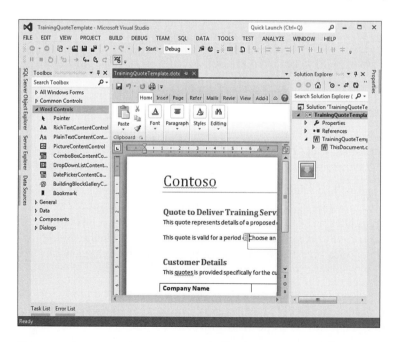

FIGURE 1.8   Designing a Word Template project in Visual Studio.

The Office templates in Visual Studio also provide design support for working with the Office ribbon. In this way, your application can behave like the rest of Office. You can embed productivity features and aids on your own tab of the Office ribbon. Figure 1.9 shows a simple example of a purchasing system surfacing purchase order actions onto the Word ribbon.

FIGURE 1.9   Creating a custom ribbon for a Microsoft Office solution.

Create SharePoint Solutions

Although not a true Windows client, SharePoint and Office have become nearly synonymous. Therefore, we thought it appropriate to discuss the SharePoint-specific capabilities of Visual Studio in this section. Companies leverage SharePoint for knowledge management, collaboration, and business process automation. Of course, this inevitably means customization and extension by developers.

Visual Studio presents a rich toolset for SharePoint developers. With it, you can create SharePoint workflows and build Web Parts based on ASP.NET. In addition, the debug experience has been streamlined. SharePoint development is now a first-class consideration inside the IDE. This should help developers more easily extend SharePoint to meet the business demand this collaboration product has generated.

There are many more advancements, however, including access to open XML formats, the capability to add features to existing Outlook forms, custom task panes in Word and Excel, data binding, and improved deployment and security.

Creating Web Clients

The vast majority of applications built these days involve some semblance of a web component (be it a full-blown browser-based, web application; a smart client that works across the Web; or a web service). In fact, the line between a traditional rich client and a web application is blurring, and technologies such as AJAX (Asynchronous JavaScript and XML), jQuery, Web Services, smart clients, XAML, and Silverlight have helped blur the line. You can now build rich user experiences as your needs dictate. Of course, Microsoft has remained suitably focused on expanding Visual Studio's capabilities with respect to web development.

Web developers want tools that help them through the common functions of building their application. Let's face it, the HTML, CSS, and XML standards can be a pain to follow by memory alone. Instead, we want tools that guide us. And, of course, as soon as we want to work with code, we want to be able to access the entire related source and massage it as necessary. Visual Studio provides an array of web development templates from which to choose. This section presents many of these possibilities.

> **NOTE**
>
> We cover many aspects that follow in greater detail in both Chapter 16 and Chapter 17.

Building Websites with ASP.NET

Visual Studio provides a rich set of tools and controls for the web developer. It supports standard controls for building server-side ASP.NET and emitting standard HTML. Controls include labels, text boxes, buttons, and related data-entry controls. In addition, there are controls for validation, working with data, doing personalization with Web Parts, and managing the user process with the login controls.

You create an ASP.NET site in Visual Studio by either creating a new website (File, New, Web Site) or by selecting the ASP.NET Web Application template in the New Project dialog. The website template should be used to create projects that mimic basic, file-centric websites. This typically means all files (your markup and code) deployed to the website and managed as files. Figure 1.10 shows an example of a new site created with this basic project template. This template should feel comfortable to most developers who are used to working on file-driven websites.

A Web Application template, in contrast, provides a project model similar to other .NET applications. You can generate dynamic link libraries (DLLs), set references, sign assemblies, manage build properties, and do similar tasks in a familiar manner as writing other .NET applications. Figure 1.11 shows an example. Your template choice ultimately depends on the manner in which you plan to build and manage your site.

FIGURE 1.10   The ASP.NET website project template.

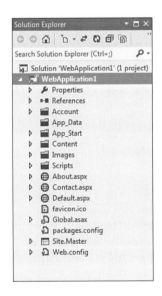

FIGURE 1.11   The ASP.NET Web Application project template.

Develop and Design at the Same Time

You develop ASP.NET pages by editing the design and connecting code to that design.
The design is referred to as markup. This is XHTML that defines the controls, their layout,
and their look on your page. Visual Studio includes both a markup editor and a visual,
WYSIWYG designer for laying out your page. Most web form developers switch between

the source (XHTML) and the design (WYSIWYG) view of a web form many times during development. The source view allows you full access to editing the XHTML of the page. Design view lets you see the page develop and gives access to the many shortcuts attached to controls in the designer. Visual Studio makes switching between these views simple. It provides a split view. With it, you can see both the XHTML and the visual designer. Figure 1.12 shows an example.

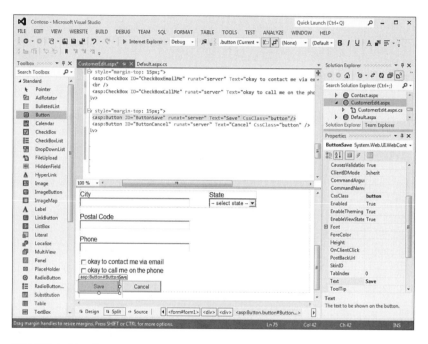

FIGURE 1.12   The Web Form Designer Split view.

Split view tries to keep both the source and the design in sync. This works when you drag items from the Toolbox to either the source or the design view panes. However, the design view can get out of sync when you are doing a lot of edits to your source. In these cases, the design view indicates that it is out of sync. Click on the designer and everything is back in sync.

Centrally Manage Navigation and Design

Visual Studio 2005 first introduced the capability to create master pages. These pages centralize the management of a site's design and navigation elements. In addition, master pages are supported by the designer, which allows for a richer design experience. A developer can see the page in the context of the site's central design while in design mode.

You create a master page by selecting the Master Page template from the Add New Item dialog. You then define your site navigation, header and footer information, styles, and anything else that should apply to each page in the site (or subarea of a site). After you define the navigation, you can create new web forms that provide specific content that should be enclosed inside a master page. Figure 1.13 shows an example of working with a web form whose outer header content is based on a master page.

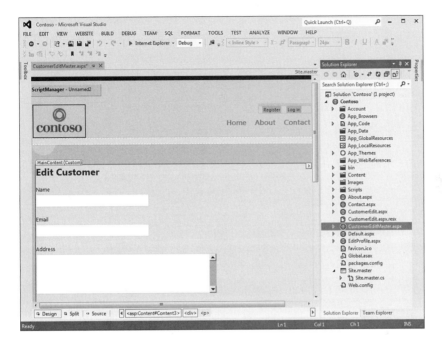

FIGURE 1.13   Creating pages that use a master page.

Building Loosely Coupled Web Applications with ASP.NET MVC

Visual Studio supports an alternative to building your application using standard web forms. This alternative is based on the Model-View-Controller (MVC) design pattern. The purpose of this pattern is to separate the application's logic and data (model), its user interface display (view), and the code that helps the user interact with the UI and the data (controller).

Sites built using MVC are typically easier to maintain as there is decreased dependency between the application layers. They also support test-driven development as you can write tests for each layer. In addition, you can use the MVC construct to separate the duties by developer where you might have designers creating views while other developers are working on models or controllers. Another advantage of MVC is that developers have more fine control over the processing as a web page.

The ASP.NET implementation of the MVC is both a set of namespaces (System.Web.Mvc) and project templates. You create a site in which you intend to use MVC by selecting the ASP.NET MVC Web Application project template in the New Project dialog. Note that you can mix sites that use both MVC and standard web forms. In addition, ASP.NET MVC supports most ASP.NET constructs such as master pages, sessions, caching, profiles and membership, configuration, and the like. However, it does not support ASP.NET view state. Figure 1.14 shows an example of the ASP.NET MVC site template inside Visual Studio. See Chapter 17 for a detailed discussion of ASP.NET MVC.

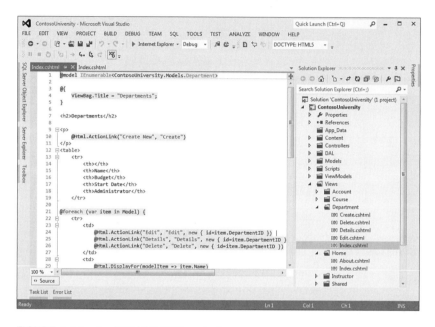

FIGURE 1.14   An ASP.NET MVC project.

Adding Richer Features with AJAX

AJAX represents the capability to leverage the ubiquitous support for JavaScript in web browsers to create a more interactive user experience. Client applications built to leverage AJAX still have a client-server paradigm. However, with AJAX the client can update portions of a given page without appearing to have posted back to the server (of course, it typically does). In addition, most AJAX-enabled applications put more processing on the client for things such as toggling sections of a page, working with tabs, autocompleting data entry, popping up dialogs, and more. The result is a step forward in interactivity for a user.

AJAX is not a Microsoft-specific technology. Instead, it is a programming model. However, Microsoft created a set of controls called the AJAX Extensions for Visual Studio. These controls allow developers to more easily create AJAX experiences. Figure 1.15 shows the controls inside the Visual Studio Toolbox.

FIGURE 1.15   The AJAX Extensions Controls in Visual Studio.

The AJAX Extension Controls enable you to create a page that can receive partial, asynchronous updates (using `UpdatePanel`) and show update progress (using `UpdateProgress`). They also allow you to create your own controls and features that implement AJAX without having to write the client-side JavaScript.

In addition to these controls, Visual Studio supports IntelliSense, code comment documentation, and client-side debugging for JavaScript. It also contains the Microsoft AJAX Library, which is a JavaScript common library that supports object-oriented development for JavaScript. Finally, many of the ASP.NET controls have AJAX features built in to give you control over partial postbacks versus full-page refresh.

Developing for Silverlight

Microsoft's Silverlight is another exciting client technology for the Web. Silverlight allows for an even richer user experience than AJAX. You use it to create media-rich (images, video, graphic scaling), highly interactive experiences. Silverlight requires a browser add-on (or plug-in). It works with Windows, Mac, and Linux in a variety of browsers. Silverlight is based on WPF; it enables you to leverage XAML skills inside a browser and across platforms.

You create a Silverlight application in Visual Studio by selecting the Silverlight Application project template in the New Project dialog. When doing so, you need to select a host for your application. This can be an ASP.NET web project or you can let Visual Studio generate a test page upon build. You can also set the target version of Silverlight on which you intend your application to be deployed. This is based on the versions of Silverlight you have installed. Figure 1.16 shows an example of configuring these two settings upon project creation.

FIGURE 1.16   Targeting a specific Silverlight version.

You create a Silverlight application like you might a WPF application. You have a designer for laying out a page. You can also edit the XAML directly. In addition, the Silverlight controls are available to you from the Toolbox. The real difference is the application host. This is typically an ASP.NET web project. You can see in Figure 1.17 that there is both a host project (generated by the Visual Studio template) and the Silverlight project.

Designers and Developers
When discussing Silverlight (or even WPF), it's important to note the work that went into the technology and tools to support a strong designer-developer workflow. It's understood that traditionally developers have been left to try to "design" the UI. It goes without saying that many developers have not exactly shined as UI designers.

However, even in scenarios where designers are employed on projects, the design often falls short or the implementation is an arduous process. Designers have their own tools that often do not talk with those of the developers. Instead, a design is often provided to the development team as a picture or some basic HTML. Developers are left to try to realize the intricacies of the design while having to concern themselves with coding the solution. This can cause the design to never be exactly what was envisioned and developers to spend too much time trying to get the look right.

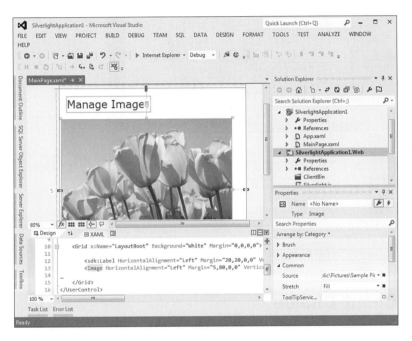

FIGURE 1.17   A Silverlight Page Inside Visual Studio.

Silverlight and WPF try to right this wrong by keeping the UI markup (XAML) totally separate from the implementation code (C# or VB). In addition, Microsoft has provided design tools that let designers create real user interfaces that can be leveraged by the development team. There are no more "lost in translation" issues. Instead, a designer can create or open a XAML-based UI element, edit it using the power of Expression Blend (they do not have to learn Visual Studio), and save it back to the solution or send it to a developer. The developer can then open the same item inside of Visual Studio and begin responding to key UI events with their code. This back-and-forth can continue as the UI builds up over time. Nobody's code gets stepped on; everyone focuses on his or her strength.

Figure 1.18 shows a sample of the Expression Blend 4.0 tool. Notice that the same XAML file that was in the Silverlight example is also open here. Designers can use a tool with which they are more familiar to lay out the UI and apply visual techniques such as 3D and animation. Also notice that the C# project file is being used to maintain continuity between the solutions. After the designers are finished, their save goes right back to the development team. They can even test their UI in the context of the application by building and running the project.

FIGURE 1.18   Designing a WPF form inside of Expression Blend.

Making the Client Choice

The many options for developing rich user experiences on Windows invariably leads to this question: What is the right UI technology for my next application? Of course, the answer depends on your specific scenario. When making your decision, keep the intent of each technology in mind. The following should help you make the right decision:

▶ Windows forms still has a place in creating installed business applications that connect with the operating system, leverage resources on the client, connect to databases, and more. They offer standard, workman-like user experiences for data entry, file manipulation, configuration, and related task-oriented solutions. Windows forms are easy to develop and do not typically involve much work from a design perspective. We suggest you continue with WinForms if you already have a significant investment in them. If you are building from scratch, however, take a good look at WPF because that is where Microsoft has focused its innovation.

▶ WPF is a Windows technology that requires the .NET Framework on the client. It can run in a browser sandbox or as a full-feature Windows application. You should leverage WPF when you need to create a rich user experience with high design aesthetics (3D, animations, vector-scaled graphics), want a low cost of installation and update, and require distributed connectivity.

▶ Silverlight runs inside a browser. Silverlight is a very lightweight, cross-platform version of WPF. It provides many of the rich features of WPF, but it allows you to run on different platforms (Windows, Mac, Linux) and different browsers. Of course, Silverlight does require a browser plug-in. The browser plug-in runs a mini version of the CLR on the client. In this way, you still can write your code in C# or VB and have access to bits of the .NET Framework. However, clients must have the plug-in to run your application. Think of Silverlight as an alternative to Adobe's Flash product.

▶ ASP.NET web applications are a great solution for creating functionality that runs ubiquitously. The only requirement is a web browser. Therefore, Web Form applications are still a great solution when you need to reach the widest possible audience and you do not want to deal with client installations. In addition, most modern browsers support JavaScript. Therefore, you can still get some interactive features using AJAX in your ASP.NET application.

▶ Microsoft Office solutions are applicable when users tend to work directly with productivity documents. In these cases, you can combine the power of Word, Excel, or another Office product with your LOB data to create a rich solution. For instance, you might define an Excel document for creating an invoice or a timesheet. You could connect that document to a SharePoint library for managing approvals and workflow. All the while, the document can be built to get data from backend systems and write out results to the same.

Coding for the Cloud

Most of the distributed applications we write are deployed onto one or more servers for hosting and delivery out to the user base. This hosted environment might contain multiple web servers, a database server, and other servers as necessary. The environment then needs to be monitored and managed either internally or through a hosting provider. The management of this environment can be costly. Servers require repair and updates; as the demand for your application increases, you often have to add new hardware to scale with the demand.

Cloud computing is meant to help address these issues. In its basic form, cloud computing represents a hosting environment for your entire application (user interface, logic, database, and so on). The environment is meant to automatically scale with your demand and free you from hardware management and monitoring tasks. This is accomplished through massive amounts of distributed, automatically managed computing power.

Visual Studio developers that want to take advantage of cloud computing can do so via Windows Azure. You can think of this technology as the server operating system for hosting your application. The difference is that Azure is not a single server OS you install; rather, it is an OS that sits atop massive amounts of shared computing power. You can develop, deploy, manage, and scale your application using the Windows Azure cloud as the single host for your application. Adding scale to that host is then simply a configuration change.

Creating a Cloud Application

You create an application destined for the cloud by selecting the Cloud Service template from Visual Studio's New Project dialog. Doing so brings up the New Cloud Service Project dialog shown in Figure 1.19. Here, you select a role (or type) for your application. The ASP.NET Web Role, for example, tells Visual Studio to create a standard ASP.NET website for deploying in the cloud. This is also the role you would use to move your existing ASP.NET sites to the cloud.

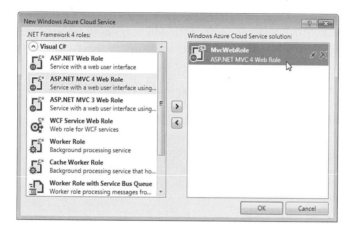

FIGURE 1.19   Selecting the role for your cloud service project.

Developing for the cloud is very similar to developing standard .NET applications. In the case of the Web Role, you simply develop your website as you might otherwise do it. This means adding pages, using standard controls, and coding to the ASP.NET event model. The Visual Studio solution template keeps the cloud service application and your ASP.NET site as separate projects in the solution. Figure 1.20 shows an example. Notice that the website looks like (and is) a standard ASP.NET site. The cloud service application serves as the configuration point for defining how the site should be deployed into the cloud.

Running a Cloud Application

You can run and debug your cloud-bound application from your client machine. That is, you are not required to deploy it into the cloud in order to run it at development time. This experience is very similar to debugging any local project. The primary difference is that the cloud is simulated locally. An application called the development fabric runs on your machine to host your application. The development fabric executes your application as if it were running on the Azure cloud. You can actually view and control this fabric by clicking on its icon in the taskbar. Figure 1.21 shows a website running in the development fabric.

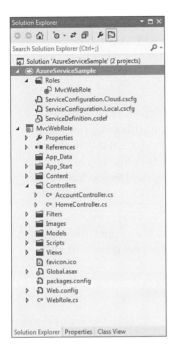

FIGURE 1.20   An ASP.NET website and its cloud configuration project.

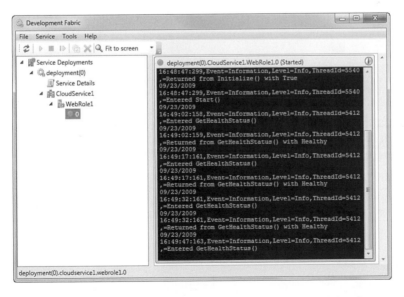

FIGURE 1.21   An application running locally inside the cloud development fabric.

Publishing to the Cloud

When you are ready to push your application into the actual cloud, you can do so directly within Visual Studio. You first must publish your solution by right-clicking the cloud service and selecting Publish. This creates a package file (.cspkg) and a configuration file inside your applications bin\Publish directory.

To deploy, you must have an Azure services account (http://windows.azure.com). In Azure, you define and manage your projects and their services. In this case, you would create a hosted service under a specific project you name. The hosted service must map to a URL that provides access to your service. After your service is defined, you can then deploy. You can deploy a staged or production version. Clicking the Deploy button for either Production or Stage takes you to a screen where you can upload your application package and configuration file. Figure 1.22 shows an example.

After deployment, you can start, suspend, configure, or upgrade the application from the Windows Azure management site. Of course, you can also now access it from its URL.

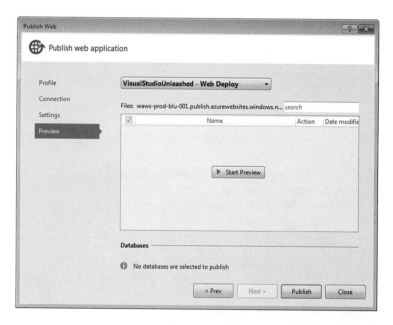

FIGURE 1.22   Deploying a hosted service (website) to the Azure cloud.

Working with Data

Data is the domain of the business developer. It makes sense then that the number one tool and framework for business development continues to provide new and better ways of accessing and exposing that data. Data access is everywhere inside Visual Studio and the .NET Framework. Here we highlight some of the things you encounter when working with data inside Visual Studio.

> **NOTE**
>
> Data access is covered in detail in Chapter 20, "Working with Databases."

Design Your Data

A typed data set allows you to create a .NET class that is based on your database table semantics but works as a data set behind the scenes. This can simplify your programming as you are working with a class. Visual Studio can generate all the code for you. Typed data sets have been part of Visual Studio for a while now. You can autogenerate them based on your actual table schemas and edit the code that is generated to query, update, insert, and delete data.

Visual Studio provides design-time support for typed data sets. You create a typed data set file (.xsd) by adding it to your project. You can then use the Toolbox and Server Explorer to build the data set. Figure 1.23 shows an example. Tables from the Server Explorer were added to the design surface to build the data set (and generate the underlying class code).

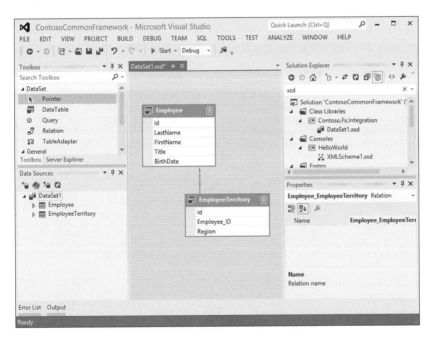

FIGURE 1.23　Building a typed data set with the data set designer.

After you create the data set, you can program against the actual class that represents your data. The class manages the task of working with your database. In addition, typed data sets support hierarchical updates. This feature allows you to save data in multiple, related tables through the typed data set class. In Figure 1.23, this would mean you could edit both the employee details and the related territories and update both as a single process.

Separate Data Design from Storage Schema

Most business applications rely on data that is stored in relational databases. Databases have a well-known structure of tables, columns, and relationships. This structure makes for a nice storage and reporting mechanism. However, the needs of an object-oriented, .NET developer and the database technology are often mismatched. The object developer thinks in terms of objects, properties, methods, relationships, encapsulation, and the like. A lot of time is spent (and a lot of code is written) to convert data from a database into an object-oriented structure and back again.

Visual Studio provides the Entity Data Model (EDM) as a means for mapping objects to database schemas. The EDM and Entity Framework allow you to design the data classes that are used by your application independent of the actual storage mechanism used to persist those classes to a database. You can program against these data classes (the design schema) in your application. You can then define a separate schema for doing the actual persistence (called the storage schema). You create a mapping specification to indicate how the design and storage schema are connected. In this way, the EDM allows your application data to evolve independent of your database schema. They are not coupled. If either schema changes, you change the map to keep them connected.

You create an EDM by selecting the ADO.NET Entity Data Model item from the Add New Item dialog (see Figure 1.24). Selecting this template launches the Entity Data Model Wizard.

FIGURE 1.24   ADO.NET Entity Data Model.

The EDM Wizard enables you to start with an empty model, which is great if you intend to model first and then build data storage. You can also generate an EDM from an existing database (as shown in Figure 1.25). This creates a set of class files that mimic your current database structure. However, your class files can then evolve independent of the underlying storage.

FIGURE 1.25   The Entity Data Model Wizard enables you to generate a model from an existing database or start with an empty model.

The EDM is a file (.edmx) in your solution. You can open it inside a designer for editing. Figure 1.26 shows an example. Notice the storage schema is being mapped to the design schema using the mapping details pane (at the bottom of the figure). There are also options for handling relationships (Toolbox) and browsing the model (Model Browser on the left). Once your EDM is complete, you can code directly against it inside your application as you would any class object.

Build Occasionally Connected Applications

Many applications written these days require access to data both online and offline. For example, you might need report data or customer service records when traveling or at a customer site. You cannot always rely on being connected. Developers have been dealing with this issue in various ways. Visual Studio provides data synchronization services to provide a common, easy solution to this difficult problem.

Data synchronization allows you to sync and cache data between a central database and a user's client system. The cache is a version of SQL Server Compact Edition (CE). Microsoft takes advantage of these services in Windows 7, Vista, Office, and even its Zune software. You, too, can take advantage of these services in your applications.

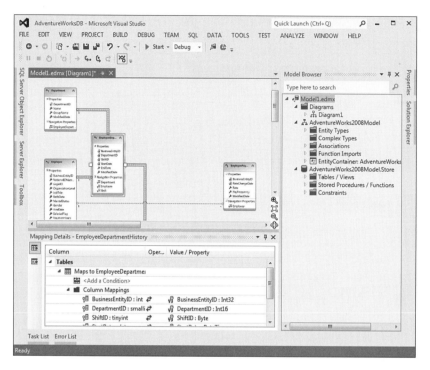

FIGURE 1.26   Mapping design schema to storage schema in the EDM designer.

You can add a local database cache to a WinForms or WPF application. You do so through the Local Database Cache item template. With it, you create a .sync file to configure how synchronization should happen between a local data store and a server. Opening the local database cache file in Visual Studio opens the Configure Data Synchronization dialog. Here you can set up tables that should be cached on a client, set up the server database, and configure the client database information. Figure 1.27 shows an example of configuring this dialog to sync certain tables between a server and a client database cache.

Write Connected, Service-Oriented Solutions

Many business applications involve specific processes, or workflows, around documents, records, and related data. These business processes typically involve staged review and approval by business personnel; they might also require communication between various systems. A business process is also typically long-running, meaning the process is not a simple, single execution but rather a multistep process that has to "wait" before moving to the next step.

Building these processes in to business application typically required a lot of custom development work with little guidance, or it meant tying your application to third-party tools. Web Services helped, but developers lacked an easy way to build them with support for multiple protocols, different transports, strong security, and transactional support.

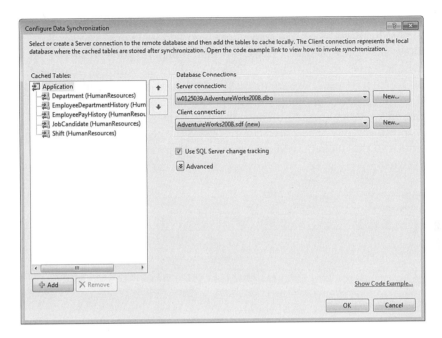

FIGURE 1.27   Configuring data synchronization.

Visual Studio provides in-the-box support for building business processes as workflows and reliably integrating them with other applications, systems, and partners. This section takes a look at Windows Workflow (WF) for defining reusable business process and Windows Communication Foundation (WCF) for unlocking that business process across system boundaries.

Develop an Application/Business Process

A workflow represents a set of actions (called activities) that typically model a business process and often involve user interaction. WF provides the framework, tools, and an execution engine for enabling workflows in your application. With it, you can create a workflow and know that it runs wherever the .NET Framework is installed.

You create a workflow model to describe the order and logic of how activities are to be executed based on the data in the workflow, your business rules and conditions, and system and user actions. A workflow is executed and managed by a workflow instance object. This object is run in process with your application and controls the execution and current state of the workflow. You interact with your workflows from within your application. This could be any type of application (Windows, ASP.NET, console, service, and so on). You typically submit data to the workflow and you might get a response, or you might use the workflow to kick off certain tasks or activities in your business process. The workflow can also persist itself during long-running transactions and then rehydrate on demand.

Building a workflow is a visual process. The thought behind this is that workflows themselves are traditionally illustrated as a set of steps (boxes) and connections (arrows). For this reason, workflows are represented as a FlowChart item template. You can add activities (or a sequence of activities) to a flowchart and connect them accordingly. Activities are added from the Toolbox items. There are many standard activities for handling things such as branching, looping, error handling, and compensation. You will most likely also code your own, custom activities and add them to the workflow. Figure 1.28 shows an example workflow in the designer. There are activities listed in the toolbox on the left. Notice that once added to the diagram, you can code the activity (including IntelliSense) from within the designer.

FIGURE 1.28   The workflow designer inside Visual Studio.

A workflow can also have both variables and arguments. These concepts are similar to programming .NET C# or VB. A variable is used to store state (or data) inside the workflow (or activity). An argument is used to pass data into and out of a workflow. Notice the variable and arguments editor at the bottom of Figure 1.28. Here, you define the name, type, direction, and default value for variable or argument used by your given workflow.

Finally, notice the various workflow activities listed on the Toolbox inside Figure 1.28. The Messaging activities allow you to define a receive/send port for the workflow. This enables your workflow to be listening for messages and then kick-off a hosted instance after a message is received. You can also use the send shape to communicate with other hosted services.

> **NOTE**
>
> See Chapter 22, "Embedding Workflow in Your Applications," for a more detailed discussion of Windows Workflow.

Create and Consume Services

Most organizations have multiple systems, each designed for a specific purpose. They might have systems for finance, HR, order management, inventory, customer service, and more. Each application houses specific business processes. However, most organizations need to unlock these business processes from their applications and reuse them as part of an integrated solution. This is where service-oriented solutions have helped. By exposing an application's business process as a service, multiple clients can take advantage of that process.

The promise of code reuse has been with us a long time. However, service-oriented code reuse became very popular with the advent of Web Services. The ubiquitous nature of HTTP and port 80 coupled with XML-based interfaces allowed for a new level of communication between application boundaries. Developers began wrapping key business functions as services and calling them from multiple clients.

Visual Studio and the .NET Framework 4.0 represent another step forward in this service-oriented paradigm. With these tools, you can create services based on Microsoft's Windows Communication Foundation. WCF is a framework that recognizes that developers need multiple layers of communication (not just the SOAP protocol carried over an HTTP transport), require strong security, often need to support transactions, and do not want to write all the plumbing code to do so.

You create WCF services as a code library, as a workflow, or as a Web Service application. Figure 1.29 shows the available WCF project types. From here you can indicate that your Web Service contains a workflow or simply create a service library that calls custom code you write.

You can also still create XML Web Services (.asmx) through the web project templates. This same template area also provides access to the WCF Service Application template. With it, you can create a WCF service that is configured similarly to a standard Web Service (and hosted in ASP.NET).

WCF is all about configuration. It frees you from having to write all the service plumbing code. Instead, you can focus on the functionality of your service. For example, you can add service endpoints to your service depending on which communication stack you intend to support (HTTP, TCP/IP, MSMQ, named pipes, and so on). Figure 1.30 shows the WCF configuration editor. Notice how the binding support for an endpoint is a configuration (and not coding) task.

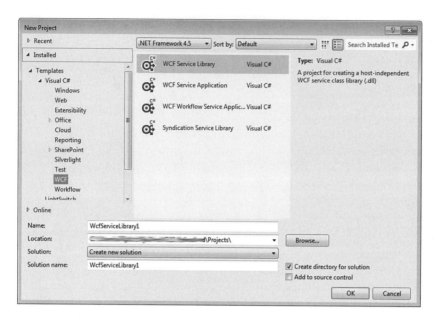

FIGURE 1.29   The WCF project templates.

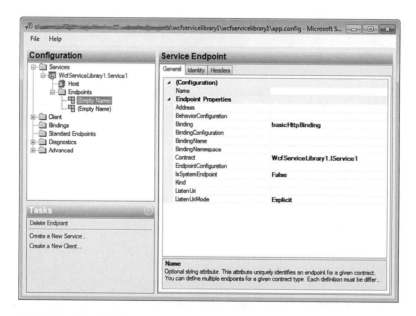

FIGURE 1.30   Configuration of a WCF service.

After you've built your service, you need to host it so that consumers (clients) can find it and call it. You have a lot of hosting options available to you including self-hosted, Windows service, Internet Information Services (IIS), and Windows Process Activation Service (WAS). Actually consuming the WCF service requires you to define a service reference and configure how you are going to talk with the service and pass messages. We discuss creating, hosting, and consuming services in detail later in this book (see Chapter 21, "Service-Oriented Applications").

Summary

A new release of Visual Studio means a lot to all the various development camps out there. Visual Studio touches developers who write code in C++, C#, Visual Basic, and many other languages. Literally millions of developers boot and launch their favorite tool every day. They spend the vast majority of their working hours, days, weeks, and months architecting and building solutions with the tool. We hope this chapter oriented you to the many possibilities available for building your next application.

CHAPTER 2

The Visual Studio IDE

When you're traveling over new ground, it's often wise to consult a guide. At a minimum, a quick check of the map is in order before you set out for new adventures. The same holds true for approaching a new development tool the size and breadth of Visual Studio 2012. It is wise to familiarize yourself a bit with the tool before starting that first project off on the wrong foot.

This chapter is your quick, to-the-point guide. It serves to orient you before you set out. We cover the basics of installation; configuration; booting the IDE; and getting to know the layout of the tool in terms of projects, menus, tools, editors, and designers. Let's get started.

Installing Visual Studio

The installation of Visual Studio 2012 remains similar to that of earlier versions. The application plays host to many tools. Depending on your purchase, a subset of these items is available during install. (See Chapter 1, "A Quick Tour of Visual Studio 2012," for a comparison of Visual Studio editions.) If you are fortunate enough to own Visual Studio Ultimate, you are presented with the full set of options for installation. For those with Visual Studio Professional, however, you choose one or more development languages, determine if you want to install unit testing, decide whether you need the features of Microsoft Office Development, and perhaps install SQL 2012 Express. Figure 2.1 shows the setup options selection page for Visual Studio Professional.

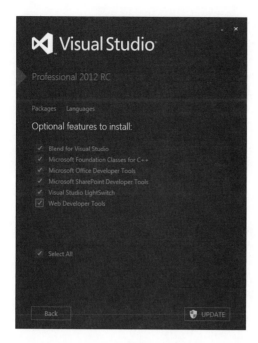

FIGURE 2.1   Visual Studio 2012 setup options page.

Choosing a Language

Setting up your development machine should be relatively straightforward. We suggest that most developers keep language installs to a primary language and perhaps one backup. You might use a secondary language for viewing sample code from Microsoft Developer Network (MSDN) or similar sites. Typically, this means if your primary language is Visual Basic, you install C# as a secondary language (and vice versa). Choosing to install many languages, most of which you do not intend to use, not only takes up hard drive space but also can clutter your environment with too many choices. Having a backup language, however, helps solve the problem of finding a great bit of code you want to learn more about only to discover you can't give it a test run because it is not available in your chosen language.

Whether to install the additional tools is entirely up to you (and the projects you will be working on). For example, if you intend to work with a lot of local database code, you want SQL Server 2008 or 2012 Express. If your project requires you to unit test your code, be sure to install the Unit Testing Tools.

TIP

You might change your mind about your installation selections at a later date. In this case, you can always go back and rerun setup. Rerunning setup gives you the Add or Remove Features, Repair/Reinstall, and Uninstall options.

Configuring Your Development Environment Settings

Booting the new IDE for the first time results in a dialog box asking you to choose your environment settings. As Visual Studio becomes the central tool for so many developers, testers, architects, and even project managers, it's harder and harder to satisfy them all with a single tool. To aid in this dilemma, Microsoft has created an entire set of environment settings that are configured for the usual developer type. For instance, if you set your environment to C#, the New Project dialog box automatically highlights C# projects above other languages. Figure 2.2 shows the available environment settings options.

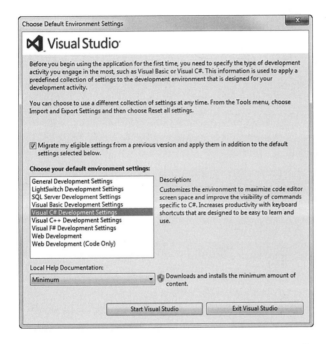

FIGURE 2.2   The Environment Settings options dialog box.

Managing Your Settings

Only your first use of Visual Studio launches the default settings dialog box. On subsequent visits, you go straight to the tool. However, you might consider switching your environment settings if you do a lot of switching from one language to another or if you switch roles. For example, C# developers might use the C# development settings most of the time. They might then toggle to another collection of settings when switching to VB or developing a web-only application.

You manage your environment settings from the Tools menu's Import and Export Settings option. Figure 2.3 shows the first screen in this wizard. This screen enables you to choose to execute a settings export, import, or total reset.

TIP

If you are like most developers, you are probably particular about your environment setup. There is nothing worse than having to work on a machine that has a different IDE configuration. You can be thankful that you can use the Import and Export Settings Wizard to take your IDE settings with you.

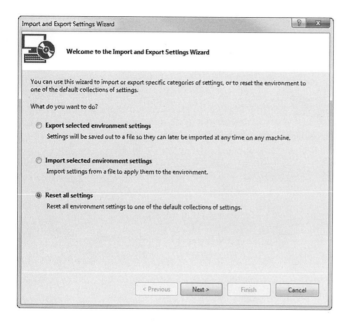

FIGURE 2.3   The Import and Export Settings Wizard.

You can choose from several setting collections when importing. There are a few default collections, including those based on language and role (such as web developer or tester in the case of Team Systems). In addition, you can select a custom settings file. Figure 2.4 shows the import settings collection options.

Another key screen to the Import and Export Settings Wizard is the settings selection screen. On this screen, you decide which options are important for export or import. This enables you to pick and choose settings you plan to either export or import. For example, you might love the way a friend has configured her code editor in terms of font and contrasting colors, but you do not want all her other settings, such as her keyboard configurations. You can accomplish this by selecting to import only her code editor settings. Figure 2.5 provides a glimpse at the granular level to which you can manage your environment settings during import and export.

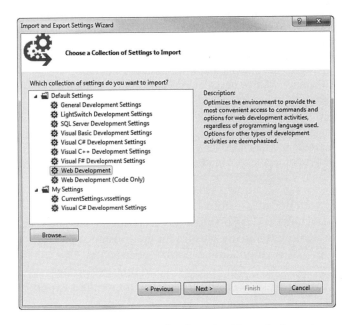

FIGURE 2.4   Choosing a collection of settings for import.

FIGURE 2.5   Choosing settings to export.

TIP

A great feature of the import and export settings tool is the capability to export/import any of your IDE customizations, including fonts and colors, Start Page customizations, menu and keyboard customizations, and more. These items can travel with you from machine to machine, so you do not have to spend valuable development time resetting them each time you rebuild or switch machines.

In Figure 2.5, note the warning icon next to the Import and Export Settings selection. Some settings may contain sensitive data (for instance, a folder path that includes domain information or your user name), and this icon flags those items that should be treated with care to avoid disclosing what might be confidential information.

By default, settings are exported to your documents folder. In Windows 7, you typically find this folder at C:\Users\[user]\Documents\Visual Studio 2012\Settings. Here you can find a .vssettings XML file representing the many settings for your instance of Visual Studio. This includes CurrentSettings.vssettings and any exported settings files. The .vssettings files can be shared among users. They can also be used to migrate settings from one PC and one IDE version to another. You do so through the Import and Export Settings Wizard.

Getting Started

When you first launch Visual Studio 2012, you are presented with the Start Page for the IDE (see Figure 2.6).

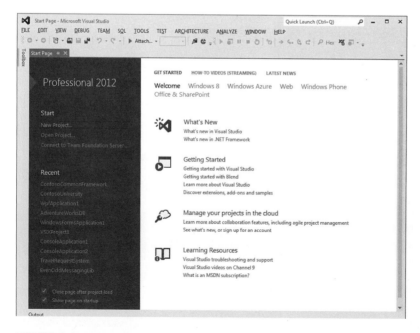

FIGURE 2.6   The Visual Studio Start Page.

The Start Page contains a number of useful links to get you moving quickly. Starting from the upper left, you have three primary options: Connect to TFS, New Project, and Open Project. You also can launch a recent project from the left side of the screen. Across the top are tabs for getting started, guidance and resources, and latest news. These all provide access to online content. See Chapter 7, "The .NET Community: Interacting Online," for more information on working with the Start Page.

> **TIP**
>
> You can highlight a project in the list and pin it to ensure it stays in the list. You can also easily delete projects from this list.

Startup Options

If you just don't like the Start Page or prefer to launch directly into the project you'll be spending the next few months of your life working on, you can customize what happens when the IDE boots. From the Options dialog box (Tools, Options or the Settings link on the Start Page), choose the Environment node and then the Startup leaf. Figure 2.7 shows some of the options available to you at startup.

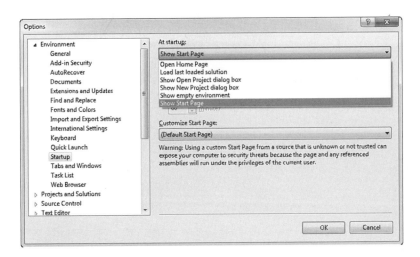

FIGURE 2.7   Startup options.

From here, you can configure where to get your Start Page news (Start Page news channel). You set this to a valid RSS feed URL. You can also use the At Startup option to tell the environment to load the last solution, show the new or open project dialog boxes, open your browser's home page, or do nothing (show an empty environment). You can also configure how often your content is automatically refreshed from the server. Finally, you have the option here to use a custom Start Page. For more information on custom start pages, click the Customize the Start Page link on the Welcome screen of the Start Page.

Creating Your First Project

The next, natural step is to create your first project. You might have an existing project you want to open or you might be starting fresh. In either case, creating or opening a project quickly exposes you to some of the basic project and file management features within the IDE.

To get started, you can click the File menu or the Projects link on the Start Page. Assuming you are using the File menu, you see the options to create a new project or website under the New submenu. Projects are simply templates that group files for Windows, Office, web, and similar applications. A website creates a set of web files that get promoted and managed as files (and not complied code).

You might have multiple projects grouped together to form a single application. In this case, each project might be grouped under a single solution. Figure 2.8 shows an example of the New Project dialog box. Notice that a Visual C#, ASP.NET Web Application is being created along with a new solution to house the project. For more information on this, see Chapter 4, "Solutions and Projects."

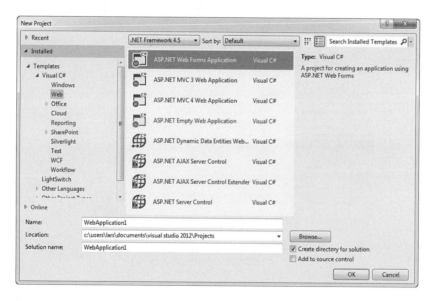

FIGURE 2.8   Creating a new project.

Targeting Your Environment

Many of us work in environments that include applications built on various versions of the .NET Framework. You might be building your new applications on .NET 4.5 but still need to support one or more .NET 3.5 applications. Of course, this becomes even more prevalent as more versions are released. You do not, however, want to have to keep multiple versions of Visual Studio on your machine. Instead, you should be able to target the version of the Framework for which the application is written. This way you can work in a single IDE and take advantage of the latest productivity enhancements.

Visual Studio 2012 supports the ability to target a specific version of the .NET Framework for an application. This means you can use a single tool to develop against many applications built on various .NET Framework flavors. Setting the .NET Framework version of an application appropriately sets the toolbox, project types, available references, and even IntelliSense inside the IDE to be in sync with the chosen .NET Framework version. Figure 2.9 shows the New Project dialog box again; this time, the .NET Framework version selection (top center) has been highlighted.

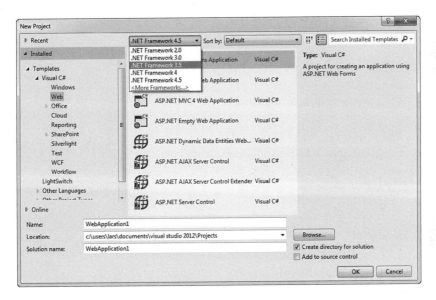

FIGURE 2.9   Creating an application to target a specific version of the .NET Framework.

After you select a Framework version, the IDE automatically adjusts the available project types, IntelliSense, reference-able libraries, and similar features. For instance, if you choose to add a reference to your project, only those libraries from the target version of the Framework are available to you in the Add Reference dialog box.

You can also decide to move your application to a different (hopefully newer) version of the .NET Framework at a later date. You can do so inside the project properties dialog box (right-click your project file inside of Solution Explorer and select Properties). Figure 2.10 shows an example. Notice the Target Framework drop-down. You can change this and the IDE then resets IntelliSense, references, your toolbox, and more to the newly selected target framework.

NOTE

The Framework setting is per project. Therefore, you can create a single solution that contains multiple projects and each can target a different version of the .NET Framework.

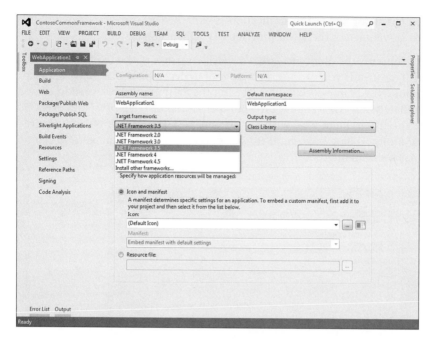

FIGURE 2.10   Resetting the target Framework of a web application.

Of course, you can use Visual Studio 2012 to open an existing application built on an earlier version of the .NET Framework. When doing so, you have the option of upgrading or keeping it tied to its current.NET Framework version. You can choose to upgrade the target Framework version or continue to target an earlier version.

Many environments include developers using different versions of Visual Studio. You do have to be careful about opening these older applications inside of a newer version of Visual Studio. Although the code itself is not affected, the actual solution file is converted to 2012 (and thus rendered useless to earlier versions). If this is your environment, we recommend creating multiple versions of the solution file: one for each version of Visual Studio in use by the team.

Navigating the IDE

After you've created your first project, you should get started adding features to your application. This, of course, requires that you have some base understanding of the many components of the IDE. Figure 2.11 shows a sample website inside the IDE. Notice that the IDE layout is relatively generic: Toolbox on the left, Solution Explorer on the right, and code in the middle. You should expect a similar experience for your applications (at least until you've customized things).

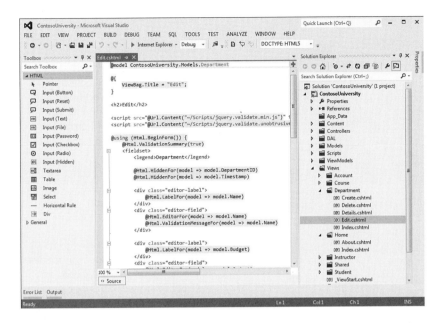

2

FIGURE 2.11   A simple web application in the IDE.

Getting around inside the IDE is the first step to being productive. The following sections break down the many items shown in Figure 2.11; it might be useful to refer to this graphic to provide overall context a given item is discussed.

The Menus

If you've been working with earlier versions of Visual Studio, you should find the Visual Studio 2012 menu bar to be standard fare. Although cosmetically speaking Visual Studio 2012 looks very different from its predecessors, its general layout has remained unchanged. It is very intuitive; options are where you would expect them; and new menus appear depending on your place within the IDE, the tools you've chosen to install, and your default programming language. For example, a Refactor menu appears when you are in the C# code editor, the Project menu shows up when you have a project open, and the File menu configures itself differently depending on the programming language you are using.

Table 2.1 lists (from left to right across the IDE) some of the more common menus, along with a description of each.

TABLE 2.1   Visual Studio 2012 Menus

Menu	Figure	Description
File	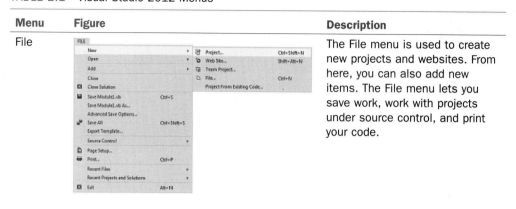	The File menu is used to create new projects and websites. From here, you can also add new items. The File menu lets you save work, work with projects under source control, and print your code.
Edit		The Edit menu is used for managing items on your Clipboard and fixing mistakes with Undo and Redo. In addition, the Edit menu provides access to important tools such as Find and Replace and IntelliSense. The fly-out menu in the graphic shows some of the advanced options available from the Edit menu, such as Format Document, which is useful to apply your formatting settings to the code with which you are working.

Menu	Figure	Description
View	**VIEW** Code — F7 Solution Explorer — Ctrl+W, S Team Explorer — Ctrl+\, Ctrl+M Server Explorer — Ctrl+W, L SQL Server Object Explorer — Ctrl+\, Ctrl+S Call Hierarchy — Ctrl+W, K Class View — Ctrl+W, C Code Definition Window — Ctrl+W, D Object Browser — Ctrl+W, J Error List — Ctrl+W, E Output — Ctrl+W, O Start Page Task List — Ctrl+W, T Toolbox — Ctrl+W, X Find Results ▸ Other Windows ▸ Toolbars ▸ Full Screen — Shift+Alt+Enter All Windows — Shift+Alt+M Navigate Backward — Ctrl+- Navigate Forward — Ctrl+Shift+- Next Task Previous Task Properties Window — Ctrl+W, P Property Pages — Shift+F4 Other Windows fly-out: Command Window — Ctrl+W, A Web Browser — Ctrl+W, W Page Inspector Load Test Runs Source Control Explorer Data Tools Operations Windows Azure Activity Log Bookmark Window — Ctrl+W, B Package Manager Console Document Outline — Ctrl+W, U History Pending Changes Property Manager Resource View — Ctrl+W, R F# Interactive — Ctrl+Alt+F Code Analysis Code Metrics Results	The View menu provides access to the multitude of windows available in Visual Studio. If you lose your way (or window) in the tool, the View menu is the best place to look to find your bearings. From here, you can access the Server Explorer, Solution Explorer, Task List, and other key windows of the IDE. The fly-out menu shows the Other Windows option (the many, many windows of Visual Studio 2012).
Refactor	**REFACTOR** Rename... — F2 Extract Method... — Ctrl+R, M Encapsulate Field... — Ctrl+R, E Extract Interface... — Ctrl+R, I Remove Parameters... — Ctrl+R, V Reorder Parameters... — Ctrl+R, O	The Refactor menu (C# only) provides access to options such as renaming code elements, extracting code from a method to a new method, and promoting local variables to parameters. See Chapter 10, "Refactoring Code," for more information on refactoring.
Website	**WEBSITE** Add New Item... — Ctrl+Shift+A Add Existing Item... — Shift+Alt+A New Folder New Virtual Directory... Add ASP.NET Folder ▸ Copy Web Site... Nest Related Files Unload Project Add Windows Azure Cloud Service Project Add Reference... Add Service Reference... Set as StartUp Project Project Dependencies... Use Visual Studio Development Server... Project Build Order... Manage NuGet Packages... Enable NuGet Package Restore Refresh Project Toolbox Items Start Options... ASP.NET Configuration Configure Code Analysis for Web Site	The Website menu is available only when you're working with websites (and not web applications or other project types). It provides access to add new items, add references, copy your website to a deployment location, and work with project dependencies. You can also set the Start Page for the application and access ASP.NET configuration options for the given website.

2

Menu	Figure	Description
Project		The Project menu is similar to the Website menu but is available to both web and non-web-based projects. From here, you can add new items and references to your projects, set the startup project, and change the build order for projects in your solution. In addition, you can access the properties for a given project. This enables you to set things such as the version of the .NET Framework you are targeting, the default namespace, and many more items.
Build		The Build menu enables you to invoke the given compilers for your solution. From here, you can force a build or rebuild on the entire solution or an individual project within the solution. You can also access the Configuration Manager from the Build menu. This dialog box enables you to control your target build in terms of debug versus release, CPU, and so on.
Debug		The Debug menu provides developers access to the debug commands for Visual Studio. These commands include options for starting your project inside a debugging session and attaching a new debug session to an existing, executing process. In addition, you can manage debug breakpoints from this menu. The fly-out menu shows some of the other debug windows available from this menu. For more information, see Chapter 11, "Debugging Code."

Menu	Figure	Description
Data	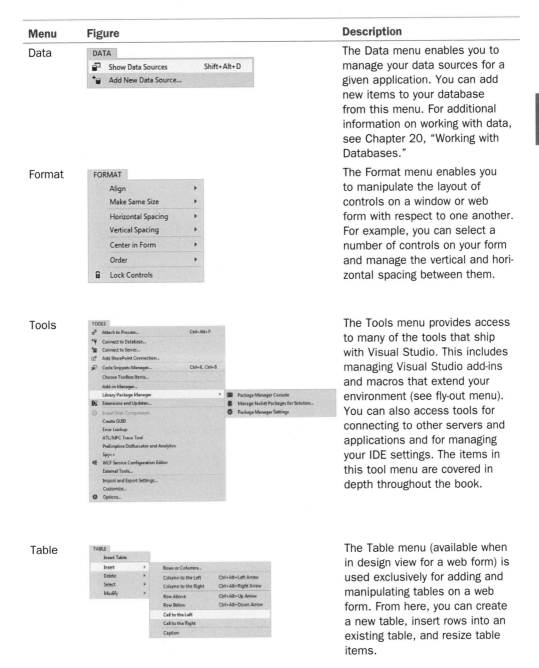	The Data menu enables you to manage your data sources for a given application. You can add new items to your database from this menu. For additional information on working with data, see Chapter 20, "Working with Databases."
Format		The Format menu enables you to manipulate the layout of controls on a window or web form with respect to one another. For example, you can select a number of controls on your form and manage the vertical and horizontal spacing between them.
Tools		The Tools menu provides access to many of the tools that ship with Visual Studio. This includes managing Visual Studio add-ins and macros that extend your environment (see fly-out menu). You can also access tools for connecting to other servers and applications and for managing your IDE settings. The items in this tool menu are covered in depth throughout the book.
Table		The Table menu (available when in design view for a web form) is used exclusively for adding and manipulating tables on a web form. From here, you can create a new table, insert rows into an existing table, and resize table items.

Menu	Figure	Description
Test	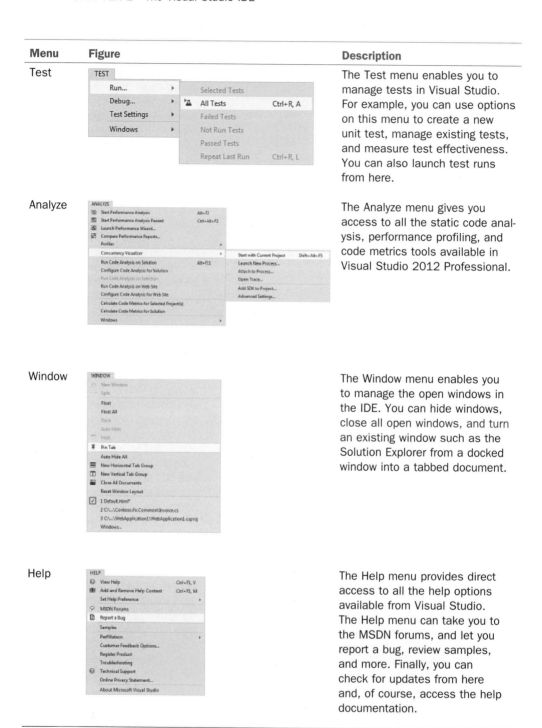	The Test menu enables you to manage tests in Visual Studio. For example, you can use options on this menu to create a new unit test, manage existing tests, and measure test effectiveness. You can also launch test runs from here.
Analyze		The Analyze menu gives you access to all the static code analysis, performance profiling, and code metrics tools available in Visual Studio 2012 Professional.
Window		The Window menu enables you to manage the open windows in the IDE. You can hide windows, close all open windows, and turn an existing window such as the Solution Explorer from a docked window into a tabbed document.
Help		The Help menu provides direct access to all the help options available from Visual Studio. The Help menu can take you to the MSDN forums, and let you report a bug, review samples, and more. Finally, you can check for updates from here and, of course, access the help documentation.

Note that each menu screenshot in Table 2.1 was taken using the C# menu default settings. In each case, Visual Basic has an equivalent, albeit slightly different, menu. In addition, the keyboard shortcut callouts in the menu items are also those of C#. Visual Basic developers should recognize a lot of them as the same. All menus can be customized to an individual developer's preference.

The Many Toolbars

Visual Studio 2012 includes close to 30 toolbars in just the professional edition. If you use a set of commands often, there is a good chance that there is a matching toolbar to group those commands. As a result, a large percentage of the toolbars are highly specialized. For example, if you are working with the Class Designer, you use the Class Designer toolbar to manage classes or change screen magnification. Or if you are building a SQL Query, you use the Query Designer toolbar. We do not cover each of these toolbars here because they are highly specialized. Instead, we stick to a quick tour to cover the common ground.

The Standard Toolbar

The Standard toolbar is present at all times during your IDE sessions (unless, of course, you customize things or turn it off). It provides quick access to all the commands you use over and over. The standard commands are on the top left: Back and Forward, Create New Project, Open, Save, and Save All. These are followed by Undo and Redo. Figure 2.12 shows the Standard toolbar in the IDE.

FIGURE 2.12   The Standard toolbar in Visual Studio 2012.

TIP

We suggest you learn the keyboard equivalents for such standard commands as cut, copy, paste, undo, and the like. In fact, most standard toolbar items have a shortcut you should learn. You can then remove many of these toolbar icons from the toolbar to save precious screen real estate for commands that have you reaching for the mouse anyway (and have harder-to-remember shortcut keys). Keep in mind that toolbars can, and will, change configurations depending on the project type currently loaded in the IDE.

The button to the right of the undo/redo commands (the one that is a green start arrow) is often called the Run or Play button. This initiates a build of your project and launches you into debug mode. Moving to the right, you see options for initiating a search within your code. This capability can be handy for quickly finding the place where you left off or the place you are looking for. And finally, to the right of this is a drop-down that enables you to add or remove buttons to/from the Standard toolbar. As you will see later, you can, in fact, customize any of the toolbars in the IDE.

Customizing Toolbars

If the standard toolbars that ship with Visual Studio don't meet your needs, you can create custom toolbars that do. Select the Tool menu's Customize item or right-click a toolbar in the IDE and select Customize to launch the Customize dialog box shown in Figure 2.13. From here, select which toolbars to show, indicate icon size for toolbar items, turn on and off tips and shortcut keys, and more.

FIGURE 2.13   The Customize dialog box in Visual Studio 2012.

You make customizations to the toolbar by selecting an item and choosing one of the option buttons on the right (move up, move down, delete, and so on). If things get messed up, you can use the Reset All button for a selected toolbar to revert to the default state.

The Toolbars tab on the Customize dialog box enables you to select which toolbars are visible. This dialog box also includes the New button, which enables you to create new toolbars to group existing commands. This gives you a great deal of customization options. After you've click the New button, you name your new toolbar and use the Commands tab (see Figure 2.14) to add items to your custom toolbar.

You can also configure your keyboard shortcut combinations from the Customize dialog box. Use the Keyboard button (the bottom of Figure 2.13) to bring up the Options dialog box to the environment's keyboard options screen. Figure 2.15 shows an example. First, you find a command in the list; next, you press a shortcut key to map (or remap) a combination. Notice that if the option is already assigned a shortcut key, Visual Studio warns you before you make the reassignment.

FIGURE 2.14   Adding commands.

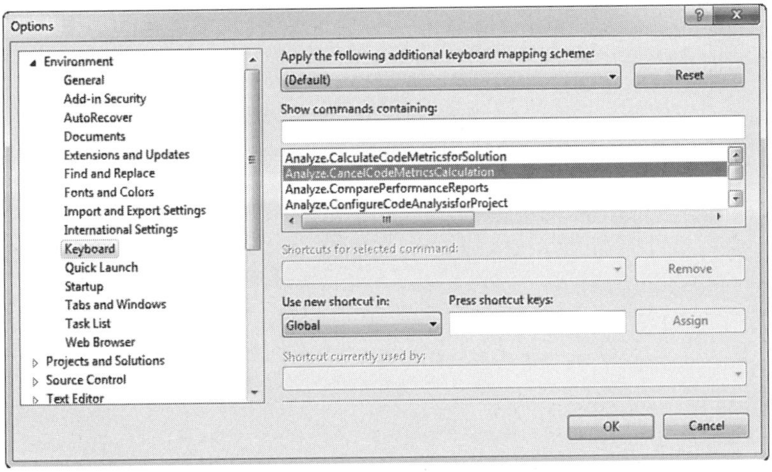

FIGURE 2.15   Options dialog box keyboard assignments.

You should do some exploration of your own into the many toolbars (and toolbar customization options) within Visual Studio. Often their usefulness presents itself only at the right moment. For instance, if you are editing a Windows form, having the Layout toolbar available to tweak the position of controls relative to one another can be a valuable timesaver. Knowing that these toolbars are available increases the likelihood that you can benefit from their value.

The Solution Explorer

The Solution Explorer enables you to group and manage the many files that make up your application. A solution simply contains multiple projects (applications). A project groups files related to its type. For instance, you can create a website, Windows Forms application, class library, console application, and more. The files inside the project containers represent your code in terms of web pages, forms, class files, XML, and other related items.

Figure 2.16 shows the Solution Explorer undocked from the IDE. Note that a single solution is open (you might only have one solution open at a time), and the solution contains a few applications (called projects). For instance, there is a Windows Forms (WinForms) application (OrderEntry), a web application (WebApplication1), and others.

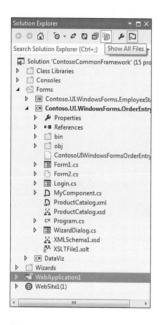

FIGURE 2.16   The Visual Studio 2012 Solution Explorer.

You use the Solution Explorer to navigate the many items in your project. You can access an item by first selecting it and then double-clicking it. Solution Explorer opens the given designer or editor associated with the type of file you request. For example, opening a file with the extension .cs opens the C# code editor. You can also add a new item (class, image, form) to your application from here by right-clicking a project or folder and selecting the Add menu. Finally, you also use the Solution Explorer during source control scenarios to check items in and out of the source database. The Solution Explorer is covered in depth in Chapter 4.

The Text Editors

Visual Studio 2012 has several text editors or word (code) processors. Each text editor is based on a common core that provides the basic set of functionality for each editor such as the selection margin, the capability to collapse nested items, and colorization. Each editor derives from this core and is customized to give you the editors for code (C#, VB, and so on), the XML editor, the XAML editor, the HTML (or ASPX) editor, the style sheet editor, and more.

The Code Editors

The code editor, for our money, is where the magic happens. It is here that you get down to business leveraging your favorite language to define objects and their functionality. Of course, you can write code outside the Visual Studio editor, but why would you? You can also write a novel using Notepad or do your taxes by hand. A good code editor means higher productivity, plain and simple. And Visual Studio has some of the best code editors around.

The code editor is front and center when you're writing the guts of your application. It handles indentation and whitespace to make your code clean and readable. It provides IntelliSense and statement completion to free you from having to look up (or memorize) every object library and keyword. It provides shortcut snippets to help you quickly generate common code such as property definitions. It groups code into blocks, it provides color codes for keywords and comments, it highlights errors, and it shows new code relative to previously compiled code. All in all, the Visual Studio code editor does quite a bit to keep you focused, organized, and productive.

The C# Code Editor

Figure 2.17 shows the C# code editor. Some items to note include the following:

▶ The code is grouped into logical sections along the left side. You can use the minus signs to close a whole class, method, property, or similar group. This capability enables you to hide code you are not working on at the moment. You can also create your own custom, named regions to do the same thing.

▶ Code lines are numbered along the left edge of the editor. You can turn this feature on or off for different code editors in the tool.

▶ New code is signaled inside the section groups with a colored line. Yellow is used for new code that has yet to be saved. The highlighted line turns green after a save and disappears after you close and reopen the file. This feature enables you to track where you have made changes to code during your current session.

▶ The name of the open code file is listed as the code window's tab across the top. The asterisk indicates that the code has changed since the last time it was saved.

▶ IntelliSense is invoked as you type. You can use the arrow keys to quickly find the item in the list. Hovering over the item shows details for the given item (tip text to the right). You can press the Tab key to complete the item from IntelliSense.

▶ The code is highlighted in various colors. By default, keywords are navy blue, comments are green, text is black, types you create are light blue, string values are red, and so on.

▶ The two drop-downs at the top of the code editor enable you to navigate between the classes in the file (left-side drop-down) and methods, fields, and properties within a given class (right-side drop-down).

FIGURE 2.17   The C# code editor.

The Visual Basic Code Editor

The Visual Basic code editor works much the same way as the C# editor. Figure 2.18 shows the code editor, this time with a Visual Basic file loaded. Some of the differences between the editors are as listed here:

▶ Horizontal lines are used to separate methods and properties within the editor.

▶ The IntelliSense drop-down list is filtered into a common subset and all the possible values.

▶ The code navigation drop-downs at the top of the code editor enable you to navigate the entire, active object hierarchy (including events). The left-side drop-down shows namespaces, objects, and events. The right-side drop-down shows all methods for the given type, including those you have not yet overridden. The items you have implemented are highlighted as bold within the list.

Of course, Visual Studio contains many more text editors. There are other language editors (C++ and F#), XML editors, XHTML editors, and more. Each has similar features to the two code editors shown here. We cover many of the specifics of these additional editors throughout the rest of this book.

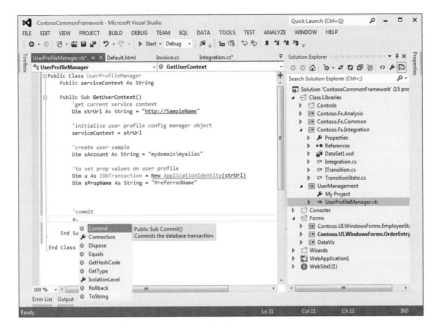

FIGURE 2.18   The Visual Basic code editor.

Editor Customizations

You can customize nearly every aspect of the many code editors to your every whim. From our experience, it seems no two developers see their code the same way. You can use the Options dialog box (Tools, Options) to change the editor's background color or the color and font of various text elements within the editor. You can also turn on line numbering and manage indenting (tabs) and whitespace. You can set options based on language and editor. The full list of customizations for the editors is large.

Figure 2.19 shows the Options dialog box set for Fonts and Colors. From here, you can tweak the many display items in the editor in terms of their color, font, and font size.

If you dig a little deeper in the Options dialog box, you come across the Text Editor node in the option tree. From here, you can manipulate even more settings for the text editor in general for language-specific editors. For example, you can remove the horizontal procedure separators in the Visual Basic editor or turn off the automatic reformatting of code by the editor.

One common change we see developers make is controlling how the editor automatically formats code inside the C# editor. It seems granular control of curly braces is a big deal to those who look at code all day. For instance, you might like to see all your curly braces on separate lines or you might prefer them to start on the line that starts the given code block. Fortunately, you can control all of that from the Options dialog box. Figure 2.20 shows some of these options available for formatting C# inside the editor. Notice how the option also shows an example of how the code is formatted by the editor.

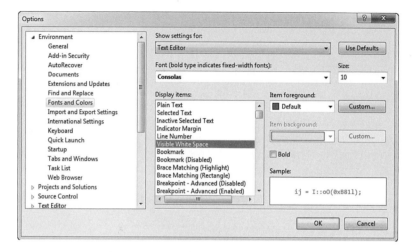

FIGURE 2.19   The Options dialog box set to Fonts and Colors.

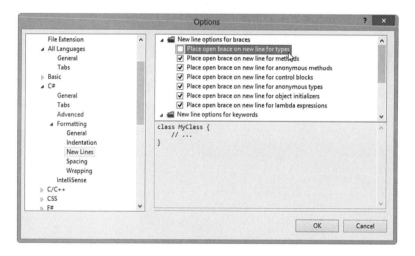

FIGURE 2.20   Controlling code formatting from the Options dialog box.

The Visual Designers

Visual Designers are the canvases that you work on using the mouse to create items such as forms via drag, drop, move, resize, and the like. Visual Studio 2012 ships with many such visual designers. Together, they enable you to build the items that make up your application. Items include Windows forms, web forms, class diagrams, XML schemas, and more.

The visual designers all work in a similar way. First, they take center stage within the IDE as tabbed windows surrounded by various menus, toolbars, and panes. Second, you use the Toolbox (discussed in a moment) as a palette from which you place items (such as controls) onto the given designer. You then configure each item's many properties using the Properties window.

Figure 2.21 shows the WPF Form Designer in action (the middle, highlighted tab). Note that the Toolbox is on the left and the Properties window is on the bottom right. In addition, note that this figure shows the Layout toolbar. This toolbar enables you to easily position controls relative to one another. We cover the majority of the visual designers in depth in the coming chapters. You can also get a better overview from Chapter 6, "Introducing the Editors and Designers."

FIGURE 2.21   The WPF/XAML Designer.

The Toolbox

The Visual Studio 2012 Toolbox provides access to the many controls when you're building web and Windows forms. It also provides access to nearly anything that can be dragged onto one of the many designers used for creating forms, XML schemas, class diagrams, and more. As an example, if you are building a web form, the Toolbox provides the many controls, grouped for easier access, which can be added to the form. Furthermore, if you are working with a text editor, the Toolbox enables you to save clips of text for quick access.

Figure 2.22 shows the Toolbox in a standard configuration (undocked from the IDE) for building a web form. Note that the Standard group of controls is closed to highlight some additional control groups. The many controls inside this Toolbox are covered throughout the rest of the book. The bulk of the Toolbox controls are covered in Part 5, "Creating Enterprise Applications."

FIGURE 2.22   The Visual Studio Toolbox configured for a web form.

TIP

You can customize the Toolbox to your liking. For example, you can add your own groups (called tabs). You can also configure the Toolbox to show more icons on the screen at a time. As you familiarize yourself with the various standard controls, you can turn off their text descriptions and simply show them as icons. To do so, right-click the control group (tab) and uncheck List View. Figure 2.23 illustrates the additional screen real estate you gain by turning off the text descriptions.

FIGURE 2.23   The Visual Studio Toolbox configured for more screen real estate.

The Properties Window

It seems that with every new release and every new tool, programming becomes less and less about writing code and more and more about dragging, dropping, and configuring. The many tools, controls, and rich designers that free us from the repetitive code also now require our attention in the form of maintenance. This work is typically done through the manipulation of the literally hundreds of properties that work in concert to define our application. This is where the Properties window comes into play. It enables us to control the size, appearance, and behavior of our controls. Furthermore, the Properties window groups common properties into sets for easier access. Finally, the Properties window also gives us access to connecting the events for a given control to the code inside our application.

Figure 2.24 shows the Properties window (undocked from the IDE) for a web button control. Note that the window can group similar properties into sections via banded categories, such as Appearance. You can also list properties in alphabetic order by clicking the AZ icon on the Properties window toolbar. Another item worth noting is the lightning bolt icon also on the toolbar (C# only). This gives you access to the events for the given control. From the list of events, you can select an event and wire it to code in your project (or double-click it to generate an event handler).

FIGURE 2.24   The Properties window.

Managing the Many Windows of the IDE

To round out our whirlwind tour, we thought it important to provide you with guidance on customizing and managing the plethora of windows available within the IDE (lest they leave you with a postage-stamp-size window in which to write your code). To manage these windows, you really need to know only two skills: pinning and docking.

Pinning

Pinning refers to the process of making a window stick in the open position. It is called pinning in reference to the visual cue you use to perform the act: a pushpin. Pinning is a key concept because you sometimes want full-screen real estate for writing code or designing a form. In this case, you should unpin (auto hide) the various extraneous windows in your IDE. Note that when a window is unpinned, a vertical tab represents the window (see the highlighted Toolbox tab in Figure 2.25). Moving the mouse near this tab results in the window unfolding for your use. After you use it, however, it goes back to its hiding spot. Alternatively, you might be working to drop controls on a form. In doing so, you might want to pin (stick open) the Toolbox window (refer back to Figure 2.22).

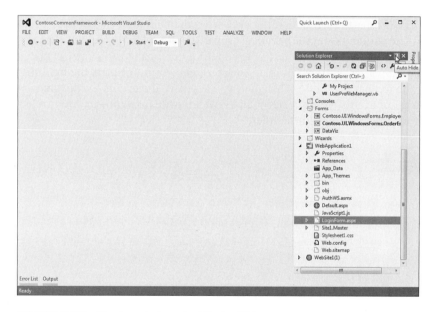

FIGURE 2.25   Pinning windows inside the IDE.

Docking

Docking is the process of connecting windows to various sticky spots within the IDE. Typically, this means docking to the left, top, right, or bottom of the IDE. For example, the Toolbox is, by default, docked to the left side of the IDE. You might prefer to put it at the bottom of the screen, docked below the active designer. You might also want to dock the Solution Explorer to the top of the screen and then unpin it for quick access. You can see an example of this docking approach in Figure 2.26.

You can also dock windows to one another. For example, you might want to dock the Properties window below the Solution Explorer. Or you might want the Properties window to be a tab within the same window to which the Solution Explorer is docked (see Figure 2.27).

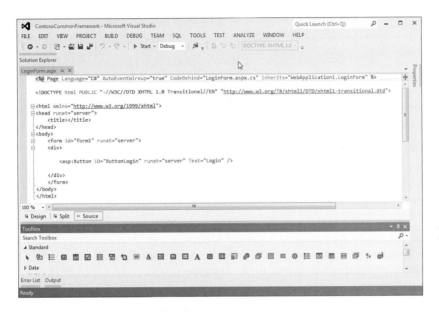

FIGURE 2.26   Horizontally docking windows in the IDE.

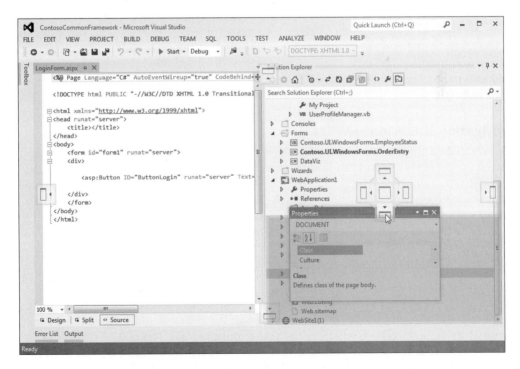

FIGURE 2.27   A window being docked to another window.

To help with docking, Visual Studio 2012 has provided visual cues and helpers. First, click and hold the title bar with the mouse, and then drag the window to where you want to dock it. Visual Studio displays some docking icons.

Four icons are at the edge of the IDE, one each at the left, top, right, and bottom. These icons are used for docking the window at the given edge of the IDE. Using these icons results in the window being docked across the full length (or width) of the IDE. Figure 2.27 shows each of these icons as the Properties window is being docked.

There is also an icon that shows over the top of a window to which you might want to dock. This icon is used for docking the selected window relative to another window in the IDE. For example, you might want to dock the Properties window under the Solution Explore window (as shown in Figure 2.27). You do so with the bottom icon inside this icon group.

Of course, you can also undock items. This is simply the process of floating windows off by themselves (outside, or on top of, the IDE). To do so, you simply grab (click with the mouse) a window by the title bar and move it off to the side of the IDE or just don't choose a docking icon.

Finally, when working with a window, you can right-click the title bar and tell Visual Studio how the window should behave. Figure 2.28 shows the available options. The down-arrow icon on the window provides access to the same features. The Float option indicates that the window floats wherever you put it, on top of the IDE. This can be useful if you find yourself moving windows about or need to use multiple monitors. You turn off this option by choosing Dock. You can also use the Dock as tabbed Document option to add a window to the center of your IDE (just like the default positioning of a designer or code editor).

Navigating IDE Windows

You can navigate open windows in the IDE without touching a mouse. This keeps your fingers on the keyboard and can lead to greater productivity. Visual Studio 2012 provides a couple of options here. The first is a simple window-switching hotkey. Suppose you have a number of code windows open in the IDE. To navigate forward (left to right) through them, you can use the key combination Ctrl+- (minus sign). This is for the standard development settings in the IDE; your settings might differ. To go backward (right to left), you use Ctrl+Shift+- (minus sign). This provides faster window switching without requiring that you scroll with the mouse or search through your solution.

You can get similar results using a visual aid called the IDE Navigator. This tool is similar to the Alt+Tab feature of Windows that allows for fast application switching. To access it, you use Ctrl+Tab (and Ctrl+Shift+Tab). You use this key combination to open the dialog box and navigate open code windows and active tool windows. Figure 2.29 shows the result. Notice that active files are cycled through on the right. You can jump between the active tools and active file lists using the right- and left-arrow keys.

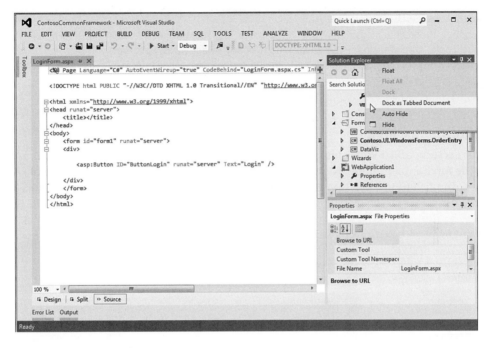

FIGURE 2.28   The IDE window options.

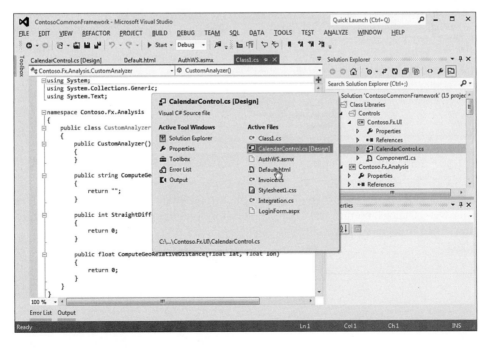

FIGURE 2.29   The IDE Navigator in action.

NOTE

To change the keyboard combinations assigned to the IDE navigator, select the menu option Tools, Options. Under the Environment node, select Keyboard. Here you can set keyboard shortcut keys. You should change the settings assigned to Window.NextDocumentWindowNav and Window.PreviousDocumentWindowNav.

Customize Your Font

There is a setting called Environment Font inside the Options dialog box (Tools menu) under the Environment node, Fonts and Colors. This option enables you to set the font for the entire IDE to the selection of your choice. Figure 2.30 shows selecting this option from the list.

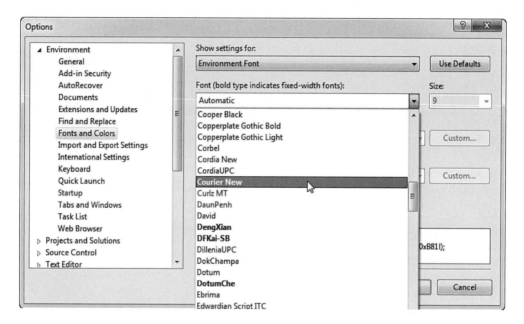

FIGURE 2.30   Setting the environment font.

Changing this font changes your IDE. For example, suppose you set the Environment Font to Courier New. Dialogs, menus, the Toolbox, Solution Explorer, and more change. Figure 2.31 shows the results of such a change.

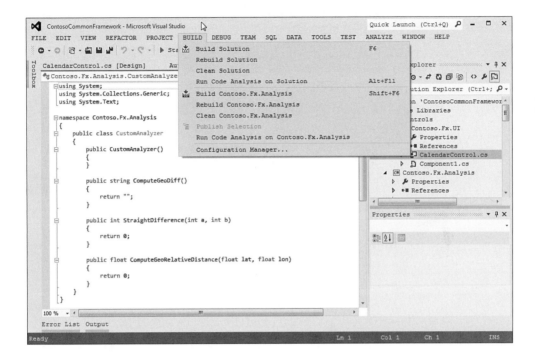

FIGURE 2.31   The IDE with a new font setting.

Summary

The whirlwind tour is over. We've covered the basics of installation, creating your first project, and the standard items you encounter when journeying out on your own. You should now be oriented to the basic set of menus, toolbars, settings, and window management inside Visual Studio. Now that you have your bearings, you can push onward.

CHAPTER 3

The .NET Languages

Unlocking the productivity promises of the Visual Studio IDE is at the heart of this book. The IDE, of course, also ships from Microsoft in concert with new versions of the .NET languages and Framework. You need to have a solid grasp of programming the Visual Basic or C# language using the .NET Framework to take advantage of everything Visual Studio has to offer.

In this chapter, we set aside the IDE (for the most part) and focus on the foundations of .NET programming. We start with a language primer on the basics; we then cover some more in-depth programming features and language-related IDE enhancements. The chapter concludes with an overview and map of the .NET Framework class library.

Language Primer

You have a few language choices available to you as a .NET programmer: Visual Basic, C#, C++, or F#. Which you choose is typically a result of your history, style, and intent. Developers who have worked with past incarnations of VB or another basic language will find they are at home inside Visual Basic. The language (including templates, tools, wizards, and so on) is all about developer productivity. Developers whose roots are in a C-based language (C++, Java, and so on) and want similar productivity in a straightforward way gravitate toward C#. Of course, some developers will just want to stay in C++ even for their .NET applications.

Visual Studio 2010 saw the introduction of the F# language. This language has been available in various states previously; however, it is now part of the full Visual Studio product line. Similar to other .NET languages, F# supports object-oriented programming. What makes it different is that it is also a functional programming language. Functional programming elevates functions to first-class values. (The *F* in F# is for functional.) For example, a functional language allows you to easily pass functions as parameters, return functions as the result of a function, chain functions together to create new functions, create recursive functions, and more. These powerful features in F# allow you to more easily tackle complex algorithms with less code (and often less pain) than it would take with the standard object-oriented (OO)-only languages of Visual Basic and C#. Having F# inside of Visual Studio also means that you can leverage the .NET Framework, get the benefits of the Common Language Runtime (CLR) (including calling to and from other .NET code), and have debugging and other related tools support.

NOTE

F# is both a new language and new way of programming. You need to spend time to be able to "think" in F#. There is not room in this book to present the language. In addition, most .NET developers still write most of their code in Visual Basic or C#. Therefore, we focus on those two languages throughout this book.

Programming Objects

Programming in .NET is an object-oriented experience. You write your own classes and leverage those created by Microsoft (forms, controls, and libraries). In fact, every .NET application has at least one class, and more often it has hundreds. You can extend classes with new functionality (inheritance), define classes based on a contract (interface), and override the behavior of existing classes (polymorphism). This section looks at defining objects with .NET code.

Classes

Think of classes as the container for your code. Classes define how you hold data (properties) and perform actions (methods); they communicate how your class works after it's created (instantiated). When you create an instance of the class, it is an object and can then actually maintain data and execute code.

You define a class using the `Class` keyword. The following shows an example:

C#

```
public class Employee
{
}
```

VB

```
Public Class Employee

End Class
```

Fields and Properties

You add code to a class to define its data and behavior. Data for your class can be stored in fields or properties. Fields and properties are similar; both define data that is contained in the class. The difference is that properties can provide a means to protect the access (setting and getting) to field data. Fields are typically private variables defined at the class level and are thus defined as follows:

C#

```
public class Employee
{
  private string _name;
}
```

VB

```
Public Class Employee
   Private _name As String
End Class
```

You can define public fields on your class. In this case, they are accessible members from the class. However, it is a best practice to encapsulate public data inside a property. This way you can control whether to expose the ability to read or write a property. You then also control the reading and writing of the data. Properties are typically backed by an internal, private field. This is called data hiding and is implemented with the `Private` keyword. For example, the previously defined field can be encapsulated into a property as follows:

C#

```
public class Employee
{
  private string _name;

  public string Name
  {
    get { return _name; }
    set { _name = value; }
  }
}
```

VB

```
Public Class Employee
    Private _name As String

    Public Property Name() As String
        Get
            Return _name
```

```
        End Get
        Set(ByVal value As String)
            _name = value
        End Set
    End Property
End Class
```

You can also create read-only properties. This is useful when you want to reserve the writing of the property's value to code running inside the class. You create a read-only property by not implementing the set statement in the property definition. In VB, you also have to add the ReadOnly keyword. For example, suppose you want to add an Id property to the Employee class defined previously. This Id can be read but only set by internal class code. You could implement a read-only property as follows:

C#

```
private int _id;

public int Id
{
  get { return _id; }
}
```

VB

```
Private _id As Integer
Public ReadOnly Property Id() As Integer
  Get
    Return _id
  End Get
End Property
```

Methods

Methods represent the blocks of code in your class that, when called, perform some specific action. This action could be reading or writing from a database, calling other methods, calculating a value, processing some business rules and returning a result, or whatever you need your code to do.

Methods are defined by their names and access levels; see the next section for more details on access levels. In VB, you also need to add the Sub keyword to define a method that does not return a value. In C#, this is done by indicating the return type of void before the method name. For example, if you were to add a Save method to the Employee class previously defined, the code would look like this:

C#

```csharp
public void Save()
{
  //implementation code goes here
}
```

VB

```vb
Public Sub Save()
  'implementation code goes here
End Sub
```

Methods often return values to the code that called the method. To define a method that returns a value, you must indicate the method's return type (the class type of the returned data). In VB, you also use the keyword Function (instead of Sub). You use the Return keyword to indicate the value to return from your code. For example, if you were to add a method to calculate an employee's remaining sick day, you would do so as follows:

C#

```csharp
public int GetRemainingSickDays()
{
  int _sickDays = 0;

  //calculate remaining sick days

  return _sickDays;
}
```

VB

```vb
Function GetRemainingSickDays() As Integer

  Dim _sickDays As Integer = 0

  'code to calculate remaining sick days

  Return _sickDays

End Function
```

In this example, note the return type defined in the method signature (first line of the method). Also note the use of the keyword Return to return a value from the method. In this case, that value is stored inside a variable defined as internal to the method.

Member Accessibility

The properties, fields, and methods in your application are referred to as class members. Each member in your class is defined to have a specific access level. As you've seen, if you want others to be able to access a member you must declare that member as public. If you want to reserve the member for accessibility only within the class, you declare it as private. These are two of the member accessibility levels available to you. The full complement of accessibility levels are described in Table 3.1.

TABLE 3.1   Member Accessibility Level in .NET

Level	Description
Public	Indicates that a member is publicly available to any code that has access to the class.
Private	Indicates that the member is hidden and private to the class that contains the member. No code outside the class can directly access members defined as private.
Protected	Protected is similar to private. It indicates that the member is not exposed publicly. Rather, it is private to the class. However, protected members are also made available to any class that derives from the class that contains the protected method. (See the "Inheritance" section for more details.)
Internal	Indicates that a member is available to all code within the assembly that contains it. This means other classes within a compiled .dll or .exe can access the member. However, other assemblies that reference a given .dll cannot access internal members.
Protected Internal	Indicates that the member is accessible by all code within an assembly and any code that derives from a class that contains the given member.

In addition to class-member accessibility, classes themselves also use the same accessibility levels. You can declare a class as public, private, protected, and so on to define your intended usage. You want to make many classes private or protected to the class and deriving types. The classes you make public define the functionality you want to expose to other code.

Constructors

A constructor is code that is called when a new instance of your class is created. This code is used to define how you want your class created, typically by setting default values or some related initialization code. You create a constructor as you would a method. The difference is that you give the constructor the same name as the class. The following code shows an example for the Employee class:

C#

```
public Employee()
{
  //init default values of an empty employee object
}
```

VB

```
Public Sub Employee()
  'init default values of an empty employee object
End Sub
```

A class can have multiple constructors to change the way in which the object is created. In these instances, each constructor is defined with a different set of parameters. The version of the constructor that does not take parameters is referred to as the default constructor. The following shows a couple additional constructors added to the `Employee` class. One initializes an `Employee` object based on the calling code passing in an `id` parameter; the other uses the employee's email address to initialize the object:

C#

```
public Employee(int id)
{
  //init default values for the employee defined by the given id
}

public Employee(string emailAddress)
{
  //init default values for the employee defined by the given email
}
```

VB

```
Public Sub Employee(ByVal id As Integer)
  'init default values for the employee defined by the given id
End Sub

Public Sub Employee(ByVal emailAddress As String)
  'init default values for the employee defined by the given email
End Sub
```

Static (Shared in VB) Members and Objects

Sometimes you do not want the full behavior of a class for all of your methods. Instead, you might want to define certain methods that are not part of an object. These methods often retrieve information or calculate values but are not part of a specific object. In these cases, you can create entire classes or just specific methods of a class as static (or shared in VB).

The `Shared` and `Static` keywords, when applied to a method, indicate that the method can be called without creating an instance of the class that contains it. `Shared` and `Static` can also be defined at the class level. In this case, you are indicating that the class only contains shared and static methods, and it cannot be created as an instance. For example, you might add a static helper method to the `Employee` class to check to see whether an employee is active in the system before you create an instance. This declaration would look like this:

C#

```csharp
public static bool IsActive(string emailAddress)
{
  //check to see if an employee has been added to the system
}
```

VB

```vb
Public Shared Function IsActive(ByVal emailAddress As String) As Boolean
  'check to see if an employee has been added to the system
End Function
```

Enumerations

Enumerations enable you to create a group of named values that help improve your code readability. Each item in an enumeration is a unique integer value. You can pass the enumeration value around as a name rather than an actual value. In this way, your code doesn't rely on arbitrary, "magic" numbers. Instead, the code is sensible and readable.

You create an enumeration using the enum keyword. For example, you might add an enumeration to the Employee class to store the employment status of an employee. This would enable you to make decisions in your code based on the specific status of an employee. To define this enumeration, you add code as follows to the Employee class:

C#

```csharp
enum EmploymentStatus
{
  Salaried,
  Hourly,
  Contract,
  Other
}
```

VB

```vb
Enum EmploymentStatus
  Salaried
  Hourly
  Contract
  Other
End Enum
```

Inheritance

You can define a new class based on an existing class, which is called inheritance. You use inheritance to extend (or add to) the functionality of a base class. Classes that that extend a base class are said to derive their functionality from another class. That is, they contain all the functionality of the base class plus any additional functionality added to the new class.

You indicate inheritance in VB by using the `Inherits` keyword; in C# you add a colon and the base class name following the name of the new class. For example, suppose you implement a `Manager` class that derives from `Employee`. The `Manager` class contains all the members of an `Employee` but might add special properties and methods specific to a `Manager`. You define this new class as follows:

C#

```
class Manager: Employee
{
}
```

VB

```
Public Class Manager
   Inherits Employee

End Class
```

Note that you can actually define a base class that cannot be created. Instead, it only exists to form the basis for a new class. Other classes can derive from it, but you cannot create a direct instance of just the base class. This is done by adding the `MustInherit` (VB) or `Abstract` (C#) keyword in front of the class definition. The keyword `NotInheritable` (VB) or `Sealed` (C#) indicates that the class cannot be used as the basis for a new class.

> **NOTE**
>
> .NET programmers can only derive from a single class. They cannot inherit from multiple base classes. However, they can implement multiple interfaces (as discussed next).

Overriding Behavior

When you design your classes, you might want to consider how other developers might extend them. That is, your classes might serve as the base class for future derived classes. If this is the case, you might also consider which (if any) features of your base class you want to allow a derived class to override. The derived class may then implement a new version of one of your base methods, for example. This process is often referred to as polymorphism in OO programming.

To change the data or behavior of a base class you can either add to the base class or you can override an existing member of the base class. Doing the latter gives you alternate behavior for the same function in your new class. You decide which members of your base class are available for override. You do so by marking them as virtual members; this indicates a derived class may fully replace your base class functionality.

For example, suppose that you want to enable the `CalculateYearlyCost` method of the `Employee` class to be overridden when the `Employee` is used as the base for the `Manager` class. In this case, the calculation for a `Manager` is different for that of an `Employee`. You therefore mark the method inside the `Employee` class as `virtual` (C#) or `Overridable` (VB), as follows:

C#

```
public class Employee
{
  public virtual float CalculateYearlyCost()
  {
  }
}
```

VB

```
Public Class Employee
    Public Overridable Function CalculateYearlyCost() As Single

    End Function
End Class
```

You can then override this method in the derived class. You do so using the `override` (C#) or `Overrides` (VB) keyword. You can still call the method on the base class if you need to by using the `base` (C#) or `MyBase` (VB) keyword. The following shows an example:

C#

```
class Manager : Employee
{
  public override float CalculateYearlyCost()
  {
    //add new functionality, access underlying method using base keyword
  }
}
```

VB

```
Public Class Manager
    Inherits Employee

    Public Overrides Function CalculateYearlyCost() As Single
```

```
    'add new functionality, access underlying method using MyBase
  End Function

End Class
```

Hiding Members

There is a second way you can override the functionality of a base class. This involves using the keyword new (C#) or Shadows (VB) to redefine the base method. Overriding in this manner hides the base class members. However, the base class member is still called if an instance of the derived class gets down-cast to an instance of the base class. This type of overriding is referred to as hiding by name. For example, you could replace the C# keyword override with new or the VB Overrides with Shadows to implement this type of behavior.

You need to be careful about hiding members versus overriding because down-casting can occur often. For example, you might be working with a collection of Employee objects (some of type Manager and some of type Employee). If you iterate over the list using the base class (for each employee), you get a different method called on the Manager class depending on if you hid the member (in which case, the base class method is called) or override the member (in which case, the derived class method is called).

Overloading Members

You can also create multiple versions of the same procedure. All versions of a procedure can be defined inside the same class or you can have a few versions in a base class and yet other versions in a derived class. This is useful when you need to preserve the name of the procedure but need to create different versions that each take different parameters. Creating multiple versions of a procedure is called overloading or hiding by signature (as in the method's calling signature).

Overloading a method must follow rules designed to make each overload somehow different from all the others. Of course, each overload has the same name. However, you must change either the number of parameters the method accepts, the data type of one or more of those parameters, or the order of the parameters. You create a valid overload by changing one or more of these items to make the overload signature unique. Note that changing the return type, if the method returns a value, or a parameter modifier is not sufficient to create an overload.

For example, suppose you were creating a method to return the number of vacation days left for an employee. You might allow the users of this method to get the vacation days left for the current year, a supplied month, or a supplied month and year. In this case, the users of your method see a single method with multiple overloads. You implement this overloading similar to the following code:

C#

```
public short GetVacationUsed()
{
  //returns all vacation used in the current year
```

```
}

public short GetVacationUsed(short monthNumber)
{
  //returns all vacation used in the given month of the current year
}

public short GetVacationUsed(short monthNumber, short year)
{
  //returns all vacation used in the given month and year
}
```

VB

```
Public Function GetVacationUsed() As Short
  'returns all vacation used in the current year
End Function

Public Function GetVacationUsed(ByVal monthNumber As Short) As Short
  'returns all vacation used in the given month of the current year
End Function

Public Function GetVacationUsed(ByVal monthNumber As Short, ByVal year As Short) _
  As Short
  'returns all vacation used in the given month and year
End Function
```

Defining Interface Contracts

An interface is used to define a class contract. An interface does not contain any actual functioning code. Rather, it indicates a common structure for code that can be implemented by another class. This enables you to create common contracts and use those contracts across multiple objects. You can then trust that each class that implements the interface does so completely and in the same manner.

An interface can define different types of class members including fields, properties, methods, events, and the like. To create an interface, you use the Interface keyword. For example, suppose you want to define a basic interface for a person. The Employee class might then be required to implement this interface. Other objects (such as User and Customer) might also implement the same interface. The following shows an example of how you might define this interface:

C#

```
interface IPerson
{
    string Name();
    DateTime DateOfBirth();
```

```
    string EyeColor();
    short HeightInInches();
}
```

VB

```
Public Interface IPerson

  Property Name As String
  Property DateOfBirth As DateTime
  Property EyeColor As String
  Property HeightInInches As Short
End Interface
```

You implement the interface by adding the interface to the class definition on the class where you intend to implement the interface. In VB, this is done by adding the `Implements` keyword under the class definition (similar to inheritance). In C#, you add the interface to the class definition the same way you would indicate a base class (using a colon). You can separate multiple implemented interfaces by a comma.

> **NOTE**
>
> You implement an interface when you want to define the structure of a base class but do not intend to implement any base functionality. If you have common base functionality for which you provide for extension, you should consider using inheritance.

Creating Structures

So far we have talked about programming classes. There is another type of class available to .NET programmers called a structure. Structures are similar to classes; they can contain properties, fields, enumerations, and methods; they can implement interfaces; they can have one or more constructors. The differences lie in how structures are managed by .NET.

Structures are considered value types. This means that when structures are used, the entire class is passed around as a value and not a reference. A class is a reference type. When you use a class and pass it around your application, you are actually passing a reference to a class. Not so with a structure. This also changes how .NET manages the memory used for structures and classes. Structures use stack allocation and classes are managed on the heap. To put this in perspective for .NET developers imagine you have an instance of an `Employee` class. This instance might be created inside one object and passed to another object's method. If the second object makes a change to the `Employee` instance, this change is reflected inside all objects that maintain a reference to the instance. If this were a structure, however, there would be copies of that object passed around, and changes would be isolated to each copy.

There are other differences between classes and structures. For one, structures cannot be inherited from. They also have an implicit public constructor that cannot be redefined. For these reasons, structures are best used when you need a lightweight container for data values and do not need the features of a reference type. Structures are often used to define custom data types.

You define a structure much like you define a class. In place of the `class` keyword, however, you use `struct` (C#) or `structure` (VB). For example, imagine you want to define a data type that represents a paycheck. You could create a structure to hold this information. The following shows an example:

C#

```
public struct PayCheck
{
  private double _amount;

  public double Amount
  {
    get { return _amount; }
  }

  //add additional structure elements ...
}
```

VB

```
Public Structure Paycheck

  Private _amount As Double
  Public ReadOnly Property Amount() As Double
    Get
      Return _amount
    End Get
  End Property

  'additional structure elements ...

End Structure
```

Organizing Your Code with Namespaces

A namespaces is used to group code that is specific to a company, an application, or a given library. Namespaces help .NET programmers overcome naming conflicts for classes and methods. For instance, you cannot have two classes with the same name in the same namespace because it would confuse the .NET runtime and developers. Instead, your class names are unique inside your namespace.

You declare a namespace at the top of your code using the keyword namespace. Alternatively, you can set the default namespace inside your project properties. In this way, you do not have to see the outer namespace definition inside each code file. A common practice for defining namespaces includes using your company name followed by the application being written and then perhaps the library to which the code belongs. For example, you might define the namespace grouping for the Employee class as follows:

C#

```
namespace MyCompany.MyApplication.UserLibrary
{
  public class Employee
  {
  }
}
```

VB

```
Namespace MyCompany.MyApplication.UserLibrary

  Public Class Employee

  End Class

End Namespace
```

You do not have to add this namespace information at the top of every code file in your project. This can become redundant and is error prone as a developer might forget to include the namespace definition. As an alternative, you can set the root namespace for your entire project using the project properties window (right-click the project file and choose Properties). Figure 3.1 shows an example. This is a similar experience in both C# and VB. Note that you can define a root namespace here and still add additional namespace groupings in your code as necessary. Of course, those additional namespace definitions fall inside the root namespace.

You access code inside a namespace by using the fully qualified definition of the namespace. For example, the .NET root namespace is System. If you were to access the String class, you would do so by calling System.String. This is true for your code, too. To access the GetVacationUsed method, you might call out as follows:

```
MyCompany.MyApplication.User.Employee.GetVacationUsed()
```

As you can see, accessing code using the fully qualified namespace can be cumbersome in terms of typing and reading your code. Thankfully, you can import (with the using statement in C#) a namespace inside your code. This frees you from having to fully qualify each type call. Instead, the compiler resolves class names based on your imported namespaces. Of course, the namespaces themselves are still required to prevent ambiguity in the compiler. Importing namespaces also help trim IntelliSense to those imported libraries.

In most cases, you do not get conflicts with imported namespaces. Type names are typically different enough in a given library that they do not overlap. If names do overlap, you can add qualification to eliminate the conflict.

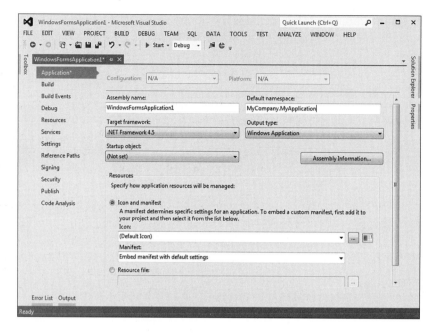

FIGURE 3.1   Setting the root namespace at the project level.

You import namespaces using the `using` statement (C#) or `imports` (VB) keyword. For example, the following shows namespaces imported into a class file for a Windows Forms application. The code includes the `import` statements for referencing the `Employee` class library:

C#

```
using System;
using System.Collections.Generic;
using System.ComponentModel;
using System.Data;
using System.Drawing;
using System.Linq;
using System.Text;
using System.Windows.Forms;
using MyCompany.MyApplication.UserLibrary;

namespace TestHarnessCSharp
{
  public partial class Form1 : Form
  {
    public Form1()
    {
```

```
      InitializeComponent();
    }

    private void Form1_Load(object sender, EventArgs e)
    {
      Employee emp = new Employee();
      //do work
    }
  }
}
```

VB

```
Imports MyCompany.MyApplication.UserLibrary

Public Class Form1

  Private Sub Form1_Load(ByVal sender As System.Object, _
    ByVal e As System.EventArgs) Handles MyBase.Load

    Dim emp As New Employee()
    'do work ...

  End Sub

End Class
```

Notice in the preceding example that the C# code has a number of additional `using` (or `imports`) statements at the top of the file. This is because VB files automatically import many of the default namespaces in .NET.

Types, Variables, and Constants

All classes and interfaces you create in .NET are considered types. That is, they define a specific type of data. The underlying classes in the .NET Framework are also all strong types. In fact, the .NET languages of both C# and VB are based on strongly typed objects. This means when you define a variable you create an instance of a strongly typed class. The .NET runtime can then rely on this type information for handling casting, comparisons, and other rules.

Data Types

A number of built-in types (classes) are used for common programming needs. These built-in types are referred to as data types and represent things such as a string of characters or a numeric value. You work with these data types like you would any structure or class. You can declare a variable of a certain type, create a new instance, or execute a method off of the type.

Most of the simple data types you use are value types (structures). There are a couple reference data types (classes). These are string (System.String) and object (System.Object). Recall that value types store data (and copies of data) and that reference types are used to provide a reference to underlying data. Table 3.2 lists many of the common value types used in .NET programming; there are more than what is in this list. The list shows the underlying .NET Framework class, the range allowed in the data type, and the C# and VB data type names.

TABLE 3.2   Value Data Types by Language

.NET Framework	C# Data Type	VB Data Type	Range
System.Byte	byte	Byte	0 to 255
System.Int16	short	Short	-32,768 to 32,767
System.Int32	int	Integer	-2,147,483,648 to 2,147,483,647
System.Int64	long	Long	−9,223,372,036,854,775,808 to 9,223,372,036,854,775,807
System.Single	float	Single	$\pm 1.5 \cdot 10{-}45$ to $\pm 3.4 \cdot 1038$
System.Double	double	Double	$\pm 5.0 \cdot 10{-}324$ to $\pm 1.7 \cdot 10308$
System.Decimal	decimal	Decimal	$\pm 1.0 \cdot 10{-}28$ to $\pm 7.9 \cdot 1028$
System.Boolean	bool	Boolean	true or false

Many of the data types listed in Table 3.2 include unsigned versions. These are preceded with a *u*. The System.Byte data type is the exception. It is unsigned. The signed version is called sbyte. Signed values include both the negative and positive numbers in their range. Unsigned value types start and zero and include only positive numeric values.

Declaring Variables

When you declare a variable using a simple type, you typically want to declare the variable using the type that represents the lowest possible range for your situation. For example, if you were to define a variable to hold the month value you might use System.Byte. If you were to define the year, you might use System.Int16. In this way, the lowest possible overhead is used for these types.

You declare a variable in C# by preceding the name of the variable with its type. In VB, you use the Dim statement. The type then comes after the variable's name. The following code shows an example of declaring variables in each language:

C#

```
byte month;
short year;
float paycheckAmount;
```

VB

```
Dim month As Byte
Dim year As Short
Dim paycheckAmount As Single
```

Of course, you can also define variables of other (more complex) types in the .NET Framework or types defined in your own class libraries. When you declare a variable, you can also assign it a default value or instantiate a new instance. The following shows an example:

C#

```
byte month = 1;
short year = 2010;
float paycheckAmount = 0;
string name = "test";
Employee emp = new Employee();
```

VB

```
Dim month As Byte = 1
Dim year As Short = 2010
Dim paycheckAmount As Single = 0
Dim name As String = "test"
Dim emp As Employee = New Employee()
```

Type Conversion

Again, both VB and C# are strongly typed languages. Therefore, the variables you declare cannot be reused by assigning different type values. Rather, they must always represent the underlying type to which they were declared. This can be problematic. Sometimes, for instance, you have an integer that you need to pass to a method that only accepts a double. Or you need to parse a string value into an integer for a calculation. You might also have to convert a class to an interface type in order to use it with a specific method. These are all instances where you need to convert one type to another.

There are two conversions that you can make: implicit and explicit. An implicit conversion happens when you pass a smaller value type into a larger type that can contain the smaller value. In this case, if no data is lost the conversion is allowed. For example, you can pass a short into a long without issue. However, passing a float (or double) into an integer might result in data loss and is thus not allowed as an implicit conversion; you need to explicitly convert. For example, the following code converts an integer value to a double. This code does not throw a type conversion error. Rather, it converts using implicit conversion:

```
ıntVal = 100;
ɔuble doubleVal = intVal;
```

VB

```
Dim intVal As Integer = 100
Dim doubleVal As Double = intVal
```

If there is a chance that the conversion results in data loss, you must explicitly indicate your intention to convert types. This is called casting. You can also cast values that might otherwise be implicitly converted. In fact, this often makes your code more readable.

In C#, you cast a variable to another type by putting the type to which you are casting in parentheses in front of the type (or value) being cast as in the following:

C#

```
double doubleVal = 12.345;
int intVal = (int)doubleVal;
```

In VB, you cast a variable to another type using conversion keywords. These keywords have a *C* (for cast) in front of them followed by the type to which you are casting. For example, you can cast to an integer using `CInt`, or a double using `CDbl`, or a string using `CStr`. The following shows an example:

VB

```
Dim doubleVal As Double = 12.345
Dim intVal As Integer = CInt(doubleVal)
```

There are times when you have a string value and need to convert it into a numeric. This cast is not allowed. However, most of the numeric types include the method `Parse` that enables you to parse a string into a numeric value. There is also `TryParse` that returns a Boolean indicating whether the parse will work. The following code shows an example:

C#

```
string stringVal = "1234";
int intVal;
intVal = int.Parse(stringVal);
```

VB

```
Dim stringVal As String = "1234"
Dim intVal As Integer
intVal = Integer.Parse(stringVal)
```

The framework also includes the `Convert` class that enables you to convert one type to almost any other (including strings). This class is available to both VB and C# programmers.

Defining Constants

You might need to define values in your application that will not (and cannot) change during the execution of the application. In this case, you need to declare a constant. A constant in .NET is said to be an immutable value. That is, they cannot change values. You declare a constant in your code (typically at the class level) using the keyword, const. Like fields, they can be private or public. The following shows an example:

C#

```
private const int CompanyTaxNumber = 123456;
```

VB

```
Private Const CompanyTaxNumber As Integer = 123456
```

Understanding Operators

Operators are indicators in your code that express an operation to perform. An operator might be an assignment from one variable to another, a comparison between two values, or a mathematical calculation among values. There are many operators available to .NET programmers. We do not cover them all here, but many of the more common operators are discussed in the following sections.

Assignment

Assignment operators are used to assign one variable or value to another. The most simple example is the equal (=) operator. This simply assigns the value on the right of the operator to the variable on the left side of the assignment (as in x = y). Other operators enable you to do assignment with addition (+=), assignment with subtraction (-=), assignment with multiplication (*=), and assignment of a string value with concatenation (&=). There are also assignment operators for division, arithmetic shifting, and more. The following shows a few assignment code examples:

C#

```
public double CalculatePaycheck(double gross, double commission,
  double deductions)
{
  double paycheck = gross;   //define paycheck as gross pay
  paycheck += commission;    //add commission
  paycheck -= deductions;    //subtract deductions

  return paycheck;
}
```

```
  ᷄c Function CalculatePaycheck(ByVal gross As Double, _
ByVal commission As Double, ByVal deductions As Double)

  Dim paycheck As Double = gross    'define paycheck as gross pay
  paycheck += commission            'add commission
  paycheck -= deductions            'subtract deductions

  Return paycheck
End Function
```

Arithmetic

The arithmetic operations enable you to perform calculations on variables and using values. For example, you can use the multiplication operator (*) to multiply two numbers (x * y). The operators you expect are all available, such as addition (+), subtraction (-), division to return an integer (\), division to return a floating point (/), multiplication (*), and dividing for remainder (mod in VB, % in C#). There are other less-common operators, too.

You typically use assignment with arithmetic operators, as in x = y * z. However, you can use the value of the calculation when making decisions in your code (without first assigning it to a variable); there's more on this in the coming sections. As an example of basic arithmetic in code with assignment, the following code shows how you might calculate an employee's accrued vacations days at the given point in the year. (The AccrualRate is either a constant or set based on the number of days of vacation an employee has.)

C#

```
double accruedVacation = DateTime.Today.DayOfYear * AccrualRate;
```

VB

```
Dim accruedVacation as Double = DateTime.Today.DayOfYear * AccrualRate
```

Comparison

The comparison operators enable you to determine whether values are equal to one another, greater than, or less than. You typically use these operators comparing two variables, values, or expressions. The results of the comparison indicate whether or not (true or false) the comparison is valid (as in is x > y). The comparison operators include less than (<), less than or equal to (<=), greater than (>), greater than or equal to (>=), equal (= in VB and == in C#), and does not equal (<> in VB and != in C#). The following shows an example of assigning a variable of type Boolean to a comparison result:

C#

```
bool check = accruedVacation > vacationTakenToDate;
```

VB

```
Dim check As Boolean = accruedVacation > vacationTakenToDate
```

You can also do type comparison to check to see whether two objects point to the same reference (or not). In C#, this type of comparison is still done with the equal (=) and not equal (!=) operators. In VB, you use the keywords Is and IsNot, as in check = Employee1 Is Employee2.

Concatenation

The concatenation operations enable you to combine string values. In VB, the concatenation operator is an ampersand (&) sign used with two string variables or values. In C#, the plus (+) sign is used. The following shows an example:

C#

```
string fullName = firstName + " " + lastName;
```

VB

```
Dim fullName as String = firstName & " " & lastName
```

Logical and Conditional

The logical and conditional operators enable you to combine comparisons in different ways to help make decisions in your code. (See the next section for even more details.) For example, you might combine two comparisons to make sure they are both true. Alternatively, you might need to determine if at least one of the two comparisons is true. You can do this and more with the logical operators. Table 3.3 lists many of the logical operators. (For code examples, see the next section.)

TABLE 3.3   Logical and Conditional Comparison Operators

Purpose	C#	VB	Pseudo Code Example
Join two Boolean expressions and get the result, as in result is true if both this and that are true.	&	And	VB: check = (x>Y) And (x>0) C#: check = (x>Y) && (x>0)
Negate a Boolean value or expression, as in results equal the opposite of an evaluation.	!	Not	VB: check = Not someVal C#: check = !someVal
Choose between one or another values, as in result is true if that or that is true.	|	Or	VB: check = (x>y) Or (x>0) C#: check = (x>y) | (x>0)
Two values must evaluate to opposite values, as in result is true if this is true and that is false.	^	Xor	VB: check = True Xor False C#: check = true ^ false

	C#	VB	Pseudo Code Example
...ort-circuited version of And ...here if the first condition does not pass evaluation, the second condition does not get executed.	&&	AndAlso	VB: `check = (x>Y) AndAlso (x>0)` C#: `check = (x>Y) && (x>0)`
A short-circuited version of Or where if the first condition does not pass evaluation, then the second condition does not get executed.	||	OrElse	VB: `check = (x>y) OrElse (x>0)` C#: `check = (x>y) | (x>0)`

Making Decisions and Branching Code

You can use the operators discussed previously to test for specific conditions in your code. These tests are then evaluated in order to make a decision on what code to execute or where to branch off in your application. There are three primary decision structures in .NET programming: If...Then...Else, Select...Case, and Try...Catch...Finally (as covered in the "Handling Errors" section later in this chapter).

If...Then...Else

You can use the If syntax in your code to test one or more conditions. Based on the results of your test, you might decide to execute one set of code if the condition proves true and another set of code if the condition proves false. You can also get into more complex scenarios by nesting If statements and using the logical operators discussed in the prior section.

In VB, you use the explicit `If...Then` statements nested with `End If`. In C#, you put your If conditions inside parentheses and the statements nested inside brackets. For example, the following shows code to determine whether an employee can get her vacation request approved. In this code, there is a nested if statement and an example of combining two conditions with and:

C#

```csharp
public bool CanApproveVacationRequest(int daysRequested, int daysTaken,
  int daysAllowed, int daysAccruedToDate)
{
  //rule: employee can take vacation if it is accrued and not used
  if ((daysRequested < daysAllowed) & (daysTaken < daysAllowed))
  {
    if ((daysTaken + daysRequested) < daysAccruedToDate)
    {
      return true;
    } else {
      return false;
    }
```

```
  } else {
    return false;
  }
}
```

VB

```
Public Function CanApproveVacationRequest(ByVal daysRequested As Integer,
  ByVal daysTaken As Integer, ByVal daysAllowed As Integer,
  ByVal daysAccruedToDate As Integer) As Boolean

  'rule: employee can take vacation if it is accrued and not used
  If daysRequested < daysAllowed And daysTaken < daysAllowed Then
    If (daysTaken + daysRequested) < daysAccruedToDate Then
      Return True
    Else
      Return False
    End If
  Else
    Return False
  End If
End Function
```

Note that in VB if you have a single line that executes based on an if condition you can write that as a single line of code, as in If x > 500 Then doSomething. In C#, if you have a single line that executes, you can eliminate the need for the braces, and the statement following the If condition is executed based on the condition's evaluation.

Select...Case (Switch)

The Select...Case (switch in C#) code construct enables you to evaluate a single statement for a value. Based on this condition, you then can execute blocks of code depending on the value.

In C#, you define the condition inside parentheses following the keyword switch. You then define each case block with the keyword case, the value you are checking on, and a colon. You must then add a break statement at the end of the case to indicate the end of the case. You can use the default keyword to execute code if no case was realized. The following code shows an example:

C#

```
private void CalculateAdditionalCompensation()
{
  switch (this.Status)
  {
    case EmploymentStatus.Contract:
      //code for contract employees
      break;
```

```
    case EmploymentStatus.Hourly:
      //code for hourly employees
      break;
    case EmploymentStatus.Salaried:
      //code for salaried employees
      break;
    case EmploymentStatus.SalariedCommissioned:
      //code for commissioned employees
      break;
    case EmploymentStatus.Other:
      //code for other employees
      break;
    default:
      //code that runs if bad status was set
      break;
  }
}
```

In VB, you write case Select...Case statements using the keyword Select followed by Case followed by the condition. Each condition is then preceded with Case. You can use Case Else to run code when no other condition value evaluates. Here is a code example:

VB

```
Private Sub CalculateAdditionalCompensation()

  Select Case Me.Status
    Case EmploymentStatus.Contract
      'code for contract employees

    Case EmploymentStatus.Hourly
      'code for hourly employees

    Case EmploymentStatus.Salaried
      'code for salaried employees

    Case EmploymentStatus.SalariedCommissioned
      'code for commissioned employees

    Case EmploymentStatus.Other
      'code for other employees

    Case Else
      'code that runs if bad status was set

  End Select

End Sub
```

Looping

There are many times in your code when you need to execute a set of statements more than once. In these cases, you need to create a loop. The most common scenarios are looping through code a set number of times, looping until a condition becomes true or false, or looping through code once per element in a collection of objects. (See the section "Working with Groups of Items" later in this chapter.)

For...Next

The For...Next construct enables you to execute a block of code statements a set number of times. This is accomplished through a counter that increments a set number of steps each time the loop executes. After the counter has reached a max value, the looping completes.

In C#, you write a `for` statement inside parentheses. The `for` statement has three parts: counter declaration, condition for the counter, and counting step. Each part is separated by a semicolon. The following code shows an example of executing a code block once for each employee's direct report:

C#

```
for (int i = 0; i < numDirectReports; i++)
{
  //update employee based on num of direct report
}
```

In VB, your `For` statement is a little more readable. You indicate the counter, the initial value, and the `To` value. Optionally, you can add the `Step` keyword to indicate how many times you want to increment the counter each time through the loop. Here is a code example:

VB

```
For i As Integer = 1 To numDirectReports
  'update employee based on num of direct reports
Next
```

For...Each (Iterators)

Like For...Next, the For...Each construct enables you to execute a group of statements. However, For...Each executes once for each element in a group of elements (or a collection). For instance, if you add a block of code to the `Employee` class that needs to execute once for each `DirectReport` you could do so using the For...Next (as shown previously) and the execute based on the count of `DirectReports`. However, using For...Each allows you to iterate over each object in a collection. As you do, you get a reference to the given object that you can use in your code. This makes coding a little easier to write and to understand.

You implement For...Each similar as For...Next in both C# and VB. The following shows code that executes once for each `Employee` instance inside the collection `DirectReports`:

C#

```
foreach (Employee emp in DirectReports)
{
  //execute code based on each direct report
  //  using the item as in emp.Name
}
```

VB

```
For Each emp As Employee In DirectReports
  'execute code based on each direct report
  '  using the item as in emp.Name
Next
```

Do...While/Until

Sometimes you need to repeat a block of code as many times as required until a condition evaluates to `true` or `false`. You might be looking for a specific value or might be using a counter that increments based on logic (instead of standard steps). In these cases, you can use a Do...While or a `While` loop. A Do...While loop executes once before the condition is evaluated to determine whether it should execute a second time. A `While` loop evaluates the condition first and then only executes if the condition evaluates to `true`.

In C#, you can create Do...While loops using the `do` keyword followed by your block of code in braces. The `while` statement is written at the end of the code block indicating that the statements are executed once before looping. (Use a `while` loop to evaluate a condition before looping.) The following shows an example:

C#

```
do
{
  //get next project and calculate commission
  projectCommission = GetNextProjectCommision(empId);
  calculatedCommission += projectCommission;
  if (projectCommission == 0)
  break;
} while (calculatedCommission < MaxMonthlyCommission);
```

Notice in this code the use of the `break` keyword. This indicates that the code should break out of the Do...While loop. You can also use the `continue` keyword to skip remaining code in your code block and jump right to the `while` statement to force a condition evaluation (and possible another loop).

In VB, you can define the `while` (or `until`) statement at the top or bottom of the loop. If defined at the top, your statement is evaluated before the loop executes once. If at the bottom, the loop executes at least once before the statement is evaluated. The `While` keyword indicates that you want to loop while a condition is `true` (until it becomes `false`). The `Until` keyword allows you to loop until a condition evaluates to `true` (while it is `false`). The following shows an example:

VB

```
Do
  'get next project and calculate commission
  projectCommission = GetNextProjectCommision(empId)
  calculatedCommission += projectCommission
  If projectCommission = 0 Then Exit Do
Loop While calculatedCommission < MaxMonthlyCommission
```

As mentioned before, there is also the basic `While` loop (without `do`). This simply loops a block of code while a condition evaluates to true. Also, like all looping constructs, you can nest Do...While loops to handle more complex situations.

Working with Groups of Items

A common scenario in computer programming is managing a group of similar items. For example, you might need to work with a set of values, such as ZIP Codes to which a sales representative is assigned. Alternatively, you might need to work with a group of objects such as the paychecks an employee has received in a given year. In cases where you need to work with a group of elements, you can do so using an array or a collection class. The former is great for working with a set sequential list of items of the same type. The latter is more applicable for managing a variable-sized group of objects.

Arrays

An array is a group of items of the same type (either value or reference types). For instance, you might create an array that contains all integer values or all string values. You also have to define the number of elements contained in your array when you first initialize it. There are ways to expand or contract this size, but these typically involve copying the array into another array. If you need the flexibility of adding and removing items in a group, you want to use a collection class and not an array.

When you define an array's size, you need to know that they are zero-based arrays. That is, the first element in the array is item zero. Therefore, if you dimension an array as `myArray(6)`, it contains seven items (0 through 6). Each item is contiguous and sequential. This enables you to set and access items quickly using the items index.

The typical array you create is one dimensional, meaning that it contains a single group of indexed items. You declare this type of an array by indicating the number of elements in the array either on the declaration of the variable or before the array's first use. There are a few valid syntaxes for defining an array. The standard way in C# is to use the `new` keyword to set the size of the array. In VB, you can set the size of the array without using the keyword `new`. The following shows an example:

C#

```
short[] salesRegionCodes = new short[numRegions];
```

VB

```
Dim salesRegionCodes(numRegions) As Short
```

You access an array through its index value. Array objects inherit for the `System.Array` class. This gives you a number of properties and methods you can use including getting the type of values in the array (`GetType`), getting the total number of elements in all dimensions of an array (`Length`), and getting the upper-bound value for a single dimension (`GetUpperBound`). The following code shows an example of using this last method and accessing an array through its index:

C#

```
for (int i = 0; i < salesRegionCodes.GetUpperBound(0); i++)
{
  short code = salesRegionCodes[i];
  //additional processing ...
}
```

VB

```
For i = 0 To salesRegionCodes.GetUpperBound(0)

  Dim code As Short = salesRegionCodes(i)
  'additional processing ...
Next
```

You can also initialize the values in an array inside the declaration statement. In this case, the number of elements you define sets the size of the array. The following is an example:

C#

```
double[] salesFigures = new double[] {12345.98, 236789.86, 67854.12};
```

VB

```
Dim salesFigures() As Double = {12345.98, 236789.86, 67854.12}
```

You can define arrays that have more than a single dimension (up to 32). A common scenario is a two-dimensional array where one dimension is considered rows and the other columns. You can use the `Rank` property to determine the number of dimensions in an array.

For example of a multidimensional array, consider one that contains sales figures for each sales representative (rows) in each region (columns). You might define this array as follows:

C#

```
double[,] salesByRegion = new double[6, 5];
```

VB

```
Dim salesByRegion(6, 5) As Double
```

Note that an array can also contain other arrays. These type of arrays are called jagged arrays (or arrays of arrays). They are considered jagged because each element in the array might contain an array of different size and dimension; therefore, there might be no real uniformity to the array.

Collection Classes and Generics

A collection class can give you more flexibility when working with objects. For example you can have objects of different types in a single collection; collections can be of varying lengths; you can easily add and remove items in a collection.

The standard collection classes are defined inside the System.Collections namespace. The classes in this namespace include a base class for creating your own, custom collections (CollectionBase), and more specific collections such as ArrayList, Stack, SortedList, Queue, and HashTable.

For example, you might create a simple, dynamic ArrayList to contain a set of sales figures. The following code shows how you can create a new ArrayList, add items to it, and loop through those items:

C#

```
ArrayList salesFigures = new ArrayList();

salesFigures.Add(12345.67);
salesFigures.Add(3424.97);
salesFigures.Add("None");

for (int i = 0; i < salesFigures.Count; i++)
{
  object figure = salesFigures[i];
  //process figures ...
}
```

VB

```
Dim salesFigures As New ArrayList()

salesFigures.Add(12345.67)
salesFigures.Add(3424.97)
salesFigures.Add("None")
```

```
For i As Integer = 0 To salesFigures.Count - 1
 Dim figure As Object = salesFigures(i)
  'process sales figure data ...
Next
```

Of course, many additional properties and methods are available to you through the `ArrayList` and related collection classes. You should explore these for your specific scenarios.

Notice in the preceding code that the collection class has two types of objects inside it: double and string. This can be problematic if you need to rely on a collection of objects all being of the same type. For example, you might want all your sales figures to be of type double; or you might want a collection of only `Employee` objects. In these cases, you need a strongly typed collection class. You can create these by coding your own, custom collection classes (inheriting from `CollectionBase` and implementing the interfaces specific to your needs). However, .NET also provides a set of classes called generics that allow for strongly typed groups of objects.

Generic collections can be found inside the `System.Collections.Generic` namespace. A generic collection class enables you to define the type that the class contains when you initialize it. This then restricts what types the class can contain. You can rely on this information within your code.

You define a generic list in C# using angle brackets (<>) with the type defined inside those brackets. In VB, you define the generic type inside parenthesis using the `Of` keyword. For example, the following defines a simple, generic list of items that can only include values of type double:

C#

```
List<double> salesFigures = new List<double>();
```

VB

```
Dim salesFigures As New List(Of Double)
```

There are many generic collection classes available to you, including `Dictionary`, `HashSet`, `LinkedList`, `List`, `Queue`, `SortedList`, `Stack`, and more. You can also write your own generic collection classes.

Tuples

The `System.Tuple` class enables you to create a set, ordered list of items and work with that list. After you've created the list, the list cannot be changed. This makes for easy storage (and access) of sequential items.

For example, if you wanted to create a `Tuple` to store the month names in the first quarter you could do so using the static member `Tuple.Create`. Each item you want to add to the list you add inside parentheses (and separated by commas). You can then access the items in your `Tuple` using the `Item1`, `Item2`, `Item3` syntax. Note that the `Tuple` only exposes item properties for the number of items that exist inside the group. The following code shows an example:

C#

```
var q1Months = Tuple.Create("Jan", "Feb", "Mar");
string month1 = q1Months.Item1;
```

VB

```
Dim q1Months = Tuple.Create("Jan", "Feb", "Mar")
Dim month1 As String = q1Months.Item1
```

The `Tuple` class is based on generics. You define the type of object you enable for each member in the list. The `Create` method shown infers this type for you. However, you might want to be explicit. In this case, you can declare your types using the constructor as follows:

C#

```
Tuple<int, string, int, string, int, string> q1MonthNumAndName =
        Tuple.Create(1, "Jan", 2, "Feb", 3, "Mar");
```

VB

```
Dim q1MonthNumAndName As Tuple(Of Integer, String, Integer, String,
                               Integer, String) =
  Tuple.Create(1, "Jan", 2, "Feb", 3, "Mar")
```

Programming with Attributes

Sometimes you need to provide metadata about the capabilities of your code. This metadata is meant to tell other code that is inspecting your code (through reflection) specific things about what the code might do. This includes information for the .NET runtime such as how you want your code compiled. There are many attributes available in the .NET Framework. You can also create your own, custom attributes to be applied to your code. In this case, you can write code to examine the metadata about your own application.

Declarative attributes can be applied to classes, properties, methods, parameters, and other elements inside your code. You can apply a single attribute or multiple attributes to an application. Some attributes also might take parameters to indicate additional information to the attribute code.

Note that by convention all attributes end with the word `Attribute` in their names, such as `SerializableAttribute`. You typically leave the word *attribute* off your declaration, however, as it is not required.

In C#, attributes are placed on code using square brackets ([]). For example, you can use the `ConditionalAttribute` to indicate to the compiler which code should be compiled based on environment variables or command-line options. You would apply this attribute to your code as shown:

C#

```
[System.Diagnostics.Conditional("DEBUG")]
public void EmployeeCalculationsTestMethod()
{
  //code that compiles in the debug version of the assembly
}
```

In VB, you decorate your code elements with an attribute by putting the attribute in angle brackets (<>) in front of the code element, as follows:

VB

```
<Conditional("DEBUG")> Public Sub EmployeeCalculationsTestMethod()
  'code that compiles in the debug version of the assembly
End Sub
```

Exception Handling

A lot of programming time is spent eliminating exceptions from our code. However, you can't always eliminate all scenarios that might cause an exception. In these cases, you need a way to anticipate the exception and then, if possible, handle the exception in your code. There is where the Try...Catch...Finally construct comes into play.

You put a Try statement around a block of code you expect might cause an exception. You typically do so if you intend to handle the error. If you are not intending to handle the error, you can let the error bubble up to the calling code. Of course, you need to have an outer-error handler (or manager) inside your outer code to prevent errors from bubbling up to users in nasty ways.

When an exception actually occurs inside your Try block, execution is immediately passed to a Catch block. This might be a general catch of all errors or a catch meant for a specific exception type. The code inside the catch block is then meant to handle the error. Handling an error might include logging the error, sending it to a message system, or actually trying something different (or trying again using a jump statement) as the result of the error.

The following shows a basic example. Inside the Try block is a calculation that does division. This Try block has the possibility of raising an exception in the case where the division is done by zero. This condition raises the specific exception DivideByZeroException. There is a Catch block that consumes this (and only this) type of exception. You can add code to the Catch block to either eat the exception (do nothing) or process it somehow. Also, if you want to rethrow the exception after handling it, you can do that, too:

C#

```
try
{
  averageSales = salesToDate / avgRate;
}
catch (System.DivideByZeroException e)
{
  //handle the exception ...
  // if re-throwing use: throw e;
}
```

VB

```
Try
  averageSales = salesToDate / avgRate

Catch ex As System.DivideByZeroException
  'handle the exception ...
  ' if re-throwing use: Throw ex
End Try
```

You can have multiple catch blocks be both specific and generic. Note that if no exception type is found in a catch block, the exception is actually not handled but gets bubbled up to the calling code (or to the runtime).

Note that you can also rethrow the error from your catch block using the Throw keyword. If you do not rethrow the exception, the runtime assumes you have handled the error and moves on. You can also use throw anywhere in your application where you want to raise an exception.

There is also a Finally block that you can write. This bit of code goes after your catch blocks. It runs regardless of whether an exception is raised. It is useful for cleaning up any resources that might have been allocated inside the Try block.

Creating and Raising Events

There is not much functionality you can build using the .NET languages without events. Events enable one piece of code to notify another bit of code that something has just happened. Code that raises events are said to publish an event and those that receive the event notice are said to subscribe to events. A simple example is when you write a user interface for the Web or Windows. In these cases, you are consistently adding code that subscribes to events published by the UI such as a user clicking a button control. Of course, an event may have more than a single subscriber and subscribers may be subscribed to multiple events.

Create an Event

When you create an event you need to determine whether you need to pass custom data to the subscribers. This custom data is referred to as event arguments (or args). If you do not need to pass custom data, you simply declare the event using the keyword event and the existing delegate EventHandler. For example, if you were to define a simple event that you would raise when an employee class is updated, you might define that event as follows:

C#

```csharp
public event EventHandler RaiseEmployeeUpdatedEvent;
```

VB

```vb
Public Event RaiseEmployeeUpdatedEvent As EventHandler
```

By declaring the event, you have effectively published it. Subscribers that have a reference to your class can then set up a subscription to your event. You then need to raise the event in the same class where you published it. This notifies the subscribers that the event has fired.

It is slightly more complicated to define events where you need to pass custom data. In this case, you must first create a custom class to maintain your event data. This class must inherit from the EventArgs base class. For example, you might create a custom event arguments class to contain the employee ID for the employee-updated event. In this case, your custom class contains a property to hold the Id value and a constructor for passing in this value, as in the following code:

C#

```csharp
public class EmployeeUpdatedEventArgs : EventArgs
{
  public EmployeeUpdatedEventArgs(string id)
  {
    _id = id;
  }

  private string _id;
  public string EmployeeId
  {
    get { return _id; }
  }
}
```

VB

```vb
Public Class EmployeeUpdatedEventArgs
  Inherits EventArgs
```

```
Public Sub New(ByVal id As String)
  _id = id
End Sub

Private _id As String
Public ReadOnly Property EmployeeId() As String
  Get
    Return _id
  End Get
End Property

End Class
```

When you use a custom event argument, you need to declare your event to use the custom event argument class. You can do so using the version of the EventHandler class that is defined as a generic. In this case, you indicate the class that contains the argument as part of the generic definition of EventHandler. This class also automatically contains the sender argument (typically a copy of the object publishing the event). The following shows an example of defining this custom event handler:

C#

```
public event EventHandler<EmployeeUpdatedEventArgs> RaiseEmployeeUpdatedCustomEvent;
```

VB

```
Public Event RaiseEmployeeUpdatedCustomEvent As _
  EventHandler(Of EmployeeUpdatedEventArgs)
```

Raise an Event

You raise the event in the same class where the event is defined. An event is raised as the result of some action. In the case of the example, the action is the employee class has been updated. To raise the event, you simply call it in the right spot and pass the appropriate parameters. In the case of the employee-updated custom event, you pass an instance of the employee class as the sender and then the employee Id as part of an instance of the EmployeeUpdatedEventArgs, as shown here:

C#

```
public void UpdateEmployee()
{
  //do work to update employee ...

  //raise event to notify subscribers of the update
  RaiseEmployeeUpdatedCustomEvent(this, new EmployeeUpdatedEventArgs(this.Id));
}
```

VB

```
Public Sub UpdateEmployee()
  'do work to update employee ...

  'raise event to notify subscribers of update
  RaiseEvent RaiseEmployeeUpdatedCustomEvent(Me, _
    New EmployeeUpdatedEventArgs(Me.Id))
End Sub
```

Subscribe to and Handle an Event

The final step is to actually listen for (or subscribe to) the event. Here, you need to do two things. First, you must write a method that mimics the signature of the event. The content of this method is yours to write. It is called when the event fires. The following shows an example of a method (inside a class that subscribes to the employee class) that gets called when the event fires. Notice how this method uses the custom event type and must therefore match that signature:

C#

```
private void OnEmployeeUpdate(object sender, EmployeeUpdatedEventArgs e)
{
  //do something in response to employee update
  string empId = e.EmployeeId;
}
```

VB

```
Private Sub OnEmployeeUpdate(ByVal sender As Object, _
  ByVal e As EmployeeUpdatedEventArgs)

  Dim empId As String = e.EmployeeId
  Console.WriteLine("Event Fired: id=" & empId)
End Sub
```

Second, you must register your event handler with the actual event. This is done by adding a pointer to the event using the += (C#) or AddHandler (VB) syntax. You typically add your handlers inside the subscribing class's constructor or initialization code. The following shows code to connect the OnEmployeeUpdate handler to the RaiseEmployeeUpdatedCustomEvent event:

C#

```
Employee _emp = new Employee();
_emp.RaiseEmployeeUpdatedCustomEvent += this.OnEmployeeUpdate;
```

VB

```
AddHandler _emp.RaiseEmployeeUpdatedCustomEvent, AddressOf OnEmployeeUpdate
```

When the code is run, you undoubtedly access features of the class that fire the event (in this case, `Employee.UpdateEmployee`). When you hit a method that triggers the event, your subscribing code is called accordingly.

Language Features

Thus far, you've looked at the basics of programming with the .NET languages, including building objects and solving common coding issues with respect to looping, handling logic, and creating and consuming events. This section points out some additional elements that make the .NET languages special. Many of these items are not necessarily things you might use every day; however, they can provide you with additional skills when writing code and better understanding when reading it. The .NET language features covered here include the following:

- ▶ Local type inference (also called implicit typing)
- ▶ Object initializers
- ▶ Collection initializers
- ▶ Extension methods
- ▶ Anonymous types
- ▶ Lambda expressions
- ▶ Partial methods
- ▶ Language Integrated Query (LINQ)
- ▶ Friend assemblies
- ▶ XML language support
- ▶ Unused event arguments
- ▶ Automatically implemented properties
- ▶ Implicit line continuation in VB
- ▶ Work with dynamic language / objects
- ▶ Covariance and contravariance
- ▶ Intrinsic support for async operations (new)
- ▶ Type equivalence support

Infer a Variable's Data Type Based on Assignment

In the later versions of Visual Basic and C# (2008 and later), you can define variables without explicitly setting their data type. And, when doing so, you can still get the benefits of strongly typed variables (compiler checking, memory allocation, and more). The compilers actually infer the data type you intend to use based on your code. This process is called local type inference or implicit typing.

For example, consider the following lines of code. Here you create a variable of type String and assign a value:

C#

```
string companyName = "Contoso";
```

VB

```
Dim companyName As String = "Contoso"
```

Now, let's look at the same line of code using type inference. You can see that you do not need the `string` portion of the declaration. Instead, the compiler is able to determine that you want a string and strongly type the variable for you. In C#, this is triggered by the keyword `var`. This should not be confused with the `var` statement in languages such as JavaScript. Variables defined as `var` are strongly typed. In VB, you still simply use the `Dim` statement but omit the data type:

C#

```
var companyName = "Contoso";
```

VB

```
Dim companyName = "Contoso"
```

These two lines of code are equivalent in all ways. Although in the second example no data type was declared, one is being declared by the compiler. This is not a return to a generalized data type such as `Variant` or `Object`. Nor does this represent late-binding of the variable. Rather, it is simply a smarter compiler that strongly types the variable by choosing a data type based on the code. You get all the benefits of early-bound variables while saving some keystrokes.

For example, take a look at Figure 3.2. This is the C# compiler in action. (The VB compiler does the same thing.) You can see that even at development time, the compiler has determined that this variable is of type `System.String`.

There are a few things for you to be aware of when using type inference. The first is that it requires your local variable to be assigned a value to do the compiler typing. This should not be a big deal, because if your variable is not assigned, it is not used.

The second item you should consider is that type inference works only with local types. It does not work with class-level variables (also called fields) or static variables. In these cases, using local type inference results in an error being thrown by the compiler in C#. In VB, you would get the same error provided that Option Strict is set to On. If you are not using Option Strict in your VB code, the variable is not strongly typed. Instead, the variable is assigned the generic `Object` data type.

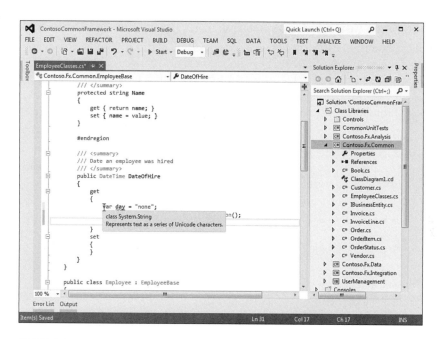

FIGURE 3.2   Type inference in action.

Local type inference can be useful in other declaration scenarios as well. This includes defining arrays, creating variables during looping, defining a variable inside a `Using` statement, and defining a variable that contains the result of a function call. In each of these cases, the compiler can infer your data type based on the context of the code.

As another example, the following code creates a `Using` statement and infers the type of the variable `cnn` (as a `SqlConnection` object). Note that a `Using` block defines a block of code for which a given resource is being used. The use of a `Using` block guarantees that the runtime disposes of the used object (in this case, the database connection) when done:

C#

```csharp
using (var cnn = new System.Data.SqlClient.SqlConnection()) {
  //code to work with the connection
}
```

VB

```vb
Using cnn = New System.Data.SqlClient.SqlConnection
  'code to work with the connection
End Using
```

In Visual Basic, you can turn local type inference off and on for a given file. By default, a new VB code file is set to allow type inference. However, if you want to turn it off at the file level, you can do so by setting Option Infer Off at the top of the code file.

Create an Object and Set Its Properties with a Single Line of Code

There is a shortcut for both declaring an instance of a class and setting the initial value of all or some of its members. With a single line of code, you can instantiate an object and set a number of properties on that object. During runtime, the object is first created, and then the properties are set in the order in which they appear in the initialization list. This feature is called object initializers.

Let's look at an example. Suppose you have a class called Employee that has a number of properties such as FirstName, LastName, FullName, Title, and the like. Using object initialization, you can both create an instance of this class and set the initial values of some (or all) of the Employee instance's properties. To do so, you first construct the object. In Visual Basic, you follow this construction with the With keyword. (C# does not require an equivalent indicator.) You then place each property initialization inside a set of curly braces. Examples are as shown here:

C#

```
Employee emp = new Employee { FirstName = "Joe",
  LastName = "Smith", Title = "Sr. Developer" };
```

VB

```
Dim emp As New Employee With {.FirstName = "Joe", _
  .LastName = "Smith", .Title = "Sr. Developer"}
```

This single line of code is the equivalent of first creating an Employee class and then writing a line of code for each of the listed properties. Notice that in VB, you need to precede the initialization using the With keyword; you also access each property using a dot. In C#, you do not need the dot or a keyword indicator.

Of course, you can also use object initialization with parameterized constructors. You simply pass the parameters into the constructor as you normally would. You then follow the constructor with the initialization. For example, suppose that the Employee class had a constructor that took the first and last name respectively. You could then create the object with the parameters and use object initialization for the Title, as shown here:

C#

```
Employee emp = new Employee("Joe", "Smith")
  { Title = "Sr. Developer" };
```

VB

```
Dim emp As New Employee("Joe", "Smith") With _
  {.Title = "Sr. Developer"}
```

Object initialization also enables you to write some code in the initialization. In addition, with VB you can use properties of the object you are initializing to help initialize other properties. This is not valid in C#. The C# compiler does not allow you to access the variable until the assignment is complete. To see an example of this, the following code initializes an `Employee` object and sets the `Employee.FullName` property by concatenating the first and last names. Notice that the VB code uses the object itself:

C#

```csharp
Employee emp = new Employee { FirstName = "Joe",
  LastName = "Smith", FullName = "Joe" + " Smith"};
```

VB

```vb
Dim emp As New Employee() With {.FirstName = "Joe", _
  .LastName = "Smith", _
  .FullName = .FirstName & " "" & .LastName}
```

You can also nest object initialization. That is, if a given property represents another object, you can create the other object as part of the initialization. You can also nest an initialization of the other object within the initialization of the first object. A simple example makes this clear. Suppose that the `Employee` class has a property called `Location`. The `Location` property might point to a `Location` object that includes the properties for `City` and `State`. You could then create the `Employee` object (along with the nested `Location` object) as shown here:

C#

```csharp
Employee emp = new Employee { FirstName = "Joe",
  LastName = "Smith", Location = new Location
  { City = "Redmond", State = "WA" } };
```

VB

```vb
Dim emp As New Employee() With {.FirstName = "Joe", _
  .LastName = "Smith", _  .
  .Location = New Location With _
  {.City = "Redmond", .State = "Washington"}}
```

Define a Collection and Initialize Its Values

You can now define a collection class or an array and, at the same time, set the initial values in your object. This turns multiple lines of code calling simple add methods into a single line. This is especially useful if you have a list of items that your application works with and you need to both declare the list and initialize these values.

For example, you might need to define an array to contain the geographic locations for your sales office. You could define this array and initialize it as follows:

C#

```csharp
string[] salesGeos = {"South", "Mid Atlantic", "Mid West"};
```

VB

```
Dim salesGeos() As String = {"South", "Mid Atlantic", "Mid West"}
```

You can use similar syntax to define and initialize a collection class including those based on a generic. For example, the following defines a list of Employee objects and adds two new Employee classes to that list. Note that the VB code requires the From keyword:

C#

```
List<Employee> empList = new List<Employee>
  {new Employee("1234"), new Employee("3456")};
```

VB

```
Dim empList As New List(Of Employee) From _
  {New Employee("1234"), New Employee("3456")}
```

Creating an Instance of a Nonexistent Class

The .NET languages enable you to create an object that does not have a class representation at design time. Instead, an unnamed (anonymous) class is created for you by the compiler. This feature is called anonymous types. Anonymous types provide crucial support for LINQ queries. With them, columns of data returned from a query can be represented as objects (more on this later). Anonymous types are compiled into class objects with read-only properties.

Let's look at an example of how you would create an anonymous type. Suppose that you want to create an object that has both a Name and a PhoneNumber property. However, you do not have such a class definition in your code. You could create an anonymous type declaration to do so, as shown here:

VB

```
Dim emp = New With {.Name = "Joe Smith", _
  .PhoneNumber = "123-123-1234"}
```

C#

```
var emp = new { Name = "Joe Smith",
  PhoneNumber = "123-123-1234"};
```

Notice that the anonymous type declaration uses object initializers (see the previous discussion) to define the object. The big difference is that there is no strong typing after the variable declaration or after the New keyword. Instead, the compiler creates an anonymous type for you with the properties Name and PhoneNumber.

There is also the Key keyword in Visual Basic. It is used to signal that a given property of an anonymous type should be used by the compiler to further define how the object is treated. Properties defined as Key are used to determine whether two instances of an anonymous type are equal to one another. C# does not have this concept. Instead, in C# all properties are treated like a VB Key property. In VB, you indicate a Key property in this way:

```
Dim emp = New With {Key .Name = "Joe Smith", _
  .PhoneNumber = "123-123-1234"}
```

You can also create anonymous types using variables (instead of the property name equals syntax). In these cases, the compiler uses the name of the variable as the property name and its value as the value for the anonymous type's property. For example, in the following code, the Name variable is used as a property for the anonymous type:

VB

```
Dim name As String = "Joe Smith"
Dim emp = New With {name, .PhoneNumber = "123-123-1234"}
```

C#

```
string name = "Joe Smith";
var emp = new {name, PhoneNumber = "123-123-1234" };
```

Add Methods to Existing Classes

You can add custom features to an existing type as if the type always had the custom features. In this way, you do not have to recompile a given object, nor do you have to create a second derived object to add these features. Rather, you can add a method to an existing object by using a new compiler feature called extension methods.

Adding methods varies between VB and C#. In VB, you first import the System.Runtime.CompilerServices namespace into your code file. Next, you mark a given Sub or Function with the ExtensionAttribute directive. Lastly, you write a new Sub or Function with the first parameter of the new method being the type you want to extend. The following shows an example. In this example, we extend the Integer type with a new method called DoubleInSize:

VB

```
Imports System.Runtime.CompilerServices

Public Module IntegerExtensions
  <Extension()> _
  Public Function DoubleInSize(ByVal i As Integer) As Integer
    Return i + i
  End Function
End Module
```

The C# compiler does not require the same import or method attribute. Instead, you first create a static class. Next, you create a static method that you intend to use as your extension. The first parameter of your extension method should be the type you want to extend. In addition, you apply this modifier to the type. Notice the following example. In it, we extend the int data type with a new method called DoubleInSize:

C#

```
namespace IntegerExtensions
{
  public static class IntegerExtensions
  {
    public static int DoubleInSize(this int i)
    {
      return i+i;
    }
  }
}
```

To use an extension method, you must first import (using in C#) the new extension methods into a project. You can then call any new method as if it had always existed on the type. The following is an example in both VB and C#. In this case, a function called DoubleInSize that was added in the preceding example is being called from the Integer (int) class:

VB

```
Imports IntegerExtensions

Module Module1
  Sub Main()
    Dim i As Integer = 10
    Console.WriteLine(i.DoubleInSize.ToString())
  End Sub
End Module
```

C#

```
using IntegerExtensions;

namespace CsEnhancements
{
  class Program
  {
    static void Main(string[] args)
    {
      int i = 10;
      Console.WriteLine(i.DoubleInSize().ToString());
    }
  }
}
```

Add Business Logic to Generated Code

A partial method (like a partial class) represents code you write to be added as a specific method to a given class upon compilation. This enables the author of a partial class to define a method stub and then call that method from other places within the class. If you provide implementation code for the partial method stub, your code is called when the stub would be called (actually the compiler merges your code with the partial class into a single class). If you do not provide a partial method definition, the compiler goes a step further and removes the method from the class along with all calls to it.

The partial method (and partial class) was created to aid in code generation and should generally be avoided unless you are writing code generators or working with them because they can cause confusion in your code.

Of course, Visual Studio has more and more code generation built in. Therefore, it is likely you will run into partial methods sooner or later. In most cases, a code generator or designer (such as LINQ to SQL) generates a partial class and perhaps one or more partial methods. The `Partial` keyword modifier defines both partial classes and partial methods. If you are working with generated code, you are often given a partial class that allows you to create your own portion of the class (to be merged with the code-generated version at compile time). In this way, you can add your own custom business logic to any partial method defined and called by generated code.

Let's look at an example. The following represents an instance of a partial class `Employee`. Here there is a single property called `Salary`. In addition, there is a method marked `Partial` called `SalaryChanged`. This method is called when the value of the `Salary` property is modified:

VB

```vb
Partial Class Employee

  Private _salary As Double

  Property Salary() As Double
    Get
      Return _salary
    End Get
    Set(ByVal value As Double)
      _salary = value
      SalaryChanged()
    End Set
  End Property

  Partial Private Sub SalaryChanged()
  End Sub

End Class
```

C#

```
partial class Employee {

  double _salary;

  public double Salary {
    get {
      return _salary;
    }
    set {
      _salary = value;
      SalaryChanged();
    }
  }


  partial void SalaryChanged();
}
```

The preceding code might represent code that was created by a code generator. The next task in implementing a partial method then is to create another partial Employee class and provide behavior for the SalaryChanged method. The following code does just that:

VB

```
Partial Class Employee
  Private Sub SalaryChanged()
    Dim newSalary As Double = Me.Salary
    'do something with the salary information ...
  End Sub
End Class
```

C#

```
partial class Employee
{
  partial void SalaryChanged()
  {
    double newSalary = this.Salary;
    //do something with the salary information ...
  }
}
```

When the compiler executes, it replaces the SalaryChanged method with the new partial method. In this way, the initial partial class (potentially code generated) made plans for a method that might be written without knowing anything about that method. If you decide to write it, it gets called at the appropriate time. However, it is optional. If you do not provide an implementation of the partial method `SalaryChanged`, the compiler strips out the method and the calls to the method (as if they had never existed).

Access and Query Data Using the .NET Languages

Visual Studio 2008 introduced the language feature set called Language-Integrated Query (LINQ). LINQ is a programming model that takes advantage of many of the features discussed in this section. It provides language extensions that change the way you access and work with data. With it, you can work with your data using object syntax and query collections of objects using VB and C#.

You can use LINQ to map between data table and objects (see Chapter 20, "Working with Databases"). In this way, you get an easier, more productive way to work with your data. This includes full IntelliSense support based on table and column names. It also includes support for managing inserts, updates, deletes, and reads.

The last of these, reading data, is a big part of LINQ, in that it has built-in support for easily querying collections of data. Using LINQ features, you can query not only your data but also any collection in .NET. There are, of course, new keywords and syntax for doing so. Query operators that ship with Visual Basic, for example, include `Select`, `From`, `Where`, `Join`, `Order By`, `Group By`, `Skip`, `Take`, `Aggregate`, `Let`, and `Distinct`. The C# language has a similar set of keywords. And, if these are not enough, you can extend the built-in query operators, replace them, or write your own.

You use these query operators to query against any .NET data that implements the IEnumerable or IQueryable interface. This may include a `DataTable`, mapped SQL Server objects, .NET collections (including Generics), `DataSets`, and XML data.

Let's look at an example. Suppose you had a collection of employee objects called `employees` and you wanted to access all the employees at a specific location. To do so, you might write the following function:

C#

```
public static List<Employee> FilterEmployeesByLocation
   (List<Employee> employees, string location)
{
   //LINQ query to return collection of employees filtered by location
   var emps = from Employee in employees
              where Employee.Location.City == location
              select Employee;

   return emps.ToList();
}
```

VB

```
Public Function FilterEmployeesByLocation( _
   ByVal employees As List(Of Employee), _
   ByVal location As String) As List(Of Employee)
```

```
'LINQ query to return collection of employees filtered by location
Dim emps = From Employee In employees _
           Where Employee.Location.City = location

Return emps.ToList()
End Function
```

Take a look at what is going on in the previous listing. The function takes a list of employee objects, filters it by a region passed to it, and then returns the resulting list. Notice that to filter the list we create a LINQ in-memory query called `emps`. This query can be read like this: Looking at all the employee objects inside the employees collection, find those whose city matches the city passed into the function. Finally, the `emps.ToList()` method call in the `Return` statement converts the in-memory query results into a new collection.

This is just a brief overview of LINQ. There are many things going on here, such as compile-time checking and schema validation (not to mention the LINQ language syntax). You will undoubtedly want to spend more time with LINQ.

Write Simple Unnamed Functions Within Your Code

The latest versions of the .NET languages (2008 and later) enable you to write simple functions that might or might not be named, execute inline, and return a single value. These functions exist inside your methods and not as separate, standalone functions. These functions are called *lambda expressions*. It's useful to understand lambda expressions because they are used behind the scenes in LINQ queries. However, they are also valid outside of LINQ.

Let's take a look at an example. Suppose that you want to create a simple function that converts a temperature from Fahrenheit to Celsius. You could do so within your Visual Basic code by first using the keyword `Function`. Next, you can indicate parameters to that function (in this case, the `Fahrenheit` value). Lastly, you write an expression that evaluates to a value that can be returned from the lambda expression. The syntax is as follows:

VB

```
Dim fahToCel = Function(fahValue As Integer) ((fahValue - 32) / 1.8)
```

The C# syntax is a bit different. In C#, you must explicitly declare a delegate for use by the compiler when converting your lambda expression. Of course, you declare the delegate at the class-level scope. After you have the delegate, you can write the expression inside your code. To do so, you use the => operator. This operator is read as "goes to." To the left side of the operator, you indicate the delegate type, a name for the expression, and then an = sign followed by any parameters the expression might take. To the right of the => operator, you put the actual expression. The following shows an example of both the delegate and the expression:

C#

```
//class-level delegate declaration
delegate float del(float f);

//lambda expression inside a method body
del fahToCel = (float fahValue) => (float)((fahValue - 32) / 1.8);
```

Notice that in both examples, we assigned the expression to a variable `fahToCel`. By doing so, we have created a delegate (explicitly converting to one in C#). We can then call the variable as a delegate and get the results, as shown here:

VB

```
Dim celcius As Single = fahToCel(70)
```

C#

```
float celcius = fahToCel(-10);
```

Alternatively, in Visual Basic, we could have written the function inline (without assigning it to a variable). For example, we could have written this:

VB

```
Console.WriteLine((Function(fahValue As Integer) ((fahValue - 32) / 1.8))(70))
```

Notice in this last example that the function is declared and then immediately called by passing in the value of 70 at the end of the function.

The C# language has its own quirk, too. Here you can write multiple statements inside your lambda expression by putting the statements inside curly braces and setting off each statement with a semicolon. The following example has two statements inside the lambda expression. The first creates the new value; the second writes it to a console window. Notice, too, that the delegate must be of type void in this instance and that you still must call the lambda expression for it to execute:

C#

```
//class level delegate declaration
delegate void del(float f);

del fahToCel = (float fahValue) => { float f =
  (float)((fahValue - 32) / 1.8); Console.WriteLine(f.ToString()); };
fahToCel(70);
```

Lambda expressions are used in LINQ queries for things such as the `Where`, `Select`, and `Order by` clauses. For example, using LINQ, you can write the following statement:

VB

```
Dim emps = From emp In db.employees
  Where(emp.Location = "Redmond")
  Select emp
```

C#

```
var emps = from emp in db.employees
  where emp.Location == "Redmond"
  select emp;
```

This LINQ code gets converted to lambda expressions similar to this:

VB

```
Dim emps = From emp In db.employees.Where(Function(emp) emp.Location = _
  "Redmond").Select(Function(emp) emp)
```

C#

```
var emps = from emp in db.employees
  where (emp => emp.Location == "Redmond")
  select (emp => emp);
```

Splitting an Assembly Across Multiple Files

The 2005 version of C# introduced the concept of friend assemblies; the feature was added to VB in 2008. It enables you to combine assemblies in terms of what constitutes internal access. That is, you can define internal members but have them be accessible by external assemblies. This capability is useful if you intend to split an assembly across physical files but still want those assemblies to be accessible to one another as if they were internal.

> **NOTE**
>
> Friend assembles *do not* allow for access to private members.

You use the attribute class `InternalsVisibleToAttribute` to mark an assembly as exposing its internal members as friends to another assembly. This attribute is applied at the assembly level. You pass the name and the public key token of the external assembly to the attribute. The compiler then links these two assemblies as friends. The assembly containing `InternalsVisibleToAttribute` exposes its internals to the other assembly (and not vice versa). You can also accomplish the same thing by using the command-line compiler switches.

Friend assemblies, like most things, come at a cost. If you define an assembly as a friend of another assembly, the two assemblies become coupled and need to coexist to be useful. That is, they are no longer a single unit of functionality. This can cause confusion and increase management of your assemblies. It is often easier to stay away from this feature unless you have a specific need.

Working with XML Directly Within Your Code (VB Only)

You can embed Extensible Markup Language (XML) directly within your Visual Basic code. This can make creating XML messages and executing queries against XML a simple task in VB. To support this feature, VB enables you to write straight XML when using the data types called `System.Xml.Linq.XElement` and `System.Xml.Linq.XDocument`. The former enables you to create a variable and assign it an XML element. The latter, `XDocument`, is used to assign a variable to a full XML document.

> **NOTE**
>
> What we cover here is how VB enables you to write XML code. The two objects (`XElement` and `XDocument`) are still important to C# developers. However, C# developers work with the properties and methods of these objects directly and not write and parse XML directly within a code editor.

Writing XML within your code is a structured process and not just simple strings assigned to a parsing engine. In fact, the compiler uses LINQ to XML behind the scenes to make all of this work. Let's look at a simple example. The following code creates a variable `emp` of type `XElement`. It then assigns the XML fragment to this variable:

```
Dim emp As XElement = <employee>
                        <firstName>Joe Smith</firstName>
                        <title>Sr. Developer</title>
                        <company>Contoso</company>
                        <location state="WA">Redmond</location>
                      </employee>
```

You can create a similar fragment as an `XDocument`. You simply add the XML document definition (`<?xml version="1.0"?>`) to the header of the XML. In either scenario, you end up with XML that can be manipulated, passed as a message, queried, and more.

In most scenarios, however, you do not want to hard-code your XML messages in your code. You might define the XML structure there, but the data comes from other sources (variables, databases, and so on). Thankfully, Visual Basic also supports building the XML using expressions. To do so, you use an ASP-style syntax, as in `<%= expression %>`. In this case, you indicate to the compiler that you want to evaluate an expression and assign it to the XML. For XML messages with repeating data, you can even define a loop in your expressions. For example, let's look at building the previous XML using this syntax. Suppose that you have an object `e` that represents an employee. In this case, you might write your `XElement` assignment as shown here:

```
Dim e As Employee = New Employee()
Dim emp As XElement = <employee>
                        <firstName><%= e.FirstName %></firstName>
```

```
<lastName><%= e.LastName %></lastName>
<title><%= e.Title %></title>
<company><%= e.Company %></company>
<location state=<%= e.Location.State %>>
    <%= e.Location.City %>
</location>
</employee>
```

Removing Unused Arguments from Event Handlers (VB Only)

Visual Basic now enables you to omit unused and unwanted arguments from your event handlers. The thought is that this makes for code that reads more cleanly. In addition, it enables you to assign methods directly to event handlers without trying to determine the proper event signature.

For example, suppose you had the following code to respond to a button click event:

```
Private Sub Button1_Click(ByVal sender As System.Object, _
  ByVal e As System.EventArgs) Handles Button1.Click


  'your code here


End Sub
```

You could remove the arguments from this code (or never put them in). Your new code functions the same and looks like this:

```
Private Sub Button1_Click() Handles Button1.Click
  'your code here
End Sub
```

Creating an Automatically Implemented Property

Beginning with the 2008 version, C# allows for a simplified property declaration called auto-implemented properties. With this feature, you can declare a property without having to declare a local private field to back the property. Instead, the compiler does this for you. This can be useful when you do not need logic inside the property's assessors. This feature has been added to VB as well with the release of Visual Studio 2010.

For example, suppose you want to define the property Name on the Employee class. You can declare this property without setting a private field variable, as shown here:

C#

```
public string Name { get; set; }
```

VB

```
Public Property Name As String
```

Notice that there is no logic in the `get` or `set` statements. Instead, the compiler creates an anonymous field to back the property for you.

Dropping the Underscore in VB for Line Continuation (New)

The latest version of VB now has a feature for implicit line continuation. This enables you to drop the need for the underscore (_) commonly used to indicate line continuation. For example, the following code shows a valid method signature without the need for the underscore required for line continuation:

```
Private Sub OnEmployeeUpdate(ByVal sender As Object,
  ByVal e As EmployeeUpdatedEventArgs)
```

There are many places in VB where you can eliminate the underscore and instead allow the compiler to use implicit continuation. These include after commas, after an open parenthesis, after an open curly brace, after concatenation, and more. For a full list, see "Statements in Visual Basic" inside the Microsoft Developer Network (MSDN).

Working with Dynamic Languages/Objects (New)

To date, everything in .NET has been about strongly typed languages where the compiler knows in advance the properties and methods that a given class exposes. However, there are objects (and languages) out there that do not have a static structure against which you can program. Instead, they are designed to get their information at runtime based on data inside an HTML form, a text file, XML, a database, or similar. These objects and languages are said to be dynamic, in that they get their structure only at runtime. These items have been mostly off limits to .NET developers until now. Dynamic support has been added to .NET for the purpose of simplifying the access to dynamic application programming interfaces (APIs) provided by languages such as IronPython and IronRuby, or even those found in Office Automation.

The Dynamic Data Type

The C# language has a new data type called dynamic. This type is similar to object in that it might contain any actual type. (In fact, in VB you simply use object to get dynamic-like behavior.) The difference in C#, however, is that any value defined as dynamic only has its actual type inferred at runtime (and not at compile time). This means you do not have type checking against valid methods and properties. (That is, the compiler does not stop you from writing code against methods it cannot see at design time.) Instead, type checking is only done when the code executes. Of course, this means that your dynamic type should be an actual type at the right time or you get errors.

You can define dynamic fields, properties, variable, or return types of methods. For example, the following shows a property defined as a dynamic:

```
public dynamic DyProperty { get; set; }
```

At first glance, it would seem that the `dynamic` keyword simply makes the type behave like types declared as object. In fact, the differences are so slight that VB combines the concept of object and dynamic. However, in C#, the keyword `dynamic` indicates that the property can contain any value and that no type checking is done at compile time regardless of what the code looks like that uses the property. That is in contrast to types declared as object where the compiler evaluates expressions that use the type and prevents certain code (such as doing arithmetic with objects), whereas dynamic types do not get this scrutiny by the compiler and therefore either execute properly or throw an error if a problem exists.

Dynamics are useful for dealing with types and code outside of .NET such as IronPython (discussed later). However, you have to be careful when using them for your own needs. Because no resolution is done until runtime, you do not get strong type checking by the compiler or with IntelliSense. Figure 3.3 shows an example of the experience inside Visual Studio. In this case, the new `Employee` type is being declared as a dynamic. This can be problematic because you have to know the method you want to call and the parameters you want to pass. You could get the method right and not provide the right number of parameters in your call. The compiler allows it but an exception is thrown at runtime.

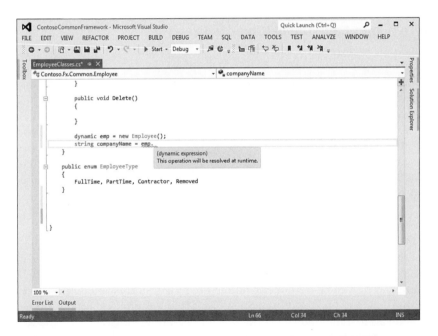

FIGURE 3.3   Using dynamics means no type checking even in IntelliSense.

Creating a Custom Dynamic Object

A dynamic object is one that gets its type information for things such as properties and methods at runtime. This is typically due to the fact that the object is meant to represent dynamic information such as that contained in an HTML or XML script file. In both cases, the underlying HTML and XML files you create are unique to your needs. Therefore, you cannot code directly against these models. Instead, you often have to code against static objects and write syntax such as `MyXml.GetElement("EmployeeId")`. In this example, the `GetElement` method then searches for the given XML element and returns the same. With a dynamic object, the object can be written to interrogate your XML (or similar data) and enables developers to code against the dynamic object as if it contained the `EmployeeId` property. For example, they could use your dynamic object to write their code as `MyXml.EmployeeId`. The dynamic object still has to interrogate the underlying structure for an `EmployeeId`, but this does simplify the coding for those working with your object and a dynamic structure such as XML or HTML.

You can create dynamic objects using either VB or C#. To do so, you inherit from the `DynamicObject` class inside the `System.Dynamic` namespace. You then override the members inside this class. These members serve as the basis for your dynamic items. For example, you can override the `TrySetMember` and `TryGetMember` to indicate the code that should be run when a user attempts to set or get a dynamic property on your object (such as calling `MyXml.EmployeeId`). In this case, if a user is trying to return a dynamic property, the `TryGetMember` method is called. Your code then determines how to return information for the dynamic property. (You might interrogate a file, for instance.)

There are many members on `DynamicObject` for which you can provide functionality. In addition to the two aforementioned members, the other notables include `TryInvokeMember` for invoking dynamic methods and `TryCreateInstance` for creating new instances of a dynamic object.

You might also add your own methods and properties to a dynamic object. In this case, the dynamic object first looks for your property or method before calling out to the appropriate `Try` member.

Let's look at an example. Suppose that you were to write a dynamic object to represent an `Employee`. In this case, perhaps you get data scraped from a web page or inside an XML file. You therefore want to convert this data to an object for easier programming. In this case, you can create a new class called `Employee` and make sure it inherits from `DynamicObject`. In our example, we use a simple `HashTable` of key value pairs to simulate the employee data. When a user creates an instance of this class, he is expected to pass the employee data to the dynamic class in the constructor. The skeleton of this class might then look like this:

C#

```
class Employee : System.Dynamic.DynamicObject
{
  Hashtable _memberData;

  public Employee(Hashtable employeeData)
  {
    _memberData = employeeData;
  }
}
```

VB

```
Public Class Employee
  Inherits System.Dynamic.DynamicObject

  Dim _memberData As Hashtable

  Public Sub New(ByVal employeeData As Hashtable)
    _memberData = employeeData
  End Sub

End Class
```

The next step is to override one or more of the `Try` members of `DynamicObject` to add our own functionality. In this simple example, we override the `TryGetMember` method to provide functionality for reading a property. This method takes two parameters: `binder` and `result`. The `binder` parameter is an object that represents the dynamic call made to your object (such as its name). The `result` parameter is an outbound parameter of type object. You use it to pass back any value you intend to pass as the property read. Finally, the method returns a `bool`. This indicates `true` if the member was determined to exist; otherwise you return `false`.

In the example, we simply look inside the `HashTable` for a given key (based on the `binder.Name` property). If it exists, we set the result to its value and return `true`. Otherwise, we set the result to `null` and return `false`. The following shows the code for this additional member of our `Employee` class (assumes you're using [imports in VB] `System.Dynamic`):

C#

```
public override bool TryGetMember(
  GetMemberBinder binder, out object result)
{
  if (_memberData.ContainsKey(binder.Name))
  {
    //set the out parameter, results to the value in the
    //  hash table for the given key
    result = _memberData[binder.Name];

    //indicate that member existed
    return true;
  }
  else
  {
    //property does not exist in hash table
    result = null;
    return false;
  }
}
```

VB

```
Public Overrides Function TryGetMember(ByVal binder As GetMemberBinder,
  ByRef result As Object) As Boolean

  If _memberData.ContainsKey(binder.Name) Then
    'set the out parameter, results to the value in the
    '  hash table for the given key
    result = _memberData(binder.Name)

    'indicate that member existed
    Return True
  Else
    'property does not exist in hash table
    result = Nothing
    Return False
  End If

End Function
```

> **NOTE**
>
> Note that classes that inherit from `DynamicObject` can be passed as instances to other languages that support the dynamic interoperability model. This includes IronPython and IronRuby.

Using the Dynamic Object

You use a dynamic object like you would any other. You can create an instance, call methods and properties, and so on. However, you do not get type checking by the compiler. Again, this is because the object is late bound at runtime. In C#, you indicate a late-bound dynamic object using the keyword `dynamic`. In VB, you simply declare your type as `object`. VB figures out whether you are using late binding.

For example, suppose that you want to use the dynamic version of the `Employee` class created in the previous section. Recall this class simulates converting data into an object. In this case, this simulation is handled through a `HashTable`. Therefore, you need to declare an instance of the `Employee` class as dynamic (or object in VB) and then create an instance passing in a valid `HashTable`. You can then call late-bound properties against your object. Recall that these properties are evaluated inside the `TryGetMember` method you overrode in the previous example. The following shows a Console application that calls the dynamic `Employee` object:

C#

```
class Program
{
  static void Main(string[] args)
```

```
  {
    Hashtable empData = new Hashtable();
    empData.Add("Name", "Dave Elper");
    empData.Add("Salary", 75000);
    empData.Add("Title", "Developer");

    dynamic dyEmp = new Employee(empData);

    Console.WriteLine(dyEmp.Name);
    Console.WriteLine(dyEmp.Salary);
    Console.WriteLine(dyEmp.Title);
    Console.WriteLine(dyEmp.Status);

    Console.ReadLine();
  }
}
```

VB

```
Module Module1

  Sub Main()

    Dim empData As New Hashtable()
    empData.Add("Name", "Dave Elper")
    empData.Add("Salary", 75000)
    empData.Add("Title", "Developer")

    Dim dyEmp As Object = New Employee(empData)

    Console.WriteLine(dyEmp.Name)
    Console.WriteLine(dyEmp.Salary)
    Console.WriteLine(dyEmp.Title)
    Console.WriteLine(dyEmp.Status)

    Console.ReadLine()

  End Sub

End Module
```

This code all passes the compiler's test and executes accordingly. However, the last call to
dyEmp.Status is not valid. In this case, the dynamic object returns false and thus throws
an error. Figure 3.4 shows the results, including the Console output and the error message
trying to access a bad member.

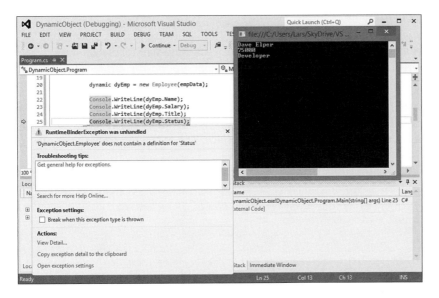

FIGURE 3.4   The dynamic object executing in the Console and throwing an error in Visual Studio.

TIP

You can use the features discussed here to load a dynamic language library such as IronPython. In this case, you load the dynamic language library and can then use this library inside your code. For more on this, see "Creating and Using Dynamic Objects (C# and Visual Basic)" inside MSDN.

Covariance and Contravariance (New)

The latest versions of the .NET languages support the concepts of covariance and contravariance. These concepts enable you to reduce restrictions on strong typing when working with delegates, generics, or generic collections of objects. In certain situations, decreasing the type restrictions might increase your ability to reuse code and objects and decrease the need to do a lot of casting or converting to provide the right type to a method.

Covariance is the ability to use a more derived type than that which was originally specified by an interface or function signature. For example, you could assign a list of strings to a generic list that only takes objects if that list supports covariance (as strings inherit from objects and are thus more derived). Contravariance is similar; it is the ability to use a less-derived type for a given parameter or return value. That is, you might assign an object type as the return type for a method that returns a string (provided that method supports contravariance).

It is important to note that the target object has to support covariance or contravariance. This is not a change to the entire language. Instead, it introduces a couple new keywords to allow support for these concepts when appropriate.

Variance in Generic Collections

Many of the generic interfaces in the latest version of the .NET Framework now support variance. This includes the interfaces IEnumerable<T> and IEnumerator<T> (among others) that support covariance. This means you can have support for variance inside your collections.

For example, you might have a list of Manager objects. Recall that Manager derives from Employee. Therefore, if you need to work with the Manager list as an Employee collection, you can do so using List and the IEnumerable interface. The following code shows an example:

C#

```
IEnumerable<Manager> managers = new List<Manager>();
IEnumerable<Employee> employees = managers;
```

VB

```
Dim managers As IEnumerable(Of Manager) = New List(Of Manager)()
Dim employees As IEnumerable(Of Employee) = managers
```

The preceding code compiles and executes because Manager inherits from Employee and is thus more derived. Using covariance, you can use a list of Manager objects with a list of Employee objects. For example, you might have a method that takes a list of Employee objects as a parameter. Using covariance support, you can pass the Manager list instead.

Additional Considerations

Support for variance has additional ramifications for your coding. These include the following:

- ▶ **Custom generic classes**—If you create your own custom generic classes, you can declare support for variance. You do so at the interface level using the out (covariant) and in (contravariant) keywords on generic type parameters.

- ▶ **Delegate variance**—Using variance, you can assign methods to delegates that return more derived types (covariance). You can also assign those methods that accept parameters that have a less-derived type (contravariance).

- ▶ **Func and Action**—The generic delegates Func and Action now support variance. This enables you to more easily use these delegates with other types (and thus increase the flexibility of your code).

Asynchronous Programming

Most of the time, developers write code that processes a series of commands sequentially. For instance, we can envision a simple routine (TallyExpenseReport) that accepts an ID, calls a second routine (GetExpenseReport) to call a service with that ID to retrieve an expense report, grabs the total dollar amount of the expense report, and then updates a database before finally giving the user a message indicating the status of the operation:

C#

```csharp
public void TallyExpenseReport(string id)
{
    // get the expense report
    ExpenseReport rpt = GetExpenseReport(id);
    UpdateDataStore(id, rpt.TotalAmt);

}

public ExpenseReport GetExpenseReport(string id)
{

    // code to fetch an expense report goes here
    return new ExpenseReport();

}
```

VB

```vb
Public Sub TallyExpenseReport(id As String)
    ' get the expense report
    Dim rpt As ExpenseReport = GetExpenseReport(id)
    UpdateDataStore(id, rpt.TotalAmt)

End Sub

Public Function GetExpenseReport(id As String) As
    ExpenseReport

    ' code to fetch an expense report goes here
    Return New ExpenseReport()

End Function
```

But in this top-down sequential process, we have actually sacrificed a bit of the user's experience; because of its sequential nature, each time we make a call, the application is blocked until the call completes. If we are talking to a service, this might be anywhere from fractions of a second to minutes. The same is true when we go to update the database. The entire time that the application is waiting for a task to complete, the application (and the user) cannot do anything else.

A better approach is an asynchronous one: We still issue a request for information from the service, and we still make a call to update the database, but in this case the application makes the call and then continues on its merry way. That, in essence, is an asynchronous application: The application doesn't block on any of the calls we chose to make asynchronous. These types of applications are fraught with complexity. But even the syntax to create and work with asynchronous calls has been complex and a tad arcane. The .NET Framework 4.5 has added two keywords, async and await, to both Visual Basic and C# that help make asynchronous programming a bit easier.

Async is used as a modifier to indicate that a method is asynchronous. The await keyword is used to mark any calls within an async method that should be waited on for completion. For the runtime wiring to work, all of your async function calls also need to have their return values modified to Task<originaltype> (C#) or Task(of originaltype).

If we were to take another stab at writing our expense report code, we might end up with two routines that look something like this:

C#

```
public async void TallyExpenseReport(string id)
{
    // get the expense report
    ExpenseReport rpt = await GetExpenseReport(id);
    UpdateDataStore(id, rpt.TotalAmt);

}

public async Task<ExpenseReport> GetExpenseReport(string id)
{

    // code to fetch an expense report goes here
    return new ExpenseReport();

}
```

VB

```
Public Async Sub TallyExpenseReport(id As String)
    ' get the expense report
    Dim rpt As ExpenseReport = Await GetExpenseReport(id)
    UpdateDataStore(id, rpt.TotalAmt)

End Sub

Public Async Function GetExpenseReport(id As String) As
    Threading.Tasks.Task(Of ExpenseReport)

    ' code to fetch an expense report goes here
    Return New ExpenseReport()

End Function
```

Our "await" call to `GetExpenseReport` will cause the `TallyExpenseReport` routine to block until a value is returned; meanwhile, execution control will be passed back to the original method that called `TallyExpenseReport` in the first place. In other words, the application will continue on, it won't block, and it may elect to do other things such as processing more user input, making additional expense report calls, and so on.

> **NOTE**
>
> Obviously, these simple code examples barely scratch the surface of async programming. The best place to start in terms of really understanding the overall patterns and syntactical sugar of async applications is with a publication titled "Task-Based Asynchronous Pattern," which you can find at the Microsoft Download Center (http://www.microsoft.com/en-us/download/default.aspx).

The .NET Framework

The .NET Framework continues to evolve. This latest version layers on top of the many earlier versions that brought us support for generics, AJAX web extensions, LINQ, Windows Presentation Foundation (WPF), Windows Communication Foundation (WCF), Windows Workflow Foundation (WF), SQL Synch Services, and more. Version 4.0 added to this list to include support for parallel computing, improved security, better performance, the Dynamic Language Runtime (DLR), and improvements in web, WPF, and WCF applications. And finally, version 4.5 of the .NET Framework brought asynchronous programming capabilities to Visual Basic and C#, the concept of portable class libraries, and a multitude of core improvements to the compiler and runtime.

A Map to the .NET Framework

We cannot begin to cover all the features of the .NET Framework in this limited space. Therefore, we simply highlight some of the key areas that fuel the current version of the .NET Framework. Think of this section as a high-level map to help guide you when exploring the Framework. Many of these items are also covered in more depth throughout the book:

- ▶ `System.AddIn` (**add-in framework**)—Provides classes and methods for developers looking to build applications that can be extended based on a common add-in framework. For example, the `AddInStore` class allows for the discovery and management of add-ins. The framework also provides versioning, isolation, activation, and sandboxing. If you are building a new application and hope to allow for add-ins, you should dig deeper on this namespace.

- ▶ `System.CodeDom`—Includes the classes used to represent the structure of a code file. The classes in this namespace can be used to generate and compile code.

- ▶ `System.Collections`—Provides the collection classes inside the Framework, including `ArrayList`, `HashTable`, `SortedList`, and others. Use the `System.Collections.Generic` namespace to get generic type-safe equivalent collections.

▶ **System.ComponentModel**—Provides classes used to help with the runtime and design time execution of .NET controls including data-binding and progress monitoring.

▶ **System.Configuration**—Provides classes for reading, writing, and managing application configuration information.

▶ **System.Data (ADO.NET)**—Provides the classes required to work with data and databases. This includes the `DataTable` and `DataSet`. There is also the namespace `System.Data.SqlClient` for working with SQL databases. For more information on working with ADO.NET, see Chapter 21.

▶ **System.Diagnostics**—Contains classes for working with diagnostic information about your application. This includes and `EventLog` and `Process` class. There is also the `EventSchemaTraceListener` class to allow for cross-domain, cross-thread, cross-computer, end-to-end, lock-free logging, and tracing.

▶ **System.Diagnostics.Contracts**—Provides support for code contracts, including preconditions and other data that is not typically defined inside a method signature.

▶ **System.Drawing**—Provides classes (like `Pen`, `Brush`, and `Graphics`) related to drawing with GDI+.

▶ **System.Dynamic**—Provides support for dynamic objects that get their members are runtime. (See content earlier in this chapter for more details.)

▶ **System.EnterpriseServices**—Provides the services architecture for creating serviced components that run under COM+.

▶ **System.Globalization**—Used to define language and culture information for writing multilingual, multicultural applications.

▶ **System.IO**—Provides classes for reading and writing file and data streams. This includes classes such as `File`, `Directory`, and `Stream`. Note there is also the `System.IO.Pipes` namespace that provides support for writing code that communicates at the pipe level across processes and across computers.

▶ **System.Linq (LINQ)**—Defines standard LINQ query operators and types. The `System.Data.Linq` namespace holds the connection between databases and the LINQ subsystem. There are more LINQ-related namespaces, too. These include `System.Data.Linq.Mapping` for handling the O/R mapping between SQL and LINQ and `System.Xml.Linq` for working between XML and the LINQ subsystem.

▶ **System.Media**—Used for accessing and playing sounds and music.

▶ **System.Messaging**—Provides support for working with message queues.

▶ **System.Net**—Provides support for programming with network protocols, including the HTTP, FTP, and TCP/IP. It also includes peer-to-peer networking support found in the `System.Net.PeerToPeer` namespace.

▶ **System.Security**—Provides the classes used to implement security inside the .NET runtime.

▶ **System.ServiceModel (WCF)**—Encapsulates what is known as WCF. With it you can easily create service-based applications that work across multiple protocols, transports, and message types. WCF is covered more in Chapter 21, "Service-Oriented Applications."

▶ **System.Threading**—Provides support for writing muultithreaded applications. This includes System.Threading.Tasks, which provides support for parallel computing on multiple threads and multiple cores. This namespace simplifies the task of writing for these environments.

▶ **System.Web (ASP.NET)**—Includes many classes and controls. For example, the framework directly supports AJAX programming with the ScriptManager and UpdatePanel controls. There are also controls for displaying data, such as ListView. For more on the ASP.NET framework, see Chapter 16, "Creating ASP.NET Applications."

▶ **System.Windows (WPF)**—Provides the WPF presentation technology for Windows applications. This technology is spread throughout the namespace and includes support for creating Windows applications based on XAML, XBAP, vector graphics, and both 2D and 3D scenarios. For more information, see Chapter 19, "Creating Richer, Smarter User Interfaces."

▶ **System.Workflow.Activities and System.Activities (WF)**—Provides classes for writing workflow applications and the custom activities found inside a workflow application. For more on WF, see Chapter 22, "Embedding Workflow in Your Applications."

▶ **System.Xml**—Provides support for working with XML and XSL.

Summary

This chapter provided a primer on the .NET languages. It should serve to get you running on the many features and programming constructs made possible by these languages. Our intent is to help you write more and better code during your development day. This chapter also presented a high-level roadmap of the .NET Framework. This Framework is becoming so large that developers (and books) are often forced to specialize in a particular area. We suggest that you look at our list and then jump off to your own specialty area for further exploration.

CHAPTER 4

Solutions and Projects

Solutions and projects are the containers Visual Studio uses to house and organize the code you write within the IDE. Solutions are virtual containers; they group and apply properties across one or more projects. Projects are both virtual and physical in purpose. Besides functioning as organizational units for your code, they also map one to one with compiler targets. Put another way, Visual Studio turns projects into compiled code. Each project results in the creation of a .NET component (such as a DLL or an EXE file).

This chapter covers the roles of solutions and projects in the development process. You learn how to create solutions and projects, examine their physical attributes, and discover how to best leverage their features.

Understanding Solutions

From a programming perspective, everything that you do within Visual Studio takes place within the context of a solution. As mentioned in this chapter's introduction, solutions in and of themselves don't do anything other than serve as higher-level containers for other items. Projects are the most obvious items that can be placed inside solutions, but solutions can also contain miscellaneous files that may be germane to the solution itself, such as "read me" documents and design diagrams. Really, any file type can be added to a solution. Solutions can't, however, contain other solutions. In addition, Visual Studio loads only one solution at a time. If you need to work on more than one solution concurrently, you need to launch another instance of Visual Studio.

So what do solutions contribute to the development experience? Solutions are useful because they allow you to treat different projects as one cohesive unit of work. By grouping multiple projects under a solution, you can work against those projects from within one instance of Visual Studio. In addition, a solution simplifies certain configuration tasks by enabling you to apply settings across all the solution's child projects.

You can also "build" a solution. As mentioned previously, solutions themselves aren't compiled, per se, but their constituent projects can be built using a single build command issued against the solution. Solutions are also a vehicle for physical file management: Because many items that show up in a solution are physical files located on disk, Visual Studio can manage those files in various ways (delete them, rename them, move them). So it turns out that solutions are very useful constructs within Visual Studio.

The easiest way to explore solution capabilities and attributes is to create a solution in the IDE.

Creating a Solution

To create a solution, you first create a project. Because projects can't be loaded independent of a solution within Visual Studio, creating a project causes a solution to be created at the same time.

NOTE

There actually is a way to create a blank, or empty, solution without also creating a project. If you expand the Other Project Types node that appears in the Installed Templates list, you will see an option for Visual Studio Solutions. This contains a Blank Solution template. Blank solutions are useful when you are creating a new solution to house a series of already existing projects; the blank solution obviates the need to worry about extra, unneeded projects being created on disk.

Launch the New Project dialog box by using the File menu and selecting the New, Project option (shown in Figure 4.1) or by using the Ctrl+Shift+N keyboard shortcut.

The New Project dialog box is displayed with defaults for the project name, location, and solution name (see Figure 4.2). We take a detailed look at the various project types offered there when we discuss projects later in this chapter. Notice that a Solution Name field is displayed at the bottom of the dialog box. In this field, you can customize the name of your solution before you create the solution. Clicking OK at this point does two things: A project of the indicated type and name is created on disk (at the location specified), and a solution, with links to the project, is also created on disk using the provided name.

If you have selected something other than the Blank Solution project type, Visual Studio now displays the newly created solution and project in the Solution Explorer window. (You will learn about Solution Explorer in depth in Chapter 5, "Browsers and Explorers.") In effect, Visual Studio has created the solution hierarchy shown in Figure 4.3.

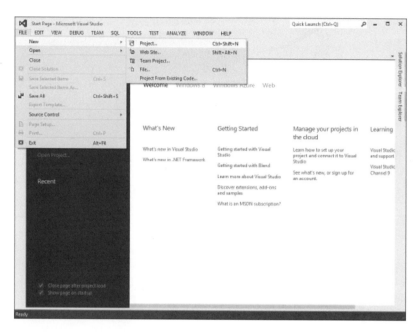

FIGURE 4.1   The File, New, Project menu.

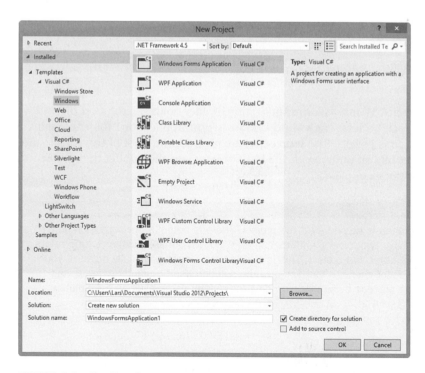

FIGURE 4.2   The New Project dialog box.

FIGURE 4.3   A simple solution hierarchy.

Assuming that you have accepted the default locations and left the Create Directory for Solution box checked, the physical directory/file structure is created, as shown in Figure 4.4.

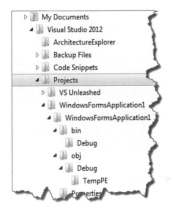

FIGURE 4.4   The solution file hierarchy.

In this example, the first WindowsFormsApplication1 folder holds the solution file and has a subfolder for each project. The second WindowsFormsApplication1 folder contains the new Windows Forms project. The source files are placed in the root of this folder, and any compiled output files sit underneath the bin directory and then under the specific build configuration (for example, Debug or Release).

> **CAUTION**
>
> By default, the solution is named after the project. There is potential for confusion here because you now have two folders/entities named WindowsFormsApplication1. One refers to the solution; the other, the project. This is not an ideal way to physically organize your code on disk. It is recommended that you give the solution itself a unique name during the project creation process by simply overriding the default name given in the Solution Name field (see Figure 4.2).

The Solution Definition File
Visual Studio stores solution information inside two separate files: a solution definition file and a solution user options file. For the preceding example, Visual Studio created the

solution definition file WindowsFormsApplication1.sln and the solution user options file WindowsFormsApplication1.suo in the indicated folder.

The solution definition file is responsible for actually describing any project relationships in the solution and for storing the various solution-level attributes that can be set. The solution user options file persists any customizations or changes that you, as a Visual Studio user, might have made to the way the solution is displayed within the IDE (such as whether the solution is expanded or which documents from the solution are open in the IDE). In addition, certain source control settings and other IDE configuration data are stored here.

The solution user options file is, by default, marked as a hidden file, and its content is actually binary. Because its internal structure is not publicly documented, we do not attempt to dissect it here. The solution definition file, however, is simply a text file. Listing 4.1 shows the file content for a fairly complex sample solution.

LISTING 4.1   Sample Solution File

```
Microsoft Visual Studio Solution File, Format Version 12.00
# Visual Studio 2012
Project("{FAE04EC0-301F-11D3-BF4B-00C04F79EFBC}") = "Contoso.Fx.Integration",
"ClassLibrary1\Contoso.Fx.Integration.csproj", "{DA0BA585-76C1-4F5E-B7EF-
➥R57254E185BE4}"
EndProject
Project("{FAE04EC0-301F-11D3-BF4B-00C04F79EFBC}") = "Contoso.Fx.Common",
"Contoso.Fx.Common\Contoso.Fx.Common.csproj", "{A706BCAC-8FD7-4D8A-AC81-
➥R249ED61FDE72}"
EndProject
Project("{FAE04EC0-301F-11D3-BF4B-00C04F79EFBC}") = "Contoso.Fx.Analysis",
"Contoso.Fx.Analysis\Contoso.Fx.Analysis.csproj", "{EB7D75D7-76FC-4EC0-
➥A11E-2B54849CF6EB}"
EndProject
Project("{FAE04EC0-301F-11D3-BF4B-00C04F79EFBC}") = "Contoso.Fx.UI",
"Contoso.Fx.UI\Contoso.Fx.UI.csproj", "{98317C19-F6E7-42AE-AC07-72425E851185}"
EndProject
Project("{2150E333-8FDC-42A3-9474-1A3956D46DE8}") = "Architecture Models",
"Architecture Models", "{60777432-3B66-4E03-A337-0366F7E0C864}"
    ProjectSection(SolutionItems) = postProject
        ContosoSystemDiagram.sd = ContosoSystemDiagram.sd
    EndProjectSection
EndProject
Project("{FAE04EC0-301F-11D3-BF4B-00C04F79EFBC}") = "Contoso.UI.WindowsForms.
OrderEntry", "Contoso.UI.WindowsForms.OrderEntry\Contoso.UI.WindowsForms.
OrderEntry.csproj", "{49C79375-6238-40F1-94C8-4183B466FD79}"
EndProject
Project("{2150E333-8FDC-42A3-9474-1A3956D46DE8}") = "Class Libraries", "Class
Libraries", "{E547969C-1B23-42DE-B2BB-A13B7E844A2B}"
```

```
EndProject
Project("{2150E333-8FDC-42A3-9474-1A3956D46DE8}") = "Controls", "Controls",
"{ED2D843C-A708-41BE-BB52-35BFE4493035}"
EndProject
Global
    GlobalSection(SolutionConfigurationPlatforms) = preSolution
        Debug|Any CPU = Debug|Any CPU
        Release|Any CPU = Release|Any CPU
    EndGlobalSection
    GlobalSection(ProjectConfigurationPlatforms) = postSolution
        {DA0BA585-76C1-4F5E-B7EF-57254E185BE4}.Debug|Any CPU.ActiveCfg = Debug|
        Any CPU
        {DA0BA585-76C1-4F5E-B7EF-57254E185BE4}.Debug|Any CPU.Build.0 = Debug|
        Any CPU
        {DA0BA585-76C1-4F5E-B7EF-57254E185BE4}.Release|Any CPU.ActiveCfg = Release
        |Any CPU
        {DA0BA585-76C1-4F5E-B7EF-57254E185BE4}.Release|Any CPU.Build.0 = Release|
        Any CPU
        {A706BCAC-8FD7-4D8A-AC81-249ED61FDE72}.Debug|Any CPU.ActiveCfg = Debug|
        Any CPU
        {A706BCAC-8FD7-4D8A-AC81-249ED61FDE72}.Debug|Any CPU.Build.0 = Debug|
        Any CPU
        {A706BCAC-8FD7-4D8A-AC81-249ED61FDE72}.Release|Any CPU.ActiveCfg = Release
        |Any CPU
        {A706BCAC-8FD7-4D8A-AC81-249ED61FDE72}.Release|Any CPU.Build.0 = Release
        |Any CPU
        {EB7D75D7-76FC-4EC0-A11E-2B54849CF6EB}.Debug|Any CPU.ActiveCfg = Debug| Any
        CPU
        {EB7D75D7-76FC-4EC0-A11E-2B54849CF6EB}.Debug|Any CPU.Build.0 = Debug|
        Any CPU
        {EB7D75D7-76FC-4EC0-A11E-2B54849CF6EB}.Release|Any CPU.ActiveCfg =
        Release |Any CPU
        {EB7D75D7-76FC-4EC0-A11E-2B54849CF6EB}.Release|Any CPU.Build.0 = Release
        |Any CPU
        {98317C19-F6E7-42AE-AC07-72425E851185}.Debug|Any CPU.ActiveCfg = Debug|
        Any CPU
        {98317C19-F6E7-42AE-AC07-72425E851185}.Debug|Any CPU.Build.0 = Debug|
        Any CPU
        {98317C19-F6E7-42AE-AC07-72425E851185}.Release|Any CPU.ActiveCfg =
        Release |Any CPU
        {98317C19-F6E7-42AE-AC07-72425E851185}.Release|Any CPU.Build.0 = Release
        |Any CPU
        {49C79375-6238-40F1-94C8-4183B466FD79}.Debug|Any CPU.ActiveCfg = Debug|
        Any CPU
        {49C79375-6238-40F1-94C8-4183B466FD79}.Debug|Any CPU.Build.0 = Debug|
        Any CPU
```

```
    {49C79375-6238-40F1-94C8-4183B466FD79}.Release|Any CPU.ActiveCfg =
        Release |Any CPU
    {49C79375-6238-40F1-94C8-4183B466FD79}.Release|Any CPU.Build.0 =
        Release |Any CPU
    EndGlobalSection
    GlobalSection(SolutionProperties) = preSolution
        HideSolutionNode = FALSE
    EndGlobalSection
    GlobalSection(NestedProjects) = preSolution
        {ED2D843C-A708-41BE-BB52-35BFE4493035} = {E547969C-1B23-42DE-B2BB-
        ➥A13B7E844A2B}
        {EB7D75D7-76FC-4EC0-A11E-2B54849CF6EB} = {E547969C-1B23-42DE-B2BB-
        ➥A13B7E844A2B}
        {A706BCAC-8FD7-4D8A-AC81-249ED61FDE72} = {E547969C-1B23-42DE-B2BB-
        ➥A13B7E844A2B}
        {DA0BA585-76C1-4F5E-B7EF-57254E185BE4} = {E547969C-1B23-42DE-B2BB-
        ➥A13B7E844A2B}
        {98317C19-F6E7-42AE-AC07-72425E851185} = {ED2D843C-A708-41BE-BB52-
        ➥35BFE4493035}
    EndGlobalSection
EndGlobal
```

At the beginning of the file are references to the projects that belong to the solution. The references contain the project's name, its globally unique identifier (GUID), and a relative path to the project file itself (more on project files in a bit):

```
Project("{FAE04EC0-301F-11D3-BF4B-00C04F79EFBC}") = "Contoso.Fx.Integration",
"ClassLibrary1\Contoso.Fx.Integration.csproj",
➥"{DA0BA585-76C1-4F5E-B7EF-R57254E185BE4}"
EndProject
```

You can also see some of the various configuration attributes applied to the solution; the Debug and Release settings, for instance, show up here. Note that this project contains several solution folders: Architecture Models, Class Libraries, and Controls. They are represented in the solution file in much the same way as projects. In fact, the only difference is that they do not have a relative file path associated with them.

Working with Solutions

After you have created a solution, the primary vehicle is in place for interacting with your code base. In essence, this boils down to controlling the way its constituent projects and files are built and deployed. Solutions also provide functionality outside the scope of projects. The primary tool for manipulating solutions and projects is the Solution Explorer. This tool is discussed in depth in Chapter 5. Here, we look at the general procedures used to manage solutions by using the menu system in Visual Studio; keep in mind that most of the commands and actions discussed here can be initiated from the Solution Explorer.

Solution Items

In practice, the content you add most often to a solution is project related. But items can be added directly to a solution as well. Collectively, the term *solution items* refers to any nonproject file that is attached to a solution. Because we know that solutions can't be compiled, it stands to reason that files added at the solution level serve no practical purpose from a compilation perspective. There are various reasons, however, that you might want to add solution items to your solution. For instance, adding solution items to your solution is a convenient way to store documentation that applies to the solution as a whole. Because you can add any type of file to a solution, this could take the form of documents, notes to other developers, design specifications, or even source code files from other solutions that could have some effect or bearing on the work at hand.

By default, Visual Studio supports a few types of solution items that can be created directly from within the IDE. They are grouped within three categories. Within each category are various file types that can be generated by Visual Studio. Table 4.1 shows the supported General types.

TABLE 4.1   File Types Supported Within a Solution by Add New Item

Category	Item Type	File Extension
General	Text file	.txt
	Style sheet	.css
	XML schema	.xsd
	Bitmap file	.bmp
	Cursor file	.cur
	Visual C# class	.cs
	Visual Basic class	.vb
	HTML page	.html
	XML file	.xml
	XSLT file	.xsl
	Icon file	.ico
	Sql file	.sql
	F# Script file	.fsx
	F# Source file	.fs
	Shader file	.hlsl
	Directed Graph Document	.dgml
	Native resource template	.rct

> **NOTE**
>
> Keep in mind that you are in no way limited as to the type of file you can add to a solution. Even though Visual Studio supports only a limited number of file types that can be created within the IDE, you always have the option of creating a file *outside* the IDE and then adding it to a solution by using the Add Existing Item command.

Figure 4.5 shows the Add New Item - Solution Items dialog box that appears when you try to add a new item to a solution.

FIGURE 4.5   Adding a new solution item.

Solution Folders

To assist in organizing the various files in your solution, you can use solution folders. Solution folders are virtual folders implemented entirely within Visual Studio. Creating a solution folder does not cause a physical file folder to be created on disk; these folders exist solely to provide another grouping level within the solution. Solution folders can be nested and are especially useful in large solutions that contain many different projects and miscellaneous files. For example, you might want to group all of your web service projects under a single solution folder called Services and group the Windows forms elements of your solution under a UI folder. On disk, files added to a virtual folder are physically stored within the root of the solution directory structure.

> **NOTE**
>
> Visual Studio creates solution folders automatically if you add a nonproject item to an existing solution. For instance, if we want to add a text file to the current solution, Visual Studio automatically adds a solution folder titled Solution Items to contain the text file. Similarly, you might see a Misc Files folder in some solutions. This is simply a solution folder as well.

Beyond providing a way to visually group items, solution folders also allow you to apply certain commands against all the projects contained within an individual folder. For example, you can "unload" all the projects within a virtual folder by issuing the unload command against the virtual folder. (This makes the projects temporarily unavailable within the solution, and can be useful when trying to isolate build problems or solution problems.) After unloading the projects in a folder, another right-click on the solution folder allows you to reload the projects.

Solution Properties

You can set several solution-level properties from within the IDE. The Solution Property Pages dialog box gives you direct access to these properties and enables you to do the following:

▶ Set the startup project of the solution (This project runs when you start the debugger.)

▶ Manage interproject dependencies

▶ Specify the location of source files to use when debugging

▶ Modify the solution build configurations

You launch this dialog box by clicking the solution in the Solution Explorer window and then clicking View, Property Pages, or right-clicking the solution and selecting Properties, or you can use the Shift+F4 keyboard shortcut. On this dialog box, the property page categories are represented in a tree view to the left; expanding a tree node reveals the individual property pages available.

Specifying the Startup Project   Figure 4.6 shows the Startup Project property page. The Startup Project property page indicates whether the startup project should be the currently selected project, a single project, or multiple projects.

The default, and most typically used option, is to specify a single startup project. The project to run is specified in the drop-down box. If Current Selection is selected, the project that currently has focus in the Solution Explorer is considered the startup project.

You can also launch multiple projects when the debugger is started. Each project currently loaded in the solution appears in the list box with a default action of None. Projects set to None are not executed by the debugger. You can also choose from the actions Start and Start Without Debugging. As their names suggest, the Start action causes the indicated project to run within the debugger; Start Without Debugging causes the project to run, but it is not debugged.

Setting Project Dependencies   If a solution has projects that depend on one another—that is, one project relies on and uses the types exposed by another project—Visual Studio needs to have a build order of precedence established among the projects. For example, consider a Windows application project that consumes types that are exposed by a class library project. The build process fails if the class library is not built first within the build sequence.

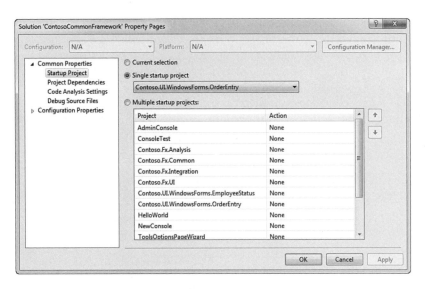

FIGURE 4.6   The Startup Project property page.

Most of the time, Visual Studio is able to determine the correct sequence. You might sometimes need to manually indicate that a project is dependent on other specific projects. For instance, a UI project might depend on another class library project. To supply this information, you use the Project Dependencies property page (see Figure 4.7). By selecting a project in the drop-down, you can indicate which other solutions it depends on by placing a check mark on any of the projects shown in the Depends On list.

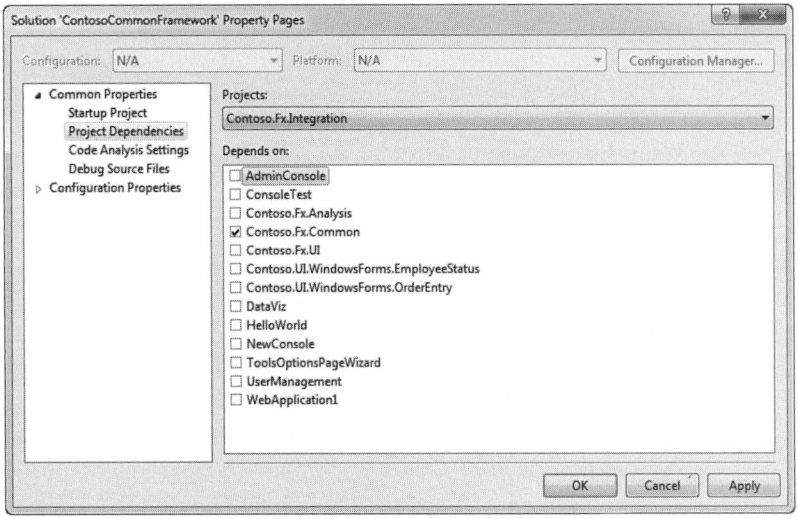

FIGURE 4.7   Project dependencies.

Code Analysis Settings   Visual Studio has a built-in capability to perform static code analysis. Put simply, this allows the IDE to analyze and report on the health of your code with regard to how well it follows a set of best practices and guidelines. Microsoft provides multiple rules libraries that can be executed against your code. These range from globalization rules to security rules to basic design guideline rules. The Code Analysis Settings property page (see Figure 4.8) is used to specify which rule set should be run against which project in your solution. Chapter 10, "Refactoring Code," covers more of the features of static code analysis.

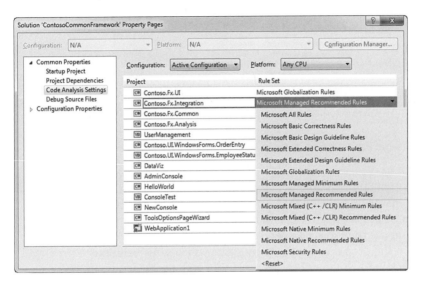

FIGURE 4.8   Code analysis settings.

Source File Location for Debugging   In certain situations, you might need to explicitly point the Visual Studio debugger at source files to use when the debugger executes. One such scenario occurs when you are trying to debug a solution that references an object on a remote machine. If the source is not available locally for that remote object, you can explicitly point Visual Studio at the source files.

The Debug Source Files property page (see Figure 4.9) has two different list boxes. The top box contains a list of folders that hold source code specific to your debugging scenario. The bottom list box enables you to indicate specific files that the debugger should ignore (that is, should not load) when debugging. This last option is useful in scenarios where you may not have all of the source code files on your local machine; you can simply tell Visual Studio to ignore files that aren't available to the debugger.

To add an entry to either box, first place your cursor within the box and then click the New Line button (upper right of the dialog box). This allows you to enter a fully qualified path to the desired folder. You remove an entry by selecting the item and then clicking the Cut Line button. The Check Entries button allows you to double-check that all entries point to valid, reachable folder paths.

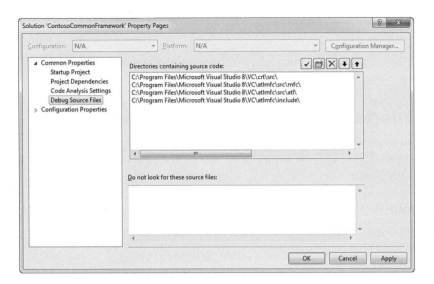

FIGURE 4.9   Source file locations.

If the loaded solution has any Visual C++ projects, you probably see several items already added into the Directories Containing Source Code list box.

Build Configuration Properties   Build configurations are covered in depth in Chapter 11, "Debugging Code." On the Build Configuration property page (see Figure 4.10), you indicate how Visual Studio builds the projects contained within the solution. For each project, you can set a configuration and platform value. In addition, a check box allows you to indicate whether to build a particular project.

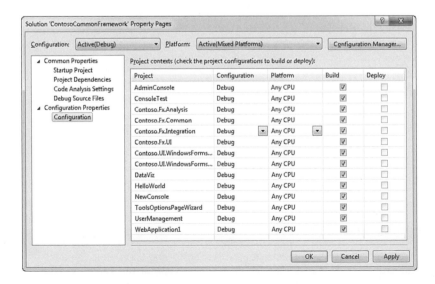

FIGURE 4.10   Build configuration properties.

See Chapter 11 for information on how to effectively use build configurations in your development.

Now that we have covered the concept of a solution in depth, let's examine the role of projects within Visual Studio.

Getting Comfortable with Projects

Projects are where all the real work is performed in Visual Studio. A project maps directly to a compiled component. Visual Studio supports various project types. Let's reexamine the project creation process.

Creating a Project

As you saw earlier during the solution creation discussion, you create projects by selecting the New, Project option from the File menu. This launches the New Project dialog box (see Figure 4.11).

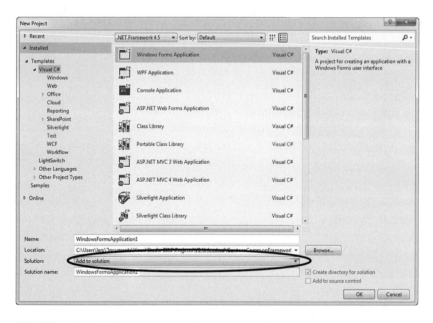

FIGURE 4.11   Adding a project to the current solution.

Table 4.2 shows some of the various project types supported in Visual Studio out of the box.

NOTE

Visual Studio supports the capability to create new project types and templates. Because Visual Studio is extensible in this fashion, the list of project types that you see in your particular copy of Visual Studio can vary greatly depending on the Visual Studio SKU you have installed and any add-ins, extensions, or "starter kits" you have installed on your PC.

For example, the Windows Azure software development kit (SDK), when downloaded and installed, adds project types under the Cloud category. Similarly, project templates for Windows Phone development are not included by default; they are installed as part of the Windows Phone SDK.

TABLE 4.2   Supported Project Types

Category	Project Type
Other Languages/SQL Server	SQL Server Database Project
Office	Excel Add-in
	Excel Template
	Excel Workbook
	InfoPath Add-in
	Outlook Add-in
	PowerPoint Add-in
	Project Add-in
	Visio Add-in
	Word Add-in
	Word Document
	Word Template
Test	Test Project
Web	ASP.NET AJAX Server Control
	ASP.NET AJAX Server Control Extender
	ASP.NET Dynamic Data Entities Web Application
	ASP.NET Empty Web Application
	ASP.NET MVC 3 Web Application
	ASP.NET MVC 4 Web Application
	ASP.NET Server Control
	ASP.NET Web Application
Windows	Class Library
	Console Application
	Empty Project
	Portable Class Library
	Windows Forms Application

4

Category	Project Type
	Windows Forms Control Library
	Windows Service
	WPF Application
	WPF Browser Application
	WPF Custom Control Library
	WPF User Control Library

NOTE

Project types are dependent on a specific version of the .NET Framework. Changing the selected entry in the framework version drop-down that you see at the top of Figure 4.11 will filter the list of project types accordingly.

As outlined previously, creating a new project also creates a new containing solution. However, if you are creating a project and you already have a solution loaded in the IDE, the New Project dialog box offers you the opportunity to add the new project to the existing solution. Compare Figure 4.11 with Figure 4.2; notice that there is a new option in the form of a drop-down box that allows you to indicate whether Visual Studio should create a new solution or add the project to the current solution.

Website Projects

Developers have two different ways to create web projects within Visual Studio 2012. Web application projects are created using the New Project dialog that we just discussed. Website projects are created in a slightly different fashion. Instead of selecting File, New, Project, you select File, New, Web Site. This launches the New Web Site dialog box (see Figure 4.12).

As with other project types, you initiate website projects by selecting one of the predefined templates. In addition to the template, you also select a target source language and the location for the website. The location can be the file system, an HTTP site, or an FTP site. Unlike other project types, websites are not typically created within the physical folder tree that houses your solution. By default, even selecting the file system object places the resulting source files in a Web Sites folder under the Visual Studio 2012 projects folder.

NOTE

The *target source language* for a website project simply represents the default language used for any code files. It does not constrain the languages you can use within the project. For instance, a website project created with C# as the target language can still contain Visual Basic code files.

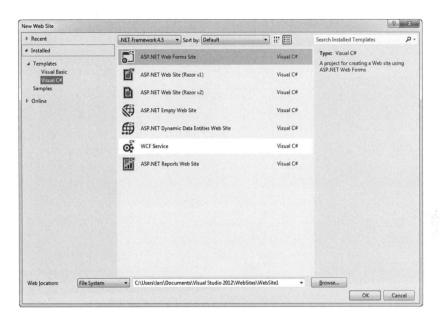

FIGURE 4.12   Creating a new website project.

After you have created the website, you manage and maintain it just like the other project types within the IDE.

You might be wondering about the difference between a web application project and a website project. One key difference is the way that these two different project types are built. Web application projects use the same build model as the other .NET project types; that is, all the code in the project is compiled into a single assembly. Website projects, however, support a dynamic build model in which the code for a particular page is generated at runtime the first time a user hits the page. In this model, each page has its own assembly. There are many other differences between the two project types, as discussed in depth in Chapter 16, "Creating ASP.NET Form-Based Applications."

Working with Project Definition Files

As with solutions, projects maintain their structure information inside a file. These files have different extensions depending on their underlying language. For instance, Visual Basic project files have a .vbproj extension, and Visual C# project files have a .csproj extension.

Each project definition file contains all the information necessary to describe the source files and the various project properties and options. This includes the following:

▶ Build configurations

▶ Project references and dependencies

▶ Source code file locations/types

Visual Basic and Visual C# project definition files are based on the same schema. Listing 4.2 contains a snippet from a Visual C# project definition file.

LISTING 4.2   Contents of a Visual C# Project Definition File

```xml
<?xml version="1.0" encoding="utf-8"?>
<Project ToolsVersion="4.0" DefaultTargets="Build"
➥xmlns="http://schemas.microsoft.com/developer/msbuild/2003">
  <Import Project="$(MSBuildExtensionsPath)\$(MSBuildToolsVersion)\
➥Microsoft.Common.props"
Condition="Exists('$(MSBuildExtensionsPath)\$(MSBuildToolsVersion)\
➥Microsoft.Common.props')" />
  <PropertyGroup>
    <Configuration Condition=" '$(Configuration)' == '' ">Debug</Configuration>
    <Platform Condition=" '$(Platform)' == '' ">AnyCPU</Platform>
    <ProjectGuid>{65C9998A-C3F7-4299-B91E-030499362F80}</ProjectGuid>
    <OutputType>WinExe</OutputType>
    <AppDesignerFolder>Properties</AppDesignerFolder>
    <RootNamespace>WindowsFormsApplication1</RootNamespace>
    <AssemblyName>WindowsFormsApplication1</AssemblyName>
    <TargetFrameworkVersion>v4.5</TargetFrameworkVersion>
    <FileAlignment>512</FileAlignment>
  </PropertyGroup>
  <PropertyGroup Condition=" '$(Configuration)|$(Platform)' == 'Debug|AnyCPU' ">
    <PlatformTarget>AnyCPU</PlatformTarget>
    <DebugSymbols>true</DebugSymbols>
    <DebugType>full</DebugType>
    <Optimize>false</Optimize>
    <OutputPath>bin\Debug\</OutputPath>
    <DefineConstants>DEBUG;TRACE</DefineConstants>
    <ErrorReport>prompt</ErrorReport>
    <WarningLevel>4</WarningLevel>
  </PropertyGroup>
  <PropertyGroup Condition=" '$(Configuration)|$(Platform)' == 'Release|AnyCPU' ">
    <PlatformTarget>AnyCPU</PlatformTarget>
    <DebugType>pdbonly</DebugType>
    <Optimize>true</Optimize>
    <OutputPath>bin\Release\</OutputPath>
    <DefineConstants>TRACE</DefineConstants>
    <ErrorReport>prompt</ErrorReport>
    <WarningLevel>4</WarningLevel>
  </PropertyGroup>
  <ItemGroup>
    <Reference Include="System" />
    <Reference Include="System.Core" />
    <Reference Include="System.Xml.Linq" />
```

```xml
      <Reference Include="System.Data.DataSetExtensions" />
      <Reference Include="Microsoft.CSharp" />
      <Reference Include="System.Data" />
      <Reference Include="System.Deployment" />
      <Reference Include="System.Drawing" />
      <Reference Include="System.Windows.Forms" />
      <Reference Include="System.Xml" />
  </ItemGroup>
  <ItemGroup>
    <Compile Include="Form1.cs">
      <SubType>Form</SubType>
    </Compile>
    <Compile Include="Form1.Designer.cs">
      <DependentUpon>Form1.cs</DependentUpon>
    </Compile>
    <Compile Include="Program.cs" />
    <Compile Include="Properties\AssemblyInfo.cs" />
    <EmbeddedResource Include="Properties\Resources.resx">
      <Generator>ResXFileCodeGenerator</Generator>
      <LastGenOutput>Resources.Designer.cs</LastGenOutput>
      <SubType>Designer</SubType>
    </EmbeddedResource>
    <Compile Include="Properties\Resources.Designer.cs">
      <AutoGen>True</AutoGen>
      <DependentUpon>Resources.resx</DependentUpon>
    </Compile>
    <None Include="Properties\Settings.settings">
      <Generator>SettingsSingleFileGenerator</Generator>
      <LastGenOutput>Settings.Designer.cs</LastGenOutput>
    </None>
    <Compile Include="Properties\Settings.Designer.cs">
      <AutoGen>True</AutoGen>
      <DependentUpon>Settings.settings</DependentUpon>
      <DesignTimeSharedInput>True</DesignTimeSharedInput>
    </Compile>
  </ItemGroup>
  <ItemGroup>
    <None Include="App.config" />
  </ItemGroup>
  <Import Project="$(MSBuildToolsPath)\Microsoft.CSharp.targets" />
  <!-- To modify your build process, add your task inside one of the targets below
➥and uncomment it.
       Other similar extension points exist, see Microsoft.Common.targets. -->
  <Target Name="BeforeBuild">
  </Target>
```

```
  <Target Name="AfterBuild">
  </Target>
  -->
</Project>
```

This project definition file would look relatively the same as a Visual Basic project. Although we don't cover Visual C++ development in this book, you might be surprised to know that project definition files in Visual C++ use an entirely different schema. For completeness, and to contrast with the Visual Basic/Visual C# content, Listing 4.3 shows a sample Visual C++ project definition file in its entirety.

LISTING 4.3   Visual C++ Project Definition File

```
<?xml version="1.0" encoding="Windows-1252"?>
<VisualStudioProject
    ProjectType="Visual C++"
    Version="10.00"
    Name="Contoso.Fx.UI.BrowserShim"
    ProjectGUID="{BE574BF5-7FDA-46F2-A42E-4A35E5E338A0}"
    RootNamespace="ContosoFxUIBrowserShim"
    Keyword="MFCActiveXProj"
    SignManifests="true">
    <Platforms>
        <Platform Name="Win32" />
    </Platforms>
    <ToolFiles>
    </ToolFiles>
    <Configurations>
        <Configuration Name="Debug|Win32" OutputDirectory="Debug"
            IntermediateDirectory="Debug" ConfigurationType="2"
            UseOfMFC="2" CharacterSet="1">
            <Tool Name="VCPreBuildEventTool" />
            <Tool Name="VCCustomBuildTool" />
            <Tool Name="VCXMLDataGeneratorTool" />
            <Tool Name="VCWebServiceProxyGeneratorTool" />
            <Tool
                Name="VCMIDLTool"
                PreprocessorDefinitions="_DEBUG"
                MkTypLibCompatible="false"
                TypeLibraryName="$(IntDir)/$(ProjectName).tlb"
                HeaderFileName="$(ProjectName)idl.h"
                ValidateParameters="false"
            />
            <Tool
                Name="VCCLCompilerTool"
                Optimization="0"
```

```
            PreprocessorDefinitions="WIN32;_WINDOWS;_DEBUG;_USRDLL"
            MinimalRebuild="true"
            BasicRuntimeChecks="3"
            RuntimeLibrary="3"
            TreatWChar_tAsBuiltInType="true"
            UsePrecompiledHeader="2"
            WarningLevel="3"
            Detect64BitPortabilityProblems="true"
            DebugInformationFormat="4"
        />
        <Tool Name="VCManagedResourceCompilerTool" />
        <Tool
            Name="VCResourceCompilerTool"
            PreprocessorDefinitions="_DEBUG"
            Culture="1033"
            AdditionalIncludeDirectories="$(IntDir)"
        />
        <Tool Name="VCPreLinkEventTool" />
        <Tool
            Name="VCLinkerTool"
            RegisterOutput="true"
            OutputFile="$(OutDir)\$(ProjectName).ocx"
            LinkIncremental="2"
            ModuleDefinitionFile=".\Contoso.Fx.UI.BrowserShim.def"
            GenerateDebugInformation="true"
            SubSystem="2"
            TargetMachine="1"
        />
        <Tool Name="VCALinkTool" />
        <Tool Name="VCManifestTool" />
        <Tool Name="VCXDCMakeTool" />
        <Tool Name="VCBscMakeTool" />
        <Tool Name="VCFxCopTool" />
        <Tool Name="VCAppVerifierTool" />
        <Tool Name="VCWebDeploymentTool" />
        <Tool Name="VCPostBuildEventTool" />
    </Configuration>
    <Configuration
        Name="Release|Win32"
        OutputDirectory="Release"
        IntermediateDirectory="Release"
        ConfigurationType="2"
        UseOfMFC="2"
        CharacterSet="1"
        >
        <Tool Name="VCPreBuildEventTool" />
```

```
<Tool Name="VCCustomBuildTool" />
<Tool Name="VCXMLDataGeneratorTool" />
<Tool Name="VCWebServiceProxyGeneratorTool" />
<Tool
    Name="VCMIDLTool"
    PreprocessorDefinitions="NDEBUG"
    MkTypLibCompatible="false"
    TypeLibraryName="$(IntDir)/$(ProjectName).tlb"
    HeaderFileName="$(ProjectName)idl.h"
    ValidateParameters="false"
/>
<Tool
    Name="VCCLCompilerTool"
    Optimization="2"
    PreprocessorDefinitions="WIN32;_WINDOWS;NDEBUG;_USRDLL"
    MinimalRebuild="false"
    RuntimeLibrary="2"
    TreatWChar_tAsBuiltInType="true"
    UsePrecompiledHeader="2"
    WarningLevel="3"
    Detect64BitPortabilityProblems="true"
    DebugInformationFormat="3"
/>
<Tool Name="VCManagedResourceCompilerTool" />
<Tool
    Name="VCResourceCompilerTool"
    PreprocessorDefinitions="NDEBUG"
    Culture="1033"
    AdditionalIncludeDirectories="$(IntDir)"
/>
<Tool Name="VCPreLinkEventTool" />
<Tool
    Name="VCLinkerTool"
    RegisterOutput="true"
    OutputFile="$(OutDir)\$(ProjectName).ocx"
    LinkIncremental="1"
    ModuleDefinitionFile=".\Contoso.Fx.UI.BrowserShim.def"
    GenerateDebugInformation="true"
    SubSystem="2"
    OptimizeReferences="2"
    EnableCOMDATFolding="2"
    TargetMachine="1"
/>
<Tool Name="VCALinkTool" />
<Tool Name="VCManifestTool" />
```

```
            <Tool Name="VCXDCMakeTool" />
            <Tool Name="VCBscMakeTool" />
            <Tool Name="VCFxCopTool" />
            <Tool Name="VCAppVerifierTool" />
            <Tool Name="VCWebDeploymentTool" />
            <Tool Name="VCPostBuildEventTool" />
        </Configuration>
    </Configurations>
    <References></References>
    <Files>
        <Filter Name="Source Files"
            Filter="cpp;c;cc;cxx;def;odl;idl;hpj;bat;asm;asmx"
            UniqueIdentifier="{4FC737F1-C7A5-4376-A066-2A32D752A2FF}">
            <File RelativePath=".\Contoso.Fx.UI.BrowserShim.cpp"></File>
            <File RelativePath=".\Contoso.Fx.UI.BrowserShim.def"></File>
            <File RelativePath=".\Contoso.Fx.UI.BrowserShim.idl"></File>
            <File RelativePath=".\Contoso.Fx.UI.BrowserShimCtrl.cpp">
            </File>
            <File RelativePath=".\Contoso.Fx.UI.BrowserShimPropPage.cpp">
            </File>
            <File RelativePath=".\stdafx.cpp">
                <FileConfiguration Name="Debug|Win32"       >
                    <Tool Name="VCCLCompilerTool"
                        UsePrecompiledHeader="1" />
                </FileConfiguration>
                <FileConfiguration Name="Release|Win32">
                    <Tool Name="VCCLCompilerTool"
                        UsePrecompiledHeader="1" />
                </FileConfiguration>
            </File>
        </Filter>
        <Filter
            Name="Header Files"
            Filter="h;hpp;hxx;hm;inl;inc;xsd"
            UniqueIdentifier="{93995380-89BD-4b04-88EB-625FBE52EBFB}">
            <File RelativePath=".\Contoso.Fx.UI.BrowserShim.h"></File>
            <File RelativePath=".\Contoso.Fx.UI.BrowserShimCtrl.h"></File>
            <File RelativePath=".\Contoso.Fx.UI.BrowserShimPropPage.h">
            </File>
            <File RelativePath=".\Resource.h"></File>
            <File RelativePath=".\stdafx.h"></File>
        </Filter>
        <Filter Name="Resource Files"
Filter="rc;ico;cur;bmp;dlg;rc2;rct;bin;rgs;gif;jpg;jpeg;jpe;resx;tiff;tif;
➥png;wav"
```

```
            UniqueIdentifier="{67DA6AB6-F800-4c08-8B7A-83BB121AAD01}">
            <File RelativePath=".\Contoso.Fx.UI.BrowserShim.ico"></File>
            <File RelativePath=".\Contoso.Fx.UI.BrowserShim.rc"></File>
            <File RelativePath=".\Contoso.Fx.UI.BrowserShimCtrl.bmp"></File>
        </Filter>
        <File RelativePath=".\ReadMe.txt"></File>
    </Files>
    <Globals></Globals>
</VisualStudioProject>
```

Working with Projects

As source code containers, projects principally act as a settings applicator. They are used to control and organize your source code files and the various properties associated with the whole build and compile process. (You learn about the build process in depth in Chapter 11.) As with solutions, projects can contain various different items that are germane to their development. Projects are language specific. You cannot mix different languages within a specific project. There is no similar limitation with solutions: A solution can contain many projects, each one in a different language.

Project Items

After a project is created, by default it contains one or more project items. These default items vary depending on the project template you selected and on the language of the project. For instance, creating a project using the C# Windows application template "results in the formation of a Form1.cs file, a Form1.Designer.cs file, and a Program.cs file. Projects are also preconfigured with references and properties that make sense for "the given project type: The Windows application template contains a reference to the System.Windows.Forms assembly, whereas the class library template does not.

> **NOTE**
>
> You might be wondering whether you can create your own project templates for you and others to use. The answer is most definitely yes! You will learn about creating and distributing custom project templates in Chapter 7, "The .NET Community: Interacting Online."

Projects, like solutions, can also have subfolders within them that you can use to better manage and group project items. Unlike solutions, the folders you create within a project are physical; they are created on disk within your project directory structure. These are examples of physical project items. Source code files are also physical in nature.

Projects can also contain virtual items (items that are merely pointers or links to items that don't actually manifest themselves physically within your project structure). They are, for example, references to other assemblies, database connections, and virtual folders. (Virtual folders are described in Chapter 5.) Figure 4.13 illustrates a fully described solution and project.

FIGURE 4.13   Project structure.

Project Properties

Like solution properties, project properties are viewed and set using a series of property pages accessed through the Project, Properties menu. These property pages are hosted within a dialog box referred to as the Project Designer. Figure 4.14 shows the Project Designer that is displayed for a sample Visual Basic class library project. Different languages and different project types actually surface different property pages within the Project Designer. For instance, the Application property page for a Visual Basic project looks different and contains slightly different information than an identical Visual C# project (although the basic intent of the page remains unchanged).

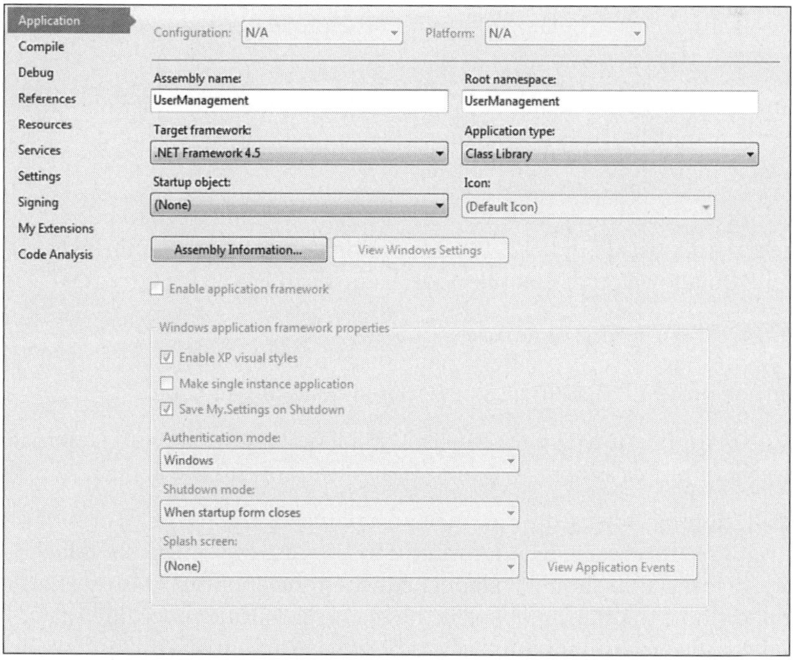

FIGURE 4.14   Setting properties using the Project Designer.

In general, you use project properties to control the following:

▶ General project attributes such as the assembly name and project type

▶ The way that the project is built/compiled

▶ Debugger configuration for the project

▶ Resources used by the project

▶ Signing and security settings

NOTE

The Project Designer is also easily accessed from the Solution Explorer window. For C# projects, you can double-click the Properties folder under the project. Visual Basic projects have a My Project item that does the same thing. And, of course, you can always right-click the project name and then select Properties from the pop-up menu.

Let's examine some of the more common project property pages and discuss briefly the options that can be set on each.

Application   The Application property page allows you to set the assembly name, root/default namespace, application/output type, and startup object. For Windows Forms applications, authentication modes and visual styles are also controlled via this property page. Note that the options available in this dialog depend on the project type and the chosen language:

▶ **Assembly Name**—This is the filename of the assembly that the project is compiled into. Typically, it defaults to the project name. The extension used is determined by the output type of the project.

▶ **Target Framework**—This is the specific version of the .NET Framework to be targeted by the project. Visual Studio 2012 adds options here for .NET Framework 4.5, but continues to allow you to compile code against earlier versions from 2.0 onward.

▶ **Root/Default Namespace**—This specifies a namespace to be used by any types declared within the project. This can also be declared manually in code.

▶ **Output Type (C#)/Application Type (VB)**—This value determines the fundamental project type (for example, class library, Windows application, console application).

▶ **Startup Object**—This object is used to set the entry point for the project. For Windows applications, this is the default form (or in the case of C#, the program entry point for the form) that should be launched when the application is executed. For console applications, the startup object is the main subroutine procedure that implements the console. Class library projects do not have an entry point and will be set to (Not set) for C# projects, and (None) for VB projects.

▶ **Icon**—This is the icon to associate with the assembly. It is not pertinent to class library or web projects.

▶ **Resource File**—This text box can be used to specify a path and filename for a resource file. Resource files contain nonexecutable content, such as strings, images, or even persisted objects, that need to be deployed along with an application.

▶ **Windows Application Framework Properties**—Visual Basic provides a series of properties that apply specifically to Windows application projects. These properties allow you to set the splash screen associated with the project, enable or disable support for XP themes/visual styles, set the authentication mode supported by the project (Windows or application-defined), and set the shutdown mode of the project. The shutdown mode specifies whether the application should shut down when the initial form is closed or when the last loaded form in the application is closed.

Build (C# Only)   The Build property page is used with Visual C# projects to tweak settings associated with build configurations. Using this dialog box, you can select whether the DEBUG and TRACE constants are turned on, and you can specify conditional compilation symbols. Settings that affect the warning and error levels and the build output are also housed here. For more exploration of the options available here, see Chapter 10.

Build Events (C# Only)   Visual Studio triggers a pre- and post-build event for each project. On the Build Events page, you can specify commands that should be run during either of these events. This page also allows you to indicate when the post-build event runs: always, after a successful build, or when the build updates the project output. Build events are particularly useful for launching system tests and unit tests against a project that has just been recompiled. If you launch a suite of, say, unit tests from within the post-build event, the test cycle can be embedded within the build cycle.

> **NOTE**
>
> If you specify commands in the pre- or post-build events, Visual Studio creates a batch file for each event and places it into the bin/debug directory. These files, PreBuildEvent.bat and PostBuildEvent.bat, house the commands you enter on the Build Events property page. In the event of an error running the build event commands, you can manually inspect and run these files to try to chase down the bug.

Compile (VB Only)   The Compile property page is used by Visual Basic projects to control which optimizations are performed during compile and also to control general compilation options for the output path and warnings versus errors raised during the compilation process. It is analogous to the C# Build property page:

▶ **Compile Options**—You use the Option Strict, Option Explicit, and Option Infer drop-downs to turn on or off these settings. You can also control whether the project performs binary or text comparisons with the Option Compare drop-down.

▶ **Compiler Conditions**—Visual Basic allows you to customize the level of notification provided upon detecting any of a handful of conditions during the compilation process. For instance, one condition defined is Unused Local Variable. If this condition is detected in the source code during the compile, you can elect to have it treated as a warning or an error, or to have it ignored altogether.

▶ **Build Events**—Visual Basic allows you to access the Build Events property page (see the preceding section for an explanation) via a Build Events button located on this screen.

▶ **Warning configurations**—You can choose to disable all compiler warnings, treat all warnings as errors, and generate an XML documentation file during the compile process. This results in an XML file with the same name as the project; it contains all the code comments parsed out of your source code in a predefined format.

Debug   The Debug property page allows you to affect the behavior of the Visual Studio debugger:

▶ **Start Action**—You use this option to specify whether a custom program, a URL, or the current project itself should be started when the debugger is launched.

▶ **Start Options**—You use this option to specify command-line arguments to pass to the running project, set the working directory for the project, and debug a process on a remote machine.

▶ **Enable Debuggers**—You use the check boxes in this section to enable or disable such things as support for debugging unmanaged code, support for SQL stored procedure debugging, and use of Visual Studio as a host for the debugger process.

Publish   The Publish property page enables you to configure many ClickOnce-specific properties. You can specify the publish location for the application, the install location (if different from the publish location), and the various installation settings, including prerequisites and update options. You can also control the versioning scheme for the published assemblies.

References (VB Only)   The References property page is used within Visual Basic projects to select the assemblies referenced by the project and to import namespaces into the project. This screen also allows you to query the project in an attempt to determine whether some existing references are unused. You do this by using the Unused References button.

Reference Paths (C# Only)   The Reference Paths property page allows you to provide path information meant to help Visual Studio find assemblies referenced by the project. Visual Studio first attempts to resolve assembly references by looking in the current project directory. If the assembly is not found there, the paths provided on this property page are used to search for the assemblies. Visual Studio also probes the project's obj directory, but only after attempting to resolve first using the reference paths you have specified on this screen.

Resources   Resources are items such as strings, images, icons, audio, and files that are embedded in a project and used during design and runtime. The Resources property page allows you to add, edit, and delete resources associated with the project.

Security   For ClickOnce applications, the Security property page allows you to enforce code access security permissions for running the ClickOnce application. Various full-trust and partial-trust scenarios are supported.

Settings   Application settings are dynamically specified name/value pairs that can be used to store information specific to your project/application. The Settings property page allows you to add, edit, and delete these name/value pairs.

Each setting can be automatically scoped to the application or to the user, and can have a default value specified. Applications can then consume these settings at runtime.

Signing   The Signing property page allows you to have Visual Studio code sign the project assembly (and its ClickOnce manifests) by specifying a key file. You can also enable Delay Signing from this screen.

Summary

Solutions and projects are the primary vehicles within Visual Studio for organizing and managing your code. They allow you to divide and conquer large solutions, and they provide a single point of access for various settings (at both the solution and project levels). Solutions are the top-level container and the first work item that Visual Studio creates when creating a new code project.

In this chapter, you learned the following about solutions:

▶ Solutions can be built (triggering a build of each of its projects) but cannot be compiled.

▶ Visual Studio can load only one solution at a time; to work on multiple solutions concurrently, you must have multiple copies of Visual Studio running.

▶ You can create folders within a solution to help group its content; these folders are virtual and do not represent physical file folders.

▶ Solutions are primarily used to group one or more projects together. Projects within a solution can be a mix of the various supported languages and project types.

▶ Solutions cannot contain other solutions.

▶ Besides projects, solutions can also contain miscellaneous files (called solution items) that typically represent information pertinent to the solution (readme files, system diagrams, and the like).

Although solutions are an important and necessary implement, it is the Visual Studio project that actually results in a compiled .NET component. Projects are created and based on templates available within the IDE that cover the various development scenarios, ranging from web application development to Windows application development to smart device development.

In this chapter, you learned the following about projects:

▶ Projects exist to compile code into assemblies.

▶ Projects are based on a project template; project templates define the various artifacts, references, and so on that make sense for the project's context.

▶ Like solutions, projects also support subfolders to help you better organize your code. These folders are actual physical folders that are created on disk.

▶ Projects contain project items. They can be source code files, references, and other items such as virtual folders and database connections.

You have seen how solutions and projects are physically manifested; the next chapter covers the primary Visual Studio tools used to interact with solutions and projects.

CHAPTER 5

Browsers and Explorers

Visual Studio provides a cohesive and all-encompassing view of your solutions, projects, and types within your projects through windows called browsers and explorers. These windows (which are confusingly also referred to as view windows) attempt to provide a visually structured representation of a large variety of elements (some code based, others not).

In general, you access and display these windows through the View menu. Some of these windows, such as the Solution Explorer and Class View, are staples of a developer's daily routine. Others touch on elements that are used during specific points within the development cycle or by more advanced Visual Studio IDE users.

This chapter examines each of the basic browser and explorer windows in detail.

Leveraging the Solution Explorer

The Solution Explorer is the primary tool for viewing and manipulating solutions and projects. It provides a simple but powerful hierarchical view of all solution and project items, and it enables you to interact with each item directly via context menus and its toolbar.

Using Solution Explorer, you can launch an editor for any given file, add new items to a project or solution, and reorganize the structure of a project or solution. In addition, the Solution Explorer provides instant, at-a-glance information as to the currently selected project; the startup project for the solution; and the physical hierarchy of the solution, its projects, and their child items.

The Solution Explorer is simply a window hosted by Visual Studio. It can be docked, pinned, and floated anywhere within the Visual Studio environment. It is composed of a title bar, a toolbar, and a scrollable tree-view region (see Figure 5.1).

The tree view provides a graphics- and text-organizational view of the currently loaded solution. Figure 5.1 shows all the various items and projects represented for a 14-project solution loaded in the IDE.

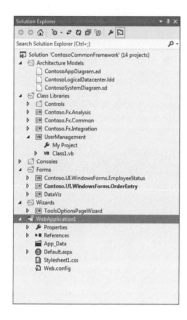

FIGURE 5.1   The Solution Explorer.

Visual Cues and Item Types

Each item in the Solution Explorer is represented by a name and by an icon. Table 5.1 shows which icon is used to represent the supported item types.

TABLE 5.1   Solution Explorer Item Types and Icons

Icon	Item	Notes
	ASP.NET Web Site	This represents the root node for an ASP.NET website project.
	Bitmap File	
	Custom Control	

Icon	Item	Notes
	DataSet	
	Folder	Solution folders or project folders.
	HTML Page	
	Icon File	
	Interface	
	Master Page	Web projects only.
	Module	Visual Basic only.
	My Project File (VB) / Properties Folder (C#)	
	Project Reference	Visual C# only.
	Site Map	Web projects only.
	Skin File	Web projects only.
	Solution	This is the topmost, root node visible within Solution Explorer.
	Style Sheet	
	Text File	
	User Control	Any class that inherits directly from the `UserControl` class.
	VBScript/JScript File	
	Visual Basic Source File	

Icon	Item	Notes
VB	Visual Basic Project	This is the root node for a Visual Basic project.
C#	Visual C# Project	This is the root node for a Visual C# project.
C#	Visual C# Source File	
	Web Configuration File	
	Web Form (.aspx)	
	Web Project	
	Web Service	
	Windows Form	Refers to a file containing a class that implements the Form class.
	XML File	
	XML Schema File	
	XSLT File	

NOTE

The icons shown in Table 5.1 are a representative list of icons that correspond to specific project and solution items within the IDE. Other files added to a project or solution are represented by the icon associated with their file types. For example, a Word document is represented by the standard Word document icon in the Solution Explorer.

Version Control and Item Status

To provide a visual cue about the status of a particular item, the Solution Explorer overlays an additional graphical element on the item icon. These overlays are called signal icons. For example, when source code control is enabled, the Solution Explorer visually indicates whether an item is checked out via a graphical overlay. Table 5.2 describes the version control signal icons used by the Solution Explorer to indicate the current version control status of the item. Note that the version control state of an item is dependent on the actual version control system you are using (for instance, Visual Source Safe or Team Foundation Source Control).

TABLE 5.2   Version Control Signal Icons

Icon	Description
🔒	Checked in. The item is under source code control and is currently checked in.
✔	Checked out (to you). The item is under source code control and is currently checked out by you.
🔒	Checked out (by someone else). The item is under source code control and is currently checked out by someone else.
⊖	Excluded. The item has been specifically excluded from version control.
✚	Pending Add. The item is scheduled to be added to the source control system during the next check-in.

Interacting with Items

The Solution Explorer supports different management actions depending on whether you are currently interacting with a solution or a project. In fact, supported commands might vary by project type as well. As an example, the Copy Web Project command button is available for web projects but not class library projects, whereas the Properties command button is available for all item types.

There are two primary interfaces for interaction within Solution Explorer: the toolbar and the context menu. Let's review the primary features.

Table 5.3 shows the various buttons hosted in the Solution Explorer's toolbar, along with their specific scope.

TABLE 5.3   Solution Explorer Toolbar Buttons

Icon	Context	Description
←	All	Back button. Moves to the prior filtering scope.
→	All	Next button. Moves to the next filtering scope.
🏠	All	Home button. Removes any existing filtering scope.

Icon	Context	Description
	All	File filter. Allows you to show only files that are open in an editor, or only files that have pending changes. You select between the two different modes (open files versus pending changes) by using the drop-down, and then you turn on or turn off the filter by toggling the button.
	All	Sync with active document. Selects the file in Solution Explorer that is open in the current/active designer/editor window.
	All	Refresh. Refreshes the contents of the solution explorer window.
	All	Collapse all. Collapses any currently expanded trees within the Solution Explorer.
	Project	Show all files. Collapses any currently expanded trees within the Solution Explorer.
	Project	Nest related files. The Solution Explorer window has the capability to group certain project item constructs together. This is most commonly done with items such as code behind files. This is a toggle button: Clicking it "on" causes related files to be nested underneath the "parent" file. Clicking it "off" causes all files to show up at the same level under the project.
	Code file	View code. Opens the currently selected item in a code editor window.
	All	Properties. Opens the properties dialog, or shows the properties window, for the currently selected item.
	All	Preview selected item. Toggles the item preview feature of Visual Studio. With preview turned on, just selecting/single-clicking an item in the Solution Explorer will cause the item to immediately load in an editor/designer tab.

Managing Solutions

Clicking the solution in Solution Explorer immediately exposes all the valid management commands for that solution. As stated earlier, you access these commands through either the Solution Explorer toolbar or the context menu for the solution (which you access by right-clicking the solution). Through the toolbar and the solution's context menu, the Solution Explorer allows you to do the following:

► View and set the properties for a solution

► Build/rebuild a solution

► Directly launch the configuration manager for a solution

▶ Set project dependencies and build order

▶ Add any of the various Visual Studio-supported solution and project items

▶ Run code analysis against all of the files in the solution

▶ View code metrics for all of the files in the solution

▶ Add the solution to the source control

You can initiate some of these actions by using the Solution Explorer toolbar; you can access the balance in the context menu for a solution, as shown in Figure 5.2.

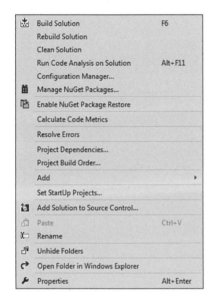

FIGURE 5.2   The solution context menu.

Managing Projects

Just as with solutions, Solution Explorer provides various ways to manage projects within a solution, including the following:

▶ Opening a project item

▶ Building or rebuilding a project

▶ Adding items to a project

▶ Adding a reference to a project

▶ Cutting, pasting, renaming, or deleting a project within the solution tree

▶ Editing project properties

▶ Running code analysis against all of the files in the project

- ▶ Viewing code metrics for all of the files in the project

- ▶ Unloading a project

- ▶ Limiting the scope of the Solution Explorer to a single project

- ▶ Launching a separate instance of the Solution Explorer window scoped to a single project

> **NOTE**
>
> The current startup project for a solution is indicated with a bold font (as is the OrderEntry project in Figure 5.1). If multiple projects are selected as startup projects, the solution name is instead bolded.

Figure 5.3 shows the project context menu for a class library project.

FIGURE 5.3　The project context menu.

The default action when you double-click an item is to open it within its default editor or designer. Multiple select and drag-and-drop operations are also supported. For instance, multiselecting several code files allows you to open them simultaneously in their editor windows.

You can move and copy items within a solution, within a project, or between projects through the standard drag and drop using the left mouse button. You can also drag certain items from within a project and drop them onto a suitable designer surface. This is an easy way, for instance, to add classes to a class diagram: Simply highlight the code files that contain the types you want to add and drag them onto the class diagram designer window.

Inspecting Objects

Visual Studio 2012 implements several improvements to the Solution Explorer from earlier versions that directly improve your ability to find and interact with objects within a solution. For instance, although the top-level hierarchies shown within the Solution Explorer are based on physical files (for example, solution files that reference project files that reference C# code files), you can also drill down directly into object definitions.

> **NOTE**
>
> The eagle-eyed developer will note that the Solution Explorer window in Visual Studio 2012 is actually not a refinement of the Visual Studio 2010 Solution Explorer, but rather is a refinement of the popular Solution Navigator tool (a Visual Studio 2010 extension made available for download by Microsoft within the Productivity Power Tools pack).
>
> If you need to still work in Visual Studio 2010, using the Solution Navigator add-on will give you nearly 100% of the functionality of the Visual Studio 2012 Solution Explorer.

Figure 5.4 illustrates how we can directly access a class, and class members, that are implemented within a specific code file. In this case, we can see three classes that are all implemented within the Integration.cs code file: `MessageMapper`, `MessageBus`, and `ContextToken`.

Further expanding a class shows its properties, private fields, methods, and nested classes. If you click any of these, a code editor window opens, and you will be placed directly within the class on that specific line of code.

> **NOTE**
>
> The Visual Studio 2012 Solution Explorer provides an improved and speedier way to open items in an editor window. Just selecting an item in the Solution Explorer window by clicking it immediately opens its associated editor within a quick tab window. No need to double-click or select and then press Enter.

Searching the Solution

The Solution Explorer search box allows you to quickly locate files and code based on simple string searches. Just type your search string into the box (using the Ctrl+; hotkey combination will get you there quickly), and as you type Solution Explorer automatically starts filtering the contents of the window to only those items that match your string.

Search can be limited to just filenames or to files and their content/code. It will even search files that are external to the solution (for example, external dependencies). The option of what to search is controlled by the search box drop-down (see Figure 5.5).

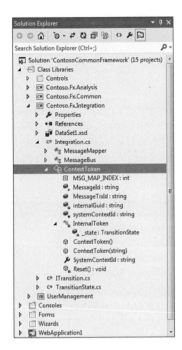

FIGURE 5.4   Examining class members.

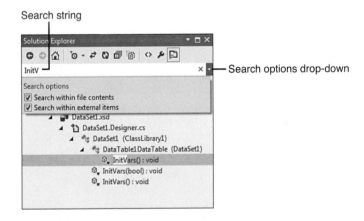

FIGURE 5.5   Searching the solution.

TIP

The search box directly supports camel casing and Pascal casing of strings. The way that it works is subtle and could be missed on initial examination. To search the contents of the solution for matches based on exact character casing, enter the string cased precisely the way that you want. For example: a class called AboutBox would be found using the search string AboutB. If you type in a search string without any casing, camel casing will not be used and the search algorithm will ignore the casing entirely. Typing in aboutb, for example, would also locate that same AboutBox class.

The search box also supports Pascal-casing breaks. This allows you to type AB and get any element Pascal cased with a capital *A* followed by a capital *B*. The AboutBox class name fits this pattern and as a result would be returned by a search of AB.

Using View Scopes and Additional Windows

Search is one way to limit the scope of what is displayed in the Solution Explorer window. There are also two other mechanisms for filtering the contents of the window to only those things you care about. By right-clicking any project or project item, you can select Scope to This in the context menu and filter the contents of the window to only that item or the things that the item contains. Scoping to a project will only show that project and its content, scoping to a code file will only show that code file and its methods/properties (and so on, and so forth). Every time you scope to a different item within the window, it is just as if another view of the Solution Explorer were added as a "page." You can then use the Back, Forward, and Home buttons on the Solution Explorer toolbar to move through these scope pages or bring you back to home, which essentially removes all scopes and shows you the entire solution again.

In a similar fashion, you can also scope to an element and launch that view within a completely separate, new Solution Explorer window. This is done by right-clicking an item (for instance, a project) and then selecting New Solution Explorer View. This is a great productivity feature if you have a lot of screen real estate on your monitor or if you have multiple monitors. You can take a very complex solution, grab the project or class that you want to focus on, and create a new Solution Explorer view, which can be floated anywhere on your screen or docked within the IDE. Figure 5.6 shows two Solution Explorer windows, one docked and one floating, existing side by side.

Class View

The Class View window is similar in design and function to the Solution Explorer window. It, too, provides a hierarchical view of project elements. However, the view here is not based on the physical files that constitute a solution or project; rather, this window provides a logical view based on the relationships of the various namespaces, types, interfaces, and enums within a project.

The Class View window is composed of four major visual components: a toolbar, a search bar, a tree view of types (called the objects pane), and a members pane, as shown in Figure 5.7.

Toolbar

The Class View window's toolbar provides easy access to command buttons for adding virtual folders, moving forward and back through the objects pane items, and controlling which objects are displayed.

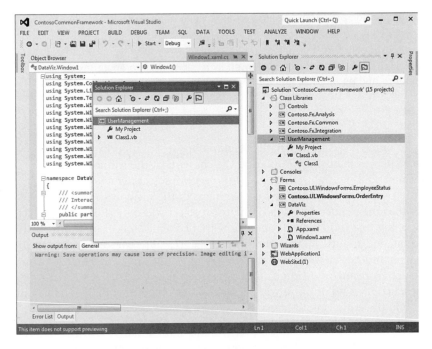

FIGURE 5.6 Creating a new Solution Explorer view.

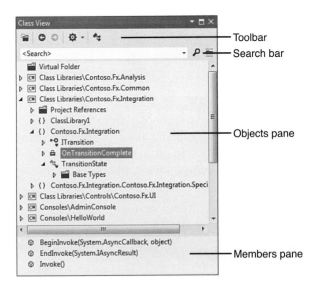

FIGURE 5.7 The Class View window.

Table 5.4 describes the various Class View toolbar buttons.

TABLE 5.4   Class View Toolbar Buttons

Icon	Description
	Class View New Folder. Creates a virtual folder used to organize objects within the objects pane.
	Back. Causes the previously selected item to become the currently selected item.
	Forward. Causes the most recently selected item to become the currently selected item. This button is available only after you've used the back button.
	Class View Settings. Displays a drop-down that allows selection of object types to display within the objects pane and the members pane. The available options include these: Show Base Types, Show Derived Types, Show Project References, Show Hidden Types and References, Show Public Members, Show Protected Members, Show Private Members, Show Other Members, and Show Inherited Members.
	View Class Diagram. Creates a class diagram project item and launches the viewer for that item. All the types contained within the project are automatically added to the diagram.

Search Bar

The search bar is a drop-down text box that provides a quick and easy way to filter the objects shown in the objects pane. When a search term (such as type name or namespace name) is entered, the Class View window clears the objects pane and then repopulates it with only those objects that match the search term. Figure 5.8 shows the results of a search for ITransition.

To restore the Objects pane and remove the filter, click the Clear Search button to the right of the Search button.

Recent search terms are saved for reuse in the drop-down list.

Objects Pane

The objects pane encloses a tree of objects grouped, at the highest level, by project. Each object is identified by an icon and by its name. Expanding a project node within the tree reveals the various types contained within that project. Further parent-child relationships are also visible, such as the namespace-to-class relationship and the type-to-parent-type relationship.

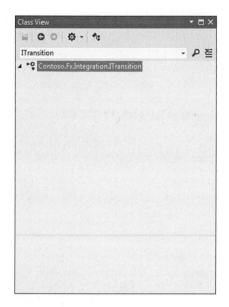

FIGURE 5.8   Filtering the objects pane.

Table 5.5 shows the icons used in the Objects pane.

TABLE 5.5   Objects Pane Icons

Icon	Description
	Class/struct
	Delegate
	Enum
{ }	Namespace
	Module
	Interface

Certain signal images are also overlaid on top of these icons to visually represent scope and access information for each object. These access type signal icons are described in Table 5.6.

TABLE 5.6   Scope/Access Signal Icons

Icon	Description
Padlock	Private
Shield	Internal/friend
(None)	Public
Star	Protected

The depth of the various levels shown for each object is dictated by the view settings in place at the time. For example, turning on the Show Base Types option appends an additional base type level to the tree for each type. The objects pane's principal duty is to allow quick and easy navigation back and forth through the object tree for each project. It exposes, in other words, an object-oriented view of each project.

Right-clicking within the objects pane displays the shortcut menu which is useful for quickly resorting and organizing items in the Class View window. These are the Sort/ Group options available:

▶ **Sort Alphabetically**—The projects, namespaces, and types in the objects pane are sorted in ascending, alphabetic order.

▶ **Sort by Object Type**—The types in the objects pane are alphabetically sorted by their general classification (for example, in the following order: classes, enums, interfaces, structs).

▶ **Sort by Object Access**—The types are sorted by their access modifiers (public, private, protected, and so on).

▶ **Group by Object Type**—Another folder level is added to the tree for each distinct object type present. For example, if a project contains both class and interface types, a class folder and an interface folder are displayed in the objects pane tree, with their correlated types contained within.

Members Pane

The members pane reacts to the selections made in the objects pane by displaying all the members (properties, events, constants, variables, enums) defined on the selected type. Each member has a distinctive icon to immediately convey information such as scope and type; even member signatures show up here (note that the same signal icons used by the objects pane, and documented in Table 5.7, are used here as well).

TABLE 5.7   Members Pane Icons

Icon	Description
▣	Constant
⬡	Method/function
🔧	Property
◆	Field

The members pane is ideal for quickly visualizing type behavior and attributes: Just select the class/type in the objects pane and browse its members in the members pane.

> **NOTE**
>
> Many developers find that the bulk of their development tasks are more easily envisioned and acted on within the Class View window rather than in the Solution Explorer window. The available actions among the two are virtually identical, but the Class View window provides a much more code-focused perspective of your projects. Developers can spelunk through inheritance trees and see, at a glance, other various members implemented on each defined type within their projects. The downside to using the Class View is that source code control information is not visually surfaced here.

The members pane also exposes a context menu that has invaluable tools for browsing and editing code. For one, you can directly apply the Rename refactoring to a selected member. Other capabilities exposed here include the capability to immediately view the definition code for a member, to find every code location where the selected member is referenced, and to launch the Object Browser with the primary node for the member already selected for you.

The capability to alter the filter and display settings is also presented here. Figure 5.9 illustrates all the available commands on this menu.

Server Explorer

The Server Explorer window serves two purposes: It exposes various system services and resources that reside on your local machine and on remote machines, and it provides access to data connection objects. As with the other Visual Studio explorer windows, the systems, services, resources, and data connections are viewed in a graphical tree format. Systems appear under a top-level Servers node (your local machine shows up by default), and data connections appear under a top-level Data Connections node.

FIGURE 5.9   The members pane context menu.

> **NOTE**
>
> The Server Explorer window content and configuration are not specific to a solution or project. Server Explorer settings are preserved as part of the IDE environment settings and are thus not subject to change on a per-solution (or project) basis.

A toolbar appears at the top of the Server Explorer window, providing one-click access to the Add Data Connection and Add Server functions (see Figure 5.10). You can also force a refresh of the window contents. (A button is also provided to cancel the refresh because querying remote machines might be a lengthy process.)

> **NOTE**
>
> The Express and Standard editions of Visual Studio do not have support for servers within the Server Explorer window; they are limited to data connections only. In fact, these versions of Visual Studio actually refer to this window as the Data Explorer window.

Data Connections

Data connections represent a physical connection to a local or remote database. Through an established connection, you can gain access to and manipulate the various objects within a database. Each category of object shows up as a folder node under the Data Connections node. The tree items under each node allow you to directly interact with their physical database counterparts through a suite of designers and editors collectively referred to as Visual Database Tools. These tools are covered in depth in Chapter 21, "Working with Databases."

FIGURE 5.10   The Server Explorer window.

The following objects are exposed in the Server Explorer:

▶ Data diagrams

▶ Tables

▶ Views

▶ Stored procedures

▶ Functions

▶ Synonyms

▶ Types

▶ Assemblies

In general, you can create new database objects, edit or delete existing ones, and, where appropriate, query data from a database object (such as a table or view).

> **NOTE**
>
> The level of functionality and the number of object types you can access through the Server Explorer depend on both the version of Visual Studio you are using and the version of the database you are connecting to. In other words, not all functions are supported across all databases. The Visual Database Tools interact most effectively with Microsoft SQL Server, although most basic functions are supported against a variety of other relational databases.

Server Components

The Servers node in Server Explorer exposes various remote or local services and resources for direct management or use within a Visual Studio project. In essence, it is a management console for server-based components. By default, your local machine is visible here as a server; to add other servers, right-click the Servers node and select Add Server or click the Connect to Server button in the Server Explorer toolbar. A dialog box prompts you for a computer name or IP address for the server; this dialog box also supports the capability to connect via a different set of credentials.

Under the Servers node, the following component categories appear as child nodes:

- ▶ Event Logs
- ▶ Management Classes
- ▶ Management Events
- ▶ Message Queues
- ▶ Performance Counters
- ▶ Services

Other component categories might also choose to register for display under the Servers node; the preceding list, however, represents the default, out-of-the-box functionality provided by Visual Studio 2012.

Event Logs

Under the Event Logs node, you can administer the separate application, security, and system event logs for the connected server. This includes clearing event log entries or drilling into and inspecting individual event log entries. Highlighting an event log or event log entry causes its properties to display in the Visual Studio property window, enabling you to view and edit their values. If you drag and drop one of the event logs into a project, a System.Diagnostics.EventLog or System.Diagnostic.EventLogEntry component instance is automatically created.

Management Classes

The items under the Management Classes node represent various Windows Management Instrumentation (WMI) classes. Each of these classes maps to a logical or physical entity associated with a server. The available classes here are shown in Table 5.8.

TABLE 5.8   WMI Management Class Nodes

Title	WMI Class
Desktop Settings	Win32_Desktop
Disk Volumes	Win32_LogicalDisk
My Computer	Win32_ComputerSystem

Title	WMI Class
Network Adapters	Win32_NetworkAdapter
Network Connections	Win32_NetworkConnection
NT Event Log Files	Win32_NTEventLogFile
Operating Systems	Win32_OperatingSystem
Printers	Win32_Printer
Processes	Win32_Process
Processors	Win32_Processor
Services	Win32_Service
Shares	Win32_Share
Software Products	Win32_Product
System Accounts	Win32_SystemAccount
Threads	Win32_Thread

A thorough discussion of WMI is beyond the scope of this chapter and this book; in summary, however, each of these nodes exposes various WMI class property groups (such as precedents, antecedents, settings, dependents), and, in turn, each of these property groups exposes a span of commands, enabling you to directly affect a resource on the server. One simple example of how you might use this capability is to set access information for a share exposed on a remote server. When you expand nodes in the Server Explorer down to the share (via the Disk Volumes node), access to the share information is gained via the shortcut menu on the share. In this example, you would select the SetShareInfo action, which initiates a WMI dialog box allowing you to change various share attributes such as the description and maximum allowed users.

Management Events

The Management Events node contains a list of event queries; essentially, these are "listeners" that you establish to periodically poll the WMI eventing system on the server. These event queries are established through a dialog box (see Figure 5.11; you launch the dialog box by selecting Add Event Query on the shortcut menu). When an event is created, a child node to the Management Events node is created, and under this node, actual event instances appear.

Message Queues

If message queuing is installed on the target server, the Message Queues node displays all the available message queues, along with any messages currently residing in each queue.

FIGURE 5.11   Creating a Management Event query.

Performance Counters

Every performance counter installed on the target computer can be viewed in the Performance Counters node. Each performance counter is displayed within its category. Performance counter instances, if available, are also displayed.

Services

Each installed service is enumerated under the Services node.

Programming with Server Explorer

Beyond enabling you to examine and manipulate data connections and server resources, the Server Explorer serves another task: By dragging and dropping items from the Server Explorer onto a Visual Studio design surface, you can quickly create components in code that directly reference the item in question. For example, dragging the Application Log node (from Servers, Event Logs) onto an existing Windows form creates a System.Diagnostics.EventLog component instance that is preconfigured to point to the application log. You can then immediately write code to interact with the event log component. You could use the same process to quickly embed message queue access into your application or read from/write to a performance counter. Table 5.9 lists the various possible drag-and-drop operations, along with their results.

TABLE 5.9   Server Explorer Drag and Drop

Under This Node	Dragging This	Does This
Event Logs	Event Log Category (for example, Application or System)	Creates a System.Diagnostics. EventLog component instance, configured for the appropriate event log
Management Classes	Management Class instance	Creates the appropriate WMI/CIMv2 component instance
Management Events	Management Event Query	Creates a System.Management. ManagementEventWatcher component instance
Message Queues	Message Queue instance	Creates a System.Messaging. MessageQueue component instance for the selected queue
Performance Counters	Performance Counter or counter instance	Creates a System.Diagnostics. PerformanceCounter component instance, configured for the appropriate counter
Services	Service	Creates a System.ServiceProcess. ServiceController, provisioned for the indicated service

NOTE

Data connection items in the Server Explorer cannot be dragged onto a design surface. For more information regarding drag-and-drop development of database solutions, see Chapter 21, "Service-Oriented Applications."

Object Browser

The Object Browser is similar in functionality and look and feel to the Class View window. It provides a hierarchical view of projects, assemblies, namespaces, types, enums, and interfaces. Unlike the Class View window, however, the Object Browser is capable of a much wider scope of objects. In addition to the currently loaded projects, the Object Browser can display items from the entire .NET Framework, up to and including COM components and externally accessible objects. This is a great tool for finding and inspecting types, regardless of where they are physically located.

Changing the Scope

You can use the toolbar's Browse drop-down to filter or change the scope of the objects displayed within the Object Browser. The scoping options offered are shown in Table 5.10.

TABLE 5.10   Object Browser Scoping Options

Scope	Effect
All Components	This is a superset of the other scopes offered. Selecting this shows all types and members within the .NET Framework, the current solution, any libraries referenced by the current solution, and any individually selected components.
.NET Framework	Shows all objects within a specific version of the .NET Framework (for example, .NET Framework 2.0, .NET Framework 3.0).
My Solution	Shows all objects with the currently loaded solution, including any referenced components.
Custom Component Set	Shows any objects specifically added to the custom component set.

Editing the Custom Component Set

A custom component set is a list of components that you manually specify. Using a custom list might be useful in situations in which you want to browse a list of components from a variety of different "buckets." Instead of wading through each of the other scopes, you could include only those types that you care about in the component list.

You add to the custom component list by selecting the Edit Custom Component Set option in the Browse drop-down or by clicking the ellipsis to the right of the drop-down. This launches an editor dialog box in which you can add or remove entries in this list (see Figure 5.12).

Adding a component to the set is as easy as selecting from one of the prepopulated object lists (available via the .NET, COM, or Projects tabs) or by browsing directly to the container assembly via the Browse tab. You can select an object or objects and then click the Add button. The current set members show up at the bottom of the dialog box. You can also select a current member and remove it from the list by clicking the Remove button.

Browsing Objects

The Object Browser consists of a toolbar and three different panes: an objects pane, a members pane, and a description pane. Again, the similarity here to the Class View window is obvious. The toolbar, objects pane, and members pane function identically to the Class View objects pane and members pane. You click down through the tree view to view each individual object's members; the toolbar aids in navigating deep trees by providing a Forward and Back button. Figure 5.13 shows the Object Browser in action.

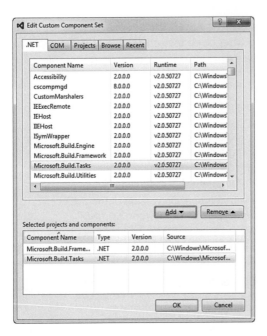

FIGURE 5.12   Editing the custom component set.

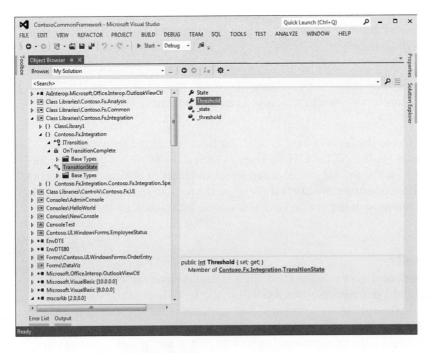

FIGURE 5.13   The Object Browser.

The hierarchical relationships, icons, and actions possible within the panes are the same (and therefore we won't rehash them here). The description pane, however, is a new concept.

Description Pane

When an item is selected in either the Object Browser's objects pane or members pane, the description pane provides detailed information about the selected item. The data provided is quite extensive and includes the following:

- The name of the selected object

- The name of the parent of the selected object

- Code comments and inline help associated with the selected object

Where possible, the description pane embeds hyperlinks within the data that it displays to enable you to easily navigate to related items. For example, a declared property of type string might show the following description:

```
public string SystemContextId { set; get; }
    Member of Contoso.Fx.Integration.ContextToken
```

Note the use of hyperlinking: Clicking the string identifier navigates to the string data type within the Object Browser window. Similarly, clicking the Contoso.Fx.Integration.ContextToken hyperlink navigates the browser to the class definition for the ContextToken class.

> **TIP**
>
> You can click an assembly in the Objects pane and quickly add it as a reference to the current project by clicking the Add to References button located on the Object Browser's toolbar.

Document Outline

The Document Outline window (opened from the View, Other Windows menu) exposes a hierarchical view of elements residing on a Windows form, a web form, or a Windows Presentation Foundation (WPF) window. This is a fantastic tool for "reparenting" form items or changing the z-order of a control within its parent. In addition, it assists with understanding the exact logical structure of a form that might have a lot happening on it from a visual perspective.

Figures 5.14 and 5.15 show the Document Outline windows for a simple web form and a slightly more complicated WPF window.

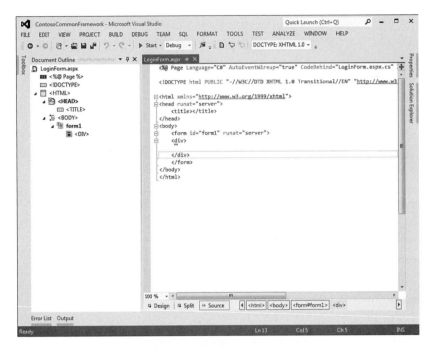

FIGURE 5.14   A web form.

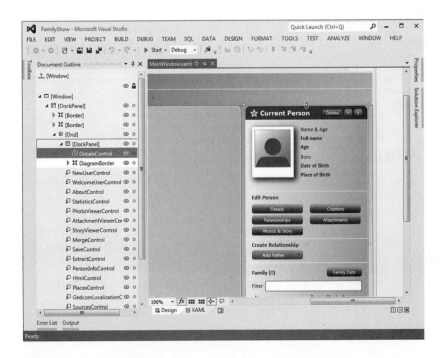

FIGURE 5.15   A WPF form.

The Document Outline toolbar allows you to control the display of the types within the tree view and also facilitates reordering and repositioning elements within the outline.

Editing Elements

The Document Outline makes it easy to instantly jump from the hierarchical element view directly to the underlying code for an item. If an item is currently being edited in the designer/code window, it is highlighted within the outline tree. Conversely, selecting an item within the outline view causes the item to be selected/highlighted within the designer/code window. Each project type has slightly different behavior within the Document Outline tool. In general, you can use drag-and-drop actions within the tree view to move elements around in the outline. Windows Forms applications actually have a toolbar you can use within the Document Outline window. Table 5.11 describes the toolbar buttons.

TABLE 5.11   Windows Forms Document Outline Toolbar Commands

Icon	Description
	Type Name Display Style. This drop-down button enables you to control how type names are displayed in the tree view: None (No type names are displayed.); Short (The local, unqualified type name is displayed.); Full (The fully qualified type name is displayed.)
	Expand All. Causes all the parent nodes to expand.
	Collapse All. Causes all the parent nodes to collapse.
	Move Down in Container. Moves the currently selected item down one place within its order in the current container.
	Move Up in Container. Moves the currently selected item up one place within its order in the current container.
	Move Out of Current Container. Moves the currently selected item out of its current container and places it in the next, higher container (or within the root level if no container exists).
	Move into Next Container. Moves the currently selected item out of its current container (or root level) and into the next container.

Summary

In this chapter, you have seen that browsers and explorers are Visual Studio windows that typically provide a hierarchical view of their content. They tend to share common interface elements (tree views, toolbars, and elements), and they are, in effect, the primary means for visualizing and interacting with project elements within the IDE.

Browsers and explorers provide simple point-and-click interfaces for the following:

▶ Visualizing and organizing your solutions and projects on a file-by-file basis

▶ Visualizing and organizing your projects on a type-by-type, class-by-class basis

▶ Querying and interacting with server resources such as databases, performance counters, and message queues

▶ Browsing through type libraries

Although certain browsers/explorers touch underlying concepts that are fairly deep and complicated (WMI, for instance), they are all geared toward a common goal: extending the reach of the IDE as a rapid application development tool for tasks beyond simple code file editing.

CHAPTER 6

Introducing the Editors and Designers

Although Visual Studio provides an impressive array of functionality for nearly all areas of the development process, its editors and designers are the real heart of the IDE. They are the bread-and-butter tools of the programmer: They enable you to write code, edit resources, design forms, and construct schemas. And, of course, each of these tools has key features designed to boost your productivity and the quality of your output.

This chapter is squarely focused on using these editors and designers to create solutions within the IDE.

Getting Started with the Basics

Broadly speaking, a Visual Studio editor is a text editor (think word processor) that enables you to write specific output efficiently (Visual Basic code, Hypertext Markup Language [HTML], Extensible Application Markup Language [XAML], and so on). A designer, in contrast, is a visual editor, enabling you to work with visual concepts directly instead of text. Many document types are supported by both designers and editors: You can build a form, for instance, by using the drag-and-drop convenience of the Windows Forms Designer or by handcrafting the code within a text editor; or you can build an Extensible Markup Language (XML) file using the same mechanisms.

The Visual Studio text editor provides the core text-editing functionality for all the editors. This functionality is then inherited and added upon to create editors specific for a given document type. Thus, you have a code editor for source code files, an XML editor for markup, a Cascading Style Sheets (CSS) editor for style sheets, and so on.

Likewise, designers manifest themselves in ways specific to their roles. The HTML designer is part text editor and part graphical tool, and the Windows and web forms designers are superb WYSIWYG form builders.

The Text Editor

There are a few text-editing features that we all take for granted: selecting parts of an existing body of text, inserting text into a document, copying and pasting text, and so on. As you would expect, the text editor window supports all of these features in a way that is familiar to anyone who has used a Windows-based word processor.

You select text, for instance, by using the following familiar actions:

1. Place the cursor at the start of the text you want to select.

2. While holding down the left mouse button, sweep the mouse to the end of the text you want to select.

3. Release the left mouse button.

In addition to this "standard" selection method, the Visual Studio text editor supports "column mode" selection. In column mode, instead of selecting text in a linear fashion from left to right, line by line, you drag a selection rectangle across a text field. Any text character caught within the selection rectangle is part of the selected text. This is called column mode because it allows you to create a selection area that captures columns of text characters instead of just lines. The procedure is largely the same:

1. Place the cursor at the start of the text you want to select.

2. While holding down the Alt key *and* the left mouse button, expand the bounds of the selection rectangle until it includes the desired text.

3. Release the left mouse button and the Alt key.

After you've selected text, you can copy, cut, or drag it to a new location within the text editor. As with text selection, the commands for cutting, copying, and pasting text remain unchanged from their basic standard implementations in other Windows applications: You first select text, and then cut or copy it using the Edit menu, the toolbar, or the text editor's shortcut menu.

By dragging a text selection, you can reposition it within the current text editor, place it in a previously opened text editor window, or even drag the selection into the command or watch windows.

Line Wrapping and Virtual Space

The default behavior of the text editor is not to automatically wrap any text for you. In other words, as you type, your text or code simply keeps trailing on to the right of the editor. If you exceed the bounds of the currently viewable area, the editor window scrolls to the right to allow you to continue typing. However, the text editor window can behave more like a word processor, in which the document content is typically constrained horizontally to its virtual sheet of paper.

TIP

With word wrapping turned on, Visual Studio automatically wraps your text onto the next line. You can also have the IDE place a visual glyph to indicate that a wrap has taken place. Both of these options are controlled on the Options dialog box, under the Text Editor, All Languages, General page (shown in Figure 6.1).

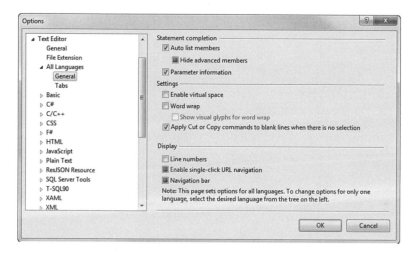

FIGURE 6.1   Editor Options dialog box.

If you override the default behavior, turn wrapping on, and then type a line of code that exceeds the editor's width, you can see that the editor window (see Figure 6.2) automatically wraps the source to fit within the boundaries of the window and provides an icon to the far right of the editor to indicate that a wrap has taken place. Word wrapping is useful for keeping all of your code in plain sight (without the need for scrolling horizontally).

The other option on the Text Editor Options dialog box, Enable Virtual Space, is a mutually exclusive feature to word wrapping. That is, you can enable virtual space or word wrapping, but not both. *Virtual space* refers to the capability to type text anywhere within the editor window without entering a bunch of spaces or tabs in the text area. This feature is useful in situations in which you want to place, for example, a code comment to the right of a few lines of code. Instead of tabbing each code comment over (or inserting padding spaces before them) to get them to indent and line up nicely, you can simply place the cursor at the exact column within the text editor where you want your comments to appear. See Figure 6.3 for an example; the code comment "floating in virtual space" that you see in the screenshot is not preceded by any spaces or tabs. It was simply typed directly into its current position.

FIGURE 6.2   Word wrapping in the editor.

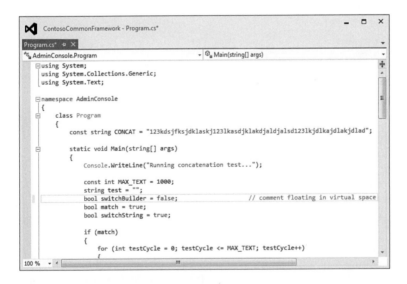

FIGURE 6.3   Virtual spacing in the editor window.

Visual Studio Designers

Designers are much more visual in nature than the text editors within Visual Studio; they provide a graphical perspective of a particular solution artifact. Thus, a form appears within a designer just as it would to the end user, as visual constructs made up of buttons, borders, menus, and frames. The code to implement the items shown in a designer is actually written by Visual Studio itself.

Like the various editors, the designers are all similar in form and function. They occupy space within the tabbed documents area of the IDE (just as the editors do). They might take on different behaviors depending on their target use. The Windows Forms Designer and the component designer appear nearly the same, but there are subtle differences in their uses.

Coding with the Code Editor

Writing code and creating other syntax-based files is really all about typing text. The text editor window is the Visual Studio tool directly on point for creating source code text files. It is the keystone of development inside the IDE. It supports text entry and basic text operations such as selecting text regions, dragging and dropping text fragments, and setting tab stops. With basic text features alone, the editor would be sufficient to code with. However, it is the advanced features layered on top for debugging, code formatting, code guidance, and customization that really make this tool shine.

As we mentioned previously, the text editor actually has a few different personalities within the IDE. The code editor is designed to support creating and editing of source code files, the XML editor is targeted at XML files, and the CSS editor is targeted at CSS files. Although there are subtle differences in the way that code or markup is displayed in these windows, they all share the user interface and the same set of editing functionality.

> **TIP**
>
> Each editor type is fully customizable. Just fire up the Options dialog box (by choosing Tools, Options) and locate the Text Editor node. Under this node are separate pages that allow customization of each editor type.

Opening an Editor

You can launch a text editor (or any other editor in the IDE, for that matter) in two ways. The first way involves using the Solution Explorer: Select an existing code file, text file, or other type file and double-click the file. If it is a code file, you can also right-click it and select View Code. The file content is loaded into a new editor window.

The second way to launch an editor window is to choose File, New, File. This launches the New File dialog box. Selecting a code template from this dialog box launches a code editor prefilled with the initial code stubs relevant to the template selected.

> **TIP**
>
> The text editor windows live as tabbed windows front and center within the IDE. If multiple code editors are open, they are each accessible by their tabs. If a lot of editors are open at one time, finding the window you are looking for by cycling through the tabs can be cumbersome. There are four ways to quickly locate and select a code editor window. First, you can use Solution Explorer. Double-clicking the code file again within the Solution Explorer selects and displays the associated code editor window. Second, you can use the Window menu. Each open code editor window is shown by name in the windows list under

the Window menu. Third, to the far right of the editor tabs, right next to the Close icon, is a small drop-down button in the image of an arrow. Clicking the arrow drops down a list of all open editor windows, allowing you to select one at will. And finally, Visual Studio has its own version of the Windows switcher: Hold down the Ctrl key and tap the Tab key to cycle through a list of all windows open in IDE.

Writing Code in the Code Editor

Because the code editor's primary purpose is "word processing" for source code, let's first look at writing the simplest of routines, a "Hello, World" function, from the ground up using the code editor.

Figure 6.4 shows a code editor with an initial stubbed-out console file. This was produced by creating a new Visual C# Console project using the Solution Explorer. Double-clicking the Program.cs file within that new project displays the source code for this console application.

FIGURE 6.4   Code template for a Console code file.

As you can see, Visual Studio, as a result of the template used for creating the project, has already filled in some code:

```
using System;
using System.Collections.Generic;
using System.Linq;
using System.Text;
using System.Threading.Tasks;
```

```
namespace ConsoleApplication1
{
    class Program
    {
        static void Main(string[] args)
        {
        }
    }
}
```

To demonstrate the code editor in action, you create a console application that outputs the "Hello, World!" string to the Console window.

Within the Main routine, add the following:

```
Console.WriteLine("Hello, World!");
```

To begin writing the code, simply place your cursor in the window by clicking within the Main routine's braces, press Enter to get some space for the new line of code, and type the Console.WriteLine syntax.

These and other productivity enhancers are discussed at great length in the next chapter. Here, we focus on the basics of editing and writing code in the editor window.

Now that you have seen the code editor in action (albeit for a very simple example), you're ready to dig more into the constituent components of the editor window.

TIP

Visual Studio supports "zooming" within any open code editor/text editor. Hold down the Ctrl key and then use the mouse scroll wheel to zoom the editor view in or out.

Anatomy of the Code Editor Window

Editor windows, as you have seen, show up as tabbed windows within the IDE and are typically front and center visually in terms of windows layout. As you can see with the code editor window in Figure 6.5, each text editor window consists of three primary regions: a code pane, a selection margin, and an indicator margin. There are also both horizontal and vertical scrollbars for navigating around the displayed file.

These regions, and their functionality, remain the same for all editor types within the IDE.

The code editor adds an additional set of UI elements that are not present with the other editors: Two drop-down boxes at the top of the code editor window enable you to quickly navigate through source code by selecting a type in the left drop-down and then selecting a specific type member (property, field, function, and so on) in the right drop-down (these drop-downs are called class and method name, respectively, in Visual Basic). This jogs the current cursor location directly to the indicated type.

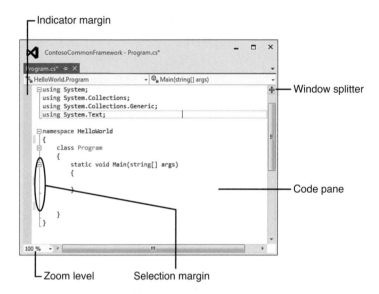

FIGURE 6.5   The components of the code editor window.

The Type drop-down displays only those types that are declared in the file currently displayed in the editor; it won't display a list that is global to the entire solution, project, or even namespace. Likewise, the Type Member drop-down displays only members for the selected type.

The Code Pane

The code pane is the place where the document (source code, XML, and so on) is displayed and edited. This region provides basic text-editing functionality, in addition to the more advanced productivity features of the editor, such as IntelliSense.

Right-clicking within the code pane provides a shortcut menu (see Figure 6.6) that includes standard cut, copy, and paste tools along with an assortment of other handy editing actions.

The Indicator Margin

The indicator margin is the slim gray-colored margin to the far left of the editor. This margin area is used to mark a line of code that contains a breakpoint or bookmark.

Figure 6.7 shows the "Hello, World" example with a bookmark placed on the Main routine and a breakpoint placed on the Console.WriteLine command.

Clicking within the indicator margin toggles a breakpoint on or off for the line of code you have selected. (You will learn more about breakpoints later in this chapter and in Chapter 11, "Debugging Code.")

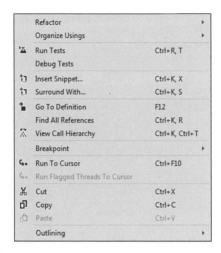

	Refactor	▶
	Organize Usings	▶
⚑	Run Tests	Ctrl+R, T
	Debug Tests	
↑⟩	Insert Snippet...	Ctrl+K, X
↑⟩	Surround With...	Ctrl+K, S
↑⟩	Go To Definition	F12
	Find All References	Ctrl+K, R
⟳	View Call Hierarchy	Ctrl+K, Ctrl+T
	Breakpoint	▶
↳•	Run To Cursor	Ctrl+F10
↳•	Run Flagged Threads To Cursor	
✂	Cut	Ctrl+X
⧉	Copy	Ctrl+C
⧉	Paste	Ctrl+V
	Outlining	▶

FIGURE 6.6   Code editor shortcut menu for a WinForms file.

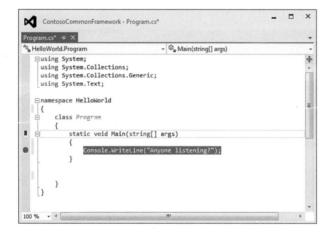

FIGURE 6.7   A bookmark and a breakpoint.

The Selection Margin

The selection margin is a narrow region between the indicator margin and the editing area of the code pane. It provides the following:

▶ The capability to select an entire line of text by clicking within the selection margin.

▶ A visual indication, via colored indicator bars, of those lines of code that have changed during the current editing session.

▶ Line numbers (if this option has been turned on). See the following section in which we discuss customizing the text editor's behavior.

You can clearly see the "changed text" indicator and line numbers in action in Figure 6.8.

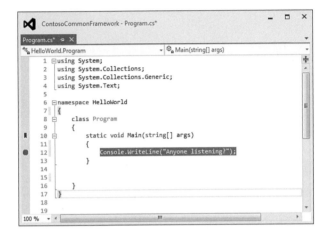

FIGURE 6.8　Changed text indicators and line numbers.

TIP

Visual Studio provides a dedicated toolbar for the text editor. You can view this toolbar by selecting View, Toolbars, Text Editor. It exposes buttons for the Member List, Quick Info, Parameter List, and Word Completion IntelliSense features, in addition to indenting buttons, commenting buttons, and bookmark navigation buttons. The navigation buttons are arguably the most useful because they provide easily accessible forward and back navigation through your code.

Code Navigation Tools

As the lines of code in any given project increase, effectively navigating through the code base (that is, quickly and easily finding lines of interest among the potentially thousands or even millions of lines of code) becomes an issue.

The text editor comes equipped with several tools to help you mark lines of code, search and replace text across source files, and, in general, maintain your situational awareness from within a long code listing.

Line Numbering

As mentioned in the discussion of the text editor's selection margin, you can enable line numbering for any given document loaded into an editor. This option is controlled in the Options dialog box within the Text Editor, All Languages, General page, or selectively under the individual languages and their General page.

By themselves, line numbers would be fairly useless. The capability to immediately jump to a line of code completes the equation and provides some real benefit from a navigation perspective. While within a text editor, press Ctrl+G to jump to a line of code. This triggers the Go To Line dialog box (see Figure 6.9), which provides a text box for speci-fying the line number to jump to and even indicates the valid "scope" for the jump by providing a line number range for the current document. Entering a valid line number here moves the cursor position to the start of that line.

FIGURE 6.9   Jumping to a line.

Bookmarks

Bookmarks tackle the problem of navigating through large code files. By placing a book-mark on a line of code, you can instantly navigate back to that line of code at any time. When dealing with a series of bookmarks, you can jump back and forth through the bookmarked lines of code, which turns out to be a surprisingly useful feature. If you are a developer who is dealing with a large base of source code, there are inevitably points of interest within the source code that you want to view in the editor. Recall that the text editor window provides a means of navigating via type and member drop-downs; these are not, however, the best tools for the job when your "line of interest" is an arbitrary statement buried deep within a million lines of code.

Bookmarks are visually rendered in the indicator margin of the text editor. (Refer to Figure 6.8; a bookmark appears on line 10.)

To add a bookmark or navigate through your bookmarks, you use either the text editor toolbar or the Bookmarks window.

You can view the Bookmarks window, shown in Figure 6.10, by choosing View, Other Windows, Bookmark Window. Notice that this window provides a toolbar for bookmark actions and provides a list of all available bookmarks, along with their actual physical location (filename and line number within that file).

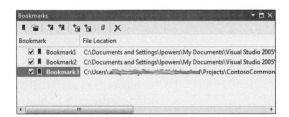

FIGURE 6.10   The Bookmarks window.

To toggle a bookmark for a given line of code, you first place your cursor on the desired line within the text editor and then click the Toggle Bookmark button. The same process is used to toggle the bookmark off. Using the Forward and Back buttons within the bookmarks window jumps the text editor's cursor location back and forth through all available bookmarks.

> **TIP**
>
> Use the Bookmarks window to navigate through code across projects. You are not limited to bookmarks placed within a single code file; they can, in fact, be in any loaded code file. The list of bookmarks in this window is also a useful mechanism for quickly toggling a bookmark on or off (via the check box next to the bookmark) and for assigning a meaningful name to a bookmark. Right-clicking a bookmark allows you to rename it something more meaningful than Bookmark7.

Bookmark Folders   One interesting feature with the Bookmarks window is the capability to create a bookmark folder. This is an organizational bucket for related bookmarks. For instance, you might want to place bookmarks for a specific math algorithm under a folder called MathFuncs. To do this, you first create a folder by using the New Folder button on the toolbar. You can rename the folder to whatever makes sense for your particular scenario. Then you can create a bookmark and drag and drop it into the folder.

See Figure 6.11 for a look at a populated Bookmarks window. Note that two folders are in use, in addition to bookmarks being shown for various source code files.

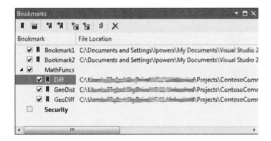

FIGURE 6.11   The Bookmarks window with folders.

Call Hierarchy

The Call Hierarchy window is yet another way to navigate through your projects. This window lets you easily follow the calls to and from every method, property, or constructor. With the code editor open, just right-click the member name and select View Call Hierarchy. This launches the Call Hierarchy window. The member name appears in a tree view in the left pane of this window; this tree view itemizes the various calls made to and from the member. If you click one of the calling sites, you can then view the calls to and from that method and so on.

Figure 6.12 shows an example of this iterative information displayed for successive callers. Clicking any of the caller or callee nodes shows you the specific location of that code in the right pane, and double-clicking that information in the right pane immediately jumps the code editor to that line of code.

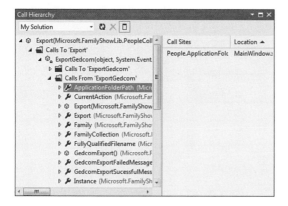

FIGURE 6.12   Using the Call Hierarchy window to explore code relationships.

> With Visual Studio 2012, the Call Hierarchy window works with both Visual Basic and C# code. In earlier versions, only C# code was supported.

The usefulness of this tool doesn't stop at caller/callee information. If you right-click any node in the tree, you can jump directly to the code that implements the method/property, find all references to the selected method/property within your code, or even directly copy the code content represented by the node. All of these commands and more are available right from a node's right-click pop-up menu.

Searching Documents

The text editor window provides an extensive search-and-replace capability. Two primary methods of searching are supported: Quick Find (ideal for finding text fragments within the current document or set of open documents), and Search In Files (ideal for finding text in a file residing anywhere within a folder structure). All of these search mechanisms are triggered through the Edit, Find and Replace menu (and more commonly, through their hotkeys).

Each search mode is also capable of doing replacement operations. That makes a total of four different functions:

- ▶ Quick Find
- ▶ Quick Replace
- ▶ Find in Files
- ▶ Replace in Files

Let's take a closer look at each of the two search-and-replace modes individually.

Quick Find/Quick Replace

Figure 6.13 shows the Quick Find window in its native position to the top right of the text editor window. Its minimalist UI allows you to very quickly start your search process by typing directly into the search box.

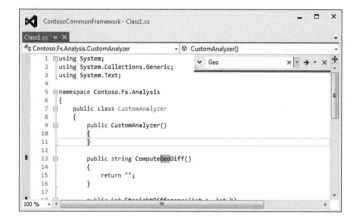

FIGURE 6.13   The Quick Find tool.

The search box drop-down holds the last 20 strings used in a find operation, making it easy to reuse a previous search. Just select the string from the list. The drop-down also lets you fine tune your search.

Fine-Tuning Your Search   The search box drop-down also hosts a set of check boxes to fine-tune your search:

▶ Match Case causes the search to be executed against the exact case you used in the Find What drop-down.

▶ Match Whole Words forces the search to match only on the entire string as entered in the Find What drop-down.

▶ Use Regular Expression changes how the search engine performs matching on the string you have entered into the search box. A standard search does a character match for the target string. By checking this box, however, you can instead use a full-blown regular expression to perform even more intricate searches. For instance, checking this box and then entering **\b[0-9]{9}\b** would return all matches for a nine-digit number.

NOTE

Although a complete discussion of regular expressions is beyond the scope of this book, you should note that the Replace With box is capable of supporting tagged expressions. For more information on how you might use this to your advantage during replace operations, consult a regular expression reference manual and look at the MSDN Regular Expressions help topic for Visual Studio.

Finding Search Results   After you have specified all the criteria for your search, the right-arrow button (or F3 as a shortcut) to the right of the search box will find the next match to the search. Any matches within the scope specified are highlighted for you within the document and will be scrolled into view. Subsequent clicks on the Find Next button move to the next match until no more matches are found.

The Find Next button also functions as a drop-down, which lets you perform a Find Previous or a Find All action.

Replacing Text   The arrow to the left of the search box will expand the Quick Find window to show a Replace text box: Type in the replacement string here, and then use one of the two buttons to the right of the box to either replace the next matching string or all matching strings with the new text (see Figure 6.14).

FIGURE 6.14   Expanding the Quick Find window to do a replacement.

Note that any replacements you make can always be undone via the Undo command under the Edit menu.

Changing the Scope of the Search   In addition to the text replacement box, the extended Quick Find window also has a place to select the exact scope of the search. Your selections here include: the current block of code, the current document, all open documents, all documents in the current project, and all documents in the entire solution.

Find in Files/Replace in Files

Figure 6.15 shows the Find in Files tool. This tool is similar to Quick Find, with one minor differences. You still have to specify the "what" (search string) and the "where" (scope) components of the search. And you still can fine-tune your search using regular expressions and by matching on case or whole word. But you also have the option of creating a custom search scope, and the way that the search results are displayed is via a separate window instead of within the code/text editor window.

Let's look at these two differences in turn.

Building Search Folder Sets   Clicking the ellipses button to the right of the Look In drop-down launches a dialog box; this dialog box allows you to build up a set of directories as the scope of the search. You can name this folder set and even set the search order for the directories. Figure 6.16 captures this dialog box as a search set called ClassLibCode is built. You can see that three directories have been added to the set and that you can add more by simply browsing to the folder with the Available Folders control and adding them to the Selected Folders list.

FIGURE 6.15   Find in Files.

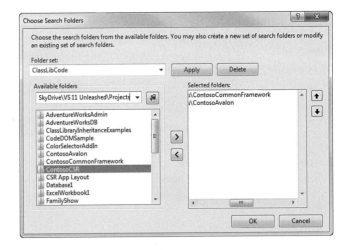

FIGURE 6.16   Building a Search Folder set.

The Find Results Window   With Quick Find, the search results are highlighted (or book-marked) right within the text editor window. The Find in Files mode displays its search results in a separate, dedicated Find Results window (see Figure 6.17). You can redirect the output to one of two results windows by selecting either the Find Results 1 Window or Find Results 2 Window option at the bottom of the Find and Replace dialog box. The two windows are identical; two options provided here allow you to keep different search results separate and avoid the confusion that the commingling of matches would cause if you were constrained to just one output window.

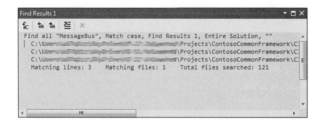

FIGURE 6.17   The Find Results window.

In Figure 6.17, you see the results of a simple search conducted across all the files in a solution. The contents of the Find Results window provides the following information:

▶ A description of the search performed (for example, Find all "MessageBus", Subfolders, Find Results 1, "Entire Solution").

▶ The matches returned from the search. Match information includes the file path and name, the line number within the file, and a verbatim repeat of the line of code containing the match.

▶ A summary of the find results, including the number of matching lines of code, the number of files containing matches, and the total number of files searched.

Double-clicking one of the results lines in the window jogs the cursor location directly to the matching line within the editor. Note that this window has a toolbar. From left to right, the buttons on this toolbar allow you to do the following:

▶ Jump to the matched line of code within the text editor. (First place your cursor on the match inside the Find Results window and then click the Go to the Location of the Current Line button.)

▶ Move back and forth through the list of matches. Each matched item is highlighted in the Find Results window and in the Text Editor window.

▶ Clear the Find Results window.

▶ Cancel any ongoing searches.

Replacing in Files   Just as with Quick Find, there is also a way to perform replacements using the Find in Files tool. This mode is entered by clicking the Replace in Files button at the top of the search window (see Figure 6.18).

We've already covered the Replace and Replace All functions. Each file that matches the search phrase is opened in a separate text editor window, and the replacements are made directly in that window. If you're performing a Replace All, the replacements are made and then saved directly into the containing file. You also have the option, via the Keep Modified Files Open After Replace All check box, to have Visual Studio keep any files touched open inside their respective text editors. This allows you to selectively save or discard the replacements as you see fit.

FIGURE 6.18   Replace in Files mode.

You can elect to skip files during the search-and-replace process by using the Skip File button. This button is available only if more than one file has been selected as part of the search scope. Clicking this button tells the search engine to skip the current file being processed and continue with the next in-scope file.

Incremental Search

Incremental Search is a special case function that works with the Quick Find window. With a text editor open, select Edit, Advanced, Incremental Search (or press Ctrl+I). While Incremental Search is active, you will see the Quick Find window and a special a visual pointer cue composed of binoculars and a down arrow. If you start typing a search string, character by character, the first match found is highlighted within the text editor window itself. With each successive character, the search string is altered and the search itself is re-executed. The current search string and search scope is displayed on the Visual Studio status bar. Figure 6.19 illustrates an Incremental Search in progress; the characters MESS have been entered, and you can see the first match flagged within the text editor.

By default, the search function works from the top of the document to the bottom, and from left to right. You can reverse the direction of the search by using the Ctrl+Shift+I key combination.

To jump to the next match within the document, use the Ctrl+I key combination.

Clicking anywhere within the document or pressing the Esc key cancels the Incremental Search.

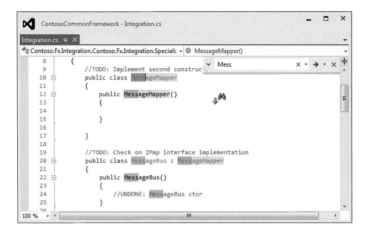

FIGURE 6.19   Incremental Search.

Debugging in the Text Editor

The text editor (more specifically, the code editor) has several interactive features that facilitate the code-debugging process. Debugging activities within the text editor primarily center on breakpoints and runtime code control. We cover general Visual Studio debugging in greater detail in Chapter 11.

A breakpoint is simply a location (a line of code) that is flagged for the debugger; when the debugger encounters a breakpoint, the currently executing program is paused immediately before executing that line of code. While the program is in this paused state, you can inspect the state of variables or even affect variable state by assigning new values. You can also interactively control the code flow at this point by skipping over the next line of code or skipping directly to another line of code and continuing from there, all without actually leaving the IDE.

Setting a Breakpoint

To set a breakpoint using the code editor, first locate the line of code you want to pause on and then click that line of code within the indicator margin. (Refer back to Figure 6.5 for the location of the indicator margin.) This sets the breakpoint, which can now be visually identified by a red ball in the indicator margin. Hovering over the breakpoint indicator margin displays a ToolTip indicating some basic information about that breakpoint: the code filename, the line number within that code file, the type you are in (if any), and the line number within that type.

In Figure 6.20, a breakpoint has been set within a class called `MessageMapper`. The ToolTip information shows that you are on line 3 in the `MessageMapper` class, but within the overall code file (Integration.cs), you are on line number 12.

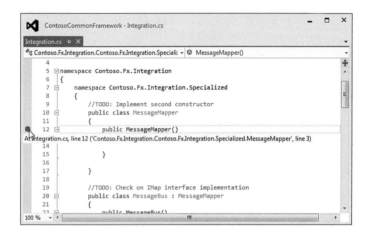

FIGURE 6.20   Setting a breakpoint.

Clicking the breakpoint again removes it.

The breakpoint we have set is a simple one in that it suspends the program on that line of code without regard for any other variable or factor. Simple breakpoints are, however, only the tip of the iceberg. Breakpoints support an extensive set of conditions used to fine-tune and control what will actually trigger the breakpoints. For instance, you can set a breakpoint to print a message, and you can specify different conditions for firing the breakpoint.

Configuring a Breakpoint

Right-clicking the breakpoint indicator reveals the context menu for configuring the breakpoint (see Figure 6.21).

FIGURE 6.21   Configuring a breakpoint.

It is from here that you can indicate special conditions for triggering the breakpoint and even disable or enable the breakpoint. Disabling the breakpoint, rather than deleting it, keeps its location intact if you ever need to reenable it.

TIP

Visual Basic actually provides a command word that allows you to programmatically trigger a breakpoint within your code. The `Stop` statement, like a breakpoint, suspends execution of the executing code. This capability is useful when you're running the application outside the IDE. Any time a `Stop` statement is encountered during runtime, the Visual Studio debugger launches and attaches to the program.

Although C# doesn't have an internal, equivalent statement to Visual Basic's `Stop` command, you can use the `Debugger` class to achieve the same thing: simply call `Debugger.Break` to force a breakpoint programmatically. The `Debugger` class lives in the `System.Diagnostic` namespace.

Controlling the Flow of Running Code

When a program is run within the IDE, it continues along its path of execution through the code base until it hits a breakpoint or Stop statement, is paused manually, or terminates either by reaching the end of its code path or by a manual stop.

TIP

The DVR-like controls and their shortcut keys (available under the Debug menu or on the Debug toolbar) are, by far, the easiest way to start, pause, or stop code within the IDE.

When a breakpoint is hit, the code editor visually indicates the line of code where execution has paused. Figure 6.22 shows a slightly modified version of the "Hello, World" program, suspended at a breakpoint. A yellow arrow in the indicator margin flags the next statement that will execute when you resume running the program. In this case, because the breakpoint is also here, the next statement indicator appears in the margin embedded within the breakpoint glyph.

When execution is paused, you can change the next line of code to be executed. By default, of course, this is the line of code where operations were paused. (Recall that execution stops just before running the line of code matched with the breakpoint.) But you can manually specify the next line of code to run by right-clicking the target line and then selecting Set Next Statement.

In Figure 6.23, this feature has been used to jump out of the `WriteLine` loop. Normal flow through the code has been circumvented, and instead of continuing to spin through the for loop, the program immediately executes the line of code just after the loop. You can see the arrow and highlighting that show the next line of code and the breakpoint are no longer at the same location within the code file.

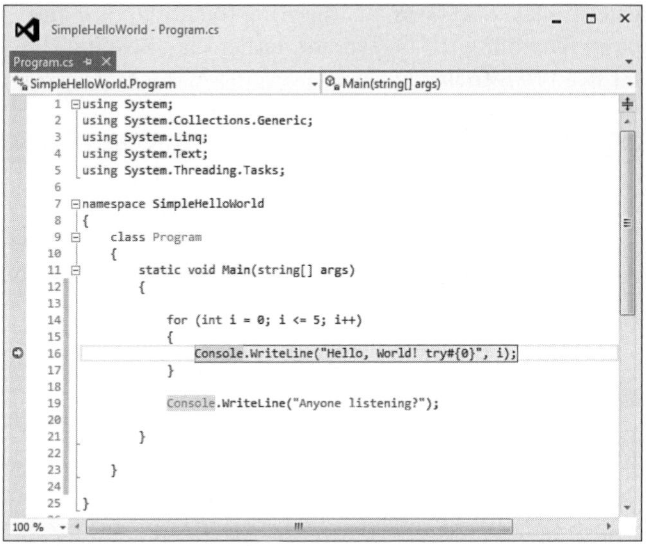

FIGURE 6.22   Stopping at a breakpoint.

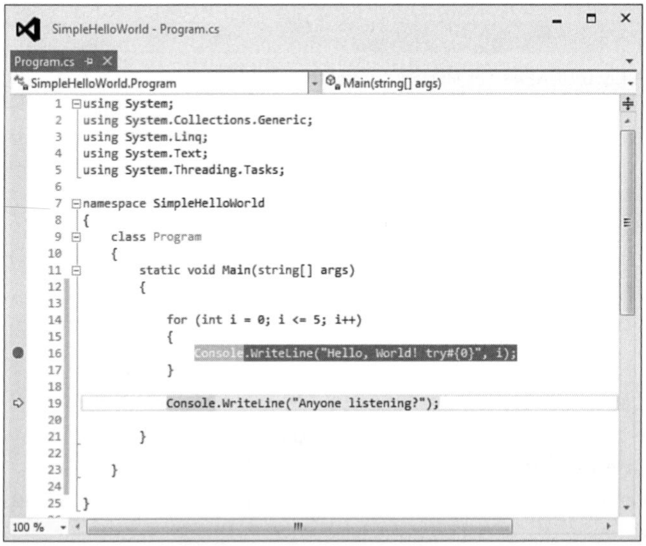

FIGURE 6.23   Setting the next Run statement.

You can also create a sort of virtual breakpoint by selecting Run to Cursor from the editor's context menu. This causes the program to run until it hits the line of code that you have selected, at which point it pauses much as if you had set a breakpoint there.

Printing Code

To print the current text editor's contents, select Print from the File menu. The Print dialog box is fairly standard, allowing you to select your printer and set basic print properties. Two Visual Studio-specific options bear mentioning here. The Print What section in this dialog box controls whether line numbers are produced in the printout and whether collapsed regions are included in the printed content.

Colors and Fonts

By default, the font colors and markup that you see in the text editor window are sent to the printer as is (assuming that you are printing to a color printer). If you so desire, you can tweak all these settings from the Environment, Fonts and Colors page in the Options dialog box (see Figure 6.24).

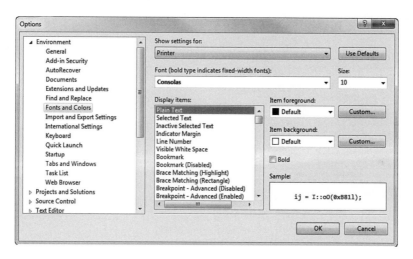

FIGURE 6.24   The Fonts and Colors Options dialog box.

This is the same dialog box used to control font and color settings for many of the IDE's constituent parts. You access the printer settings by selecting Printer in the Show Settings For drop-down at the top of the dialog box.

Figure 6.25 provides a snapshot of output produced by printing a code file.

Using the Code Definition Window

The code definition window is a "helper" window that works in close conjunction with the code editor window by displaying definitions for symbols selected within the code editor. It is actually a near clone of the code editor window, with one big exception: It is read-only and does not permit edits to its content.

The code definition window content is refreshed anytime the cursor position is moved within the code editor window. If the cursor or caret is placed in a symbol/type, the code definition window shows you how that symbol is defined.

```
c:\                                              \SimpleHelloWorld\Program.cs      1
 1 using System;
 2 using System.Collections.Generic;
 3 using System.Linq;
 4 using System.Text;
 5 using System.Threading.Tasks;
 6
 7 namespace SimpleHelloWorld
 8 {
 9     class Program
10     {
11         static void Main(string[] args)
12         {
13
14             for (int i = 0; i <= 5; i++)
15             {
16                 Console.WriteLine("Hello, World! try#{0}", i);
17             }
18
19             Console.WriteLine("Anyone listening?");
20
21         }
22
23     }
24
25 }
26
```

FIGURE 6.25   Code printout.

Figure 6.26 shows an open code editor and a code definition window; the cursor in the editor is positioned on an internal field, _state, defined within the class InternalToken.

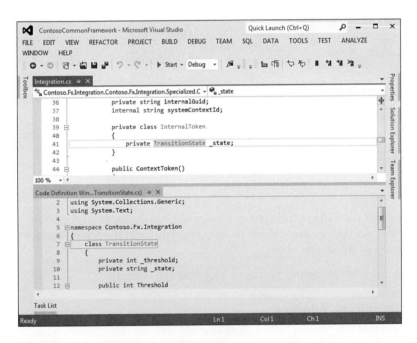

FIGURE 6.26   The code definition window.

The code definition window has reacted to the cursor position by showing the source code that actually defines the type of the _state field. You can see from the figure that the code definition window is a fairly featured adaptation of a text editor window: It supports bookmarks, breakpoints, and various navigation aids. Although you cannot edit code using this window, you are not prevented from copying code out of the window.

You can open a code definition window by using the View menu.

TIP

The code definition window also works well with the Class View window. If you single-click a class within the Class View window, the code definition window refreshes to show you the code implementation for that class.

Creating and Editing XML Documents and Schema

The text editor is equally adept, and just as productive, at editing documents with XML content, including XML schemas. The XML editor is launched whenever you open a file with the .xml extension inside of Visual Studio. It is also launched for .xsl files and .config files, and is always available when you use the Open With command in the Solution Explorer against any item in a project.

Because XML documents contain structured content involving the concepts of nodes and tags, attributes, and node containership, the XML editor supports document outlining in a similar fashion to the code editor: You can expand or collapse nodes within the editor to expose or hide a node's content (see Figure 6.27). And just as with the code editor, syntax checking and IntelliSense are fully supported by the XML editor. The XML editor is aware of the syntactical requirements for the current document and provides appropriate IntelliSense and formatting help where possible.

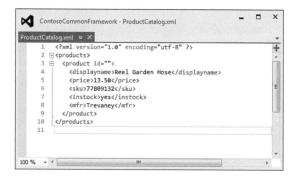

FIGURE 6.27   Editing an XML document.

Using the XML editor, you can also carry out these actions:

▶ Edit XSD schema documents

▶ Generate a schema document from an XML document

▶ Edit XSLT style sheets

▶ Edit Document Type Definition (DTD) documents and XML-Data Reduced (XDR) documents

▶ Insert XML snippets

For a proper treatment of the various editing, validation, and productivity aids available in this editor, see Chapter 8, "Working with Visual Studio's Productivity Aids." Here, let's explore two of the core XML functions: schema generation and EXtensible Stylesheet Language (XSLT) style sheet editing.

Inferring Schema

The XML editor can automatically generate an XML schema document (XSD) based on a valid XML document. While the XML document is open, select Create Schema from the XML main menu. This creates an XSD document and opens it in the XML Schema Designer (more on this in the next section). From there, you can make any necessary changes to the XSD document and save it to disk. You can also include it in your project at this point.

> **NOTE**
>
> If you run the Create Schema command against an XML document that already contains a DTD or XDR schema, the XML inference algorithm uses these schemas as the basis for the conversion as opposed to the actual data within the XML document.

Designing XML Schemas

Visual Studio has made huge strides over the years in its support for XML schema design. This is evident right off the bat when you open an XML schema file (.xsd). A visual design window and an XML Schema Explorer window, working in tandem, quickly allow you to inspect, edit, and build out your schema. Figure 6.28 shows the same schema we just inferred from our simple "product catalog" XML file opened in the Visual Studio IDE. Note the schema explorer to the right, and the schema design surface to the left. Let's examine the various views in detail.

Schema Views

Visual Studio provides five different ways to visualize/edit the information in an XML schema, delivered by three different tools. We have already covered the XML editor. Because XML schemas are verbalized using XML itself, the editor's functions apply just as well to schema editing as they do to document editing.

That leaves us with two remaining tools: the XML Schema Explorer and the XML Schema Designer. Just as you have come to expect with most explorer/designer pairs in the IDE, these two tools work hand in hand.

The XML Schema Explorer

The Schema Explorer is a tree-view representation of schema content (see Figure 6.29). Using this explorer, you can expand any of the schema container elements to view their child elements. The toolbar on this explorer window lets you search for schema elements and change the sort order as well.

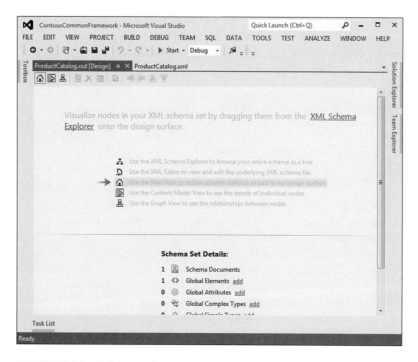

FIGURE 6.28   Editing a simple XML schema.

FIGURE 6.29   The XML Schema Explorer.

While this hierarchical view of the schema is useful in its own right, the real purpose of the explorer window is to select items to view/edit in the design window. In fact, the explorer and designer windows are inseparable pairs: closing the designer automatically closes the explorer.

The XML Schema Designer

The schema design window is where all of the schema editing takes place. You can edit or view a schema (or set of schemas) by dragging items from the XML Schema Explorer window onto the XML Schema Designer surface.

After you have added the schema to the design surface, the schema design window provides you with three different views into the schema's structure and content:

▶ The Start View is the default view. As its name implies, this is a launching page into the other views. The Start View also provides summary statistics for the XML schema (such as a count of the global elements, attributes, and types), and provides a quick and easy way to add these items to the design surface.

▶ The Graph View is a 2D view of the nodes and node relationships within a schema. The Graph View is primarily useful in visualizing the complexity and types of relationships within a schema. You can't use this to directly edit the nodes or node relationships. Use the toolbar buttons at the top of the designer to change the way that the graph is displayed: left to right, right to left, top to bottom, or bottom to top. Double-clicking a node opens the schema's XML in the XML editor, with the XML for that node highlighted. See Figure 6.30 for a picture of the Graph View with a complex schema file loaded.

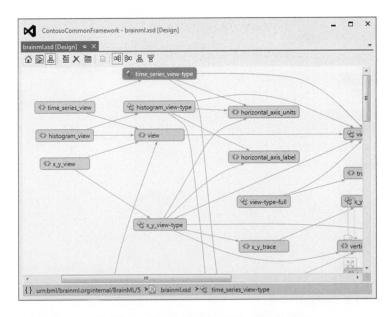

FIGURE 6.30   Using the Schema Designer's Graph View.

▶ The Content Model View is a graphical, hierarchical view of the nodes and node elements, attributes, types, and groups. This view is particularly useful if you are trying to understand the details of a particular portion of the schema. For instance, by double-clicking a type, you can quickly gain a fairly complete understanding of that type's schema, including elements, attributes, types, and groups (in addition to any constraints or relationships that are defined in the schema). This view also provides a simple way to select nodes: An A-Z list of all nodes within the schema appears in the list box to the left of the design surface. Clicking the node in this list displays the node details on the design surface (see Figure 6.31).

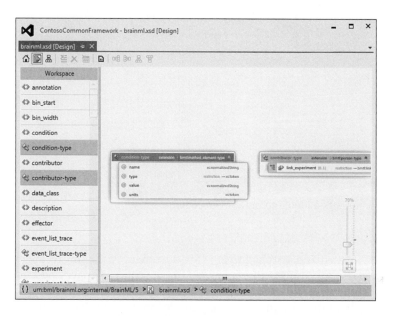

FIGURE 6.31   The Content Model View with multiple nodes selected.

TIP

Using the Content Model View, it is easy to compare and contrast two or more nodes within a schema. Just select the nodes you want to view in the node list to the left of the design surface (using Ctrl+Left mouse button to add additional nodes to your selection). You can then use the design surface's image scaler to get a high-level view of the nodes or to zoom in on specific details.

Editing XSLT Style Sheets

XSLT files are XML files, so the process of editing an XSLT style sheet is the same as that described for editing an XML document. There are, however, a few additional features specific to XSLT documents. For one, keywords are recognized and shaded appropriately in the editor just as with a code document. Second, the XML editor automatically processes the current state of the document against the standard schema for XSLT style sheets and shows any validation errors to you directly. And finally, Visual Studio is fully aware of any script embedded in an XSLT document. You can set breakpoints within a script block, and there is full debug support for script enabling you to step through code, see the current state of variables, and so forth. Figure 6.32 shows an XSLT style sheet with a breakpoint set within a section of embedded script.

FIGURE 6.32   Debugging script embedded into an XSLT document.

Running XSLT Against XML

After a style sheet has been created and attached to an XML document, you can execute that XSLT style sheet and view the output within a new editor window. To attach the XSLT sheet to the XML document, use the Properties window for the XML document and set the `Stylesheet` property. Entering the full path and filename of the XSLT in this property attaches the style sheet. Alternatively, you can manually code the style sheet into the XML document's prolog section by typing an **xml-stylesheet** Processing Instruction prolog into the document, like this:

```
<?xml-stylesheet type='text/xsl' href='myxsl.xsl'?>
```

When a style sheet is associated, selecting the Show XSLT Output option from the XML menu runs the transforms against the XML document and shows you the results in a separate editor window.

Working with Cascading Style Sheets

The CSS editor allows you to build and edit cascading style sheet documents. Because CSS documents are, at their core, text documents, the editor doesn't need to provide much more than standard text-editing features to be effective. However, a few built-in tools available from the editor enable you to add style rules and build styles using dialog boxes as opposed to free-form text entry.

Adding Style Rules

Right-click within the CSS editor to access the shortcut menu. From there, select the Add Style Rule option. The Add Style Rule dialog box allows you to input an element, class name, or class ID and even define a hierarchy between the rules. Committing the change from this dialog box injects the necessary content into the CSS editor to create the rule.

Defining Style Sheet Attributes

After you've added a style to the CSS document by either writing the style syntax manually or using the aforementioned Add Style Rule dialog box, you can edit the attributes of that style using the Style Builder dialog box. You launch this dialog box by right-clicking anywhere within the previously entered style section and then selecting the Build Style option. When you use this dialog box, it is possible to fully describe the style across several different categories from font to layout to list formatting.

Developing Windows Client Applications

There are two principal .NET technologies used to develop Windows client applications: Windows Forms (WinForms) and Windows Presentation Foundation (WPF). Both of these technologies are essentially a set of classes and user interface controls exposed by the .NET Framework that enable developers to quickly build out applications that are installed, and run, under the Microsoft Windows operating system.

> **NOTE**
>
> Microsoft has now also introduced the concept of modern UI applications that run on top of the Windows Runtime (yet another presentation layer platform introduced with Windows 8). Although we don't cover building Windows Client applications for the Windows Runtime in this chapter, we do cover those tools and technologies in depth in Chapter 25, "Writing Windows Store Applications Using the Windows Runtime Library."

WPF is unique when compared to the older Windows Forms technology because it uses a markup language called XAML (Extensible Application Markup Language) to describe application objects, property values, and behavior. In this respect, it is similar to a web application that uses HTML to describe the various elements of a web page. WPF as a technology heavily leverages vector graphics and graphics hardware acceleration to display an application's user interface.

Regardless of the type of client application you need to build, the process is much the same: Both the WinForms designer and the WPF designer enable drag-and-drop development, and both have project templates available in Visual Studio.

Creating a Windows Forms Project

The process of building a Windows Forms application starts the same as all other project types within Visual Studio: You select the Windows Application project template from the New Project dialog box and set up the location for the application's source. From there, Visual Studio stubs out an initial project, and the Windows Forms Designer loads, as shown in Figure 6.33.

FIGURE 6.33   Initial form in the Windows Forms Designer.

As you can see from the figure, a design-time "mock-up" of the actual form is visible within the designer. This is the canvas for your user interface. Using this canvas, you can add controls and visual elements to the form, tweak the look and feel of the form itself, and launch directly to the code that is wired to the form. To investigate how the designer works, start with a simple design premise: Suppose, for instance, that you want to take the blank form that Visual Studio generated for you and create a login dialog box that allows users to input a name and password and confirm their entries by clicking an OK button. A Cancel button should also be available to allow users to dismiss the form.

> **NOTE**
>
> Don't get confused about the various representations that a form can have, such as message box or dialog box. From a development perspective, they are all windows and are therefore all forms.

The designer in this exercise allows you, the developer, to craft the form and its actions while writing as little code as possible. Using drag-and-drop operations and Property dialog boxes, you should be able to customize the look and feel of the application without ever dealing with the code editor.

Customizing the Form's Appearance

There are a few obvious visual elements in the designer. For one, the form itself is shown complete with its borders, title bar, client area, and Min/Max/Close buttons. In addition, you can see grab handles at the bottom, right, and bottom-right corner of the form. The grab handles are used to resize the form. To change other attributes of the form, you use the property grid for the form. The property grid enables you to set the background color, border appearance and behavior, title text, and so on.

In Figure 6.34, the title of the form has been changed to Login, and the border behavior has been changed to match a dialog box as opposed to a normal resizable window.

FIGURE 6.34   Editing the form's size, border and title.

Adding Controls to a Form

Controls are adornments to a form that have their own user interface. (There is such a thing as UI-less controls; we cover such controls later in this chapter in the section "Authoring Components and Controls.") They provide the principal interaction mechanism method with a form. Put another way, a form is really just a container for the various controls that implement the desired functionality for the form.

You can add controls to a form quite easily by dragging and dropping them from the Toolbox. Continuing the metaphor of the designer as a canvas, the Toolbox is the palette.

The Toolbox   The Toolbox is a dockable window within the IDE; it is viewable only when you are editing a project element that supports Toolbox functionality. To make sure that the Toolbox is visible, select it from the View menu (or use the Ctrl+W, X shortcut).

The Toolbox groups the controls in a tabbed tree. Expand the tab grouping (such as Common Controls or Menus & Toolbars), and you see a list of the available controls. In this case, you want two text box controls to hold the login ID and password text, a few label controls to describe the text box controls, and the OK and Cancel buttons to commit or cancel the entries. You can find all of these controls under the Common Controls tab (see Figure 6.35).

FIGURE 6.35   The WinForms Toolbox.

To place a control on the form, drag its representation from the Toolbox onto the form. Some controls, referred to as components, don't actually have a visual user interface. The timer is one example of a component. When you drag a component to a form, it is placed in a separate area of the designer called the component tray. The component tray allows you to select one of the added components and access its properties via the Properties window.

TIP

The Toolbox is customizable in terms of its content and arrangement. You can add or remove tabs from the Toolbox, move controls from one tab to another through simple drag and drop, and even rename individual items within the Toolbox. To perform many of these actions, bring up the Toolbox context menu by right-clicking a tab or an item.

Arranging Controls   When you are designing a form, control layout becomes an important issue. You are typically concerned about ensuring that controls are aligned either horizontally or vertically, that controls and control groups are positioned with equal and common margins between their edges, that margins are enforced along the form borders, and so on.

The designer provides three distinct sets of tools and aids that assist with form layout. First, you have the options available to you under the Format menu. With a form loaded in the designer, you can select different groups of controls and use the commands under the Format menu to align these controls vertically or horizontally with one another, standardize and increase or decrease the spacing between controls, center the controls within the form, and even alter the controls' appearance attributes so that they are of equal size in either dimension.

The other layout tools within the designer are interactive in nature and are surfaced through two different modes: snap line and grid positioning. You can toggle between these two modes via the Windows Forms Designer Options dialog box (choose Tools, Options and then the Windows Forms Designer tab). The property called LayoutMode can be set to either SnapToGrid or SnapLines.

Using the Layout Grid   The layout grid is, as its name implies, a grid that is laid on top of the form. The grid itself is visually represented within the designer by dots representing the intersection of the grid squares. As you drag and move controls over the surface of the grid, the designer automatically snaps the control's leading edges to one of the grid's square edges.

TIP

Even with the grid layout turned on, you can circumvent the snapping behavior by selecting a control, holding down the Ctrl key and using the arrow keys to move the control up, down, right, or left one pixel at a time.

The size of the grid squares (and thus the spacing of these guide dots) is controlled by the GridSize property (also located in the Options dialog box). A smaller grid size equates to a tighter spacing of guide dots, which in turns equates to more finely grained control over control placement.

Figure 6.36 shows the login form with the layout grid in evidence. Note that the grid was used to confirm the following:

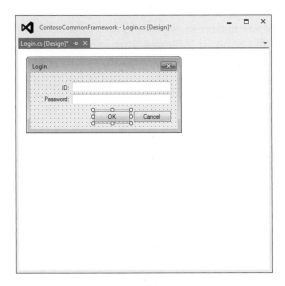

FIGURE 6.36   The layout grid.

▶ The text boxes are aligned with one another (and are the same length).

▶ The labels are aligned vertically with the text boxes and horizontally with each other.

▶ The buttons are aligned vertically and have an appropriate buffer area between their control edges and the form's border.

Using Snap Lines   Snap lines are a slightly more intelligent mechanism for positioning controls. With snap lines, no grid is visible on the form's surface. Instead, the designer draws visual hints while a control is in motion on the form.

Figure 6.37 illustrates snap lines in action; this figure shows the process of positioning the OK button.

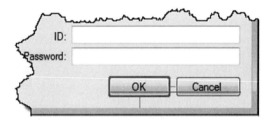

FIGURE 6.37   Using snap lines.

Note that the control (in this case, an OK button) has "snapped" into a position that is located a set distance away from the form border (indicated by the thin blue line extending down from the button to the form edge). The button snap position also sufficiently spaces the control from its neighboring Cancel button, as indicated by the thin blue line extending from the right edge of the button to the left edge of the Cancel button. The snap line algorithm has also determined that you are trying to create a row of buttons and thus need to vertically align the current control to its neighbor. This is actually done using the interior text of the buttons; the thin pink line running under the text of both buttons clearly shows that they are perfectly aligned.

The snap line algorithms automatically take into account the recommended margins and spacing distances as discussed in the Windows User Interface Guidelines written and adopted by Microsoft. This feature takes the guesswork out of many layout decisions and helps to ensure some commonality and standards adherence within the Windows Forms applications.

> **NOTE**
>
> Changes made to the layout modes of the designer typically do not take effect immediately. You might need to close the designer and reopen it after making a change (such as switching between SnapLine mode and SnapToGrid mode). If you have multiple designer windows open, you may need to close them all before your layout mode changes take effect.

Resizing Controls and Editing Attributes   When a control is in place on its parent form, you can interact with the control in various ways. You can set control properties using the Properties window. You also can alter the sizing and shape of the control by dragging the grab handles on the sides of the control.

Writing Code

Although the designer excels at enabling developers to visually construct a user interface, its capability to actually implement behavior is limited. You can use the designer to place a button, but responding to a click the button and reacting in some way are still the domain of code.

At the code level, a form is simply a class that encapsulates all the form's behavior. For simplicity and ease of development, Visual Studio pushes all the code that it writes via the designer into clearly marked regions and, in the case of Windows forms, a separate code file. The file is named after the primary form code file like this: FormName.Designer. language_extension. As an example, the login form is accompanied by a Login.Designer.cs file that implements the designer-written code.

Listing 6.1 shows what Visual Studio has generated in the way of code to implement the changes made through the designer.

LISTING 6.1   Windows Forms Designer–Generated Code

```csharp
namespace Contoso.UI.WindowsForms.OrderEntry
{
    partial class Login
    {
        /// <summary>
        /// Required designer variable.
        /// </summary>
        private System.ComponentModel.IContainer components = null;

        /// <summary>
        /// Clean up any resources being used.
        /// </summary>
        /// <param name="disposing">true if managed resources should be disposed;
        /// otherwise, false.</param>
        protected override void Dispose(bool disposing)
        {
            if (disposing && (components != null))
            {
                components.Dispose();
            }
            base.Dispose(disposing);
        }

        #region Windows Form Designer generated code
```

```csharp
/// <summary>
/// Required method for Designer support - do not modify
/// the contents of this method with the code editor.
/// </summary>
private void InitializeComponent()
{
    this.label1 = new System.Windows.Forms.Label();
    this.label2 = new System.Windows.Forms.Label();
    this.textBoxID = new System.Windows.Forms.TextBox();
    this.textBoxPassword = new System.Windows.Forms.TextBox();
    this.buttonCancel = new System.Windows.Forms.Button();
    this.buttonOk = new System.Windows.Forms.Button();
    this.SuspendLayout();
    //
    // label1
    //
    this.label1.AutoSize = true;
    this.label1.Location = new System.Drawing.Point(61, 23);
    this.label1.Name = "label1";
    this.label1.Size = new System.Drawing.Size(17, 13);
    this.label1.TabIndex = 0;
    this.label1.Text = "ID:";
    //
    // label2
    //
    this.label2.AutoSize = true;
    this.label2.Location = new System.Drawing.Point(26, 46);
    this.label2.Name = "label2";
    this.label2.Size = new System.Drawing.Size(52, 13);
    this.label2.TabIndex = 1;
    this.label2.Text = "Password:";
    //
    // textBoxID
    //
    this.textBoxID.Location = new System.Drawing.Point(85, 20);
    this.textBoxID.Name = "textBoxID";
    this.textBoxID.Size = new System.Drawing.Size(195, 20);
    this.textBoxID.TabIndex = 2;
    //
    // textBoxPassword
    //
    this.textBoxPassword.Location = new System.Drawing.Point(85, 46);
    this.textBoxPassword.Name = "textBoxPassword";
    this.textBoxPassword.Size = new System.Drawing.Size(195, 20);
    this.textBoxPassword.TabIndex = 3;
    //
```

```
// buttonCancel
//
this.buttonCancel.DialogResult =
    System.Windows.Forms.DialogResult.Cancel;
this.buttonCancel.Location = new System.Drawing.Point(205, 72);
this.buttonCancel.Name = "buttonCancel";
this.buttonCancel.Size = new System.Drawing.Size(75, 23);
this.buttonCancel.TabIndex = 4;
this.buttonCancel.Text = "Cancel";
//
// buttonOk
//
this.buttonOk.Location = new System.Drawing.Point(124, 72);
this.buttonOk.Name = "buttonOk";
this.buttonOk.Size = new System.Drawing.Size(75, 23);
this.buttonOk.TabIndex = 5;
this.buttonOk.Text = "OK";
//
// Login
//
this.AcceptButton = this.buttonOk;
this.AutoScaleDimensions = new System.Drawing.SizeF(6F, 13F);
this.AutoScaleMode = System.Windows.Forms.AutoScaleMode.Font;
this.CancelButton = this.buttonCancel;
this.ClientSize = new System.Drawing.Size(292, 109);
this.Controls.Add(this.buttonOk);
this.Controls.Add(this.buttonCancel);
this.Controls.Add(this.textBoxPassword);
this.Controls.Add(this.textBoxID);
this.Controls.Add(this.label2);
this.Controls.Add(this.label1);
this.FormBorderStyle =
    System.Windows.Forms.FormBorderStyle.FixedDialog;
this.MaximizeBox = false;
this.MinimizeBox = false;
this.Name = "Login";
this.ShowInTaskbar = false;
this.SizeGripStyle = System.Windows.Forms.SizeGripStyle.Hide;
this.Text = "Login";
this.ResumeLayout(false);
this.PerformLayout();

}

#endregion
```

```
        private System.Windows.Forms.Label label1;
        private System.Windows.Forms.Label label2;
        private System.Windows.Forms.TextBox textBoxID;
        private System.Windows.Forms.TextBox textBoxPassword;
        private System.Windows.Forms.Button buttonCancel;
        private System.Windows.Forms.Button buttonOk;
    }
}
```

Creating a Windows Presentation Foundation Project

Windows Presentation Foundation (WPF) projects behave much like WinForms projects do. In fact, one of the design goals for the WPF Designer and editor was to act in ways that would be familiar to developers who are used to Windows Forms development. Just as we previously did with our WinForms project, we start the development and design process by selecting a template (WPF Application) from the File, New Project dialog.

Two XAML files are automatically created within the project: MainWindow.xaml, which represents the main window for the app; and App.xaml (Application.xaml in Visual Basic), which represents the application itself. These are analogous to the Form1.cs/Form1.vb and Program.cs/Module1.vb files created in a new Windows Forms project.

The first difference you notice with WPF projects is that, by default, you are presented with two different panes: In one pane, you see the design surface for the window, and in another you see an editor that contains the XAML declarations for the form. This design view is actually the same that is used for web applications (which we investigate as part of the next topic). See Figure 6.38 for a look at the Window1 file loaded in the IDE.

Each of these panes is simply a different view of the same window: a visual view and a text/XML view. I can add a button to the window, for example, by dragging it from the Toolbox onto the design surface or by typing the XAML declaration directly into the XAML pane like this:

```
<Button Height="25" Name="button1" Width="75">Button</Button>
```

Both the design and the XAML view are kept in sync with one another automatically.

Because WPF is based on vector graphics, you can zoom in and out in the designer using the slider control in the upper left of the designer. Figure 6.39 shows the Window1 form, with a button, zoomed in at 10x.

Using the Split Panes

You have control over how the design and XAML panes are displayed and positioned within the IDE. There is a small button flagged with two-way arrows that, when pressed, swaps the position of the two panes. You can also change the panes from a horizontal to a vertical orientation (or vice versa) by clicking the Horizontal Split or Vertical Split button. And, finally, you can collapse either pane by clicking the Collapse/Expand Pane button.

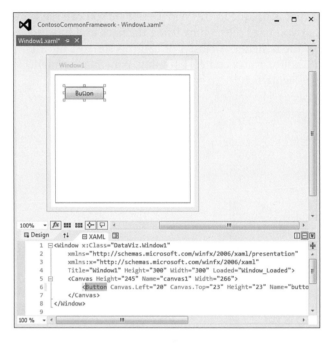

FIGURE 6.38   The initial window in the WPF Designer.

FIGURE 6.39   10x magnification in the WPF designer.

There is one other feature of interest that is unique to the WPF Designer: You can navigate back and forward through objects that you have selected by using the back and forward selectors shown in the bottom area of the designer. A cluster of controls situated on the border between the design and XAML editor panes control zooming, pane management/arrangement, and other functions (see Figure 6.40).

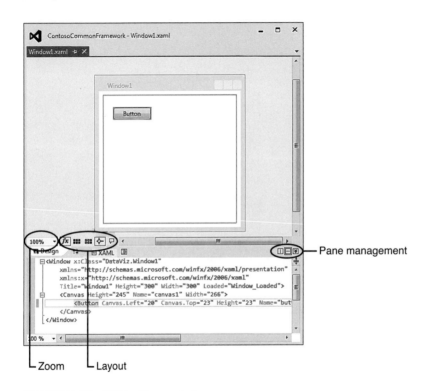

FIGURE 6.40   WPF editor controls.

Adding Controls

WPF windows are populated with controls by using the same drag-and-drop action from the Toolbox that is used with Windows Forms and web forms development. Control positioning and sizing is aided through snap lines, grid lines, and sizing boxes that look a bit different than their WinForms counterparts but perform the same tasks (see Figure 6.41).

We cover WPF development in more detail in Chapter 19, "Creating Richer, Smarter User Interfaces."

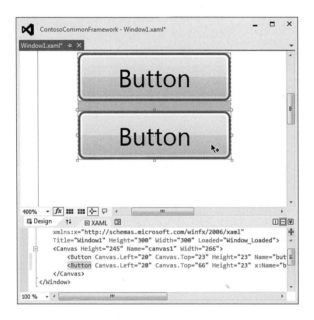

FIGURE 6.41   Positioning controls in the WPF Designer.

Developing Web Forms

Web forms represent the user interface element to a web application. Traditionally with .NET, the term *web form* is used to refer specifically to pages processed dynamically on the server (using ASP.NET). We use a broader definition here and use the term to refer to any web page, static or dynamic, that can be developed and designed within the Visual Studio IDE.

The HTML designer (also referred to as the web designer) is the sister application to the Windows Forms and WPF designers; it allows you to visually design and edit the markup for a web page. As with the two client application designers, it works in conjunction with the HTML designer and source view to cover all the bases needed for web page design. We cover the entire web application development process in depth in Chapter 16, "Creating ASP.NET Form-Based Applications"; the following sections cover the basics of the web designers and editors.

Designing a Web Form Application

Web page design starts first with a web project. As previously discussed, there are two different ways for you to construct a web page or website with Visual Studio. Both of these approaches are represented by their own unique project templates. Specifically, we are talking about "web application" versus "website" projects. In Chapter 4, "Solutions and Projects," we broached some of the core differences between these two project types; even more detail is waiting for you in Chapter 17. However, because the actual construction of a web page with the web designer remains exactly the same between the two project types, we concentrate here on illustrating our points by walking through a website project.

Select File, New Web Site, and from the dialog box select the ASP.NET Web Site option. After you set the source code directory and source language, click OK to have Visual Studio create the project and its initial web page.

The web designer looks similar to the WPF Designer; it has a design surface that acts as a canvas, allowing objects from the Toolbox to be placed and positioned on its surface. Although they look slightly different from the pane controls we saw in the WPF designer, they have the same basic functions. You can work in a "split" mode in which the designer and markup editor are visible in separate panes, or you can elect to work strictly with either the designer or the editor open.

Now examine what happens when you try to mimic the login form that was previously built using Windows forms. (There is actually a prebuilt login form component that you could use here; for the sake of demonstrating the development process, however, we will go ahead and cobble together our own simple one for comparison's sake.)

Adding and Arranging Controls

The process of adding and arranging controls doesn't change from the Windows Forms or WPF Designer process. Simply drag the controls from the Toolbox onto the designer's surface. In this case, you want two labels, two text boxes, and an OK button (because this isn't a dialog box, you can dispense with the Cancel button). Changing control properties is also handled the same way via the Properties window. You can select the labels and command buttons and set their text this way.

> **NOTE**
>
> As you add controls to a web page, note that the default layout mode is relative. That is, controls are not placed at absolute coordinates on the screen but instead are placed relative to one another. Absolute positioning is accommodated via style sheets. For instance, you can select a label control, edit its style properties, and select Absolutely Position as the position mode. This will now allow you to range freely over the form with the control.

A formatting toolbar is provided by default; it supplies buttons for common text formatting actions such as changing font styles, colors, paragraph indenting, and bulleting.

To line up control edges the way you want, you can press Shift+Enter to insert spacing between the controls as necessary. (This generates a break tag, `<br>`, in the HTML.) In this case, a break was added between the first text box and the second label, and between the second text box and the first button. Figure 6.42 shows the design in progress. The text boxes don't line up, and you probably want to apply a style for the label fonts and buttons; but the general layout and intent are evident. Note that the designer provides a box above the currently selected control that indicates both the control's type and the instance name of the control on the page.

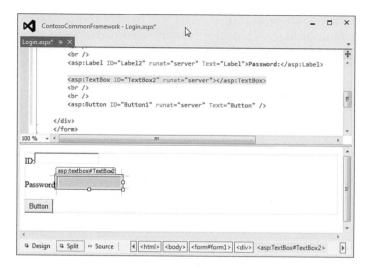

FIGURE 6.42   Creating a web form.

TIP

As a further aid for control alignment, be sure to turn on the ruler, the positioning grid, or both; they are accessed from the View menu, under Ruler and Grid.

Editing Markup

As controls and other elements are added and manipulated on the designer's surface, HTML is created to implement the design and layout. As a designer or developer, you are free to work at either the visual level with the designer or the text/source level with the HTML source editor. Like the other editors within Visual Studio, the HTML source editor supports IntelliSense and other interactive features for navigating and validating markup.

Looking back at Figure 6.42, you can see the markup generated by the designer when the controls were added to the login page.

As with the other designer/editor pairs, you can write your own HTML and see it implemented immediately in the design view. The HTML editor has a toolbar as well: The HTML source editing toolbar provides quick access to code "forward and back" navigation, commenting, and schema validation options. (We discuss schema validation in the section "Browser Output and Validation.")

One key feature realized with the HTML editor is source format preservation: The HTML source editor works hard to respect the way that you, the developer, want your markup formatted. This includes the placement of carriage returns and whitespace, the use of indentation, and even how you want to handle word and line wrapping. In short, Visual Studio never reformats HTML code that you have written!

Working with Tables   HTML tables provide a quick and easy way to align controls on a web page: A dedicated Insert Table dialog box provides extensive control over table layout and appearance. To place a table onto the design surface, select Insert Table from the Table menu. The Insert Table dialog box supports custom table layouts in which you specify the row and column attributes and the general style attributes such as borders and padding. Through this dialog box, you can also select from a list of preformatted table templates.

After you've added a table to the designer, it is fully interactive for drag-and-drop resizing of its columns and rows.

Formatting Options   In addition to preserving the format of HTML that you write, Visual Studio provides fine-grained control over how the designer generates and formats the HTML that it produces. You use the HTML page and its subpages in the Options dialog box (Tools, Options, Text Editor, HTML) to configure indentation style, quotation use, word wrapping, and tag casing (see Figure 6.43).

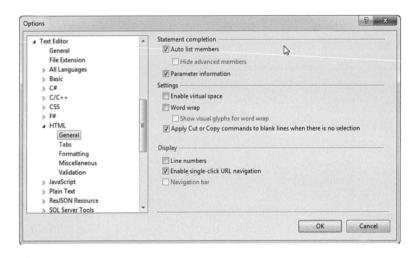

FIGURE 6.43   HTML formatting options.

Settings can be applied globally for all markup, or you can set options on a per-tag basis by clicking the Tag Specific Options button (Text Editor, HTML, Format). For example, this level of control is useful if your particular coding style uses line breaks within your table column tags (`<td>`), but not with your table row tags (`<tr>`). In Figure 6.44, the `tr` tag is being set to support line breaks before and after the tag, but not within the tag.

Managing Styles and Style Sheets

Visual Studio has a complete set of tools for managing styles and cascading style sheets. The Manage Styles and Apply Styles windows are both used to perform common style editing tasks, including applying a style to the current HTML document, or attaching/detaching a cascading style sheet file to/from the current HTML document. The third tool, the CSS Properties window, enumerates all the CSS properties for the currently selected page element, allowing for quick changes for any of the property values.

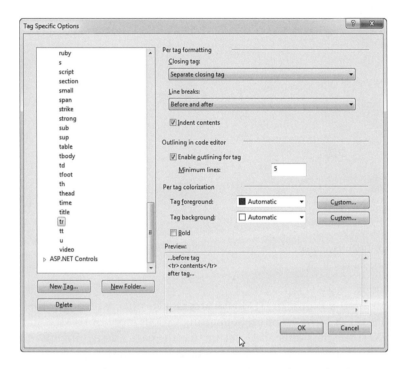

FIGURE 6.44   Setting HTML formatting options at the tag level.

A typical workflow for editing styles might look like this:

1. Open a web page.

2. Define a new style.

3. Apply the style.

4. Tweak the style.

Figure 6.45 shows the Manage Styles window and its capability to itemize and preview any of the formatting elements within a style sheet. The Options button at the upper right of the window is used to control the way that the list of elements within a style sheet is shown (by order, by type, and so on) or to filter the elements that are shown (all, only those used in the current page, and so on).

Both the Manage Styles window and the Apply Styles window are accessed from the View menu.

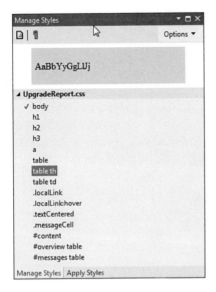

FIGURE 6.45   The Manage Styles window.

Browser Output and Validation

The result of all the design effort put into an HTML document is its final rendering within a browser. With various flavors of browsers in use supporting various levels of HTML specifications (including XHTML), it is difficult to ensure that the page's design intent actually matches reality. Visual Studio's browser target settings help with this problem by enabling you to easily target a specific HTML standard or browser. As you type HTML into the source editor, Visual Studio validates the syntax on-the-fly against your selected browser target. If a piece of markup violates the rules of your particular validation target, it is flagged by the familiar red squiggly line (complete with a ToolTip explaining the exact violation), and the error is listed within the Task List window.

The target can be selected on the HTML designer or source editor toolbar; just pick the target from the drop-down.

> **NOTE**
>
> The validation rules for a given browser or standard can actually be customized to support targets that do not ship out of the box with Visual Studio.

Standards Compliance   The HTML code generated by the HTML designer is, by default, XHTML compliant; tags, for instance, are well formed with regard to XHTML requirements. Using the various XHTML validation targets helps you to ensure that the code you write is compliant as well.

Visual Studio also focuses on providing compliance with accessibility standards (those standards that govern the display of web pages for persons with disabilities). You launch the Accessibility Checker by using the Check Page for Accessibility button on the HTML Source Editing or Formatting toolbars.

Figure 6.46 shows the Accessibility Validation dialog box. You can select the specific standards you want to have your HTML validated against. You can also select the level of feedback that you receive (errors, warnings, or a text checklist). Each item flagged by the checker appears in the Task List window for resolution. For more details on the two standards supported here (WCAG and Access Board Section 508), see their respective websites: http://www.w3.org/TR/WCAG10/ and http://www.access-board.gov/508.htm.

FIGURE 6.46   Setting accessibility validation options.

Authoring WinForms Components and Controls

Referring to our earlier discussion of Windows forms, components are nonvisual controls or classes. This is a good generic definition, but a more specific one is this: A component is any class that inherits from `System.ComponentModel.IComponent`. This particular interface provides support for designability and resource handling. If you need a designable control that does not have a user interface of its own, you work with a component. Controls are similar in function but not form; a control is a reusable chunk of code that does have a visual element to it.

Because Visual Studio provides a dedicated design surface for creating Windows Forms components, we cover this separately in this section. WPF projects also allow for custom controls and components, but in a fashion that is much more streamlined and integrated with the overall development of forms in the WPF world. We cover some of that content in our WPF chapter later in the book (Chapter 19).

Creating a New Component or Control

Starting from an existing WinForms project, you kick off the process of authoring a component by using the Add New Item dialog box (from the Project menu). Selecting Component Class in this dialog box adds the stub code file to your current project and launches the component designer. To start control development, you use the Add New User Control dialog box.

Both the control and the component designers work on the same principles as the Windows Forms Designer: The designers allow you to drag an object from the Toolbox onto the design surface.

Assume that you need a component that sends a signal across a serial port every *x* minutes. Because Visual Studio already provides a timer and a serial port component, which are accessible from the Toolbox, you can use the component designer to add these objects to your own custom component and then leverage and access their intrinsic properties and methods (essentially, using them as building blocks to get your desired functionality).

Figure 6.47 shows the component designer for this fictional custom component. Two objects have been added: a serial port component and a timer component.

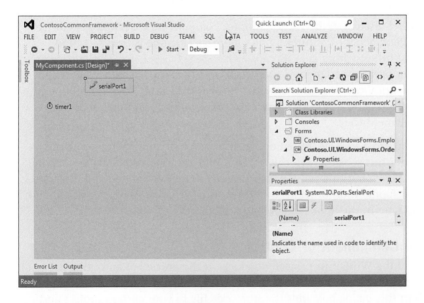

FIGURE 6.47   The component designer.

A similar scenario can be envisioned with a user control. You can take the example of a login "form," consisting of two text boxes, two labels, and two buttons, and actually make that a control (one that can be easily included in the Toolbox and dropped onto a Windows form or web form).

Further Notes on Writing Component Code

Because the component has no visual aspect to it, you don't have the layout and formatting features that you see with the Windows Forms Designer. However, the concept of drag-and-drop programming is alive and well. Visual Studio, behind the scenes, injects the code to programmatically add the given class to the component's container. From there, you can edit the various objects' properties, double-click an object to get to its code, and so on.

When you drag the timer and process objects over from the Toolbox, Visual Studio aggregates these objects into the component by automatically writing the code shown in Listing 6.2.

LISTING 6.2   Component Designer–Generated Code

```
namespace Contoso.UI.WindowsForms.OrderEntry
{
    partial class Component1
    {
        /// <summary>
        /// Required designer variable.
        /// </summary>
        private System.ComponentModel.IContainer components = null;

        /// <summary>
        /// Clean up any resources being used.
        /// </summary>
        /// <param name="disposing">true if managed resources should be
        /// disposed; otherwise, false.</param>
        protected override void Dispose(bool disposing)
        {
            if (disposing && (components != null))
            {
                components.Dispose();
            }
            base.Dispose(disposing);
        }

        #region Component Designer generated code

        /// <summary>
        /// Required method for Designer support - do not modify
        /// the contents of this method with the code editor.
```

```
/// </summary>
private void InitializeComponent()
{
    this.components = new System.ComponentModel.Container();
    this.timer1 = new System.Windows.Forms.Timer(this.components);
    this.serialPort1 = new System.IO.Ports.SerialPort(this.components);

}

#endregion

private System.Windows.Forms.Timer timer1;
private System.IO.Ports.SerialPort serialPort1;



    }
}
```

Writing code "behind" one of the objects placed on the component designer canvas is easy: Double-click the object's icon, and the code editor is launched. For instance, double-clicking the timer icon on the designer surface causes the timer1_Tick routine to be created and then launched in the code editor.

Creating Classes with the Class Designer

The final designer we cover in this chapter is the class designer. The class designer, via its class diagram, allows you to get a view of your code as it exists statically (or at rest). You also get real-time synchronization between the model and the actual code. You should think of the class designer more as a visual code editor and less like a diagram. If you make a change to code, that change is reflected in the diagram. When you change the diagram, your code changes too.

Creating a Class Diagram

There are a couple of ways to create a class diagram. The first is to add a class diagram to your project from the Add New Item dialog box. Here, you select a class diagram template (.cd) and add it to the project. You can then add items to this diagram from the Toolbox or from existing classes in the Solution Explorer.

The second way to add a class diagram to a project is to choose View Class Diagram from the context menu for a given project. In this way, Visual Studio generates a class diagram from an existing project. This option is shown in Figure 6.48.

In either case, you end up with a .cd file in your project that represents the visual model of your classes. Clearly the View Class Diagram option saves you the time of dragging everything onto the diagram. Figure 6.49 shows an example of the class designer file. We cover each window shown in this designer.

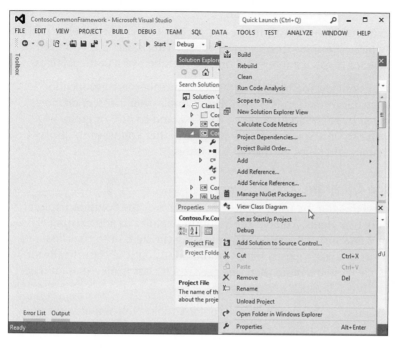

FIGURE 6.48   Launching the class designer.

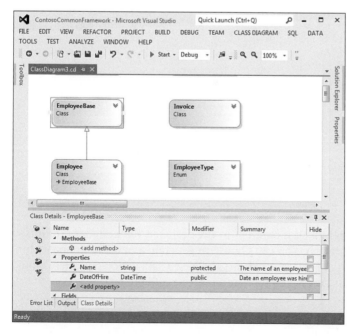

FIGURE 6.49   The class designer.

Displaying Members

You use the arrow icon (points up or down) in the upper-right corner of each object in the designer to toggle whether to show or hide its members. This is useful if you need to conserve screen real estate or if you are interested only in members of a particular class.

You can also use the class designer toolbar to indicate how members are grouped for display and what additional information is shown. For example, you can sort members alphabetically, group them by their kind (property, method, and so on), or group by access (public, private, and so on). You can then indicate whether you want to display just member names, their names and types, or the full signatures.

Adding Items to the Diagram

You add items to the class designer by using either the Toolbox or the Solution Explorer. The Toolbox is for adding new items. You use the Solution Explorer to add existing classes to the diagram. In both scenarios, you simply drag and drop the item onto the class designer window. If the item already exists, Visual Studio builds out the class details for you. In fact, if the class file contains more than one class, each class is placed as an object on the diagram.

Figure 6.50 shows an example of the class designer Toolbox tools. Notice that you can define all object-oriented concepts here, including classes, interfaces, inheritance, and so on.

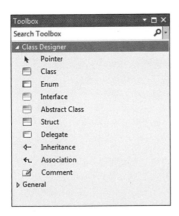

FIGURE 6.50   The class designer Toolbox.

When you add a new item such as a class or struct to the designer, the designer prompts you for the item's name and location. You can choose to generate a new file to house the item or place it in an existing file. Figure 6.51 shows the New Class dialog box. Here, you can give the class a name, set its access modifier, and indicate a filename.

FIGURE 6.51   Adding a new class to the class designer.

> **TIP**
>
> The class designer can automatically add related classes to the diagram. For example, suppose you add a class from the Solution Explorer. If you want to show classes that inherit from this class, you can right-click the class and choose Show Derived Classes. This adds to the model all classes that derive from the selected class.

Defining Relationships Between Classes

One of the biggest benefits of the class diagram is that it visually represents the relationships between classes. These relationships are much easier to see in a diagram than through code. The following relationships can be represented:

▶ **Inheritance**—Indicates whether a class inherits from another class

▶ **Interface**—Indicates whether a class implements one or more interfaces

▶ **Association**—Indicates an association between classes

Let's look at implementing each of these relationships through an example.

Inheritance

First, let's look at inheritance with the class designer. Suppose that you have a base class called `EmployeeBase`. This class represents a generic employee in your system. You then want to create a concrete `Employee` class that inherits from `Product`. If you look back at Figure 6.49, you can see that both of these classes are connected with an arrow leading from the implementing class to the base or parent class. This is simply a visualization of the inheritance that we had already set up in our code. But you can also wire classes together through inheritance by just using the class diagram window and the class designer Toolbox. Select the Inheritance tool from the class designer Toolbox, click the inheriting class (in this example, Employee), and then extend the line up to the base class and click it. And just like that, you have inherited a class, with Visual Studio writing the code for you. Figure 6.52 shows the two classes being connected via the inheritance tool.

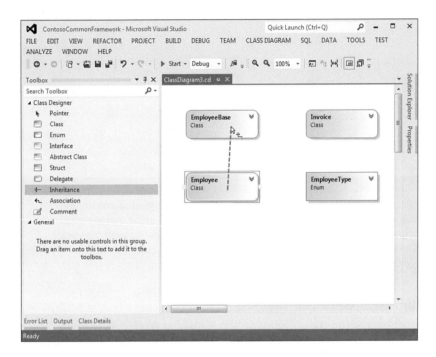

FIGURE 6.52   Class inheritance.

Interface

The next visual relationship we look at is an interface. For this example, suppose that all the business entities in your system implement a similar contract. This contract might define properties for ID and name. It might also define methods such as Get, Delete, and Save.

To implement this interface, you again use the Inheritance tool from the class designer Toolbox. You drag it from the class doing the implementation toward the interface. Figure 6.53 shows the result of an implemented interface. Notice the lollipop icon above the Customer class; it denotes the interface implementation.

Association

The final relationship to look at is association. This relationship is typically a loose one in the Unified Modeling Language (UML) world. However, in the class designer, an association is very real. Typically, this means that two classes have an association through the use of one of the classes. This relationship is also optional in terms of viewing. It can exist, but you do not have to show it in the diagram.

FIGURE 6.53   Implementing an interface.

For example, suppose that you have an `Order` object. This object might expose an `OrderStatus` property. Suppose that it also has a property for accessing the `Customer` record associated with the order. These two properties are associations. You can leave them as properties, or you can choose to show them as associations.

You can also draw these property associations on the diagram. To do so, you select the Association tool from the Toolbox. This tool has the same icon as Inheritance. You then draw the association from the class that contains the association to the class that is the object of the association. You can also right-click the actual property that represents the association and choose Show as Association from the context menu (or Show as Collection Association for associations that are part of a collection).

The result is that the association property is displayed on the association arrow. This indicates that the class from where the association originates contains this property (it is shown only on this line, however). Figure 6.54 illustrates this.

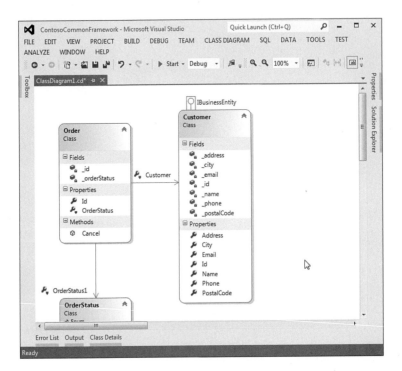

FIGURE 6.54   Creating an association.

Defining Methods, Properties, Fields, and Events

The most exciting part of the class designer is that it allows you to do more than define classes and relationships. You can actually stub out code and do refactoring. (See Chapter 10, "Refactoring Code," for details.)

There are two ways to add code to your classes, structs, interfaces, and the like. The first is to type directly into the designer. For example, if you are in the Properties section of a class, you can right-click and choose to add a new property. This places the property in your class and allows you to edit it in the diagram. This method works for other class members as well. It does have a couple of drawbacks, however. You can't, for instance, define a full method signature or indicate access levels. For that, you need the Class Details window.

The Class Details window allows you to fully define methods, fields, properties, and events for a class. It also works with other constructs such as interfaces, delegates, and enums. To use this window, right-click a class and choose Class Details from the context menu. Selecting this menu item brings up the Class Details editor for the selected class. Figure 6.55 shows the Class Details window in action.

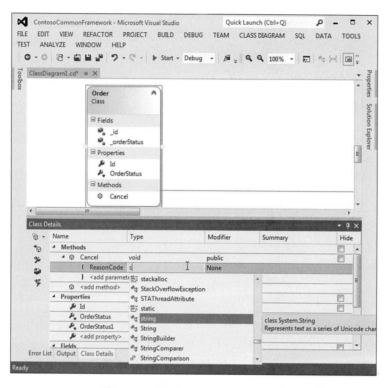

FIGURE 6.55   Creating a method in the Class Details window.

Notice that when working in the Class Details window, you still get IntelliSense. In this example, the `Cancel` method is being added to the `Order` class. You can indicate a return type for the method with the Type column. You can define the access modifier with the Modifier column. You can also set the parameters of the method. In this case, the method takes the parameter `ReasonCode`.

Finally, there are the Summary and Hide columns. The Hide column indicates whether you want to show an item on the diagram. This capability allows you to hide various members when printing or exporting as an image. The Summary column allows you to add your XML documentation to the class. Clicking the ellipsis button (not shown) in this field brings up the Description dialog box. Here, you can enter your XML summary information for the given member. Figure 6.56 shows an example for the Cancel method.

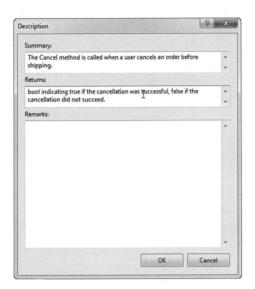

FIGURE 6.56   Creating code comments for a method.

Summary

Visual Studio provides a full array of editors and designers. They cover the gamut of solution development activities from WYSIWYG positioning of graphical controls to finely tuned text editing for a certain language, syntax, or markup.

This chapter described how to leverage the basics within these editors and designers. It also described how the editor and designer relationship provides two complementary views of the same solution artifact, in effect working together to provide you, the developer, with the right tool for the right task at hand.

In subsequent chapters, we look at the more advanced options and productivity features available within these tools and even look at end-to-end development efforts involved in building a web application with ASP.NET or Silverlight, and building a Windows application using Windows Forms or Windows Presentation Foundation.

CHAPTER 7

The .NET Community: Interacting Online

The image of a developer coding away, disconnected from others and from vast amounts of information on the Internet, is an anachronism. Instead, development is now a very connected experience. It is common when programming to expect to take advantage of the large and diverse .NET community. Take a quick look across the Internet and you can find countless bits of content and help for building applications. Microsoft continues to add community features to Visual Studio. These features connect developers with the content in the cloud. They help you quickly gain access to information, sample code, and productivity aids provided by other developers and communities. Visual Studio helps to package this content, manage it, and streamline access to it.

This chapter covers how developers can take advantage of the community capabilities of Visual Studio 2010. You see how to gain access to community content that is right for you, how to get community-driven support, and how to find and consume code from the developer community. Finally, you also learn how you can bundle your own code samples and productivity aids for sharing with the .NET community.

The Community Features of Visual Studio

Software development has become a more connected experience. Web services, RSS feeds, websites, and the like provide access to rich content well beyond what was once stored on a local hard drive or network. This content is no longer simply supplied by and managed by Microsoft.

Microsoft provides a huge amount of developer help, samples, and information, but it also recognizes the contributions of the greater .NET community. Visual Studio provides links to all of this content. The intent is to provide developers with important (and targeted) product, development, and learning information where developers will find it: in their IDE. Taking advantage of this content helps you increase your productivity and use of best practices.

The Visual Studio team has refined the community connections and features in the IDE over the years, so it is intuitive and unobtrusive (yet readily available). You do not have to go searching to find and connect to your community. Rather, these communities are delivered to you through your development tool. If you are looking to find specific information, explore what is available, or publish your own community content, you can do so directly from within Visual Studio. The following sections illustrate what is available from the IDE in terms of the Visual Studio Start Page and the Help menu.

The Visual Studio Start Page

Developers new to Visual Studio first encounter the IDE through the Start Page. The Start Page acts as a simple portal to your development experience and includes links to community content.

The Start Page is divided into two primary sections. On the left is the projects area, which includes links for creating a new project, opening an existing one, or clicking a recent project. The right side contains a lot of information within tabs:

▶ **Get Started**—This tab provides links to content for starting with Visual Studio, Windows, web, and cloud applications. This is also one place where you can link to community inside the Community and Learning Resources link.

▶ **Latest News**—This tab is an RSS reader and can be connected to the latest news on all things .NET related.

Within each primary tab, content is usually further categorized with a second order of tabs. Figure 7.1 shows a sample of the Start Page in the IDE. Notice that the sample Start Page (or portal) shown in Figure 7.1 is for a developer who has set default settings in the IDE to Visual C# Development Settings (Tools, Import and Export Settings). The Start Page (and other items in the IDE such as toolbars and layout) change to reflect the setup of your default profile in the IDE (see Chapter 2, "The Visual Studio IDE"). For example, if you select Visual Basic Development Settings, your Start Page content would contain links targeted to a Visual Basic developer.

Projects Area

The projects section of the Start Page provides quick links to connecting to a Team Foundation Server (TFS) to open a project from source control, create a new project, or open an existing one. Using these links, you can quickly start a new project, create a new website, or browse to another project not listed here. Having quick access to these features makes the Start Page more useful as a launch point for your daily development work.

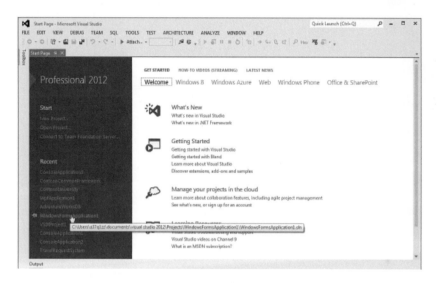

FIGURE 7.1   The Visual Studio Start Page.

This area also includes a list of projects you have been working on. This allows you to easily access one or more projects in which you are currently engaged. Clicking a project in this list opens that project for editing. Figure 7.2 shows an example of a projects area on the Start Page.

Get Started

The Get Started tab on the Start Page provides developers who are new to Visual Studio (or those looking to learn something new) a common place to start. The links in this list typically revolve around creating a new project, using a template or starter kit, answering a question, or learning something new. This feature can be a great launch point for doing your own exploration. Figure 7.3 shows an example of the Get Started tab with the Windows 8 subtab selected.

The links that appear within the various sections could link directly to Microsoft Developer Network (MSDN) pages or to community-related websites.

FIGURE 7.2   The Projects area on the Visual Studio Start Page.

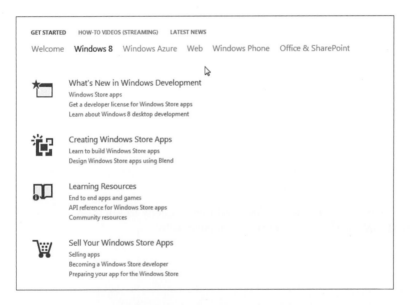

FIGURE 7.3   The Get Started tab on the Visual Studio Start Page.

Latest News

The Latest News tab on the Start Page provides links to all the current news and important information about Visual Studio development. This information includes announcements on training, new betas, new tools, webcasts, and more. It helps keep you informed even if you do not have time for browsing the MSDN website. Figure 7.4 shows an example of some of the news captured when the release candidate of Visual Studio 2012 was first released.

Content for the news channel comes to the IDE via an RSS feed. For those of you unfamiliar with the term *RSS*, it stands for *Really Simple Syndication*. RSS is provides an Extensible Markup Language (XML)-structured list that contains summaries and links to key information found within a particular website. Note that when you first use this tab, you will have to use the Enable RSS Feed button to turn on this feature; it is off by default.

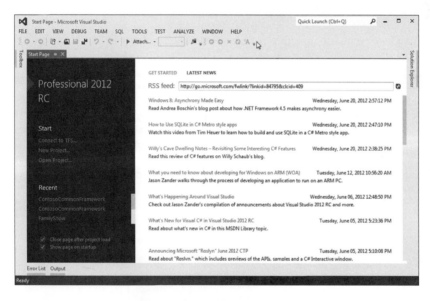

FIGURE 7.4   The Latest News tab on the Visual Studio Start Page.

Setting a Custom News Channel

You can customize which RSS feed is displayed by default in the Latest News tab. To do so, you use the Options dialog box (Tools, Options). You select the Environment node from the tree view on the left side of the dialog box. Under Environment, you select the Startup page and you are presented with a few options regarding the Start Page. Figure 7.5 shows these options.

The second option inside the Startup options dialog box is Start Page news channel. Here you can set a URL to a default RSS feed. This option allows for easy customization and connection to any RSS channel. Changing this setting changes the default RSS data that is displayed in the Latest News tab of the Start Page.

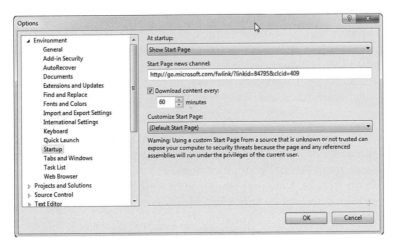

FIGURE 7.5   You can use the Startup node to set Start Page settings.

Some common MSDN RSS feeds and their URLs can be found inside the MSDN developer centers from Microsoft. You can access the list of developer centers at http://msdn.microsoft.com/en-us/aa937802.aspx. From this page, select a developer center. You can then look for a list of information that has an RSS logo associated to it (as shown in Figure 7.6, next to the Visual Studio Highlights section). Click the RSS logo. Copy the resulting URL from the address bar to the Start Page news channel inside the Options dialog box (shown in Figure 7.5).

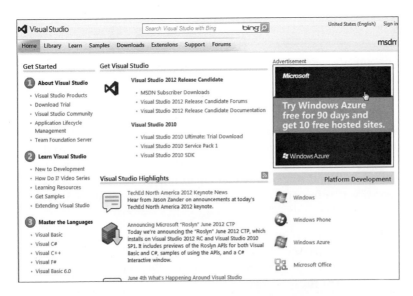

FIGURE 7.6   An RSS link inside one of the MSDN developer centers.

Selecting What to Do at Startup

You can choose what Visual Studio does at the time of application startup. Referring back to Figure 7.5, notice the first option, At Startup. This drop-down list enables you to choose to either show the default Start Page supplied by the IDE, load your last solution, show the open or new project dialog box, show an empty environment, or open a home page. Most of these options are self-explanatory. The last one (open home page), however, requires a little explanation. By setting this value, Visual Studio opens to the Visual Studio MSDN home page. Figure 7.7 shows the Start Page as it looks with this option selected.

FIGURE 7.7   You can load a language-based startup home page inside the IDE.

TIP

If you choose not to see the Start Page when your IDE starts (show empty environment), or you close the Start Page and need to get back to it, you can still navigate to the Start Page. You do so by using the Start Page toolbar icon, as shown in Figure 7.8. This button is not included by default on the standard toolbar, so you will need to add it. Alternatively, you can choose View, Start Page from the IDE menu bar.

Creating a Custom Start Page

You can have full control over what is displayed when you (or your team) open the IDE. The Start Page is a .xaml WPF form that you can customize. You can either start with a blank WPF form and turn it into a Start Page or use the Start Page project template. The project template makes thing easier because it already contains a fully functioning Start Page. To get the project template, you download it from the Visual Studio Code Gallery (http://visualstudiogallery.msdn.microsoft.com). Search for "Custom Start Page Project

Template" to find this free download from Microsoft. Note that you also need the Visual Studio SDK (again found through a quick search).

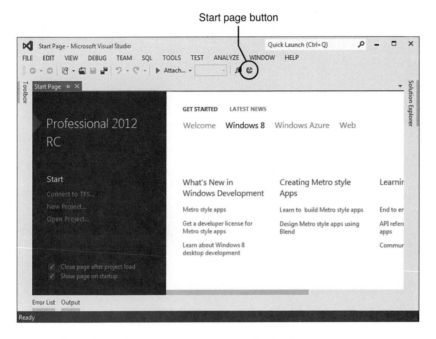

FIGURE 7.8   Accessing the Start Page using the toolbar icon.

Once installed, you can create a new Start Page project from File, New Project. Then select Other Project Types, Extensibility. There you should find the Custom Start Page template.

The Solution contains two projects: the Start Page and a Start Page control. The Start Page project contains the actual Start Page (StartPage.xaml) and creates the VSIX required for deployment (more on VSIX later in this chapter). The Start Page control is a WPF user control you use to add custom content to your Start Page. Figure 7.9 shows the default view of the two projects.

Remember, the Start Page is a WPF form. Therefore, you can create a totally custom Start Page or customize the existing Start Page.

For example, suppose you want to add a tab to the Start Page to show the current state of the project. You could edit the XAML file to add the tab group and a related control that reads a report from a website URL. For more on XAML coding, see Chapter 19, "Creating Richer, Smarter User Interfaces."

After the project is complete, you build it and use the VSIX file for deployment. When run, it will install the new Start Page. You then can then use the Options dialog box (refer to Figure 7.7) to select the new Start Page. Figure 7.10 shows an example of a project burndown chart being displayed within a custom Start Page.

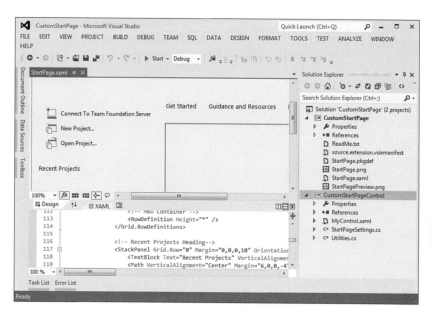

FIGURE 7.9   You can edit the Start Page displayed inside your IDE.

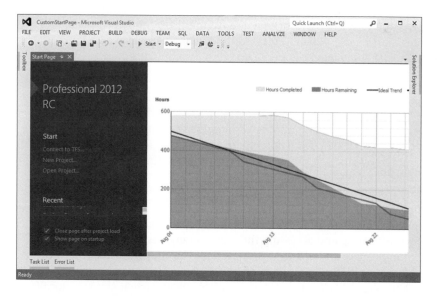

FIGURE 7.10   You can customize the IDE Start Page to show your own information.

Accessing Help

The Visual Studio Help menu is there for you when you get stuck and need to reach out for some assistance. The Help menu provides access to the Visual Studio Documentation (either local or online). It lets you quickly search for an answer to a question, access code samples, or even report a bug with Visual Studio or the Framework. Figure 7.11 shows the Help menu.

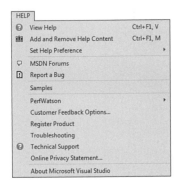

FIGURE 7.11   The Visual Studio Help menu connects you to help and your community.

Manage Your Help Settings

The Visual Studio help system was substantially redesigned with Visual Studio 2010, and Visual Studio 2012 has introduced more changes as well. The Microsoft Document Explorer application is no longer a part of the help system. Instead, Microsoft is moving to a system that creates a stronger link between the online help and your local help. You can choose to access all your help locally, online, or through a combination of the two. You can also get updates to your local help on a regular basis.

How you receive help is controlled through the Help menu link, Add and Remove Help Content. Clicking this link brings up the Microsoft Help Viewer, with an active tab for managing help content as shown in Figure 7.12. From here, you can determine whether you want to use online or local help (or a combination); you can also get updates to your help system, add and remove local content, and find content online or browse to local downloads.

Choose Between Online and Local Help

The new Help system has been simplified somewhat to use compressed XML files, which makes authoring, downloading, and accessing the help content easier. You can use the Content Manager to indicate what help you want available locally and what you want to only access via the Internet. Referring back to Figure 7.12, you can see that some of these help files have actually been downloaded and are available locally (their status is 'local').

If you want to add more content to your local machine, simply click the "add" link next to that help topic. Removing content is done in the same fashion: Click the "remove" link for any of the currently available local topics.

The Content Manager window also checks for any updates that might be available to topic contents. Adding something to your local help cache via this manager will also force the help system to automatically refresh all of your existing content with any updates.

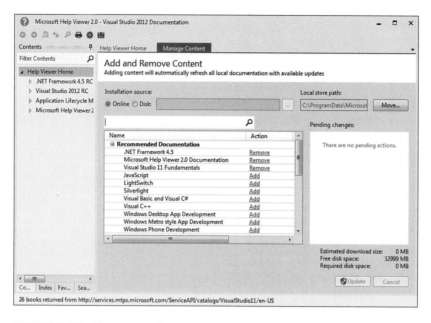

FIGURE 7.12   You can easily manage both the online and local content of your help files.

Using the Visual Studio Documentation

The Visual Studio help documentation can be rendered either in the help viewer application, or within your browser. From the Help menu, you can control which way you want to consume the help content by selecting either Launch in Browser or Launch in Help Viewer from the Set Help Preference option (see Figure 7.13).

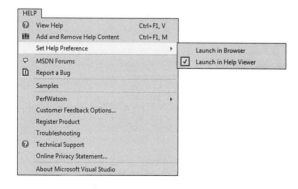

FIGURE 7.13   Switching help viewers is easy.

Using the help viewer has a few advantages over the browser. Both support searching across content, but the help viewer allows you to build lists of favorite topics, and also has a flat top to bottom index that can be consulted to locate content. Figure 7.14 shows an example of a short favorites list that has been compiled in the help viewer.

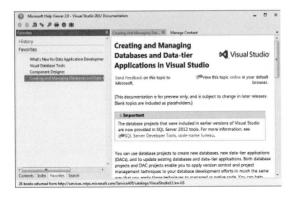

FIGURE 7.14   Using the Favorites list.

MSDN Forums

The MSDN Forums item on the Help menu allows you to search the community forums for answers to questions you have about Visual Studio or the .NET Framework and related languages. When you click this button, Visual Studio navigates to a general page for the MSDN Community Forums. This page allows you to search, browse, and log in to the forums. Figure 7.15 shows an example.

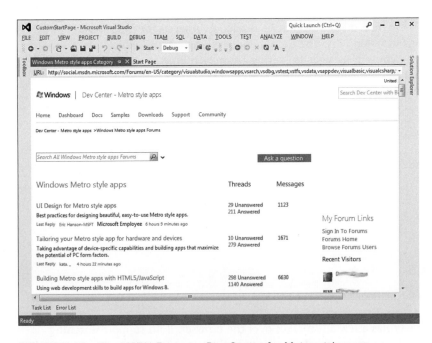

FIGURE 7.15   The MSDN Forums – Dev Center for Metro style apps.

The MSDN Forums are organized around the concept of dev centers, each one catering to a specific technology or product line. Developers can find information relevant to a common problem or to post specific issues and receive feedback from the community. The intent of these moderated forums is to provide a community of developers to aid other developers.

When you reach out to the MSDN forums, you start the process of getting an answer to your question by first searching to find out whether your question was already asked (and possibly already answered). Your search can be constrained to the current dev center that you are in or can be executed globally across all of the dev centers and forums. This is controlled by a drop-down next to the search box toward the lefthand side of the page (see Figure 7.16).

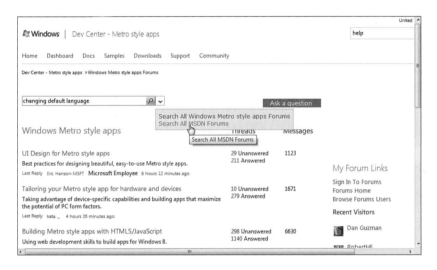

FIGURE 7.16   Searching the forums.

For example, suppose that you want to search the forums for answers to a question pertaining to changing the default language for Visual Studio. In this case, the new forums do not have much to offer (at present). However, this question was asked and answered inside earlier editions. Therefore, you can set your search settings accordingly and click the Search button. MSDN searches the community forum for relevant matches. Figure 7.17 shows the matches returned by the sample question.

Results are displayed based on Bing's (Microsoft's search engine for the Web) relevance rating to your search text. If you are specific enough, you can typically find your question in the first few search results. Note that you have a variety of even more granular options for searching, including expanding your search to MSDN help content in addition to forums, searching downloads and knowledge base entries, etc.

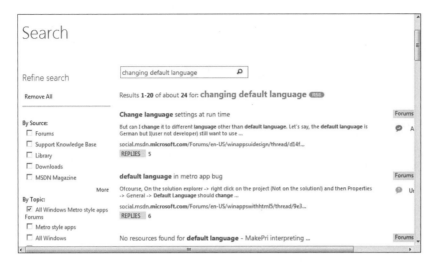

FIGURE 7.17   The sample search results from the MSDN forums.

When you select a search result from the forums, you are taken to a page showing the question and the various replies and answers (see Figure 7.18). Those replies that have been flagged as answers to the question are highlighted in green, which makes it much easier to find real answers to your questions and not have to filter through a large number of replies that did not really answer the question. You can also vote on the best answers. (You must have an account and be logged in.) Those replies that have the largest number of votes float to the top of the list.

Notice, too, on the right side of Figure 7.18 that you can see related topics. Here you can pick a topic that includes an answer (check mark) or one that still needs to be answered (question mark). Select the latter if you think you can add to the discussion of a specific question.

Finally, if you are signed in, you have access to a few more options. You can use the Alert Me button (at the top of the posted question) to receive alerts when a new post is added to the discussion thread (more on this a bit later). You can also quickly access the forums, threads, and other users in which you might have a specific interest.

Starting a New Thread

Of course, often your search does not come up with a suitable answer. In these cases, you can post the question to the appropriate community forum. You can browse forums directly and post your thread or question right there. You can also quickly post a question using the Ask a Question button from the home page (see the upper right of the page shown in Figure 7.15).

Shows related questions (both un-answered and answered)

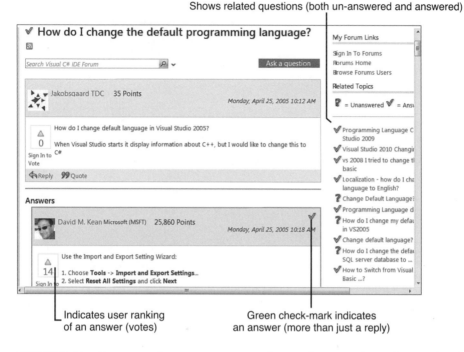

Indicates user ranking
of an answer (votes)

Green check-mark indicates
an answer (more than just a reply)

FIGURE 7.18   You can review answers to questions and vote on those that provide the best answer to a given question.

To post a question (or do much else on the forums), you must have a Windows Live account and be logged in. When you start, you decide if you want to ask a question or start a discussion. Figure 7.19 shows an example. In either case, before your new item is listed, the page shows a list of possible topics that already match your question or discussion topic.

If you end up posting a new topic or question, you need to select the correct forum and tag the content accordingly. Figure 7.20 shows tagging your content and selecting a forum. Finally, you can select the Alert Me link to make sure you are notified in the event people reply to your post.

After you've completed the form, your new question or discussion topic is added to the appropriate forum and marked unanswered. Typically, each forum has a group of people who peruse these unanswered questions and provide assistance.

Navigating Forums and Topics

The MSDN Community Forums are organized into a wide variety of high-level forum categories. These categories include web development, .NET, Visual Studio, Visual Basic, C#, and many more. Each forum category is further refined by the actual forums in the given category.

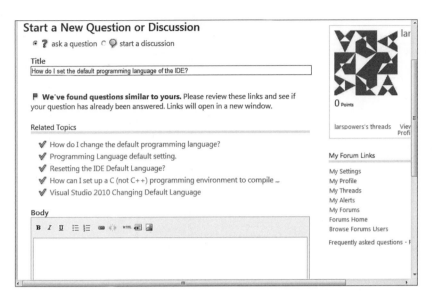

FIGURE 7.19   You can ask a question or start a discussion on the MSDN forums.

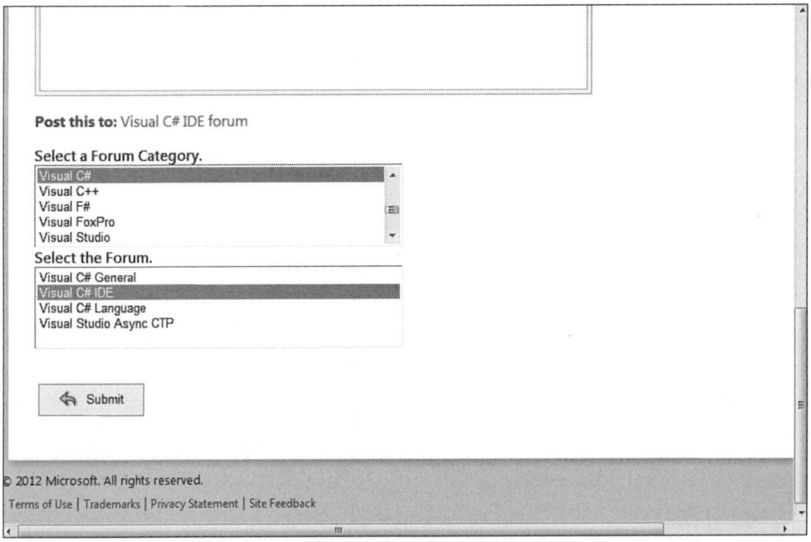

FIGURE 7.20   Completing an MSDN forum post.

You click a forum category to navigate to the forums list for the given category. You can find forums that might be of particular interest to you in the Visual Studio category (or any of the other forums on the forum home page). Figure 7.21 shows the main page for the Visual Studio vNext category.

FIGURE 7.21   The Visual Studio vNext category home page.

Selecting a given forum from a category takes you to the main page for that forum. From here, you can find announcements related to the forum and the actual discussion threads. You can browse the discussion threads, or you can filter them by most popular, posts with code, posts flagged as helpful, and posts that have no reply. You can also sort the topics by recent replies, most views, and most replies. The forums keep track of which items you have and have not read. You can mark all items as read or mark as unread. Of course, you can also search the forum.

For example, Figure 7.22 shows some of the topics found on the Visual Studio 2010 Install and Setup forum. Notice you can see which items are unanswered (designated by the question mark icon). You can also see the number of replies and views for each item.

The forums are decorated with many icons. The icons help you to navigate through topics. As you look through the topics, you quickly learn that not all topics are questions and not all questions are answered. The icons also help guide you to the content within a given topic. For instance, a check mark over a document icon indicates that the topic is an answer to a question. Helpful items have a star icon. There are many icons with which you should become familiar. Figure 7.23 shows the icons and what they mean.

Managing Your Thread Alerts

Typically, when you start a new thread or post a new question, you ask to receive alerts when someone replies to your post or answers your question. In addition, if you find a topic that is of particular interest, you can request to be alerted when new posts are made to the thread. You can also subscribe on any of the existing threads/discussions and be alerted whenever there is activity.

FIGURE 7.22   You can filter how you view the discussion topics in a given forum.

What do the Thread icons mean?

The following table lists the Thread icons and their meanings.

Icon	Legend	Icon	Legend
	Thread Has Code		All Threads
	Helpful Post	?	Unanswered Thread
	No Replies	✓	Answered Thread
	Sort By		General Discussion Thread
	Start New Thread		Proposed Answer
	User		Sticky Thread
	Alerts		Locked Thread
	Reply		Abusive Thread
99	Quote	X	Deleted Thread
	Edit	!	Escalated Thread

FIGURE 7.23   The icons used to help you understand the forums.

Your delivery options for forum alerts are managed via the My Alerts link, under the My Forum Links panel, on the forums home pages (see Figure 7.24).

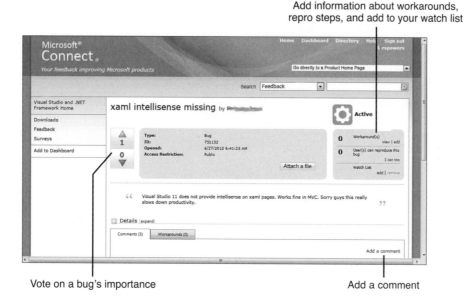

Add information about workarounds, repro steps, and add to your watch list

Vote on a bug's importance   Add a comment

FIGURE 7.24   Locating the forum alerts setting link.

Reporting a Bug and Other Customer Feedback Options

Most developers we've met love to work with cool software and are always looking for ways it might be improved. This holds especially true for their tools, the biggest of which is Visual Studio. There are a couple options to help Microsoft make this tool better. One option is to allow Microsoft to collect data about your customer experience with the product. The other includes making suggestions and reporting any issues, anomalies, or actual bugs you find in your day-to-day programming.

Help Improve Visual Studio

You can choose to participate in the Visual Studio Customer Improvement Program. This option is first presented at the time you install the product. If you ever want to change your original selection you can do so by selecting the Customer Feedback Options menu item from the Help menu. This brings up the dialog box shown in Figure 7.25. Here you can choose to participate or not. If you choose to participate, Visual Studio collects usage data from you and sends it anonymously back to Microsoft. Microsoft then uses that data to identify usage trends with Visual Studio and to help improve the overall product.

FIGURE 7.25   You can choose to help improve Visual Studio.

Report a Bug or Make a Suggestion

Often you think of something that would make for a great addition or perhaps you find a flaw (or bug) in the software. Using the Report a Bug item on the Help menu, you can post your suggestions and log any bugs you find.

The process for reporting bugs and making suggestions is similar to that of starting a new thread in the MSDN forums. After you log in, you see the Microsoft Connect website. Figure 7.26 shows the main page of this site.

The process starts by first searching for a similar suggestion or bug, which helps to reduce the creation of duplicate submissions. If you find an item similar to the one you had planned to post, you can rate the item in terms of relative importance. Adding an importance vote helps Microsoft to focus on items of highest relevance to the community. You can also add a workaround to the item (if you know one), add the item to your watch list for additional monitoring, or indicate that you can reproduce the issue. You can also add comments to a suggestion or bug. Adding your comments to an item allows you to provide similar evidence or clarification to a reported bug or suggestion. Figure 7.27 shows the screen for an active bug.

Microsoft actively monitors these lists. In fact, most items are marked with Microsoft comments and are closed or resolved in new builds and service packs. In addition, if you find a bug for which you know a workaround, you can attach your workaround to the item. This is another way the .NET community can help itself.

FIGURE 7.26   You can report a bug or make a suggestion for Visual Studio.

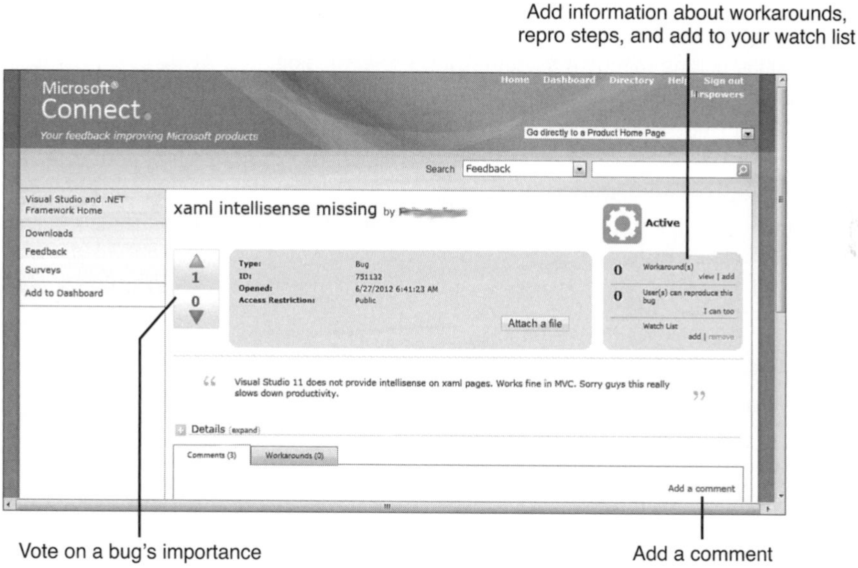

Add information about workarounds,
repro steps, and add to your watch list

Vote on a bug's importance   Add a comment

FIGURE 7.27   You can report, monitor, and comment on bugs.

Samples

Selecting the Samples link from the Help menu will launch the New Project dialog, and
show you a list of the sample applications available online.

You click a link from the samples read me page to access the sample downloads from
MSDN. This takes you to a development center on MSDN. Which developer center you go
to is based on your IDE preferences. Figure 7.28 shows the selection of a project that will
teach you the basics of building MVC 3 applications with C#.

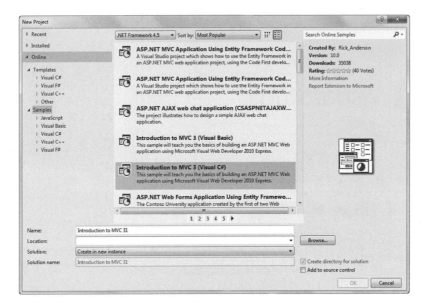

FIGURE 7.28   Accessing coding samples from the New Project dialog.

Notice in Figure 7.28 that you can click a More Information link (right side of the dialog) to get more details of the sample application template. From the sample's home page (see Figure 7.29), you can get release details about the sample, download the actual sample code, participate in discussions about the sample, and more. Of course, you can also just browse the other available samples.

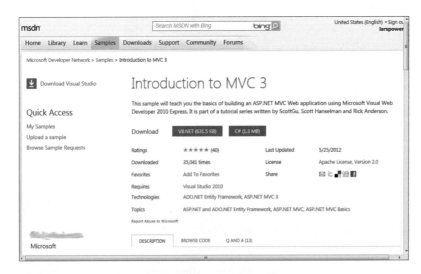

FIGURE 7.29   Coding sample information page.

Selecting a sample enables you to download it locally.

Discovering and Consuming Shared Content

We have all been given programming tasks in which we just know someone must have already tackled the problem, and we've all faced tight deadlines. In these cases, it is often wise to hit the Internet to find out whether there is community content you can use to your advantage. At a minimum, you might find a partial solution that can speed your development effort and increase your understanding of how you might solve your particular problem.

Visual Studio provides a formal mechanism for publishing, finding, and consuming shared content. In the following sections, we look at discovering and leveraging this content. We also demonstrate how you can be an active participant in this community.

Examining Shared Content Types

Visual Studio provides a number of code-sharing opportunities. For example, you might download a project template that defines an observer or singleton pattern, perhaps you find a code snippet that inserts a common method for accessing a database, or maybe you write a timesaving add-in or macro that you can share with the community. Visual Studio allows developers to write these types of extensions and more. Table 7.1 describes the many content types that provide opportunities for community sharing and consumption in Visual Studio 2010.

TABLE 7.1   Shared Content Types

Content	Description
Project Template	Project templates are the sets of files that define a new project. When you create a new project using Visual Studio, you are asked to select a project template. Visual Studio allows for the creation of your own project templates and the consumption of the same.
Starter Kit	Starter kits are just like project templates but typically include additional documentation and step-by-step instructions.
Item Template	Item templates are files that you want to be able to reuse across projects. When you use Visual Studio to add a new item to your project, you are selecting and adding an item template. Item templates define the contents and structure of new items when they are added to a project. Visual Studio allows you to create and consume custom item templates.
Code Snippet	Code snippets are bits of code that you can add to the Visual Studio IntelliSense feature. You can create your own code snippets and share them with your community. A number of useful snippets are also available for download. We cover creating a custom code snippet in Chapter 8, "Working with Visual Studio's Productivity Aids."
Sample	A number of MSDN sample applications are available for download and installation. These files are typically .zip files and come in multiple languages (C# and VB being the most common). In addition, a number of samples are available when installing Visual Studio (see the discussion in this chapter under "Samples").

Content	Description
Control	Controls can be both user and custom controls written for .NET. They might be free to the community and include source code, or they might be made for commercial purposes. You can write and share your own controls using Visual Studio.
Add-Ins	Add-ins are typically extensions and enhancements to the development environment. Visual Studio supports the creation and sharing of these items. Add-ins are covered in Chapter 14, "Writing Add-Ins and Wizards."

Finding the Right Content

As we saw in our previous discussion of code samples, the New Project dialog presents you with a list of code content available online. The first trick to leveraging the knowledge that exists out there is finding it, and using the online search capabilities of this dialog are a great way to start. The Online Templates option in the New Project dialog box enables you to find templates by technology (see the left side of Figure 7.30), sort those templates by relevance and framework version (the top middle of Figure 7.30), and do a text-based search for templates (the upper right of Figure 7.30).

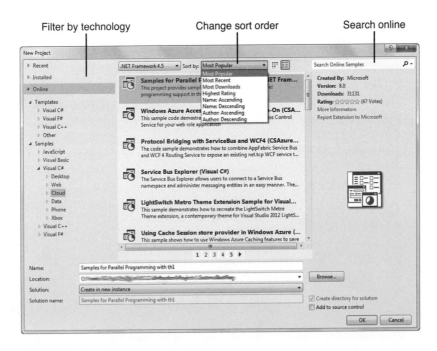

FIGURE 7.30   Finding online content.

NOTE

We are using the word *template* here because that is what they are called in the dialog box. However, by using the New Project dialog box, you are really installing *starter kits*. Starter kits are sample applications and learning tools that allow you to examine a full solution. If you need just a Visual Studio item template, you can find these, too, inside the Add New Item dialog box under the Online templates link.

TIP

Another site you should check for finding good, sample content is CodePlex (http://www.codeplex.com). This is a site used by both Microsoft and the .NET community to post open-source projects for download. You can also contribute to projects posted on this site.

Installing and Storing Shared Content

When you click OK on a selected template or starter kit in the New Project dialog, Visual Studio downloads the content and stores it accordingly in the selected folder location. You may have to first respond to a dialog box to accept any applicable license terms (see Figure 7.31).

FIGURE 7.31 You can accept license terms of the downloaded content.

Real Visual Studio project and item templates (not starter kits, add-ins, or snippets) are installed in one of the appropriate Visual Studio locations. There are paths for projects, project templates, and item templates. Figure 7.32 shows the Options dialog box that can be used to manage these paths. Note that if you have a lot of varied project and item templates, you may choose to set these paths to a network share. This enables you to share templates among a development team.

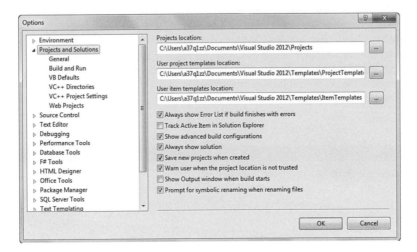

FIGURE 7.32   Setting project and item template storage locations.

Participating in the Community

No matter how good Visual Studio gets, most developers often think of great additions or extensions to the existing functionality. These extensions might be project-specific, or they might apply to all Visual Studio users. Of course, developers also like to write code. Therefore, it is not surprising that some go so far as to write their own custom extensions (add-ins, snippets, and the like). This feat is often successful for single, personal use. The trouble comes when you want to share your timesaving creation with the rest of the team. Often, you end up writing a page of installation instructions and doing one-on-one troubleshooting with each developer as he or she installs your "timesaver."

Visual Studio offers a solution in the form of a packaging mechanism that allows developers to publish, exchange, and install Visual Studio content. Previously, we looked at consuming community content. Now we demonstrate how you can package your own creations and exchange them with team members, with friends, or through community websites.

Starter Kits Versus Templates

In other chapters, we demonstrate how to create snippets and add-ins (see Table 7.1 for chapter references). What we have not covered is creating starter kits and templates (both project and item templates). These items are very useful for large teams that want to disseminate standards and provide guidance. They are also useful for providing content to the community.

A project template and a starter kit are fundamentally the same thing. They are only discussed differently to set expectations of those consuming these items. People who use a starter kit expect to use it as a learning tool and therefore you are expected to provide a high-degree of documentation and step-by-step instruction when creating something called a starter kit. Project and item templates are similar to the templates that you use inside Visual Studio to create new projects and items. In most cases, these templates provide a starting point for something that you create often. The documentation of these items is typically stored elsewhere (if at all).

Again, Visual Studio does not distinguish between starter kits and templates. Therefore, we discuss creating templates. You can use what is discussed here to package your starter kits, too.

Creating a Project Template

To review, project templates are what appear in Visual Studio's New Project dialog box. Projects are grouped by project type (C#, VB, Windows, Office, and so on). These project types are defined by a tree control.

You can create a project template manually or use the Visual Studio Export Template Wizard. The wizard simply makes the task of putting together the right XML files and zipping your project slightly easier. To create a project template, you follow these basic steps:

1. Create a project in Visual Studio (or start with an existing project).

2. Determine where (if any) parameters should exist in your template.

3. Choose the Export Template option from the File menu.

4. (Optional) Edit the .vstemplate XML.

Next, let's look at each of these steps.

Step 1: Create Your Project

Most templates you create start with an existing Visual Studio template (or an empty project). Typically, developers look to templates to enforce standards and practices and provide guidance to teams. Therefore, the hardest part of creating a project template is defining the template itself in terms of what content should go into it. For example, perhaps your team uses a common set of libraries, resources, or controls. You can define a project template that has these items either built in or referenced.

Step 2: Determine Project Parameters

Project parameters define the items that are set by default when Visual Studio sets up a new project based on the given template. For example, when you create a new project, the namespace of the code files is set to the namespace of the project. This is a project parameter. Visual Studio uses a number of reserved template parameters for this purpose. Table 7.2 provides an overview of these parameters.

TABLE 7.2   Reserved Template Parameters

Content	Description
clrversion	The version of the Common Language Runtime (CLR).
GUID[1-10]	A unique project ID. You can set up to 10 project IDs using GUID1, GUID2, and so on.
itemname	The name of the given item that the user types into the Add New Item dialog box (for example, MyNewClass.cs).
machinename	The user's computer name.
projectname	The name of the given project that the user types into the Add New Project dialog box (for example, MySmartClient).
registeredorganization	The Registry key value for the organization set during Windows installation.
rootnamespace	The namespace that is set as the root for the current project.
safeitemname	Similar to the itemname but with all unsafe characters and spaces removed.
safeprojectname	Similar to the projectname but with all unsafe characters and spaces removed.
time	The current time on the user's computer.
userdomain	The domain the user has logged in to.
username	The name of the active user.
webnamespace	The name of the website is used as the default namespace for web applications.
year	The current year as represented by the user's computer.

The Export Template Wizard helps you with these parameters. After you define them manually in your code, the Export Template Wizard picks up the settings.

For example, suppose you have a project template titled SmartClient. When a user chooses to create a project based on this template, you want the template to behave as another template in the dialog box. For instance, you want the project's namespace to be defined as the project name the user has chosen.

To implement parameters in the template, you define the parameter's position within the code. In the namespace example, you must use the reserved template parameter safeprojectname in place of the actual namespace defined throughout the code files in the project. This indicates to Visual Studio that when a new project is created the namespace should be set to the safe project name as defined by the user. The following code example shows how to define the code:

```
namespace $safeprojectname$ {
    class Framework {
```

> **NOTE**
>
> Your code will not build with these parameters in place. Therefore, it is best to debug your code before setting up parameters.

After you've defined your parameters, the Export Template Wizard picks them up and places them in the .vstemplate XML file. We look at this in the "Step 3: Export Your Template" section.

Defining Custom Parameters   In addition to the aforementioned Visual Studio parameters, you can define your own custom parameters to be passed to your templates. The process is similar to using the reserved template parameters. You first define the parameters using the $parameter$ syntax in your code, as shown here:

```
string myCustomValue = "$CustomParameter1$";
```

You then edit the .vstemplate XML (generated in the next step) to include a <CustomParameters> node in which you define your replacements. We look at this XML in more detail in the next major section; however, the following defines a custom parameter in the .vstemplate file:

```
<TemplateContent>
    ...
    <CustomParameters>
        <CustomParameter Name="$CustomParameter1$" Value="Some Custom Value"/>
    </CustomParameters>
</TemplateContent>
```

Visual Studio replaces the content of the custom parameter when a user creates a new instance of the project template. In the preceding example, the value of the variable myCustomValue is set to Some Custom Value.

> **NOTE**
>
> The Export Template Wizard does not recognize custom parameters. You have to edit the .vstemplate XML manually to include the CustomParameters node.

Step 3: Export Your Template

Now that you have defined your template and decided on template parameters, the next step is to run the Export Template Wizard. This wizard is used for both project and item templates. You access it from the File menu.

Figure 7.33 shows the first step in the wizard. Here, you are asked to choose the template type (project or item). You then must select a project from within the current, open Visual Studio solution. This project serves as the basis for your template.

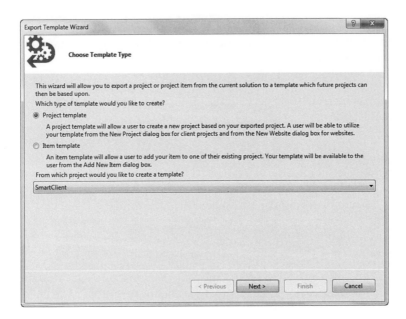

FIGURE 7.33   You use the Export Template Wizard to create a project or item template.

The next step in the Export Template Wizard allows you to define a few additional parameters for your template. You can set an icon and a preview picture for the template, indicate a name and description that show up in the New Project dialog box, and also choose the location where your template is placed. Figure 7.34 shows an example of this dialog box.

Notice that in the dialog box shown in Figure 7.34, we have not checked the Automatically Import the Template into Visual Studio option. This is for two reasons. First, before importing, we want to edit the .vstemplate file the wizard generates. Second, you might want to package the template for installation and test out that installation. (We look at this topic in the next major section.) By default, the template is output to the directory Documents\Visual Studio 10\My Exported Templates\. The exported template is a single, .zip file. All templates in Visual Studio are zip files. To edit the template before deploying, you can unzip the file and gain access to the many files defined by the template (including .vstemplate).

Step 4 (Optional): Edit the .vstemplate XML
A fourth (optional) step in the process is to edit the .vstemplate XML. The Export Template Wizard generates a default .vstemplate for you. You can open the .zip file, edit the XML, rezip (compress) the file, and place it directly into the template folder or package for installation. Listing 7.1 shows a sample .vstemplate file.

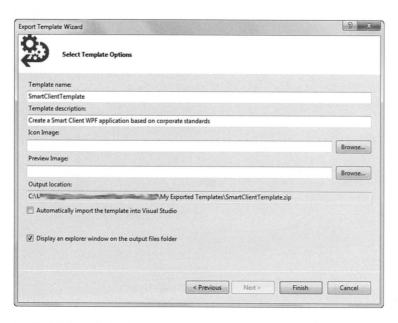

FIGURE 7.34   Define the export template options.

LISTING 7.1   A Sample .vstemplate File

```xml
<VSTemplate Version="3.0.0"
  xmlns="http://schemas.microsoft.com/developer/vstemplate/2005" Type="Project">
  <TemplateData>
    <Name>SmartClientWpf Template</Name>
    <Description>A Smart Client WPF App based on corporate standards</Description>
    <ProjectType>CSharp</ProjectType>
    <ProjectSubType>
    </ProjectSubType>
    <SortOrder>1000</SortOrder>
    <CreateNewFolder>true</CreateNewFolder>
    <DefaultName>SmartClientWpf Template</DefaultName>
    <ProvideDefaultName>true</ProvideDefaultName>
    <LocationField>Enabled</LocationField>
    <EnableLocationBrowseButton>true</EnableLocationBrowseButton>
    <Icon>__TemplateIcon.bmp</Icon>
    <PreviewImage>__PreviewImage.bmp</PreviewImage>
  </TemplateData>
  <TemplateContent>
    <Project TargetFileName="SmartClientWpf Template.csproj"
      File="SmartClientWpf Template.csproj" ReplaceParameters="true">
      <ProjectItem ReplaceParameters="true"
        TargetFileName="Framework.cs">Framework.cs</ProjectItem>
```

```
    <Folder Name="Properties" TargetFolderName="Properties">
      <ProjectItem ReplaceParameters="true"
        TargetFileName="AssemblyInfo.cs">AssemblyInfo.cs</ProjectItem>
      <ProjectItem ReplaceParameters="true"
        TargetFileName="Resources.resx">Resources.resx</ProjectItem>
      <ProjectItem ReplaceParameters="true"
        TargetFileName="Resources.Designer.cs">Resources.Designer.cs</ProjectItem>
      <ProjectItem ReplaceParameters="true"
        TargetFileName="Settings.settings">Settings.settings</ProjectItem>
      <ProjectItem ReplaceParameters="true"
        TargetFileName="Settings.Designer.cs">Settings.Designer.cs</ProjectItem>
    </Folder>
    </Project>
  </TemplateContent>
</VSTemplate>
```

Notice that the wizard added the `ReplaceParameters` attribute to the `Project` and `ProjectItem` nodes and set its value to `true`. This setting indicates to Visual Studio that it should swap any parameters in the target file during project creation. In the example, Framework.cs is the target file that contains the parameter `$safeprojectname$`.

TIP

You can actually create templates that contain multiple projects. To do so, you still create a .vstemplate file for each project in the solution. You then create a .vstemplate root file that describes the multiproject template. The data inside this XML is used by the New Project dialog box. The file also contains pointers to each individual project's .vstemplate file.

Installing the Template

The simple way to install your template on a local machine is to copy it to the templates directory (Documents\Visual Studio 2012\Templates\). You can put the template inside one of the folders found in this location depending on the language you used, etc. It is then available for use. Figure 7.35 shows an example of the SmartClientWpf Template project ready for use.

When the project is generated, Visual Studio inserts the safe filename for the project namespace. Recall that this was the reserved parameter you had set. The following code is inserted into Framework.cs:

```
namespace SmartClient_Template1 {
    class Framework {
```

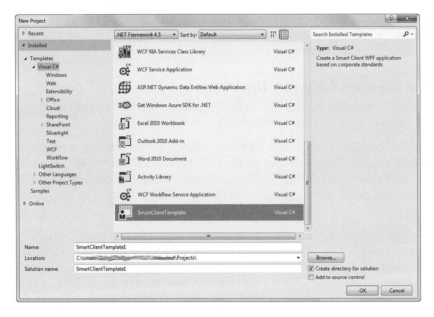

FIGURE 7.35   The installed template in the New Project dialog box.

> **TIP**
>
> You can package templates for installation. This allows you to distribute them to other developers and post them on the Visual Studio Gallery. We look at creating a packaged solution and installing it the "Packaging Your Creation for Wider Distribution" section.

Creating Item Templates

Item templates represent the various items or files you can add to Visual Studio projects. Selecting Add New Item opens a dialog box that enables you to select from the various Visual Studio items (class files, for example). You can also create your own, custom items. Examples of custom items are timesaving devices that stub out the shell of a class or a fully implemented specific type of class.

The good news is that you create item templates the same way you create project templates. You start with an existing item, edit it, and then use the Export Template Wizard to create an item template from the item. In Step 1 of the wizard, you choose Item Template (refer to Figure 7.33).

There are a couple of additional steps to creating an item template. You must select the files in your project that you want to use to generate item templates. Each item template is based on a single file. You then select any references you want to add to a project when someone uses your new item template. The list of available references from which to choose is built based on the project from which you are exporting.

Note that you can also define the same set of parameters for item templates that you can for project templates. Also, item templates are copied to the same location as project templates (but inside a different folder).

Packaging Your Creation for Wider Distribution

You can package your content for distribution in three primary ways: VSIX, MSI, and VSI. Each of these has their place depending on your needs:

▶ **VSIX**—The Visual Studio Extension file format (.vsix) is used for creating content that you intend to publish to the Visual Studio Gallery. The VSIX items are then installed and managed via the Visual Studio Extension Manager (Tool, Extension Manager). The VSIX projects are also available in the Online Templates in the New Project Dialog.

VSIX can package project and item templates, toolbox controls, and more. You cannot, however, use VSIX to deploy add-ins or code snippets; you use VSI for that. In addition, you cannot write to the GAC or Registry with VSIX. (It is a file-based deployment.) In order to create a VSIX project with Visual Studio, you will need to download and install the Visual Studio 2012 SDK. The SDK will add the required project and item templates to your Visual Studio installation.

▶ **MSI**—The Windows Installer (MSI) is used to create custom setup packages. These are great for deploying your applications. They can write to the Global Assembly Cache (GAC) and the Registry (among other things). MSIs, however, cannot be used to deploy project and item templates to Visual Studio.

▶ **VSI**—The Visual Studio Content Installer (VSI) is great for deploying macros, add-ins, and code snippets. However, it cannot write to the GAC or Registry. In addition, VSI packaged content cannot be deployed to the Visual Studio Gallery. You can still create item and project templates with VSI. (You just cannot deploy them into the gallery.)

The VSIX and VSI deployment methods are the primary means for distributing your community content. Of course, VSIX is the preferred option if you intend to use the Visual Studio Gallery. We look at both of these options in greater detail.

Packaging Content with VSI

The VSI helps developers install content that is targeted at the Visual Studio IDE. This includes add-ins, and code snippets. A VSI file has the .vsi extension and bundles the other files that make up the package. After it has been created, a VSI can be easily installed into the right directories on a developer's computer to make that macro, add-in, or snippet available at runtime.

> **NOTE**
>
> As mentioned, VSI packages can be used to deploy macros. But Visual Studio 2012 has actually dropped all support for macros. This means that while you can develop and distribute macros using earlier versions, they will not install in Visual Studio 2012.

The good news is that creating these files is a relatively straightforward process. Of course, the first step is to define and debug your creation. When you are ready to share your creation, you need to follow these steps (we elaborate on them later):

1. Create a VSContent file that contains XML describing your content.

2. Gather the file or files that define your creation.

3. Compress your files into a .zip file.

4. Rename the .zip file using the .vsi extension.

5. (Optional) Add an end-user license agreement (EULA) to your VSI.

6. (Optional) Sign your .vsi file.

This process is the same no matter the content type. The install tool gets its information regarding your contents through the settings of your .VSContent XML file.

The Elements of a VSContent XML File   The VSContent file is an XML structure that contains elements for all pertinent items needed by the Visual Studio Content Installer. Your content is defined by a `Content` node (or element). This element is meant to define a single item of content you want to share (such as a macro file or control defined in a .dll file). Listing 7.2 presents the high-level structure of the VSContent file. This is neither a real example nor the official XSD. Rather, it serves to present the elements and their relations to one another.

LISTING 7.2   The Structure of a VSContent File

```
<VSContent xmlns="http://schemas.microsoft.com/developer/vscontent/2005">
  <Content>
    <FileName></FileName>
    <DisplayName></DisplayName>
    <Description></Description>
    <FileContentType></FileContentType>
    <ContentVersion></ContentVersion>
    <Attributes>
      <Attribute name="" value=""/>
    </Attributes>
  </Content>
</VSContent>
```

> **TIP**
>
> The actual XSD that defines the structure of a VSContent file is a bit lengthy to reprint here. However, if you would like to examine the XSD file that defines the structure for valid VSContent XML, you can do so. The file is stored at C:\Program Files (x86)\ Microsoft Visual Studio 11.0\Xml\Schemas\1033\ and is named vscontent.xsd.

You can point to multiple content types and their associated files using a single .vsi file. You do so by creating multiple instances of the Content element, one for each item you want to share. For example, a single .vsi file could contain a Content node that installs a code snippet and another Content node that points to a .vsmacro file containing macros.

Each element inside Listing 7.2 is covered in depth in Table 7.3. We walk through an actual example of creating and using a VSContent file in a coming section.

TABLE 7.3   Elements of a VSContent file

Element	Description
FileName	This element represents the name of the file that contains the item to be installed as the content. A single Content element can contain multiple FileName elements, depending on the situation. For example, you may define a VSContent file to install an add-in. The add-in might contain both an .Addin file and a .dll file.
DisplayName	This is the name of your content. The Visual Studio Content Installer displays this name when users install your creation.
Description	This element is used as the ToolTip text for your content inside the Visual Studio Content Installer.
FileContentType	This represents the type of content defined by the given Content node. This value is enumerated and therefore must be one of the following settings: Addin, Macro Project, Code Snippet, VSTemplate, Toolbox Control.
ContentVersion	This element represents a version number for your content. The only valid setting at this time is 1.0. All other settings result in an error.
Attributes	This element is used to group Attribute elements.
Attribute	You can use attributes to further define code snippet and VSTemplate content. These settings are discussed further in the next section.

Using Attributes to Define VSTemplates and Code Snippets   The Attribute element inside the VSContent file provides the Visual Studio Content Installer additional information for your given content type that include project templates, item templates, and code snippets. The Attributes node is not used for the content types Addin, Macro Project, and Toolbox Control.

The Attribute element consists of a name/value pair. You set the name and value of the element using XML attributes in the following format:

```
<Attribute name="" value=""/>
```

Both the name and the value attributes are defined with enumerated values. These enumerated values define the possible setting combinations you can define for code snippets and templates.

For code snippets, only the value lang is applicable for the name attribute. Setting the lang attribute on code snippets allows you to indicate the development language to which the snippet applies. Possible entries for the value attribute when defined with `lang` include `csharp`, `jsharp`, `vb`, and `xml`. For example, if your code snippet is meant to work with Visual Basic, you define your attribute as shown here:

```
<Attribute name="lang" value="vb"/>
```

When defining content of type `VSTemplate`, you can use the following enumerated items for the name attribute:

- ▶ `TemplateType`—Defines the type of template your content represents. Values are either Project for project templates or Item for item templates.

- ▶ `ProjectType`—Defines the type of project contained in your template. Possible enumerated items for the value attribute are Visual Basic, Visual C#, Visual J#, and Visual Web Developer.

- ▶ `ProjectSubType`—Defines the subcategory in which your template is placed in the New Project dialog box. Possible entries include Windows, Office, Smart Device, Database, Starter Kits, and Test.

Recall the Smart Client project template you created earlier. Listing 7.3 represents the VSContent file used to define the installation for the Smart Client. Notice the three attribute definitions used to define template, project, and project subtype.

LISTING 7.3   The VSContent File for the Smart Client Example

```
<VSContent xmlns="http://schemas.microsoft.com/developer/vscontent/2010">
  <Content>
    <FileName>Smart Client.zip</FileName>
    <DisplayName>Smart Client</DisplayName>
    <Description>Install a smart client project template</Description>
    <FileContentType>VSTemplate</FileContentType>
    <ContentVersion>1.0</ContentVersion>
    <Attributes>
      <Attribute name="TemplateType" value="Project"/>
      <Attribute name="ProjectType" value="Visual C#"/>
      <Attribute name="ProjectSubType" value="Windows"/>
    </Attributes>
  </Content>
</VSContent>
```

An Example: Packaging an Add-In   Let's examine how we might package and distribute a Visual Studio add-in (.dll) using a VSI.

After you've debugged and tested your extension, the first step in packaging it is to define the VSContent file. For this example, we've created a simple Visual Studio add-in. (Add-ins are compiled into .dll files.) We use the add-in .dll file as content for our package. The name of the macro file is MyFirstAddin.dll.

An easy way to define the VSContent file is to create an XML file inside Visual Studio (File, New, File), which opens the New File dialog box. From here, select XML File. Remember, the VSContent file is simply an XML file with a special extension in the filename (.VSContent). In this way, you can create and edit your VSContent file directly in Visual Studio. You have to edit the filename from .xml to VSContent. However, using Visual Studio enables you to take advantage of the built-in XML editor that includes IntelliSense.

The first step in defining the content of this file is to set the XML namespace (xmlns) to the proper schema. You do this by adding the following root node to the file:

```
<VSContent xmlns="http://schemas.microsoft.com/developer/vscontent/2005">
```

After you've done this, Visual Studio recognizes the intended structure for the XML and guides you through defining additional elements. Figure 7.36 shows an example of creating the VSContent file inside the IDE. Note that for the example, you define two FileName elements to point to the required add-in files. This is your primary payload for the VSI. You also must set the `FileContentType` to the value `Addin`. This ensures that the example is installed in the proper location.

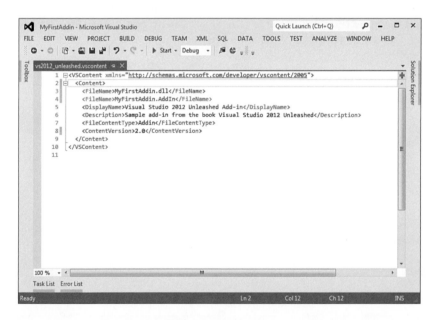

FIGURE 7.36   Defining the VSContent file inside the Visual Studio IDE.

The next step is to place all your files into a single directory where they can easily find each other. You need to include in your bundle any files that are called out in the VSContent file (.vsmacros, .dll, .addin, and so on) and the VSContent file itself. For some files and projects, you might have to dig a little.

In this example, create a folder named VS2012 Unleashed Addin. In it, you place the .dll file named MyFirstAddin.dll, the .addin file MyFirstAddin.addin, and the VSContent file named VS2012_Unleashed.vscontent.

The third step is to compress (.zip) your files. The process of compressing the files should be familiar to all developers. You can use Windows's built-in capability to compress files, or you can use a compression tool. In this example, use the Windows compression tool. You select the .AddIn, .dll, and VSContent files, right-click, and then choose Send To, Compressed (Zipped) Folder.

The result of Step 3 is the creation of a file named MyFirstAddin.zip. Now you're ready for the easiest step. Right-click the .zip file and choose Rename from the context menu. Remove the .zip extension and replace it with .vsi. Of course, you need to be showing file extensions for this to work. You can do so in Windows 7 using Windows Explorer, Organize, Folder and Search Options. That's it. If you are on a machine with Visual Studio installed, the new file takes on the .vsi icon (used for both .vsi and VSContent files).

All that remains is to distribute the .vsi file to the intended audience. Of course, it would be prudent to do a couple of test installations first. Let's look at the Visual Studio Content Installer tool in action.

Both the .vsi and the VSContent files are Visual Studio Content Installer (VSContentInstaller.exe) files. They have the same icon. The reason is that both can be used to install the content.

There are some differences between the two, however. The .vsi file is fully self-contained. It does not require additional files for installation, whereas the VSContent file must exist in a directory that also contains the related content files. In addition, when you run the VSContent file, you are not warned about the lack of a signature (if one is lacking). Therefore, you might think that there is a bug or that these files are more appropriate for internal installations. The .vsi file, in contrast, prompts you with a security warning dialog box if the content is not signed by a publisher. This, along with the single file and compression factor, seems to make the .vsi file ideal in larger, distributed scenarios.

Let's examine the installation process for the .vsi file. First, you double-click the file to invoke the Visual Studio Content Installer. Figure 7.37 shows the example loaded in the tool.

From this screen, you can select View Files in Windows Explorer to examine the files that will be installed by the .vsi. Also, notice that the Publisher Information section is blank. The reason is that the bundle is not signed. When you click the Next button, the tool prompts you with a warning regarding the lack of signature. Again, this warning is not shown if you are installing from the VSContent file directly. For now, click Yes and move on. In the sidebar, we discuss signing your work.

Next, the installer prepares you to finish the installation. When you click the Finish button, the installer writes the files to the appropriate folders based on content type. If the given file already exists, the installer prompts you to find out whether you want it left as is or overwritten. Finally, the installer finishes its job and reports back. Figure 7.38 shows a successful installation.

FIGURE 7.37   The first step in the Visual Studio Content Installer.

FIGURE 7.38   A successful installation.

SIGNING YOUR WORK

To sign your .vsi files with Authenticode, you must get a valid software publisher certificate (.spc) from a certificate authority (CA). Of course, this requires that you have a company set up and that you fill out an application as such. Visual Studio does have a few test tools to help developers understand the process before working with a CA. These tools include the following:

Zip to Exe Conversion Tool (MakeZipExe.exe)

Certificate Creation Tool (MakeCert.exe)

Software Publisher Certificate Test Tool (Cert2spc.exe)

Sign Tool (SignTool.exe)

The vision for these tools is as follows: You use the MakeZipExe.exe tool to convert your .zip file to an .exe file (because code signing requires an .exe or a .dll). You then use the SignTool.exe to sign the resulting .exe. You then convert this file into a .vsi file for publication.

If you do not have a valid certificate from a CA, you can create a test certificate (not to be used for publishing) with the MakeCert.exe tool. You then must convert this certificate into a software publisher certificate (.spc) using the Cert2spc.exe.

Packaging Content with VSIX

You can use Visual Studio to create Visual Studio Extension projects that can then be distributed within VSIX files. These projects are used to distribute project and item templates as well as sample applications you might distribute for learning purposes. You can also package Visual Studio controls you want to share (or sell).

Recall that the first step toward creating community content is to code it, build it, debug it, and export it. This process puts your shared content in a .zip file that will add to the VSIX project. Refer to the prior section if you need to refresh. Remember that you must have the Visual Studio 2012 SDK in order to see the VSIX project template in your New Project dialog.

Step 1: Create a VSIX Project   Using the VSIX project template (found inside the Extensibility node on the New Project dialog box in both VB and C#), create a new project in Visual Studio (see Figure 7.39).

Step 2: Add Your Content   The next step is to add to the project the content you want to share. Again, this is a .zip file of a project you created and exported. (See the preceding section for more details.) You can add this content to your project by right-clicking your project and selecting Add, Existing Item. Recall that your exported template should be in your documents directory (Documents\Visual Studio 2012\My Exported Templates). You may have to show all files to find the .zip file.

After your exported template is added to the project, use the Properties dialog box to set its Copy to Output Directory property to Copy Always. This ensures that an install of your shared template is always deployed to the output directory. Figure 7.40 shows an example of this property.

FIGURE 7.39   The Visual Studio VSIX project.

FIGURE 7.40   Set the Copy to Output Directory property to Copy Always.

Step 3: Edit the VSIX Manifest   Before you deploy you should add information about your project for those looking to browse before they download. You can do this by editing the source.extension.vsixmanifest file. You can open this file in an XML editor (right-click and choose Open With). Alternatively, you can open the file inside the Visual Studio VSIX manifest editor. This editor is shown in Figure 7.41.

FIGURE 7.41   You can edit the VSIX manifest inside a designer.

The editor allows you to set nearly all of the values of the manifest. This includes the project's unique ID, the author, version, product name, description, and much more. Notice in Figure 7.50, you can also select your project's icon and preview image. You can also provide a link to a website for more information and a link to any documentation.

The manifest editor also contains a number of additional options. The References section allows you to indicate a payload, installed extension, or other reference on which your project depends. This is an advanced option for those creating toolbox controls and other Visual Studio extensions (beyond project templates).

The Assets tab of the designer is where you indicate content you want to deploy as part of your VSIX project. The Add Content dialog box is shown in Figure 7.42. You first select a content type (project or item template, toolbox control, and so on). You then select the actual file that contains this content.

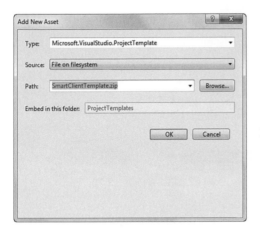

FIGURE 7.42   You must add your content to the VSIX manifest.

On the Install Targets tab, you indicate the editions of Visual Studio to which your extension applies. To add a new version definition, click the New button and then edit the values accordingly (see Figure 7.43).

FIGURE 7.43   You can select the editions of Visual Studio for which your extension should apply.

Step 4: Build the Project   The next step is to compile your code. Visual Studio validates your manifest and raises any errors that invalidate the XML schema.

Step 5: Test Your Install   You can find your compiled project inside the Bin folder of your project. The file has a .vsix extension. Double-click this file to test the installation. This launches the Visual Studio Extension Installer. Figure 7.44 shows an example of this dialog box. The Visual Studio Extension Installer gives the same experience someone would get if the project has been downloaded from the Visual Studio Gallery. Click the Install button to install the extension. After the installation is complete, your new project template (or related extension) should be available for use inside Visual Studio.

FIGURE 7.44   The Visual Studio Extension Installer.

Step 6: Share Your Content on the MSDN Code Gallery (Optional)   You can distribute your VSIX file to other developers in many ways. If you want to expose it to the larger Visual Studio community, you can post it on the MSDN Code Gallery (http://code.msdn.microsoft.com). Recall that putting your code here makes it accessible inside the Online Templates section of the New Project dialog box, the Extension Manager, and elsewhere in Visual Studio.

To use this site, you must have a Windows Live ID, sign in, create a unique username, and agree to the terms and conditions. You then click the Upload link on the home page. This takes you through a wizard in which you create a resource page for your extension. This page allows you to upload your files and determine when to publish them to the world (see Figure 7.45).

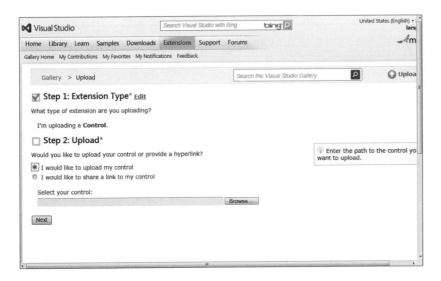

FIGURE 7.45   Defining your upload.

Summary

This chapter presented the many community options inside Visual Studio. Developers can expect to feel part of a larger community that surrounds .NET. Microsoft has built in a community to .NET. You see it with the Start Page inside Visual Studio, in the options on the Help menu, and within the capability to search for, use, and create community content.

Don't forget that being part of the developer community means giving back to it once in a while. Visual Studio provides the tools to make that happen. You can create and share project and item templates, code snippets, add-ins, and controls. After you've created these items, Visual Studio provides the Visual Studio Content Installer framework and the VSIX project template (in the SDK) to package your shared content for distribution. Now, the next time you write a great timesaving macro, snippet, or project template, you have the know-how to package it up and share it with others.

CHAPTER **8**

Working with Visual Studio's Productivity Aids

In Chapter 6, "Introducing the Editors and Designers," we discussed the basic capabilities of the designers and editors in Visual Studio 2012. In this chapter, we delve a bit deeper into their capabilities and those of other Visual Studio tools by examining the many productivity aids provided by the IDE. Many of these productivity enhancers are embedded within the text editors. Others are more generic in nature. But they all have one common goal: helping you, the developer, write code quickly and correctly.

If you recall from Chapter 6, in our coverage of the editors, we used a very basic code scenario: a console application that printed "Hello, World!" to the console. In Figure 8.1, you see what the final code looks like in the code editor window.

If you have followed along by re-creating this project and typing the "Hello, World!" code in Visual Studio, you notice that the productivity features of the code editor have already kicked into gear. For one, as you start to type code into the template file, the code editor has tabbed the cursor in for you, placing it at a new location for writing nicely indented code.

Second, as you type your first line of code, Visual Studio reacts to your every keystroke by interpreting what you are trying to write and extending help in various forms (see Figure 8.2). You are given hints in terms of completing your in-progress source, provided information on the members you are in the process of selecting, and given information on the parameters required to complete a particular method. These features are collectively referred to as IntelliSense, and we explore its forms and functions in depth in this chapter.

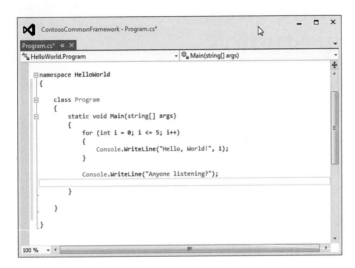

FIGURE 8.1   "Hello, World" in the code editor.

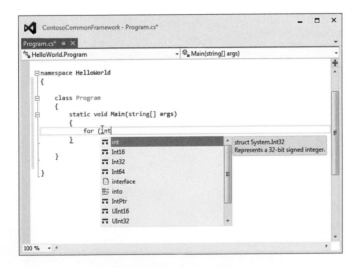

FIGURE 8.2   IntelliSense in action.

As you type, the IDE is also constantly checking what you have written with the compiler. If compile errors exist, they are dynamically displayed for you in the output window.

So, for this one simple line of code, Visual Studio has been hard at work improving your coding productivity by doing the following:

▶ Intelligently indenting the code

▶ Suggesting code syntax

▶ Displaying member descriptions to help you select the correct code syntax

▶ Visually matching delimiting parentheses

▶ Flagging code errors by constantly background compiling the current version of the source code

These features subtly help and coach you through the code-writing process and accelerate the act of coding itself.

Basic Aids in the Text Editor

The text editor user interface has several visual constructs that help you with common problem areas encountered during the code-writing process. These basic aids provide support for determining what has changed within a code document and what compile problems exist in a document. In addition, the discrete syntax elements for each individual language are visually delineated for you using colored text.

Change Tracking

When you are in the midst of editing a source code file, it is tremendously useful to understand which lines of code have been committed (that is, saved to disk) and which have not. Change tracking provides this functionality; a yellow vertical bar in the text editor's selection margin spans any lines in the editor that have been changed but not saved. If content has been changed and subsequently saved, it is marked with a green vertical bar in the selection margin.

By looking at the yellow and green tracking bars, you can quickly differentiate between the following:

▶ Code that hasn't been touched since the file was loaded (no bar)

▶ Code that has been touched and saved since the file was loaded (green bar)

▶ Code that has been touched but not saved since the file was loaded (yellow bar)

Change tracking is valid only for as long as the editor window is open. In other words, change tracking is significant only for the current document "session"; if you close and reopen the window, the track bars disappear because you have established a new working session with that specific document.

Figure 8.3 shows a section of a code file displaying the change tracking bars.

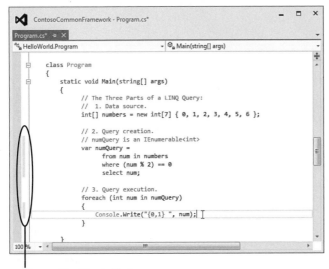

Change Tracking Indicators

FIGURE 8.3   Change tracking.

Coding Problem Indicators

The Visual Studio compiler works in conjunction with the code editor window to flag any problems found within a source code document. The compiler can even work in the background, enabling the editor window to flag problems as you type (as opposed to waiting for the project to be compiled).

Coding problems are flagged using "squiggles" (wavy, color-coded lines placed under the offending piece of code). These squiggles are the same mechanism Microsoft Word uses to flag spelling and grammar problems. The squiggle colors indicate a specific class of problem. Table 8.1 shows how these colors map to an underlying problem.

TABLE 8.1   Coding Problem Indicator Colors

Color	Problem
Red	Syntax error; the code will not compile because of the syntax requirements and rules of the language.
Blue	Semantic error; this is the result of the compiler not being able to resolve the type or code construct within the current context. For instance, a type name that doesn't exist within the compiled context of the current project is flagged with a blue squiggle. Typically, these are good indicators for typos (for example, misspelling a classname).
Purple	Warning; the purple squiggle denotes code that has triggered a compiler warning.

Hovering the mouse pointer over the problem indicator reveals the actual compiler error or warning message, as demonstrated in Figure 8.4.

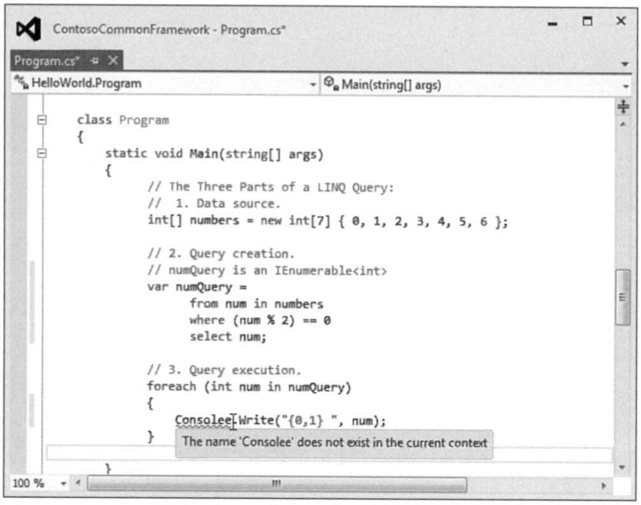

FIGURE 8.4   Coding problem indicators.

Active Hyperlinking

Text editors support clickable hyperlinks within documents; clicking a link launches a browser redirected at the URL. One great use of this feature is to embed URLs for supporting documentation or other helpful reference information within code comments.

Syntax Coloring

The text editor can parse and distinctly color different code constructs to make them that much easier to identify on sight. As an example, the code editor window, by default, colors any code comments green. Code identifiers are black, keywords are blue, strings are colored red, and so on.

In fact, the number of unique elements that the text editor is capable of parsing and coloring is immense: The text editor window recognizes more than 100 different elements. And you can customize and color each one of them to your heart's content through the Fonts and Colors section, under the Environments node in the Options dialog box. Do you like working with larger fonts? Would a higher contrast benefit your programming activities? How about squeezing more code into your viewable screen real estate? These are just a few reasons you might stray from the defaults with this dialog box.

Figure 8.5 shows the fonts and colors page in the Options dialog box that allows you to specify foreground and background colors for code, HTML, CSS, or other elements. Select the element in the Display Items list and change its syntax coloring via the Item Foreground and Item Background drop-downs.

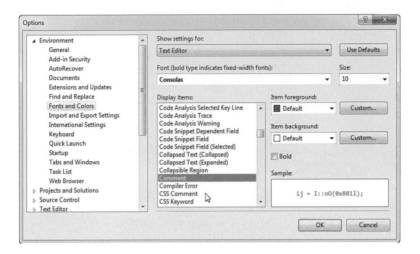

FIGURE 8.5   Setting font and color options.

NOTE

We first explored this dialog back in Chapter 2, "The Visual Studio IDE." The dialog box shown in Figure 8.5 enables you to control much more than the syntax coloring for the text editor; you can change the coloring schemes used in all the different windows within Visual Studio. The item you select in the Show Settings For drop-down determines the portion of the IDE you are customizing and alters the list of items in the Display Items list.

You can always click the Use Defaults button at the upper right of the dialog box to restore the default coloring schemes.

Outlining and Navigation

Certain documents, such as source code files and markup files, have a natural parent-child aspect to their organization and syntax. Extensible Markup Language (XML) nodes, for instance, can contain other nodes. Likewise, functions and other programming language constructs such as loops and try/catch blocks act as a container for other lines of code. Outlining is the concept of visually representing this parent-child relationship.

Code Outlining

Code outlining is used within the code editor; it allows you to collapse or expand regions of code along these container boundaries. A series of grouping lines and expand/collapse boxes are drawn in the selection margin. These expand/collapse boxes are clickable, enabling you to hide or display lines of code based on the logical groupings.

TIP

Both Visual Basic and C# provide a way to manually create named regions of code via a special region keyword. Use `#region/#endregion` (`#Region` and `#End Region` for Visual Basic) to create your own artificial code container that is appropriately parsed by the code outliner. Because each region is named, this is a handy approach for organizing and segregating the logical sections of your code. In fact, to use one example, the code generated for you by the Windows Forms Designer is automatically tucked within a "Windows Forms Designer generated code" region.

One quick way to implement a region is with Surround With. In the editor, highlight the code that you want to sit in a new region, right-click the highlighted text, select Surround With from the context menu, and then select #region (or #Region for VB).

Code outlining is best understood using a simple example. First, refer to Figure 8.1. This is the initial console application code. It contains a routine called Main, a class declaration, a namespace declaration, and several `using` statements. The code outline groupings that you see in the selection margin visually indicate code regions that can be collapsed or hidden from view.

Because the class declaration is a logical container, the selection margin for that line of code contains a collapse box (a box with a minus sign). A line is drawn from the collapse box to the end of the container (in this case, because you are dealing with C#, the class declaration is delimited by a curly brace). If you click the collapse box for the class declaration, Visual Studio hides all the code contained within that declaration.

Figure 8.6 shows how the editor window looks with this code hidden from view. Note that the collapse box has changed to a plus sign, indicating that you can click the box to reshow the now-hidden code and that the first line of code for the class declaration has been altered to include a trailing box with an ellipsis.

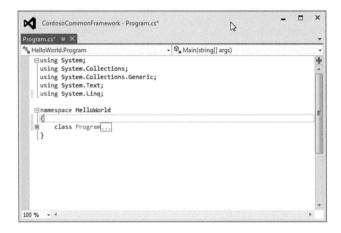

FIGURE 8.6   A collapsed outlined region.

The HTML Editor also supports outlining in this fashion. HTML elements can be expanded or collapsed to show or hide their containing elements.

Using the Outlining Menu

Several code outlining commands are available under the Edit, Outlining menu (see Figure 8.7):

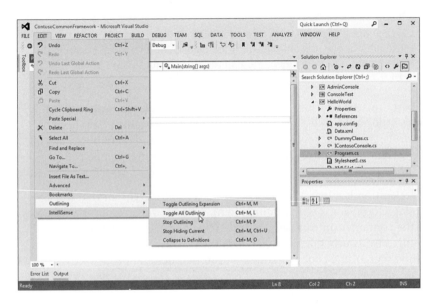

FIGURE 8.7   The Edit, Outlining menu.

- ▶ **Toggle Outlining Expansion**—Based on the current cursor position in the editor window, hides or unhides the outline region.

- ▶ **Toggle All Outlining**—Hides or unhides all outline regions in the editor.

- ▶ **Stop Outlining**—Turns off automatic code outlining (any hidden regions are expanded). This command is available only if automatic outlining is turned on.

- ▶ **Stop Hiding Current**—Removes the outline for the currently selected region. This command is available only if automatic outlining has been turned off.

- ▶ **Collapse to Definitions**—Hides all procedure regions. This command is useful for distilling a type down to single lines of code for all of its members.

- ▶ **Start Automatic Outlining**—Enables the code outlining feature. This command is available only if outlining is currently turned off.

Code outlining is a convenience mechanism: By hiding currently irrelevant sections of code, you decrease the visible surface of the code file and increase code readability. You can pick and choose the specific regions to view based on the task at hand.

> **TIP**
>
> If you place the mouse pointer over the ellipsis box of a hidden code region, the contents of that hidden region are displayed to you in a ToolTip-style box; this is done without having to expand and reshow the code region.

Tag Navigation

One problem with large or complex code files, be they web forms, Windows Presentation Foundation (WPF) windows, or XML documents, is navigation through the multiple levels and layers of nested tags. Envision a web page containing a button within a table within a table within a table. When you are editing the HTML (through either the designer or the editor), how can you tell exactly where you are? Put another way, how can you tell where the current focus is within the markup hierarchy?

Using the Tag Navigator

The tag navigator is Visual Studio's answer to this question. The navigator appears as a series of buttons at the bottom of the WPF, Web, and XML Schema designers. A breadcrumb trail of tags is shown that leads from the tag that currently has focus all the way to the outermost tag. If this path is too long to actually display within the confines of the editor window, it is truncated at the parent tag side; a button enables you to display more tags toward the parent.

Figure 8.8 shows the tag navigator as implemented by the web designer. While you're editing the OK button in the sample login page, the tag navigator shows the path all the way back to the parent enclosing `<html>` tag.

FIGURE 8.8   The Web designer's tag navigator in action.

Each tag button displayed by the navigator can be used to directly select the inclusive or exclusive contents of that tag. A drop-down triggered by the tag button contains options for selecting the tag or selecting the tag content. The former causes the tag itself, in addition to all of its enclosed content, to be selected. The latter excludes the tag begin and end, but still selects all of its enclosed content.

The navigator is a great mechanism for quickly moving up and down within a large tag tree.

Using the Document Outline Window

The document outline window displays a tree-view representation of the elements on a web page, WPF window, or Windows form. This hierarchical display is a great navigation tool because it enables you to take in the entire structure of your document in one glance and immediately jump to any of the elements within the page.

To use the document outline window, choose Document Outline from the View, Other Windows menu. Figure 8.9 shows a sample outline for a WPF window.

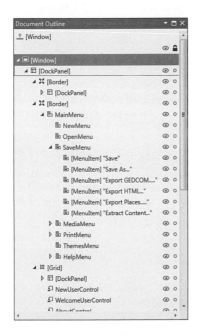

FIGURE 8.9   The document outline of a WPF window.

Clicking an element navigates to that element (and selects it) within the designer window, and, of course, you can expand or collapse the tree nodes as needed.

> **NOTE**
>
> The features and look and feel of the document outline window change by document type. For instance, the WPF document outline shows a thumbnail image of the UI element when you hover over the node in the outline window. The Windows Forms outline window actually allows you to move and reparent items within the form. Using just the outline window, you could move a button from within one tab container and place it within another by just dragging the corresponding node and dragging it to the new parent in the outline.

Smart Tags and Smart Tasks

Smart tags and smart tasks (the terms can essentially be used interchangeably) are menu- or IntelliSense-driven features for automating common control configuration and coding tasks within the IDE. Designers and editors both implement smart tags in various scenarios. In the following sections, we examine a few of the ways that smart tags make your life easier, starting first with the HTML designer.

HTML Designer

As controls are placed onto the HTML designer, a pop-up list of common tasks appears. These tasks, collectively referred to as *smart tasks*, allow you to "set the dials" for a given control to quickly configure it for the task at hand.

You use the common tasks list to quickly configure a control's properties, as well as walk through common operations you might perform with it. For example, when you add a GridView control to a web page, a common task list appears that allows you to quickly enable sorting, paging, or editing for the GridView. When you add a TextBox control to a web page, a common task list appears that enables you to quickly associate a validation control with the control.

The Windows Forms Designer also plays host to smart tags.

Windows Forms Designer

With the Windows Forms Designer, the functionality of smart tags remains consistent; they do, however, take a slightly different form. A form control that supports this functionality shows a smart tag glyph somewhere within its bounds (typically to the top right of the control). This glyph, when clicked, opens a small drop-down of tasks. Figure 8.10 contains a snapshot of the smart tag in action for a tab control.

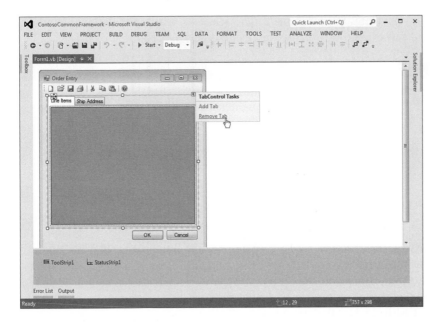

FIGURE 8.10   A Windows Forms TabControl smart tag.

Code Editor

Smart tags can also appear within code. You can find one example on interfaces. Normally, implementing an interface is a fairly code-intensive task. You have to individually create a member to map to each member defined on the interface. The smart tag in this case allows you to automatically create those members using two different naming modes:

▶ **Explicit naming**—Members have the name of the derived interface.

▶ **Implicit naming**—Member names do not reference the name of the derived interface.

See Figure 8.11 to view this smart tag in action.

In general, this type of smart tag is called a Generate From Usage smart tag. It's meant to solve a fairly common workflow issue: With certain development styles (especially, test-driven development or TDD), it is often the case that you are referencing members and types that have not yet been created. In the preceding example, this is an interface, but it could just as easily be another class, a property, or a method. As you type the name of the interface (in this example, `'IContosoConsole'`), notice that the first letter of the interface will be decorated with an underline glyph. Hovering over this glyph reveals the smart tag drop-down, which displays the implementation options. The Generate From Usage smart tag enables you to automatically stub out the required type or member so that you can continue with your current coding task without having to switch context and develop, in full, the referenced item.

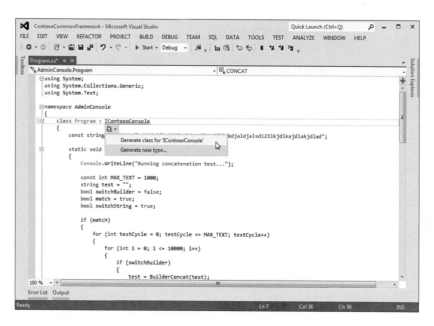

FIGURE 8.11   An implement interface smart tag.

Visual Studio supports the following Generate From Usage scenarios:

▶ Properties

▶ Methods

▶ Interfaces

▶ Classes

▶ Structs

▶ Enums

IntelliSense

IntelliSense is the name applied to a collection of different coding aids surfaced within the text editor window. Its sole purpose is to help you, the developer, write a syntactically correct line of code *quickly*. In addition, it tries to provide enough guidance to help you write lines of code that are correct *in context* (that is, code that makes sense given the surrounding lines of code).

As you type within the text editor, IntelliSense is the behind-the-scenes agent responsible for providing a list of code fragments that match the characters you have already entered, highlighting/preselecting the one that makes the most sense given the surrounding context, and, if so commanded, automatically inserting that code fragment in-line. This saves you the time of looking up types and members in the reference documentation and saves time again by inserting code without your having to actually type the characters for that code.

We spend a lot of time in this section discussing IntelliSense in the context of editing code, but you should know that IntelliSense also works with other document types such as XML documents, HTML documents, and EXtensible Stylesheet Language (XSLT) files.

TIP

Attaching a schema to an XML document is beneficial from an IntelliSense perspective. The schema is used to further enhance the capabilities of the List Members function. (See the "List Members" section later in this chapter.)

Many discrete pieces to IntelliSense seamlessly work in conjunction with one another as you are writing code. You can trigger all of these IntelliSense features directly from the Edit, IntelliSense menu or by pressing Ctrl+Space. Many of the features can be found as well on the text editor's context menu or by right-clicking anywhere in the editor window. Let's look at them one by one.

Complete Word

Complete Word is the basic timesaving kernel of IntelliSense. After you have typed enough characters for IntelliSense to recognize what you are trying to write, a guess is made as to the complete word you are in the process of typing. This guess is then presented to you within a list of possible alternatives (referred to as the *completion list*) and can be inserted into the code editor with one keystroke. This is in contrast to your completing the word manually by typing all of its characters.

Figure 8.12 illustrates the process: Based on the context of the code and based on the characters typed into the editor, a list of possible words is displayed. One of these words is selected as the most viable candidate; you may select any entry in the list (via the arrow keys or the mouse). Pressing the Tab key automatically injects the word into the editor for you.

NOTE

Complete Word takes the actual code context into account for various situations. For instance, if you are in the midst of keying in the exception type in a `try/catch` block, IntelliSense displays only exception types in the completion list. Likewise, typing an attribute triggers a completion list filtered only for attributes; when you're implementing an interface, only interface types are displayed; and so on.

This IntelliSense feature is enabled for all sorts of content: Beyond C# and Visual Basic code, IntelliSense completion works for other files as well, such as HTML tags, JavaScript, XAML, CSS style attributes, .config files, and HTML script blocks, just to name a few. Visual Basic offers functionality with Complete Word that C# does not: It provides a tabbed completion list, in which one tab contains the most commonly used syntax snippets, and the other contains *all* the possible words.

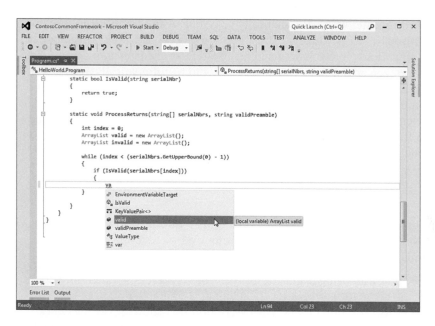

FIGURE 8.12   IntelliSense: Complete Word.

You can manually invoke Complete Word at any time by using the Ctrl+Space or Alt+right-arrow key combinations.

TIP

Holding down the Ctrl key while the completion list is displayed makes the list partially transparent. This is useful if, during the process of selecting an item from the list, you need to see any of the lines of code that are hidden behind the list.

Completion Versus Suggestion Mode

Two different modes drive how IntelliSense displays its Complete Word list. These modes are toggled with a hotkey combination, Ctrl+Alt+Space, or via the Edit, IntelliSense, ToggleCompletionMode menu. When invoked, this command toggles the behavior of Complete Word (and its derivatives such as List Members) between completion and suggestion modes. Completion mode works as previously described: Visual Studio offers you the closest matches to what you are typing; the current closest match is highlighted in the completion list. You can easily insert the highlighted item by pressing Enter, or you can select to insert another item from the list.

Suggestion mode is subtly different: It also displays the closest matches to your typed text, but instead of highlighting an item in the completion list, it simply places a focus rectangle on the closest match. It preserves your current typing at the top of the list. The net result is that hitting enter won't automatically place one of the completion list items into your code; instead, it places whatever you are in the process of typing. This mode is meant to cater to scenarios where you are referencing a type or member that doesn't (yet) exist. In this scenario, you actually *don't want* Visual Studio to automatically assume that you are trying to reference a code construct that currently exists. In this mode, you have the explicit option to select an existing code element, or to continue typing and enter the name for a code element that has yet to be created. This gives you more flexibility while sacrificing a bit of the speed of standard mode. (If you are referencing an existing item, consume-first mode requires an extra mouse click to insert the item because it won't be highlighted in the completion list.)

Quick Info

Quick Info displays the complete code declaration and help information for any code construct. You invoke it by hovering the mouse pointer over an identifier; a pop-up box displays the information available for that identifier.

Figure 8.13 shows Quick Info being displayed for the `Console.ReadLine` function. You are provided with the declaration syntax for the member, a brief description of the member, and a list of its exception classes. The description that shows up in the Quick Info balloon also works for code that you write: If you have a code comment associated with a member, IntelliSense parses the comment and uses it to display the description information.

FIGURE 8.13   IntelliSense: Quick Info.

List Members

The List Members feature functions in an identical fashion to Complete Word; for any given type or namespace, it displays a scrollable list of all valid member variables and functions specific to that type. To see the List Members function in action, perform the following steps in an open code editor window:

1. Type the name of a class. (Ctrl+Space gives you the IntelliSense window with possible classnames.)

2. Type a period; this indicates to IntelliSense that you have finished with the type name and are now "scoped in" to that type's members.

3. The list of valid members is displayed. You can manually scroll through the list and select the desired member at this point, or, if you are well aware of the member you are trying to code, you can simply continue typing until IntelliSense has captured enough characters to select the member you are looking for.

4. Leverage Complete Word by pressing the Tab key to automatically insert the member into your line of code (thus saving you the typing effort).

This feature also operates in conjunction with Quick Info: As you select different members in the members list, a Quick Info pop-up is displayed for that member.

As noted earlier in our discussion of Complete Word, List Members can function in either standard or consume-first modes.

> **NOTE**
>
> IntelliSense maintains a record of the most frequently used (selected) members from the List Members and Complete Word functions. This record is used to help avoid displaying or selecting members that you have rarely, if ever, used for a given type.

Parameter Info

Parameter Info, as its name implies, is designed to provide interactive guidance for the parameters needed for any given function call. This feature proves especially useful for making function calls that have a long list of parameters or a long overload list.

Parameter Info is initiated whenever you type an opening parenthesis after a function name. To see how this works, perform these steps:

1. Type the name of a function.

2. Type an open parenthesis.

3. A pop-up box shows the function signature. If there are multiple valid signatures (for example, multiple overloaded versions of this function), you can scroll through the different signatures by using the small up- and down-arrow cues. Select the desired signature.

4. Start typing the actual parameters you want to pass in to the function.

As you type, the parameter info pop-up continues coaching you through the parameter list by bolding the current parameter you are working on. As each successive parameter is highlighted, the definition for that parameter appears. If the function in question has multiple overloads, the pop-up box will contain up and down arrows that can be used to cycle between the different parameter definition sets.

In Figure 8.14, we are entering a parameter for the `Console.ReadKey` method. Note that we are using an overload of this function, and the presence of the up and down arrows for cycling between the two defined function definitions for `ReadKey`.

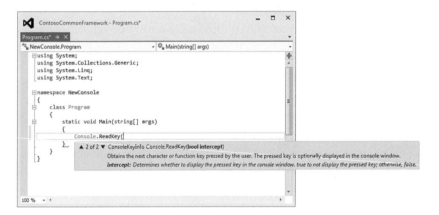

FIGURE 8.14   IntelliSense: Parameter Info.

Organize Usings

Organize Usings is a C#-only IntelliSense item. It provides two separate functions: Remove Unused Usings and Sort Usings. It also provides a third command, Remove and Sort, which combines the two actions into one. All three commands live under the Organize Usings menu item on the editor shortcut menu, or under the main Edit, IntelliSense menu.

The Remove Unused Usings function is a great aid for uncluttering your code. It parses through the current body of code and determines which Using statements are necessary for the code to compile; it then removes all other Using statements. The Sort command is straightforward as well; it simply rearranges all of your Using statements so that they appear in *A–Z* alphabetic order by namespace.

Code Snippets and Template Code

Code snippets are prestocked lines of code available for selection and insertion into the text editor. Each code snippet is referenced by a name referred to as its alias. Code snippets are used to automate what would normally be non-value-added, repetitive typing. You can create your own code snippets or use the default library of common code elements provided by Visual Studio.

Using the Code Snippet Inserter

You insert snippets by right-clicking at the intended insertion point within an open text editor window and then selecting Insert Snippet from the shortcut menu. This launches the Code Snippet Inserter, which is a drop-down (or series of drop-downs) that works much like the IntelliSense Complete Word feature. Each item in the inserter represents a snippet, represented by its alias. Selecting an alias expands the snippet into the active document.

Each snippet is categorized to make it easier to find the specific piece of code you are looking for. As an example, to insert a constructor snippet into a C# class, we would right-click within the class definition, select Insert Snippet, select Visual C# from the list of snippet categories, and then select ctor. Figure 8.15 shows this workflow in process; note that as you select a snippet category, a placeholder is displayed in the text editor window to help establish a breadcrumb trail.

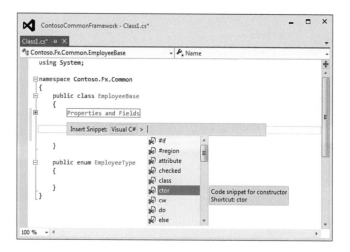

FIGURE 8.15   The C# ctor code snippet.

After the constructor snippet is expanded into the text editor, you still, of course, have to write meaningful code inside of the constructor; but, in general, snippets eliminate the process of tedious coding that really doesn't require much intellectual horsepower to generate.

Figure 8.16 shows the same process being followed for a Visual Basic code window. The process is identical with the exception that Visual Basic makes more extensive use of categories.

TIP

If you are coding in Visual Basic, a quick, alternative way to display the Code Snippet Inserter is to type a question mark and then press the Tab key.

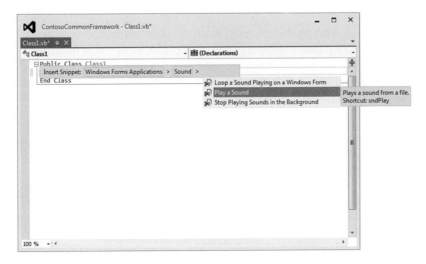

FIGURE 8.16 Visual Basic code snippet.

Visual Basic also exhibits slightly different behavior than C# after a snippet has been expanded into the code window. Figure 8.17 shows the results of drilling down through multiple categories and, in this example, selecting the Create Transparent Windows Form snippet. Notice that the inserter has injected the template code into the Visual Basic code for you, but the inserter (at least in this case) wasn't intelligent enough to know the name of the form you are trying to make transparent.

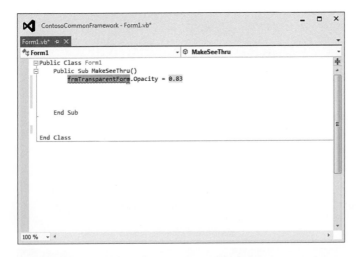

FIGURE 8.17 A Visual Basic form transparency snippet.

The snippet code has the form name filled in with a default, dummy name that is already highlighted. You merely start typing the form name you need and it replaces the dummy name. The opacity value is also a dummy value that you can quickly correct at this time.

TIP

Snippets may have one or more placeholder values: fragments of code that you will want and probably need to change. You can cycle through each of the placeholder values by pressing the Tab key. When a placeholder is highlighted (in blue), you can start typing to replace the syntax with something that makes sense for your specific code context.

Surrounding Code with Snippets

C# and XML documents have one additional style of code snippets that bears mentioning: Surround With snippets. Surround With snippets are still snippets at their core (again, these are simply prestocked lines of code), but they differ in how they are able to insert themselves into your code.

Using a Surround With snippet, you can stack enclosing text around a selection with the text editor. As an example, perhaps you have a few different class declarations that you would like to nest within a namespace. Using the Surround With snippet is a simple two-step process: Highlight the class definitions and fire up the Code Snippet Inserter. This time, instead of selecting Insert Snippet from the shortcut menu, you select Surround With. The insert works the same way, but this time has applied the snippet (in this case, a namespace snippet) in a different fashion. Compare the before and after text shown in Figures 8.18 and 8.19. We have encapsulated the class definitions within a new namespace that sits within yet another namespace (all with just a few mouse clicks).

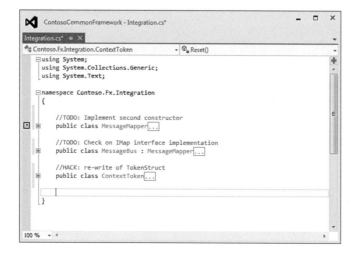

FIGURE 8.18   Before inserting a Surround With snippet.

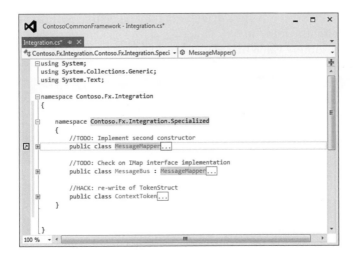

FIGURE 8.19   After inserting a Surround With snippet.

Creating Your Own Code Snippets

Because code snippets are stored in XML files, you can create your own snippets quite easily. The key is understanding the XML schema that defines a snippet, and the best way to do that is to look at the XML source data for some of the snippets included with the IDE.

Snippets are stored on a per-language basis under the install directory for Visual Studio. For example, with a U.S. English installation of Windows 7, the Visual Basic snippets can be found, by default, in the folders under the C:\Program Files\Microsoft Visual Studio 11.0\Vb\Snippets\1033 directory. Although snippet files are XML, they carry a .Snippet extension.

The XML Snippet Format   Listing 8.1 provides the XML for the C# constructor snippet.

LISTING 8.1   C# Constructor Snippet

```xml
<?xml version="1.0" encoding="utf-8" ?>
<CodeSnippets xmlns="http://schemas.microsoft.com/VisualStudio/2005/CodeSnippet">
    <CodeSnippet Format="1.0.0">
        <Header>
            <Title>ctor</Title>
            <Shortcut>ctor</Shortcut>
            <Description>Code snippet for constructor</Description>
            <Author>Microsoft Corporation</Author>
            <SnippetTypes>
                <SnippetType>Expansion</SnippetType>
            </SnippetTypes>
        </Header>
```

```
    <Snippet>
        <Declarations>
            <Literal Editable="false">
                <ID>classname</ID>
                <ToolTip>Class name</ToolTip>
                <Function>ClassName()</Function>
                <Default>ClassNamePlaceholder</Default>
            </Literal>
        </Declarations>
        <Code Language="csharp"><![CDATA[public $classname$ ()
{
    $end$
}]]>
        </Code>
    </Snippet>
  </CodeSnippet>
</CodeSnippets>
```

The basic structure of this particular snippet declaration is described in Table 8.2. A more complete schema reference is available as a part of the Visual Studio Microsoft Developer Network (MSDN) library; it is located under Visual Studio 2012, Reference, XML Schema References, Code Snippets Schema Reference.

TABLE 8.2   XML Snippet File Node Descriptions

XML Node	Description
<CodeSnippets>	The parent element for all code snippet information. It references the specific XML namespace used to define snippets within Visual Studio.
<CodeSnippet>	The root element for a single code snippet. This tag sets the format version information for the snippet. Although multiple CodeSnippet elements are possible within the parent <CodeSnippets> element, the convention is to place one snippet per file.
<Header>	A metadata container element for data that describes the snippet.
<Title>	The title of the code snippet.
<Shortcut>	Typically, the same as the title, this is the text that appears in the code snippet insertion drop-downs.
<Description>	A description of the snippet.
<Author>	The author of the snippet.
<SnippetTypes>	The parent element for holding elements describing the snippet's type.
<SnippetType>	The type of the snippet: Expansion, Refactoring, or Surrounds With. You cannot create custom refactoring snippets. This property is really used to tell Visual Studio where the snippet can be inserted within the editor window: Expansion snippets insert at the current cursor position, whereas Surrounds With snippets are inserted before and after the code body identified by the current cursor position or selection.

8

XML Node	Description
`<Snippet>`	The root element for the snippet code.
`<Declarations>`	The root element for the literals and objects used by the snippet.
`<Literal>`	A string whose value can be interactively set as part of the snippet expansion process. The Editable attribute on this tag indicates whether the literal is static or editable. The `ctor` snippet is an example of one without an editable literal; contrast this with the form transparency snippet that you saw (an example of a snippet with an editable literal that allows you to set the form name as part of the snippet insertion).
`<ID>`	A unique ID for the literal.
`<ToolTip>`	A ToolTip to display when the cursor is placed over the literal.
`<Function>`	The name of a function (see Table 8.3) to call when the literal receives focus. Functions are available only in C# snippets.
`<Default>`	The default string literal to insert into the editor.
`<Code>`	An element that contains the actual code to insert.

The trick to writing a snippet is to understand how literals and variable replacement work. Suppose, for instance, that you want to create a C# snippet that writes out a simple code comment indicating that a class has been reviewed and approved as part of a code review process. In other words, you want something like this:

```
// Code review of ContextToken.
//    Reviewer: Lars Powers
//    Date: 6/1/2012
//    Approval: Approved
```

In this snippet, you need to treat four literals as variable; they can change each time the snippet is used: the classname, the reviewer's name, the date, and the approval. You can set them up within the declarations section like this:

```
<Declarations>
    <Literal Editable="False">
        <ID>classname</ID>
        <ToolTip>Class name/type being reviewed</ToolTip>
        <Function>ClassName()</Function>
        <Default>ClassNameGoesHere</Default>
    </Literal>
    <Literal Editable="True">
        <ID>reviewer</ID>
        <ToolTip>Replace with the reviewer's name</ToolTip>
        <Default>ReviewerName</Default>
    </Literal>
    <Literal Editable="True">
        <ID>currdate</ID>
```

```
        <ToolTip>Replace with the review date</ToolTip>
        <Default>ReviewDate</Default>
    </Literal>
    <Literal Editable="True">
        <ID>approval</ID>
        <ToolTip>Replace with Approved or Rejected</ToolTip>
        <Default>Approved</Default>
    </Literal>
</Declarations>
```

Notice that you are actually calling a function to prepopulate the class name within the snippet. Functions are available only with C#; they are documented in Table 8.3. The rest of the literals rely on the developer to type over the placeholder value with the correct value.

TABLE 8.3   Code Snippet Functions

Function	Description
GenerateSwitchCases (enumliteral)	Creates the syntax for a switch statement that includes a case statement for each value defined by the enumeration represented by enumliteral (C#/J#).
ClassName()	Inserts the name of the class containing the code snippet (C#/J#).
SimpleTypeName(typename)	Takes the type name referenced by typename and returns the shortest name possible given the using statements in effect for the current code block. For example, SimpleTypeName(System.Exception) would return Exception if a using System statement is present (C#).
CallBase(parameter)	Is useful when stubbing out members that implement or return the base type: When you specify get, set, or method as the parameter, a call will be created against the base class for that specific property accessor or method (C#).

You should also provide some basic header information for the snippet:

```
<Header>
    <Title>review</Title>
    <Shortcut>review</Shortcut>
    <Description>Code review comment</Description>
    <Author>L. Powers</Author>
    <SnippetTypes>
        <SnippetType>Expansion</SnippetType>
    </SnippetTypes>
</Header>
<Snippet>
```

The last remaining task is to implement the `<Code>` element, which contains the actual text of the snippet and references the literals that we have previously defined:

```
<Code Language="csharp">
    <![CDATA[// Review of $classname$
    //    Reviewer: $reviewer$
    //    Date: $currdate$
    //    Approval: $approval$]]>
</Code>
```

When the code snippet is executed, our literals (bracketed by the $ symbols in the preceding code) are replaced by their specified default values and are highlighted to allow the snippet user to easily replace them after they are in the editor. Our `$classname$` literal is a bit different in that it places a call to the `ClassName()` function to get the name of the current, enclosing class.

At this point, the snippet is syntactically complete. Although this snippet is writing comments into the editor, the same exact process and structure applies for emitting code into the editor. If you want to write a Surround With snippet, you change the `<SnippetType>` to `SurroundsWith`.

Now, you need to make Visual Studio aware of the snippet.

Adding a Snippet to Visual Studio   You can use Visual Studio's own XML editor to create the XML document and save it to a directory. (A big bonus for doing so is that you can leverage IntelliSense triggered by the XML snippet schema to help you with your element names and relationships.) The Visual Studio installer creates a default directory to place your custom snippets located in your Documents folder: *user*\My Documents\Visual Studio 2012\Code Snippets\Visual C#\My Code Snippets. If you place your XML template here, Visual Studio automatically includes your snippet for use.

TIP

If you have placed your snippet file in the correct folder and it still doesn't show up within the Code Snippets Manager dialog box, you probably have a syntax error within the file. A good way to check this is to try to import the snippet file using the Import button. Visual Studio immediately tells you whether the snippet file is valid.

The Code Snippets Manager, which is launched from the Tools menu, is the central control dialog box for browsing the available snippets, adding new ones, or removing a snippet (see Figure 8.20). As you can see, the review snippet shows up under the My Code Snippets folder.

You can also opt to include other folders besides the standard ones. To do so, click the Add button to enter additional folders for Visual Studio to use when displaying the list of snippets.

Figure 8.21 shows the results of the custom snippet.

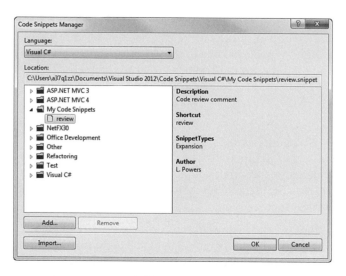

FIGURE 8.20   The Code Snippets Manager.

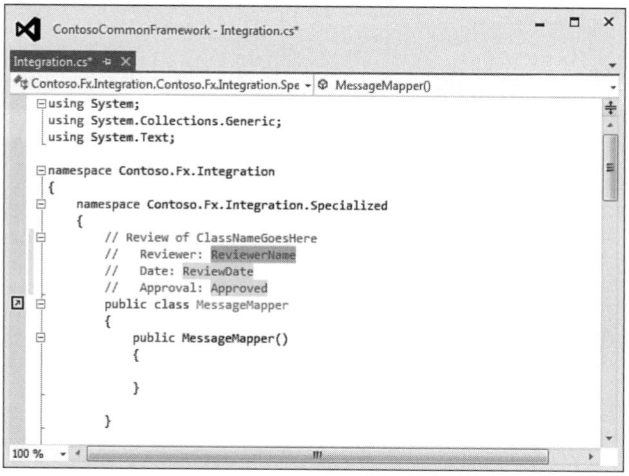

FIGURE 8.21   The results of a custom code snippet.

Snippets can also be browsed and shared online (see Chapter 7, "The .NET Community: Interacting Online," for a discussion of online communities). A great way to further your understanding of code snippet structure and functions is to browse your way through the snippet files included in Visual Studio, as well as those created by the developer community as a whole.

Snippets in the Toolbox

Although this capability is technically not part of the official code snippet technology within Visual Studio, you can also store snippets of code in the Toolbox. First, select the text in the editor and then drag and drop it onto the Toolbox. You can then reuse this snippet at any time by dragging it back from the Toolbox into an open editor window.

Brace Matching

Programming languages make use of parentheses, braces, brackets, and other delimiters to delimit function arguments, mathematical functions/order of operation, and bodies of code. It can be difficult to visually determine whether you have missed a matching delimiter—that is, if you have more opening delimiters than you have closing delimiters—especially with highly nested lines of code.

Brace matching refers to visual cues that the code editor uses to make you aware of your matching delimiters. As you type code into the editor, any time you enter a closing delimiter, the matching opening delimiter and the closing delimiter are briefly highlighted. In Figure 8.22, brace matching helps to indicate the matching delimiters for the interior `for` loop.

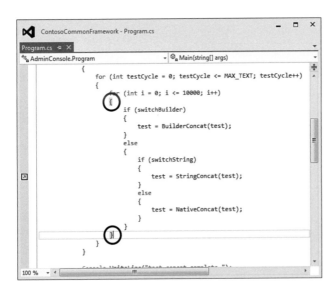

FIGURE 8.22   Brace matching.

> **TIP**
>
> You also can trigger brace matching simply by placing the cursor directly to the left of an opening delimiter or the right of a closing delimiter. If you are browsing through a routine congested with parentheses and braces, you can quickly sort out the matching pairs by moving your cursor around to the various delimiters.

Although this feature is referred to as brace matching, it actually functions with the following delimiters:

- Parentheses: ()
- Brackets: [], <>
- Quotation marks: ""
- Braces: {}

In the case of C#, brace matching also works with the following keyword pairs (which essentially function as delimiters using keywords):

- `# region, #endregion`
- `#if, #else, #endif`
- `case, break`
- `default, break`
- `for, break, continue`
- `if, else`
- `while, break, continue`

Customizing IntelliSense

Certain IntelliSense features can be customized, on a per-language basis, within the Visual Studio Options dialog box. If you launch the Options dialog box (located under the Tools menu) and then navigate to the Text Editor node, you find IntelliSense options confusingly scattered under both the General and IntelliSense pages.

Figure 8.23 shows the IntelliSense editor Options dialog box for Visual C#.

Completion Lists in this dialog box refer to any of the IntelliSense features that facilitate autocompletion of code, such as List Members and Complete Word. Table 8.4 itemizes the options available in this dialog box.

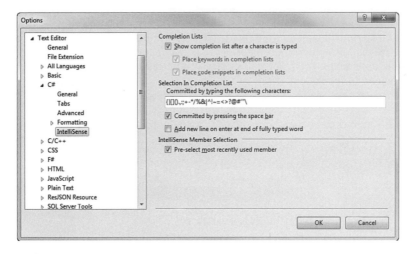

FIGURE 8.23   IntelliSense options.

TABLE 8.4   IntelliSense Options

Option	Effect
Show Completion List After a Character Is Typed	This causes the Complete Word feature to automatically run after a single character is typed in the editor window.
Place Keywords in Completion Lists	If this box is checked, language keywords are displayed within the completion list. As an example, for C#, this would cause keywords such as class or string to be included in the completion list.
Place Code Snippets in Completion Lists	Checking this box places code-snippet alias names into any displayed completion lists.
Committed by Typing the Following Characters	This check box contains any of the characters that cause IntelliSense to execute a completion action. In other words, typing any of the characters in this text box while a completion list is displayed causes IntelliSense to insert the current selection into the editor window.
Committed by Pressing the Space Bar	Checking this adds the space character to the list of characters that fire a completion commit.
Add New Line on Enter at End of Fully Typed Word	Checking this box causes the cursor to advance down an entire line if you fully type a word in the IntelliSense list box. This is useful for those scenarios in which fully typed keywords are unlikely to be followed on the same line with other code.

Option	Effect
Pre-Select Most Recently Used Member	If this box is checked, IntelliSense maintains and use a historical list of the most frequently used members for a given type. This "MFU" list is then used to preselect members in a completion list.

The Task List

The Task List is essentially an integrated to-do list; it captures all the items that, for one reason or another, need attention and tracking. The Task List window then surfaces this list and allows you to interact with it. To show the window, select the View menu and choose the Task List entry. Figure 8.24 illustrates the Task List window displaying a series of user tasks. Tasks belong to one of three categories: comment tasks, shortcut tasks, and user tasks. Only one category can be displayed at a time.

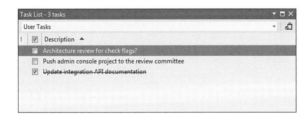

FIGURE 8.24   The Task List window.

You can sort the tasks by any of the columns shown in the list. Right-clicking the column headers provides a shortcut menu that allows you to control the sort behavior, as well as which columns (from a list of all supported columns) should be displayed. This shortcut menu is also how you will delete, cut, copy, or paste tasks from the list.

User Tasks

User tasks allow for rudimentary action item lists to be created. Each task has a description, a completion indicator, and a priority indicator. You add tasks to the list by clicking the Create User Task button to the right of the category drop-down (refer to Figure 8.24). You can type directly into the description column to add the task's title. To mark a user task as complete, place a check mark in the check box provided to the left of each line in the Task List window. Tasks are marked as high, normal, or low priority by using the left-most priority column (again, refer to Figure 8.24).

Shortcut Tasks

Shortcut tasks are very similar to user tasks. But shortcut tasks are directly tied to a line of code, and they are added by first putting your cursor on the line of code you want to associate with the task, and then selecting Edit, Bookmarks, Add Task List Shortcut. (We covered the similar concept of bookmarks back in Chapter 6.)

In addition to the description, completion indicator, and priority indicator columns, they show the file, and line number for the shortcut. Double-clicking the shortcut task opens the associated file and puts your cursor back on the associated line of code.

Comment Tasks

Comment tasks, like shortcut tasks, are associated with lines of code. But unlike shortcut tasks or user tasks, comment tasks are created by placing a code comment with a special string literal/token in a code file. There are three tokens defined by default by Visual Studio: HACK, TODO, and UNDONE.

There is no check box in the Task List to mark a comment task as complete. Instead, you simply remove the comment token from your code to remove the task from the list.

For example, the following C# code results in four different comment tasks in the Task List:

```
namespace Contoso.Fx.Integration.Specialized
{
    //TODO: Implement second constructor
    public class MessageMapper : IMessageSink
    {
        public MessageMapper()
        {
        }
    }

    //TODO: Check on IMap interface implementation
    public class MessageBus : MessageMapper
    {
        public MessageBus()
        {
            //UNDONE: MessageBus ctor
        }
    }

    //HACK: rewrite of TokenStruct
    public class ContextToken
    {
        public ContextToken()
        {
        }
        public ContextToken(string guid)
        {
        }
    }
}
```

Double-clicking the comment task takes you directly to the referenced comment line within the editor window.

Custom Comment Tokens

If needed, you can add your own set of tokens that are recognized as comment tasks. From the Tools, Options dialog box, select the Task List page under the Environment section; this dialog box provides options for adding, editing, or deleting the list of comment tokens recognized by the Task List.

TIP

The UI for adding a comment task token is not that intuitive. To add a token, you first type in a name for the token using the Name text box. At this point in time, the Add button becomes enabled. Click the Add button to add the token to the list, and then you can edit its priority and so on. Similarly, if you want to change a token's name or priority, you would select the token, make the change to either the priority or name, and then click the Change button to commit the change to the list.

In Figure 8.25, a Review token has been added to the standard list. Note that you can also set a priority against each of the tokens and fine-tune some of the display behavior by using the Task List Options check boxes, which control whether task deletions are confirmed, and by setting whether filenames or complete file paths are displayed within the task list.

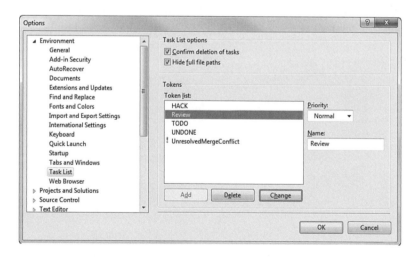

FIGURE 8.25   Adding a custom comment task token.

> **NOTE**
>
> Visual Studio's automation model provides complete control over task lists. Using the exposed automation objects such as `TaskList` and `TaskListEvents`, you can, for example, programmatically add or remove tasks from the list; respond to a task being added, edited, or even selected; and control the linking between a task and an editor.

Summary

Visual Studio carries a staggering number of features designed to boost your productivity. This chapter described the many facets of the IntelliSense technology, ranging from statement completion to the new code snippet technology, and you learned how to work with the various IntelliSense features to both write code faster and improve the quality of your code.

We covered how to navigate and browse through sometimes complicated and congested code files.

We also introduced code snippets and discussed the different types of code snippets and their usefulness.

Finally, we covered how to use the Task List window to its fullest potential, to help organize and track the various to-do items inherent with any programming project.

From a productivity standpoint, Visual Studio truly is more than the sum of its parts: In synergy with one another, each of these features knocks down substantial hurdles and eases pain points for developers, regardless of their backgrounds, skill levels, or language preferences.

Developers have always been responsible for testing their code before it is released to testers or users. In years past, this meant walking through every line of code in the debugger (including all conditions and errors). To do so, you often had to create test-harness applications that mimicked the functionality required to execute your code. Stepping through all your code in a debugger made for a fine goal but was not always realized (and very difficult to verify). In fact, the entire exercise was often skipped during code changes and updates. In addition, this process made it difficult to see if your code changes affected other parts of the system. The result was lower-quality builds sent to testers and users and thus higher defect rates and wasted time going back and forth between developers and testers.

This method of developer testing (and its results) highlighted a need to provide more robust, automated unit testing of code. As a result, unit test frameworks were developed. The first such framework for .NET was NUnit (http://nunit.org). This framework is available as open source for most .NET languages. It allows you to write code that tests other code. A similar framework was built into Visual Studio 2005 and has been carried forward through the current edition.

The unit test framework in Visual Studio enables you to build tests as you build your application. Alternatively, if you subscribe to test-driven development, you can write your tests before you write your code. In either case, a disciplined approach to unit testing can lead toward building a full set of tests in unison with your application.

This full set of tests can often represent a regression test for most components or even the entire system. The result is increased confidence in activities that were previously high-risk, such as last-minute fixes, refactoring, and late additions. When these activities occur, you can leverage your full set of unit tests to find out what, if anything, was broken as a result of the change.

This chapter covers the many tools, technologies, and techniques for developer testing. With this information in hand, you are able to begin realizing the many benefits of auto-mated, developer testing including fewer bugs, easier to understand code, and additional confidence in code changes.

Unit Testing Basics

Unit testing in Visual Studio is about creating tests that test the code inside the working layers of your application. This includes the many classes that make up your business and data domain. The user interface, on the other hand, is typically tested using alternate methods of automated testing. These methods are targeted more at testers. These features and products are included in the Premium Edition of Visual Studio and therefore not covered here. Our focus is the code you write to test the code you write. Of course, this assumes you follow good, layered architecture techniques when writing your applications. In this section, we cover the basics of writing unit tests. We drill in on these basics in coming sections.

Creating a Test Project

Your developer test must exist inside a test project. This is a project that has the right references to the unit testing framework and the configuration required to be run via the test tool built inside of Visual Studio. There are two primary ways you can initiate the creation of a unit test project: You can create a test project from within the IDE, or you can automatically generate unit tests into a new test project for existing code. We start with the first option.

The Test Project Template

You create a new test project in Visual Studio through the New Project dialog box (File, New, Project). Inside this dialog box, you navigate to the Test Projects node in the Installed Templates tree. Figure 9.1 shows an example. Notice that you can select to put your test project inside a new solution or an existing solution. In most cases, you add test projects to existing solutions as they must reference the projects within your solution.

> **NOTE**
>
> You should define a policy on how many test projects you want to create for your solution. Typically, you create a test project as a one-to-one ratio with a project you want to test. For example, if you have a project for your business objects and another project for your data services, you might create two test projects (one for each). This is not required. It just makes for an easily understood organization of your code.

A similar approach holds true for test classes. You should create a single test class for each class you have in your target project you want to test. For example, if you are creating a test project for your business domain objects that includes a `Customer` and an `Order` object, you should create a `CustomerTest` and `OrderTest` class. Again, this is not required; rather, it makes for a good, logical organization of your code.

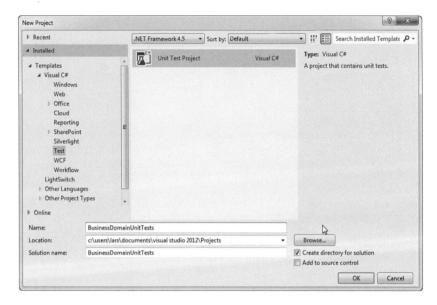

FIGURE 9.1   You can create a new test project for your solution from the New Project dialog box.

The Test Project

Visual Studio sets a reference to the unit test framework (`Microsoft.VisualStudio.QualityTools.UnitTestFramework`) when you create a new test project. In addition, it creates a test class for you to use to encapsulate your unit tests. Figure 9.2 shows the default project files included in the unit test project.

You can add additional test files to your test project by right-clicking the test project and choosing Add, Unit Test or Add, Ordered Test (see Figure 9.3):

▶ **Unit Test**—This template creates a simple test class with a blank test method.

▶ **Ordered Test**—This template enables you to create a sequential list of tests to be executed as a group (see "Creating Ordered Tests" later in this chapter).

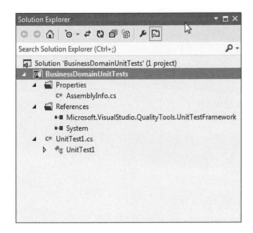

FIGURE 9.2   The Test Project (and related items) inside the Solution Explorer.

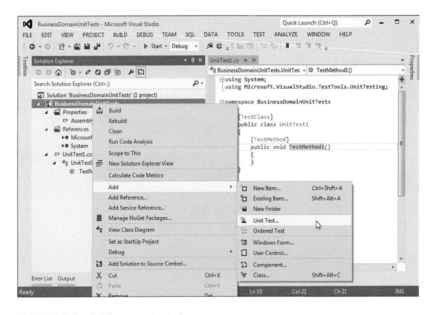

FIGURE 9.3   Adding new test classes.

The Test Menu

The Test menu, and the test toolbar, access the common testing features including running tests, managing test settings, and accessing the Test Explorer window. Figure 9.4 shows the Test menu open in the IDE. We touch on the details of all of these actions shortly. But next, let's explore how to create tests.

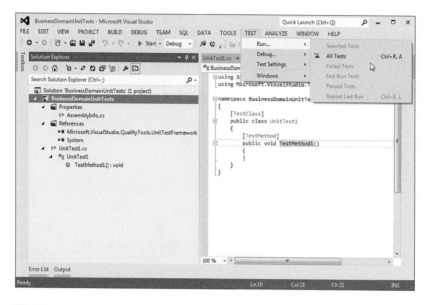

FIGURE 9.4   The Visual Studio Test menu can be used to access developer testing features in Visual Studio.

Writing a Unit Test

Recall that a unit test is simply test code you write to call your application code. This test code asserts that various conditions are either true or false as a result of the call to your application code. The test either passes or fails based on the results of these assertions. If, for example, you expect an outcome to be true and it turns out to be false, that test would be a failed test.

In broad strokes, there are three steps to creating a typical unit test:

1. Apply the TestMethod attribute to the test code.

2. Execute the code in question passing in known values if there are parameters.

3. Use assertions to evaluate the test results.

Let's look more closely with a real example.

Consider an Invoice class that has all the properties implemented that we normally associate with an invoice: It is associated to a Customer object, it has a collection of invoice line items (represented by a List<InvoiceLine> collection), and it has a method that you can use to add line items to the invoice itself. Figure 9.5 shows the class as implemented.

Let's dig into the AddLines method:

```
public void AddLine(InvoiceLine line)
    {
        _lines.Add(line);
```

```
    _total = ComputeTotal();
    _totalItems = CountItems();
}
```

FIGURE 9.5   A simple `Invoice` class.

The method is simple enough: It takes a `LineItem` object in as a parameter, and adds it to the `Invoice` object's internal `List` array (called `_lines`). The method also updates a few running tallies of both the total number of items accounted for in the Invoice (this is just the sum total of all quantity fields), and a total dollar amount represented by all of the lines.

Now let's see how we can add a unit test that will validate whether the item count property is updated correctly on the `Invoice` object when we add a line item. To do that, we create a new unit test project as previously discussed. With the project created, we need to first add a reference from the unit test project back to the project containing our `Invoice` object. (Right-click References, select Add Reference, and then pick the Invoice project from within the list of projects.)

> **NOTE**
>
> You don't need to have access to a target object's project or source code to write a unit test. You can add a reference instead to an assembly that implements the code you want to test.

With the initial structure setup, now we can actually write the unit test. One approach to organizing a unit test is to use the arrange, act, and assert pattern (AAA). This pattern advocates a code structure that first initializes the necessary objects and fields (arrange), then calls the method that you want to test (act), and finally verifies that everything has worked as expected (assert).

Listing 9.1 shows our test method, organized with the AAA pattern.

LISTING 9.1   Testing the `Invoice` Class with a Unit Test

```csharp
using System;
using Microsoft.VisualStudio.TestTools.UnitTesting;
using Contoso.Fx.Common;

namespace CommonUnitTests
{
    [TestClass]
    public class InvoiceTest
    {
        [TestMethod]
        public void Adding_Lines_Changes_Total_Qty()
        {
            //arrange -------------------------
            Invoice invoice = new Invoice();

            // line 1
            int qty1 = 2;
            string desc1 = "line 1";
            double price1 = 2.5;


            InvoiceLine line1 = new InvoiceLine();
            line1.Qty = qty1;
            line1.Description = desc1;
            line1.Price = price1;


            // line 2
            int qty2 = 3;
            string desc2 = "line 2";
            double price2 = 1.75;


            InvoiceLine line2 = new InvoiceLine();
            line2.Qty = qty2;
            line2.Description = desc2;
            line2.Price = price2;

            double expectedQty = qty1 + qty2;

            //act -------------------------
            invoice.AddLine(line1);
            invoice.AddLine(line2);
```

6

```
//assert -------------------------
Assert.AreEqual(expectedQty, invoice.TotalItems,
    "Total quantity not computed correctly.");

        }
    }
}
```

Notice that there is nothing special with respect to this code. It looks like any other method that you would craft with C#. This is because unit testing with Visual Studio is attribute driven. What distinguishes your unit test code, and signals it as an actual unit test to Visual Studio, are the attributes (`TestClass` and `TestMethod`) added at the class and method level. These attributes are automatically added for you when you create a unit test project, but there is nothing stopping you from writing a unit test class from the ground up and just adding them manually.

Running Your Tests

As you saw back in Figure 9.4, the Test menu is used to run your unit tests. You can select individual tests within a project, or you can run them all. The Debug selection on this menu will run tests with the debugger activated. This allows you to break into the debugger if a test fails, and is obviously useful if you are actively troubleshooting code through tests. Many times, however, you simply want an itemized list of test results. This is accomplished via the Run selection on the menu.

> **NOTE**
>
> When you run a test project, any referenced projects are recompiled along with your test project.

Viewing Test Results

When you run your tests, the results are shown in the Test Explorer window (typically docked to the bottom of the IDE). The Test Results window provides an overview of which tests passed and which failed. Figure 9.6 shows the results of running our Invoice unit test: It passed!

Note that the Test Explorer window is not only a tool for exploring test results, it is also the primary way within Visual Studio to categorize/organize tests, and can also directly run tests (arguably an easier way to execute tests instead of using the Test menu).

If you click a test, you see its details in the right pane of the Test Explorer window. You can see information regarding the test name, whether it passed or failed, the duration of the test, and the start and end time. The results pane also shows you the stack trace for any failed unit test code, and includes a link to the unit test source code file as well.

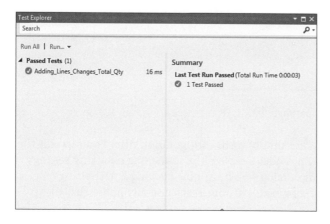

FIGURE 9.6   The Test Explorer window with the results of our Invoice unit test.

Controlling Advanced Test Settings

Visual Studio provides a settings file that provides control over how your tests execute. In most cases, you can leave this setting file in its default mode. However, in many instances, you might need to edit the settings such as running deployment scripts that are part of tests, controlling test timeouts, and more.

The test settings files is added at the solution level inside Solution Explore. Each of your test settings files has the extension .testsettings. You can configure which .testsettings file is active at any given time through the menu by using the menu Test, Test Settings. Figure 9.7 illustrates the process of adding a test setting file to the solution, and Figure 9.8 shows the menu option for selecting the test setting file.

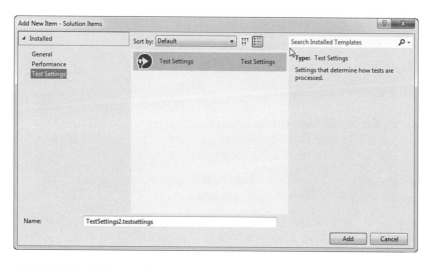

FIGURE 9.7   Adding test settings.

FIGURE 9.8   Selecting the active test settings file.

The .testsettings files in Visual Studio are simply XML configuration files. You can edit the XML directly. However, Visual Studio provides a dialog box to making changing settings easier. You can launch the Test Settings dialog box by double-clicking a .testsettings file. Figure 9.9 shows an example of the dialog box with the Test Timeouts node selected.

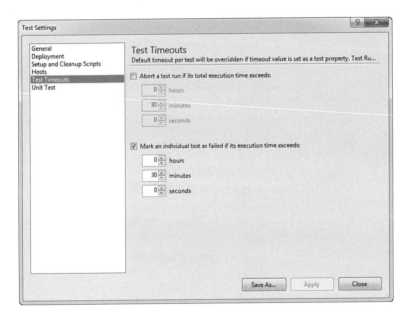

FIGURE 9.9   Using the test settings designer.

Selecting a node on the left of the Test Settings dialog box enables you to configure various settings associated with that node. The following provides an overview of the settings you can manage for each of the Test Settings nodes:

▶ **General**—Provides options for naming the settings file, providing a description, creating a naming scheme for each of your test runs.

▶ **Deployment**—Enables you to specify additional files and folders to deploy as part of running your tests. By default, the assemblies being tested automatically deploy to the test bin, which enables you to add any additional items you might want to deploy before running tests (such as a file-based database).

▶ **Setup and Cleanup Scripts**—Enables you to select a script to run either before or after your tests run (or both). This is different than running code before a test class runs. Here, you can define code to run before (or after) any test groups run.

▶ **Hosts**—Enables you to specify a host on which the tests can execute. Typically this is the default host (Visual Studio). You might also need to configure your tests to run inside an ASP.NET server host.

▶ **Test Timeouts**—Enables you to indicate how long Visual Studio (or your host) should wait before aborting a long-running test. You can also mark tests that run too long as failures (as shown in Figure 9.9).

▶ **Unit Test**—Provides advanced options for loading additional assemblies that are required for your tests to execute.

The Unit Testing Framework

The unit testing framework is part of Visual Studio (and not the .NET Framework itself). Unit testing in Visual Studio includes a set of framework classes, the tools, and the execution host. You can find the namespace that contains the unit testing framework classes at `Microsoft.VisualStudio.TestTools.UnitTesting`. Developers are most interested in the attribute classes and the `Assert` class in this namespace. This section highlights the core usage scenarios for both the attribute and assertion classes (among others).

The `TestContext` Class

The unit test framework contains a class that is used to store information pertaining to executing tests. This class is called `TestContext`. You use the properties of this class to get information about your running tests including the path to the test directory, a URL to the executing test (in the case of ASP.NET unit tests), and data-binding information such as the data connection or the current row of data for the executing test. The test context information is stored inside properties of this class. The key properties and their use are defined inside Table 9.1.

TABLE 9.1   TestContext Key Properties

Property	Description
CurrentTestOutcome	Enables you to determine the outcome of the last test that executed. This is useful inside methods marked as `TestCleanup` (see "The Test Attribute Classes").
DataConnection	Enables you to view the connection string used by any data-driven unit tests (see "Creating Data-Driven Unit Tests").
DataRow	Enables you to access columns in a row of data when working with data-bound unit tests (see "Creating Data-Driven Unit Tests").
RequestedPage	Provides access to the `Page` object for the requested page in an ASP.NET unit test (see "Writing ASP.NET Hosted Unit Tests").

Property	Description
TestDeploymentDir	Enables you to view the path to the directory where your unit tests are deployed and executing. This is useful if you need to read or write a file in that directory.
TestLogsDir	Enables you to view the path to the directory where your test results are written.
TestName	Enables access to the name of the currently executing test.

TestContext is not accessible to your code by default. You access TestContext by first defining a field, and a property named TestContext. The unit test framework automatically creates an instance of a TestContext object when it runs your tests. It then looks for a TestContext property in your source code. If it finds it, the framework assigns an instance of TestContext to your property. You can then use your property to access information about the executing test context. The following code shows how you might define the TestContext property in a C# unit test:

```
private TestContext testContextInstance;

public TestContext TestContext {
  get {
    return testContextInstance;
  }
  set {
    testContextInstance = value;
  }
}
```

NOTE

Some attribute classes require that you define a parameter of type TestContext to your decorated method. This is true for ClassInitialize (as discussed later). In this case, the unit test framework automatically passes an instance of a TestContext object to your method when it executes.

The Test Attribute Classes

The unit tests you write are run by Visual Studio using the unit test execution host. This host has to examine your code and find the unit tests within in it and run them accordingly. To do so, it relies on attributes. Recall that an attribute is used to provide metadata about your code. Other code (such as the unit test host) can use reflection to determine various bits of information about your code.

As you've seen in the brief samples thus far, you signify unit tests by decorating your code with the attribute classes defined inside the unit namespace. For example, a test class has the TestClass attribute; a test method is indicated using the TestMethod attribute.

Table 9.2 presents a list of the most common attribute classes found in the unit testing namespace.

TABLE 9.2   Visual Studio Test Attribute Classes

Test	Description
AssemblyCleanup	Used to define a method that should be run after all the tests in a given assembly have been executed by the framework. This is useful if you need to clean up resources after all tests have executed.
	Note that only one method in a given assembly can contain this attribute.
AssemblyInitialize	Used to define a method that should be run before any tests in a given assembly have been executed by the framework. This is useful if you need to initialize resources for all tests in an assembly.
	Note that only one method in a given assembly can contain this attribute.
ClassCleanup	Used to indicate a method that should be run once after all tests are executed in a given test class. This can be useful if you need to reset the system state (such as a database) after your tests have completed.
ClassInitialize	Used to indicate a method that should be run once by the test execution host before any other tests are run in the given test class. This can be useful if you need to reset a database or execute any code to prepare the test environment.
	Requires that your method take a parameter of type TestContext.
DataSource	Used to provide connection information for a data-driven unit test (see "Creating Data-Driven Unit Tests").
DeploymentItem	Used to indicate any additional files (.dll, .txt, or otherwise) that need to be deployed to the folder in which your tests run.
ExpectedException	Used to indicate that a given test method is expected to receive a certain exception for the code called within the test method. This type of test method is considered successful if the given exception type is received as part of the test execution; otherwise the test fails. This capability is useful for testing expected error conditions in your code (see "Testing Your Exceptions").
HostType	Used if you want to override the default test host (Visual Studio). In most test scenarios, you do not need to use this attribute. If, however, you write tests to run in another host process (such as ASP.NET) you can use this attribute (along with UrlToTest and AspNetDevelopmentServerHost).
Ignore	Added to a TestMethod to indicate that method should be ignored when run by the test execution host.
TestClass	Used to indicate that a given class is a test class that contains one or more unit tests (test methods).

9

Test	Description
TestCleanup	Used to indicate a method that should be run once after each test method is executed. You can use this method to do any cleanup after each test method runs in a given test class. Cleanup at the class level can be done via the ClassCleanup attribute.
TestInitialize	Used to indicate that a given method should be run once before each test method is executed. This capability is useful if you need to reset the system state before each test method within a given test class. If you only need to initialize for all the methods in a given test class, use ClassInitialize.
TestProperty	Used to define a property (name and value pair) attribute to a test method. This property information can be read inside the code of the test method.
TestMethod	Used to decorate a method as a unit test inside a test class. Test methods must have no return value (void). They succeed or fail based on error conditions and assertions. Test methods cannot take parameters as the host cannot pass parameters to the method. There are ways to simulate parameters, however. See "Creating Data-Driven Unit Tests" for more information.
Timeout	Used to indicate a timeout (in milliseconds) for a given test method. If the test exceeds this timeout period, it is stopped and considered failed.

You can see from Table 9.2 that a number of attribute classes give you control over your unit tests. Listing 9.2 shows a further refinement of our Invoice unit test class, demonstrating the many attributes you might typically use. Notice the methods to initialize the test class and clean up following the test run.

The next step is to write code inside each of these test methods. The code should make calls to the Customer object and then make assertions with respect to the results. These assertions are made using the Assert class, which we cover next.

LISTING 9.2   Using the Unit Test Framework Classes

```
using System;
using Microsoft.VisualStudio.TestTools.UnitTesting;
using Contoso.Fx.Common;

namespace CommonUnitTests
{
    [TestClass]
    public class InvoiceTest
    {

        private TestContext _testContext;
        public TestContext TestContext
```

```
{
    get { return _testContext; }
    set { _testContext = value; }
}


[ClassInitialize()]
public static void InitTests(TestContext testContext)
{
    //call code to reset the test db (Utilities.ResetTestDb();)

}


[ClassCleanup()]
public static void CleanupPostTests()
{
    //call code to reset the test db (Utilities.ResetTestDb();)

}



[TestMethod]
public void Adding_Lines_Changes_Total_Qty()
{
    //arrange ------------------------
    Invoice invoice = new Invoice();

    // line 1
    int qty1 = 2;
    string desc1 = "line 1";
    double price1 = 2.5;


    InvoiceLine line1 = new InvoiceLine();
    line1.Qty = qty1;
    line1.Description = desc1;
    line1.Price = price1;


    // line 2
    int qty2 = 3;
    string desc2 = "line 2";
    double price2 = 1.75;


    InvoiceLine line2 = new InvoiceLine();
    line2.Qty = qty2;
    line2.Description = desc2;
```

```
        line2.Price = price2;

        double expectedQty = qty1 + qty2;

        //act ------------------------
        invoice.AddLine(line1);
        invoice.AddLine(line2);

        //assert ------------------------
        Assert.AreEqual(expectedQty, invoice.TotalItems,
            "Total quantity not computed correctly.");


    }



    [TestMethod]
    public void Invoice_Has_A_Customer()
    {
        //arrange ------------------------


        // line 1
        int qty1 = 2;
        string desc1 = "line 1";
        double price1 = 2.5;


        InvoiceLine line1 = new InvoiceLine();
        line1.Qty = qty1;
        line1.Description = desc1;
        line1.Price = price1;


        //act ------------------------
        Invoice invoice = new Invoice();
        invoice.AddLine(line1);


        //assert ------------------------
        Assert.IsNotNull(invoice.Customer,
            "Invoice does not have an associated customer.");


    }
  }
}
```

Unit Test Setup and Teardown

A good practice for your unit tests is to write them for a known state of the system; this includes the database, files, and anything that makes up the entire system. This ensures that developers can rely on these items being there when they write their tests. Of course, the tests themselves often disrupt this state. You might have a test that deletes data, changes it, adds new records, and the like. In this case, you need to be able to reinitialize the state of the system prior to executing your tests (or after executing your tests) to ensure both a steady state to test against and a one-click test run experience for developers (another good practice for unit testing).

You typically need to write code to keep your system in a steady state. This code might copy a known good test database down to the test directory (you could also do this with a DeploymentItem attribute); reset your database using SQL; use a data generation plan to create your database; copy files; or verify other deployment items.

The code to reset your system is specific to your environment. However, to ensure this code is called when your tests run you have a few attribute classes with which to work: ClassInitialize and ClassCleanup, or TestInitialize and TestCleanup. The former set are run at the start (or end) of a test run in the entire unit test class. The latter are run before (or after) each test executes in a given test class.

In most cases, you run initialize and cleanup at the class level. As an example, if you had a Utilities class that included a method to reset your database you could ensure it is called by marking a method as ClassInitialize. Note that this method takes a TestContext object (which is passed to it by the unit test framework). A good practice is to reset the system again after the unit tests execute. The following code shows an example of two test methods doing both setup and cleanup:

```
[ClassInitialize()]
public static void InitTests(TestContext testContext) {
  Utilities.ResetTestDb();
}

[ClassCleanup()]
public static void CleanupPostTests() {
  Utilities.ResetTestDb();
}
```

Controlling Setup and Cleanup at the Test Execution Level

Sometimes your setup and cleanup needs to be executed at a higher level than just the running test class. Your scripts might need to run before any test classes execute. In this case, you can use your .testsettings file (see the earlier section "Controlling Advanced Test Settings") to define a script to execute when any tests are run (and after they have run).

Figure 9.10 shows an example of the Test Settings dialog box, Setup and Cleanup Scripts node. You can use this area to define setup and cleanup scripts to execute when any test in your solution executes.

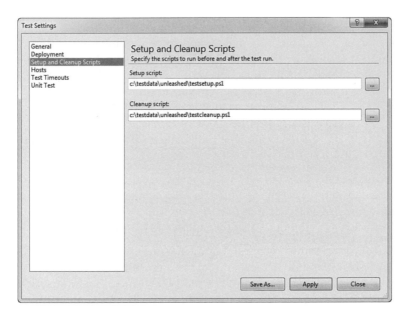

FIGURE 9.10   You can define setup and cleanup scripts to execute when any test in your solution executes.

The `Assert` Classes

The `UnitTesting` namespace also includes the `Assert` static type. This object contains methods for evaluating whether the results of a test were as expected. You call these static methods and expect a true/false condition. If the Boolean condition fails, the assertion fails. The assertions do not actually return results. Rather, they automatically notify the unit test framework at runtime if the assertion fails or succeeds.

As an example, you might write a unit test to load a known record from the database. You would then write assertions about this known record to prove that you can retrieve the data from the database and properly call the right sets and gets on a specific object. The following shows a simple assertion for testing that two variables contain the same value. If the values match (`AreEqual`), the assertion passes without issue. If the values don't match, the assertion fails and the unit test framework marks the test as failed:

```
Assert.AreEqual(cust.Id, customerId);
```

The `AreEqual` method is just one example of the many assertion methods available to you from the `Assert` class. For the most part, these assertion methods are variations on a concept: compare two values and determine the results. Table 9.3 provides a more complete list.

TABLE 9.3 Test Assertions

Test	Description
AreEqual/AreNotEqual	Used to test whether two values are equal to one another.
AreSame/AreNotSame	Used to test whether two objects are the same object.
Fail	The `Assert.Fail` method is used to fail a condition without doing any evaluation. This might be useful if your evaluation is based on logic and you get to a point in your code where the logic represents a failed test.
Inconclusive	Used to indicate that a given test has not failed or succeeded (but has inconclusive results).
IsInstanceOfType/ IsNotInstanceOfType	Used to determine whether an object is of a specified type.
IsNull/IsNotNull	Used to test whether an object contains a null reference.
IsTrue/IsFalse	Used to test whether a condition is true.

Each assertion method has a number of overloads. These overloads enable you to compare various data types, such as strings, numeric values, objects, and generic collections of objects, to one another. In addition, there are overloads that enable you to simply do the assertion and those that both do the assertion and enable you to enter a message that is displayed when the assertion fails.

The `Assert` class also contains a version of the `AreEqual/AreNotEqual` methods that uses a generic data type. These methods enable you to compare two generic types against one another for equality. In this case, you indicate the generic type using standard generic notation, `<T>` (or `(of T)` in VB) and pass the two generic types you want to compare. The following shows an example:

```
Assert.AreEqual<Invoice>(cust1, cust2);
```

Verifying Collections of Objects

The `UnitTesting` namespace also contains the assertion classes, `CollectionAssert`. With it, you can verify the contents of collection classes. For instance, you can call the `Contains` method to assert whether a given collection contains a specific element (or `DoesNotContain`). You can use the `AllItemsAreInstancesOfType` to check that a collection only contains like instances. You can compare two collections to see if they are equal (`AreEqual/AreNotEqual`) or that they are simply equivalent; they have the same elements but might be in a different order (`AreEquivalent/AreNotEquivalent`).

Verifying Strings

The `StringAssert` class contains methods for verifying strings and portions of strings. For example, the `Contains` method enables you to check that a string contains a specific substring. You can use the `StartsWith` method to assert whether a string begins with a certain set of characters, or EndsWith to check the ending of a string. Finally, the

`Matches/DoesNotMatch` methods enable you to check whether a string matches a regular expression you define.

Testing Your Exceptions

You should write unit tests to verify your code behaves as expected in both positive and negative conditions. The positive conditions can be verified using the Assert methods as discussed previously. However, many times you want to verify that your code returns the correct exception when you call or use it in a certain manner. In this case, you can use the `ExpectedException` attribute to test for specific error conditions.

You use the `ExpectedException` attribute by adding it to a test method. The attribute takes the type of expected exception as a parameter. If the test method results in an exception being thrown and the type of that exception is as you defined in the attribute, the test is considered a success. If an exception is not thrown or an exception of a different type is thrown, the test is considered as failed.

As an example, suppose that you want to test what happens when you try to create a new invoice that has incomplete details. In this case, your code might be written to throw a custom exception of type `InvalidInvoiceException`. You would then decorate your test method as follows:

```
[TestMethod()]
[ExpectedException(typeof(InvalidInvoiceException),
  "The Invalid Invoice Exception was not thrown.")]
public void Invoice_Is_Valid() {

  //create a bad, new invoice instance to test against
}
```

Notice that in this code, if the exception is not thrown, there is an error message provided as the result of the test ("The Invalid Invoice Exception was not thrown."). This error message is an optional parameter of the `ExpectedException` attribute.

You can combine assertions with the `ExpectedException` attribute. In this case, both the assertions need to pass and the exception needs to be thrown for the test method to be considered passed.

> **NOTE**
>
> The resulting exception must be of the exact same type as the expected exception. The resulting exception cannot, for instance, inherit from the expected exception. In this case, the test is considered as failed.

Creating Data-Driven Unit Tests

Let's build on our knowledge now of both basic unit testing concepts and the unit testing framework attribute classes and examine how to create a unit test that feeds off of a data source.

Looking back at Listing 9.1, you can see that we are doing a lot of setup work in terms of initializing objects and fields in our "arrange" section of the test. This works out fine for the limited data we are dealing with here, but would quickly become unmanageable if we wanted or needed a more expansive data set. In other words, instead of just testing with a scenario of adding two invoice lines, what if we wanted to add hundreds? And what if we wanted to dynamically populate those line items instead of hard-coding them in the test method? In these cases, you want to author the unit test in such a way that it derives its values from an actual data source.

The basic process for authoring the unit test remains the same, with the following tweaks:

1. Create the data source that will store the values to inject into the unit test.

2. A `TestContext` property (public) and field (private) need to be added to the unit test class.

3. The data source will be wired to the unit test method by adding a `DataSource` attribute to the method.

Let's put the data-driven scenario into action by adding another unit test method. This one tests whether the `InvoiceLineItem` object is successfully producing line item totals (that is, the product of the price and the qty of each line).

Adding a Data Source

Any .NET accessible data source will work: a table in SQL Server, an object collection, an Excel file, a CSV file, a XML file, and so on. Because it is quick and easy to implement, let's store our invoice test data in a CSV file.

First we add a text file to the test project (right-click the project, select Add New Item, and then select the Text File item template); name the file InvoiceTestData.csv.

With the file open in the Visual Studio editor, enter the following values and save the file:

```
1,"line 1",2,2.50
525,"line 2",0,100
78,"line 3",10,1.25
1001,"line 4",3,3.33
1002,"line 5",1000,10
2,"line 6",2,5
901,"line 7",1,9.10
700,"line 8",5,5
221,"line 9",8,9.75
442,"line 10",20,2000
```

Because we have chosen to use a file to store our test data, we want to make sure that the file gets deployed along with the unit test binaries as part of any build. The CSV file needs to be marked as `'content'`, and it needs its build action set to `'Copy Always'`. To do this, right-click the file in the Solution Explorer window, and use the property window to change the Build Action and Copy to Output Directory values to the mentioned values.

With the file setup complete, let's write the data source attribute. The `DataSource` attribute class has three overloads. The first simply takes a single parameter, `dataSourceSettingName`. In this case, you are expected to pass the name of the data source settings as defined inside a configuration file. The second overload takes both a `connectionString` and a `tableName`. In this case, you pass a valid connection string to the `DataSource` and indicate the name of the table you intend to bind to the unit test. The final overload takes `providerInvariantName`, `connectionString`, `tableName`, and `dataAccessMethod`. The provider name is used to indicate the type of provider such as a CSV provider, SQL Server, or similar. The connection string is based on your chosen provider and indicates how you access the data. The table name is the name of the table (or file) that contains your data. Finally, the data access method determines how your data is bound to the unit test: sequentially or randomly:

```
[DataSource("Microsoft.VisualStudio.TestTools.DataSource.CSV",
   "InvoiceTestData.csv", "InvoiceTestData#csv",
   DataAccessMethod.Sequential)]
```

> **NOTE**
>
> The first parameter is using the built-in CSV data source parser that exists in the unit testing framework. The way you would configure this data source for other sources, such as SQL tables or even Excel files, will vary. You should consult the Microsoft Developer Network (MSDN) documentation to determine exactly how to construct this attribute for your data source.

Notice that in the preceding code example, the first parameter of the `DataSource` call defines the `.csv` provider. The next parameter is a connection string to the actual data file. The third parameter (`InvoiceTestData#csv`) simply indicates that the table name does not exist; it is the filename. The last parameter, the enumeration `DataAccessMethod.Sequential`, indicates that each row should be bound to the unit test in sequential order.

Because we are deploying a file as a data source here, we need one additional attribute, `DeploymentItem`, to tell the unit testing framework what specific deployed file it should look for:

```
[DeploymentItem("InvoiceTestData.csv")]
```

With those in place, we can write our test method. See Listing 9.3 for our final product. Each row within our data source is accessed via the `TestContext` property, which we added to our unit test class. Because we have attributed our method correctly, it will be called once for every row in our data source. We extract the values from the row (item number, description, quantity and price) within the "arrange" section, and then we create a new `InvoiceLine` object using those values. Within the "act" section, we create the `LineItem` instance, and store off the line item total that it produced. And finally, in the "assert" section, we compare the total from the `LineItem` object with the total that we manually computed. If they are equal, our code has passed the unit test.

LISTING 9.3   Driving a Unit Test Using a CSV File

```
using System;
using Microsoft.VisualStudio.TestTools.UnitTesting;
using Contoso.Fx.Common;

namespace CommonUnitTests
{
    [TestClass]
    public class InvoiceTest
    {
        [TestMethod]
        [DataSource("Microsoft.VisualStudio.TestTools.DataSource.CSV",
           "InvoiceTestData.csv", "InvoiceTestData#csv",
           DataAccessMethod.Sequential)]
        [DeploymentItem("InvoiceTestData.csv")]
        public void LineItem_Total_Is_Correct()
        {
            //arrange ------------------------
            int itemNbr = Convert.ToInt32(TestContext.DataRow[0]);
            string desc = Convert.ToString(TestContext.DataRow[1]);
            int qty = Convert.ToInt32(TestContext.DataRow[2]);
            double price = Convert.ToDouble(TestContext.DataRow[3]);

            double expected = qty * price;

            //act
            InvoiceLine line = new InvoiceLine(itemNbr, desc, qty, price);
            double actual = line.LineTotal;

            //assert ------------------------
            Assert.AreEqual(expected, actual,
               "Line total is incorrect.");

        }
    }
}
```

Figure 9.11 shows the results of newly minted unit tests, including our data-driven unit test that will be executed once for every row in the data source CSV file.

Connecting Using a Configuration File   In another example, you might have your connection information stored inside a configuration file. This is useful if you do not want to hard-code this information in your unit tests. You might, for instance, have a test database that is used across many unit tests. It might change between development and test environments. In this case, having your connection information inside a configuration file makes it easier to manage.

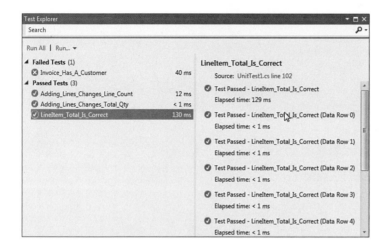

FIGURE 9.11   Data-driven unit test results in Test Explorer.

The first step in this scenario is to define a configuration file. To do so, you simply add an app.config file to your unit test project. (Right-click the project file and select Add, New Item.) Getting the format of the configuration file right is the only trick. You have to add a configuration section specific to the Visual Studio test tools. Note that this configuration section must indicate version 10 of the unit test framework. The following shows an example:

```
<configSections>
  <section name="microsoft.visualstudio.testtools"
    type="Microsoft.VisualStudio.TestTools.UnitTesting.TestConfigurationSection,
Microsoft.VisualStudio.QualityTools.UnitTestFramework, Version=10.0.0.0, Culture=
neutral,
PublicKeyToken=b03f5f7f11d50a3a" />
</configSections>
```

You then add a connection string section. You give your connection string a name and provide information on both the connection and the data provider. The specifics of your connection string, of course, depend on your provider and the type of data. Data stored in XLSX, CSV, XML files, Access, Oracle, or SQL databases all have their own connection string idiosyncrasies. For example, the following uses the OleDb provider to define a connection string to a delimited text file (CSV):

```
<connectionStrings>
  <add name="InvoiceTestDataConn"
    connectionString="Provider=Microsoft.Jet.OLEDB.4.0; Data Source=
```

```
|DataDirectory|TestData\; Extended Properties='text;HDR=Yes;FMT=Delimited'"
    providerName="System.Data.OleDb" />
</connectionStrings>
```

The last step is to create a data source section embedded inside a test tools section. The data source defines a name for your test data source and points to your connection string. You can also indicate the data access method here (sequential or random) and the table name (if applicable). Your final configuration file should look similar to Listing 9.4.

LISTING 9.4   A Unit Test Configuration File Example

```
<?xml version="1.0" encoding="utf-8" ?>
<configuration>
  <configSections>
    <section name="microsoft.visualstudio.testtools"
      type="Microsoft.VisualStudio.TestTools.UnitTesting.TestConfigurationSection,
Microsoft.VisualStudio.QualityTools.UnitTestFramework, Version=10.0.0.0, Culture=
neutral, PublicKeyToken=b03f5f7f11d50a3a" />
  </configSections>
  <connectionStrings>
    <add name=" InvoiceTestDataConn"
      connectionString="Provider=Microsoft.Jet.OLEDB.4.0; Data Source=
|DataDirectory|TestData\; Extended Properties='text;HDR=Yes;FMT=Delimited'"
      providerName="System.Data.OleDb" />
  </connectionStrings>
  <microsoft.visualstudio.testtools>
    <dataSources>
      <add name=" InvoiceTestDataSource"
        connectionString=" InvoiceTestDataConn" dataTableName="InvoiceTestData#csv"
        dataAccessMethod="Sequential"/>
    </dataSources>
  </microsoft.visualstudio.testtools>

</configuration>
```

NOTE

Note that you can have multiple connection strings defined in a single configuration file (each named uniquely of course).

You can then use your configured test data source inside your test method. To do so, you simply indicate the data source name inside the `DataSource` attribute of the test method. This makes for cleaner code, reusable connection strings, and central management of the connection in case it changes from machine to machine. The following shows an example of the data source being used:

```
DataSource("InvoiceTestDataSource")
public void My_Unit_Test() {

  //unit test code goes here

}
```

Writing ASP.NET Hosted Unit Tests

You can choose to have your unit tests hosted and run inside of ASP.NET instead of the default VSTest host process. This is useful if you're writing tests that work with ASP.NET objects such as `Page` and `Session`. You might want to test a Web Service or some other application logic specific to your web interface. In either case, you have the option to host your ASP.NET unit tests in either Internet Information Services (IIS) or the Visual Studio development server. Doing so ensures your test has full access to the ASP.NET environment variables.

Defining ASP.NET Attributes

You indicate a unit test should be run inside of ASP.NET by adding attributes to the test method. Many of these attributes are found in the `UnitTesting.Web` namespace. Therefore, you should first add a using statement (imports in VB) to the top of any test class file you intend to use with ASP.NET. This statement should read as follows:

```
using Microsoft.VisualStudio.TestTools.UnitTesting.Web;
```

You should also set a reference from your unit test application to your website. This ensures you can access the classes in the site. This includes the pages themselves and any other class files you might have in the App_Code directory or elsewhere.

You define three primary attributes when creating ASP.NET unit tests: `UrlToTest`, `HostType`, and `AspNetDevelopmentServerHost`. The `UrlToTest` attribute allows you to indicate a page that should be called for the execution of the given unit test. This page is called by the test framework and the context of that web request is available to your unit test (via the `Page` object). You can code against the ASP.NET environment inside your unit test as if you were writing code in a web page's code-behind file.

The `HostType` attribute allows you to change the host type to ASP.NET. You do so by passing ASP.NET as a string value to the attribute.

If you are using IIS as your host, you need only set `UrlToTest` and `HostType`. If you are using the ASP.NET Development Server (that works with Visual Studio), however, you must also add the attribute `AspNetDevelopmentServerHost`. You pass the path to the web application as a parameter of the attribute. You also pass the name of the web application root.

Listing 9.5 shows an example of using all three attributes to define an ASP.NET unit test that runs against a local development server. Notice that you obtain a reference to the

ASP.NET objects from the `TestContext` object's `RequestedPage` property. You can use this property to cast directly to the type of the requested page (in this case, `ShoppingCartPage`). Of course, the `RequestedPage` property is of type `System.Web.UI.Page` and therefore gives you access to objects such as `Server`, `Session`, `Request`, and `Response`.

LISTING 9.5   An ASP.NET Unit Test

```
[TestMethod()]
[HostType("ASP.NET")]
[AspNetDevelopmentServerHost("C:\\CODE\\Unleashed\\Contoso\\ContosoWeb", "/")]
[UrlToTest("http://localhost:55136/ShoppingCart.aspx")]
public void AddShoppingCartItemTest() {

  //get the requested page
  Page reqPage = TestContext.RequestedPage;
  Assert.IsTrue(reqPage.Title == "Shopping Cart", "Page title does not match.");

  //cast to actual page type
  ShoppingCartPage actualPage = (ShoppingCartPage)reqPage;
  Assert.IsNotNull(actualPage.Cart, "There is no cart on the page.");

  //validate cart usage
  actualPage.Cart.AddItem("Product 1", 1, 12.75);
  actualPage.Cart.AddItem("Product 2", 2, 26.95);
  Assert.IsTrue(actualPage.Cart.Items.Count == 2, "Item count does not match.");
  Assert.AreEqual(actualPage.Cart.CalculateCartTotal(), 66.65);

}
```

Configuring Your Test Project Host

A common scenario is to have a separate unit test project for working with your website. This project can focus on tests specifically related to the functions of your site. You can create additional test projects to work with other code libraries. This type of separation makes the writing and running of unit tests a more straightforward process.

You can also configure your test project settings to be specific to your host. In this way, you do not have to define the many ASP.NET attributes on each unit test. Instead, you can configure your .testsettings file to work with a specific host, as shown in Figure 9.12.

TIP

If your solution contains multiple unit test projects, you might want multiple versions of the .testsettings file. You can then easily switch between configurations for ASP.NET and the standard VSTest hosts.

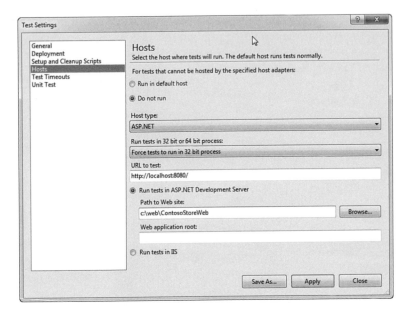

FIGURE 9.12   You can use a .testsettings file to configure your entire test project to work with an ASP.NET site.

Creating Ordered Tests

Visual Studio enables you to group unit tests together, set their sequence of execution, and treat the results as if a single test was run. This can be useful if you need to write unit tests that are dependent on one another. For example, you might insert a record in one test and rely on that record being there in a later test. Of course, this goes against a good practice for unit testing; each test should be able to execute independently. Thankfully, you can create an ordered test that groups the individual unit tests into a new, self-contained test.

You add an ordered test to your test project by right-clicking the unit test project and selecting Add, Ordered Test. You can also select the Ordered Test template from the Add New Test dialog box.

An ordered test is simply an XML file based on the OrderedTest schema. You do not, however, need to hand-edit the XML. Instead, Visual Studio gives you the ordered test designer to help you. Figure 9.13 shows an example of this designer.

The left side of the dialog box is where you find all your tests in your solution. Tests are shown by their parent project. You select individual tests from the left side and use the arrow (>) to include the tests in your ordered test. You can use the up and down arrows on the right side to change the order in which your tests execute.

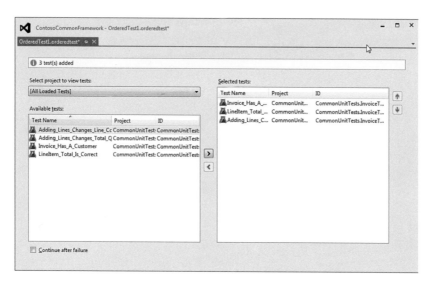

FIGURE 9.13   You add existing unit tests to an ordered to test to create a new test that executes two or more tests in a specific order.

When you run your ordered test, Visual Studio executes each unit test in the order you defined. If any fail, the entire ordered test fails unless you have checked the Continue After Failure check box (located on the bottom of the dialog). You can view the details of the failed ordered test to see which tests passed and which failed.

Summary

This chapter showed how you can use the unit test framework to define test projects and create test class files using the `TestClass` attribute. Each test method should include the `TestMethod` attribute. You can also data-bind unit tests using the `DataSource` attribute class.

You can write unit tests that are hosted by ASP.NET (either in IIS or the Visual Studio development server). An ASP.NET unit test uses the `TestContext` object to access information about the ASP.NET environment including the executing page, session, and server variables.

Writing unit tests can lead to fewer issues found in production. Having a suite of tests for your code makes that code easier to understand and more reliable. You will also gain confidence with code changes as you will be able to tell what code was broken as a result of a change.

CHAPTER 10

Refactoring Code

Whether or not you realize it, if you are like most developers, you are always refactoring code. Every time you change your code to reduce duplication or rename items for the sake of clarity, you are refactoring. Refactoring is simply putting a name to a common development task. The strict definition of the term is "a change made to the internal structure of software to make it easier to understand and cheaper to modify without changing its observable behavior." That is, refactoring does not add features to the application. Instead, it improves the general maintenance of the code base.

The term *refactoring* has received a large amount of attention. A number of good books have been written touting the many benefits of refactoring code as you are building your application. This is when you are closest to the code and thus able to quickly make these maintenance-type changes. Many of these books are on the subject of agile development. Refactoring has become one of the key tenets of the agile developer. In agile development, your code base builds feature by feature to satisfy a series of tests. This can result in code that works wonderfully but does not look as though it was designed as a cohesive unit. To combat this problem, you would be wise to go over the code base at frequent intervals and thus improve the general quality of the code (remove duplication, create common interfaces, rename items, put things into logical groups, and so on).

A new set of features has been developed inside code editors to aid with refactoring. These features have their basis in a real need. No developer wants to introduce errors into a relatively stable code base simply for the sake of improving maintenance, especially when running a tight schedule. Imagine explaining to your manager or client that the large spike in bugs is a result of sweeping changes you made to the code to improve future maintenance and readability. We can be thankful that the C# editor inside Visual Studio provides a reliable set of refactoring tools.

These tools let you make changes to the code base without the concern of creating more problems than you are solving.

> **NOTE**
>
> There are a couple of features built in to Visual Studio for refactoring database elements. We cover these in Chapter 20, "Working with Databases."

Visual Studio Refactoring Basics

The Visual Studio refactoring tools work to ensure that you see the promises of refactoring: increased reuse of your code, fewer rewrites, reduced duplication, and better readability. These tools work to instill confidence in the edits they make to your code. They do so by using a common refactoring engine based on the C# compiler rather than string matching and search-and-replace. The engine and compiler work together to cover the entire code base (and its references) to find all possible changes that need to be made as part of a given refactor operation. The engine even searches out code comments and tries to update them to reflect new type names. In addition, you can preview changes to your code before they happen. This adds further to your comfort level with the modifications these tools are making to your code.

Table 10.1 presents a high-level overview of the many refactoring operations that are possible with the C# editor. We cover each of them in detail in the coming sections. First, however, we cover some of the common elements of the refactoring process. These elements include both invoking a refactoring tool inside Visual Studio and previewing the refactoring changes as they happen.

TABLE 10.1   Refactoring Tools Inside the Visual Studio C# Editor

Tool	Description
Rename	Renames fields, properties, namespaces, methods, types, and local variables
Extract Method	Creates a new method using existing code within an existing method
Reorder Parameters	Changes the order of parameters for a given method and updates all callers
Remove Parameters	Removes a parameter from a method and updates callers
Encapsulate Field	Quickly creates a property from an existing field
Extract Interface	Creates an interface from an existing class or structure

Invoking the Refactoring Tools

The refactoring tools are available from wherever you work on your C# code inside Visual Studio. You can invoke them in several ways. For example, if you are working inside the code editor, you can invoke the Rename tool using a smart tag. You can also select and right-click code to reveal the refactoring options; these same options are available on the menu bar through the Refactor menu. Finally, you can refactor directly from the class designer as you edit and change various items within a given class.

Using the Refactor Menu (and Right-Click)

The most common place to invoke the refactoring commands is from the actual refactoring menu. This menu item, located under the top-level Edit menu, is added to the IDE when you have a C# code window open and active. Figure 10.1 shows the menu being invoked. Note that the portion of code you are trying to refactor is highlighted in the IDE. In this case, we want to reorder the parameters within the constructor for an InvoiceLine class.

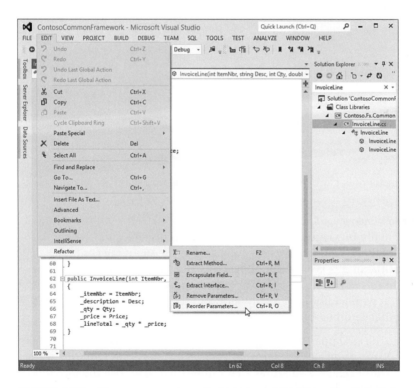

FIGURE 10.1   You can access a refactoring operation from the Refactor menu.

The same Refactor menu is available via a right-click within the code editor. In this case, you highlight a word or section of code (or simply position the cursor accordingly) and then right-click inside the editor, which brings up the context version of the Refactor menu, as shown in Figure 10.2. Notice that the first item in this menu is Refactor. Selecting this option reveals the fold-out version of the refactor menu.

FIGURE 10.2   The Refactor menu invoked via a right-click with the mouse.

Refactoring in the Code Window via Smart Tags

The smart tag was originally introduced in Microsoft Office. As discussed in Chapter 8, "Working with Visual Studio's Productivity Aids," the goal of the smart tag is simple: try to understand what the user is typing and offer additional "smart" functionality. For example, as you type in the word editor, it tries to understand what you've typed. The editor then provides you with additional functionality and the ability to control formatting options based on that information.

The C# code editor provides a similar smart tag feature. The editor detects your typing and understands when you have made a change to your code that is the equivalent of a refactor. In these cases, the editor creates a smart tag that can be used to invoke the refactoring tool. This allows you to stay in the code editor but still take advantage of the increased productivity and reduced error rate that the refactoring tool can provide.

As an example, suppose you have a property named Id. You want to rename this item to Identifier. You open the class file and position your cursor near the property name. You then type the new property name. The C# code editor detects your change and underlines the final character of the changed name. Figure 10.3 shows an example of this. Notice the small rectangle beneath the property name.

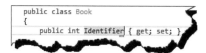

```
public class Book
{
    public int Identifier { get; set; }
```

FIGURE 10.3   Renaming a property invokes a smart tag for refactoring.

This small rectangle hovering under the change is your visual cue that the C# code editor thinks it can help you. You can position your mouse cursor next to the rectangle to reveal an in-line menu that indicates how the editor might help. Figure 10.4 shows the smart tag as it is invoked when after renaming Id to Identifier.

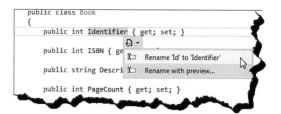

```
public class Book
{
    public int Identifier { get; set; }

    public int ISBN { ge
                        Rename 'Id' to 'Identifier'
    public string Descri    Rename with preview...

    public int PageCount { get; set; }
```

FIGURE 10.4   The rename smart tag menu in action.

TIP

You can also invoke smart tags without grabbing for the mouse by pressing the key combination Shift+Alt+F10.

Using the Class Designer to Refactor

The class designer enables you to view the contents of your classes and their relationships. It can also be used as a productivity tool: You can create new classes and modify existing classes directly within the designer.

NOTE

The class designer is covered in Chapter 6, "Introducing the Editors and Designers."

The Visual Studio class designer exposes the refactoring tool when you're working with C# classes. This ensures that code modifications made using this Visual Designer take full advantage of refactoring. For instance, suppose you want to rename a property from within the class designer but also want to make sure that the references to that property are automatically updated. You can do so by right-clicking the property within the class designer and choosing the Refactor menu's Rename option. Figure 10.5 shows refactoring (renaming the `Creator` property to `Author`) from directly within the class designer.

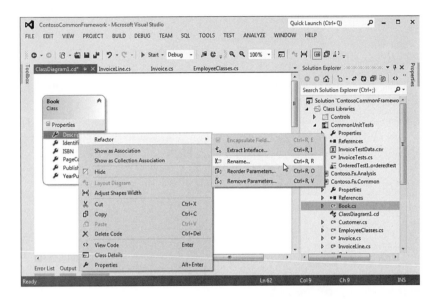

FIGURE 10.5   Invoking refactoring from within the Visual Studio class designer.

Previewing Changes

As you become comfortable with the refactoring tools, you might decide to simply let them do their thing without much oversight on your part. However, if you are like most developers, no one (or no tool) touches your code without your consent. Fortunately for us, the refactoring tools provide a preview option. This option lets you follow the tool through its changes and, in turn, accept or reject a given change.

The Preview Changes dialog box is invoked as an option (check box) on a given refactoring operation (or, in the case of a smart tag, from a second menu item on the smart tag menu). Figure 10.6 provides an example of selecting the Preview Reference Changes option from the Rename refactor operation.

After the refactoring operation is invoked with Preview Changes, Visual Studio presents you with the Preview Changes dialog box. The top portion of this dialog box lists all the changes the given refactor operation intends to make. This list is presented as a tree, with the outer branch representing where you intend to originate the change. The leaves under this branch are all files where changes happen. Nested beneath the filenames are the actual places within the code where a change is made. You use this list to select each item you would like to preview. Figure 10.7 shows an example of the changes required in a simple example of changing the `PageCount` property of the `Book` object.

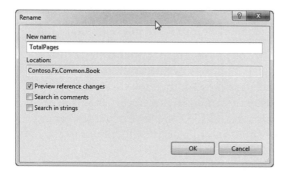

FIGURE 10.6   Invoking a refactor operation with Preview reference changes checked.

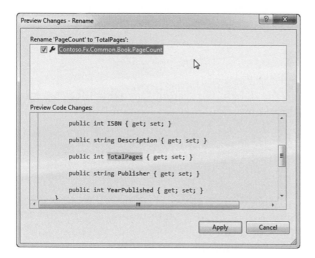

FIGURE 10.7   Previewing changes of a Rename operation.

As each item in the Preview Changes tree is clicked, the corresponding code is displayed below the tree in the Preview Code Changes section of the dialog box. This enables developers to quickly review where changes are being made. To prevent a given change, you can simply uncheck the item in the tree view. Of course, you can prevent entire file changes by unchecking farther up in the hierarchy at the file level. When you are finished with your preview and satisfied with the proposed changes, you simply click the Apply button to commit the changes to your code.

Renaming Code

Renaming code elements is the most common refactoring operation. In fact, while Rename is part of the refactoring support in the C# editor, a similar rename feature exists in the VB editor. Database projects also now include the ability to reliably rename elements in your database schema. Here we stick to our coverage of the C# refactoring tools. However, both the VB and database rename operations work in a similar fashion.

Most developers do not typically wait until the code base is operational and say to themselves, "Okay, now I will go back and rename items for clarity." Although this does happen on some teams as part of a set code refactoring step, the more likely scenario is that as you build your application, you consistently rename items to correct mistakes or make things clearer and more readable. Of course, as the code base builds, renaming classes, methods, fields, and the like becomes more and more difficult without introducing new bugs into your code.

The capability to rename items with the confidence that you are not introducing bugs into your code is paramount. With the C# editor, you can rename all relevant code items including namespaces, classes, fields, properties, methods, and variables. The compiler helps make sure that your code does not get broken and that all source code references are found. In fact, the Rename operation can even search through your code comments and update them accordingly.

Accessing the Rename Operation

You can rename from many places within the IDE. In the section "Invoking the Refactoring Tools," earlier in this chapter, we looked at accessing Rename from the Refactor menu, a right-click, a smart tag, and the class designer. You can also access Rename from the Object Browser, Solution Explorer, and Class View window. In addition, if you use the Properties dialog box to change the name of a control you've placed on a form, the Rename operation is invoked behind the scenes, and the control is renamed appropriately.

From the Object Browser, you can access the Rename operation only from the Refactor menu. Of course, you need to be browsing your own types in your solution. You select the item you want to rename and then click the Refactor menu. Figure 10.8 shows an example of the Object Browser and Rename operation working together.

You can rename within the Solution Explorer for filenames that equate to classnames. For instance, suppose you have a file named Customer and want to change the classname and filename to Shopper. You do so by right-clicking and choosing Rename. Visual Studio enables you to rename the file. When you do so, it prompts you to see whether you also want to rename the class. If you choose yes, Visual Studio searches the code within the file for any class that has the same name as the file. So if you have a `Customer` class and a Customer.cs file, a Rename operation to `Shopper` will rename the file as well as the class if you give it permission to (and will also refactor all references to the previous classname).

NOTE

Although an undo on the Rename operation rolls back a change, in the case of a filename change, Undo reverts the code but does not change the filename back to its original name.

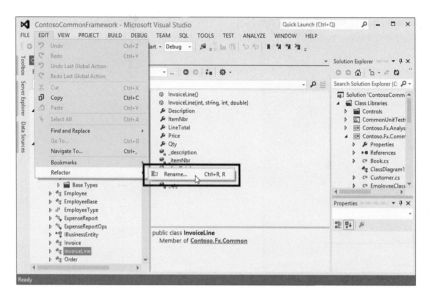

FIGURE 10.8   Accessing the Rename operation from the Object Browser.

Finally, you can also rename from within Class View window (View, Class View). This can be helpful if you look at your code from a namespace and object perspective (rather than a file-based perspective). To do so, you right-click the item you want to rename and select the Rename option. Figure 10.9 shows an example of renaming the State property of the Order object (to Status) from within Class View. Note that renaming a class from within Class View has no effect on the filename for the file that contains the class.

TIP

You can access the Rename operation from a set of command keys. Earlier versions of Visual Studio introduced the concept of chords. They are like traditional keyboard commands, but you press (or play) them in sequence. For instance, to invoke the Rename operation without touching your mouse, position your cursor over what you want to rename. Then press the sequence Ctrl+R, R (where you continue to hold Ctrl when pressing the second R). Pressing this combination in sequence will bring up the Refactoring, Rename dialog box relative to the code element behind your cursor.

Working with the Rename Dialog Box

The Rename dialog box enables you to specify a few options when invoking a given Rename refactor operation. Refer to Figure 10.6 for an example of the dialog box. The text box on the form enables you to define the rename itself. In the New Name section, you indicate the new name of the element to be renamed. The Location text box indicates the namespace of the element to be renamed. Of course, all referenced locations are also searched. The Rename dialog box presents developers with a few options when doing a rename. The three check boxes below the Location text box enable you to set the options described in Table 10.2.

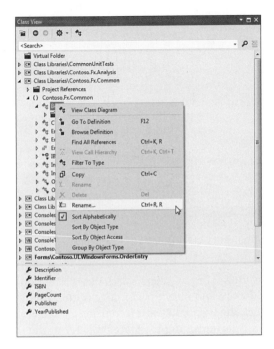

FIGURE 10.9 Accessing Rename from the Class View window.

TABLE 10.2 The Rename Dialog Box Options

Option	Description
Preview Reference Changes	This option enables you to indicate whether you want to preview the changes before they are applied to your code. This capability can be especially useful if you are renaming for the first time or you intend to rename items inside strings or comments.
	Renaming strings and comments does not use the compiler. Instead it uses string matching (see Figure 10.10 for an example). In this case, previewing a change before applying it can be especially helpful. For example, you may want to rename a type, but not similar text in a label.
Search in Comments	This option enables you to indicate whether the Rename operation should search your comments for possible textual references that should be renamed. Comments often refer to types and hence need to be synced with changes.
	Figure 10.10 shows the Preview Changes – Rename dialog box with both a `Strings` folder and a `Comments` folder expanded in the tree. Note that the string matching is case-sensitive. Therefore, you might want to be vigilant when writing comments that refer to types.

Option	Description
Search in Strings	This preference enables you to indicate whether the Rename operation should search inside your literal strings for references to a given item name. String literals include constants, control names, form names, and so on. This capability is most useful if there is a tight coupling between your code and the elements within your user interface. Again, this too is case sensitive.

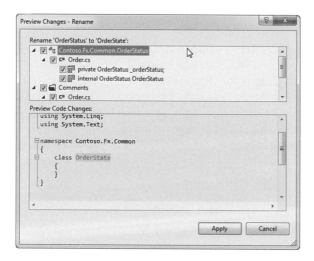

FIGURE 10.10   The Preview Changes – Rename dialog box.

Extract Method

When developers go back and take a look at their code, perhaps during a periodic code review or after a particularly long session of heads-down development, they often find methods that are too long or coarse-grained, contain duplicate code, or are just poorly organized. A common thing to do is pass over the code and create fine-grained, discrete methods to reduce these issues and make for a more readable, reusable, and maintainable code base.

The problem, of course, is that doing this is time-consuming and often introduces bugs into the code. The C# code editor in Visual Studio provides an Extract Method refactoring tool to ensure a quick, bug-free experience when you're working to better organize your code. With this tool, you can create a new method using existing code.

Accessing the Extract Method Refactor

To access the Extract Method refactor operation, you first must select a portion of code to refactor. You then can use the Refactor menu and select the Extract Method menu item. You can also invoke the Extract Method from the context menu via a right-click.

10

TIP

To invoke the Extract Method operation from the keyboard, first select the section of code you want to extract. Next, play the chord Ctrl+R, Ctrl+M.

Extracting Methods

With the Extract Method operation, you can create (or extract) a new method from multiple lines of code, a single line, or an expression within a given line of code. In each case, the method is created immediately following the method from which the code was extracted. The extracted code is replaced by a call to the new method.

Listing 10.1 provides an example of a method that is unnecessarily long. We've added line numbers for reference purposes. When you're reviewing code, methods such as these are common and exactly what you should be looking for. The method is designed as a static call that returns a given customer's `Order` object based on the customer's ID number and the order ID number. However, the order, the order line items, and the customer details are all retrieved from discreet database calls and stored in domain-specific objects. These objects are then stored on the order as properties.

LISTING 10.1   A Long Static Method

```
01   public static Order GetCustomerOrder(int customerId, int orderId) {
02
03     DataAccess.DAL dal = new DataAccess.DAL();
04     Order order = new Order();
05
06     //get order details
07     System.Data.DataTable dtOrder = dal.GetData("customerOrder", orderId);
08
09     //validate order against customer
10     if (customerId != (int)dtOrder.Rows[0]["customer_id"]) {
11       throw new ApplicationException("Invalid order for the given customer.");
12     }
13     order.Id = (int)dtOrder.Rows[0]["id"];
14
15     //get order items
16     List<OrderItem> items = new List<OrderItem>();
17     System.Data.DataTable dtItems = dal.GetData("orderItems", orderId);
18     foreach (System.Data.DataRow r in dtItems.Rows) {
19       OrderItem item = new OrderItem((int)r["product_id"], orderId);
20       item.Name = (string)r["name"];
21       item.Description = (string)r["description"];
22       item.Quantity = (int)r["quantity"];
23       item.UnitPrice = (double)r["unit_price"];
24       items.Add(item);
25     }
```

```
26    order.Items = items;

27

28    //get customer details
29    System.Data.DataTable dtCustomer = dal.GetData("customer", customerId);
30    Shopper cust = new Shopper(customerId);
31    order.Customer = cust;

32

33    return order;

34 }
```

Opportunities for method extraction inside this one method are numerous. You might consider extracting the call to initialize the Order object, the call to get order items, and the call to get customer details, which results in better organized code (thus, more read-able), more opportunities for reuse, and an easier-to-maintain code base. Let's look at doing these extractions.

First, you extract the call that sets up the order. Knowing what to select for extraction requires a bit of experience with the tool. In this case, extract lines 3 through 13, which is the code from the DataAccess setup through the order initialization. However, doing this confuses the Extract Method operation somewhat because you are setting up both a DataAccess object and an Order object in the first two operations. The Extract Method understands you need these two objects later in your method. Therefore, it creates both objects as out parameters of the method. What you want is the method to return an instance of the Order object and set up its own DataAccess object. You can accomplish this with the following steps:

1. Select lines 4 though 13 (order creation through initialization).

2. Select the Extract Method refactor operation (menu, right-click, or keyboard chord).

3. Visual Studio presents the Extract Method dialog box shown in Figure 10.11. This dialog box presents the new method name (NewMethod by default) and the method signature. If the method signature does not look right, you can cancel the operation and refine your code selection. In this case, the method is private; static; returns an Order object; and takes customerId, orderId, and DataAccess objects. We do not want the latter in our function signature but deal with this momentarily.

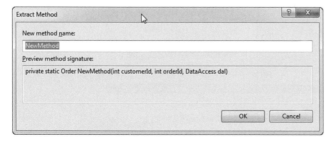

FIGURE 10.11   Extracting code from an existing method to a new method.

4. Rename the method to something meaningful. In this case, rename it to **InitCustomerOrder**.

5. Click the OK button to allow the method to be extracted.

6. The new method is created, and the old method is replaced by the following call:

```
Order order = InitCustomerOrder(customerId, orderId, dal);
```

You still have one issue with the extracted method: It takes an instance of `DataAccess` when you would prefer that it created its own instance. Fortunately, you can use another refactoring operation to deal with this issue. In this case, use the Remove Parameters refactor. This refactoring operation is covered later in this chapter. It is important to point out that removing the parameter results in removing it from both the method signature and the call to the method. It does not, however, put the call to create that `DataAccess` object inside the new method (nor does it remove it from the old method). You must take these steps manually.

Next, let's extract the call to get order items. Begin by selecting lines 16 through 25 (see Listing 10.1). Note that we do not want to select the call to set the order's property (line 26); we simply want to return an object that represents all line items for a given order. Figure 10.12 shows the selection and method extraction. In this case, name the new method **GetOrderItems**. After the method is extracted, it is replaced by the following call to the new method:

```
List<OrderItem> items = GetOrderItems(orderId, dal);
```

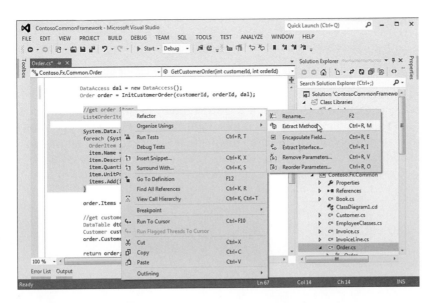

FIGURE 10.12   Extracting code to a method to return order items.

Again you have the issue with the DataAccess object being passed into the new method. You solve this issue in the same manner as you did previously.

Finally, let's look at extracting the portion of the method that gets the customer details. By now, this procedure should be reasonably straightforward. You select the code (lines 29 and 30) and choose the Extract Method operation. You name the new method **GetShopper** and deal with the extracted DataAccess parameter.

The newly organized (and much shorter) method looks like Listing 10.2. In addition, you now have three new tight, discrete methods that you may be able to reuse in the future (and perhaps make public). These new methods are in Listing 10.3.

LISTING 10.2   The Static Method After the Extractions

```
public static Order GetCustomerOrder(int customerId, int orderId) {

  Order order = InitCustomerOrder(customerId, orderId);

  //get order items
  List<OrderItem> items = GetOrderItems(orderId);
  order.Items = items;

  //get customer details
  Shopper cust = GetShopper(customerId);
  order.Customer = cust;

  return order;

}
```

LISTING 10.3   The Extractions

```
private static Shopper GetShopper(int customerId) {

  DataAccess.DAL dal = new DataAccess.DAL();

  System.Data.DataTable dtCustomer = dal.GetData("customer", customerId);
  Shopper cust = new Shopper(customerId);
  return cust;
}

private static List<OrderItem> GetOrderItems(int orderId) {

  DataAccess.DAL dal = new DataAccess.DAL();

  List<OrderItem> items = new List<OrderItem>();
  System.Data.DataTable dtItems = dal.GetData("orderItems", orderId);
```

```
  foreach (System.Data.DataRow r in dtItems.Rows) {
    OrderItem item = new OrderItem((int)r["product_id"], orderId);
    item.Name = (string)r["name"];
    item.Description = (string)r["description"];
    item.Quantity = (int)r["quantity"];
    item.UnitPrice = (double)r["unit_price"];
    items.Add(item);
  }
  return items;

}


private static Order InitCustomerOrder(int customerId, int orderId) {

  DataAccess.DAL dal = new DataAccess.DAL();
  Order order = new Order();

  //get order details
  System.Data.DataTable dtOrder = dal.GetData("customerOrder", orderId);

  //validate order against customer
  if (customerId != (int)dtOrder.Rows[0]["customer_id"]) {
    throw new ApplicationException("Invalid order for the given customer.");
  }
  order.Id = (int)dtOrder.Rows[0]["id"];
  return order;

}
```

> **NOTE**
>
> Extract Method does not allow you to choose where to put the extracted method. Many times, you might find a bit of code that really needs to be extracted into a method of another, different class. For this, you have to extract the method and then move things around manually.

Extracting a Single Line of Code

Sometimes, you might want to extract a single line of code or a portion of a line of code as its own method. For example, you might have a calculation that is done as part of a line of code but is common enough to warrant its own method. Alternatively, you might need to extract an object assignment to add additional logic to it. In either case, the C# code editor supports this type of extraction.

Let's look at an example. Suppose you have the following line of code that calculates an order's total inside a loop through the order items list:

```
total = total + item.Quantity * item.UnitPrice;
```

You might want to extract the portion of the assignment that calculates a line item's total (quantity * unit price). To do so, you select the portion of code and invoke the Extract Method refactor. Figure 10.13 shows this operation in action.

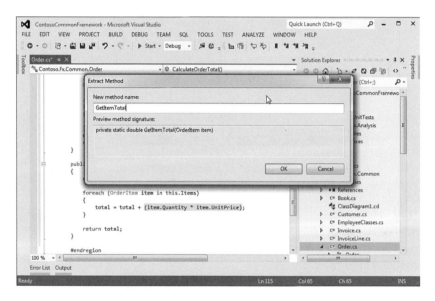

FIGURE 10.13   Extracting a portion of a line of code.

Notice that, by default, the new method would like an instance of OrderItem. You might prefer to pass both quantity and unit price instead. You would have to make this change manually. Alternatively, if quantity and unit price were assigned to variables before the extraction was done, you would get a new method that accepted these parameters (instead of an OrderItem instance). Figure 10.14 demonstrates this fact.

The resulting refactor replaces a portion of the line of code with the following:

```
total = total + GetItemTotal(qty, unitPrice);
```

It also adds the new method as follows:

```
private static double GetItemTotal(int qty, double unitPrice) {
  return qty * unitPrice;
}
```

10

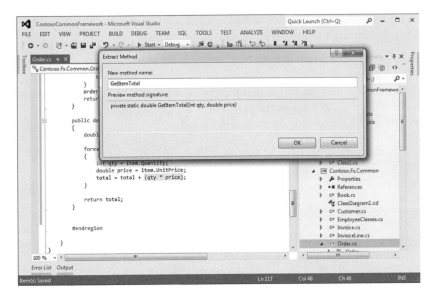

FIGURE 10.14   An alternative extraction of a portion of a line of code.

Generate Method Stub

You can get Visual Studio to automatically generate a method stub for you. This is not strictly a refactoring operation but can provide some similar increases in productivity. The scenario where this is applicable is as follows. Suppose you are writing code that calls a method from one of your objects. However, that method does not exist. You can still write code to make the call to the nonexistent method. Visual Studio then recognizes that this method does not exist and provides you with a smart tag (see Figure 10.15) to create the method.

Clicking the smart tag results in Visual Studio extracting the method call to a newly generated method in the target assembly and class. Figure 10.16 shows the new method. Note that Visual Studio provides a readable name for the method's parameter provided you used a variable inside the calling method.

Extract Interface

When classes contain the same subset of members, defining a common contract that each class shares can be useful. You do this, of course, via an interface. Some basic advantages to defining interfaces are that your code becomes more readable, is easier to maintain, and operates the same for like members. However, developers often don't realize the commonality between their classes until after those classes are coded. This sometimes makes creating interfaces a painful operation.

The C# editor in Visual Studio provides the Extract Interface refactoring operation to make this process easier. It enables you to take an existing class or struct and automatically generate a matching interface that the existing class then implements.

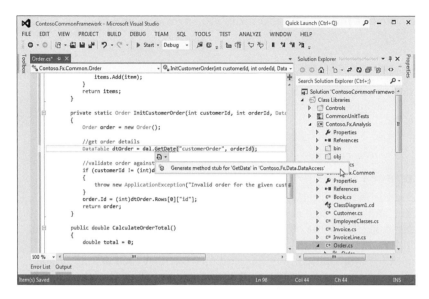

FIGURE 10.15   Generate a method stub for a nonexistent method.

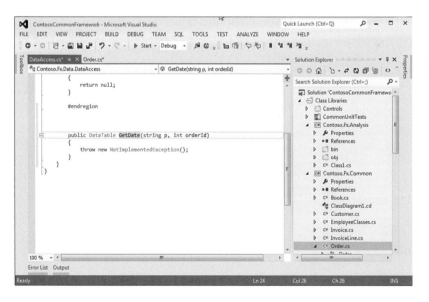

FIGURE 10.16   The generated method stub.

Accessing the Extract Interface Refactor

To access the Extract Interface refactor operation, you first must position your cursor in a class, a struct, or another interface that contains the members you want to extract. You then can use the Refactor menu and select the Extract Interface menu item. You can also invoke Extract Interface from the context menu via a right-click and from the class designer.

Extracting Interfaces

To better understand the Extract Interface operation, let's look at an example. Suppose you review your code and notice that a number of your domain objects share similar properties and methods. Let's say the objects Customer, Vendor, and Employee all contain properties for Id and Name, and methods for Save and Delete. In this case, you should consider extracting this commonality into a standard interface that each of your domain objects would implement. Let's look at how the Extract Interface refactoring operation aids in this regard.

First, you position your cursor on the target class whose members you want to extract. In the example, choose the Vendor class. Invoking the Extract Interface operation presents a dialog box named the same. Figure 10.17 shows this dialog box relative to the example.

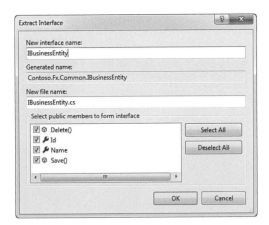

FIGURE 10.17   Extracting an interface.

Notice that you first define a name for the interface. By default, the tool names the interface with the name of the class preceded by the letter *I* for *interface* (in this case, IVendor). Of course, we are going to use our interface across our domain, so we change this to **IBusinessEntity**.

The Extract Interface dialog box also shows the generated name and the new filename for the interface. The generated name is simply the fully qualified name of the interface.

This is used by the class for implementation of the interface. The New File Name text box shows the C# filename for the interface. All extracted interfaces result in the creation of a new file. The tool tries to keep the filename in sync with the interface name.

The last thing to do is select which members of the object you want to publish as an interface. Of course, only public members are displayed in this list. For this example, select all of the available public members: Id, Name, Save, and Delete.

Clicking the OK button generates the interface. The only change that is made to the Vendor class is that it now implements the new interface, as in the following line of code:

```
public class Vendor : IBusinessEntity
```

The interface is then extracted to a new file. Listing 10.4 shows the newly extracted interface.

LISTING 10.4   The Extracted Interface

```
using System;
namespace Contoso.Fx.Common
{
    interface IBusinessEntity
    {
        void Delete();
        string Description { get; set; }
        int Id { get; set; }
        string Name { get; set; }
        void Save();
    }

}
```

The next step in the example is to go out to each additional domain object and implement the new interface. This has to be done without the benefit of refactoring. However, Visual Studio provides a smart tag for implementing an interface. Figure 10.18 shows the smart tag that results from typing IBusinessEntity after the Vendor class declaration.

In this case, you have two options: Implement the interface or explicitly implement the interface. The former checks the current class to see whether there are implementations that apply. The latter generates code that explicitly calls the interface items. It puts all this code inside a region for the given interface. This capability can be very useful if you're stubbing out a new class based on the interface. The following lines of code provide an example of an explicit interface member declaration:

```
void IBusinessEntity.Save() {
  throw new NotImplementedException();
}
```

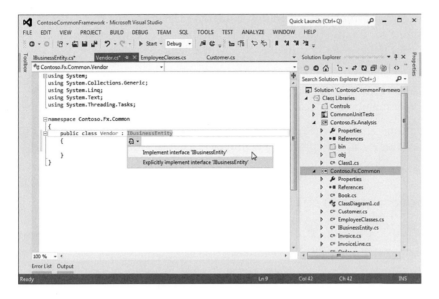

FIGURE 10.18   Implementing an interface.

Refactor Parameters

You sometimes need to change your method signatures by removing an item, by adding a local variable as a parameter, or by reordering the existing parameters. These changes require that all calls to the method also be changed. Doing this manually can introduce new bugs into the code. For example, suppose you want to swap the order of two parameters with the same type (int, for example). If you forget to change a call to the method, it might still work; it just won't work right. These bugs can be challenging to find. Therefore, Visual Studio provides refactoring operations for removing, promoting, and reordering parameters.

Remove Parameters

The Remove Parameters refactor operation enables you to select one or more parameters from a given method, constructor, or delegate and have it or them removed from the method. It also works to update any callers to the method and remove the value passed to the parameter.

You invoke the Remove Parameters operation by positioning your cursor inside the method signature and then selecting the Remove Parameters menu item from the Refactor menu. You can also get to this operation through the context menu (right-click). In addition, this operation is available from the class designer from inside both the class designer and the Class Details window.

To invoke the Remove Parameters operation from the keyboard, first position your cursor in the method that contains the parameters you want to remove. Next, play the keyboard chord Ctrl+R, Ctrl+V.

Let's look at an example. Suppose you have a method with the following signature:

```
public static Order GetCustomerOrder(int customerId, int orderId)
```

This method returns an `Order` object based on both a customer and an order identification number. Suppose you determine that the order ID is sufficient for returning an order. In this case, you invoke the Remove Parameters refactor and are then presented with the Remove Parameters dialog box (see Figure 10.19). Method parameters are listed at the top. To remove one, you select it and click the Remove button. The item to be removed is then updated with strikethrough. If you change your mind, you can use the Restore button to cancel individual parameter removals.

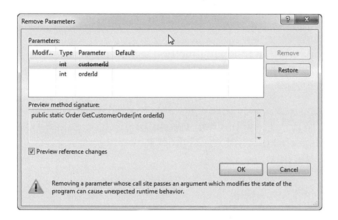

FIGURE 10.19   The Remove Parameters dialog box.

When you are ready to make the removal, you can choose to preview the changes or simply apply them all simultaneously. The preview option works the same as other previews. It shows you each change in a tree view and enables you to see the details behind the change. You can, of course, also uncheck specific changes. When finished, you apply the final set of removals to your code.

It is common to declare a local variable inside a method and pass that local variable in a call to another method. If you use the refactoring operation to remove the parameter on the method you are calling, the local variable still exists in your calling method. Be careful to make sure that this is what you intended; if not, you have to remove the local variable manually.

Reorder Parameters

You move parameters around in a method typically just for readability and maintenance. You might want the more important parameters to appear first on the method signature, or you might try to keep the order similar across like methods or overloads. The Reorder Parameters refactor operation enables you to change the order in which parameters exist on a given method, constructor, or delegate. It also works to update any callers to the method and rearrange the parameters passed on the call.

You invoke the Reorder Parameters operation by positioning your cursor inside the method signature that contains the parameters you want to reorder and then selecting the Reorder Parameters menu item from the Refactor menu. You can also get to this operation through the context menu (right-click). In addition, this operation is available from the class designer.

TIP

To invoke the Reorder Parameters operation from the keyboard, first position your cursor in the method that contains the parameters you want to rearrange. Next, play the keyboard chord Ctrl+R, Ctrl+O.

Let's look at an example. Suppose you have the following method signature:

```
private static Order InitCustomerOrder(int customerId, int orderId, DataAccess dal)
```

This method is called `InitCustomerOrder`. Suppose that you want to make the first parameter `orderId` instead of `customerId`. To do so, you position the cursor on the method and invoke the Reorder Parameters refactor. This presents the Reorder Parameters dialog box (see Figure 10.20).

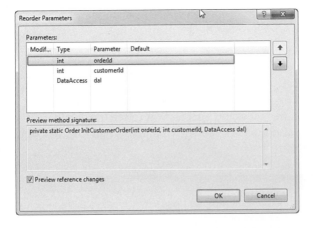

FIGURE 10.20   The Reorder Parameters dialog box.

This dialog box enables you to modify the order of the parameters on the given method. At the top, it lists all the parameters of the method. To the right of this list, there are two buttons. The up-arrow button moves the selected parameter in the list up. The down-arrow button does the opposite. You use these buttons to get the order of the parameters the way you want them. Figure 10.20 shows this example loaded into the Reorder Parameters dialog box.

Notice that as you change parameter order, the resulting method signature is displayed below the parameter list. You also have the option to preview any changes that are made to callers of the method. Clicking the OK button applies the changes to both the method and its callers.

Encapsulate Field

It's common to have a private field in your object from which you need to create a property. These fields might have been built as private because they were used only internally to the object. Alternatively, a developer might have simply defined a public field instead of encapsulating it as a property. In either case, if you need to make an actual property out of a field, you can do so with the Encapsulate Field refactor operation.

Accessing Encapsulate Field

The Encapsulate Field operation enables you to quickly generate properties from a given field. Properties, of course, enable you to protect the field from direct access and to know when the given field is being modified or accessed. To encapsulate a field, you position your cursor over the field and select the Encapsulate Field option from the Refactor menu. You can also do use the context menu (right-click) or the class designer.

> **TIP**
>
> To invoke the Encapsulate Field operation from the keyboard, first position your cursor on the field that you want to encapsulate. Next, play the keyboard chord Ctrl+R, Ctrl+F.

The Encapsulate Field Dialog Box

The Encapsulate Field dialog box, shown in Figure 10.21, enables you to set a few options for this refactor. First, it presents the field you are refactoring in a read-only text box. Next, it enables you to define a name for the new property. The good news is that the tool tries to name your property correctly. For example, if you have a private field named _rating, the tool chooses Rating for the property name by default.

An additional option on this dialog box is the choice of which references you would like to have updated. This refers to existing references to the field. Suppose you have a public field. This field might be called both from within the object that defines the field and by other, external objects. You might want to force external callers to use the new property.

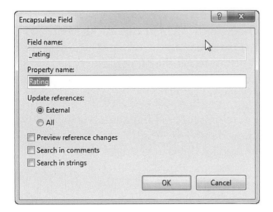

FIGURE 10.21   The Encapsulate Field dialog box.

For this, you would use the External setting. In this case, the object that contains the field would still reference the local, private field (and not the property). Setting the Update Reference option to All results in both the external and internal callers using the property.

When you apply the encapsulation, the tool changes your internal field to private (if it was not already private) and then generates a property. The property includes both `get` and `set` accessors for the field. If the field was declared as read-only, the encapsulation generates only a `get` accessor.

Let's look at the code. Suppose you have the following field declaration:

```
private int _rating;
```

You want to encapsulate this private into a public property. The code that is generated is as follows:

```
private int _rating;
public int Rating {
    get { return _rating; }
    set { _rating = value; }
}
```

In addition, should you choose the All value for the update references option in the Encapsulate Field dialog box, your internal callers to the field (the field was private) would be updated to use the property internally.

Summary

This chapter showed how the refactoring tools built in to the C# editor for Visual Studio can greatly increase productivity and decrease unwanted side effects (bugs) when you're making sweeping changes to your code to improve maintenance, reuse, and readability. The refactoring tools don't simply make changes using text searches and replacements;

they use the Visual Studio compiler to make and validate the code changes and this improves confidence in, and reliability of, the tools.

These tools can be accessed using the keyboard, the Refactor menu, a context menu, the class designer, and elsewhere. The refactoring tools enable you to change your code in many ways. You can easily rename items in your code. You can take existing lines of code and extract them to new methods. Your objects can be used as the basis to define new interfaces. You can modify method signatures using the Remove and Reorder refactoring operations. Finally, you can take existing fields and quickly encapsulate them into properties.

CHAPTER 11

Debugging Code

Today's developers might spend as much time debugging their code as they do writing it. This is due in some part to the nature of today's highly dependent and distributed applications. These applications are built to leverage existing functionality, frameworks, building blocks, libraries, and so on. In addition, they often communicate with other applications, services, components, databases, and even data exchanges. Developers also demand more assistance from their debugger to help increase their productivity. The Visual Studio debugger addresses these needs by enabling some great debugging scenarios. Some highlights include the following:

▶ Breakpoint and tracepoint management

▶ Visualizers and debugger DataTips

▶ Edit and Continue

▶ Just-my-code debugging

▶ The Exception Assistant

▶ Debugging support at design time

▶ Client-side script debugging

▶ Support for debugging WCF applications

▶ Debugging support for LINQ

▶ Debugging multithreaded and parallel code

▶ Remote debugging

We cover all of these features and more in this chapter. Of course, if you are just getting started with .NET, more than just this list is new to you. The Visual Studio debugger has been evolving since the first release of .NET, which provided a unified debugger with the capability to debug across languages. In this chapter, we start by covering the basics of debugging an application. We then discuss the Visual Studio debugger in depth.

Debugging Basics

A typical scenario for a developer is to start building a web page or form and build up the code that surrounds it. In addition, the developer might rely on a framework or a few building blocks that provide added functionality. The application might also communicate with a services layer and most often a database. Even the most typical applications have a lot of moving parts. These moving parts make the task of finding and eliminating errors in the code all the more complex. The tools that help you track down and purge errors from your code not only have to keep up with this complexity, but also must ease the effort involved with the debugging process. In the following sections, we cover how a developer uses the tools built into Visual Studio to debug a typical development scenario.

The Scenario

We want to define an application scenario that we can use both to introduce the basics of debugging and to function as a base for us to build on throughout the chapter when demonstrating the many features of the debugging tools. In this scenario, imagine you are writing a web application with all of the typical moving parts:

▶ It stores data in a SQL database.

▶ A data access library abstracts all access to the database.

▶ A variety of different technologies are involved in the solution, including JavaScript, an MVC-based web user interface (UI), and class libraries written in C#.

Even though we concentrate on C#, the debugging tools in Visual Studio are equally applicable to Visual Basic development. Everything we discuss here applies to both languages unless specified otherwise.

The Many Phases of Debugging

Nearly every time developers open the IDE, they are in some way debugging their code. The line between debugging and writing code, in fact, is becoming more and more blurred. For example, the code editor helps eliminate errors in your code as you write it. It highlights items where errors are present and enables you to fix them. You are then both writing and debugging simultaneously.

In addition, the compiler acts as another debugging tool. The first time you click the Run button, the compiler checks your code and reports a list of errors for you to fix before continuing. This is debugging. The steps or phases of the debugging process include the following:

- **Coding**—The editor helps you by pointing out issues and possible resolutions.

- **Compiling**—The compiler checks your code and reports errors before continuing.

- **Self-checking**—You run the application in debug mode and step through screens and code to verify functionality.

- **Unit testing**—You write and run unit tests to check your application (see Chapter 9, "Testing Code").

- **Code analysis**—You run the Static Code Analyzer to verify that your application meets project standards (requires Visual Studio Premium).

- **Code review**—Your code is reviewed by a peer or an architect and issues are logged accordingly.

- **Responding to bug**—When a bug has been logged against the code, you must re-create and debug a specific scenario.

In this chapter, we concentrate on two of these phases: self-checking and responding to bugs. These are the two phases in which developers get the most use of the debugging tools built in to Visual Studio. For the purposes of this chapter, we assume that the code is written and that it compiles. Let's start by looking at how to self-check the code.

Debugging the Application (Self-Checking)

In this scenario, you have just started writing a web page to edit a customer's profile. Assume that you've laid out the page, connected to the profile web service, and written the code to save a user's profile to the database. You now need to start self-checking your work to make sure that everything operates as you expect.

> **NOTE**
>
> If you want to follow along, the code we have used in this chapter comes predominantly from the Contoso University sample application that Microsoft provides to demonstrate construction of an MVC-based web application. Search for "Contoso University" on the Microsoft Developer Network (MSDN) site to find the download location for the entire Visual Studio solution.

The first step is to start your application in debug mode. This allows you to break into your code if an error occurs. In development, this is typically your default setting. You first invoke debug mode by clicking the Run button (the green arrow on either the Standard or the Debug toolbar). Figure 11.1 shows the sample application about to be run in debug mode for the first time. Notice that for web applications, you can choose which browser to use out of all the installed browsers on your machine. In this case, we are selecting Internet Explorer.

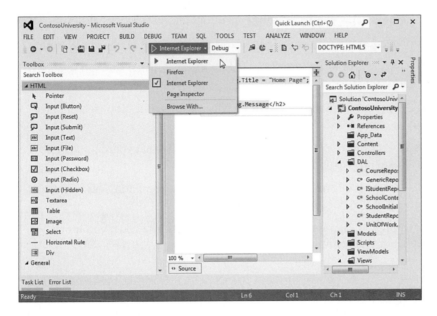

FIGURE 11.1   Use the Run button to start the application in debug mode.

Enabling Debugging on a Website

This example is a web application. Therefore, it requires you to set up debugging on server-side code whose errors and information are output to a remote client. Of course, in the vast majority of cases, developers code and debug on a single development machine. However, sometimes you might have to debug a process on a test server.

In either case, you have to enable debugging through a setting in the configuration file (web.config) for your application. If debugging isn't currently enabled for the web application, and you run the application with debugging, then Visual Studio prompts you to enable debugging. Figure 11.2 shows this prompt. Clicking the OK button adds the appropriate configuration information to the file and starts the debugging session.

FIGURE 11.2   You can choose to allow Visual Studio to enable debugging of an ASP.NET site (and thus modify the Web.config for you).

> **NOTE**
>
> It is important that you turn off debugging in your config file before deploying your web application to production. Having debugging enabled in a production environment is a security risk. With debugging enabled, ASP.NET writes the details of your errors to a web page. These details provide valuable clues to would-be attackers about how your application is put together. In some instances, the error could include user credentials that are being used to access secured resources.

To turn off debug mode, you must edit the web configuration file. Specifically, you edit the Compilation element under the system.web node. You set debug equal to false (as in off). The following is an example of the XML with debug mode turned on:

```
<system.web>
  <compilation debug="true" targetFramework="4.0"/>

    ...

</system.web>
```

Starting in Debug Mode

The most typical scenario for starting a debug session is just clicking the Run button on the toolbar. This works with all application types including Windows and ASP.NET. This action instructs Visual Studio to compile the application and bring up the initial form or page.

Applications can also be started without debugging; this includes both Windows and ASP. NET applications. This capability is useful if you intend to attach to a running process or simply want to walk through an application as a user might see it (without breaking into the IDE). You use the Debug menu, Start Without Debugging option to start your application without attaching it to the Visual Studio Debugger. Figure 11.3 shows an example of invoking this action.

You can also start by stepping into code, line by line. This approach is useful if you want to see all of your code as it executes (rather than just errors). You might desire this if you are getting some unexpected behavior. Stepping line by line gives you an exact understanding of what is going on with your code (rather than just your assumed understanding).

Stepping into code on a web form is typically done by first opening the main source. You then right-click and select the Run to Cursor option from the shortcut menu. Figure 11.4 shows an example. This command tells Visual Studio to run the application until it gets to this point. At that time, the IDE opens into debug mode, where you can step through each line of code (or continue, and so on).

Breaking on an Error

Not everything you find in debug mode is an error that results in a break in the code. Often, issues arise just because you're looking at the behavior of the application. For example, a control could be out of place, the tab order could be wrong, and so on. For these items, you still have to rely on your eyes. The debugging tools in Visual Studio help you respond to hard errors in your code.

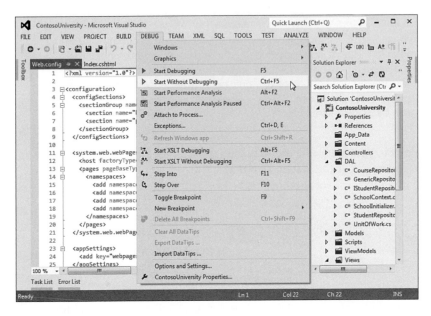

FIGURE 11.3   You can start an application without debugging turned on.

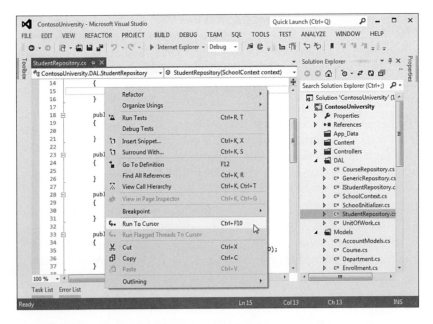

FIGURE 11.4   You can have Visual Studio run your application up to the current line of code and then break into debugging.

By default, when unhandled exceptions occur in your code, the IDE will break into the debugger and highlight the offending code. The key in that sentence is "unhandled exceptions." They represent places in your code where you do not have try-catch blocks to manage an exception. This is typically a good default setting. However, you often need to see handled exceptions as well.

Fortunately, the errors that result in a break in the IDE are a configurable set. For example, you might handle a specific exception in your code and not want to be dumped to the IDE every time it occurs. Rather, you want to be notified only of those exceptional conditions. The Exceptions dialog box allows you to manage the set of exceptions you're concerned with. You access this dialog box by choosing Debug, Exceptions (or pressing Ctrl+D, E in C# or Ctrl+Alt+E in VB). Figure 11.5 shows the dialog box.

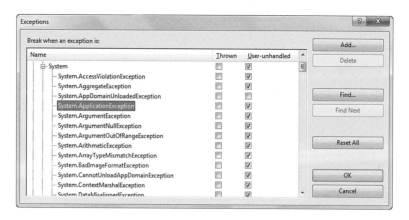

FIGURE 11.5   You can select the exceptions on which you want Visual Studio to break.

In the Exceptions dialog box, the various exceptions are categorized by namespace for easy access. (There is also a Find feature.) The two columns of check boxes are of primary interest: one for Thrown and one for User-unhandled. Notice that, by default, the setting for nearly all exceptions in the .NET Framework is User-unhandled. This indicates that the debugger should break execution only when a given exception is thrown and it is not handled by your code.

Adding Thrown to the mix tells the debugger to break execution even if you have code to handle a given exception. The debugger reacts by breaking on the line of the exception, before your handler is called. If you intend to use this option, you should consider simply setting it at the category level. For example, you might toggle Thrown for the entire category Common Language Runtime Exceptions. Setting up more granularity is certainly possible. However, doing so often results in more confusion as the debugger breaks in different places depending on the given exception thrown.

Debugging an Error

The first step in debugging your application is to click the Run button. Your application is then running in debug mode. As it happens, the sample application we discussed in our scenario throws an exception upon its initial startup. The debugger responds by breaking into the code and showing the offending line. Figure 11.6 shows a typical view of the editor when it breaks on an error.

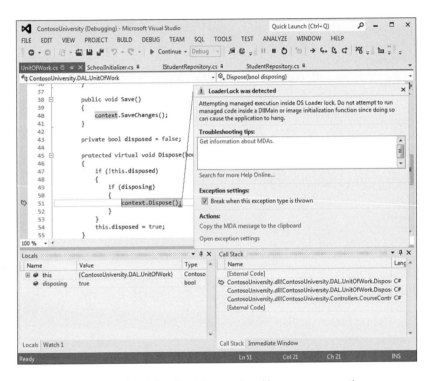

FIGURE 11.6   The Visual Studio debugger breaking on an exception.

There are a few items of interest about the standard debug session shown in Figure 11.6. First, Visual Studio has highlighted the line on which the error was thrown. You can see this clearly by the arrow and the highlighted text.

Next, notice the window in the upper right of the image. This is the Exception Assistant. It provides details on the exception and offers tips for troubleshooting and fixing the given issue. From this window, you can access a few actions, including searching online help for more information on the exception.

At the bottom of the screen are a few additional helpful windows. The Locals window on the left automatically shows the value assigned to all local variables in the code where the exception was thrown. This gives you easy access to key information that might be contributing to the issue. Notice that to the right of this window is an inactive tab called Watch 1 (bottom of screen). This is a watch window; it keeps track of any custom watch scenarios you set up (more on this later).

The window on the bottom right of the screen is the call stack. It shows the order in which various components of an application were called. You can look at the call stack to find out how you got to where you are. You can also use it to navigate to any code referenced in the stack. (See the section "Debugging Multithreaded Applications" later in this chapter for more on the call stack.) Finally, the inactive tab next to this gives you access to the Immediate Window. The Immediate window allows you to type in code commands and get the results in the editor (more on this to come).

Debugging Different Processes   After you examine the error in this example (Figure 11.6), you can see that it is being thrown inside the web service process. The code called by the web service is being run in a separate process from that of the startup application (the web user interface). When you debug an application, you debug (or shadow) a running process such as an executable (.exe). Visual Studio, by default, considers the startup application's process as the primary process being debugged.

To debug code that is running in a different process (such as the web service process), you must both have the source code and be attached to the executing process (running a debug build). If all the code for a given application is in a single solution, Visual Studio automatically attaches to each process. In the example, this includes both the web user interface process and the web service process. Therefore, in this case, you do not need to manually attach to another process.

The debugger does not, however, automatically break into the IDE on errors raised outside of the startup process. Instead, it respects breakpoints you set inside code executing in other processes. If an error is thrown in a separate process (and no related breakpoints exist in that process), the debugger breaks into the IDE inside the process that called into the process that threw the error.

For example, if you have both a web UI application and a web service, each of these could run in a separate process. Therefore, even if both code projects are in the same solution, when the IDE encounters the error from the web service, it would break in the web UI application (and not on the web service) as the web UI application was the startup (and attached-to) process. To debug the error in the web service, you would need to set a breakpoint in the web service code (or step into that code from the web UI application).

> **NOTE**
>
> Recall that you need to enable debugging for web applications using the configuration file (web.config). This holds true for web service applications as well. Refer to Figure 11.2 for details.

Sometimes you need to manually attach to an already-running process. You might want to attach the IDE to a running web server, or you might have a web service application (as in the example) to which you want to bind debugging. Whatever the scenario, Visual Studio allows you to attach to the process and begin a debug session. To attach to a running process, like a web server, you choose the Attach to Process option from the Debug menu. This brings up the dialog box shown in Figure 11.7.

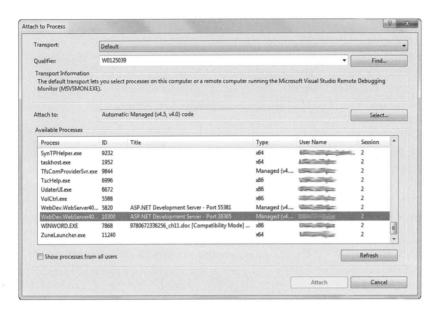

FIGURE 11.7   You can attach the debugger to a running process (such as a web server).

To connect the Visual Studio debugger to a process, you simply highlight it and click the Attach button (as shown in Figure 11.7). Note that any currently attached processes are grayed out. This is a visual indicator that you are already attached to a given process. In this example, the web UI process is grayed out. You can see that you can add the service process to the debug session. Clicking attach means that you are debugging both processes. Therefore, if you attach to the web service process prior to making a call to it, the IDE also breaks inside the web service code (provided it contains errors).

Setting a Breakpoint   To get the debugger to break into your code when it reaches a specific line, you set a breakpoint on that line. You do so by clicking on the indicator bar for the given line. Alternatively, you can right-click on the line and choose Insert Breakpoint from the Breakpoint context menu (see Figure 11.8).

Continuing the Debugging   If you have navigated off the executing code during a debug session, it can often be hard to find your way back. The line that was executing could be buried in any one of the open code windows. Thus, Visual Studio provides the Show Next Statement button (yellow arrow icon) on the Debug toolbar to take you back, effectively returning you to the line of code that was executing when the debugger broke.

In our example, we want to rerun a call to the data access layer without restarting the application. This allows you to hit your new breakpoint and step through the code. You must move the current execution point in the code by right-clicking the line where you want execution to start (or rerun) and selecting Set Next Statement from the context menu. Figure 11.9 shows this menu option.

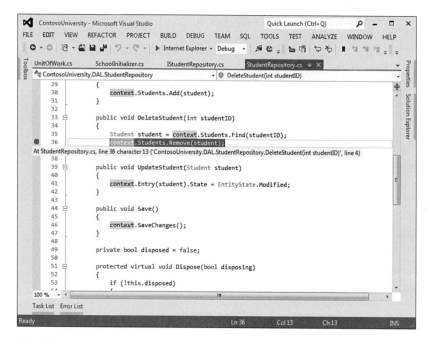

FIGURE 11.8   You can set a breakpoint on a specific line of code.

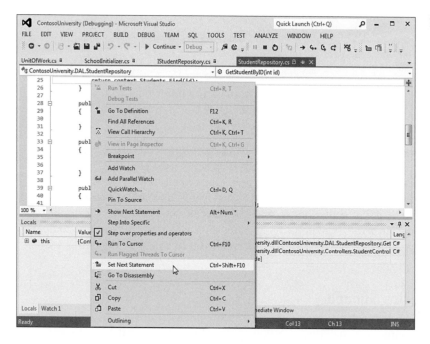

FIGURE 11.9   You can back up in your code using Set Next Statement.

Now that you have backed up the execution point, you are ready to continue the debugging by clicking the Run button again. This is essentially indicating that you are done with the break and want to continue execution (until an error is caught or a breakpoint is hit).

Stepping to Find the Error   In the example, the debugger now breaks execution as soon as it hits the breakpoint in the data access layer. This allows you to step through the code. To step line by line through the code, you can click the Step Into button on the Debug toolbar (or press the F11 function key). This executes the code one line at a time, enabling you to view both execution flow and the state of the application as code executes.

In most scenarios, you can make a fix to bugs found during the debug session and continue stepping through or running the code; this is referred to as Edit and Continue. However, there are certain scenarios where this is not supported. You cannot invoke Edit and Continue when the debugger has been attached to an already running process. Figure 11.10 shows the message you get when you try.

FIGURE 11.10   Visual Studio throws an Edit and Continue error when trying to edit code in a process that it did not start (and you attached to).

Instead of using Edit and Continue, you can bookmark the line where you want to make the change using the Text Editor toolbar. You then click the Stop button on the Debug toolbar to stop the debug session. The code change can now be made.

To continue through self-checking, you restart the debugging process. However, before restarting, you might want to clear the breakpoint you set by selecting the Debug menu, Windows, and then Breakpoints. (you can also add a Breakpoints command button to your debug toolbar to accomplish the same task). This brings up the Breakpoints window shown in Figure 11.11. From this window, you can view all breakpoints in the application. Here, you select and clear the breakpoint by clicking the Delete button from the toolbar on the Breakpoints pane. Finally, you click the Run button to continue the debug self-check session.

Debugging Basics Summary

This scenario walked through the many phases of debugging a simple error, and introducing basics of debugging in Visual Studio. If you are familiar with prior IDE versions, you probably noticed a lot of similarities.

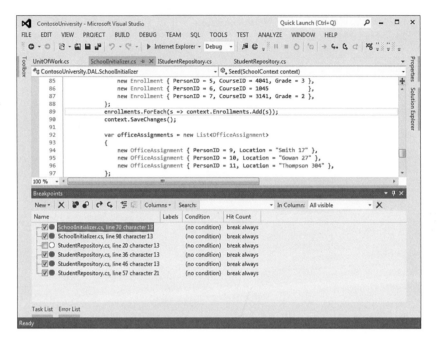

FIGURE 11.11   You can manage your breakpoints using the Breakpoints window.

Walking through the scenario demonstrated the many tools inside the debugging environment, including the Debug toolbar and menu, the Breakpoints window, the watch window, and so on. Now that you have a grasp of the basics, in the next section we intend to explore these debug elements in greater detail.

The Visual Studio Debugger

The debugger built in to Visual Studio 2012 is one of the largest and most complex tools in the IDE. With such a large feature-set area, we cannot possibly cover every scenario you might encounter. In this next section, however, we hope to expose the most commonly applicable features.

The Debug Menu and Toolbar

The Debug menu and its related toolbar provide your first-level access to starting debug sessions, stepping into code, managing breakpoints, and accessing the many features of debugging with Visual Studio. There are two states to the debug menu: at rest (or inactive) and in debug mode. Figure 11.12 shows the menu in the at-rest state.

In the at-rest state, the Debug menu provides features to start a debug session, attach code to a running process, or access some of the many debug windows. Table 11.1 lists all the features available from the Debug menu at rest.

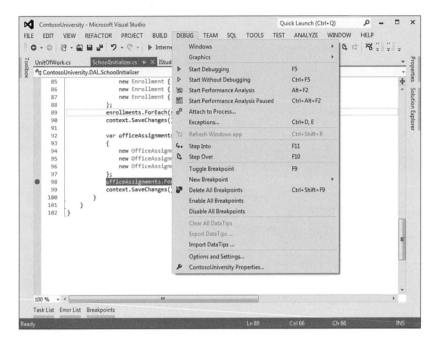

FIGURE 11.12   The Debug menu outside of a debug session.

TABLE 11.1   Debug Menu Items at Rest

Menu Item	Description
Windows, Breakpoints	Opens the Breakpoints window in the IDE. This window provides access to all the breakpoints in the option solution.
Windows, Output	Shows the Output window in the IDE. The Output window is a running log of the many messages that are emitted by the IDE, the compiler, and the debugger. Therefore, the information transcends just debug sessions.
Windows, Immediate	Opens the Immediate window in the IDE. This window allows you to execute commands. For example, during application design, you can call your methods directly from the Immediate window. This will start the application and enter directly into a debug session.
Start Debugging	Starts your application in debug mode.
Start Without Debugging	Starts your application without connecting the debugger to the executing process. In this mode, the developer sees what users would see (instead of breaking into the IDE for errors and breakpoints).
Start Performance Analysis	Starts your application and connects the Visual Studio profiler to the process.

Menu Item	Description
Start Performance Analysis Paused	Same as above, but immediately pauses the performance profiler. This is useful if you first want to perform a set of actions within the application, and then unpause the profiler to capture performance information about a specific function or feature.
Attach to Process	Allows you to attach the debugger (and your code) to a running process (executable). If, for example, you started the application without debugging, you could then attach to that running process and begin debugging.
Exceptions	Opens the Exceptions Option dialog box. This dialog box enables you to choose how the debugger breaks on any given exception.
Refresh Windows app	Reloads your application process without restarting the debugger itself. This allows you to make a change to your applications source code, refresh the app process with the new code, and not interrupt the debugger itself.
Step Into	Starts the application in debug mode. For most projects, clicking the Step Into command invokes the debugger on the first executing line of the application. In this way, you can step into the application from the first line.
Step Over	When not in a debug session, the Step Over command simply starts the application the same way as clicking the Run button would.
Toggle Breakpoint	Toggles the breakpoint on or off for the current, active line of code in a text editor. The option is inactive if you do not have a code window active in the IDE.
New Breakpoint, Break at Function	Brings up the New Breakpoint dialog box. This dialog box enables you to indicate a function name to define for which to create a breakpoint. This can be useful if you know a function's name but do not want to search your code files for it.
New Breakpoint, New Data Breakpoint	This option is available only for native, C++ applications. It allows you to define a breakpoint that breaks into the IDE when a value in a specific memory location changes.
Delete All Breakpoints	Removes all breakpoints from your solution.
Enable All Breakpoints	Enables all the breakpoints in your solution.
Disable All Breakpoints	Disables (without removing) all the breakpoints in your solution.
Clear All DataTips	Enables you to clear any data tips you might have pinned to the IDE (including comments). See "DataTips" later in this chapter.
Export DataTips	Allows you to export your data tips as an XML file for sharing with other developers. See "DataTips" later in this chapter.

11

Menu Item	Description
Import DataTips	Allows you to import an XML data tips file for use inside your debug sessions. See DataTips later in this chapter.
Options and Settings	Brings up the Options dialog box for debugging. See "Debug Options" later in this chapter.
(project) Properties	Brings up the Properties dialog box for the current project.

When the debugger is engaged and you are working through a debug session, the state of the Debug menu changes. It now provides several additional options over those provided by the at-rest state. These options include those designed to move through the code, restart the session, and access even more debug-related windows. Figure 11.13 shows the Debug menu during a debug session.

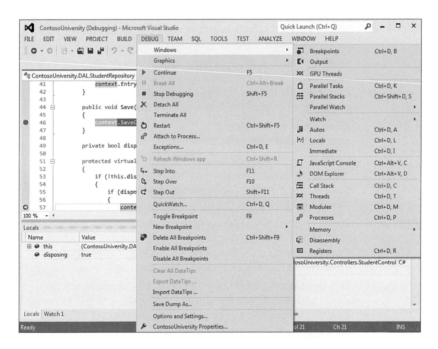

FIGURE 11.13   The Debug menu during a debug session.

Let's look at the many options provided by the Debug menu during a debug session. Table 11.2 presents the many items available from the debug menu in this state. When reading through the table, refer to the preceding figures to get context on any given item.

TABLE 11.2   Debug Menu Items for an Active Debug Session

Menu Item	Description
Windows, Breakpoints	Allows you to open the Breakpoints window during a debug session.
Windows, Output	Opens the Output window during an active debug session in order to read output messages emitted by the compiler and debugger.
Windows, GPU Threads	Opens a window for inspection of any active GPU threads spawned by your application.
Windows, Parallel Tasks	Enables you to view parallel tasks in a visual window. See "Debugging Parallel Applications" later in this chapter.
Windows, Parallel Stacks	Enables you to view executing threads and tasks in a visual window. See "Debugging Parallel Applications" later in this chapter.
Windows, Parallel Watch	Enables you to evaluate watch expressions spanning multiple or even all available threads.
Windows, Watch	Opens one of many possible watch windows in the IDE. Watch windows represent items and expressions you are keeping a close eye on through a debug session.
Windows, Autos	Opens the Autos window. This window shows variables (and their values) in the current line of code and the preceding line of code.
Windows, Locals	Opens the Locals window in the IDE. This window shows variables in the local scope (function).
Windows, Immediate	Opens the Immediate window where you can execute a command.
Windows, Immediate	Opens the Immediate window where you can execute a command.
JavaScript Console	Available for web applications, this launches the JavaScript Console window. This console enables you to execute JavaScript against the currently loaded Document Object Model (DOM).
DOM Explorer	Allows you to drill down into the currently loaded Document Object Model (DOM), and easily view property settings at any point within the DOM tree.
Windows, Call Stack	Shows the list of functions that are on the stack. Also indicates the current stack frame (function). This selected item is what defines the content from the Locals, watch, and Autos windows.
Windows, Threads	Shows the Threads window in the IDE. From here, you can view and control the threads in the application you are debugging.
Windows, Modules	Shows the Modules window in the IDE. This window lists the DLLs and EXEs used by your application.
Windows, Processes	Shows the Processes window in the IDE. This window lists the processes to which the debug session is attached.

Menu Item	Description
Windows, Memory	Opens the Memory window for a view at the memory used by your application. This is valid only when address-level debugging is enabled from the Options dialog box.
Windows, Disassembly	Opens the Disassembly window. This window shows the assembly code corresponding to the compiler instructions. This is valid only when address-level debugging is enabled from the Options dialog box.
Windows, Registers	Opens the Registers window so that you can see register values change as you step through code. This is valid only when address-level debugging is enabled from the Options dialog box.
Continue	Continues executing the application after broken into the IDE. The application continues running on the active line of code (the breakpoint, a line that threw an error, or a line set using Set Next Statement).
Break All	Enables you to break the application into the debugger manually (without having to hit a breakpoint) during a debug session. The application breaks on the next line that executes. This capability is useful to gain access to the debug information such as watch windows. It can also be used to gain access to the debug session when your application appears to have hung.
Stop Debugging	Terminates the debugging session. It also terminates the process you are debugging, provided that the process was started by Visual Studio.
Detach All	Detaches the debugger from the executing process. This enables your application to continue running after the debugger is through with it.
Terminate All	Stops debugging and terminates all processes to which you are attached.
Restart	Stops the debugging session and restarts it. Similar to clicking both Stop Debugging and Start Debugging in sequence.
Attach to Process	Enables you to attach the active debug session to one or more additional processes such as an executing web server or a Windows service.
Exceptions	Brings up the Exceptions dialog box, which enables you to manage how the IDE breaks on specific exception types in the .NET Framework and other libraries.
Step Into	Advances the debugger a line. If you choose to "step into" a function, the debugger does so line by line.
Step Over	Functions the same as Step Into with one major difference: If you choose to "step over" a function, the line calling the function is executed (along with the function), and the debugger sets the next line after the function call as the next line to be debugged.

Menu Item	Description
Step Out	Tells the debugger to execute the current function and then break back into debugging after the function has finished. This capability is useful if you step into a function but then want to have that function just execute and yet return you to debug mode when it is complete.
QuickWatch	Brings up the QuickWatch window when the debugger is in break mode. The QuickWatch window shows one variable or expression you are watching and its value.
Toggle Breakpoint	Turns an active breakpoint on or off.
New Breakpoint	Brings up the New Breakpoint dialog box (see Table 11.1 for more information).
Delete All Breakpoints	Deletes all breakpoints in your solution.
Enable All Breakpoints	Enables all breakpoints in your solution.
Disable All Breakpoints	Disables breakpoints in the solution without deleting them. You can also disable individual breakpoints. This capability is very useful if you want to keep the breakpoints around for later but simply don't want to hit that one at the moment.
Clear All DataTips	Allows you to clear any data tips you might have pinned to the IDE (including comments). See "DataTips" later in this chapter.
Clear All DataTips Pinned to	Clear only those DataTips pinned to the active file. See "DataTips" later in this chapter.
Export DataTips	Enables you to export your DataTips as an XML file for sharing with other developers. See "DataTips" later in this chapter.
Import DataTips	Enables you to import an XML DataTips file for use inside your debug sessions. See "DataTips" later in this chapter.
Save Dump As	Enables you to save a memory dump for the active debug session.
Options and Settings	Brings up the Options dialog box for debugging. See "Debug Options" later in this chapter.
(project) Properties	Brings up the Properties dialog box for the current project.

The Debug Toolbar

The Debug toolbar provides quick access to some of the key items available on the Debug menu. From here, you can manage your debug session. For example, you can start or continue a debug session, stop an executing session, step through lines of code, and so on.

TIP

There are a variety of buttons that aren't visible within the debug toolbar by default. We recommend adding all of the available debug commands to this toolbar. There aren't many, and they turn out to be tremendously useful during debugging sessions.

Figure 11.14 presents the Debug toolbar during an active debug session. In design mode, the Continue button reads Start Debugging, and a number of these items are disabled. We have added callouts for each item on the toolbar. You can cross-reference these callouts to Table 11.2 for further information.

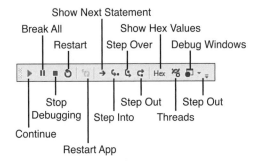

FIGURE 11.14   The Debug toolbar during an active debug session (break mode).

> **NOTE**
>
> In Figure 11.14, the Breakpoints window icon on the right of the figure with the callout "Debug Windows" actually is a drop-down menu. This menu provides access to the many debug windows that are available to developers. See Figure 11.13 for a sample of the menus you can access from this toolbar item.

Debug Options

You can control the many debugging options in Visual Studio through the Options dialog box. You can access these options from the Tools menu (Tools, Options) and then select the Debugging node from the left-side of the dialog box. Alternatively, you can open the options right to Debugging from the Debug menu (Debug, Options and Settings).

Six sets of options available are under the Debugging node:

▶ **General**—Provides access to the many debugging switches (more than 20) to turn on and off Visual Studio debugging behavior. This includes enabling and disabling breakpoint filters, using just-my-code debugging, creating breakpoint filters, handling warnings, and many other options (see Figure 11.15).

▶ **Edit and Continue**—Enables you to enable and disable edit-and-continue as a feature.

▶ **Just-In-Time**—Enables you to indicate the type of code (managed, native, and script) for which you want to enable or disable Visual Studio debugging (also called just-in-time debugging).

▶ **Native**—Enables you to control native (non-managed) code debugging.

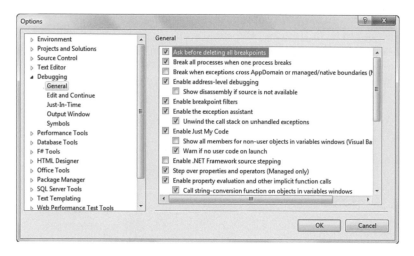

FIGURE 11.15 You can use the Options dialog box to control how Visual Studio behaves during a debugging session.

▶ **Output Window**—Provides management features for the Output window such as which messages are shown.

▶ **Symbols**—Enables you to choose which debug symbols are loaded for your debug session. You can also choose additional debug symbol files (.pdb and .dbg). These files can be helpful if you do not have the source code associated with a particular library you need to debug, such as the .NET Framework itself or a third-party component.

The majority of the settings you manage can be found on the General screen. Figure 11.15 shows the many options for this dialog box. We cover the features behind these options throughout the remainder of this chapter.

These many options help you customize your debug experience. However, as we debug code in this chapter, we are assuming the default options for the debugger.

Stepping In, Out, and Over Code

Probably the most common debug operation for developers is stepping through their code line by line and examining the data emitted by the application and the debugger. Code stepping is just that, examining a line, executing the line, and examining the results (and then repeating the process over and over). Because this is such a dominant activity, becoming efficient with the step operations in Visual Studio is important for maximizing the use of your time during a debug session. Here, we cover each of the stepping options and provide examples.

Beginning a Debug Session (Stepping into Code)

The Step Into command is available from the Debug menu and toolbar. (You can also press F11 as a shortcut.) Two behaviors are commonly associated with this one command.

The first is related to when you invoke the command for an application that is not currently running in debug mode. In this case, the application is compiled and started, and the first line is presented to you in the debug window for stepping purposes. This is, in essence, stepping into your application. Figure 11.16 shows a Windows Presentation Foundation (WPF) application in debug mode as the result of a call to Step Into.

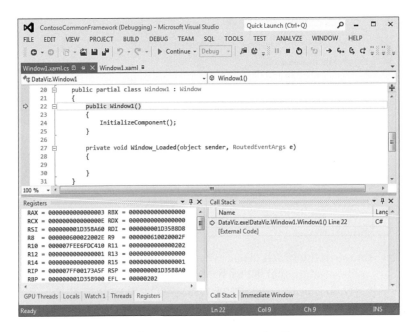

FIGURE 11.16   Using Step Into to start an application.

> **NOTE**
>
> For web applications, using Step Into or Step Over does not work the same as with other applications. Instead, your application simply runs in debug mode in the case of websites. The debugger does not break on the first line of your application. To do this, you must set a breakpoint or choose the Run to Cursor option (see the following section).

A call to the Step Over command (Debug menu, toolbar, or F10) while your application is at rest results in the same behavior as Step Into. That is, your application (provided it is not a website) is compiled and started in a debug session on the first line of code.

Run to Cursor   One of the more handy (and overlooked) features of the debug toolset is Run to Cursor. This feature works the way it sounds. You set your cursor position on some code and invoke the Run to Cursor command (right-click or Ctrl+F10). The application is compiled and run until it hits the line of code where your cursor is placed. At this point, the debugger breaks the application and presents the line of code for you to step through. This capability is especially handy because this is how many developers work. They are looking at a specific line (or lines) of code and want to debug this line. They do not need to start from the first line and might not want to be bothered with breakpoints. The Run to Cursor feature is therefore an efficient means to get the debugger on the same page as you. Figure 11.17 shows this feature being invoked from the context menu.

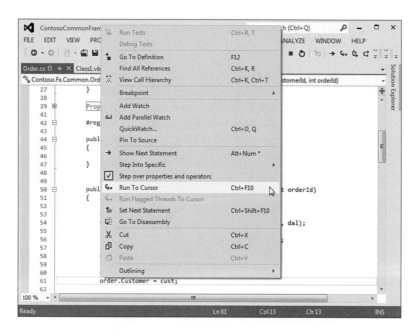

FIGURE 11.17   You can tell the debugger to stop when it hits a given line of code using the Run to Cursor command.

Run to Cursor works even if the user is required to activate some portion of the code prior to the code's reaching the cursor position. In this way, it acts like an invisible, temporary breakpoint. For instance, consider an example in which users are presented with a default web page. From here, they can select to edit their profiles. If you set the Run to Cursor command on a line inside the edit profile screen, the debugger still executes the application and waits until the user (tester or developer) invokes the given line of code.

Start Debugging   You can also start your debug session by selecting the Start Debugging option (green "play" arrow) from the Debug menu or toolbar (or F5). This starts a debug session but does not break into code unless an exception occurs or a breakpoint is encountered. This is a common operation for developers testing their code without wanting to walk through it or those who use a lot of breakpoints.

Break All   If your application is already running in a debug session and you want to enter break mode, you can do so at any time by invoking the Break All command from the Debug menu or toolbar (or Ctrl+Alt+Break). The Break All feature is represented by the pause icon on the toolbar. Clicking this button stops your application on the next executing line and enables you to interrogate the debugger for information. The Break All command is especially useful if you need to break into a long-running process or a loop that seems to have stalled your application.

Walking Through Your Code

During a debug session, you have basically three options for moving through your code. You can step into a line or function, step over a given function, or step out of a function. Let's look at each option.

Step Into   The Step Into command (F11 for C# and F8 for VB) enables you to progress through your code one line at a time. Invoking this command executes the current line of code and positions your cursor on the next line to be executed. The important distinction between stepping into and other similar commands is how Step Into handles lines of code that contain method calls. If you are positioned on such a line, calling Step Into takes you to the first line inside that method.

For example, look at Figure 11.18. It shows an example of a Order object making a call to a data access method named GetCustomer. In this case, both projects are loaded in the solution; thus, you have access to their debug symbols. Therefore, a call to Step Into results in your stepping into the first line of GetCustomer.

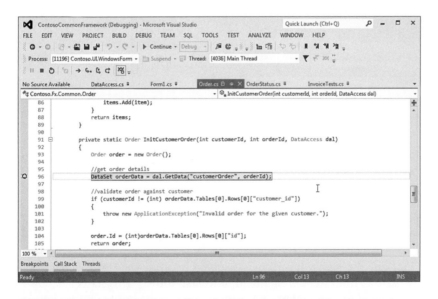

FIGURE 11.18   Stepping into a line of code can take you into another class.

Figure 11.19 shows stepping into this method. Notice that you are now positioned to step line by line through the method (line 18). Of course, when you reach the end of this method, the debugger returns you to the next line in the calling function (back to line 96, as depicted in Figure 11.18).

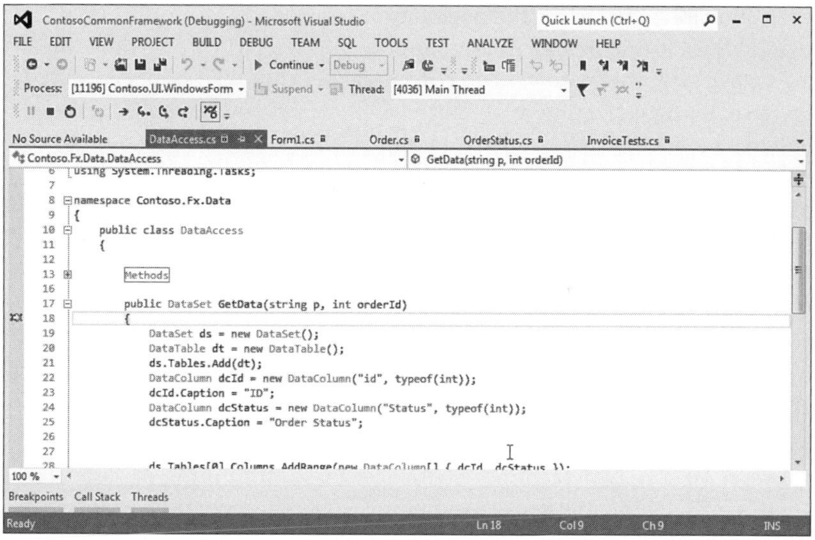

FIGURE 11.19   The results of stepping into a function.

Step Over   The Step Over command (F10 for C# and Shift+F8 for VB) enables you to maintain focus on the current procedure without stepping into any methods called by it. That is, calling Step Over executes line by line but does not take you into any function calls, constructors, or property calls.

For example, consider Figure 11.18. Here, the debugger is positioned on the call to GetData. If you call the Step Over command, the GetData function executes in its entirety without your stepping through it. Instead, the next line to execute in step mode is the line following the call to GetData (line 99). Of course, any exception thrown by the function you step over results in the debugger breaking into your code (and the function) as normal.

Step Out   The Step Out command (Shift+F11 and Ctrl+Shift+F8 for VB) is another useful tool. It allows you to tell the debugger to finish executing the current method you are debugging but return to break mode as soon as it is finished. This is a great tool when you get stuck in a long method you wish you had stepped over. In addition, you might step into a given function only to debug a portion of it and then want to step out.

For example, refer again to Figure 11.19. Recall that you stepped into this method from the code in Figure 11.18. Suppose that you start stepping through a couple of lines of code. After you take a look and verify that a connection is made to the database, you simply want to have the function complete and return to debugging back in the calling function (line 99 of Figure 11.18). To do so, you simply invoke Step Out.

Continuing Execution

When you are in a debug session, the Start Debugging (or Run) command changes to Continue. The Continue command is available when you are paused on a given line of code in the debugger. It enables you to let the application continue to run on its own without stepping through each line. For example, suppose you walked through the lines of code you wanted to see, and now you want to continue checking your application from a user's perspective. Using Continue, you tell the application and debugger to keep running until either an exception occurs or a breakpoint is hit.

Ending a Debug Session

You can end your debug session in several ways. One common method is to kill the currently executing application. This might be done by closing the browser window for a web application or clicking the Close button of a Windows application. Calls in your code that terminate your application also end a debug session.

You also have a couple of options available to you from the Debug window. The Terminate All command kills all processes that the debugger is attached to and ends the debug session. There is also the Detach All option. Figure 11.20 shows both options from the Debug menu. Detach All simply detaches the debugger from all running processes without terminating them. This capability can be useful if you've temporarily attached to a running process, debugged it, and want to leave it running.

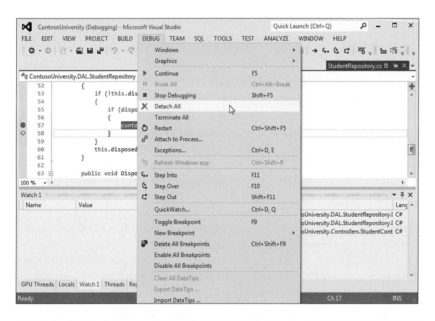

FIGURE 11.20   You can detach from a running process but leave the process running.

Indicating When to Break into Code

You control the debugger through breakpoints and tracepoints. With these, you can tell the debugger when you are interested in breaking into code or receiving information about your application. Breakpoints enable you to indicate when the debugger should stop on a specific line in your code. Tracepoints were first introduced in Visual Studio 2005. They are a type of breakpoint that enables you to perform an action when a given line of your code is reached. This typically involves emitting data about your application to the output window. Mastering the use of breakpoints reduces the time it takes to zero in on and fix issues with your code.

Setting a Breakpoint

The most common method of setting a breakpoint is to first find the line of code on which you want the debugger to stop. You then click in the code editor's indicator margin for the given line of code. Doing so places a red circle in the indicator margin and highlights the line of code as red. Of course, these are the default colors; you can change the look of breakpoints in the Tools, Options dialog box under the Environment node, Fonts and Colors.

There are a few additional ways to set breakpoints. For instance, you can right-click a given line of code and choose Insert Breakpoint from the Breakpoint context menu. You can also choose New Breakpoint from the Debug menu (or press Ctrl+D, N in C# or Ctrl+B in VB) to open the New Breakpoint dialog box in which you can set a function breakpoint.

Setting a Function Breakpoint   A function breakpoint is just a breakpoint that is set through the New Breakpoint dialog box. It is called a function breakpoint because it is typically set at the beginning of the function (but does not need to be). From the New Breakpoint dialog box, you can manually set the function on which you want to break, the line of code in the function, and even the character on the line.

If your cursor is on a function or on a call to a function when you invoke this dialog box, the name of the function is automatically placed in the dialog box, or you can type a function name in the dialog box. Figure 11.21 shows the New Breakpoint dialog box in action. Notice that you can manually set the line and even the character on the line where the breakpoint should be placed (for lines of code that include multiple statements).

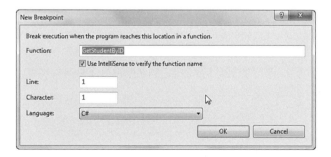

FIGURE 11.21   You can set a function breakpoint for a given function by name.

NOTE

If you specify an overloaded function in the New Breakpoint dialog box, you must specify the actual function on which you want to break. You do so by indicating the correct parameter types for the given overload. For example, the `GetCustomer` function in the example takes a `customerId` parameter (as an int). If you have an overload that also looks up a customer by name (as a string), you indicate this overload in the Function field as `LoadCustomer(string)`.

Recognizing the Many Breakpoints of Visual Studio

Visual Studio has a number of breakpoint icons. These icons enable you to easily recognize the type of breakpoint associated with a given line of code. For instance, a round, filled circle is a common breakpoint, whereas a round, hollow circle represents a common breakpoint that has been disabled. We've provided Table 11.3 for reference purposes. It shows some of the more common icons associated with breakpoints and presents a description of each.

TABLE 11.3   The Breakpoint Icons

Icon	Description
●	This icon indicates a standard, enabled breakpoint. When the debugger encounters this line of code, it stops the application and breaks into debug mode.
◆	This icon indicates a standard tracepoint. When the debugger hits this line of code, it performs the action associated with the tracepoint.
⊕	The plus icon inside the breakpoint indicates an advanced breakpoint that contains a condition, hit count, or filter.
◈	The plus icon inside the tracepoint indicates an advanced tracepoint that contains a condition, hit count, or filter.
○	An empty or hollow breakpoint indicates a disabled breakpoint. The breakpoint is still associated with the line of code. However, the debugger does not recognize the disabled breakpoint until it has been reenabled.
	Hollow icons are associated with types of breakpoint icons such as tracepoints, advanced items, and even breakpoint errors and warnings. In all conditions, the hollow icon indicates that the item is disabled.
⇨	Indicates that the breakpoint is also the next line to be executed by Visual Studio (step into).

Working with the Breakpoints Window

The Breakpoints window in Visual Studio provides a convenient way to organize and manage the many conditions on which you intend to break into the debugger. You access this window from the Debug menu or toolbar (or by pressing Ctrl+D, B in C# or Ctrl+Alt+B in VB). Figure 11.22 shows the Breakpoints window inside Visual Studio.

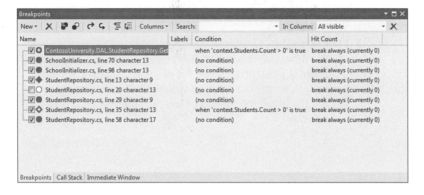

FIGURE 11.22   The Breakpoints window.

The Breakpoints Window Toolbar   The Breakpoints window has its own toolbar that enables you to manage the breakpoints listed in the grid below the toolbar (refer to Figure 11.22). The commands available from the toolbar are described in detail in Table 11.4.

TABLE 11.4   The Breakpoints Window Toolbar

Icon	Description

New ▾
    Break at Function...   Ctrl+D, N
    New Data Breakpoint...
	Brings up the new Breakpoints window, enabling you to set a breakpoint at a function.

✕	Enables you to delete the selected breakpoint in the list.
✕⊙	Deletes all breakpoints in the window.
⊙	Toggles all breakpoints as either on or off. If even one breakpoint in the list is enabled, clicking this icon the first time disables it (and all others that are enabled). Clicking it a second time (or when all breakpoints are disabled) enables all breakpoints.
↱	Enables you to export your breakpoints to an XML file. This can be useful if you have a lot of breakpoint information you want to share. You can share your breakpoints to allow others to debug your code.
↰	Enables you to import breakpoints from an XML file.
⇥	Enables you to go to the source code associated with the selected breakpoint.
⊑	Enables you to go to the disassembly information associated with the selected breakpoint.

11

Icon	Description
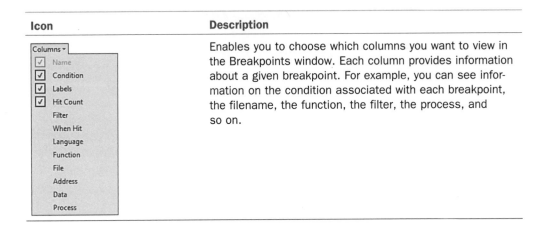	Enables you to choose which columns you want to view in the Breakpoints window. Each column provides information about a given breakpoint. For example, you can see information on the condition associated with each breakpoint, the filename, the function, the filter, the process, and so on.

Managing Each Individual Breakpoint   The Breakpoints window also gives you access to each individual breakpoint. It serves as a launching point for setting the many options associated with a breakpoint. For example, you can disable a single breakpoint by toggling the check box associated with the breakpoint in the list. In addition, you can set the many properties and conditions associated with a breakpoint. Figure 11.23 shows a disabled tracepoint and a disabled breakpoint; it also shows the context menu associated with an individual breakpoint.

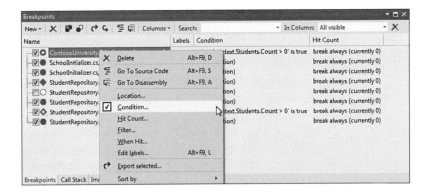

FIGURE 11.23   You can manage individual breakpoints inside the Breakpoints window.

Notice that from this context menu, you can delete the breakpoint and navigate to its related source code (Go to Source Code). More important, however, is the access to setting the conditions and filters associated with the breakpoint. We cover using each of these options next.

Labeling Breakpoints   You can provide labels for your breakpoints, which enables you to define categories of breakpoints and quickly find them in the Breakpoints window. For example, you might want to set a number of breakpoints and tracepoints related to a specific scenario in your code such as managing a customer profile or creating a new order. These breakpoints are useful when you need to modify and review this code. However, when you are working on unrelated code, you might want to turn a whole group of breakpoints off. Breakpoint labels support this scenario.

You label a breakpoint by selecting Edit Labels from the breakpoint context menu (refer to Figure 11.23 to see an example). The Edit Breakpoint Labels dialog box opens, as shown in Figure 11.24. Here you can add a new label and apply that label to the selected breakpoint. Alternatively, you can select one or more labels from the existing labels previously defined.

FIGURE 11.24   You can use the Edit Breakpoint Labels dialog box to label breakpoints to make them easier to find and work with as a group.

You can work with the breakpoint labels inside the Breakpoints window. You can sort the list by the Labels column, as shown in Figure 11.25. In addition, you can use the Search feature to find breakpoints based on keywords contained in the labels.

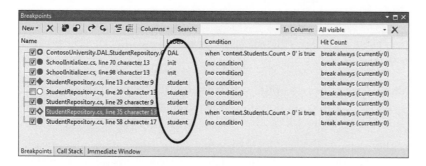

FIGURE 11.25   You can sort or search breakpoints based on their labels.

Breaking Based on Conditions

Often, setting a simple breakpoint is not sufficient (or efficient). For instance, if you are looking for a particular condition to be true in your code (a condition that seems to be causing an exception), you would prefer to break based on that condition. This saves the time of constantly breaking into a function only to examine a few data points and determine that you have not hit your condition.

You can add five types of conditions to a breakpoint: Location, Condition, Hit Count, Filter, and When Hit. You add a condition to a breakpoint from within the Breakpoints window. Select a given breakpoint and then right-click to open the context menu for the given breakpoint. Refer to Figure 11.23 for an example. You can see that each possible condition is listed for the breakpoint. The following sections highlight the conditional options available for breakpoints.

Setting a Breakpoint Condition   A breakpoint condition enables you to break into the debugger or perform an action (tracepoint) when a specific condition is either evaluated as true or has changed. Often, you know that the bug you are working on occurs only based on a very specific condition. Breakpoint conditions are the perfect answer for troubleshooting an intermittent bug.

To set a condition, you select the breakpoint on which you want to apply a condition. You then choose the Condition option from the context (right-click) menu to open the Breakpoint Condition dialog box, as shown in Figure 11.26. Notice that when setting the condition, you have access to IntelliSense.

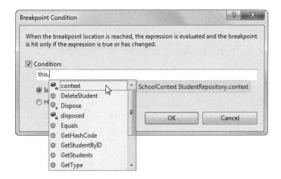

FIGURE 11.26   You can use the Breakpoint Condition dialog box to set a Boolean code condition that tells the debugger when to stop on your breakpoint.

When you set a condition, you have two options: Is True and Has Changed. The Is True option enables you to set a Boolean condition that, when evaluated to true, results in the debugger's breaking into the given line of code.

For example, suppose that you are notified of an error that happens when populating a collection of student objects. You might go to the data access layer class and set a breakpoint inside the function that returns students from the database. You might then add the Is True condition context.Students.Count > 0 to the breakpoint. This tells the debugger not to stop on this line of code unless this condition is met. Figure 11.27 shows this condition in the dialog box. It also shows the two options available for conditions at the bottom of the dialog box.

FIGURE 11.27   An example of a breakpoint condition.

The option Has Changed tells the debugger to break when the value of an expression changes. The first pass through your code sets the value for the first evaluation. If the value changes after that, the debugger breaks on a given line. This capability can be useful when you have fields or properties with initial values and you want to track when those values are being changed. In addition, Has Changed can be useful in looping and if...then scenarios in which you are interested in only whether the results of your code changed a particular value.

> **TIP**
>
> Your breakpoint information is persisted between debug sessions. That is, when you close Visual Studio for the day, your breakpoints are still there when you return. This validates the time you might spend setting some sophisticated debugging options because they can remain in your application and be turned on and off as required. The options can also be exported to a file and shared with other developers or other computers.

Breaking on Location   You can edit a breakpoint to break based on a specific location in a file. Most breakpoints already work this way. That is, they automatically know the file, line number, and character on which to break. However, there are times when you might want to edit this information. For example, suppose your code is slightly out of sync with the running build. You might need to edit your breakpoints to break on a different line of code.

Figure 11.28 shows an example of the File Breakpoint window as accessed from the Location option on the breakpoint context menu. You might also use this feature to quickly set a breakpoint on a specific line without searching your source code.

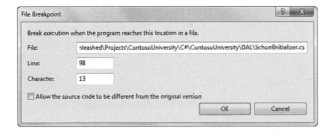

FIGURE 11.28   The File Breakpoint window enables you to set a breakpoint at a specific location in your code.

Setting a Breakpoint Filter   Breakpoint filters enable you to specify a specific machine, process, or thread on which you want to break. For instance, if your error condition seems to happen only on a certain machine or within a certain process, you can debug this condition specifically with a filter. Filters are most useful in complex debugging scenarios in which your application is highly distributed.

To use this feature, you can specify the machine by name, the process by name or ID, or the thread by name or ID. You can also specify combinations with & (and), || (or), and ! (not). This allows you to get to a specific thread on a specific process on a certain machine. Figure 11.29 shows the dialog box in which you set breakpoint filters. In this figure, the breakpoint is being configured to stop provided that the running process is the development web server (WebDev.WebServer.EXE).

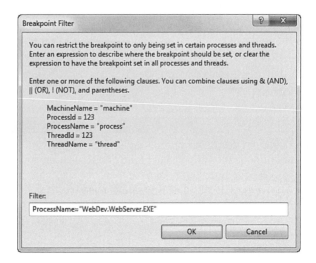

FIGURE 11.29   You can set a breakpoint filter to stop the debugger inside a specific process or thread, or on a specific machine.

Using a Hit Count with a Breakpoint   Using the Hit Count command, you can tell the debugger that you want to break when a given line of code is reached a number of times. Typically, you can find a better condition than breaking based on Hit Count. However, this feature is useful in those cases in which you can't determine the actual condition but know that when you pass through a function a certain number of times, something bad happens. In addition, the Hit Count option might be more useful in tracepoint scenarios in which you are emitting data about what is happening in your code. You might want to write that data only periodically.

Figure 11.30 shows the Breakpoint Hit Count dialog box.

You have the option of clicking the Reset button and turning the hit count back to zero and continuing debugging from that point. Note that you can add any condition to a breakpoint during an active debug session.

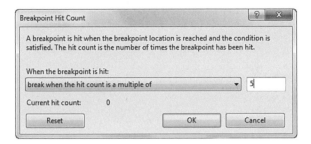

FIGURE 11.30   You can set the debugger to break when it hits a line of code a set number of times.

This dialog box also provides a few options for setting the actual hit count. In the drop-down list under When the Breakpoint Is Hit, the following options are available:

▶ Break Always (the default and does not invoke the hit count option)

▶ Break When the Hit Count Is Equal To

▶ Break When the Hit Count Is a Multiple Of

▶ Break When the Hit Count Is Greater Than or Equal To

TIP

You can combine all the breakpoint conditions we've discussed on a single breakpoint. For example, you may add a condition and a filter to a given breakpoint. Doing so allows you to create even more specific scenarios for debugging your application using break-points.

Working with Tracepoints (When Hit Option)

Tracepoints enable you to emit data to the Output window or run a Visual Studio macro when a specific breakpoint is hit. You then have the option to break into the debugger (like a regular breakpoint), process another condition, or just continue executing the application. This capability can be very useful if you want to keep a running log of what is happening as your application runs in debug mode. You can then review this log to get valuable information about specific conditions and order of execution when an exception is thrown.

You can set tracepoints explicitly by right-clicking a line of code and choosing Insert Tracepoint from the Breakpoint menu. In addition, selecting the When Hit command from the context menu (refer to Figure 11.25) for a breakpoint in the Breakpoints window opens a tracepoint dialog box, named When Breakpoint Is Hit, as shown in Figure 11.31.

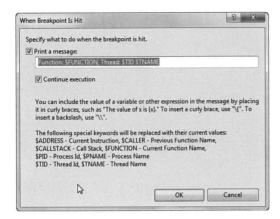

FIGURE 11.31   You can set a tracepoint using the When Breakpoint Is Hit dialog box.

The options available for the When Breakpoint Is Hit dialog box include printing a message to the output window and continuing execution. The first option, printing a message, enables you to output data about your function. You can use a number of keywords to output data, such as $FUNCTION for the function name and $CALLER for the name of the calling function. A list of keywords is shown in the instructional text within the dialog box in Figure 11.29. You can also output your specific variable values. You do so by enclosing the variable names in curly braces.

The Continue execution option enables you to indicate whether this is a true tracepoint or a breakpoint that contains a tracing action. If you choose to continue, you get only the trace action (message/macro). If you indicate not to continue, you get the trace action, plus the debugger stops on this line of code, just as with a regular breakpoint. This is essentially applying a When Hit action to a standard breakpoint.

You can also combine tracepoint actions with conditions. When you do so, the action fires only when the breakpoint condition is met.

For example, suppose a tracepoint is set inside the web service GetCustomerProfile. Imagine this tracepoint prints a message to the output window when the line of code is hit and simply continues executing the application. The message we intend to print is as follows:

```
Function: $FUNCTION, Thread: $TID $TNAME, Id: {id}
```

This message prints the function name, the thread ID and name (if any), and the value of the variable, id. Figure 11.32 shows two passes through the tracepoint output in the Output window (Debug, Windows, Output).

Viewing Data in the Debugger

After the debugger has thrown you into break mode, the next challenge is to filter all the data your application is emitting. Getting to the right data helps you find problems faster and fix them faster. Visual Studio tries to make the data available where you want it. For example, DataTips show you variable values right in the code editor. There are many similar examples in the way Visual Studio shows debugging data when and where you need it, which are covered throughout the following sections.

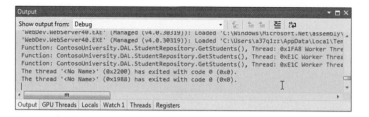

FIGURE 11.32   You can view the results of tracepoints inside the Output window.

Watching Variables

A common activity in a debug session is to view the values associated with the many types in your application. Various windows are available to help you here. The two most obvious are the Locals and Autos windows.

Locals Window   The Locals window shows all the variables and their values for the current debug scope, which gives you a view of everything available in the current, executing method. The variables in this window are set automatically by the debugger. They are organized alphabetically in a list by name. In addition, hierarchy is also shown. For example, if a given variable relates to an object type, that object's members are listed inside the variable (as a tree-based structure).

Figure 11.33 shows an example of the Locals window. In it, you can see the sample Contoso University application paused while executing calls to retrieve data. Notice that the `StudentRepository` instance (`this`) is expanded to show the various properties and fields associated with this object. As values are set, the results are shown in the Value column.

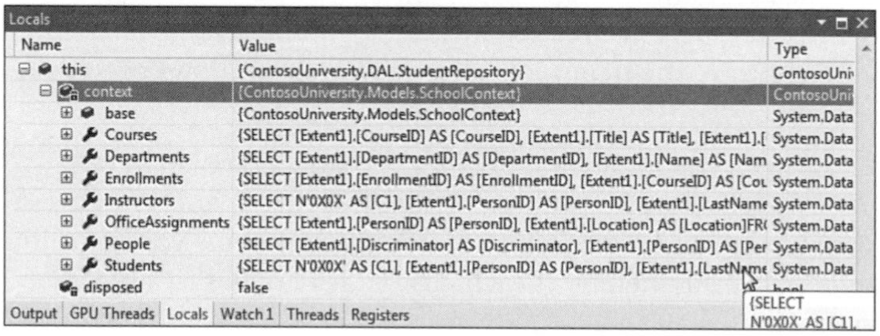

FIGURE 11.33   The Locals window shows you variable values for the currently executing method.

TIP

You can edit a value in the Locals or Autos window by right-clicking the variable and choosing Edit Value from the context menu. You can then change the value of the variable directly from within the window (similar to changing variable values using the Immediate window).

The Autos Window   Often, viewing all the locals provides too many options to sort through. This can be true when there is just too much in scope in the given process or function. To home in on the values associated with the line of code you are looking at, you can use the Autos window, which shows the value of all variables and expressions that are in the current executing line of code or in the preceding line of code. This allows you to really focus on just the values you are currently debugging.

Figure 11.34 shows the Autos window for the same method as was shown in Figure 11.33. Notice the difference in what is shown: The Autos window tries to anticipate the items you might need to review and shows their values.

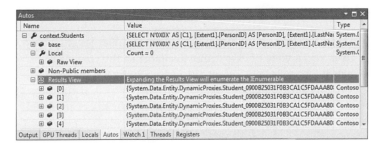

FIGURE 11.34   You can use the Autos window to automatically get variable values for the last executed and the currently executing line of code.

The Watch Windows   The Visual Studio Watch windows enable you to set a custom list of variables and expressions that you want to keep an eye on. In this way, you decide the items in which you are interested. The Watch windows look and behave just like the Locals and Autos windows. In addition, the items you place in Watch windows persist from one debug session to another.

You access each Watch window from the Debug menu (Debug, Windows, Watch) or toolbar. The four Watch windows are named Watch 1, Watch 2, Watch 3, and Watch 4. Having four Watch windows enables you to set up four custom lists of items you want to monitor. This capability can be especially helpful if each custom list applies to a separate scope in your application.

You add a variable or an expression to the Watch window from either the code editor or the QuickWatch window. If you are in the code editor, select a variable or highlight an expression, right-click, and choose the Add Watch menu item. This takes the highlighted variable or expression and places it in the Watch window. You can also drag and drop the highlighted item into a Watch window.

QuickWatch   The QuickWatch window is similar to the other Watch windows. However, it enables you to focus on a single variable or expression. The QuickWatch window has been used less often since DataTips were introduced in 2005. From the QuickWatch window, you can write expressions and add them to the Watch window. When writing your expression, you have access to IntelliSense. Figure 11.35 shows the QuickWatch window.

FIGURE 11.35   The QuickWatch window enables you to define expressions and monitor their results during a debug session.

The item you add to QuickWatch is evaluated when you click the Reevaluate button. Clicking the Add Watch button sends the variable to the Watch 1 window.

DataTips

DataTips enable you to highlight a variable or an expression in your code editor and get watch information right in the editor. This feature is more in tune with how developers work. For example, if you are looking at a line of code, you might highlight something in that line to evaluate it. You can do this by creating a QuickWatch. However, you can also simply hover over the item and its data is unfolded in a DataTip. In addition, Visual Studio lets you pin your data tips directly to your code window so that they are always visible during a debug session inside your code editor.

Figure 11.36 shows a DataTip active in a debug session. Here, the cursor is positioned over an object. Clicking on the plus sign to expand this variable unfolds the many properties and fields of the object. If the member list is long, you can scroll through it using an arrow at the bottom of the window. You can also right-click any member in the list and edit its value, copy it, or add it to the watch window (as shown). Also, notice the magnifying glass icon next to the items in the list; it allows you to select a specific visual-izer for a given item (more on visualizers shortly).

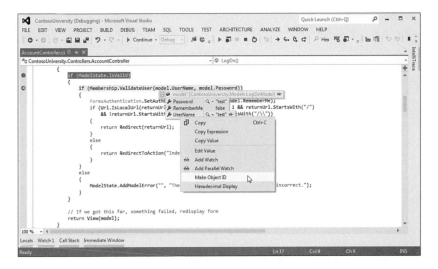

FIGURE 11.36   You can use DataTips to quickly visualize your object data in the debugger.

TIP

The DataTips window can often get in the way of viewing code. Sometimes, you need to see the DataTips and the code underneath. In this case, pressing the Control (Ctrl) key makes the DataTips window transparent for as long as you hold the key.

Pinning a Data Tip   In Figure 11.36, the highlighted member "model" has a pin icon on the far right of the window. This icon enables you to pin your DataTip to the code window, which ensures this DataTip is displayed each time you pass through the code in the debugger. This is a faster, more accessible version of a Watch window.

You can pin all sorts of code items as DataTips. You can pin an entire object, or, in the case of the example, a single member. You can also move pinned DataTips around in the editor to position them accordingly. After a DataTip is pinned, you can highlight it to remove it, unpin it, or add your own comment to the DataTip. In Figure 11.37, we have pinned a DataTip to the code editor.

TIP

Recall that you can use the export and import options from the Debug menu to save your DataTips to an XML file and re-use them on another computer.

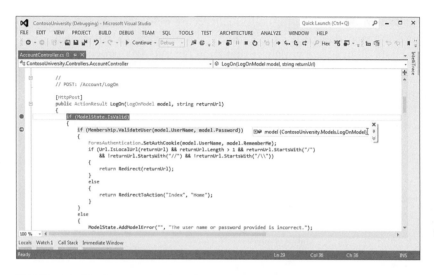

FIGURE 11.37   You can pin DataTips to the code editor to provide easier variable watching during a debug session.

Visualizing Data

When you are looking at variable values, what you really want to get to is the data behind the object. Sometimes this data is obscured by the object model itself. For example, suppose you are looking for the data that is contained in a `DataSet` object. To find it, you have to dig many layers deep in a watch window or a DataTip. You have to traverse the inner workings of the object model just to get at something as basic as the data contained by the object. If you've spent much time doing this, you know how frustrating it can be.

Visual Studio offers a quick, easy way to access the data contained in an object. It does so through a tool called a visualizer. Visualizers are meant to present the object's data in a meaningful way.

A few visualizers ship with Visual Studio by default, including the following:

> ▶ **HTML**—Shows a browser-like dialog box with the HTML interpreted as a user might see it.

> ▶ **XML**—Shows the XML in a structured format.

> ▶ **Text**—Shows a string value in an easy-to-read format.

> ▶ **WPF Tree Visualizer**—Enables you to view the WPF application events in a meaningful way. We cover WPF applications in Chapter 19, "Creating Richer, Smarter User Interfaces."

> ▶ **DataSet**—Shows the contents of the `DataSet`, `DataView`, and `DataTable` objects.

There is also a framework for writing and installing visualizers in Visual Studio so that you can write your own and plug them into the debugger. You can also download additional visualizers and install them. The possibilities of visualizers are many, as many ways as there are to structure and view data. A few ideas might be a tree-view visualizer that displays hierarchical data or an image visualizer that shows image data structures.

You invoke a visualizer from one of the many places you view data values, including Watch windows and DataTips. Visualizers are represented by a magnifying glass icon. Refer to Figures 11.36 or 11.37 to see an example of launching a visualizer using the icon. Instead of digging through the object hierarchy to get at the data, you can invoke the DataSet visualizer right from a DataTip. Figure 11.38 shows the visualizer in action for an order DataSet.

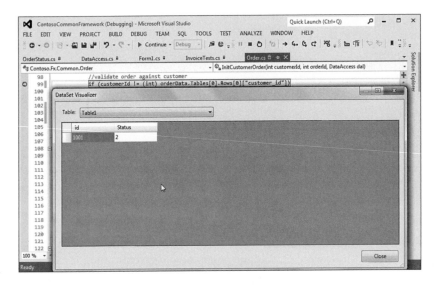

FIGURE 11.38   You can use the DataSet visualizer to quickly view the contents of a data table inside a grid.

Using the Edit and Continue Feature

Edit and Continue enables you to change code as you debug without killing your debug session. You can make a modification to a line of code or even fix a bug and keep working in break mode. Visual Basic developers who worked in versions prior to .NET should recall this powerful tool. Its absence in .NET made it one of the most requested features. The good news is that Edit and Continue was added in 2005 to both Visual Basic and C#. In 2008, this feature was also added to Visual C++.

There is no trick to invoking Edit and Continue. You simply make your code change during a debug session and then keep running through your code with a Step command or Continue.

The feature is turned on by default. If it is turned off, you can reenable it using the Options dialog box available from the Tools menu.

Not all code changes you make are eligible for Edit and Continue. In fact, it should be used only in minor fixes. As a best practice, any major additions to your code should not be done in debug mode. If your change is within the body of a method, it has a higher likelihood of passing the Edit and Continue test. Most code changes outside the method body require the debugger to restart. Common changes that are not eligible for Edit and Continue include the following:

▶ Changing code on the current, active statement

▶ Changing code on any calls on the stack that lead to the current, active statement

▶ Adding new types, methods, fields, events, or properties

▶ Changing a method signature

For a more exhaustive list, search MSDN for "Edit and Continue." From there, you can link to the Edit and Continue documentation for your chosen language. You can then select the link, titled "Supported Code Changes." Here you can review the full list of supported and unsupported changes for your chosen language.

Advanced Debugging Scenarios

Debugging can sometimes be a complex process. We've looked at many of the straightforward scenarios presented by Windows and web applications. However, debugging remote processes, multithreaded applications, and multicore (parallel) applications, for example, present their own needs in terms of configuration and tools. This section presents a few of the more common, advanced debugging scenarios you will encounter.

Remote Debugging

Remote debugging allows you to connect to a running application on another machine or domain and debug that application in its environment. This is often the only way to experience errors that are occurring on specific hardware. We've all heard this developer's cry: "Works on my machine." Remote debugging helps those developers figure out why their application doesn't work in other environments.

Remote debugging makes a lot of sense in various scenarios, such as debugging SQL server-stored procedures, web services, web applications, remote services or processes, and so on.

The hardest part about remote debugging is getting it set up properly. The actual debugging is no different from the debugging we've discussed thus far. However, the setup requires you to jump through a lot of hoops in terms of installation and security. These hoops are necessary because you do not, by default, want developers to easily connect debug sessions to applications on your servers.

There is some good news. Visual Studio tries to minimize and simplify the setup and configuration of remote debugging. Microsoft has written the Remote Debugging Monitor (msvsmon.exe) for this purpose. However, developers still find the setup tasks somewhat arduous (but rewarding when finished). We do not cover the setup in great detail here because it is often environment-specific. We suggest querying MSDN for "Remote Debugging" to get the full walk-through and troubleshooting advice for your specific situation.

We do offer the following, however, as a set of high-level tasks that you need to complete to get remote debugging working:

1. Install the remote debugging monitor (msvsmon.exe) on the remote machine being debugged. You install it using the setup application, rdbsetup.exe. You can also run it from a file share.

2. Configure remote debugging permissions. Typically, this means one of two things. You can set up identical accounts (username and password) on both machines (debugging and server). The debugging account may be local or a domain account. However, the server account should be a local account. Alternatively, you can give your user account administrative access to the machine being debugged, but this is often a security risk that should not be taken lightly.

3. Run the remote debugging monitor on the remote machine. This is a Windows application (with a GUI). You can also set the monitor to run as a Windows service. This capability can be useful for specific server scenarios and ASP.NET remote debugging.

4. If your debug machine is running XP with SP2, you have to configure your security policy and firewall for remote debugging (see the MSDN documentation "How to: Set Up Remote Debugging"). If you are running Windows 7 or Vista, you might have to elevate privileges when running Visual Studio (run as Administrator).

5. Run Visual Studio on your debug machine as you would to debug any process. Open the project that contains the source for the process you want to debug.

6. Attach to the running process on the remote machine using Attach to Process. You have to browse to the machine you want to debug and find the process running on that machine.

As you can see, getting remote debugging set up can be a challenge. However, if you have a test environment that you typically debug, the setup should be a one-time operation. From there, you should be able to debug in a more realistic environment as well as walk through SQL-stored procedures.

Debugging WCF Services

For the most part, you debug a web service (or Windows Communication Foundation [WCF] service) using the same tools and techniques we've discussed to this point. The key to debugging services is properly attaching to them. There are basically two options for this. The first option is to step into a service directly from within code you are debugging (a client calling a service). The second option is to attach to a service that has already been called by a client. Let's look at these options.

Stepping into a WCF Service

You can step directly into a WCF service provided that your calling code (or client) has a two-way contract with the service. This is called a Duplex Contract and it enables the client and the service to communicate with one another. Each can initiate calls. This is useful when your server needs to call back to the client or raise events on the client. You use the `ServiceContractAttribute` to set this up. (See Chapter 21, "Service-Oriented Applications," for more information.)

Your client must also be synchronous for this to work. That is, the client cannot make a call to the WCF service asynchronously and then begin doing something else. Instead, it must call and wait.

Attaching to a WCF Service

You can use the Attach to Process option (covered earlier) to debug both WCF and Web Services (.asmx). In these cases, the service is already running typically in a process outside of your current debug environment. To attach and debug to this process, you must make sure you have the code for the service loaded inside of Visual Studio. Next, the service process must be hosted by IIS or the ASP.NET Development Server. Finally, the service must have been invoked by a WCF-based client to gain access to its execution.

Debugging Multithreaded Applications

A multithreaded application is one in which more than a single thread is running in a given process. By default, each process that runs your application has at least one thread of execution. You might create multiple threads to do parallel processing. This can significantly improve performance, especially when run on today's multicore processors and hyperthreading technology. However, multithreading comes at a cost. The code can be more complex to write and more difficult to debug. If you've ever written a multithreaded application, you already know this. For example, just stepping line by line through a multithreaded application to debug it might have you jumping from one thread to another. You would then have to keep track of this flow in your head to make sense of the diagnostic information you see.

Fortunately, Visual Studio provides a few tools that make the job a bit easier. We do not cover coding a multithreaded application here. Instead, we cover the debug options available to you for debugging one, such as the following:

▶ The ability to view threads in your source during a debug session

▶ The Debug Location toolbar used to view processes, threads, and flagged threads

▶ The Thread window used to work with a list of threads in your application

▶ Breakpoint filters that enable you to set a breakpoint for an individual thread

Let's look at each of these features in more detail.

NOTE

MSDN provides a simple code sample that is useful for working through debugging a multithreaded application. Search for the topic "Walkthrough: Debugging a Multithreaded Application." We use that code sample here to help drive home the key debugging concepts.

Discovering and Flagging Threads

Visual Studio enables you to visualize the threads in your application in debug mode. When you are stopped on a breakpoint, your application is paused and all threads in that application are halted. The threads are still there. They are put in a suspended state so you can examine their statuses. They do not continue until you continue the execution of your code. However, in a multithreaded scenario, threads outside the one on which your code broke might not be easily visible in the debugger. To see them in the Debug menu, you can use the Show Threads in Source option from the Debug menu, as shown in Figure 11.39.

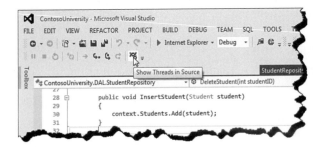

FIGURE 11.39   Select the Show Threads in Source icon from the Debug toolbar to tell Visual Studio to visually display threads in the debug session.

Selecting Show Threads in Source highlights other threads that exist in your code in the indicator margin (or gutter) of the code window during a debug session. The icon used to highlight these items looks like two wavy lines (or cloth threads). Figure 11.40 shows an example of a multithreaded application in a debug session.

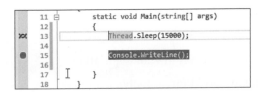

FIGURE 11.40   The thread icon indicates that a thread is stopped on a line of code in the debug session.

11

Most debug scenarios are single threaded. Therefore, you will not see another thread executing. You must write an application that uses more than one thread to see the thread icon in the debugger.

Notice the graphic on the left of line 13. This indicates that a thread exists at this location in your source code. Hovering over the indicator shows the thread (or threads) that are referenced by the indicator. Each thread is shown by its ID number (in brackets) and name (if any).

TIP

Naming threads can help you better identify them when debugging. To name a thread, you use the `Threading` namespace. Specifically, call the `Name` property of the `Thread` class.

Now that you've found a thread, you might want to flag it for further monitoring. This simply helps group it with the threads you want to monitor versus those you do not care about. You can flag a thread right from the indicator margin. To do so, right-click the indicator and choose the Flag option on the context menu. Figure 11.41 shows an example.

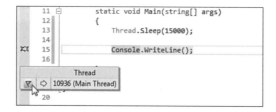

FIGURE 11.41   You can flag a thread to help you keep track of it in the Thread window.

Flagged threads show up highlighted in the Threads window (Debug, Windows, Threads). You can use this window to flag additional threads (or unflag them). Flagged threads provide special grouping in both the Thread window and the Debug Location toolbar. We cover these features next.

Managing Debug Processes and Threads

You can switch between the processes you are debugging and the threads within those processes by using the Debug Location toolbar. (You might have to right-click the toolbar area and add this toolbar to the IDE.) This toolbar is shown in Figure 11.42. On the left is the Process list. Here you can select a process to view details about that process, including executing threads. Many multithreaded applications are run within a single process, however.

FIGURE 11.42 The Debug Location toolbar.

The Thread list (see Figure 11.43) on the toolbar shows a list of threads for the selected process. Notice that the threads are shown with their IDs, names, and flag indicators. You can select a thread in this list to jump to source code associated with the thread. If no source code is associated with a selected thread, the thread name is shown as red when you select it. You can filter the list to show only flagged threads by toggling the second button to the right of the Thread list (shown with two flags). The first button to the right flags (or unflags) the current, active thread. Finally, the list on the right shows the call stack. The active stack frame in the call stack is what is shown in the debug windows (Watch, Local, Autos, and so on).

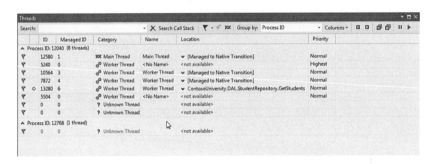

FIGURE 11.43 The Threads window provides total control over the threads in a debug session.

You can also manage threads from within the Threads window (Debug, Windows, Threads). Here you see all threads listed for a given process. Figure 11.43 shows an example. Notice that the left of the list shows flagged threads. We have flagged a thread in a sample application. Notice also that these threads can be named. This allows for easy recognition in the Name column.

You have several options available when you right-click a thread in the window, as shown in the context menu in Figure 11.43. Notice the Switch to Thread option, which allows you to switch the active thread being debugged. The active thread is shown with a yellow arrow in the thread list (to the right of the flag). Switching active threads changes the debug context and content in the debug windows. You can also Freeze (or pause) threads using this context menu. (Of course, you can then thaw [or resume] them, too.) Freezing a thread is equivalent to suspending it. The icons for freezing and thawing selected threads are on the far right side of the toolbar in the Threads window. The Threads window has a number of other features. You can use it to search the calls stack, group threads by process, id, category, priority, suspended state, and more.

TIP

When debugging multithreaded applications, it's often easier to freeze all but one thread. This allows you to focus on what is happening with the given thread.

Inspecting Individual Threads   When your application hits a breakpoint, all executing threads are paused. This enables you to inspect them individually. As you've seen, you can use the Debug Locations toolbar (refer to Figure 11.42) to change the selected thread. Doing so reconfigures the debug windows. This includes the call stack and watch windows (including Autos and Locals).

For example, imagine you are working on an application that has a main thread of execution. It might then create two additional threads on which it does work. When you break into the application, you can inspect the main thread and its current state or any of the other threads spawned by the application. Figure 11.44 shows an example. Notice that a worker thread is selected in the Debug Locations toolbar. Next, notice the Locals window pertains to this main thread information. The call stack also includes information about the lifetime of this main thread.

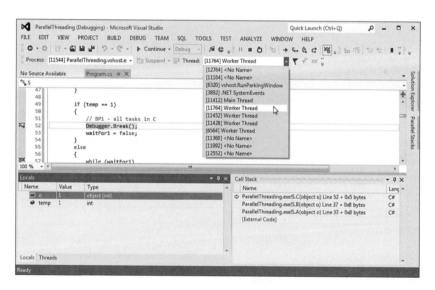

FIGURE 11.44   You can use Visual Studio to inspect individual threads during a debug session.

As further illustration, suppose that you selected another thread from the Debug Locations toolbar. Figure 11.45 shows a different thread selected. Notice that the code window changes to the current line being executed by this thread. Because this is not the active thread, this icon is a different type of arrow and the selection is green (by default). In addition, the Locals window now shows values for this thread and the call stack shows the lifeline of this code.

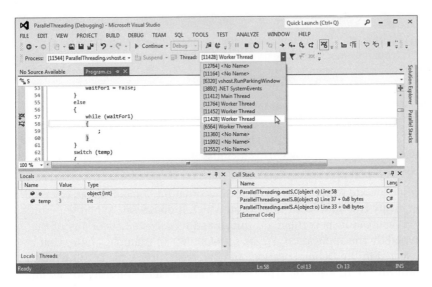

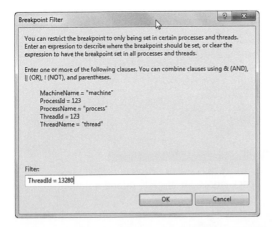

FIGURE 11.45   Selecting another thread in a debug session allows you to view the call stack for that thread and inspect its variables.

Breaking Based on a Specific Thread   You can also break on a line of code when it hits a thread. To do so, set a breakpoint in your code and choose a breakpoint filter (covered earlier). Figure 11.46 shows an example. You can choose to break based on the thread ID or its name. In this case, the breakpoint is hit based on the thread ID.

FIGURE 11.46   You can add a breakpoint filter to stop Visual Studio on a specific thread.

Debugging Parallel Applications

A parallel application is one that executes code simultaneously. This includes multithreading applications. Therefore, the multithreading debugging discussed thus far is applicable to parallel applications. However, there are additional features of the .NET languages, the framework, and the Visual Studio Debugger to help support parallel coding scenarios. These features are an attempt to take advantage of the recent proliferation of many-core processors. Developers want to take advantage of this computer power, which means developers need to begin changing the way they write their applications to take advantage of the multiple cores, each capable of running one or more threads in parallel.

This section covers two of the new debugging features that help support parallel programming: Parallel Stack and Parallel Tasks. Some of these features also apply to multithreaded applications. However, the main focus of these features is parallel applications written for multicore. Recall that parallel programming means task-based programming using the new features of .NET 4.0. You can refer to Chapter 3, "The .NET Languages," for a short discussion on parallel programming (System.Threading.Task, Parallel.For, and so on).

The Parallel Stacks Window

As more cores become available and more programming is done to support those cores, more threads will be executing. You therefore need additional support for debugging the processing complexities of your application. The Parallel Stacks window provides some help. It gives you a view of either all threads or all tasks executing at any given moment in time. The view is a diagram that shows the threads or tasks in your application, how they were created, and full call stack information for each thread or stack.

Parallel Stacks Threads View   You access the Parallel Stacks window in an active debug session from the Debug menu (Debug, Windows, Parallel Stacks). This window provides a visual diagram of the threads executing in your application. Figure 11.47 shows an example of the threads view in the Parallel Stacks window.

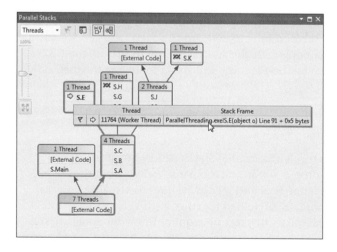

FIGURE 11.47   Use threads view of the Parallel Stacks window to visualize your threads.

In this example, notice that there are seven threads in the application. As you can see, if you hover over one of the thread call stack boxes, you can see the thread IDs and their names (if they have been named). Hovering over the initial grouping (7 Threads) shows all seven threads represented by the code in this application.

> **TIP**
>
> You can visualize external code (including that being executed by the framework) in the Parallel Stacks Window by right-clicking in the window and selecting Show External Code.

The arrows in the diagram indicate how the threads are spawned within the application, and provides information such as the thread ID, name, and call stack. You can use each thread's call stack information to switch to the code associated with a thread (and thus debug its context) by double-clicking.

Notice the toolbar in this window has the Threads option selected (as opposed to tasks). You can toggle between tasks (see the next section) and threads. The other options for this toolbar are shown in Figure 11.48.

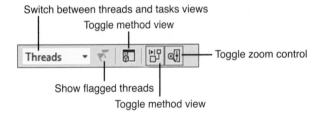

FIGURE 11.48   The toolbar in the Parallel Stacks window.

Switching to method view using the toolbar (refer to Figure 11.48) changes the diagram to highlight (or pivot on) a specific method in your code. In this view, you can see all threads that enter the given method along with their call stacks up to that method. You can then see the exit points from the method and the call stacks following the method's exit.

Figure 11.49 shows an example of method view. You can clearly see the active threads and their method call stacks as they chain together.

Parallel Stacks Task View   You can toggle the Parallel Stacks window to show tasks instead of threads. You can use the drop-down in the toolbar to switch from threads to tasks. You can then use the same diagram tool and related features to visualize tasks as you would threads. Both tasks and threads are joined together in this same tool window as they are such similar concepts. Of course, this feature requires that your application is coded to use tasks.

Recall that tasks are bits of work that can be executed in parallel by two or more processor cores. You code tasks using the task scheduling service in the .NET Framework's parallel task library (`System.Threading.Task` namespace). The task scheduler provides a number of services such as managing thread pools on each core and providing synchronization services for your code. This is an additional layer of abstraction over simply managing your own threads or using the `ThreadPool` class. Instead, the framework handles cores and threads. Therefore, trying to debug task-based applications at the thread level is a challenge given the fact that the framework (and not your code) is typically managing the threads.

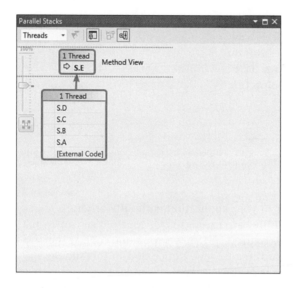

FIGURE 11.49   Use the method view to show all threads that enter and exit a method along with the related call stack information.

Visual Studio provides two principal windows for looking at the task-level abstraction of multi-core development: Parallel Stacks (in tasks view) and the Parallel Tasks window. We discuss the latter in a moment. First, let's look at what can be done to view tasks using the Parallel Stacks window.

TIP

If you are debugging unfamiliar-but-parallel code and are unsure if it uses tasks or threads, you can enable external code in the Parallel Tasks window (right-click, select Show External Code). In threads view, you can see whether there are calls to the `Task` class. This indicates the code was written using multitask (and not simply multithreads).

You switch to task view by selecting Tasks in the drop-down of the Parallel Stacks toolbar. This shows the call stacks for each task being executed. It also shows you the status of the task (waiting, running, scheduled). Figure 11.50 shows you an example.

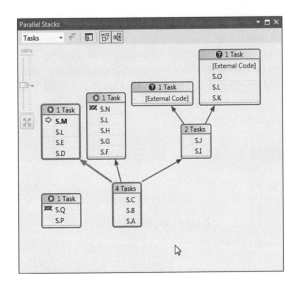

FIGURE 11.50   You can switch the Parallel Stacks window to Tasks view to view the tasks running in your debug session.

This abstracted view helps you see the tasks in your application without worrying so much about on which processor and thread they are executing. Of course, you can switch to threads view to see this information, too. Figure 11.51 shows the same code at the same breakpoint in the same window but for threads view. Notice that in this simple example, the parallel framework has created threads that are very similar to the tasks (two main threads executing the work). If you start to add a lot more work to this application, however, you start to see inactive threads that are sitting in the pool waiting to do work. You also start to see a single thread executing larger call stacks (due to reuse) that do not align with your task view.

The Parallel Tasks Window

Another way to look at the tasks running in your application is through the Parallel Tasks window (Debug, Windows, Parallel Tasks). This window is actually similar to the Threads window (refer to Figure 11.43) but it shows the abstraction layer of tasks for those developers doing multicore task-based development.

Figure 11.52 shows an example of this window running for a parallel application. Notice that for each task (in this case there are seven) you can view the task ID, status, location, the task (or entry point for the task), the thread assignment, and application domain. Note that this example groups the tasks by their status (active, blocked, etc.). This is done by right-clicking the status column and selecting Group by Status from the context menu.

You can also use the parallel tasks window to flag tasks for viewing. You do so using the arrows on the left side of each task in the dialog box. You can also right-click a task to freeze or thaw its associated thread. Alternatively, you can use the right-click command Freeze All Threads But This to focus in on a specific thread and task.

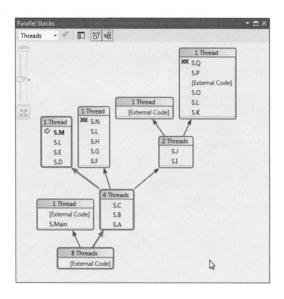

FIGURE 11.51   The Threads view of the same spot in a debug session depicted by the Tasks view shown in Figure 11.50.

	ID	Status	Location	Task	Thread Assignment	AppDomain	Process
^ Status: Active (2 tasks)							
▼ ⇨	1	⏵ Active	S.E	A	9836 (Worker Threac	1 (ParallelThr	4304
▼	2	⏵ Active	S.H	A	9324 (Worker Threac	1 (ParallelThr	4304
^ Status: Blocked (2 tasks)							
▼	3	❷ Blocked	S.J	A	11820 (Worker Threa	1 (ParallelThr	4304
▼	4	❷ Blocked	S.K	A	6276 (Worker Threac	1 (ParallelThr	4304

FIGURE 11.52   You can use the Parallel Tasks window in a similar manner as you would the Threads window.

The location column shows the current location of the task. If you hover over this location, you see the call stack for the task. This is all code called thus far in the given task. This mouseover is actually actionable. It is called a stack tip. The stack tip enables you to switch between stack frames and view the code inside a given call in the stack. Figure 11.53 shows an example of selecting an item from a stack tip. You can double-click this item to be taken to the code and change the debug context to focus on this call.

Debugging a Client-Side Script

Visual Studio lets you debug your client-side script (JavaScript and VBScript) by enabling script debugging in the browser. This can be done in Internet Explorer using the Internet Options dialog box (Tools, Internet Options). From this dialog box, select the Advanced tab and then navigate to the Browsing category (see Figure 11.54). Here you need to uncheck the Disable Script Debugging option (checked by default). This tells IE that if it encounters a script error, it should look for a debugger (such as Visual Studio).

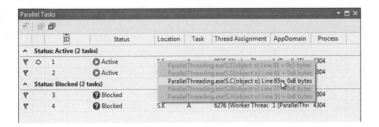

FIGURE 11.53 The Location column includes an actionable stack tip window that represents the call stack for the given task.

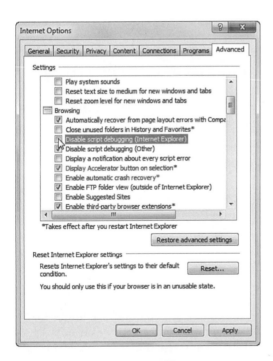

FIGURE 11.54 You can enable client-side script debugging from IE's Options dialog box.

Next, set breakpoints inside your .aspx or .html files within your `<script>` blocks. You can then stop on these lines and debug them with Visual Studio. There are some limitations, however. If you are having trouble, review "Limitations on Script Debugging" in the MSDN documentation.

Debugging Crash Information (Dump Files)

It is often not possible to re-create all environment- or user-specific scenarios in a development environment. Of course, many application bugs or crashes happen without the developer present, or a copy of Visual Studio running. In these cases, you can output a dump file of the application state at the time of the issue.

Dump files save information about the state of your application. Dump files are typically created in response to a major bug or an application failure (crash). The dump file can then be sent to a developer. A developer can open the file, connect it with the source code and debug symbols, and debug the state of the application at the time of the issue.

Dumping Debug Information

You can save running (but paused or on a breakpoint) .NET managed code as mini dump files. You have a few options for creating these files. In a debugging setting, you can use Visual Studio to create these files and share them with other developers as necessary. Of course, other applications can also create mini dump files, which then can be opened by Visual Studio for debugging. Your options for creating dump files include the following:

▶ Use the Save Dump As option from the Debug menu in an active debug session of Visual Studio.

▶ Attach to a running (or crashed) remote process from Visual Studio (see the information about attaching to a process earlier in this chapter). You can then break into that process and save the dump file using the Save Dump As option.

▶ Microsoft provides the utility UserDump as part of their OEM Support Tools. You can use this utility to create dump files that Visual Studio can read.

▶ Microsoft provides the Autodump+ utility as part of the Microsoft Debugging Tools for Windows. It, too, creates dump files for use by Visual Studio.

We focus on how Visual Studio creates dump files. A quick web search will lead you to the download for other dump-creating utilities.

Using Visual Studio to Create a Dump File   Creating a dump file with Visual Studio is straightforward. You stop (or break into) the application at the point you want to capture. This might be at a place in the testing where there is a known issue. You then select the Save Dump As option from the Debug menu. The Save Dump As dialog box is then displayed, as shown in Figure 11.55.

Notice that when you save a dump file, you can choose between creating the file with heap information and without. The heap information is often not required for many managed code debugging scenarios. Thus, you can save your file without it and conserve hard drive space.

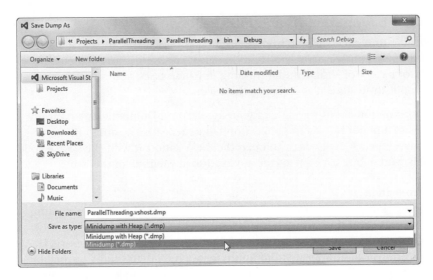

FIGURE 11.55   You can save a mini dump file with or without heap information.

Debugging with a Dump File

The first step to debugging with a dump file is to open the file from the File menu (File, Open, File) or by double-clicking the dump file. When you open a dump file, the new Dump File summary page appears. This page displays information about the dump file, such as when the dump file was created, the version of the OS and CLR that was running when the dump file was written, and the versions of the various other components (modules) that were running at the time. Figure 11.56 shows an example of this new summary page. Notice that you can use the modules search box to determine if a specific .dll or .exe was loaded at the time of the dump.

The summary page shown in Figure 11.56 represents a dump file from a break in the Contoso application discussed earlier in the chapter. Recall that this application includes a page that allows a customer to manage her profile that's stored in a database. In this case, an error has occurred. Imagine a scenario where the developer looking at the error could not debug it. Therefore, he might create a dump file and pass it to another developer to take a look. Alternatively, the dump could have come from a tester that encountered the error or from the web server.

The dump summary page provides a few actions. The two developers use the most are Set Symbol Paths and Debug with Mixed. The Set Symbol Paths option enables you to indicate the paths to the symbol files (.pdb) that match the build of the application from which the dump originated. By default, Visual Studio looks for symbol files in the location where your code executed. Therefore, if you dump and open that dump on the same machine, you have nothing more to set up. Visual Studio finds your symbol files. If, however, symbol files are created on a per-build basis and dumps can originate from anywhere, you have to use Set Symbol Paths to indicate where Visual Studio should find your latest symbols.

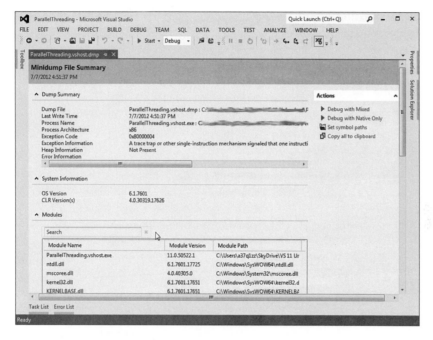

FIGURE 11.56   The mini dump summary page shows you both detailed information and next steps (actions) when you open a dump file.

IMPORTANT

Symbol files (.pdb) are important if you intend to debug a built application. For this reason, we recommend you store your symbol files in a safe location along with the compiled versions of your deployed code to make debugging a production issue using a dump much easier.

Figure 11.57 shows an example of the Options, Debugging, Symbols dialog box. In the top part of the dialog box, you can set up a symbol location, which might be a server where builds are dropped or a local folder on your machine. Notice, too, that you can load the Microsoft Public Symbols from their servers. The middle section of the dialog box, Cache Symbols in This Directory, enables you to set up a local folder for caching symbols downloaded from a server, which saves time in that the files can load from a local source. You indicate which modules of your symbol files should be loaded (or excluded) in the last part of the dialog box. You can set this option to All Modules.

The other option available on the mini dump page (refer back to Figure 11.56), Debug with Mixed, enables you to start the debugger using the data found in the mini dump file. It is helpful to know that a .NET symbol file (.pdb) essentially contains information about your source files, variable names, and code line numbers. When you debug a dump file, Visual Studio looks at the .pdb files it finds (searching your code or your symbol directory) and tries to use this information to find your code files on your machine. If it can locate your code, it opens the code file and gives you a rich debugging experience.

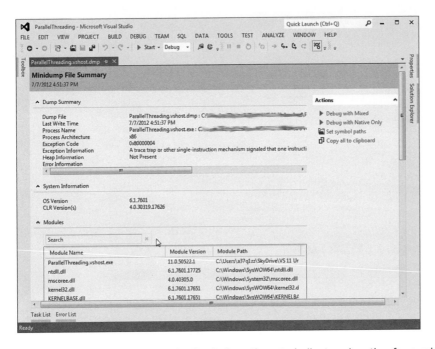

FIGURE 11.57 You can use the Symbols options to indicate a location for symbol files and set up a local cache.

Summary

This chapter presented the Visual Studio 2012 debugger. We covered setting breakpoints in code as well as setting conditions for when those breakpoints are hit. We discussed stepping through code after hitting that breakpoint. In addition, we presented tracepoints, which perform an action (such as printing a message to the output window) when a line of code is hit in the debugger. The chapter also examined the many ways you can see the data presented by the debugger, including the Watch windows, visualizers, and DataTips.

The advanced debugging scenarios covered included remote processes, web services, multi-threaded applications, multicore, and client-side script. In this chapter, you also learned how to use the mini dump features to take a snapshot of a running application and debug it at a later time on a different machine.

Although the debugger itself is large and, in some areas, complicated, mastering its features is a critical skill to have for all Visual Studio developers.

CHAPTER 12

Deploying Code

Visual Studio is primarily a coding and development tool. But after you have built an application, the next problem you face is how to get it into the hands of the users. This is not an insignificant problem space. Applications might have a variety of prerequisites that need to be verified: Is the right version of the .NET Framework installed? Does the target machine have SQL Server installed? Is a supported operating system detected?

In addition to prerequisites, the actual install process involves myriad variables. Some applications are simple enough to enjoy the ability to do "xcopy deployment." In other words, you just copy the executable over to the target machine and away you go. But there are certainly more complicated scenarios as well. For instance, your application might store some data in the Registry and might require Registry values to be set upon install. Or there might be a particular folder structure required. Or maybe a database schema needs to be configured, and data populated, during the deployment process.

Visual Studio can help with all of these scenarios. In this chapter, we examine how you can use Visual Studio to package and deploy .NET client applications. We also investigate how you can deploy server-based, ASP.NET web applications.

An Overview of Client Deployment Options

Two primary installation and deployment are technologies available within Visual Studio: ClickOnce and InstallShield. Both of these vehicles are similar in that they enable you to move binaries and components from one location and install them onto a target client machine. But there are definitely pros and cons to dealing with each.

Introducing ClickOnce Deployments

ClickOnce was created to try and match the low-deployment factor of web applications. With web applications, users can merely open a browser and click a link to access functionality. In a similar fashion, with ClickOnce, you can publish a set of binaries to a web server or file share, and users can simply click a link to the ClickOnce package to have the application installed onto their machine.

You can deploy an application using ClickOnce in three ways:

▶ **Web/Share deployment**—In this model, your application executables or DLLs are first published to a web server or network share. You can then provide a link (either a web URL or network path) to binaries. Users can click this link to have the applications automatically installed onto their current machine (thus the moniker *ClickOnce*). No further interaction is required from the user.

▶ **CD deployment**—With this method, binaries are packaged and copied onto a CD or DVD. Users then browse the content of the media and launch the install process with one click. This method is primarily used for situations where users are isolated and do not have the required Internet access or network access to make the web/ share deployment method useful.

▶ **Web/share execution**—This scenario is nearly identical to the first method discussed. Binaries are published to a web location or network share, and a link to that location is then provided to users. When the user clicks that link, the binaries are immediately copied over and the application starts without making a permanent home for the app on the user's PC. After a user closes the application, it is like it was never there in the first place; all the application binaries are removed, there are no entries placed within the Start menu or within the Add or Remove Programs list in the Control Panel, and so on. To the user, it appears as if the application has been run directly from the Internet (or network share), although in fact the binaries have been cached on to the local machine.

ClickOnce applications are extremely easy to deploy for developers, and they are extremely easy for users to install because little interaction is required and there is little overall footprint on the client. However, this simplicity comes with a price. Generally speaking, ClickOnce deployments cannot do any of the more complicated things we referenced in the introduction to this chapter, such as modifying registry settings, or installing third-party software. If your install scenario is too complicated for ClickOnce to handle, you have to turn to Windows Installer.

Introducing Windows Installer and InstallShield Deployments

InstallShield is an installer technology created by Flexera; Visual Studio 2012 ships with a version of this software called InstallShield Limited Edition. InstallShield generates installation packages (MSI files), which contain all the information that the Windows Installer runtime needs to execute and support the installation process for that particular payload.

The basic process looks like this:

1. InstallShield, based on your input, bundles your application and its resources within a setup package, typically referred to as an MSI file because of its default .msi file extension. MSI files are a cohesive unit of deployment that is understood by the Windows Installer runtime.

2. The MSI file is delivered to the end users.

3. Running the MSI file launches a wizard that guides the user through the install process. This typically includes querying for information such as where the software should be installed on the hard drive and specifying various options that the software might support in terms of feature set selection.

> **NOTE**
>
> Earlier versions of Visual Studio offered a dedicated project template for generating MSI packages. With Visual Studio 2012, this approach has been deprecated in favor of InstallShield Limited Edition. Even though the InstallShield project template is integrated directly into Visual Studio 2012, you must still register, download, and install the software to use it. If you have Windows Installer setup projects created in earlier versions of Visual Studio, you can import those for use with InstallShield and Visual Studio 2012.

With few limitations, you can craft a setup wizard to handle a variety of situations, including different payloads based on the running OS version, adding a shortcut to the Windows startup group, adding Registry entries, and installing device drivers.

> **NOTE**
>
> Certain applications have special deployment requirements. We reexamine the topic of deployment for the other major application types within each chapter that covers those types. For example, for Azure cloud-based applications, read Chapter 24, "Developing Applications in the Cloud with Windows Azure."

Publishing a Project with ClickOnce

You create a ClickOnce install by first configuring the correct "publish" options for your project. These are all located on the project properties dialog box, under the Publish tab (see Figure 12.1).

You can see that this property page holds a variety of settings including where to host the ClickOnce installation, and how we want to handle the offline versus online aspects of ClickOnce. To make things easy for our first deployment, we let the Publish Wizard walk us through setting these options. Click the Publish Wizard button at the bottom of the Publish property page to get started.

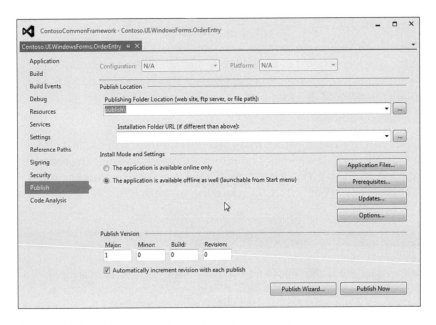

FIGURE 12.1   Setting ClickOnce publication properties.

The first page of the wizard captures where we want to publish our application. This can be a path to a file share, or it can be a URL pointing to a website or FTP site directory.

Page two of the wizard (see Figure 12.2) identifies how users install the application. You have three choices here: via a website, via a network share, or from physical media (CD/DVD).

The first two selections require you to enter the exact location where users can download the software. At first glance, it's not clear what is different about the location specified here and the location specified on page one. Let's clarify what is happening with an example. Let's assume, for instance, that we want users of our application to be able to install the Windows Forms client by visiting a link on the Contoso website. In this scenario, we might end up with the following values:

▶ **Publishing folder location**—c:\inetpub\wwwroot\ContosoCSRInstall

▶ **Installation folder location**—http://www.contoso.com/CSR/Install.htm

The first path is the physical path that Visual Studio uses to copy the installation files to their home. The second path is the path (in this case, a URL) that the world uses to access those installation files.

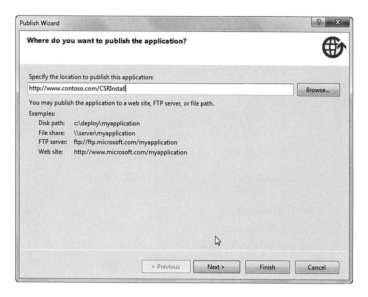

FIGURE 12.2   Setting the install type in the Publish Wizard.

The third and final page of the wizard varies slightly depending on the install option we selected on page two. For website and network share installs, we must indicate whether the application should be available online and offline or just online. Offline capable applications have a shortcut added to the Start menu and can be uninstalled through the normal Add/Remove Programs control panel. Online-only applications are run directly from the Installation folder location. If we select the CD/DVD installation option, we have the opportunity to specify whether the application updates itself when online.

After the wizard finishes, the project builds and immediately tries to publish using the information collected. If you have specified that an installation web page be created (click the Options button, and then specify a web page such as Install.htm on the Deployment tab), Visual Studio creates a basic ClickOnce install web page (see Figure 12.3). You can easily customize the look and feel of a ClickOnce page by editing the HTML.

> **NOTE**
>
> You don't need to go through the entire Publish Wizard every time you want to deploy or redeploy your application. After you have the options set the way you want them on the Publish property page, you can republish using those settings by selecting Publish from the Visual Studio Build menu.

Now let's move on and see discuss how to accomplish the same end result using Visual Studio and the Windows Installer technology.

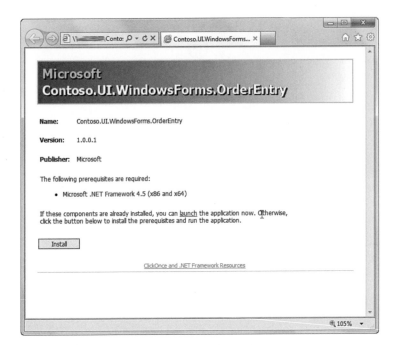

FIGURE 12.3   A ClickOnce install point (web page).

Publishing a Project with InstallShield Limited Edition

Just as with ClickOnce, Visual Studio directly supports deployment of applications using the Windows Installer technology. The approach is different (as are the underlying technologies); Windows Installer deployments are created with the use of a separate project template and application (InstallShield). The first step is to add a deployment project to our existing Contoso order entry solution.

> **NOTE**
>
> For deploying complicated installations, the Windows Installer is a great approach. For those situations where you want to get an application up and running in a short time with minimal user interaction, the Windows Installer can be overkill. This is where ClickOnce can be a better option.

Right-click the solution, select Add, New Project, and then find the InstallShield Limited Edition Project template by first expanding Other Project Types and then InstallShield Limited Edition (see Figure 12.4). Give your setup project a name, and click OK to add it to the solution.

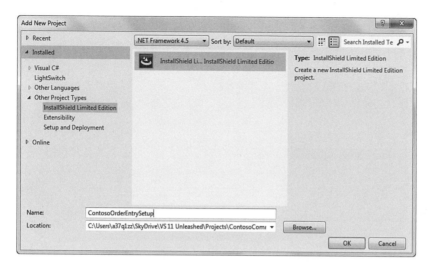

FIGURE 12.4   The InstallShield project template.

InstallShield projects are highly specialized projects within Visual Studio, and as such have their own unique layout and organization. Each setup project contains several nodes that are numbered to correspond to the high-level activities each setup project will perform. Figure 12.5 shows an example of an InstallShield project inside of the Solution Explorer.

You can visit each of the nodes and use the designers/editors they contain to manually tweak your installs, but by default InstallShield will guide you through the entire process via the Project Assistant (see Figure 12.6).

To get started, click the right-arrow button at the bottom right of the Project Assistant window. There are seven different areas of the Project Assistant. Let's visit each in turn, starting with Application Information.

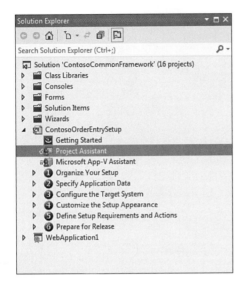

FIGURE 12.5   An InstallShield setup project.

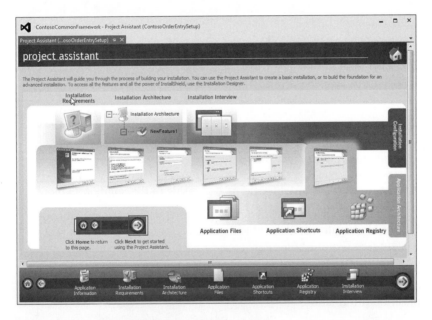

FIGURE 12.6   The InstallShield Project Assistant.

Application Information

The first page of the Project Assistant gathers general information related to the application you are packaging for deployment. On this screen, you provide the name of your company, the application name, the version of the application, and your company's website address (see Figure 12.7). This information is displayed during the install process, and also shows up within the Windows Control Panel if a user visits the Add/Remove Programs application.

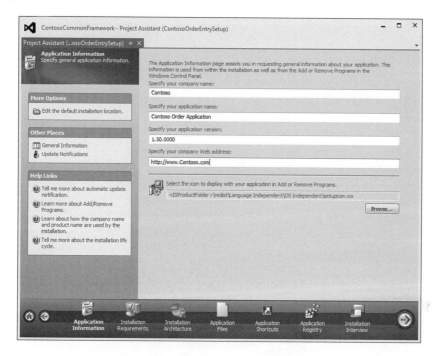

FIGURE 12.7   Providing general application information.

Installation Requirements

Most application installers need to check for a set of preexisting conditions. For example, you might support only certain operating systems, or you might require certain other third-party software components to be already installed on the target machine. Figure 12.8 shows the Installation Requirements screen.

Two primary pieces of information are captured here: OS requirements and additional software requirements. If our sample Contoso application requires Windows 8, Windows 7, or Windows Vista, we indicate that by checking those OS values in the top list box.

We also want to indicate that our application requires the .NET Framework 4.0 Client profile package, and it requires SQL Server 2008 Express. Both of these are indicated by checking the appropriate entries in the bottom list box.

Checking for Other Conditions

Besides the stock list of prerequisites that can be checked, you also have the option to specify your own custom set of conditions to be checked by the installer. As an example, perhaps we require another piece of Contoso software to be already registered in the system prior to setup. One approach is to check the system Registry for a specific key indicating this condition. To look for the presence of a Registry key or value, we use a custom software condition. InstallShield has a wizard for defining these conditions. They aren't limited to Registry key checks. You can also set up conditions based on the existence of folder paths, files, or even INI file contents.

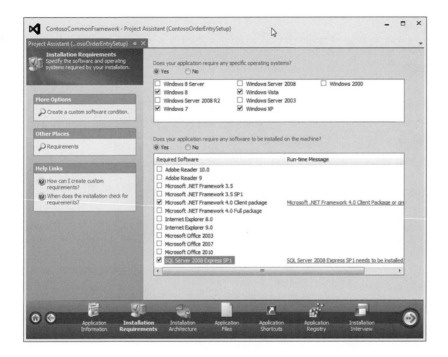

FIGURE 12.8   The Installation Requirements screen.

To launch the wizard and specify custom conditions, click Create a Custom Software Condition link under More Options on the left pane of the assistance screen.

Application Files

Because installation, at its heart, involves copying files onto the target machine, we need a way to indicate which files are to be included as part of our application installation. The Application Files screen is where this happens.

The interface for this editor is meant to mimic the folder structure on the target system, so a left pane shows the various default folders we can copy files to, and the right pane identifies the files to copy into each folder. Typically, you simply add the output of a particular project in your solution to the right pane by clicking the Add Project Outputs button. Then, in the selection dialog, you just navigate to the project that you want to deploy and select the appropriate file categories for inclusion. In our case, we have a Windows

Forms project; we want to deploy the actual binaries, any localized resources in use by the application, any files marked as content files (these might be data files, help files, and so on), and finally documentation files. Figure 12.9 shows these selections made within the Output Selector dialog, and Figure 12.10 shows the Application Files screen after adding the selections. To add files to your setup that aren't necessarily project output files, you click the Add Files or Add Folders button instead.

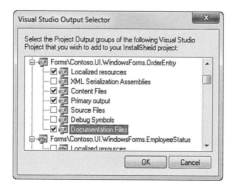

FIGURE 12.9   Adding project files to the deployment package.

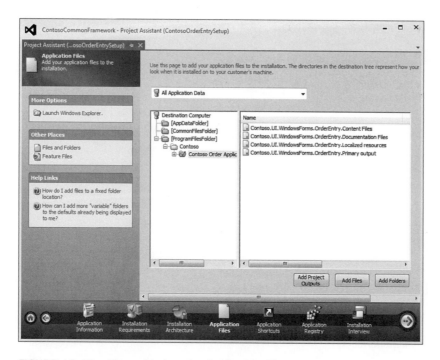

FIGURE 12.10   Files added on the Application Files screen.

You can see that the folders that are listed in the left pane are actually predefined alias names for physical directories. For instance, the ProgramFilesFolder maps to the actual program files directory on the target computer. The DesktopFolder, for example, physically represents C:\Users\username\Desktop on Windows 7, and the System Folder represents C:\Windows\System32.

You can add additional folders to the existing predefined list by right-clicking the Destination Computer root node and selecting New Folder. Similarly, you can display more predefined folders by selecting them from the Show Predefined Folders fly-out menu (also available via right-clicking the Destination Computer node).

Application Shortcuts

On the next screen in the Project Assistant, you can specify how and where shortcuts will be created to your application. You can create shortcuts within the Windows Start menu, and you can place them on the desktop as well. To indicate that a shortcut is to be configured as part of your setup process, you first add the file to which the shortcut will point by clicking the New button. For each file that you add, use the check boxes to the right of the screen to indicate where to create the shortcuts. Figure 12.11 shows a set of shortcuts added to the list.

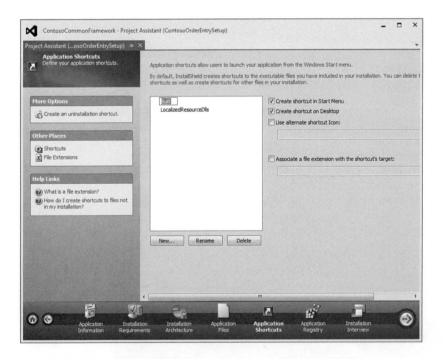

FIGURE 12.11   Adding shortcuts.

Note that you can also use this page to create a shortcut for uninstalling your application. See the option Create an Uninstallation Shortcut under More Options (left side of the window).

Application Registry

The Application Registry screen is used to create or modify Registry entries on the target computer during the setup process. The left pane of the editor shows the four HKEY "hives" and the User/Machine hive. You can walk down through the Registry folder structure, find the location for your Registry key, and then right-click in the right pane to specify the key name and default value (see Figure 12.12).

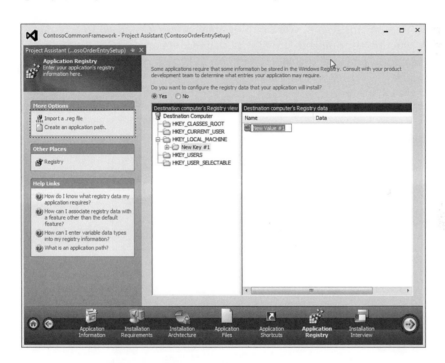

FIGURE 12.12   Setting up Registry entries.

TIP

A quick and easy way to get your Registry changes into the setup project is to import them from a machine that already has a Registry configured the correct way for your application. First, export, regedit.exe, the appropriate Registry entries to a REG file. Then use the option Import a .reg File on the left pane of the Application Registry screen to import the keys from the REG file into the Registry Editor.

Installation Interview

The Installation Interview screen, the last in the Project Assistant workflow, enables you to customize the basic set of prompts that the Install Wizard will display. You can think of the Installer Wizard as a series of dialog boxes that are meant to either collect information from the user (such as an install path or installation options) or relay information to the user (such as a progress indicator for keeping track of the install process). The Windows Installer provides a basic set of these screens that are grouped into the three phases of an install. The Start phase consists of an initial Welcome screen, a dialog box to capture the installation folder, and a confirmation screen. The Progress phase has just one screen with a progress bar that measures current progress. And the End phase has a summary Finished screen.

Using the radio buttons on this screen, you can indicate whether users need to accept a license agreement, whether they need to provide username and company information, and whether the wizard should give the user the option to launch the application as soon as it has been installed (see Figure 12.13).

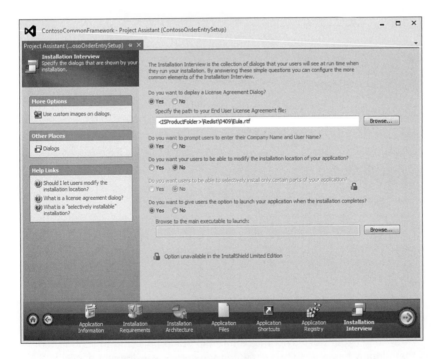

FIGURE 12.13   Configuring installer prompts.

Customizing the Installer Dialogs

If you need to exercise finer-grained control over the look and feel of your application's installer, this is accomplished via the InstallShield dialog editor. To access this feature from the Installation Interview screen, click Dialogs under Other Places. The Dialogs designer (see Figure 12.14) controls which dialog pages will appear during the setup process and enables you to set various properties on those pages. For instance, adding a Contoso-specific bitmap for use as a splash screen is accomplished by first enabling the Splash Bitmap option and then entering the correct path to the image file for the screen.

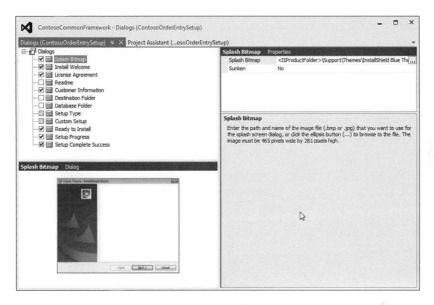

FIGURE 12.14   Selecting and customizing a dialog box to add to the installer.

> **NOTE**
>
> Some of the more advanced functionality in terms of editing and designing dialogs is available only within the Premier or Professional editions of InstallShield, and is not available for use in the edition bundled with Visual Studio.

So, you have now learned the two principal ways to deploy client applications. You can also deploy ASP.NET applications from the IDE.

Publishing an ASP.NET Web Application

Visual Studio 2012 provides an improved tool, the Web Publish tool, for deploying ASP.NET web applications. Using this tool, you can take an existing web application project, compile it, bundle all the folders, files, settings, and databases that are used by that application into a web package, and then deploy that package to a web server. One advantage to compiling your website before deploying is that the compiler finds compile-time errors for you before deploying onto the target server. Another advantage you gain by compiling your application is increased page performance. Because all the pages within the site are precompiled, the need to compile dynamically during the first page hit is removed.

> **NOTE**
>
> As mentioned, the Web Publish tool is designed to deploy websites, as opposed to web applications. For a thorough treatment on the differences between these two project types, see Chapter 4, "Solutions and Projects," and Chapter 16, "Creating ASP.NET Form-Based Applications."

Let's continue with a brief walkthrough of the publishing process. The Web Publish process is kicked off via the Build menu via the Publish command (see Figure 12.15) or by right-clicking on the web application project in Solution Explorer and selecting Publish.

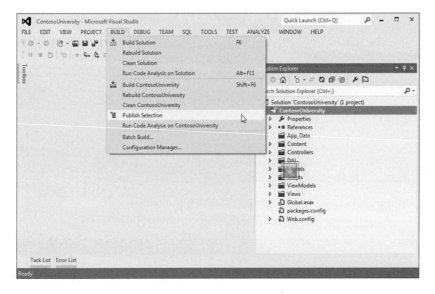

FIGURE 12.15   Launching the Web Publishing tool from within the IDE.

The very first screen asks for a profile to use.

Creating a Profile

The publishing process is driven by a profile. This is a collection of settings that define the publishing process and all of its associated variables. You can either create your own profile (as you would if you were publishing to an internal web server, or to your own development machine, or to a corporate IT/enterprise asset), or you can use a profile provided by a third party (as would be the case if you were publishing your web application to a third-party hosting provider).

If you are using a third-party hosting provider, and they have a profile file available, you can import it at this stage by using the Import button. Otherwise, you can create your own profile by clicking New in the drop-down box (see Figure 12.16).

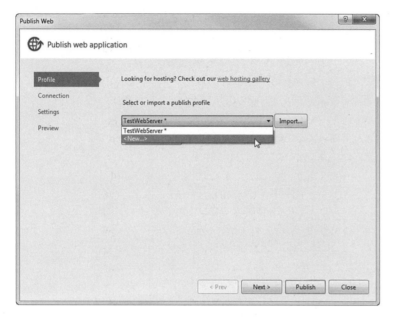

FIGURE 12.16   Creating a publishing profile.

With a blank profile created, let's move on to the next step: specifying connection information.

Configuring a Connection

The next page in the Publish Wizard captures the method of deployment and connection information. The method of deployment is selected by using the Publish Method drop-down. Prior to Visual Studio 2010, we could select one of three different deployment methods: FTP, FrontPage Server Extensions (FPSE), or a file system path. Visual Studio 2010 added a fourth option: One-Click Publishing. And now, with Visual Studio 2012, One-Click Publishing has undergone a name change to Web Deploy. Out of all the options available, Web Deploy is the best in terms of leveraging Visual Studio to do the heavy lifting. This method uses Internet Information Services (IIS) remote management services to copy the relevant application files to a remote or local server. As mentioned in the discussion about profile settings, some web hosting providers directly support One-Click Publishing/Web Deploy, which makes this method particularly attractive for targeting off-site web servers that are being maintained by a third party.

The rest of the options on this page of the wizard are dynamic and depend on the method you choose. For FTP deployments, for example, you must need to provide the appropriate FTP login information. For Web Deploy profiles, you must provide a service URL and an application URL (see Figure 12.17).

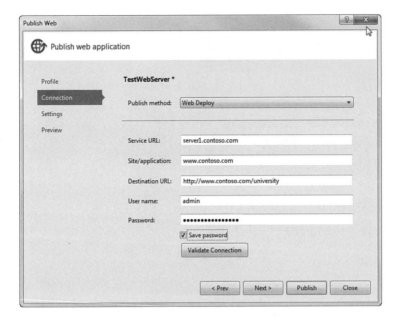

FIGURE 12.17   The Web Deploy connection settings.

Configuring Deployment Settings

The next to last step in the Publish Wizard captures the build configuration that you want to deploy (for example, Release or Debug). Also, for each database connection used by the web application, it configures the corresponding connection string to use on the target server.

In the Contoso University sample application, two database connections are used, one called SchoolContext, and the other called ApplicationServices. If you look at Figure 12.18, you can see that the wizard shows us a section for each of these connections. Use the drop-down box to enter the connection string that the application should use on the target server (that is, the server on the receiving end of the publish operation).

Deploying the Database

Under each connection string drop-down, you'll find an Update Database check box. Placing a check here tells the Web Deploy engine to also package up your physical database (in this case, a SQL Express database) and deploy it to the target server as well. The publishing engine automatically updates or creates the destination database schema as needed.

You can also provide custom SQL scripts to be used as part of the deployment process. To do this, click the Configure Database Updates link located to the right of the Update Database check box. In the dialog, click the Add SQL Script link at the top (see Figure 12.19).

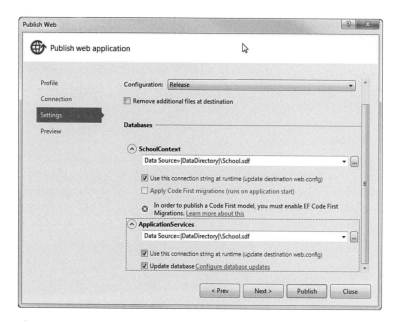

FIGURE 12.18   Deployment configuration and database connection information.

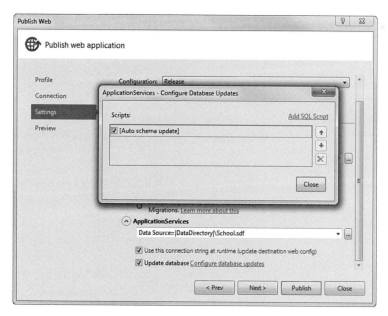

FIGURE 12.19   Deploying referenced databases with custom SQL script.

From there, click the Add Script button, and then navigate to the script file. Notice that there is already a script entry in the list; this is the script that the deployment tool generates based on the settings you have provided. Custom scripts that are added are executed in the order they are listed. For instance, if you need a script to execute *before* the general schema and data script that the tool generates, you add the script to the list and then use the arrow keys to the right of the list to move it above the default script.

Previewing the Publication

After all the required properties and settings have been provided, the final page of the wizard shows you a preview of the actions that will be performed (see Figure 2.20). This is a smart preview and not just a restatement of your earlier settings. In other words, the publishing tool actually reaches out to the target server at this stage and visually shows you a list of files that will be copied or deleted, database schemas that will be created, and so forth. You can make last-minute changes on this screen by opting to not copy or delete specific files.

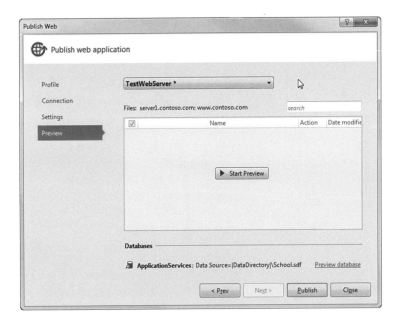

FIGURE 12.20   Previewing the deployment.

If everything looks okay, click the Publish button to initiate the deployment.

Summary

This chapter introduced you to the various tools available within Visual Studio for deploying both client applications and server-side ASP.NET web applications. For client applications, you learned about the two principal deployment technologies (ClickOnce and InstallShield) and the specific reasons why you might choose one over the other. This chapter explored these two technologies in depth by examining how to use Visual Studio to publish a WinForms application using both methods.

This chapter also covered the tools available for deploying ASP.NET web applications from a local machine off to a web server and demonstrated the tools within the IDE for accomplishing the same.

12

CHAPTER 13

Introducing the Automation Object Model

Visual Studio is built to be extensible. It ships with its own application programming interface (API) to enable you, the developer, to control many of the pieces of the IDE.

This API is called the Visual Studio automation object model, and understanding its capabilities is the key to unlocking your ability to program and control the IDE itself by writing code in the form of add-ins (discussed in Chapter 14, "Writing Add-Ins and Wizards").

In this chapter, we discuss the layout and structure of the automation object model. We map the various objects in the object model to their IDE counterparts, delve into the various ways to interact with these objects through managed code, and show the possibilities in terms of Visual Studio customization.

To drive home the object model concepts and place them in context, we have provided various code snippets and listings, nearly 100% of which are written in the context of a C# add-in. This chapter is, in essence, a reference chapter for learning about the automation objects, their properties, and their methods. In Chapter 14, we move beyond the object model and work to understand how to use, write, and run add-ins.

So for now, don't worry too much about the mechanics of writing an add-in; concentrate instead on understanding the automation objects and how they are referenced and used. For the ambitious, know that the code listings here can be pasted directly into an add-in class and run as is.

An Overview of the Automation Object Model

The automation object model is a structured class library with a top-level root object called DTE (or DTE2; more on this in a bit), which stands for Development Tools Environment. By referencing the assembly that implements the DTE/DTE2 object, you can instance this root object and use its members and child classes to access the IDE components.

Object Model Versions

The automation object model is actually implemented across four different, complementary primary interop assemblies (PIAs): EnvDTE, EnvDTE80, EnvDTE90, and EnvDTE100. EnvDTE is the original automation assembly distributed with Visual Studio .NET 2003. EnvDTE80 was the library distributed with Visual Studio 2005. EnvDTE90 is distributed with Visual Studio 2008 (yet another assembly, EnvDTE90a is installed with Visual Studio 2008 Service Pack 1). And finally, EnvDTE100 made its first appearance with Visual Studio 2010. Each version of Visual Studio ships with the cumulative set of libraries. Visual Studio 2012, which did not introduce a new version, comes with all four PIAs.

The reason for multiple assemblies is simple: They help balance the need for new features against the need to preserve backward compatibility. For instance, with Visual Studio 2008, Microsoft was faced with a common design decision: replace or upgrade the previous assembly shipped with Visual Studio 2005 (EnvDTE80) and risk introducing incompatibilities with current macros and add-ins, or ship a new assembly that could be leveraged in cases in which the new functionality was desired (existing code would still target the previous, unchanged library).

The latter path was chosen, and thus EnvDTE100 (100 represents version 10.0) contains automation types and members that are new to Visual Studio 2010, while EnvDTE90 (for Visual Studio 2008) and EnvDTE80 (for Visual Studio 2005) provide the base level of functionality and backward compatibility.

Within the EnvDTE100 assembly, you find types that supersede their predecessors from the EnvDTE90 assembly, and the same is true for types within EnvDTE90 that supersede types implemented in EnvDTE80, all the way back to the original EnvDTE assembly. In these cases, the type name has been appended with a number to indicate the revised version. Therefore, we have DTE and DTE2; Solution, Solution2, and Solution3; and so on.

Table 13.1 provides a side-by-side listing of some of the most important types implemented in the EnvDTE libraries. This type list is incomplete; it should be considered for reference only. This table is useful, however, for identifying some of the newly minted types in the new automation assembly; in the next section, we see how these types can be organized into broad Visual Studio automation categories and how they map onto physical IDE constructs.

TABLE 13.1 Partial List of Automation Types

Type	Description
AddIn	Represents a VS add-in.
Breakpoint, Breakpoint2	Represents a debugger breakpoint.
BuildDependencies	For the selected project, represents a collection of `BuildDependency` objects.
BuildDependency	For the selected project, the projects that it depends on for a successful build.
BuildEvents	Exposes a list of events relevant to a solution build.
Command	Represents a command action in the IDE.
Commands, Commands2	A collection of all commands supported in the IDE.
CommandWindow	Represents the command window.
Configuration	Represents a project's configuration properties.
Debugger, Debugger2, Debugger3, Debugger4, Debugger5	Represents the Visual Studio debugger.
DebuggerEvents	Exposes events from the debugger.
Document	Represents an open document in the IDE.
Documents	A collection of all open documents in the IDE.
DTE	Represents the IDE; this is the top-level, root object for the automation object model.
EditPoint	Represents a text operation point within a document.
Events	Exposes all automation events.
ExceptionGroups	Represents the exception grouping categories supported by Visual Studio.
Find	Represents the Find capability for text searches in the IDE.
HTMLWindow, HTMLWindow3	Represents an HTML document window.
OutputWindow	Represents the Output window.
Program, (Process2)	Represents a program running within the IDE; useful for examining processes and threads within the program. EnvDTE80 functionality is provided by the `Process2` object.
Project	Represents a project loaded in the IDE.
ProjectItem	Represents an item contained within a given project.
ProjectItems	A collection of all items contained within a project.

13

Type	Description
Property	Represents a generic property for an object. (This can be used across various objects in the automation library.)
SelectedItem	Represents projects or project items that are currently selected in the IDE.
Solution, Solution2, Solution3, Solution4	Represents the solution currently loaded in Visual Studio.
SourceControl, SourceControl2	Represents the source control system of record within Visual Studio.
TaskItem	Represents an item in the Task List window.
TaskItems, TaskItems2	A collection of all items in the Task List window.
TaskList	Represents the Task List window.
Template	Represents a Visual Studio template.
TextDocument	Represents a text file open in the IDE.
TextPane, TextPane2	Represents a pane within an open text editor window.
TextWindow	Represents a text window.
ToolBox	Represents the Toolbox window.
ToolBoxItem, ToolBoxItem2	Represents an item within the Toolbox window.
ToolBoxTab, ToolboxTab2, ToolboxTab3	Represents a tab of items on the Toolbox window.
Window, Window2	Represents, generically, any window within the IDE.
Windows, Windows2	A collection of all windows within the IDE.

Automation Categories

Because any automation effort with Visual Studio starts with the object model, you should first understand how it maps onto the IDE constructs and determine the exact capabilities it exposes.

In general, you can think of the object model classes as being organized into categories that directly speak to these IDE concepts:

▶ Solutions and projects

▶ Windows and command bars (toolbars and menu bars)

▶ Documents

▶ Commands

▶ Debugger

▶ Events

Each of the objects in these categories touches a different piece of the IDE, and access to each object is typically through the root-level DTE2 object.

The DTE/DTE2 Root Object

The DTE/DTE2 object represents the tip of the API tree. You can think of it as representing Visual Studio itself, with the objects under it mapping to the various constituent parts of the IDE.

As mentioned previously, DTE2 is the most current version of this object, with DTE providing compatibility with earlier versions. In this chapter, unless we specifically need to differentiate between their capabilities, we generically refer to the DTE and DTE2 objects as simply DTE.

The DTE properties are used to gain a reference to a specific IDE object (or collection of objects). Methods on the object are used to execute commands in the IDE, launch wizards, or close the IDE.

Table 13.2 shows the major properties and methods defined on the DTE2 object; they have been organized within the six object categories itemized in the preceding section.

TABLE 13.2   DTE2 Properties and Methods for IDE Access

Category	Property	Description
Commands	Commands	Returns a collection of Command objects; in general, a command is an action that can be carried out within the IDE such as opening or saving a file.
Debugger	Debugger	Returns the debugger object.
Documents	ActiveDocument	Returns a Document object representing the currently active document.
Documents	Documents	Returns a collection of Document objects representing all open documents.
Event Notification	Events	Returns the Events object for handling event notifications.
Solutions and Projects	ActiveSolutionProjects	Returns a collection of the Project objects representing the projects that are currently selected within the Solution Explorer.
Solutions and Projects	Solution	Returns the Solution object for the currently loaded solution.
Windows and Command Bars	ActiveWindow	Returns a Window object representing the window within the IDE that currently has focus.

13

Category	Property	Description
Windows and Command Bars	CommandBars	Returns a collection of CommandBar objects representing all the toolbars and menu bars.
Windows and Command Bars	MainWindow	Returns a Window object representing the IDE window itself.
Windows and Command Bars	StatusBar	Returns a StatusBar object representing Visual Studio's status bar.
Windows and Command Bars	ToolWindows	Returns a ToolWindows instance, which in turns provides access to a few of the most prominent tool windows: the command window, error list, output window, Solution Explorer, task list, and Toolbox.
Windows and Command Bars	WindowConfigurations	Returns a collection of WindowConfiguration objects; these objects represent the various window layouts in use by Visual Studio.

Category	Method	Description
Commands	ExecuteCommand	Executes an environment command.
—	LaunchWizard	Starts the identified wizard with the given parameters.
—	Quit	Closes Visual Studio.

> **NOTE**
>
> The mechanics of referencing and instancing a DTE object are covered in detail in Chapter 14.

In summary, the DTE object is a tool for directly interacting with certain IDE components and providing access to the deeper layers of the API with its property collections. If you move one level down in the API, you find the major objects that form the keystone for automation.

Solution and Project Objects

The `Solution` object represents the currently loaded solution. The individual projects within the solution are available via `Project` objects returned within the `Solution.Projects` collection. Items within a project are accessed in a similar fashion through the `Project.ProjectItems` collection.

As you can see from Figure 13.1, this hierarchy exactly mirrors the solution/project hierarchy that we first discussed in Chapter 4, "Solutions and Projects."

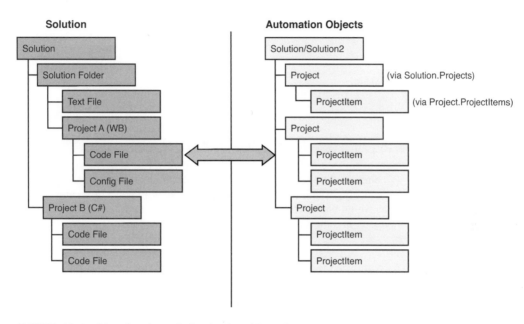

FIGURE 13.1 Mapping the solution/project hierarchy.

There are some mismatches here (solution folders, for instance, are treated as projects), but for the most part, the object model tree closely resembles the solution project tree that you are used to.

The Solution object and members enable you to interact with the current solution to perform common tasks such as these:

▶ Determining the number of projects in the solution (Count property)

▶ Adding a project to the solution based on a project file (AddFromFile method)

▶ Creating a new solution or closing the current one (Create and Close methods)

▶ Saving the solution (SaveAs method)

▶ Removing a project from the solution (Remove method)

You can also directly retrieve a reference to any of the projects within the currently loaded solution by iterating over the Solution.Projects collection. As an example of interacting with the Solution and Project objects, this C# code snippet removes the first project from the current solution:

```
Solution solution = _applicationObject.Solution;
Project project = solution.Projects.Item(0) as Project;

if (project.Saved)
{
```

```
    solution.Remove(project);
}
else
{
    //
}
```

> **NOTE**
>
> Most of the code snippets you see in this chapter are merely meant to reinforce how you would access the API component being discussed. We get into the specifics of exactly how to leverage these concepts within the next chapter. If you want to get a head start by playing with the code as we go along, you will need to skip ahead to Chapter 14, create a Visual Studio add-in project, and then return back here to follow along.

Table 13.3 provides the combined list of the most commonly used properties and methods implemented by the Solution objects.

TABLE 13.3   Primary Solution/Solution2/Solution3 Type Members

Property	Description
AddIns	Returns a collection of AddIn objects associated with the current solution.
Count	A count of the project within the solution.
DTE	A reference to the parent DTE object.
FullName	The full path and name of the solution file.
Globals	Returns the Globals object, a cache of variables used across the solution.
IsOpen	Indicates whether a solution is open.
Projects	Returns a collection of Project objects representing all the projects within the solution.
Properties	Returns a collection of Property objects that expose all the solution's properties.
Saved	Indicates whether the solution has been saved since the last modification.
SolutionBuild	Returns a reference to a SolutionBuild object. This is the entry point to the build automation objects applicable for the current solution.

Method	Description
AddFromFile	Adds a project to the solution using an existing project file.
AddFromTemplate	Takes an existing project, clones it, and adds it to the solution.
AddFromTemplateEx	Adds an existing project to a solution using the solution name.

Property	Description
AddSolutionFolder	Creates a new solution folder in the solution.
Close	Closes the solution.
Create	Creates an empty solution.
FindProjectItem	Initiates a search for a given item in one of the solution's projects.
GetProjectItemTemplate	Returns the path to the template used for the referenced project item.
GetProjectTemplate	Returns the path to the template used for the referenced project.
Item	Returns a `Project` instance.
Open	Opens a solution (using a specific view).
Remove	Removes a project from the solution.
SaveAs	Saves the solution.

Controlling Projects in a Solution

One of the things that the `Solution` object is good for is retrieving references to the various projects that belong to the solution. Each `Project` object has its own set of useful members for interacting with the projects and their items. By using these members, you can interact with the projects in various, expected ways, such as renaming a project, deleting a project, and saving a project.

See Table 13.4 for a summary of the most common `Project` members.

TABLE 13.4   Primary Project Object Members

Property	Description
CodeModel	Returns the `CodeModel` object associated with this project.
Collection	Returns a collection of `Project` objects for the current `Solution`.
DTE	Provides a reference back to the parent DTE object.
FullName	Provides the full path and name of the solution file.
Kind	Returns a string GUID indicating the type of project. Each project type is registered with Visual Studio using a GUID; consult the Visual Studio software development kit (SDK) documentation for a list that maps the project type GUIDs to their text description.
Name	Returns the name of the project.
ParentProjectItem	Returns an instance of the parent `Project`. Some project types within Visual Studio are able to host or contain other project types; this property can be used to identify the host project for the current project (if there is one).

Property	Description
ProjectItems	Returns a `ProjectItems` collection containing each individual object within the current project.
Properties	Returns a collection of `Property` objects that expose all the project's properties.
Saved	Indicates whether the project has been saved since the last modification.

Method	Description
Delete	Removes the current project instance from the solution.
Save	Saves the project.
SaveAs	Saves the project. This method enables you to provide a new name for the project.

Accessing Code Within a Project

Beyond the basic project attributes and items, one of the cooler things that can be accessed via a `Project` instance is the actual code within the project's source files. Through the `CodeModel` property, you can access an entire line of proxy objects representing the code constructs within a project. For instance, the `CodeClass` interface enables you to examine and edit the code for a given class in a given project.

> **NOTE**
>
> Support for the different `CodeModel` entities varies from language to language. The Microsoft Developer Network (MSDN) documentation for each `CodeModel` type clearly indicates the source language support for that element.

After grabbing a `CodeModel` reference from a `Project` instance, you can access its `CodeElements` collection (which is, not surprisingly, a collection of `CodeElement` objects). A `CodeElement` is nothing more than a generic representation of a certain code structure within a project. The `CodeElement` object is generic, but it provides a property, `Kind`. This property is used to determine the exact native type of the code object contained within the `CodeElement`.

The `CodeElement.Kind` property is an enumeration (of type `vsCMElement`) that identifies the specific type of code construct lurking within the `CodeElement` object. Using the `Kind` property, you can first determine the true nature of the code element and then cast the `CodeElement` object to its strong type. Here is a snippet of C# code that does just that:

```
if (element.Kind == vsCMElement.vsCMElementClass)
 {
         CodeClass myClass = (CodeClass)element;
 }
```

For a better grasp of the code model hierarchy, consider the C# code presented in Listing 13.1; this is a "shell" solution that merely implements a namespace, a class within that namespace, and a function within the class.

LISTING 13.1   A Simple Namespace and Class Implementation

```csharp
using System;
using System.Collections.Generic;
using System.Text;

namespace MyNamespace
{
    class MyClass
    {
        public string SumInt(int x, int y)
        {
            return (x + y).ToString();
        }
    }
}
```

If you map the code in Listing 13.1 to the code object model, you end up with the structure shown in Figure 13.2.

To get an idea of the complete depth of the code model tree that can be accessed through the CodeElements collection, consult Table 13.5; this table shows all the possible vsCMElement values, the type they are used to represent, and a brief description of the type.

TABLE 13.5   Mapping the vsCMElement Enumeration Values

Enumeration Value	Type	Description
vsCMElementAssignmentStmt		An assignment statement
vsCMElementAttribute		An attribute
vsCMElementClass	CodeClass	A class
vsCMElementDeclareDecl		A declaration
vsCMElementDefineStmt		A define statement
vsCMElementDelegate	CodeDelegate	A delegate
vsCMElementEnum	CodeEnum	An enumeration
vsCMElementEvent	CodeEvent	An event
vsCMElementEventsDeclaration		An event declaration
vsCMElementFunction	CodeFunction	A function

Enumeration Value	Type	Description
vsCMElementFunctionInvokeStmt		A statement invoking a function
vsCMElementIDLCoClass		An IDL co-class
vsCMElementIDLImport		An IDL import statement
vsCMElementIDLImportLib		An IDL import library
vsCMElementIDLLibrary		An IDL library
vsCMElementImplementsStmt		An implements statement
vsCMElementImportStmt	CodeImport	An import statement
vsCMElementIncludeStmt		An include statement
vsCMElementInheritsStmt		An inherits statement
vsCMElementInterface	CodeInterface	An interface
vsCMElementLocalDeclStmt		A local declaration statement
vsCMElementMacro		A macro
vsCMElementMap		A map
vsCMElementMapEntry		A map entry
vsCMElementModule		A module
vsCMElementNamespace	CodeNamespace	A namespace
vsCMElementOptionStmt		An option statement
vsCMElementOther	CodeElement	A code element not otherwise identified in this enum
vsCMElementParameter	CodeParameter	A parameter
vsCMElementProperty	CodeProperty	A property
vsCMElementPropertySetStmt		A property set statement
vsCMElementStruct	CodeStruct	A structure
vsCMElementTypeDef		A type definition
vsCMElementUDTDecl		A user-defined type
vsCMElementUnion		A union
vsCMElementUsingStmt	CodeImport	A using statement
vsCMElementVariable		A variable
vsCMElementVBAttributeGroup		A Visual Basic attribute group
vsCMElementVBAttributeStmt		A Visual Basic attribute statement
vsCMElementVCBase		A Visual C++ base

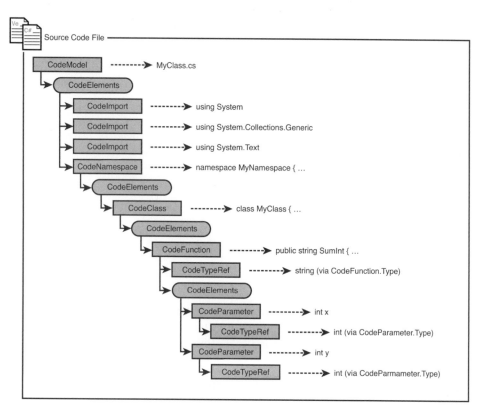

FIGURE 13.2   A simple code model object hierarchy.

Working with Windows

The visible content portion of Visual Studio is represented by `Window` objects, which are instances of open windows within the IDE such as the Solution Explorer, the Task List window, an open code editor window, and so on. Even the IDE itself is represented by a `Window` object.

Any given window is either a document window or a tool window. Document windows host documents that are editable by the Text Editor. Tool windows contain controls that display information relevant to the current context of the IDE; the Solution Explorer and Task List windows are examples of tool windows, and a VB source code file open in an editor is an example of a document window.

Referencing Windows

If you need to retrieve an instance of a specific window, you have a few different options, each optimal for a given situation. For starters, the main IDE window is always available directly from the DTE object:

```
Window IDE = _applicationObject.MainWindow;
```

Obviously, if you need to perform a specific action against the IDE window, this is your quickest route.

The DTE.ActiveWindow property also provides direct and quick access to a Window object, in this case the currently active window:

```
Window currentWindow = _applicationObject.ActiveWindow;
```

The tool windows within the IDE (that is, the command window, the error list window, the output window, the Solution Explorer, the Task List window, and the Toolbox) also have a direct way to retrieve their object model instances: You use the DTE.ToolWindows property. This property returns a ToolWindows object that exposes a separate property for each of the tool windows.

This code grabs a reference to the Task List window and closes it:

```
Window taskwin = _applicationObject.ToolWindows.TaskList;
taskwin.Close();
```

And finally, the fourth way to access an IDE window is through the DTE.Windows collection; this collection holds an entry for each IDE window. You can access a window from the collection either by using an integer representing the window's position within the collection or by providing an object or a string that represents the window you are trying to retrieve.

The following code grabs a handle to the Solution Explorer window:

```
Windows windows = _applicationObject.Windows;
Window window = windows.Item(Constants.vsWindowKindSolutionExplorer);
```

Interacting with Windows

Table 13.6 itemizes the properties and methods available on each Window object.

TABLE 13.6   Window Object Members

Property	Description
AutoHides	A Boolean flag indicating whether the window can be hidden (applies only to tool windows).
Caption	The title/caption of the window.
Collection	The Windows collection that the current Window object belongs to.
CommandBars	A CommandBars collection of the command bars implemented by the window.
ContextAttributes	A collection of ContextAttribute objects; they are used to associate the current context of the window with the Dynamic Help window.
Document	If the Window object is hosting a document, this returns a reference to the document.

Property	Description
DTE	A reference to the root DTE object.
Height	The height of the window in pixels.
IsFloating	A Boolean flag indicating whether the window is floating or docked.
Left	The distance, in pixels, between the window's left edge and its container's left edge.
Linkable	A Boolean flag indicating whether the window can be docked with other windows.
LinkedWindowFrame	Returns a reference to the Window object that is acting as the frame for a docked window.
LinkedWindows	A collection of Window objects representing the windows that are linked together within the same frame.
Object	Returns an object proxy that represents the window and can be referenced by name.
ObjectKind	A GUID indicating the type of the object returned from Window. Object.
Project	A Project instance representing the project containing the Window object.
ProjectItem	A ProjectItem instance representing the project item containing the Window object.
Selection	Returns an object representing the currently selected item in the window. (For document windows, this might be text; for tool windows, this might be an item in a list; and so on.)
Top	The distance, in pixels, between the window's top edge and its parent's top edge.
Visible	A Boolean flag indicating whether the window is visible or hidden.
Width	The width of the window in pixels.
WindowState	Gets or sets the current state of the window (via a vsWindowState enum value: vsWindowStateMaximize, vsWindowStateMinimize, vsWindowStateNormal).

Method	Description
Activate	Gives the window focus.
Close	Closes the window; you can indicate, with a vsSaveChanges enum value, whether the window's hosted document should be saved or not saved, or whether the IDE should prompt the user to make that decision.
SetSelectionContainer	Passes an array of objects to the Properties window when the Window object has focus. This property is mainly used for custom tool windows where you need to control what is displayed in the Properties window.

13

Property	Description
SetTabPicture	Specifies an object to use as a tab image; this image is displayed whenever the window is part of a tab group within the IDE.

Beyond the basics (such as using the Height and Width properties to query or affect a window's dimensions, or setting focus to the window with the SetFocus method), a few properties deserve special mention:

▶ The Document property gives you a way to programmatically interact with the document that the window is hosting (if any).

▶ The Project and ProjectItem properties serve to bridge the Window portion of the API with the Project/Solution portion; in a similar vein as the Document property, you can use these properties to interact with the project that is related to the window, or the project item (such as the VB code file, text file, or resource file).

▶ If you are dealing with a tool window, the SetTabPicture method provides a way to set the tab icon that is displayed when the tool window is part of a group of tabbed windows. (For instance, the Toolbox window displays a wrench and hammer picture on its tab when part of a tabbed group.)

▶ Again, specifically for tool windows only, the SetSelectionContainer can be used to supply one or more objects for display within the Properties window. This capability is useful if you have a custom window where you need to control what is displayed in the Properties window when the window has focus. (All the standard VS windows already do this for you.)

Listing 13.2 contains an excerpt from a C# add-in; the method QueryWindows illustrates the use of the Window object. In this example, each window is queried to determine its type, and then a summary of each window is output in a simple message box.

LISTING 13.2   A C# Routine for Querying the Windows Collection

```
using System;
using Extensibility;
using EnvDTE;
using EnvDTE80;
using Microsoft.VisualStudio.CommandBars;
using System.Resources;
using System.Reflection;
using System.Globalization;
using System.Windows.Forms;

public class Connect : IDTExtensibility2, IDTCommandTarget
{
```

```csharp
public void QueryWindows()
{
    Windows windows = _applicationObject.DTE.Windows;
    Window window;
    int count = windows.Count;

    string results =
        count.ToString()  + " windows open..." + "\r\n";

    // iterate the collection of windows
    for (int index = 1; index <= count; index++)
    {
        window = windows.Item(index);

        string title = window.Caption;

        //If the window is hosting a document, a valid Document
        //object will be returned through Window.Document
        if (window.Document != null)
        {
            //Write this out as a document window
            string docName = window.Document.Name;
            results =
                results + "Window '" + title + "' is a document window" + "/r/n";
        }
        else
        {
            //If no document was present, this is a tool window
            //(tool windows don't host documents)
            results =
                results + "Window '" + title + "' is a tool window" + "/r/n";
        }

    }


    //Show the results

    MessageBox.Show(results, "Window Documents",
        MessageBoxButtons.OK, MessageBoxIcon.Information);


}

}
```

> **NOTE**
>
> If you want to embed your own custom control inside a tool window, you have to write an add-in and use the `Windows.CreateToolWindow` method. We cover this scenario in Chapter 14.

Text Windows and Window Panes

Text windows have their own specific object abstraction in addition to the generic `Window` object: The `TextWindow` object is used to represent text editor windows. To obtain a reference to a window's `TextWindow` object, you retrieve the `Window` object's value and assign it into a `TextWindow` type:

```
TextWindow textWindow = DTE.ActiveWindow.Object;
```

The `TextWindow` object doesn't provide much functionality over and above the functionality found in the `Window` type; its real value is the access it provides to window panes.

Text editor windows in Visual Studio can be split into two panes; with a text editor open, simply select Split from the Window menu to create a new pane within the window. The `TextWindow.ActivePane` property returns a `TextPane` object representing the currently active pane in the window, and the `TextWindow.Panes` property provides access to all the panes within a text window:

```
//Get pane instance from collection
TextPane2 newPane = textWindow.Panes.Item(1);


//Get currently active pane
TextPane2 currPane = textWindow.ActivePane;
```

One of the more useful things you can do with the `TextPane` object is to scroll the client area of the pane (for example, the visible portion of the document within the pane) so that a specific range of text is visible. This is done via the `TextPane.TryToShow` method.

Here is the definition for the method:

```
bool TryToShow( [InAttribute] TextPoint Point,
            [OptionalAttribute] [InAttribute] vsPaneShowHow How,
            [OptionalAttribute] [InAttribute] Object PointOrCount)
```

The `TextPoint` parameter represents the specific location within the text document that you want visible in the text pane. (We discuss `TextPoint` objects in depth later in this chapter, in the section "Editing Text Documents.") The `vsPaneShowHow` value specifies how the pane should behave when scrolling to the indicated location:

▶ `vsPaneShowHow.vsPaneShowCentered` causes the pane to center the text/text selection in the middle of the pane (horizontally and vertically).

▶ `vsPaneShowHow.vsPaneShowTop` places the text point at the top of the viewable region in the pane.

▶ vsPaneShowHow.vsPaneShowAsIs shows the text point as is with no changes in horizontal or vertical orientation within the viewable region in the pane.

The last parameter, the PointOrCount object, is used to specify the end of the text area that you want displayed. If you provide an integer here, this represents a count of characters past the original text point; if you provide another text point, the selection is considered to be that text that resides between the two text points.

The TextPane object is also used to access the Incremental Search feature for a specific window pane. Listing 13.3 shows an add-in routine demonstrating this feature in action.

LISTING 13.3   Controlling Incremental Search

```csharp
using System;
using Extensibility;
using EnvDTE;
using EnvDTE80;

public class Connect : IDTExtensibility2
{

        private DTE2 _applicationObject;
        private AddIn _addInInstance;

        public void IncrementalSearchDemo()
        {
            // Grab references to the active window;
            // we assume, for this example, that the window
            //is a text window.
            Window window = _applicationObject.ActiveWindow;

            // Grab a TextWindow instance that maps to our
            // active window
            TextWindow txtWindow = (TextWindow)window.Object;

            // Get the active pane from the text window
            TextPane2 pane = (TextPane2)txtWindow.ActivePane;

            // Using the active pane, get an IncrementalSearch object
            // for the pane
            IncrementalSearch search = pane.IncrementalSearch;

            // Try to find our IMessageMapper interface by looking
            // for the string "IM"
            // Configure the search:
            //    search forward in the document
```

```
//   append the chars that we are searching for
//   quit the search

search.StartForward();
search.AppendCharAndSearch((short)Strings.Asc('I'));
search.AppendCharAndSearch((short)Strings.Asc('M'));


// To remove us from incremental search mode,
// we can call IncrementalSearch.Exit()...
search.Exit();

    }


}
```

The Tool Window Types

In addition to having a `Window` object abstraction, each default tool window in the IDE (the command window, output window, Toolbox window, and Task List window) is also represented by a discrete type that exposes methods and properties unique to that tool window. Table 13.7 lists the default tool windows and their underlying types in the automation object model.

TABLE 13.7   Tool Windows and Their Types

Tool Window	Type
Command window	CommandWindow
Output window	OutputWindow
Task List window	TaskList
Toolbox window	ToolBox

To reference one of these objects, you first start with its `Window` representation and then cast its `Window.Object` value to the matching type. For instance, this C# snippet starts with a `Window` reference to the Task List window and then uses that `Window` object to obtain a reference to the `TaskList` object:

```
Windows windows = _applicationObject.Windows;
Window twindow =
    _applicationObject.Windows.Item(EnvDTE.Constants.vsWindowKindTaskList);
```

Tasks and the Task List Window

The `TaskList` object enables you to access the items currently displayed in the Task List window; each item in the window is represented by its own `TaskItem` object. The

`TaskItem` object exposes methods and properties that enable you to manipulate the task items. For instance, you can mark an item as complete, get or set the line number associated with the task, and change the priority of the task.

You remove tasks from the list by using the `TaskItem.Delete` method and add them by using the `TaskItems.Add` method. The `Add` method allows you to specify the task category, subcategory, description, priority, icon, and so on:

```
TaskList tlist = (TaskList)twindow.Object;

tlist.TaskItems.Add("Best Practices", "Coding Style",
    "Use of brace indenting is inconsistent",
    vsTaskPriority.vsTaskPriorityMedium,
    vsTaskIcon.vsTaskIconUser, True,
    "S:\ContosoCommonFramework\Contoso.Fx.Common\Class1.cs", _
    7, True, True);
```

Table 13.8 provides an inventory of the `TaskItem` members.

TABLE 13.8   `TaskItem` Members

Property	Description
Category	The category of the task.
Checked	A Boolean flag indicating whether the task is marked as completed. (A check mark appears in the check box next to the task.)
Collection	The `TaskList` collection that the current `TaskItem` object belongs to.
Description	The description of the task.
Displayed	A Boolean flag indicating whether the task is currently visible in the Task List window.
DTE	A reference to the root DTE object.
FileName	The name of the file associated with the task (if any).
IsSettable	By passing in a `vsTaskListColumn` enum value to this property, you can determine whether that column is editable.
Line	The line number associated with the task.
Priority	A `vsTaskPriority` value indicating the task's priority level. Possible values include `vsTaskPriorityHigh`, `vsTaskPriorityMedium`, and `vsTaskPriorityLow`.
SubCategory	The subcategory of the task.
Method	**Description**
Delete	Removes the task from the Task List window.
Navigate	Causes the IDE to navigate to the location (for example, file and line) associated with the task.
Select	Selects or moves the focus to the task within the Task List window.

13

Listing 13.4 contains a short, C# add-in routine demonstrating the use of the `TaskList`, `TaskItems`, and `TaskItem` objects to iterate the list of user tasks and toggle their completed status.

LISTING 13.4   Toggling Task Item Completion

```csharp
using System;
using Extensibility;
using EnvDTE;
using EnvDTE80;

public class Connect : IDTExtensibility2
{
    private DTE2 _applicationObject;
    private AddIn _addInInstance;

    public void ToggleAllTasks()
    {
        // Reference the windows collection
        Windows windows = _applicationObject.Windows;

        // Pluck the task list window from the collection
        Window twindow =
        windows.Item(EnvDTE.Constants.vsWindowKindTaskList);

        // Convert the window object to a TaskList instance by
        // casting its Object property
        TaskList tlist = (TaskList)twindow.Object;

        // Iterate all of the task items in the task list
        foreach (TaskItem task in tlist.TaskItems)
        {
            // Toggle the "completed" check mark on each user task
            if (task.Category == "User")
            {
                task.Checked = !(task.Checked);
            }

        }

    }


}
```

The Toolbox

Four objects are used to programmatically interface with the Toolbox:

- ▶ `ToolBox`—An object representing the Toolbox itself

- ▶ `ToolBoxTabs`—A collection representing the tab panes on the Toolbox

- ▶ `ToolBoxItems`—A collection representing the items within a tab on the Toolbox

- ▶ `ToolBoxItem`—A discrete item displayed within a Toolbox tab

Figure 13.3 illustrates the `Toolbox` object hierarchy.

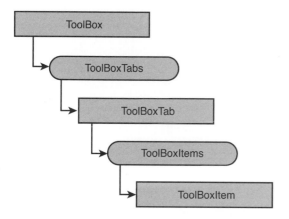

FIGURE 13.3   The `Toolbox` object hierarchy.

These objects are used primarily to add, remove, or alter the items hosted by the Toolbox. For instance, you can easily add a custom tab to the Toolbox by using the `ToolBoxTabs` collection:

```
ToolBox tbox;
ToolBoxTab myTab;
tBox = _applicationObject.Windows.Item(Constants.vsWindowKindToolbox).Object;
myTab = tBox.ToolBoxTabs.Add("My TBox Tab");
```

You can also add items to any tab with the `ToolBoxItems.Add` method, which accepts a name for the item to add, a "data" object representing the item, and a `vsToolBoxItemFormat` enum, which specifies the format of the item. The `Add` method uses the `vsToolBoxItemFormat` to determine how to interpret the data object value. For instance, if you want to add a .NET control to the tab created in the preceding code snippet, you can accomplish that with just one line of code:

```
myTab.ToolBoxItems.Add("ContosoControl",
        "C:\Contoso\Controls\CalendarControl.dll",
        vsToolBoxItemFormat.vsToolBoxItemFormatDotNETComponent);
```

Notice that the item, in this case, is represented by a path to the assembly that implements the control and that it has an item format of `vsToolBoxItemFormatDotNETComponent`.

Listing 13.5 contains a C# add-in function that adds a tab to the Toolbox, adds a control and a text fragment to the tab, and then removes the tab.

LISTING 13.5   Adding and Removing Items in the Toolbox Window

```csharp
using System;
using Extensibility;
using EnvDTE;
using EnvDTE80;
using System.Windows.Forms;

public class Connect : IDTExtensibility2
{
    private DTE2 _applicationObject;
    private AddIn _addInInstance;

    public void AddAToolboxTab()
    {

        ToolBox toolBox;
        ToolBoxTabs tabs;
        ToolBoxTab tab;
        ToolBoxItems tabItems;
        Window win;


        // Get a reference to the Toolbox
        win = applicationObject.Windows.Item(
            EnvDTE.Constants.vsWindowKindToolbox);
        toolBox = (ToolBox)win.Object;

        // Get a reference to the Toolbox tabs collection
        tabs = toolBox.ToolBoxTabs;

        // Add a new tab to the ToolBox
        tab = tabs.Add("New ToolBox Tab");

        // Make the added tab the active tab
        tab.Activate();

        tabItems = tab.ToolBoxItems;
```

```
        // Add a piece of text to the Toolbox.
        // Clicking on the text will add it to
        // the active document...
        tabItems.Add("code Comment",
          "This is some text to add to the toolbox",
          vsToolBoxItemFormat.vsToolBoxItemFormatText);

        // Now add a control to the Toolbox.
        // When adding a control, you need to specify
        // the path to the assembly; you can add all
        // classes from the assembly (shown below)
        // or just one of the classes (see MSDN
        // docs for that syntax)
        tabItems.Add("My Login Control",
              "C:\MyComponents\Contoso\LoginControl.dll",
              vsToolBoxItemFormat.vsToolBoxItemFormatDotNETComponent);

        // For demonstration purposes, let's remove
        // the items that we had just added, and then
        // remove the newly created tab...

        // Put up a messagebox to confirm the deletes
        MessageBox.Show("Click OK to delete the tab and added items.",
            "Delete Toolbox Tab Items", MessageBoxButtons.OK,
            MessageBoxIcon.Information);

        //Delete the tab
        tab.Delete();


    }
}
```

Executing Commands in the Command Window

The command window is a tool window used to execute IDE commands or aliases. IDE commands are essentially ways to tell the IDE to perform some action. Some commands map directly to menu items (such as File Open), whereas others don't have menu equivalents.

The CommandWindow object permits you to programmatically pipe commands into the command window and execute them. You can also output a text string (for informational purposes) to the window and clear its current content:

```
// Get a reference to the command window
CommandWindow cmdWindow =
    _applicationObject.Windows.Item(
```

```
Constants.vsWindowKindCommandWindow).Object;

// Display some text in the command window
cmdWindow.OutputString("Hello, World!");

// Clear the command window
cmdWindow.Clear();
```

Listing 13.6 shows how to programmatically execute commands in the `CommandWindow` object.

LISTING 13.6   Executing Commands in the Command Window

```
using System;
using Extensibility;
using EnvDTE;
using EnvDTE80;
using Microsoft.VisualBasic;
using System.Windows.Forms;

public class Connect : IDTExtensibility2
{
    private DTE2 _applicationObject;
    private AddIn _addInInstance;


    public void ExecCommandWindow()
    {
        CommandWindow cmdWindow = (CommandWindow)
        _applicationObject.Windows.Item(
            EnvDTE.Constants.vsWindowKindCommandWindow).Object;

        //Display some text in the command window
        cmdWindow.OutputString("Executing command from the automation OM...");

        // Send some command strings to the command window and execute
        // them...

        // This command will start logging all input/output in the
        // command window to the specified file
        cmdWindow.SendInput("Tools.LogCommandWindowOutput cmdwindow.log", true);

        // Open a file in a code editor:
        //    1. We use an alias, 'of', for the File.OpenFile command
        //    2. This command takes quote-delimited parameters (in this case,
        //       the name of the editor to load the file in)
```

```
    string cmd = @"of ";
    cmd = cmd + @"""C:\Contoso\ContosoCommonFramework\Integration.cs""";
    cmd = cmd + @"/e:""CSharp Editor""";

    cmdWindow.SendInput(cmd, true);

    cmdWindow.SendInput("Edit.Find MessageTrxId", true);

    // Turn off logging
    cmdWindow.SendInput("Tools.LogCommandWindowOutput /off", true);
  }

}
```

Output Window

The output window displays messages generated from various sources in the IDE. A prime example is the messages generated by the compiler when a project is being built. For a deeper look at the functionality provided by the output window, see Chapter 11, "Debugging Code."

The output window is controlled through three objects:

▶ `OutputWindow` is the root object representing the output window.

▶ `OutputWindowPanes` is a collection of `OutputWindowPane` objects.

▶ `OutputWindowPane` represents one of the current panes within the output window.

Using these objects, you can add or remove panes from the output window, output text to any one of the panes, and respond to events transpiring in the window.

The following C# code fragment retrieves a reference to the output window and writes a test string in the Build pane:

```
OutputWindow outWindow = (OutputWindow)
    _applicationObject.Windows.Item(Constants.vsWindowKindOutput).Object;

OutputWindowPane pane = (OutputWindowPane)
    outWindow.OutputWindowPanes.Item("Build");

pane.OutputString("test");
```

Using the `OutputWindowPane` object, you can also add items simultaneously to a specific output pane and the Task List window. The `OutputWindowPane.OutputTaskItemString` method writes text into the output window and simultaneously adds that text as a task to the Task List window:

```
string output = "Exception handler not found";
string task = "Add exception handler";
pane.OutputTaskItemString(output,
    vsTaskPriority.vsTaskPriorityMedium,
    "", vsTaskIcon.vsTaskIconNone,
    "", 0, task, true);
```

Because most of the output window actions are conducted against a specific pane, most of the useful methods are concentrated in the OutputWindowPane object. For your reference, the OutputWindowPane members are itemized in Table 13.9.

TABLE 13.9   OutputWindowPane Members

Property	Description
Collection	The OutputWindowPanes collection that the current OutputWindowPane object belongs to
DTE	A reference to the root DTE object
Guid	The GUID for the output window pane
Name	The name of the output window pane
TextDocument	A TextDocument object representing the window pane's content
Method	**Description**
Activate	Moves the focus to the output window
Clear	Clears the contents of the window pane
ForceItemsToTaskList	Writes all task items not yet written to the Task List window
OutputString	Writes a string to the output window pane
OutputTaskItemString	Writes a string to the output window pane and simultaneously adds a task to the Task List window

Listing 13.7 demonstrates controlling the output window by adding a new pane to the window, writing text into that pane, and then clearing its content.

LISTING 13.7   Writing to the Output Window

```
using System;
using Extensibility;
using EnvDTE;
using EnvDTE80;
using Microsoft.VisualBasic;
using System.Windows.Forms;
```

```
public class Connect : IDTExtensibility2
{

    private DTE2 _applicationObject;
    private AddIn _addInInstance;

    public void WriteToOutputWindow()
    {
        // Grab a reference to the output window
        OutputWindow outWindow = (OutputWindow)
        _applicationObject.Windows.Item(
        EnvDTE.Constants.vsWindowKindOutput).Object;


        // Create a new pane in the output window
        OutputWindowPane pane = (OutputWindowPane)
           outWindow.OutputWindowPanes.Add("New Pane");

        pane.OutputString("Text in the 'New Pane'");

        pane.Clear();
    }


}
```

Linked Windows

Tool windows can be positioned in various ways within the IDE: You can float tool windows around within the overall IDE container, you can dock a tool window to one of the sides of the IDE, you can join windows together and pin and unpin them, and so on. (See the section "Managing the Many Windows of the IDE" in Chapter 2, "The Visual Studio IDE," for an introduction to window layout.)

A linked window refers to two or more tool windows that have been aggregated together. Figure 13.4 shows one common example of this; the Toolbox and Solution Explorer window have been joined together in a common frame. Each window that is part of the frame can be viewed by clicking its tab.

FIGURE 13.4   Linked windows.

By joining together two or more tool windows, you actually create an additional window object (called a linked window or window frame) that functions as the container for its hosted tool windows and is available as a part of the `DTE.Windows` collection.

By using the `Window.LinkedWindows` and `Window.WindowFrame` properties and the `Windows2.CreateLinkedWindowFrame` method, you can programmatically link and unlink any available tool windows. The C# code in Listing 13.8 demonstrates this process by doing the following:

1. You grab the window objects for the Toolbox window and the Solution Explorer window.

2. You programmatically join these two windows, effectively creating the linked window shown in Figure 13.4.

3. After joining the windows, you get a reference to the newly created linked window and use its `LinkedWindows` property to unlink the windows that were previously linked together.

LISTING 13.8   Linking and Unlinking Tool Windows

```csharp
using System;
using Extensibility;
using EnvDTE;
using EnvDTE80;
using Microsoft.VisualBasic;
using System.Windows.Forms;

public class Connect : IDTExtensibility2
{

    private DTE2 _applicationObject;
```

```
    private AddIn _addInInstance;

    public void LinkUnLink()
    {
        Windows windows = _applicationObject.Windows;

        // Grab references to the Solution Explorer and the Toolbox
        Window solExplorer =
            windows.Item(EnvDTE.Constants.vsWindowKindSolutionExplorer);

        Window toolbox = windows.Item(EnvDTE.Constants.vsWindowKindToolbox);

        // Use the Windows2 collection to create a linked window/window
        // frame to hold the Toolbox and Solution Explorer windows
        Window windowFrame;
        windowFrame = windows.CreateLinkedWindowFrame(solExplorer,
            toolbox, vsLinkedWindowType.vsLinkedWindowTypeTabbed);

        // At this point, we have created a linked window with two tabbed
        // "interior" windows: the Solution Explorer, and the Toolbox...

        MessageBox.Show("Press OK to Unlink the windows", "LinkUnLink",
            MessageBoxButtons.OK, MessageBoxIcon.None);

        // To unlink the windows:
        //    - Use the window frame's LinkedWindows collection
        //    - Remove the window objects from this collection

        windowFrame.LinkedWindows.Remove(toolbox);
        windowFrame.LinkedWindows.Remove(solExplorer);

    }

}
```

Command Bars

A command bar is a menu bar or toolbar; from an object model perspective, these are
represented by CommandBar objects. Because menu bars and toolbars are hosted within
a window, you reference specific CommandBar objects via the Window object, through the
Window.CommandBars property. In turn, every CommandBar plays host to controls such as
buttons and drop-downs. Figure 13.5 shows the Solution Explorer tool window with its
command bar highlighted.

Note that there are six buttons hosted on the command bar (see Figure 13.6).

FIGURE 13.5 The Solution Explorer's command bar.

> **NOTE**
>
> Unlike the `Windows` collection, which holds only an instance of each open window, the `CommandBars` collection holds instances for every single registered command bar, regardless of whether the command bar is currently being shown in the window. Also note that working with the `CommandBar` and `CommandBars` objects will require a reference to `Microsoft.VisualStudio.CommandBars`. This `using` statement is not included by default with add-in project class templates.

The C# code in Listing 13.9 queries the `CommandBar` object for the Solution Explorer window and prints out the `CommandBar` objects that it finds.

LISTING 13.9 Querying the `CommandBar` Object

```
using System;
using Extensibility;
using EnvDTE;
using EnvDTE80;
using Microsoft.VisualBasic;
using System.Windows.Forms;
using Microsoft.VisualStudio.CommandBars;

public class Connect : IDTExtensibility2
{
    private DTE2 _applicationObject;
    private AddIn _addInInstance;

    public void QueryCommandBar()
    {
        Windows windows = _applicationObject.Windows;
```

```
// Grab reference to the Solution Explorer
Window2 solExplorer = (Window2)
   windows.Item(EnvDTE.Constants.vsWindowKindSolutionExplorer);


// Retrieve the Solution Explorer's command bar object

CommandBar cmdBar = ((CommandBars)solExplorer.CommandBars)[0];

// Start building our output string
string output = "Command bar contains: /r/n";

// Get a reference to the controls hosted in the
// command bar
CommandBarControls controls = cmdBar.Controls;

// Count integer
integer i = 1;

// Iterate the controls in the command bar

foreach (CommandBarControl control in controls)
{
    if (control.Enabled)
    {
        output = output + i.ToString() + @" " +
            control.Type.ToString() + ": " + control.Caption
            + "\r\n";
    }
}

MessageBox.Show(output, "Solution Explorer Command Bar",
    MessageBoxButtons.OK);
    }
}
```

13

FIGURE 13.6   Enumerating the buttons in a `CommandBar`.

Notice in Listing 13.9 that you have to explicitly cast the object returned from the `Window.CommandBars` property. This is, interestingly, not a strongly typed property, and it returns an `Object` instead of an actual `CommandBar` instance.

TIP

Use the `CommandBar.Type` property to determine whether a command bar is a toolbar or a menu bar. A value of `MsoBarType.msoBarTypeNormal` indicates that the command bar is a toolbar, whereas a value of `MsoBarType.msoBarTypeMenuBar` indicates that the command bar is a menu bar.

The `CommandBar` object properties and methods are documented in Table 13.10.

TABLE 13.10   `CommandBar` Members

Property	Description
AdaptiveMenu	For menu bars, this Boolean flag indicates whether the command bar has *adaptive menus* enabled. (Adaptive menus, sometimes referred to as *personalized menus*, are menus that alter their drop-down content based on projected or actual usage by the user; the intent is to display only those commands that are useful on the menu and hide the other nonessential commands.)
Application	An object representing the parent application to the command bar.
BuiltIn	A Boolean flag used to distinguish between built-in and custom command bars.
Context	A string indicating where the `CommandBar` is saved. (The format and expected content of this string are dictated by the hosting application.)
Controls	A `CommandBarControls` collection containing `CommandBarControl` objects; each of these objects represents a control displayed by the command bar.
Creator	An integer value that identifies the application hosting the `CommandBar`.
Enabled	A Boolean flag indicating whether the command bar is enabled.
Height	The height of the command bar in pixels.

Property	Description
Index	The index of the command bar in the command bar collection.
Left	The distance, in pixels, between the left side of the command bar and the left edge of its parent container.
Name	The name of the command bar.
NameLocal	The localized name of the command bar.
Parent	An object that is the parent of the command bar.
Position	An `MsoBarPosition` enum value used to get or set the position of the command bar (for example, `MsoBarPosition.msoBarTop`).
Protection	An `MsoBarProtection` enum value that identifies the protection employed against used modification (for example, `MsoBarProtection.msoBarNoMove`).
RowIndex	An integer representing the docking row of the command bar.
Top	The distance, in pixels, between the top of the command bar and the top edge of its parent container.
Type	The type of the command bar (as an MsobarType enum value; for example, `MsoBarType.msoBarTypeNormal`).
Visible	A Boolean flag indicating whether the command bar is currently visible.
Width	The width of the command bar in pixels.

Method	Description
Delete	Removes the command bar from its parent collection.
FindControl	Enables you to retrieve a reference to a control hosted by the command bar that fits various parameters such as its type, ID, tag, and visibility.
Reset	Resets one of the built-in command bars to its default configuration.
ShowPopup	Displays a pop-up representing a command bar.

NOTE

Earlier versions of Visual Studio actually relied on a Microsoft Office assembly for the `CommandBar` object definition (`Microsoft.Office.Core`). Visual Studio 2005 and later versions provide their own implementation of the `CommandBar` object that is defined in the `Microsoft.VisualStudio.CommandBars` namespace, although you will find some types that carry their nomenclature over from the MS Office assembly, such as the various `MsoXXX` enums.

Documents

`Document` objects are used to represent an open document in the IDE. To contrast this abstraction with that provided by the `Window` object, a `Window` object is used to represent the physical UI aspects of a document window, whereas a `Document` object is used to represent the physical document that is being displayed within that document window.

13

A document could be a designer, such as the Windows Forms Designer, or it could be a text-based document such as a ReadMe file or a C# code file open in an editor.

Just as you get a list of all open windows using the DTE.Windows collection, you can use the DTE.Documents collection to retrieve a list of all open documents:

```
Dim documents As Documents = DTE.Documents
```

The Documents collection is indexed by the document's Name property, which is, in effect, the document's filename without the path information. This makes it easy to quickly retrieve a Document instance:

```
Dim documents As Documents = DTE.Documents

Dim readme As Document = documents.Item("ReadMe.txt")
Documents documents = DTE.Documents;
Document readme = documents.Item["ReadMe.txt"];
```

Using the Document object, you can do the following:

▶ Close the document (and optionally save changes)

▶ Retrieve the filename and path of the document

▶ Determine whether the document has been modified since the last time it was saved

▶ Determine what, if anything, is currently selected within the document

▶ Obtain a ProjectItem instance representing the project item that is associated with the document

▶ Read and edit the contents of text documents

Table 13.11 contains the member descriptions for the Document object.

TABLE 13.11   Document Members

Property	Description
ActiveWindow	The currently active window associated with the document. (A null or Nothing value indicates that there is no active window.)
Collection	The collection of Document objects to which this instance belongs.
DTE	The root-level DTE object.
Extender	Returns a Document extender object.
ExtenderCATID	The extender category ID for the object.
ExtenderNames	A list of extenders available for the current Document object.
FullName	The full path and filename of the document.

Property	Description
Kind	A GUID representing the kind of document.
Name	The name (essentially, the filename without path information) for the document.
Path	The path of the document's file excluding the filename.
ProjectItem	The ProjectItem instance associated with the document.
Saved	Indicates whether the solution has been saved since the last modification.
Selection	An object representing the current selection in the document (if any).
Windows	The Windows collection containing the window displaying the document.

Method	Description
Activate	Moves the focus to the document.
Close	Closes the document. You can indicate, with a vsSaveChanges enum value, whether the window's hosted document should be saved or not saved, or whether the IDE should prompt the user to make that decision.
NewWindow	Opens the document in a new window and returns the new window's Window object.
Object	Returns an object proxy that represents the window and can be referenced by name.
Redo	Re-executes the last user action in the document.
Save	Saves the document.
Undo	Reverses the last used action in the document.

Text Documents

As previously mentioned, documents can have textual or nontextual content. For those documents with textual content, a separate object exists: TextDocument. The TextDocument object provides access to control functions specifically related to text content.

If you have a valid Document object to start with, and if that Document object refers to a text document, and then a TextDocument instance can be referenced from the Document.Object property like this:

```
TextDocument doc;
Document myDocument;

doc = myDocument.Object;
```

Table 13.12 contains the `TextDocument` members.

TABLE 13.12   `TextDocument` Members

Property	Description
DTE	The root-level DTE object.
EndPoint	A `TextPoint` object positioned at the end of the document.
Parent	Gets the parent object of the text document.
Selection	Returns a `TextSelection` object representing the currently selected text in the document.
StartPoint	A `TextPoint` object positioned at the start of the document.

Method	Description
ClearBookmarks	Removes any unnamed bookmarks present in the document.
CreateEditPoint	Returns an edit point at the specific location. (If no location is specified, the beginning of the document is assumed.)
MarkText	Bookmarks lines in the document that match the specified string pattern.
ReplacePattern	Replaces any text in the document that matches the pattern.

TIP

A text document is represented by both a `Document` instance and a `TextDocument` instance. Nontext documents, such as a Windows form, open in a Windows Forms Designer window, have a `Document` representation but no corresponding `TextDocument` representation. Unfortunately, there isn't a great way to distinguish whether a document is text based during runtime. One approach is to attempt a cast or assignment to a `TextDocument` object and catch any exceptions that might occur during the assignment.

Two `TextDocument` methods are useful for manipulating bookmarks within the document: `ClearBookmarks` removes any unnamed bookmarks from the document, and `MarkText` performs a string pattern search and places bookmarks against the resulting document lines. A simple add-in to bookmark `For` loops in a VB document is presented in Listing 13.10.

LISTING 13.10   Bookmarking `For` Loops in a VB Document

```
using System;
using Extensibility;
using EnvDTE;
using EnvDTE80;
using Microsoft.VisualBasic;
using System.Windows.Forms;
using Microsoft.VisualStudio.CommandBars;
```

```
public class Connect : IDTExtensibility2
{

    private DTE2 _applicationObject;
    private AddIn _addInInstance;

    public void BookmarkFor()
    {
        Document doc;
        TextDocument txtDoc;

        // Reference the current document
        doc = _applicationObject.ActiveDocument;

        // Retrieve a TextDocument instance from
        // the document
        txtDoc = (TextDocument)doc.Object();

        // Call the MarkText method with the 'For' string
        bool found =
            txtDoc.MarkText("For", (int)vsFindOptions.vsFindOptionsFromStart);

        // MarkText returns a boolean flag indicating whether or not
        // the search pattern was found in the textdocument
        if (found)
        {
            MessageBox.Show("All instances of 'For' have been bookmarked.");
        }
        else
        {
            MessageBox.Show("No instances of 'For' were found.");
        }

    }

}
```

The other key functionality exposed by the TextDocument object is the capability to read and edit the text within the document.

Editing Text Documents

From a Visual Studio perspective, text in a text document actually has two distinct "representations": a virtual one and a physical one. The physical representation is the straight and unadulterated code file that sits on disk. The virtual representation is what Visual Studio presents on the screen: It is an interpreted view of the text in the code file that takes into account various editor document features such as code outlining/regions, virtual spacing, and word wrapping.

Figure 13.7 shows this relationship. When displaying a text document, Visual Studio reads the source file into a text buffer, and then the text editor presents one view of that text file to you (based on options you have configured for the editor).

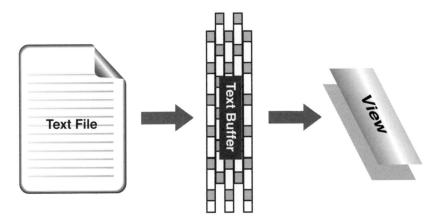

FIGURE 13.7   Presentation of text documents within the IDE.

Text in a document is manipulated or read either on the buffered text or on the "view" text that you see in the editor. Four different automation objects enable you to affect text; two work on the text buffer, and two work on the editor view.

For the text buffer:

▶ TextPoint objects are used to locate specific points within a text document. By querying the TextPoint properties, you can determine the line number of the text point, the number of characters it is offset from the start of a line, the number of characters it is offset from the start of the document, and its display column within the text editor window. You can also retrieve a reference to a CodeModel object representing the code at the text point's current location.

▶ The EditPoint object inherits from the TextPoint object; this is the primary object used for manipulating text in the text buffer. You can add, delete, or move text using edit points, and they can be moved around within the text buffer.

And, for the editor view:

▶ The VirtualPoint object is equivalent to the TextPoint object except that it can be used to query text locations that reside in the "virtual" space of the text view. (Virtual space is the whitespace that exists after the last character in a document line.) VirtualPoint instances are returned through the TextSelection object.

▶ The TextSelection object operates on text within the text editor view as opposed to the text buffer and is equivalent to the EditPoint interface. When you use the

`TextSelection` object, you are actively affecting the text that is being displayed within the text editor. The methods and properties of this object, therefore, end up being programmatic approximations of the various ways that you would manually affect text: You can page up or page down within the view; cut, copy, and paste text; select a range of text; or even outline and expand or collapse regions of text.

Because the `VirtualPoint` object is nearly identical to the `TextPoint` object, and the `TextSelection` object is nearly identical to the `EditPoint` object, we won't bother to cover each of these four objects in detail. Instead, we focus on text buffer operations using `EditPoint` and `TextPoint`. You should be able to easily apply the concepts here to the text view.

Because `EditPoint` objects expose the most functionality and play the central role with text editing, we have provided a list of their type members in Table 13.13.

TABLE 13.13 `EditPoint2` Members

Property	Description
AbsoluteCharOffset	The number of characters from the start of the document to the current location of the edit point
AtEndOfDocument	Boolean flag indicating whether the point is at the end of the document
AtEndOfLine	Boolean flag indicating whether the point is at the end of a line in the document
AtStartOfDocument	Boolean flag indicating whether the point is at the beginning of the document
AtStartOfLine	Boolean flag indicating whether the point is at the start of a line in the document
CodeElement	Returns the code element that maps to the edit point's current location
DisplayColumn	The column number of the edit point
DTE	Returns the root automation DTE object
Line	The line number where the point is positioned
LineCharOffset	The character offset, within a line, of the edit point
LineLength	The length of the line where the edit point is positioned
Parent	Returns the parent object of the `EditPoint2` object
Method	**Description**
ChangeCase	Changes the case of a range of text
CharLeft	Moves the edit point to the left the specified number of characters
CharRight	Moves the edit point to the right the specified number of characters
ClearBookmark	Clears any unnamed bookmarks that exist on the point's current line location

Property	Description
Copy	Copies a range of text to the Clipboard
CreateEditPoint	Creates a new EditPoint object at the same location as the current EditPoint object
Cut	Cuts a range of text and places it on the Clipboard
Delete	Deletes a range of text from the document
DeleteWhitespace	Deletes any whitespace found around the edit point
EndOfDocument	Moves the edit point to the end of the document
EndOfLine	Moves the edit point to the end of the current line
EqualTo	A Boolean value indicating whether the edit point's AbsoluteCharOffset value is equal to another edit point's offset
FindPattern	Finds any matching string patterns in the document
GetLines	A string representing the text between two lines in the document
GetText	A string representing the text between the edit point and another location in the document
GreaterThan	A Boolean value indicating whether the edit point's AbsoluteCharOffset value is greater than another edit point's offset
Indent	Indents the selected lines by the given number of levels
Insert	Inserts a string into the document, starting at the edit point's current location
InsertFromFile	Inserts the entire contents of a text file into the document starting at the edit point's current location
LessThan	Returns a Boolean value indicating whether the edit point's AbsoluteCharOffset value is less than another edit point's offset
LineDown	Moves the point down one or more lines
LineUp	Moves the point up one or more lines
MoveToAbsoluteOffset	Moves the edit point to the given character offset
MoveToLineAndOffset	Moves the edit point to the given line and to the character offset within that line
MoveToPoint	Moves the edit point to the location of another EditPoint or TextPoint object
NextBookmark	Moves the edit point to the next available bookmark in the document
OutlineSection	Creates an outline section between the point's current location and another location in the document
PadToColumn	Pads spaces in the current line up to the indicated column number
Paste	Pastes the contents of the Clipboard to the edit point's current location
PreviousBookmark	Moves the edit point to the previous bookmark
ReadOnly	Returns a Boolean flag indicating whether a text range in the document is read-only

Property	Description
ReplacePattern	Replaces any text that matches the provided pattern
ReplaceText	Replaces a range of text with the provided string
SetBookmark	Creates an unnamed bookmark on the edit point's current line in the document
StartOfDocument	Moves the edit point to the start of the document
StartOfLine	Moves the edit point to the beginning of the line where it is positioned
TryToShow	Attempts to display the point's current location within the text editor window
Unindent	Removes the given number of indentation levels from a range of lines in the document
WordLeft	Moves the edit point to the left the given number of words
WordRight	Moves the edit point to the right the given number of words

Now let's look at various text manipulation scenarios.

Adding Text   EditPoint objects are the key to adding text, and you create them either by using a TextDocument object or by using a TextPoint object.

A TextPoint instance can create an EditPoint instance in its same exact location by calling TextPoint.CreateInstance. With the TextDocument type, you can call the CreateEditPoint method and pass in a valid TextPoint.

Because TextPoint objects are used to locate specific points in a document, a TextPoint object is leveraged as an input parameter to CreateEditPoint. In essence, the object tells the method where to create the edit point. If you don't provide a TextPoint object, the edit point is created at the start of the document.

This code snippet shows an edit point being created at the end of a document:

```
Document doc = _applicationObject.ActiveDocument;
TextDocument txtDoc = (Textdocument)doc.Object();
TextPoint tp = txtDoc.EndPoint;
EditPoint2 ep = txtDoc.CreateEditPoint(tp);
// This line of code would have the same effect
ep = tp.CreateEditPoint();
```

After creating an edit point, you can use it to add text into the document. (Remember, you are editing the buffered text whenever you use an EditPoint object.) To inject a string into the document, you use the Insert method:

```
// Insert a C# comment line
ep.Insert("// some comment");
```

You can even grab the contents of a file and throw that into the document with the `EditPoint.InsertFromFile` method:

```
// Insert comments from a comments file
ep.InsertFromFile("C:\Contoso\std comments.txt");
```

Editing Text   The `EditPoint` object supports deleting, replacing, cutting, copying, and pasting text in a document.

Some of these operations require more than a single point to operate. For instance, if you want to cut a word or an entire line of code from a document, you need to specify a start point and end point that define that range of text (see Figure 13.8).

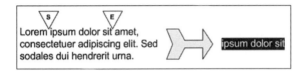

FIGURE 13.8   Using points within a document to select text.

This snippet uses two end points, one at the start of a document and one at the end, to delete the entire contents of the document:

```
Document doc = _applicationObject.ActiveDocument;
TextDocument txtDoc = (TextDocument)doc.Object();

TextPoint tpStart = txtDoc.StartPoint;
TextPoint tpEnd = txtDoc.EndPoint;

EditPoint2 epStart = txtDoc.CreateEditPoint(tpStart);
EditPoint2 epEnd = txtDoc.CreateEditPoint(tpEnd);
epStart.Delete(epEnd);
```

Besides accepting a second `EditPoint`, the methods that operate on a range of text also accept an integer identifying a count of characters. This has the effect of defining a select. For example, this snippet cuts the first 10 characters from a document:

```
epStart.Cut(10);
```

Repositioning an `EditPoint`   After establishing an `EditPoint`, you can move it to any location in the document by using various methods. The `CharLeft` and `CharRight` methods move the point any number of characters to the left or right, and the `WordLeft` and `WordRight` methods perform the same operation with words:

```
// Move the edit point four words to the right
epStart.WordRight(4);
```

The `LineUp` and `LineDown` methods jog the point up or down the specified number of lines. You can also move `EditPoints` to any given line within a document by using `MoveToLineAndOffset`. This method also positions the point any number of characters into the line:

```
// Move the edit point to line 100, and then
// in 5 characters to the right
epStart.MoveToLineAndOffset(100, 5);
```

The add-in code in Listing 13.11 pulls together some of the areas that we have covered with editing text documents. This add-in and its supporting functions illustrate the use of `EditPoints` to write text into a document. In this case, the add-in automatically inserts a comment "flower box" immediately preceding a routine. To accomplish this, the add-in goes through the following process:

1. A reference is obtained for the current document in the IDE.

2. The active cursor location in that document is obtained via the `TextDocument.Selection.ActivePoint` property.

3. An `EditPoint` is created using the `VirtualPoint` object.

4. A second `EditPoint` is then created; these two points are used to obtain the entire content of the routine definition line.

5. The routine definition is then parsed to try to ferret out items such as its name, return value, and parameter list.

6. A string is built using the routine information and is inserted into the text document using an `EditPoint`.

LISTING 13.11   Inserting Comments into a Text Window

```
using System;
using Extensibility;
using EnvDTE;
using EnvDTE80;
using Microsoft.VisualBasic;
using System.Windows.Forms;
using Microsoft.VisualStudio.CommandBars;
public class Connect : IDTExtensibility2
{

    private DTE2 _applicationObject;
    private AddIn _addInInstance;

    // This routine demonstrates various text editing scenarios
    // using the EditPoint and TextPoint types. If you place your
    // cursor on a Visual Basic subroutine or function, it will build
```

```
// a default "flower box" comment area, insert it immediately
// above the sub/function, and outline it.
//
// To use:
//    1) put cursor anywhere on the Sub/Function line
//    2) run add-in command
//    This will fail silently (e.g., will not insert any
//    comments) if it is unable to determine the start
//    of the Sub/Function
//
public void  InsertVBTemplateFlowerbox()
{
    // Get reference to the active document
    Document doc = _applicationObject.ActiveDocument;
    TextDocument txtDoc = (TextDocument)doc.Object();
    bool isFunc;

    try
    {
        EditPoint2 ep = (EditPoint2)txtDoc.Selection.ActivePoint.
➥CreateEditPoint();

        ep.StartOfLine();
        EditPoint2 ep2 = (EditPoint2)ep.CreateEditPoint();
        ep2.EndOfLine();

        string lineText = ep.GetText(ep2).Trim();

        if (lineText.IndexOf(" Function ") > 0)
        {
            isFunc = true;
        }
        else
        {
            if (lineText.IndexOf(" Sub ") > 0)
            {
                isFunc = false;
            }

            else
            {
                throw new Exception();
            }
        }

        // Parse out info that we can derive from the routine
```

```csharp
            // definition: the return value type (if this is a function),
            // the names of the parameters, and the name of the routine.
            string returnType = "";

            if (isFunc)
            {
                returnType = ParseRetValueType(lineText);
            }


            string[] parameters = ParseParameters(lineText);
            string name = ParseRoutineName(lineText);
            string commentBlock = BuildCommentBlock(isFunc, name,
                returnType, parameters);

            // Move the edit point up one line (to position
            // immediately preceding the routine)
            ep.LineUp(1);

            // Give us some room by inserting a new blank line
            ep.InsertNewLine();

            // Insert our comment block
            ep.Insert(commentBlock.ToString());
        }
        catch (Exception ex)
        {

        }


    }

    private string BuildCommentBlock(bool isFunc,
        string name,
        string returnType,
            string[] parameters)

    {
        try
        {
            string comment = "";

            // Build up a sample comment block using the passed in info
            comment += "//////////////////////////////////////////////////\r\n";
            comment += "// Routine: " + name;
```

```csharp
        comment += "\r\n";
        comment += "// Description: [insert routine desc here]";
        comment += "\r\n";
        comment += "//";
        comment += "\r\n";

        if (isFunc)
        {
            comment += "// Returns: A " +
                returnType +
                "[insert return value description here]";
        }

        comment += "\r\n";
        comment += "//";
        comment += "\r\n";
        comment += "// Parameters:";
        comment += "\r\n";

        for (int i = 0; i <= parameters.GetUpperBound(0); i++)
        {
            comment += "//     ";
            comment += parameters[i];
            comment += ": [insert parameter description here]";
            comment += "\r\n";
        }

        comment += "//////////////////////////////////////////////////\r\n";

        return comment;

    }
    catch (Exception ex)
    {
        return "";
    }

}


private string ParseRetValueType(string code)
{
    try
    {
        // Parse out the return value of a function (VB)
        // Search for //As', starting from the end of the string
```

```csharp
            int length = code.Length;
            int index = code.LastIndexOf(" As ");

            string retVal = code.Substring(index + 3, length - (index + 3));
            return retVal.Trim();

        }

        catch (Exception ex)
        {
            return "";
        }


    }

    private string[] ParseParameters(string code)
    {
        try{
            // Parse out the parameters specified (if any) for
            // a VB sub/func definition
            int length = code.Length;
            int indexStart = code.IndexOf("(");
            int indexEnd = code.LastIndexOf(")");

            string parameters = code.Substring(indexStart + 1, indexEnd -
              (indexStart + 1));

            return parameters.Split(',');

        }
        catch (Exception ex)
        {
            return null;
        }

    }

    private string ParseRoutineName(string code)

    {
        try
        {
            string name;
            int length = code.Length;
            int indexStart = code.IndexOf(" Sub ");
```

```
        int indexEnd = code.IndexOf("(");

        if (indexStart == -1)
        {
            indexStart = code.IndexOf(" Function ");
            if (indexStart != -1)
            {
                indexStart = indexStart + 9;
            }

        }
        else
        {
            indexStart = indexStart + 5;
        }

        name = code.Substring(indexStart, indexEnd - indexStart);

        return name.Trim();
    }
    catch (Exception ex)
    {
        return "";
    }

    }

}
```

Command Objects

Every action that is possible to execute through the menus and toolbars in Visual Studio is generically referred to as a command. For example, pasting text into a window is a command, as are building a project, toggling a breakpoint, and closing a window.

For each command supported in the IDE, there is a corresponding Command object; the DTE.Commands collection holds all the valid Command object instances. Each command is keyed by a name that categorizes, describes, and uniquely identifies the command. The "paste" command, for instance, is available via the string key "Edit.Paste". If you want to retrieve the Command object mapping to the paste command, you pull from the Commands collection using that string key:

```
Commands2 commands = (Commands2)_applicationObject.Commands;
Command cmd = commands.Item["Edit.Paste"];
```

You can query a command's name via its `Name` property:

```
// name would = "Edit.Paste"
string name = cmd.Name;
```

Table 13.14 contains the members declared on the `Command` interface.

The list of all available commands is extremely long (nearly 3,000 total), and it is therefore impossible to cover every one of them here, or even a large portion of them. To get an idea of the specific commands available, however, you can use the dialog box used to customize the Visual Studio toolbars. If you select the Customize option from the View, Toolbars menu and then click the Commands tab, you can investigate all the various commands by category (see Figure 13.9). Another alternative is to programmatically iterate the `DTE.Commands` collection and view them that way. In fact, in Chapter 14, we use this as one scenario for showcasing add-in development.

TABLE 13.14   Command Members

Property	Description
Bindings	The keystrokes that can be used to invoke the command
Collection	The `Commands` collection that the `Command` object belongs to
DTE	A reference to the root-level DTE object
Guid	A GUID that identifies the command's group
ID	An integer that identifies the command within its group
IsAvailable	A Boolean flag that indicates whether the command is currently available
LocalizedName	The localized name of the command
Name	The name of the command
Method	**Description**
AddControl	Creates a control for the command that can be hosted in a command bar
Delete	Removes a named command that was previously added with the `Commands.AddNamedCommand` method

FIGURE 13.9   Using the Customize dialog box to view commands.

So, although we can't cover all the commands, you can learn how to perform common tasks with the Command objects such as executing a command, checking on a command's current status, and even adding your own commands to the command library.

Executing a Command

Commands can be executed in two ways. The DTE object has an ExecuteCommand method you can use to trigger a command based on its name:

```
_applicationObject.ExecuteCommand("Window.CloseDocumentWindow");
```

The Commands collection is also a vehicle for launching commands through its Raise method. Instead of using the command's name, the Raise method uses its GUID and ID to identify the command:

```
Commands2 commands = (Commands2)_applicationObject.Commands;
Command cmd = commands.Item["Window.CloseDocumentWindow"];
object customIn;
object customOut;

commands.Raise(cmd.Guid, cmd.ID, customin, customout);
```

Some commands accept arguments. The Shell command is one example. It is used to launch an external application into the shell environment and thus takes the application filename as one of its parameters. You can launch this command by using the ExecuteCommand method like this:

```
Commands2 commands = _applicationObject.Commands;
Command cmd = commands.Item("Tools.Shell");
string arg1 = "MyApp.exe";

_applicationObject.ExecuteCommand(cmd.Name, arg1);
```

The `Raise` method also works with arguments: The last two parameters provided to the `Raise` method are used to specify an array of arguments to be used by the command and an array of output values returned from the command.

Mapping Key Bindings

Most commands can be invoked by a keyboard shortcut in addition to a menu entry or button on a command bar. You can set these keyboard shortcuts on a per-command basis by using the `Command.Bindings` property. This property returns or accepts a `SafeArray` (essentially an array of objects) that contains each shortcut as an element of the array.

Key bindings are represented as strings with the following format: "[scopename]::[modifier+] [key]".

`Scopename` is used to refer to the scope where the shortcut is valid, such as `Text Editor` or `Global`. The `modifier` token is used to specify the key modifier such as "Ctrl+," "Alt+," or "Shift+" (modifiers are not required). And the `key` is the keyboard key that is pressed (in conjunction with the modifier if present) to invoke the command.

To add a binding to an existing command, you first need to retrieve the current array of binding values, add your binding string to the array, and then assign the whole array back into the `Bindings` property like this:

```
Commands2 commands As = (Commands2)_applicationObject.Commands;
Command cmd =
    commands.Item("File.SaveSelectedItems");

object[] bindings;

bindings = cmd.Bindings;

// Increase the array size by 1 to hold the new binding
Array.Resize<object>(ref bindings, bindings.GetUpperBound(0) + 1);

// Assign the new binding into the array
bindings(bindings.GetUpperBound(0)) = "Global::Shift+F2";

// Assign the array back to the command object
cmd.Bindings = bindings;
```

> **NOTE**
>
> You can create your own named commands that can be launched from a command bar in the IDE (or from the command window for that matter). The Command object itself is added to the Commands collection by calling Commands.AddNamedCommand. The code that runs when the command is executed has to be implemented by an add-in. We cover this scenario in Chapter 14.

Debugger Objects

The automation object model provides a Debugger object that enables you to control the Visual Studio debugger. A Debugger instance can be obtained through the DTE.Debugger property:

```
Dim debugger As EnvDTE.Debugger
debugger = DTE.Debugger
```

With a valid Debugger object, you can do the following:

- ▶ Set breakpoints
- ▶ Start and stop the debugger for a given process
- ▶ Control the various execution stepping actions supported by the debugger such as Step Into, Step Over, and Step Out
- ▶ Issue the Run to Cursor command to the debugger
- ▶ Query the debugger for its current mode (for example, break mode, design mode, or run mode)

The following code starts the debugger if it isn't already started:

```
Debugger2 debugger = (Debugger2)_applicationObject.Debugger;

If (debugger.CurrentMode != dbgDebugMode.dbgRunMode)
{
    debugger.Go();
}
```

Automation Events

If your add-in needs to be notified when a certain event occurs, various event objects are supported in all the automation object categories previously discussed. There are events for windows, events for editors, events for projects, and so on. For every event supported by the IDE, a corresponding class in the automation model allows you to hook the event and take action if the event is raised. The event objects tree is rooted in the DTE.Events property, as depicted in Figure 13.10.

Because events are handled differently depending on whether you are working with code in an add-in or code in a macro, we cover the details of handling events in Chapter 14. The basic premise, however, is fairly simple: You obtain a reference to the event object that you are interested in and then write an event handler that responds to one of that object's published events.

This code, for instance, is how you might handle the "build complete" event from inside a Visual Basic add-in:

```
Dim WithEvents bldevents As BuildEvents
bldevents = DTE.Events.BuildEvents
```

After instantiating a `BuildEvents` object, you now have to write the actual event handler:

```
Private Sub bldevents_OnBuildDone(ByVal Scope As EnvDTE.vsBuildScope, _
    ByVal Action As EnvDTE.vsBuildAction) Handles bldevents.OnBuildDone
        ' Code to handle the event goes here
    End Sub
```

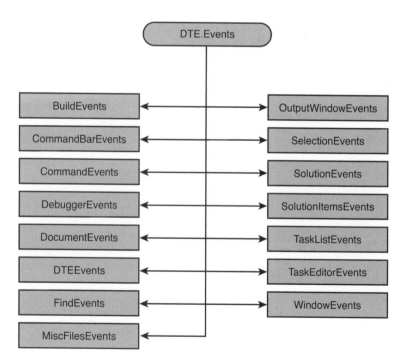

FIGURE 13.10   DTE event types.

Summary

The Visual Studio automation object model is a deep and wide API that exposes many of the IDE components to managed code running as an add-in in the IDE. This chapter documented how this API is organized and described its capabilities in terms of controlling the Visual Studio debugger, editors, windows, tool windows, solutions, and projects.

We also discussed the eventing model exposed by the API and looked at the API's capabilities with regard to accessing the underlying code structure for a project, issuing commands inside the IDE, and editing text documents programmatically.

Using the methods and properties expressed on the automation objects, you can automate common tasks in the IDE and extend Visual Studio in ways that address your specific development tool needs.

In the next chapter, we directly build on the concepts discussed here and specifically walk you through the process of writing Visual Studio add-ins.

CHAPTER 14

Writing Add-Ins and Wizards

As robust as Visual Studio is in terms of features and capabilities, its designers cannot anticipate every single possible scenario. Nor can Microsoft move at a fast enough clip to deliver enough versions of Visual Studio to satisfy all the various requirements that individual developers or companies might have. And so, Visual Studio has been constructed in a way that allows .NET developers to reach out and customize the behavior of the IDE, or even add new behaviors. Add-ins are the vehicles for accomplishing this. Add-ins are compiled projects written in Visual Basic, Visual C#, or even Visual C++ that directly leverage the object model and application programming interface (API) discussed in the preceding chapter. By writing an add-in, you can surface your own custom forms, tool windows, and designers within the IDE. Here are just a few of the things possible with add-ins:

▶ Create and display custom tool windows

▶ Expose a custom user interface to end users

▶ Implement a property page hosted in the Visual Studio Options dialog box

▶ Dynamically enable or disable menu and toolbar items in the IDE

Another related topic is that of creating and customizing Visual Studio wizards. Wizards are launched anytime you create a new project or add an item to a project. These wizards typically present one or more dialog boxes to capture preferences from the user and then use those preferences to create a project structure, generate default code, or perform even more complicated tasks. Wizards work in conjunction with template files to drive the initial structure for a code file or an entire project. The entire framework for wizards and templates is available to customize to fit your particular needs.

Creating Your First Add-In Project

The simplest way to get started with add-ins is to run the Add-In Wizard. As with the macro recorder, the wizard gives you a starting point for implementing your own add-ins. You can learn a great deal about the makeup of an add-in by examining the code the Add-In Wizard creates.

The Add-In Wizard launches whenever you try to create a new project of the type Visual Studio Add-in. From the File, New Project dialog box, select the Extensibility node in the project types tree (in Other Project Types, Extensibility). From here, you can see the Visual Studio Add-in project type (see Figure 14.1).

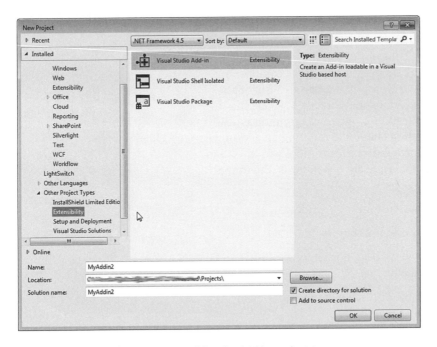

FIGURE 14.1   Selecting the Visual Studio Add-In project type.

We touch on the differences between these two project types in a bit; for now, we are interested in the Visual Studio Add-In template.

Click OK to start the Add-In Wizard.

Setting Add-In Parameters

The Add-In Wizard collects all the information necessary for defining the core parameters for the add-in project: the language you want to develop in, the application host, runtime information about the add-in (such as a description), and information for the About box. Let's briefly examine each of the wizard pages.

Selecting a Language

After an initial Welcome page, the first piece of information you need to provide is the language you want to use for developing the add-in (see Figure 14.2).

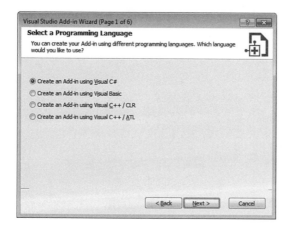

FIGURE 14.2   Picking the add-in language.

The list of languages available depends on two things:

▶ The languages installed as part of your Visual Studio package

▶ The type of add-in

Visual Studio add-ins support Visual C#, Visual Basic, and both managed and unmanaged Visual C++.

Picking an Application Host

After selecting a language, you are presented with a question about "application hosts." This screen is really just asking where you want the add-in to run. In our case, of course, this is Visual Studio 2012 (see Figure 14.3). Depending on which versions of Visual Studio you have installed on your machine, you may be able to write an add-in that targets more than one version of the IDE.

Describing the Add-In

The name and description you enter on page 3 of the wizard (see Figure 14.4) are visible in the Add-In Manager when the add-in is selected. This information is intended to give users an idea as to the add-in's functionality and purpose.

FIGURE 14.3   Selecting the application host.

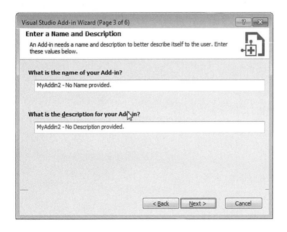

FIGURE 14.4   Providing the add-in's name and description.

Setting Add-In Options

The next wizard page, shown in Figure 14.5, enables you to specify various add-in options. You can indicate whether you want the add-in to appear in the Tools menu, when you want the add-in to load, and whether the add-in could potentially display a modal dialog box during its operation.

Setting About Box Information

The second-to-last wizard page captures the text that Visual Studio displays in its About box (see Figure 14.6).

This is the place to include details such as where users can contact the author of the add-in, support and licensing information, copyright and version information, and so on.

FIGURE 14.5   Setting add-in options.

14

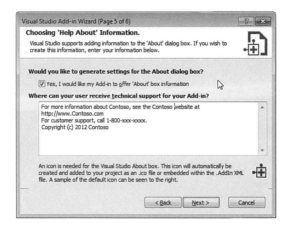

FIGURE 14.6   Setting the add-in's About box text.

Finishing the Wizard

The last page of the wizard contains a summary of the options that you have selected. After you click the Finish button, the wizard starts creating the code for your add-in based on all the selections you have made in the wizard.

Because add-ins are dynamic link libraries (DLLs), the Add-In Wizard creates the add-in source as part of a class library project in the IDE. The primary code file that is created implements a class called `Connect`. This class inherits from all the necessary COM interfaces to make the add-in work in the context of the IDE.

Listing 14.1 shows the `Connect` class as it was generated by the Add-In Wizard.

LISTING 14.1   Code Generated by the Add-In Wizard

```csharp
using System;
using Extensibility;
using EnvDTE;
using EnvDTE80;
using Microsoft.VisualStudio.CommandBars;
using System.Resources;
using System.Reflection;
using System.Globalization;

namespace MyAddin1
{
    /// <summary>The object for implementing an Add-in.</summary>
    /// <seealso class='IDTExtensibility2' />
    public class Connect : IDTExtensibility2, IDTCommandTarget
    {
        /// <summary>Implements the constructor for the Add-in object.
        /// Place your initialization code within this method.</summary>
        public Connect()
        {

        }

        /// <summary>Implements the OnConnection method of the
        /// IDTExtensibility2 interface. Receives notification that
        /// the Add-in is being loaded.</summary>
        /// <param term='application'>Root object of the host
        /// application.</param>
        /// <param term='connectMode'>Describes how the Add-in
        /// is being loaded.</param>
        /// <param term='addInInst'>Object representing this
        /// Add-in.</param>
        /// <seealso class='IDTExtensibility2' />
        public void OnConnection(object application,
          ext_ConnectMode connectMode,
          object addInInst, ref Array custom)
        {
            _applicationObject = (DTE2)application;
            _addInInstance = (AddIn)addInInst;
            if(connectMode == ext_ConnectMode.ext_cm_UISetup)
            {
                object []contextGUIDS = new object[] { };
                Commands2 commands =
                    (Commands2)_applicationObject.Commands;
```

```
string toolsMenuName = "Tools";

//Place the command on the Tools menu.
//Find the MenuBar command bar, which is the top-level
// command bar holding all the main menu items:
Microsoft.VisualStudio.CommandBars.CommandBar
  menuBarCommandBar =
  ((Microsoft.VisualStudio.CommandBars.CommandBars)
  _applicationObject.CommandBars)["MenuBar"];

//Find the Tools command bar on the MenuBar command bar:
CommandBarControl toolsControl =
  menuBarCommandBar.Controls[toolsMenuName];

CommandBarPopup toolsPopup =
    (CommandBarPopup)toolsControl;

//This try/catch block can be duplicated if you wish to
// add multiple commands to be handled by your Add-in,
// just make sure you also update the QueryStatus/Exec
// method to include the new command names.
try
{
    //Add a command to the Commands collection:
    Command command =
      commands.AddNamedCommand2(_addInInstance,
      "MyAddin1", "MyAddin1",
      "Executes the command for MyAddin1", true, 59,
      ref contextGUIDS,
      (int)vsCommandStatus.vsCommandStatusSupported+
      (int)vsCommandStatus.vsCommandStatusEnabled,
      (int)vsCommandStyle.vsCommandStylePictAndText,
      vsCommandControlType.vsCommandControlTypeButton);

    //Add a control for the command to the Tools menu:
    if((command != null) && (toolsPopup != null))
    {
        command.AddControl(toolsPopup.CommandBar, 1);
    }
}
catch(System.ArgumentException)
{
    //If we are here, then the exception is probably because
    //a command with that name already exists. If so there
    //is no need to re-create the command and we can safely
    //ignore the exception.
    }
```

```
        }
    }

    /// <summary>Implements the OnDisconnection method of the
    /// IDTExtensibility2 interface. Receives notification that the
    /// Add-in is being unloaded.</summary>
    /// <param term='disconnectMode'>Describes how the Add-in is being
    /// unloaded.</param>
    /// <param term='custom'>Array of parameters that are host application
    /// specific.</param>
    /// <seealso class='IDTExtensibility2' />
    public void OnDisconnection(ext_DisconnectMode disconnectMode,
        ref Array custom)
    {
    }

    /// <summary>Implements the OnAddInsUpdate method of the
    /// IDTExtensibility2 interface. Receives notification when the
    /// collection of Add-ins has changed.</summary>
    /// <param term='custom'>Array of parameters that are host application
    /// specific.</param>
    /// <seealso class='IDTExtensibility2' />
    public void OnAddInsUpdate(ref Array custom)
    {
    }
    /// <summary>Implements the OnStartupComplete method of the
    /// IDTExtensibility2 interface. Receives notification that the host
    /// application has completed loading.</summary>
    /// <param term='custom'>Array of parameters that are host application
    /// specific.</param>
    /// <seealso class='IDTExtensibility2' />
    public void OnStartupComplete(ref Array custom)
    {
    }

    /// <summary>Implements the OnBeginShutdown method of the
    /// IDTExtensibility2 interface. Receives notification that the host
    /// application is being unloaded.</summary>
    /// <param term='custom'>Array of parameters that are host application
    /// specific.</param>
    /// <seealso class='IDTExtensibility2' />
    public void OnBeginShutdown(ref Array custom)
    {
    }

    /// <summary>Implements the QueryStatus method of the IDTCommandTarget
    /// interface. This is called when the command's availability is
```

```
/// updated</summary>
/// <param term='commandName'>The name of the command to determine
/// state for.</param>
/// <param term='neededText'>Text that is needed for the
/// command.</param>
/// <param term='status'>The state of the command in the user
/// interface.</param>
/// <param term='commandText'>Text requested by the neededText
/// parameter.</param>
/// <seealso class='Exec' />
public void QueryStatus(string commandName,
  vsCommandStatusTextWanted neededText,
  ref vsCommandStatus status,
  ref object commandText)
  {
      if(neededText ==
        vsCommandStatusTextWanted.vsCommandStatusTextWantedNone)
      {
        if(commandName == "MyAddin1.Connect.MyAddin1")
        {
          status =
            (vsCommandStatus)vsCommandStatus.vsCommandStatusSupported
             |vsCommandStatus.vsCommandStatusEnabled;
          return;
        }
      }
  }

/// <summary>Implements the Exec method of the IDTCommandTarget
/// interface. This is called when the command is invoked.</summary>
/// <param term='commandName'>The name of the command to
/// execute.</param>
/// <param term='executeOption'>Describes how the command should
/// be run.</param>
/// <param term='varIn'>Parameters passed from the caller to the
/// command handler.</param>
/// <param term='varOut'>Parameters passed from the command handler
/// to the caller.</param>
/// <param term='handled'>Informs the caller if the command was
/// handled or not.</param>
/// <seealso class='Exec' />
public void Exec(string commandName,
  vsCommandExecOption executeOption,
  ref object varIn, ref object varOut,
  ref bool handled)
{
    handled = false;
```

14

```
            if(executeOption ==
              vsCommandExecOption.vsCommandExecOptionDoDefault)
            {
                if(commandName == "MyAddin1.Connect.MyAddin1")
                {
                    handled = true;
                    return;
                }
            }
        }
        private DTE2 _applicationObject;
        private AddIn _addInInstance;
    }
}
```

At this stage, the add-in doesn't actually do anything. You still have to implement the custom logic for the add-in. What the wizard has done, however, is implement much (if not all) of the tedious plumbing required to do the following:

▶ Wire the add-in into the IDE

▶ Expose it on the Tools menu

▶ Intercept the appropriate extensibility events to make the add-in work

Now that you have a baseline of code to work with, you're ready to examine the source to understand the overall structure and layout of an add-in.

The Structure of an Add-In

The first thing to notice is that the Connect class inherits from two different interfaces: IDTCommandTarget and IDTExtensibility2.

```
public class Connect : IDTExtensibility2, IDTCommandTarget
```

The IDTCommandTarget interface provides the functionality necessary to expose the add-in via a command bar. The code to inherit from this interface was added by the wizard because the Yes, Create a Tools Menu Item box was checked on page 4 of the add-in wizard.

The IDTExtensibility2 interface provides the eventing glue for add-ins. It is responsible for all the events that constitute the life span of an add-in.

The Lifecycle of an Add-In

Add-ins progress through a sequence of events every time they are loaded or unloaded in their application host. Each of these events is represented by a method defined on the IDTExtensibility2 interface. These methods are documented in Table 14.1.

TABLE 14.1 **IDTExtensibility2** Methods

Method	Description
OnAddInsUpdate	Called whenever an add-in is either loaded or unloaded
OnBeginShutdown	Called if Visual Studio is shut down while an add-in is loaded
OnConnection	Called when an add-in is loaded
OnDisconnection	Called when an add-in is unloaded
OnStartupComplete	Called when the add-in loads if this add-in is set to load when Visual Studio starts

The diagrams in Figure 14.7 and Figure 14.8 show how these methods (which really represent events) fall onto the normal load and unload path for an add-in.

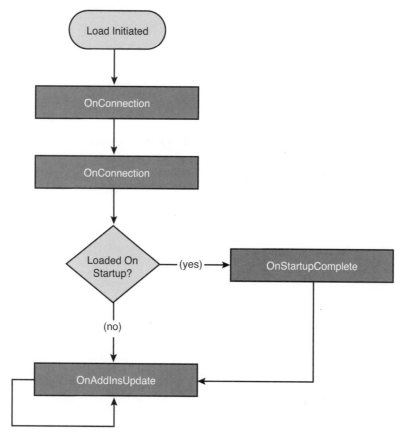

FIGURE 14.7   Load sequence of events.

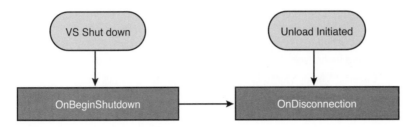

FIGURE 14.8   Unload sequence of events.

If you look back at the template code for the add-in, you can see that each one of these IDTExtensibility2 methods has been implemented. The OnDisconnection, OnAddInsUpdate, OnStartupComplete, and OnBeginShutdown methods are empty; the wizard has merely implemented the method signature. The OnConnection method, however, already has a fair bit of code to it before you even lift a hand to modify or add to the wizard-generated code.

Now you're ready to investigate what happens in each of the IDTExtensibility2 methods.

OnAddInsUpdate

The OnAddInsUpdate method is called when any add-in is loaded or unloaded from Visual Studio; because of this, the OnAddInsUpdate method is primarily useful for enforcing or dealing with dependencies between add-ins. If your add-in depends on or otherwise uses the functionality contained in another add-in, this is the ideal injection point for containing the logic that deals with that relationship.

Here is the OnAddInsUpdate method as implemented by the Add-In Wizard:

```
/// <summary>Implements the OnAddInsUpdate method of the IDTExtensibility2
/// interface. Receives notification when the collection of Add-ins has
/// changed.</summary>
/// <param term='custom'>Array of parameters that are host application
/// specific.</param>
/// <seealso class='IDTExtensibility2' />
public void OnAddInsUpdate(ref Array custom)
{
}
```

> **TIP**
>
> Because you don't know which add-in has triggered the OnAddInsUpdate method, you would need to iterate through the DTE.AddIns collection and query each add-in's Connected property to determine its current state.

OnBeginShutdown

OnBeginShutdown is called for every running add-in when Visual Studio begins its shutdown sequence. If an IDE requires any cleanup code (including perhaps resetting IDE settings that have been changed during the add-in's life), you place that code within this method.

A user may elect to cancel Visual Studio's shutdown process. OnBeginShutdown fires regardless of whether the Visual Studio shutdown process was successful. This forces you, as an add-in author, to always assume that Visual Studio has, in fact, terminated.

Here is the OnBeginShutdown method:

```
/// <summary>Implements the OnBeginShutdown method of the
///IDTExtensibility2 interface. Receives notification that the host
///application is being unloaded.</summary>
/// <param term='custom'>Array of parameters that are host
application specific.</param>
/// <seealso class='IDTExtensibility2' />
public void OnBeginShutdown(ref Array custom)
{
}
```

OnConnection

OnConnection indicates that an add-in has been loaded:

```
public void OnConnection(object application, ext_ConnectMode connectMode,
    object addInInst, ref Array custom)
```

It accepts four parameters. The first parameter, application, is the most important; it provides a reference to the DTE object representing the IDE. You know from Chapter 13, "Introducing the Automation Object Model," that the DTE object is the key to accessing the entire automation object model. For add-ins, the OnConnection method establishes the reference to this object, thus providing the crucial link between the add-in and its host IDE.

The second parameter, connectMode, is an ext_ConnectMode enumeration. It indicates exactly how the add-in was loaded. (See Table 14.2 for a list of the possible ext_ConnectMode values.)

TABLE 14.2   ext_ConnectMode Members

Member	Description
ext_cm_AfterStartup	The add-in was loaded after Visual Studio was started.
ext_cm_CommandLine	The add-in was loaded from the command line.
ext_cm_External	N/A (Visual Studio does not use this value.)
ext_cm_Solution	The add-in was loaded with a Visual Studio solution.
ext_cm_Startup	The add-in was loaded when Visual Studio started.
ext_cm_UISetup	The add-in was loaded for UI setup. (This represents the initial load of an add-in.)

The `addInInst` parameter is actually a reference to the add-in itself. And last, the custom parameter is an empty `Array` object. This array is passed by reference and can be used to pass parameters into and out of the add-in.

The Add-In Wizard has taken the first two parameters, explicitly cast them to their underlying types, and assigned them into two class fields for later reference:

```
_applicationObject = (DTE2)application;
_addInInstance = (AddIn)addInInst;
```

If you refer back to Chapter 13, you will see that many of the code examples there rely on the `_applicationObject` instance to do their work.

The next block of code examines the `ext_ConnectMode` value. If this is the first time the add-in was loaded (for example, `ext_ConnectMode` is equal to `ext_cm_UISetup`), the code does two things: It creates a Tools menu entry for the add-in, and it creates a custom named command to launch the add-in. (This named command is called when you select the add-in from the Tools menu.)

```
if(connectMode == ext_ConnectMode.ext_cm_UISetup)
{
        object []contextGUIDS = new object[] { };
        Commands2 commands = (Commands2)_applicationObject.Commands;
    string toolsMenuName = "Tools";

    //Place the command on the Tools menu.
    //Find the MenuBar command bar, which is the top-level command bar holding
    //all the main menu items:
    Microsoft.VisualStudio.CommandBars.CommandBar menuBarCommandBar = _
      ((Microsoft.VisualStudio.CommandBars.CommandBars)__
      applicationObject.CommandBars)["MenuBar"];

    //Find the Tools command bar on the MenuBar command bar:
    CommandBarControl toolsControl = menuBarCommandBar.Controls[toolsMenuName];
    CommandBarPopup toolsPopup = (CommandBarPopup)toolsControl;

    //This try/catch block can be duplicated if you wish to add multiple commands
    //to be handled by your Add-in,
    // just make sure you also update the QueryStatus/Exec method to include
    // the new command names.
    try
    {
        //Add a command to the Commands collection:
        Command command = commands.AddNamedCommand2(_addInInstance, _
                    "MyFirstAddin", "MyFirstAddin", _
                    "Executes the command for MyFirstAddin", true, 59, _
                    ref contextGUIDS,
                    (int)vsCommandStatus.vsCommandStatusSupported
```

```
            +(int)vsCommandStatus.vsCommandStatusEnabled,
            (int)vsCommandStyle.vsCommandStylePictAndText,
             vsCommandControlType.vsCommandControlTypeButton);

    //Add a control for the command to the Tools menu:
    if((command != null) && (toolsPopup != null))
    {
        command.AddControl(toolsPopup.CommandBar, 1);
    }
}
catch(System.ArgumentException)
{
    //If we are here, then the exception is probably because a command with
    //that name already exists. If so there is no need to re-create the
    //command and we can
    //  safely ignore the exception.

}
```

OnDisconnection

OnDisconnection fires when the add-in is unloaded from Visual Studio. This is the opposite action from that signaled by the OnConnection method. As with OnConnection, an enumeration (ext_DisconnectMode) is provided to this method that indicates how the unload action was initiated. For a list of the possible ext_DisconnectMode values, see Table 14.3.

TABLE 14.3   ext_DisconnectMode Members

Member	Description
ext_dm_HostShutdown	The add-in was unloaded because Visual Studio was shut down.
ext_dm_SolutionClosed	The add-in was unloaded because the solution was closed.
ext_dm_UISetupComplete	The add-in was unloaded after UI setup was complete.
ext_dm_UserClosed	The add-in was manually or programmatically unloaded. (This is used only if Visual Studio is still running; otherwise, ext_dm_HostShutdown will be used.)

Here is the `OnDisconnection` method:

```
/// <summary>Implements the OnDisconnection method of the IDTExtensibility2
///interface. Receives notification that the Add-in is being
///unloaded.</summary>
/// <param term='disconnectMode'>Describes how the Add-in is being
/// unloaded.</param>
/// <param term='custom'>Array of parameters that are host application
/// specific.</param>
/// <seealso class='IDTExtensibility2' />
public void OnDisconnection(ext_DisconnectMode disconnectMode, ref Array custom)
{
}
```

OnStartupComplete

If an add-in is set to load automatically during Visual Studio startup, the `OnStartupComplete` method fires after that add-in has been loaded.

Here is the `OnStartupComplete` method:

```
/// <summary>Implements the OnStartupComplete method of the IDTExtensibility2
/// interface. Receives notification that the host application has completed
/// loading.</summary>
/// <param term='custom'>Array of parameters that are host application
/// specific.</param>
/// <seealso class='IDTExtensibility2' />
public void OnStartupComplete(ref Array custom)
{
}
```

Reacting to Commands

Add-ins can react to commands issued within the IDE. If you recall from the discussion on commands in Chapter 13, this is done through the concept of *named commands*. A named command is really nothing more than an action that has a name attached to it. You already know that Visual Studio comes with its own extensive set of commands that cover a wide variety of actions in the IDE. Using the Commands/Commands2 collection, you can create your own named commands by using the AddNamedCommand2 method.

To repeat the dissection of the `OnConnection` method, the wizard has created a body of code responsible for creating a new named command, adding it to the Tools menu, and then reacting to the command. The `IDTCommandTarget.Exec` method is the hook used to react to an issued command. Here is its prototype:

```
void Exec (
    [InAttribute] string CmdName,
    [InAttribute] vsCommandExecOption ExecuteOption,
    [InAttribute] ref Object VariantIn,
```

```
    [InAttribute] out Object VariantOut,
    [InAttribute] out bool Handled
)
```

To handle a command issued to an add-in, you write code in the `Exec` method that reacts to the passed-in command.

`CmdName` is a string containing the name of the command; this is the token used to uniquely identify a command, and thus is the parameter you examine in the body of the `Exec` method to determine whether and how you should react to the command.

`ExecuteOption` is a `vsCommandExecOption` enumeration that provides information about the options associated with the command (see Table 14.4).

TABLE 14.4 `vsCommandExecOption` Members

Member	Description
vsCommandExecOptionDoDefault	Performs the default behavior
vsCommandExecOptionDoPromptUser	Obtains user input and then executes the command
vsCommandExecOptionPromptUser	Executes the command without user input
vsCommandExecOptionShowHelp	Shows help for the command (does not execute it)

The `VariantIn` parameter is used to pass any arguments needed for the incoming command, and `VariantOut` is used as a way to pass information back out of the add-in to the caller.

Finally, `Handled` is a Boolean that indicates to the host application whether the add-in handled the command. As a general rule, if your add-in processed the command, it sets `Handled` to `true`. Otherwise, it sets `Handled` to `false`, which is a signal to Visual Studio that it needs to continue to look for a command invocation target that will handle the command.

The code to handle the Tool menu command looks like this:

```
/// <summary>Implements the Exec method of the IDTCommandTarget
///interface. This is called when the command is invoked.</summary>
/// <param term='commandName'>The name of the command to execute.</param>
/// <param term='executeOption'>Describes how the command should
///be run.</param>
/// <param term='varIn'>Parameters passed from the caller to the command
/// handler.</param>
/// <param term='varOut'>Parameters passed from the command handler to
/// the caller.</param>
/// <param term='handled'>Informs the caller if the command was handled
/// or not.</param>
```

```
/// <seealso class='Exec' />
public void Exec(string commandName, vsCommandExecOption executeOption,
    ref object varIn, ref object varOut, ref bool handled)
{
    handled = false;
    if(executeOption == vsCommandExecOption.vsCommandExecOptionDoDefault)
    {
        if(commandName == "MyFirstAddin.Connect.MyFirstAddin")
        {
            handled = true;
            return;
        }
    }

}
```

Managing Add-Ins

Visual Studio add-ins are controlled with the Visual Studio Add-in Manager, which enables you to do two things: load and unload any registered add-in and specify how an add-in can be loaded. To access the Add-in Manager (see Figure 14.9), select Tools, Add-in Manager.

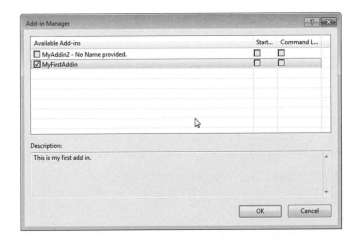

FIGURE 14.9   Managing add-ins.

This dialog box always displays a list of any available add-ins on the local machine. Checking or unchecking the box next to an add-in's name causes the add-in to immediately load or unload. The Startup check box determines whether the add-in loads automatically when Visual Studio is started. The Command Line check box performs the same action if Visual Studio is started via the command line (such as when you are launching Visual Studio as part of an automated build scenario).

Add-In Automation Objects

To programmatically manage add-ins, you use the DTE.AddIns collection, which contains an `AddIn` instance for every currently registered add-in (whether or not it is loaded).

Assuming a valid reference to the `DTE2` object, you can directly reference registered add-ins from the DTE.AddIns collection by using their names like this:

```
DTE2 _appObject;
AddIn addIn = _appObject.AddIns.Item("MyFirstAddin");
```

With a valid add-in object, you can use its properties to determine whether it is loaded, query its name, or retrieve the add-in's `ProgID`:

```
bool isLoaded = addIn.Connected;
string name = addIn.Name;

string id = addIn.ProgID;
```

> **NOTE**
>
> We use the term *registered* to denote an add-in that has been installed on the local machine and registered with Visual Studio. In versions before Visual Studio 2005, this meant that a Registry entry was created for the add-in. This concept was replaced in 2005 with XML files: Visual Studio looks for XML files with an .addin extension to determine the list of add-ins available to be loaded (an add-in is "loaded" when it has been connected to, and loaded within, an application's host process). These .addin files are created for you automatically by the Add-In Wizard, but they can be easily created or edited by hand as well. To get a feeling for the information and structure of these files, look in the Visual Studio 2012\Addins folder under your local Documents directory. Each registered add-in appears here; you can explore an add-in file by loading it into Visual Studio, Notepad, or any other text editor.

A Sample Add-In: Color Palette

To cap this discussion of add-ins, let's look at the process of developing a functioning add-in from start to finish. The add-in is a color picker. It enables users to click an area of a color palette, and the add-in emits code to create an instance of a color structure that matches the selected color from the palette. Here is a summary list of requirements for the add-in:

▶ In a tool window, it displays a visual color palette representing all the possible colors.

▶ As the mouse pointer is moved over the palette, the control displays the Red, Green, and Blue values for the point directly under the mouse pointer.

▶ If a user clicks the palette, it takes the current RGB values and emits C# or VB code into the currently active document window to create a new color structure that encapsulates the given color.

▶ The selection of language (for example, C# or VB) is a configurable property of the control.

Getting Started

To start the development process, you create a new solution and a Visual Studio Add-In project called **ColorSelectorAddIn**. The Add-In Wizard creates a code base for you inside a `Connect` class just as you saw earlier in this chapter. The `Connect` class is the place where all the IDE and automation object model-specific code goes.

In addition to the core add-in plumbing, you also need to create a User Control class that encapsulates the user interface and the processing logic for the add-in.

Creating the User Control

First, you can work on getting in place a user control that has the functionality you are looking for. After you have a workable control, you can worry about wiring that control into Visual Studio using the `Connect` class created by the Add-In Wizard.

Add a user control (called `PaletteControl`) to the add-in project by selecting Project, Add User Control. After the control is added, you place nine controls on the user control design surface. First, add a picture box (`pictureBoxPalette`), which is used to display the palette of colors, stored as a simple bitmap in a resource file. (In this case, we're using a color palette from a popular paint program as our source for the bitmap.) With the palette in place, you now need six label controls to display RGB values (call them `labelR`, `labelRValue`, `labelG`, `labelGValue`, `labelB`, and `labelBValue`) per the requirements. And finally, in the finest tradition of gold-plating, you also add a picture box (called `pictureBoxColor`) that repeats the current color selection and a label that shows the code you would generate to implement that color in a color structure.

Figure 14.10 provides a glimpse of the user control after these controls have been situated on the designer.

Handling Movement over the Palette

With the UI in place, you can now concentrate on the code. First, you can add an event handler to deal with mouse movements over the top of the palette picture box. With the `MouseMove` event handler, you can update your label controls and the secondary picture box instantly as the pointer roves over the palette bitmap:

```
public PaletteControl()
{
    InitializeComponent();
    this.pictureBoxPalette.MouseMove +=
        new MouseEventHandler(pictureBoxPalette_MouseMove);
```

```
        this.pictureBoxPalette.Cursor = System.Windows.Forms.Cursors.Cross;
}


void pictureBoxPalette_MouseMove(object sender, MouseEventArgs e)
{
        // Get the color under the current pointer position
        Color color = GetPointColor(e.X, e.Y);

        // Update the RGB labels and the 2nd pic box
        // using the retrieved color
        DisplayColor(color);

        // Generate our VB or C# code for the Color
        // structure
        SetCode(color, _generateVB);
}
```

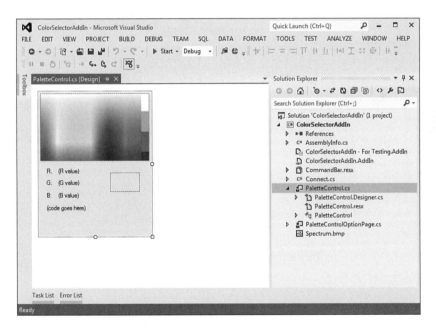

FIGURE 14.10   The PaletteControl user control.

Looking at the Code-Generation Properties

The PaletteControl class exposes two properties. Code is a string property that holds the color structure code generated when the palette is clicked on, and GenerateVB is a Boolean that specifies whether the control should generate Visual Basic code (GenerateVB = true) or C# code (GenerateVB = false). Here are the field and property declarations for these two properties:

```
string _code = "";
public string Code
{
    get { return _code; }
}


bool _generateVB = false;
public bool GenerateVB
{
   get { return _generateVB; }

}
```

Implementing the Helper Routines

Whenever the mouse pointer moves over the picture box region, you need to capture the color components of the point directly below the cursor (GetPointColor), update the label controls and the secondary picture box control to reflect that color (DisplayColor), and then generate the code to implement a matching color structure (SetCode). Here are the implementations of these routines:

```
/// <summary>
/// Returns a Color structure representing the color of
/// the pixel at the indicated x and y coordinates.
/// </summary>
/// <param name="x"></param>
/// <param name="y"></param>
/// <returns>A Color structure</returns>
private Color GetPointColor(int x, int y)
{
    // Get the bitmap from the palette picture box
    Bitmap bmp = (Bitmap)pictureBoxPalette.Image;
    // Use GetPixel to retrieve a color
    // structure for the current pointer position
    Color color = bmp.GetPixel(x, y);

    // Return the color structure
    return color;
}


/// <summary>
/// Displays the RGB values for the given color. Also sets
/// the background color of the secondary picture box.
/// </summary>
/// <param name="color">The Color to display</param>
private void DisplayColor(Color color)
{
```

```csharp
        // pull out the RGB values from the
        // color structure
        string R = color.R.ToString();
        string G = color.G.ToString();
        string B = color.B.ToString();
        // set our secondary picture box
        // to display the current color
        this.pictureBoxColor.BackColor = color;
        // display RGB values in the label
        // controls
        this.labelRValue.Text = R;
        this.labelGValue.Text = G;
        this.labelBValue.Text = B;
}


/// <summary>
/// Generates a string representing the C# or VB code necessary to
/// create a Color structure instance that matches the passed in
/// Color structure. This string is then assigned to this
/// user control's _code field.
/// </summary>
/// <param name="color">The color to represent in code.</param>
/// <param name="isVB">Boolean flag indicating the language
/// to use: false indicates C#, true indicates VB</param>
private void SetCode(Color color, bool isVB)
{
    // Read in add-in settings from registry
    SetPropFromReg();

    string code = "";

    if (isVB)
    {
        code = "Dim color As Color = ";
    }
    else
    {
        code = "Color color = ";
    }

    code = code + @"Color.FromArgb(" + color.R.ToString() + ", " +
        color.G.ToString() + ", " +
        color.B.ToString() + ");";

  _code = code;
  this.labelCode.Text = _code;
```

```
}
/// <summary>
/// Reads a registry entry and sets the language output fields
/// appropriately.
/// </summary>
private void SetPropFromReg()
{
    RegistryKey regKey =
      Registry.CurrentUser.OpenSubKey(@"Software\Contoso\Addins\ColorPalette");
    string codeVal = (string)regKey.GetValue("Language", "CSharp");

    if (codeVal == "CSharp")
    {
        _generateVB = false;
    }
    else
    {
        _generateVB = true;
    }

}
```

Signaling a Color Selection

Because you need some way for the control to indicate that a user has selected a color (for example, has clicked the palette), you also define an event on the user control class that is raised whenever a click is registered in the palette picture box:

```
public event EventHandler ColorSelected;

protected virtual void OnColorSelected(EventArgs e)
{
    if (ColorSelected != null)
        ColorSelected(this, e);
}

private void pictureBoxPalette_Click(object sender, EventArgs e)
{
    OnColorSelected(new EventArgs());

}
```

> **TIP**
>
> To isolate and test the user control, you might want to add a Windows Forms project to the solution and host the control on a Windows form for testing. Just drop the control onto the form and run the forms project.

With the user control in place, you are ready to proceed to the second stage of the add-in's development: wiring the user control into the IDE.

Finishing the Connect Class

The `Connect` class already has the basic add-in code; now it's time to revisit that code and add the custom code to drive the user control. The add-in should integrate seamlessly into the development environment, so you can use a tool window to display the user control that you previously created.

Harking back to the discussions of the automation object model, you know that the Windows2 collection has a `CreateToolWindow2` method, which allows you to create your own custom tool windows.

> **NOTE**
>
> Earlier versions of Visual Studio required you to create a shim control (using C++) that would host a control for display in a tool window. The tool window, in turn, would then host the shim. With Visual Studio 2005 and later (and the improved `Windows2.CreateToolWindow2` method), this is no longer necessary. Now you can directly host a managed user control in a tool window.

Here is the method prototype:

```
Window CreateToolWindow2 (
    AddIn Addin,
    string Assembly,
    string Class,
    string Caption,
    string GuidPosition,
    [InAttribute] out Object ControlObject


)
```

Displaying the Tool Window and User Control

Because you want the tool window to be created and displayed after the add-in has loaded, this `CreateToolWindow2` method call will be placed in the `Connect.OnConnection` method. Scroll through to the end of the OnConnection method (past all of the code that Visual Studio has generated for you), and set up a local object to point to the DTE.ToolWindows collection:

```
// The DTE.ToolWindows collection
Windows2 toolWindows= (Windows2)_applicationObject.Windows;
```

Then you need an object to hold the reference to the tool window that you create:

```
// Object to refer to the newly created tool window
Window2 toolWindow;
```

And finally, you need to create the parameters to feed to the `CreateToolWindow2` method:

```
// Placeholder object; will eventually refer to the user control
// hosted by the user control
object paletteObject = null;


// This section specifies the path and class name for the palette
// control to be hosted in the new tool window; we also need to
// specify its caption and a unique GUID.
Assembly asm = System.Reflection.Assembly.GetExecutingAssembly();
string assemblyPath = asm.Location;
string className = "ColorSelectorAddIn.PaletteControl";
string guid = "{62175059-FD7E-407a-9EF3-5D07F2B704E8}";string caption = "Palette
Color Picker";
```

Note that we have hard-coded a GUID to pass in to the `CreateToolWindow2` method. Because our user control is a managed code control, and it is hosted in a native COM component (all tool windows in Visual Studio are COM based), the add-in infrastructure needs some way to establish a viable calling interface for the control. This is done through the use of the GUID parameter.

You can use Visual Studio to generate your GUID by selecting Tools, Create GUID, and then selecting Registry Format. You can then directly copy and paste this into your code window.

With that in place, you are only a few lines of code away from creating and displaying the tool window:

```
// Create the new tool window with the hosted user control
toolWindow = (Window2)toolWindows.CreateToolWindow2(_addInInstance, assemblyPath,
    className, caption, guid, ref paletteObject);


// If tool window was created successfully, make it visible
if (toolWindow != null)
{
    toolWindow.Visible = true;
}
```

Capturing User Control Events

The add-in is missing one last piece: You need to react whenever the user clicks on the palette by grabbing the generated code (available from the `PaletteControl.Code` property) and inserting it into the currently active document. There are two tasks at hand. First, you need to write an event handler to deal with the click event raised by the `PaletteControl` object. But to do that, you need a reference to the user control. This is the purpose of the `paletteObject` object that you pass in as the last parameter to the `CreateToolWindow2` method. Because this is passed in by reference, it holds a valid instance of the `PaletteControl` after the method call completes and returns. You can then cast this object to the specific `PaletteControl` type, assign it to a field within the `Connect` class, and attach an event handler to the `PaletteControl.ColorSelected` event:

```
// retrieve a reference back to our user control object
_paletteControl = (PaletteControl)paletteObject;

// wire up event handler for the PaletteControl.ColorSelected event
_paletteControl.ColorSelected +=
    new System.EventHandler(paletteControl1_ColorSelected);
```

TIP

Getting a reference to the user control can be a bit tricky. If the user control is not a part of the same project as your add-in class, `CreateToolWindow2` will return only a `null` value instead of a valid reference to the user control. If you want to develop your user control outside the add-in project, you have to make sure that the user control is fully attributed to be visible to calling COM components. See the topic "Exposing .NET Framework Components to COM" in the Microsoft Developer Network (MSDN) for details on how this task is accomplished.

Inserting the Generated Code

You react to the `ColorSelect` event by grabbing the content of the `PaletteControl.Code` property and writing it into the currently active document. Again, you use your automation object model knowledge gained from the preceding chapter to make this happen. The `DTE.ActiveDocument` class holds a reference to the currently active document. By using an edit point, you can easily write text directly into the text document:

```
TextDocument currDoc = (TextDocument)_applicationObject.ActiveDocument.Object("");
EditPoint2 ep = (EditPoint2) currDoc.Selection.ActivePoint.CreateEditPoint();
ep.Insert(_paletteControl.Code);
ep.InsertNewLine(1);
```

Exposing Add-In Settings

The final step is to make the add-in's language choice a configurable option. Users should be able to indicate whether they want the add-in to emit C# or Visual Basic code. To do this, you need to have a user interface in the form of an Options page (that displays in the Options dialog box), and you need a place to persist the option selections.

Creating the Option Page UI

Add-ins can reference an Options page that appears in the Tools Options dialog box. Again, as you did with the custom tool window, you build a user control to implement the logic and the user interface for the Options page.

You start by adding a new user control to the existing add-in project. For this example, call this class `PaletteControlOptionPage`. Adding a label control and two radio button controls enables you to indicate the language preference for the palette add-in. Figure 14.11 shows the design surface of the Options page.

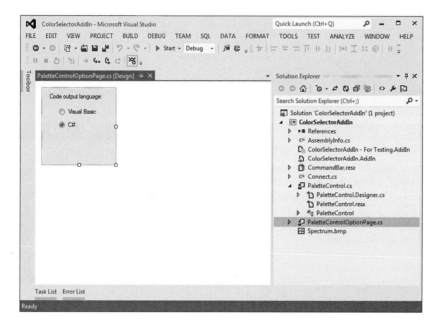

FIGURE 14.11   Designing the add-in options page UI.

The user control for the Options page needs to inherit from `IDTToolsOptionPage`:

```
public partial class PaletteControlOptionPage : UserControl, IDTToolsOptionsPage
{
    public PaletteControlOptionPage()
    {
        InitializeComponent();
    }
}
```

The `IDTToolsOptionsPage` interface defines five methods, outlined in Table 14.5.

TABLE 14.5   `IDTToolsOptionsPage` Members

Member	Description
GetProperties	Returns a properties object in response to calling `DTE.Properties` for this specific Options page
OnAfterCreated	Fires after the Tools Options page is created for the first time
OnCancel	Fires if the user clicks the Cancel button on the Tools Options dialog box

Member	Description
OnHelp	Fires if the user clicks the Help button on the Tools Options dialog box
OnOK	Fires if the user clicks the OK button on the Tools Options dialog box

These methods are called as the Options page progresses through its normal sequence of states, as you can see in Figure 14.12.

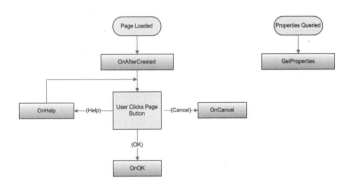

FIGURE 14.12   The Tools Options page action sequence.

By placing code within these methods, you can read in and store any configuration changes that a user makes through the Options page. In this case, you can keep things simple: Read in a value from a Registry entry as part of the OnAfterCreated method and update that same entry as part of the OnOK method:

```
public void OnAfterCreated(DTE DTEObject)
{
    // read our current value from registry
    // TODO: we should really include contingency code here for creating
    // the key if it doesn't already exist, dealing with unexpected values,
    // exceptions, etc.
    RegistryKey regKey =
        Registry.CurrentUser.OpenSubKey(@"Software\Contoso\Addins\ColorPalette");
    string codeVal = (string)regKey.GetValue("Language", "CSharp");

    if (codeVal == "CSharp")
    {
        this.radioButtonCSharp.Checked = true;
        this.radioButtonVB.Checked = false;
    }
    else
    {
```

```
        this.radioButtonCSharp.Checked = true;
        this.radioButtonVB.Checked = false;
    }
}
public void OnOK()
{
    string codeValue = "CSharp";    // our default value

    if (this.radioButtonVB.Checked)
    {
        codeValue = "VB";
    }

    // update the registry with the new setting
    RegistryKey regKey =
        Registry.CurrentUser.OpenSubKey(@"Software\Contoso\Addins\ColorPalette");
    regKey.SetValue("Language", codeValue);
}
```

NOTE

It is up to you to decide where and how you persist your add-in's settings. The Registry is one logical place; you could also elect to store your settings in an XML file that is deployed along with your binaries.

Registering the Options Page

The registration mechanism for an Options page is the same as that for an add-in: The .addin file is used. By adding a few lines of XML, you can indicate to Visual Studio that an Options page exists with the custom add-in. You can do this easily by editing the .addin file right in Visual Studio (because it is automatically created as part of the project).

To include the necessary XML registration information, edit the .addin file and place the following XML before the closing `</extensibility>` tag:

```
<ToolsOptionsPage>
  <Category Name="Color Palette">
    <SubCategory Name="Code Generation">
      <Assembly>C:\Users\lpowers\My Documents\Visual Studio 2012\Projects\

PaletteControlAddIn\PaletteControlAddIn\bin\PaletteControlAddIn.dll</Assembly>
      <FullClassName>PaletteControlAddIn.PaletteControlOptionPage </FullClassName>
    </SubCategory>
  </Category>
</ToolsOptionsPage>
```

You use the Category tag to specify the name of the option category displayed in the Tools Options dialog box. The SubCategory tag specifies the subnode under that category. The Assembly tag provides a path to the add-in's DLL file, and the FullClassName tag contains the full name for the add-in class.

With this final step complete, the add-in is fully functional. You can compile the project and then immediately load the add-in using the Add-in Manager. Figure 14.13 shows the add-in in action, and a complete code listing for the Connect, PaletteControl, and PaletteControlOptionPage classes (in that order) is provided in Listings 14.2, 14.3, and 14.4. You can download the complete source code for this add-in from the Sams Publishing website.

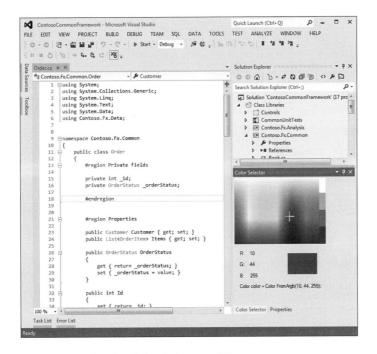

FIGURE 14.13   The Color Selector add-in.

LISTING 14.2   The Connect Class

```
using System;
using Extensibility;
using EnvDTE;
using EnvDTE80;
using Microsoft.VisualStudio.CommandBars;
using System.Resources;
using System.Reflection;
using System.Globalization;
using System.Windows.Forms;
```

```csharp
namespace ColorSelectorAddIn
{
    /// <summary>The object for implementing an Add-in.</summary>
    /// <seealso class='IDTExtensibility2' />
    public class Connect : IDTExtensibility2, IDTCommandTarget
    {
        #region Fields

        private DTE2 _applicationObject;
        private AddIn _addInInstance;
        private PaletteControl _paletteControl;

        #endregion

        /// <summary>Implements the constructor for the Add-in object.
        /// Place your initialization code within this method.</summary>
        public Connect()
        {
        }

        #region Events and Event Handlers

        private void paletteControl1_ColorSelected(object sender, EventArgs e)
        {
            try
            {
                TextDocument currDoc =
                  (TextDocument)_applicationObject.ActiveDocument.Object("");
                EditPoint2 ep = (EditPoint2)
                  currDoc.Selection.ActivePoint.CreateEditPoint();
                ep.Insert(_paletteControl.Code);
                ep.InsertNewLine(1);
            }

            catch (Exception ex)
            {
                MessageBox.Show("Exception caught: " + ex.ToString());
            }

        }

        #endregion

        /// <summary>Implements the OnConnection method of the
        /// IDTExtensibility2 interface. Receives notification that the Add-in
        /// is being loaded.</summary>
```

```
/// <param term='application'>Root object of the host application.
///</param>
/// <param term='connectMode'>Describes how the Add-in is being
/// loaded.</param>
/// <param term='addInInst'>Object representing this Add-in.</param>
/// <seealso class='IDTExtensibility2' />
public void OnConnection(object application,
    ext_ConnectMode connectMode,
    object addInInst, ref Array custom)
{
    _applicationObject = (DTE2)application;
    _addInInstance = (AddIn)addInInst;

    if(connectMode == ext_ConnectMode.ext_cm_UISetup)
    {
        object []contextGUIDS = new object[] { };
        Commands2 commands = (Commands2)_applicationObject.Commands;
        string toolsMenuName;

        try
        {
            string resourceName;
            ResourceManager resourceManager =
                new ResourceManager("ColorSelectorAddIn.CommandBar",
                    Assembly.GetExecutingAssembly());

            CultureInfo cultureInfo =
                new CultureInfo(_applicationObject.LocaleID);

            if(cultureInfo.TwoLetterISOLanguageName == "zh")
            {
                System.Globalization.CultureInfo parentCultureInfo =
                    cultureInfo.Parent;
                resourceName = String.Concat(parentCultureInfo.Name,
                                        "Tools");
            }
            else
            {
                resourceName =
                    String.Concat(cultureInfo.TwoLetterISOLanguageName,
                    "Tools");
            }
            toolsMenuName = resourceManager.GetString(resourceName);
        }
        catch
        {
```

```
            //We tried to find a localized version of the word Tools,
            //but one was not found.
            //  Default to the en-US word, which may work for the
            //  current culture.
            toolsMenuName = "Tools";
        }


        //Place the command on the Tools menu.
        //Find the MenuBar command bar, which is the top-level command
        // bar holding all the main menu items:

        Microsoft.VisualStudio.CommandBars.CommandBar
            menuBarCommandBar =
            ((Microsoft.VisualStudio.CommandBars.CommandBars)
            _applicationObject.CommandBars)["MenuBar"];

        //Find the Tools command bar on the MenuBar command bar:
        CommandBarControl toolsControl =
            menuBarCommandBar.Controls[toolsMenuName];
        CommandBarPopup toolsPopup = (CommandBarPopup)toolsControl;

        //This try/catch block can be duplicated if you wish to add
        // multiple commands to be handled by your Add-in, just make
        // sure you also update the QueryStatus/Exec method to include
        // the new command names.
        try
        {
            //Add a command to the Commands collection:
            Command command = commands.AddNamedCommand2(_addInInstance,
                "ColorSelectorAddIn", "ColorSelectorAddIn",
                "Executes the command for ColorSelectorAddIn", true, 59,
                ref contextGUIDS,
                (int)vsCommandStatus.vsCommandStatusSupported+
                    (int)vsCommandStatus.vsCommandStatusEnabled,
                (int)vsCommandStyle.vsCommandStylePictAndText,
                vsCommandControlType.vsCommandControlTypeButton);

            //Add a control for the command to the Tools menu:
            if((command != null) && (toolsPopup != null))
            {
                command.AddControl(toolsPopup.CommandBar, 1);
            }
        }
        catch(System.ArgumentException)
        {
            //If we are here, then the exception is probably because a
```

```
        //command with that name already exists. If so there is no
        //need to re-create the command and we can safely ignore the
        //exception.
    }
}

#region Create Tool Window

// The DTE.ToolWindows collection
Windows2 windows = (Windows2)_applicationObject.Windows;

// Placeholder object; will eventually refer to the user control
// hosted by the user control
object paletteObject = null;

// This section specifies the path and class name for the palette
// control to be hosted in the new tool window; we also need to
// specify its caption and a unique GUID.
Window toolWindow;
Assembly asm = System.Reflection.Assembly.GetExecutingAssembly();
string assemblyPath = asm.Location;
string className = "ColorSelectorAddIn.PaletteControl";
string guid = "{62175059-FD7E-407a-9EF3-5D07F2B704E8}";
string caption = "Color Selector";

try
{

  // Create the new tool window and insert the user control in
  // it.
    toolWindow = windows.CreateToolWindow2(_addInInstance,
        assemblyPath, className, caption, guid,
        ref paletteObject);

  // If tool window was created successfully, make it visible
  if (toolWindow != null)
  {
      toolWindow.Visible = true;
  }

  // retrieve a reference back to our user control object
  _paletteControl = (PaletteControl)paletteObject;

  // wire up event handler for the PaletteControl.ColorSelected
  //event
  _paletteControl.ColorSelected +=
```

```
                new System.EventHandler(paletteControl1_ColorSelected);

        }
        catch (Exception ex)
        {
            MessageBox.Show("Exception caught: " + ex.ToString());
        }


        #endregion

    }


    /// <summary>Implements the OnDisconnection method of the
    /// IDTExtensibility2 interface. Receives notification that
    /// the Add-in is being unloaded.</summary>
    /// <param term='disconnectMode'>Describes how the Add-in
    /// is being unloaded.</param>
    /// <param term='custom'>Array of parameters that are host
    /// application specific.</param>
    /// <seealso class='IDTExtensibility2' />
    public void OnDisconnection(ext_DisconnectMode disconnectMode,
        ref Array custom)
    {
    }


    /// <summary>Implements the OnAddInsUpdate method of the
    /// IDTExtensibility2 interface. Receives notification when
    /// the collection of Add-ins has changed.</summary>
    /// <param term='custom'>Array of parameters that are host
    /// application specific.</param>
    /// <seealso class='IDTExtensibility2' />
    public void OnAddInsUpdate(ref Array custom)
    {
    }


    /// <summary>Implements the OnStartupComplete method of the
    /// IDTExtensibility2 interface. Receives notification that
    /// the host application has completed loading.</summary>
    /// <param term='custom'>Array of parameters that are host
    /// application specific.</param>
    /// <seealso class='IDTExtensibility2' />
    public void OnStartupComplete(ref Array custom)
    {
    }


    /// <summary>Implements the OnBeginShutdown method of the
```

```
/// IDTExtensibility2 interface. Receives notification that
/// the host application is being unloaded.</summary>
/// <param term='custom'>Array of parameters that are host
/// application specific.</param>
/// <seealso class='IDTExtensibility2' />
public void OnBeginShutdown(ref Array custom)
{
}


/// <summary>Implements the QueryStatus method of the
/// IDTCommandTarget interface. This is called when the
/// command's availability is updated</summary>
/// <param term='commandName'>The name of the command to
/// determine state for.</param>
/// <param term='neededText'>Text that is needed for the
/// command.</param>
/// <param term='status'>The state of the command in the
/// user interface.</param>
/// <param term='commandText'>Text requested by the neededText
/// parameter.</param>
/// <seealso class='Exec' />
public void QueryStatus(string commandName,
    vsCommandStatusTextWanted neededText, ref vsCommandStatus status,
    ref object commandText)
{
    if(neededText ==
        vsCommandStatusTextWanted.vsCommandStatusTextWantedNone)
    {
        if(commandName ==
            "ColorSelectorAddIn.Connect.ColorSelectorAddIn")
        {
            status = (vsCommandStatus)
                    vsCommandStatus.vsCommandStatusSupported
                    |vsCommandStatus.vsCommandStatusEnabled;
            return;
        }
    }
}


/// <summary>Implements the Exec method of the IDTCommandTarget
/// interface. This is called when the command is invoked.</summary>
/// <param term='commandName'>The name of the command to
/// execute.</param>
/// <param term='executeOption'>Describes how the command should
/// be run.</param>
/// <param term='varIn'>Parameters passed from the caller to the
```

```
/// command handler.</param>
/// <param term='varOut'>Parameters passed from the command handler
/// to the caller.</param>
/// <param term='handled'>Informs the caller if the command was
/// handled or not.</param>
/// <seealso class='Exec' />
public void Exec(string commandName, vsCommandExecOption executeOption,
    ref object varIn, ref object varOut, ref bool handled)
{
    handled = false;
    if(executeOption ==
        vsCommandExecOption.vsCommandExecOptionDoDefault)
    {
        if(commandName ==
            "ColorSelectorAddIn.Connect.ColorSelectorAddIn")
        {
            handled = true;
            return;
        }
    }
}

}
```

LISTING 14.3   The `PaletteControl` Class

```
using System;
using System.Collections.Generic;
using System.ComponentModel;
using System.Drawing;
using System.Data;
using System.Runtime.InteropServices;
using System.Text;
using System.Windows.Forms;
using Microsoft.Win32;

namespace ColorSelectorAddIn
{
    [Guid("62175059-FD7E-407a-9EF3-5D07F2B704E8")]
    public partial class PaletteControl : UserControl
    {
        #region Fields
```

```csharp
string _code = "";
bool _generateVB = false;

#endregion

#region Properties

public string Code
{
    get { return _code; }
}

public bool GenerateVB
{
    get { return _generateVB; }
}

#endregion

#region Ctor(s)

public PaletteControl()
{
    InitializeComponent();
    this.pictureBoxPalette.MouseMove += new
      MouseEventHandler(pictureBoxPalette_MouseMove);
    this.pictureBoxPalette.Cursor = System.Windows.Forms.Cursors.Cross;
}

#endregion

#region Event Handlers and Delegates

void pictureBoxPalette_MouseMove(object sender, MouseEventArgs e)
{
    // Get the color under the current pointer position
    Color color = GetPointColor(e.X, e.Y);

    // Update the RGB labels and the 2nd pic box
    // using the retrieved color
    DisplayColor(color);

    // Generate our VB or C# code for the Color
    // structure
    SetCode(color, _generateVB);
}
```

14

```csharp
    public event EventHandler ColorSelected;

    protected virtual void OnColorSelected(EventArgs e)
    {
        if (ColorSelected != null)
            ColorSelected(this, e);
    }

    private void pictureBoxPalette_Click(object sender, EventArgs e)
    {
        OnColorSelected(new EventArgs());
    }

    #endregion

    #region Private Routines

    /// <summary>
    /// Returns a Color structure representing the color of
    /// the pixel at the indicated x and y coordinates.
    /// </summary>
    /// <param name="x"></param>
    /// <param name="y"></param>
    /// <returns>A Color structure</returns>
    private Color GetPointColor(int x, int y)
    {
        // Get the bitmap from the palette picture box
        Bitmap bmp = (Bitmap)pictureBoxPalette.Image;
        // Use GetPixel to retrieve a color
        // structure for the current pointer position
        Color color = bmp.GetPixel(x, y);

        // Return the color structure
        return color;
    }

    /// <summary>
    /// Displays the RGB values for the given color. Also sets
    /// the background color of the secondary picture box.
    /// </summary>
    /// <param name="color">The Color to display</param>
    private void DisplayColor(Color color)
    {
        // pull out the RGB values from the
        // color structure
        string R = color.R.ToString();
```

```csharp
        string G = color.G.ToString();
        string B = color.B.ToString();

        // set our secondary picture box
        // to display the current color
        this.pictureBoxColor.BackColor = color;

        // display RGB values in the label
        // controls
        this.labelRValue.Text = R;
        this.labelGValue.Text = G;
        this.labelBValue.Text = B;
    }


    /// <summary>
    /// Generates a string representing the C# or VB code necessary to
    /// create a Color structure instance that matches the passed in
    /// Color structure. This string is then assigned to this
    /// user control's _code field.
    /// </summary>
    /// <param name="color">The color to represent in code.</param>
    /// <param name="isVB">Boolean flag indicating the language
    /// to use: false indicates C#, true indicates VB</param>
    private void SetCode(Color color, bool isVB)
    {
        // Read in add-in settings from registry
        SetPropFromReg();

        string code = "";

        if (isVB)
        {
            code = "Dim color As Color = ";
        }
        else
        {
            code = "Color color = ";
        }

        code = code + "Color.FromArgb(" + color.R.ToString() + ", " +
            color.G.ToString() + ", " +
            color.B.ToString() + ");";

        _code = code;
        this.labelCode.Text = _code;
    }
```

```csharp
/// <summary>
/// Reads a registry entry and sets the language output fields
/// appropriately.
/// </summary>
private void SetPropFromReg()
{
    try
    {
        RegistryKey regKey =
          Registry.CurrentUser.OpenSubKey(@"Software\Contoso\Addins\
          RColorPalette");
        string codeVal = (string)regKey.GetValue("Language", "CSharp");

        if (codeVal == "CSharp")
        {
            _generateVB = false;
        }
        else
        {
            _generateVB = true;
        }
    }
    catch (Exception ex)
    {
        // error reading the registry; default to C#
        _generateVB = false;
    }
}
#endregion
}
}
```

LISTING 14.4   The `PaletteControlOptionPage` Class

```csharp
using System;
using System.Collections.Generic;
using System.ComponentModel;
using System.Drawing;
using System.Data;
using System.Text;
using System.Windows.Forms;
using EnvDTE;
using Microsoft.Win32;
```

```csharp
namespace ColorSelectorAddIn
{
    public partial class PaletteControlOptionPage : UserControl,
      IDTToolsOptionsPage
    {
        public PaletteControlOptionPage()
        {
            InitializeComponent();
        }

        #region IDTToolsOptionsPage Members

        public void GetProperties(ref object PropertiesObject)
        {
            throw new NotImplementedException();
        }

        public void OnAfterCreated(DTE DTEObject)
        {
            // read our current value from registry
            // TODO: we should really include contingency code here for
            // creating the key if it doesn't already exist, dealing with
            // unexpected values, exceptions, etc.
            RegistryKey regKey =
              Registry.CurrentUser.OpenSubKey(@"Software\Contoso\Addins\
              RColorPalette");
            string codeVal = (string)regKey.GetValue("Language", "CSharp");

            if (codeVal == "CSharp")
            {
                this.radioButtonCSharp.Checked = true;
                this.radioButtonVB.Checked = false;
            }
            else
            {
                this.radioButtonCSharp.Checked = true;
                this.radioButtonVB.Checked = false;
            }
        }


        public void OnCancel()
        {
            throw new NotImplementedException();
        }
```

```csharp
public void OnHelp()
{
    throw new NotImplementedException();
}


public void OnOK()
{
    string codeValue = "CSharp";    // our default value

    if (this.radioButtonVB.Checked)
    {
        codeValue = "VB";
    }

    // update the registry with the new setting
    RegistryKey regKey =
        Registry.CurrentUser.OpenSubKey(@"Software\Contoso\Addins\
        RColorPalette");

    regKey.SetValue("Language", codeValue);

}

    #endregion
    }
}
```

NOTE

If you have add-ins that were written for Visual Studio 2005, you need to make some minor updates to the source code to fully migrate features over to later versions of Visual Studio. Detailed migration steps are provided in the Visual Studio MSDN documentation. Search for the article "How to: Update Visual Studio 2005 Add-ins to Visual Studio 2008."

Creating a Visual Studio Wizard

Visual Studio makes heavy use of wizards to help guide developers through various tasks. The Add-In Wizard discussed in the previous sections is one such example of a New Project Wizard. (It is launched when you try to create a new add-in project.) There are also wizards for adding new items to projects. You can modify the existing Project/Add New Item wizards or create your own wizard complete with its own user interface. Finally, there are custom wizards that, like the other wizards, are responsible for generating code but are not called from a Visual Studio dialog box.

In the following sections, we focus on understanding the wizard landscape by creating a custom Add New Item Wizard.

Examining the Wizard Structure

Each wizard consists of two major components: a class that contains the code (and user interface) for the wizard and a .vsz file that provides information about the wizard to Visual Studio.

The IDTWizard Interface

To hook into Visual Studio's wizard engine, your Wizard class must implement the EnvDTE.IDTWizard interface. The IDTWizard defines a single method, Execute, that is called by Visual Studio whenever the wizard is launched. Here is the prototype for the IDTWizard.Execute method (in C#):

```
void Execute (
    Object Application,
    int hwndOwner,
    ref Object[] ContextParams,
    ref Object[] CustomParams,
    out wizardResult retval
)
```

The arguments passed to the Execute method are used to link the wizard to the Visual Studio environment and to pass relevant data to the wizard:

- ▶ **Application**—A DTE instance for the Visual Studio IDE.

- ▶ **hwndOwner**—A handle to the parent window; this window "parents" any user interface elements created by the wizard.

- ▶ **ContextParams**—For New Project/Add New Item wizards, an array of objects used to pass information about the type of wizard that was launched and various data necessary for the wizard to function, such as project name and install directory.

- ▶ **CustomParams**—An array of objects used to carry any custom parameters you define for your wizard.

- ▶ **wizardResult**—An enumeration value that indicates the results of the wizard.

The ContextParams parameter's content varies depending on the type of wizard. For instance, for a New Project Wizard, the third value in the ContextParams array represents the location where the project file is stored (called the LocalDirectory). But for an Add Item Wizard, the third value in the array is a pointer to a ProjectItems collection. Table 14.6 maps the various array elements to the three different wizard types.

To determine the results of the wizard, you look at the value placed in the wizardResult parameter. Table 14.7 lists the wizardResult enum values.

TABLE 14.6   `wizardResult` Enumeration Values

Index	NewProject Wizard	AddSubProject Wizard	AddItem Wizard
0	WizardType enum	`WizardType` enum	`WizardType` enum
1	Project name	Project name	Project name
2	Local directory	`ProjectItems` object	`ProjectItems` object
3	VS install directory	Local directory	Local directory
4	`FExclusive` flag (create new solution or use current)	Name of added item	Name of added item
5	Solution name	VS install directory	VS install directory
6	Silent flag (run with or without UI)	Silent flag	Silent flag

TABLE 14.7   `wizardResult` Enumeration Values

Member	Description
`wizardResultBackOut`	The user exited the wizard by clicking the Back button.
`wizardResultCancel`	The wizard was canceled.
`wizardResultFailure`	The wizard startup failed.
`wizardResultSuccess`	The wizard startup succeeded.

The core content of the `Execute` method is entirely up to you. Within the body of the `Execute` method, you need to implement all the code necessary to do the work of the wizard and display its UI to the user.

> **NOTE**
>
> Although you probably think of wizards as a series of pages accessed by Next and Back navigation buttons, a wizard in Visual Studio's terms is nothing more than a COM object that implements `IDTWizard`. In fact, a wizard doesn't need to display a user interface at all. It could, for instance, merely use the parameters passed to it to do some work and then quit.

The .vsz and .vsdir Files

If you recall from our discussion of add-ins, every add-in uses an .addin file to register the add-in with Visual Studio. The .vsz files are the equivalent for wizards; they make Visual Studio aware of the wizard and its implementing class.

Here is a complete sample .vsz file:

```
VSWizard 10.0
Wizard=ContosoWizard.AddNewClassWizard

Param=
```

The VSWizard line in this file identifies the version information for the wizard. The number 10.0 equates to Visual Studio 2010, and earlier version numbers map to earlier Visual Studio releases.

After the version number, a class ID is provided for the wizard. And finally, there are one or more (optional) Param lines. These lines define any custom parameters that you want sent to the wizard. Any parameters defined here come across in the CustomParams parameter in the Execute method.

Visual Studio has a specific folder hierarchy that it uses for storing wizard .vsz files; the folder where you place the .vsz file dictates exactly where the option to launch the wizard appears. As an example, if you want to create an Add Item Wizard for both Visual Basic and Visual C#, you need to place a copy of the .vsz file into both the Visual Basic and the C# folders. If Visual Studio 2012 is installed in its default location, you place the wizard files here:

```
C:\Program Files\Microsoft Visual Studio 11.0\VC#\CSharpProjectItems
C:\Program Files\Microsoft Visual Studio 11.0\VB\VBProjectItems
```

If you are creating a New Project Wizard, the files are placed in the VC#\CSharpProjects and the VB\VBProjects folders.

Wizard folders may also contain a .vsdir file. This file is used to provide Visual Studio with icon and other resource information about a particular wizard. The .vsdir file is also a plain-text file. Each line in the file represents a specific .vsz file/wizard and provides multiple fields (separated by the pipe character, |) with optional information about the wizard. Table 14.8 documents the valid fields for each .vsdir line, in order of their appearance. The optional fields are noted.

TABLE 14.8   .vsdir Options

Sort Priority	A number used to provide a relative grouping number for the wizard in the display dialog boxes. A wizard with a value of 1 is displayed next to other 1 wizards, and so on.
Description	The description of the wizard. This will appear whenever the wizard is selected in the Add Item dialog box.
DLL Path	A full path to the assembly containing the wizard's icon.
Icon Resource ID	A resource identifier that points within the DLL to the icon to be displayed.

| Flags | One or more bitwise values used to control certain wizard behaviors. See the MSDN documentation for a complete list. Optional. |
| Name | The name of the wizard to be displayed in the Name field of the dialog box. (Unlike the Localized Name, this field is required.) |

Here is a simple .vsdir file example with one wizard record:

```
CSharpContosoDataClass.vsz | | |1|Create a new Contoso storage
class|c:\ContosoFramework\Wizards\DataClassWizard.dll| | |Contoso Data Class
```

> **TIP**
>
> The .vsdir record provides a way to associate an icon resource to the wizard by enabling you to specify a DLL path and an icon resource ID. There is also a simpler way to accomplish this: Just create an .ico file, give it the same name as the wizard's .vsz file, and place it in the same directory.

Creating an Add New Item Wizard

Here are the basic steps for creating a wizard:

1. Create a new class library project; in this project, create a new class that implements the IDTWizard interface.

2. In the wizard class, write the code in the `Execute` method to perform the wizard's tasks and display its UI.

3. Create a .vsz file for the wizard.

4. Create or edit a .vsdir file to reference the new wizard and the .vsz file.

To solidify these concepts, let's look at them in action. We follow the development of a wizard from start to finish. In this case, the wizard is a C# Add Item Wizard. Its purpose is to collect some basic data from the user and then create a Tools Options page class (much like you manually did earlier in the chapter) that has been customized in accordance with the user's input into the wizard dialog box.

Implementing the Execute Method

The `Execute` method needs to do two things: display a Windows Forms dialog box to capture preferences such as class name; and process those preferences, generate a class that implements a Tools Options page, and add that class to the current project.

Creating the Dialog Box   First, the dialog box: It should look roughly like the dialog box in Figure 14.14. (There is nothing special about the implementation of this form, so we won't bother to detail all of its code here.)

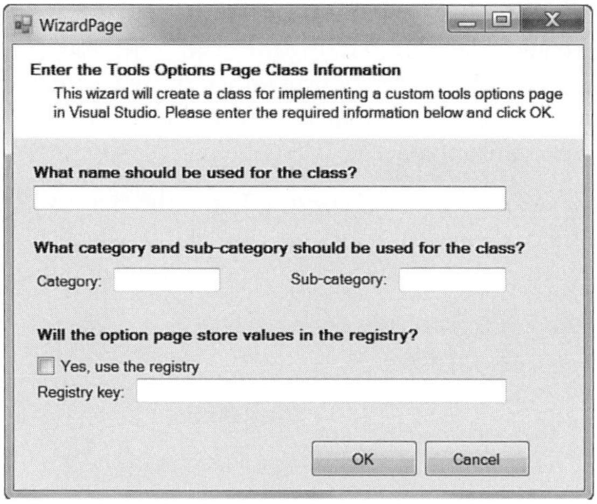

FIGURE 14.14   The wizard form.

When the user clicks the OK button, you should set several properties on the form that mirror the selections made on the dialog box. For instance, if you implement this form as a class called WizardDialog, you need a WizardDialog.ClassName property, a WizardDialog.Category property, and so on. The last thing to do when the OK button is clicked is to set the form's DialogResult property. The Execute method on the wizard (which we examine in a moment) queries the DialogResult property to determine whether the user has committed the wizard or canceled it. Here is a look at the OK and Cancel button click event handlers:

```csharp
private void buttonOK_Click(object sender, EventArgs e)
{
    // assign screen control values to our public
    // fields
    this.ClassName = this.textBoxClassName.Text;
    this.Category = this.textBoxCategory.Text;
    this.SubCategory = this.textBoxSubCategory.Text;
    this.UseRegistry = this.checkBoxUseRegistry.Checked;
    this.RegKey = this.textBoxRegKey.Text;

    // indicate dialog was accepted
    this.DialogResult = DialogResult.OK;
}

private void buttonCancel_Click(object sender, EventArgs e)
{
    // indicate dialog was cancelled
    this.DialogResult = DialogResult.Cancel;
}
```

Using a Template File   Remember, the purpose of this wizard is to generate some class code for us. There are two approaches we could take to generating the class code: You can generate every line of code using either the Code DOM API or brute-force string creation/concatenation, or you can use a template file. The template file approach is a bit simpler, and probably more efficient as well, so that is the approach we describe here.

The class template is a file that looks just like any other user control. Using the standard code created for a user control class, you substitute key areas with string placeholders. For instance, the class name is specified within the wizard, and thus something you should replace in the template class:

```
public class %TemplateClassName% : UserControl, IDTToolsOptionsPage
{
    ...
}
```

You also need the `IDTToolsOptionsPage` members (such as `OnAfterCreated`, `OnOK`, and so on) represented in the class. For most of these methods, you leave a simple `System.NotImplementedException` as a reminder to fill in code as necessary. For `OnAfterCreated` and `OnOK`, however, you need the option of including a line of code to open the indicated `Registry` key:

```
public void OnAfterCreated(DTE DTEObject)
{
    // read our current value from registry
    // TODO: Include code to read from registry here
    %StartRegistryCode%
    RegistryKey regKey = Registry.CurrentUser.OpenSubKey(@"%TemplateRegKey%");
    %EndRegistryCode%
}
public void OnOK()
{
    //TODO: include code to save options
    // update the registry with the new setting
    %StartRegistryCode%
    RegistryKey regKey = Registry.CurrentUser.OpenSubKey(@"%TemplateRegKey%");
    %EndRegistryCode%
}
```

Again, you use placeholders here: The `%StartRegistryCode%` and `%EndRegistryCode%` delimit the `OpenSubKey` line of code. If the user unchecks the User Registry check box in the wizard, you eliminate everything between these two placeholders (including the placeholders themselves). The `%TemplateRegKey%` is used as a token for the `Registry` key value; this is something else that you collect from the user in the wizard's dialog box.

Executing the Wizard   The `Execute` method opens the wizard form and, if the user has not canceled the dialog box, uses the form's properties to call into a few internal routines responsible for generating the output class:

```
public void Execute(object Application, int hwndOwner, ref object[] ContextParams,
    ref object[] CustomParams, ref wizardResult retval)
{
    // instance the dialog for the wizard
    WizardDialog dlg = new WizardDialog();

    // show the dialog
    dlg.Show();

    // process the wizard results
    if (dlg.DialogResult == DialogResult.OK)
    {
        // Load template file, replace tokens, return content
        // as string
        string classContent = ReplaceTokens(dlg.ClassName, dlg.Category,
            dlg.SubCategory, dlg.UseRegistry, dlg.RegKey);

        // Put the returned string content into a file and
        // add the file to the current project
        // (3rd element of ContextParams is the current project's
        // items collection)
        ProjectItems projItems = (ProjectItems)ContextParams[2];
        AddFile(this.ClassName, classContent, projItems);

        retval = wizardResult.wizardResultSuccess;

    }
    // wizard was canceled; no action required
    else
    {
        retval = wizardResult.wizardResultCancel;
    }
}
```

To react to the user clicking OK, you call three separate internal routines. The first, ReplaceTokens, opens the template class file and replaces the tokens. (Because this is a simple string substitution process, we won't reproduce the code here.)

The second routine, AddFile, writes the new class content into a new file and adds it to the current project. Because this code might not be entirely obvious, here is one approach:

```
private void AddFile(string className, string classContent,
    ProjectItems projItems)
{
    // determine path to project files
    string fileName =
        Path.GetDirectoryName(projItems.ContainingProject.FileName);
```

```
    // use path and class name to build file name for class
    fileName = fileName + className + ".cs";

    // save class file into project folder
    using (TextWriter writer = new StreamWriter(fileName, false))
    {
        writer.Write(classContent);
        writer.Close();
    }

    // add the newly created file to the current project
    projItems.AddFromFile(fileName);

}
```

Last, you call `UpdateXML`; this routine opens the .addin file and adds the appropriate `<ToolsOptionsPage>` node to the XML content:

```
private void UpdateXml(ProjectItems projItems, string category,
    string subCategory)
{
    // create string XML snippet
    string xml = "";
    xml += "<ToolsOptionsPage>\r\n";
    xml += "    <Category Name=\"" + category + "\">\r\n";
    xml += "        <SubCategory Name=\"" + subCategory + "\">\r\n";
    xml += "            <Assembly></Assembly>\r\n";
    xml += "            <FullClassName></FullClassName>\r\n";
    xml += "        </SubCategory>\r\n";
    xml += "    </Category>\r\n";
    xml += "</ToolsOptionsPage>\r\n";
    xml += "</Extensibility>";

    // iterate items in the project, looking for the
    // .addin file
    string projName = projItems.ContainingProject.FullName;
    foreach (ProjectItem itm in projItems)
    {
        if (itm.Name == projName + ".addin")
        {
            // open the .addin file's document object
            itm.Document.Activate();
            TextDocument txtDoc = (TextDocument)itm.Document.Object("");
            TextRanges nullObj = null;
            // add in the cat/sub-cat XML snippet
            txtDoc.ReplacePattern("</Extensibility>", xml,
```

```
            (int)vsFindOptions.vsFindOptionsFromStart,
            ref nullObj);


      }
    }
}
```

At this point, the wizard code is complete.

Creating the .vsz and .vsdir Files

All that is left to do is to "register" the wizard by creating the .vsz file and adding an entry to the .vsdir file. The .vsz file is straightforward:

```
VSWizard 8.0
Wizard=ContosoWizards.ToolsOptionsPageWizard
Param=
```

The record you add to the .vsdir file looks like this:

```
ToolsOptionsPageWizard.vsz | | |1|Create a new Tools Options Page
class|c:\ContosoFramework\Wizards\ToolsOptionsPageWizar dd.dll| | |Contoso Options
Page Class
```

With that, the wizard is fully functional and should be selectable from the Add Item dialog box.

Summary

This chapter described how to leverage the power of Visual Studio's automation APIs to create add-ins and wizards.

You investigated the nearly unlimited potential for extending Visual Studio by using add-ins that call into the automation API and expose their interfaces in a variety of ways, including custom tool windows and dialog boxes.

And you also saw how to once again leverage the ubiquitous automation object model and the built-in wizard engine to create your own custom wizards for adding new projects, adding new project items, or executing nearly any other type of step-by-step process within Visual Studio.

In the next chapter, we explore another (and final) way to extend Visual Studio using the Managed Extensibility Framework.

CHAPTER 15

Extending the Code Editor Using Managed Extensibility Framework

You have seen in the preceding two chapters that there are many different opportunities, and approaches, for extending Visual Studio functionality. The add-in model, in particular, is a powerful way to implement fairly robust applications within the Visual Studio IDE. But Visual Studio 2010 introduced a brand-new technology for extending Visual Studio that has been further refined with Visual Studio 2012 and .NET 4.5: the Managed Extensibility Framework (MEF).

MEF is actually a generic architecture pattern, application programming interface (API), and .NET class library for enabling easy "plug-in" extensions for any .NET application. Visual Studio allows for MEF-based extensions in the code editor, and will likely embrace MEF more broadly across the entire IDE as time goes one.

This chapter introduces Microsoft's MEF and how the framework can be applied to extend the Visual Studio code editor.

The Extensibility Problem

Before getting into the architecture and code-level details of MEF, it is useful to understand the problem or question that MEF is trying to answer. Put simply, that question is how can developers allow their applications to be easily extended by others, or conversely how can developers extend existing applications in a simple way?

A variety of hurdles have to be overcome in this space. For instance, how can an application be open for extensions and yet closed so that its core functionality cannot be usurped against the intentions of its designers? What developers are really after is a consistent solution that enables dynamic applications to be created and thus enables other developers to extend those dynamic applications using well-known and understood mechanisms.

Creating Dynamic Applications

Prior to MEF, the work required to create a so-called open-ended .NET application (that is, an application that allows others to contribute code and alter or add to its functionality) was far from a trivial effort. The main issue here is one of discovery and instantiation. The "host" application (the application that supports extensions) needs to have a standard way of identifying and validating code meant to extend the host. And there needs to be a runtime activation approach as well: How is the plug-in code executed, and what portions of the host app can be affected by the plug-in?

This is where MEF enters the scene. It provides an architecture pattern and framework/API that host application developers and plug-in developers can use to enable these dynamic application scenarios.

In fact, MEF explicitly targets developers who are creating any of three different classes of applications:

▶ **Extensions**—Chunks of compiled code that enhance the functionality of an existing application. Extension developers need to be able to implement their components without having either access to the host applications' source, or even specialized knowledge of that source.

▶ **Extensible frameworks/host applications**—Applications that need to support the dynamic addition of functionality via extensions.

▶ **Programming model**—The least common scenario; in this case, a developer is interested in creating a potentially new way of developing against an application platform. In this case, MEF can provide the building blocks that developers need to build their own extensible application platform.

Visual Studio is merely one example of a host application that clearly benefits from its ability to support rich add-ins that add value to the core feature areas delivered out of the box by Microsoft.

MEF Architecture

MEF achieves its goals through three different, but related, mechanisms:

▶ Dependency injection

▶ Structural matching

▶ Naming and activation

Let's walk through each of these concepts in an abstract sense and then see how they are physically implemented with MEF.

MEF Principles

Dependency injection is a software architecture term that refers to the concept of a framework or runtime "injecting" an external dependency into another piece of software. Handling this process is a core requirement for an extensibility framework.

Structural matching, also sometimes referred to as *duck typing*, is a style of feature discovery and typing in which a host determines the type of an object based on the properties and methods it exposes as opposed to its actual type in the object-oriented sense.

Finally, *naming and activation* is the "last-mile" feature that puts all of the pieces together and enables an application to load and run the plug-in code in a predictable fashion.

When all three of these mechanisms are in place, you have a reasonable platform for building applications that can be dynamically composited at runtime. In other words, by exploiting an extensibility framework, you can deliver a flexible application that is capable of leveraging new features that are added dynamically over time; functionality that does not, in fact, require a wholesale replacement or upgrade of a core, monolithic executable.

Working with MEF

MEF applications are based around a small set of core concepts: the composition container, catalog, and parts. These are both abstract concepts and a physical API that you can interact with from managed code. All of the MEF classes live within the `System.ComponentModel.Composition` namespace and its children namespaces such as `System.ComponentModel.Composition.Hosting`.

Parts

An MEF *part* is the primary unit of functionality. Parts have a set of features that they provide (called exports); parts might also depend on features that other parts provide (termed imports).

Parts verbalize their exports and imports through contracts. At the code level, contracts are specified by using declarative attributes to declare their imports and exports (`System.ComponentModel.Composition.ImportAttribute` and `System.ComponentModel.Composition.ExportAttribute`, respectively).

Here is an example of a C# class declaring an export:

```
[Export(typeof(IMyExtensionProvider))]
internal class TestExtensionProvider
```

Composition Container

The *composition container* is the core of an MEF application and does all of the heavy lifting. It holds all the available parts, handles the instantiation of those parts, and is the primary composition engine in MEF. In this context, composition can be thought of as the process of matching required services (imports) with published services (exports).

Host applications can instantiate a container via the `System.ComponentModel.Composition.Hosting.CompositionContainer` class like this:

```
private CompositionContainer _container;
```

Catalog

The *catalog* is a sort of Registry and discovery mechanism for parts, and is used by the composition container. MEF provides a default set of catalogs, each one designed to discover parts from a particular source or target: there is a type catalog for discovering parts from a given .NET type (via the `TypeCatalog` class), an assembly catalog for discovering parts from an assembly (via the `AssemblyCatalog` catalog), and a directory catalog (via the `DirectoryCatalog` class) for discovering parts that exist in a specified folder.

A fourth class, `AggregateCatalog`, enables you to combine multiple catalogs so that parts from multiple catalog sources can be combined into one master catalog.

A catalog instance can be passed into the constructor for a `CompositionContainer` object. You could write the following code to both create a new composition container and specify a catalog of parts that are to be discovered from within the specific assembly:

```
var catalog = new TypeCatalog(typeof(MyExtension));

CompositionContainer container =
    new CompositionContainer(catalog);
```

Figure 15.1 shows a diagram of the abstract MEF architecture.

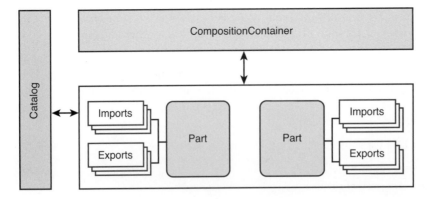

FIGURE 15.1   A simplified view of MEF architecture.

The Visual Studio Editor and MEF

Although the MEF is a general-purpose extensibility framework applicable across a wide range of application scenarios, it is particularly applicable to extending the Visual Studio code editor for one simple reason: The editor itself was built by Microsoft using MEF. In other words, the code editor consists of a series of MEF parts. Adding additional parts to extend and change editor behavior is simply a matter of using the MEF design patterns and writing your own MEF parts to be discovered and used by the editor.

Chapter 14, "Writing Add-Ins and Wizards," during the discussion about Visual Studio add-in development, talked about the need to understand two pieces of information to be successful with add-in development: You need to understand both the add-in process, and you need to understand the API that Visual Studio exposes to add-ins.

With the editor (and with MEF), the same concepts apply. If you are to embark on an editor extension endeavor, you need to understand the extensibility mechanism (MEF) and the specific extensibility points (MEF exports) offered by the editor. Now that you understand the MEF process, it's time to examine how to create an MEF-based project within Visual Studio and can review the numerous extension points the editor exposes.

If you want to extend the editor, you need to know the exact editor extensibility points; in other words, you need to know which editor feature areas can be easily replaced or enhanced using your own MEF parts.

15

Editor Extension Points

The Visual Studio code editor has its own sort of API that it exposes via MEF. In MEF terms, the editor publishes a set of exports that you can then use within your own MEF parts to extend the editor in virtually unboundless ways.

With nearly 100% coverage of the editor's features, the following feature areas are valid extension points exposed by the Visual Studio editor:

▶ **Content types**—A content type in the context of a Visual Studio code editor is the type of text and syntax that can be parsed and understood by the editor. If you think about this from a languages perspective, Visual Studio content types map directly to the various syntax and text formats that Visual Studio understands, such as C#, plain text, HTML, XML, XAML, and so on.

▶ **Classification types and classification formats**—Classification types are the types of text, appearing within a document, which the VS editor understands and looks for. In a typical C# file, for example, the editor recognizes numerical and string instances within the document because those are default classification types built in to Visual Studio. For each classification type, a format can be defined as well. A classic example of this is the highlighting and text coloring that you see within the editor for things like string literals or comments.

▶ **Margins and scrollbars**—If you think of the physical layout of a code editor, its visual surface is dominated by the text area where the code actually lives, and this is surrounded by scrollbars and by a margin area (for instance, the area where you see breakpoint information). Those margins and scrollbars are both artifacts that can be customized with MEF parts.

▶ **Tags**—Tags are objects that enable you to associate data with different recognized types of text within an editor. For instance, the SquiggleTag is implemented by Visual Studio to associate things like syntax errors with a chunk of text that is un-recognized. In this case, the data associated with the squiggle is the actual syntax error generated by the compiler; this data is manifested as a tooltip when you hover the mouse over the squiggle.

▶ **Adornments**—Adornments are visual objects that can appear within an editor. Physically, they are implemented as Windows Presentation Foundation (WPF) objects, and they can exist at several different "layers" within the editor, so the adornment can actually occupy the same physical space as the text within the editor or float above text within the editor.

▶ **Mouse processors**—Mouse processors are extension points that enable you to capture and handle mouse input.

▶ **Drop handlers**—Drop handlers enable you to react to different types of objects as they are dropped on the editor surface. Visual Studio has a library of stock format types that it recognizes, including files, pen data, XAML, and TIFF or bitmap images.

▶ **Options**—Using MEF, it is possible to define, store, and react to your own set of custom options within the editor.

▶ **IntelliSense**—Chapter 8, "Working with Visual Studio's Productivity Aids," discusses IntelliSense extensively. You can write your own IntelliSense functionality using MEF.

Using the Visual Studio SDK

Besides understanding the editor extension points, there is another crucial step to take: installation of the Visual Studio software development kit (SDK). The Visual Studio SDK, generally speaking, is a collection of tools and project templates that help developers customize the IDE. The SDK is particularly germane to the topic of editor extensions because it ships with a set of project templates and code samples that help kick-start your extension development efforts.

The SDK download links for Visual Studio 2012 are located at the Visual Studio Extensibility center on MSDN: http://msdn.microsoft.com/vstudio/vextend.

After downloading and installing the SDK, you see a new set of project templates available when you launch the New Project dialog box (see Figure 15.2).

FIGURE 15.2   Project templates added by the Visual Studio SDK.

These templates all live under the Extensibility category. For the purposes of this chapter, four editor templates are of interest: the Editor Classifier, Editor Margin, Editor Text Adornment, and Editor Viewport Adornment templates.

Based on their names, and the prior list of extension points, you can get a good idea for the specific capabilities of each template. Seeing the extensions in action is as simple as running the template project; a new instance of Visual Studio launches with the extension running.

Every time you compile an extension project, the extension is copied over to Visual Studio's local folder where extensions are kept: %LocalAppData%\Microsoft\ VisualStudio\11.0\Extensions\. Keep in mind that extensions can be deployed by simply copying their binaries; they do not need to be deployed to the Global Assembly Cache (GAC) or otherwise registered. The default mechanism for deployment of extensions is the VSIX file. (To refresh your memory on what VSIX is, see Chapter 12, "Deploying Code.") The VSIX file, when run, automatically creates the correct folder in the correct location and copies the extension binaries.

After an extension has been deployed in this fashion, you can manage via the Extensions and Updates window (located under the Tools menu), discussed later in this chapter.

Editor Classifier

The Editor Classifier template creates an MEF part that exports a classifier that handles syntax highlighting within the editor. This is implemented with a set of default classes that can be customized to implement your own classifier. By using this project as a starting point, you can direct the editor to recognize certain syntax and display the matching text in a certain way.

> **NOTE**
>
> As you examine the content generated by these extension projects, notice that the code generated for you maps directly back to the extension points previously discussed. For example, the Editor Classifier template relates directly back to the classification types/ formats extension point.

The Editor Classifier project exports a new classifier type that is used by the editor when loaded in the IDE. The definition of the classifier (that is, the type of text that the classifier recognizes) is implemented in the EditorClassifier1 class. This class implements the IClassifier interface, and has a GetClassificationSpans property that is responsible for recognizing a certain class of text. By default, this template simply recognizes any text; but you are free to tweak this code to parse out and match any sort of text pattern that you want.

> **NOTE**
>
> All of these MEF extension templates end up creating classes and types that are named after the project. By using the default EditorClassifier1 project name, you end up with classes such as EditorClassifier1, EditorClassifier1Form, and so on. If you have used a different name for your project, your type names should look different from those presented here.

Besides recognizing a class of text, a classifier is also responsible for how that text is displayed within the editor. For instance, keywords are shaded a different color, comments are colored, and so on. All of this work is performed within the EditorClassifier1Format class. The code generated for us sets the background color to a color (blue violet), and underlines the text, but you can change those details to whatever you want:

```
/// <summary>
/// Defines the visual format for the "EditorClassifier1" classification type
/// </summary>
public EditorClassifier1Format()
{
    this.DisplayName = "EditorClassifier1"; //human readable version of the name
    this.BackgroundColor = Colors.BlueViolet;
    this.TextDecorations = System.Windows.TextDecorations.Underline;
}
```

Editor Margin

The Editor Margin template creates a project that exports a margin that is displayed on one of the editor's borders. The main class here is the EditorMargin1 class, which derives from the WPF `Canvas` class and places a canvas with a child textbox (with the text "Hello, World!") at the bottom of the editor window (see Figure 15.3).

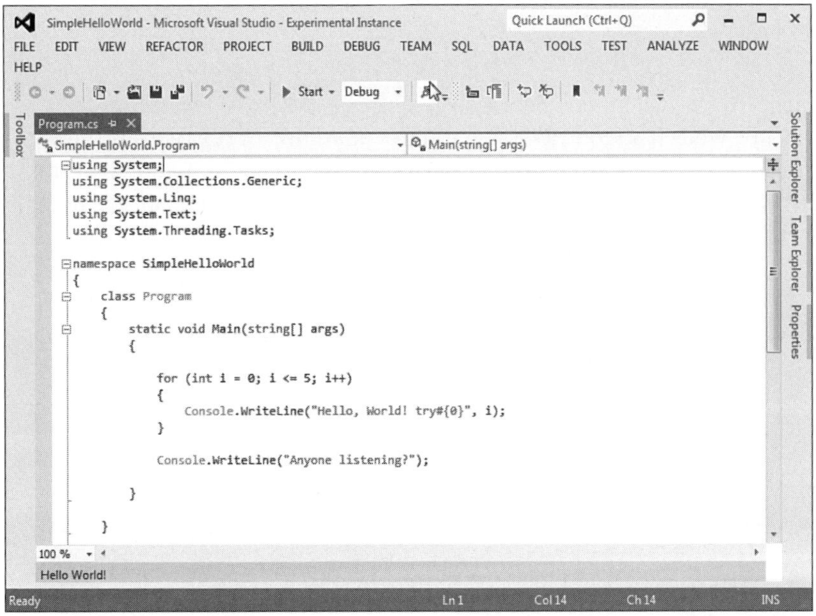

FIGURE 15.3   A "Hello World" margin added to the bottom of the code editor.

Here is the code responsible for displaying the margin. Again, if you had a need to display meaningful data within a margin (code review comments? bug counts?), you can easily use the code here as a building block:

```
/// <summary>
/// Creates a <see cref="EditorMargin1"/> for a given <see cref="IWpfTextView"/>.
/// </summary>
/// <param name="textView">The <see cref="IWpfTextView"/> to attach the margin
 to.</param>
public EditorMargin1(IWpfTextView textView)
{
    _textView = textView;

    this.Height = 20;
    this.ClipToBounds = true;
    this.Background = new SolidColorBrush(Colors.LightGreen);

    // Add a green colored label that says "Hello World!"
    Label label = new Label();
```

```
    label.Background = new SolidColorBrush(Colors.LightGreen);
    label.Content = "Hello world!";
    this.Children.Add(label);
}
```

Editor Text Adornment

A text adornment is just what it sounds like: a graphical "markup" of text within the editor window. The Editor Text Adornment template creates a project that adorns every instance of the character A with a purple background and a red bordered box (see Figure 15.4). As with the editor margin project, you use WPF objects.

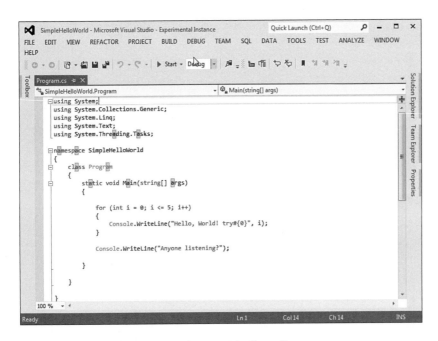

FIGURE 15.4   Creating a text adornment in the editor.

Adornments reside on different "layers" within the editor. In this case, the adornment is implemented on the same layer that the text is rendered in, and that's what makes this specifically a text adornment implementation. Note that this isn't actually a case of the editor changing the font of those A's to include the background decoration. The adorner uses WPF to paint a red block behind the text. This block is then synced to any movements of the text within the editor (by re-creating its visuals every time the layout of the editor window changes):

```
public TextAdornment1(IWpfTextView view)
{
    _view = view;
    _layer = view.GetAdornmentLayer("TextAdornment1");
```

```
//Listen to any event that changes the layout (text changes, scrolling, etc)
_view.LayoutChanged += OnLayoutChanged;

//Create the pen and brush to color the box behind the A's
Brush brush = new SolidColorBrush(Color.FromArgb(0x20, 0x00, 0x00, 0xff));
brush.Freeze();
Brush penBrush = new SolidColorBrush(Colors.Red);
penBrush.Freeze();
Pen pen = new Pen(penBrush, 0.5);
pen.Freeze();

_brush = brush;
_pen = pen;
}
```

Editor Viewport Adornment

The viewport adornment project is similar to the text adornment project, but it applies to a different layer of the editor (one where the text does not reside, which is a small but important distinction). Adorning the viewport in this fashion enables you to introduce visuals within the editor that aren't tied to any particular piece of text and can float in front or in back of the text layer.

The sample effect produced by this template places a simple purple box in the upper-right corner of the editor (see Figure 15.5).

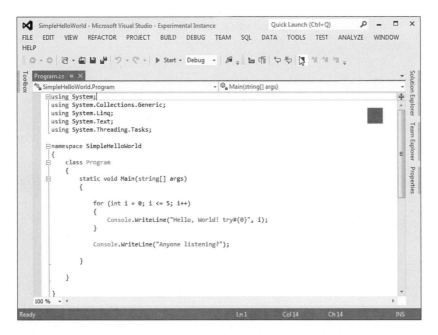

FIGURE 15.5   An editor viewport adornment.

Structurally, the code differs only slightly from the code for the text adornment sample. The adornment class (ViewportAdornment1) uses the same WPF brush objects to paint its adornment. The key difference is the visual layer used by the factory class (ViewportAdornment1Factory). To compare and contrast the two, first examine the previous project's factory:

```
[Export(typeof(IWpfTextViewCreationListener))]
[ContentType("text")]
[TextViewRole(PredefinedTextViewRoles.Document)]
internal sealed class TextAdornment1Factory : IWpfTextViewCreationListener
{
    /// <summary>
    /// Defines the adornment layer for the adornment. This layer is ordered
    /// after the selection layer in the Z-order
    /// </summary>
    [Export(typeof(AdornmentLayerDefinition))]
    [Name("TextAdornment1")]
    [Order(After = PredefinedAdornmentLayers.Selection,
        Before = PredefinedAdornmentLayers.Text)]
    [TextViewRole(PredefinedTextViewRoles.Document)]
    public AdornmentLayerDefinition editorAdornmentLayer = null;

    /// <summary>
    /// Instantiates a TextAdornment1 manager when a textView is created.
    /// </summary>
    /// <param name="textView">The <see cref="IWpfTextView"/> upon which the
    /// adornment should be placed</param>
    public void TextViewCreated(IWpfTextView textView)
    {
        new TextAdornment1(textView);
    }
}
```

And now, here is the viewport adornment factory:

```
[Export(typeof(IWpfTextViewCreationListener))]
[ContentType("text")]
[TextViewRole(PredefinedTextViewRoles.Document)]
internal sealed class PurpleBoxAdornmentFactory : IWpfTextViewCreationListener
{
    /// <summary>
    /// Defines the adornment layer for the scarlet adornment. This layer is ordered
    /// after the selection layer in the Z-order
    /// </summary>
    [Export(typeof(AdornmentLayerDefinition))]
    [Name("ViewportAdornment1")]
    [Order(After = PredefinedAdornmentLayers.Caret)]
```

```
[TextViewRole(PredefinedTextViewRoles.Document)]
public AdornmentLayerDefinition editorAdornmentLayer = null;


/// <summary>
/// Instantiates a ViewportAdornment1 manager when a textView is created.
/// </summary>
/// <param name="textView">The <see cref="IWpfTextView"/> upon which the
///     adornment should be placed</param>
public void TextViewCreated(IWpfTextView textView)
{
    new ViewportAdornment1(textView);
}
}
```

Note the different layer order defined by each via the Order attribute
([Order(After = PredefinedAdornmentLayers.Caret)] versus [Order(After =
PredefinedAdornmentLayers.Selection, Before = PredefinedAdornmentLayers.Text)]).

Managing Extensions and Updates

Before we detailed the editor extension points, we briefly mentioned the Extensions and
Updates window. This dialog is launched via the Tools menu, Extensions and Updates.
The UI used by the extension manager is clean and simple (see Figure 15.6).

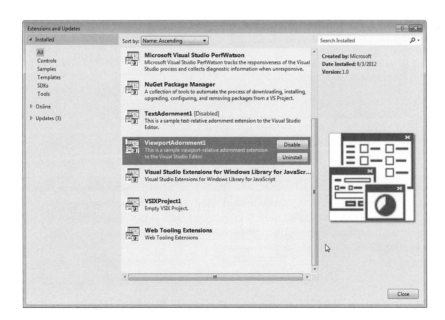

FIGURE 15.6   The Visual Studio Extension Manager.

You can manage installed extensions, browse extensions available online, or view updates available to any currently installed extensions. The left pane selects the location/category of the extensions or updates you want to manage. The center pane provides a list of the appropriate extensions; from here you can disable or enable an extensions, and install or uninstall an extension. In Figure 15.6, you can clearly see all the extensions that were installed as a result of running the four different extension template projects. The right pane provides general information about the currently selected extension.

Selecting Online in the left pane enables you to browse and install extensions that are hosted online (see Figure 15.7). You can post your own extensions online as well by visiting http://visualstudiogallery.msdn.microsoft.com/.

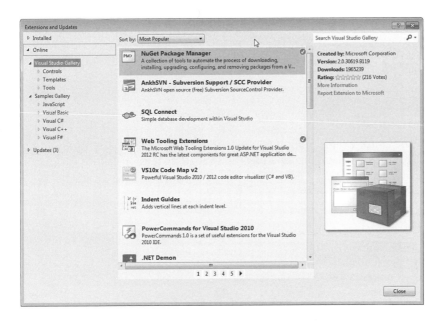

FIGURE 15.7   Browsing the extensions available online.

> **NOTE**
>
> The Visual Studio gallery and Visual Studio only fully support extensions packaged with VSIX. MSI-based extensions can be viewed here and installed, but Visual Studio doesn't have the ability to enable or disable them through this UI. VSI-based extensions are not supported at all via the Extensions and Updates window.

Creating Your Own MEF-Based Editor Extension

You have now learned all the ingredients necessary to build your own extension. Let's walk through a simple example, end to end, and build an extension that displays some basic code metrics in a window in the corner of the editor. Functionally, you need to accomplish the following:

▶ Compute the required code stats by parsing the currently loaded code file

▶ Expose a set of properties on a WPF user control to hold those metrics (and which also displays those metrics)

▶ Display the WPF user control as an editor viewport adornment

Because this involves creating a new adornment pegged to the editor's viewport, you have the luxury of starting with the code produced for us by the Viewport Adornment template.

Create a new project using this template and name the project **CodeMetricAdornment**. Then, add a WPF user control title **CodeMetricDisplayControl**. Your baseline project structure should look like Figure 15.8.

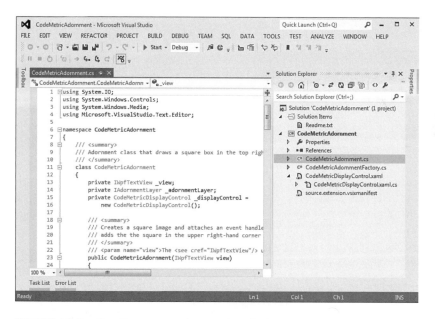

FIGURE 15.8   Creating a new adornment project.

Now, open the `CodeMetricAdornment` class itself. Within the class, you add a field to hold a WPF user control object, and you get rid of the current Image field that is used by the template code:

```
private CodeMetricDisplayControl _displayControl =
        new CodeMetricDisplayControl();
```

We'll get to our code counting algorithm in a bit. Let's first focus on creating a simple WPF user control to display our code metric information using the CodeMetricDisplayControl. You need to display the three metrics, and their three labels, within the control; a grid works nicely for this.

Because the grid is already included by default as the root arrangement element of our control, you just need to tweak its display a bit. Add three rows and two columns to the grid:

```
<Grid>
    <Grid.ColumnDefinitions>
        <ColumnDefinition Width="auto" />
        <ColumnDefinition Width="*" />
    </Grid.ColumnDefinitions>
    <Grid.RowDefinitions>
        <RowDefinition />
        <RowDefinition />
        <RowDefinition />
    </Grid.RowDefinitions>
</Grid>
```

Within the grid, add six TextBlock objects, three to hold the labels, and three to hold the actual counts:

```
<TextBlock Grid.Column="0" Grid.Row="0"
           VerticalAlignment="Center"
           x:Name="TextBlockLOC"
           Padding="5">Total Lines of Code:</TextBlock>
<TextBlock Grid.Column="0" Grid.Row="1"
           x:Name="TextBlockComments"
           VerticalAlignment="Center"
           Padding="5">Comment Lines:</TextBlock>
<TextBlock Grid.Column="0" Grid.Row="2"
           x:Name="TextBlockWhitespace"
           VerticalAlignment="Center"
           Padding="5">Whitespace Lines:</TextBlock>

<TextBlock Grid.Column="1" Grid.Row="0"
           VerticalAlignment="Center">0</TextBlock>
<TextBlock Grid.Column="1" Grid.Row="1"
           VerticalAlignment="Center">0</TextBlock>
<TextBlock Grid.Column="1" Grid.Row="2"
           VerticalAlignment="Center">0</TextBlock>
```

Within the `CodeMetricDisplayControl` class, add a property for each of these integers as well:

```
public partial class CodeMetricDisplayControl : UserControl
{
    private int _loc = 0;    // total lines of code
    private int _whitespace = 0; // whitespace (empty) lines
    private int _comments = 0; // total lines that are comments

    public int LinesOfCode
    {
        get { return _loc; }
        set { _loc = value; Refresh(); }
    }


    public int CommentLines
    {
        get { return _comments; }
        set { _comments = value; Refresh(); }
    }


    public int WhitespaceLines
    {
        get { return _whitespace; }
        set { _whitespace = value; Refresh(); }
    }

    public CodeMetricDisplayControl()
    {
        InitializeComponent();
    }

}
```

Note that in each setter, you are calling a `Refresh` routine. Let's write that routine, which updates the value of our `TextBlocks` to the current value held by our field for each of the code metrics:

```
private void Refresh()
{
    this.TextBlockComments.Text = _comments.ToString();
    this.TextBlockLOC.Text = _loc.ToString();
    this.TextBlockWhitespace.Text = _whitespace.ToString();
}
```

Disregarding any look and feel refinements, the WPF user control is now ready to go. Let's turn our attention back to the adorner class and write the code to actually count our lines of code, comments, and whitespace lines.

In `CodeMetricAdornment`, strip out all of the current WPF drawing code from the constructor. In its place, add three lines that set the user control's properties based on the return values from a few private routines (which we implement next):

```
public CodeMetricAdornment(IWpfTextView view)
{
    _view = view;

    _displayControl.LinesOfCode = CountLOC(view);

    _adornmentLayer =
        view.GetAdornmentLayer
        ("CodeMetricAdornment");

    _view.ViewportHeightChanged += delegate { this.onSizeChange(); };
    _view.ViewportWidthChanged += delegate { this.onSizeChange(); };
}
```

The code to actually count our lines of code is straightforward. We take the `IWpfTextView` object provided by our adorner and get the string representation for all of the current text in the editor window like this:

```
string code = view.TextSnapshot.GetText();
```

Now we can parse that string and return the various counts:

```
private int CountLOC(IWpfTextView view)
{
    string code = view.TextSnapshot.GetText();

    int count = 1;
    int start = 0;
    while ((start = code.IndexOf('\n', start)) != -1)
    {
        count++;
        start++;
    }

    return count;
```

```csharp
}

private int CountWhitespaceLines(IWpfTextView view)
{
    string code = view.TextSnapshot.GetText();
    int count = 0;

     using (StringReader reader = new StringReader(code))
    {
        string line;

        while ((line = reader.ReadLine()) != null)
        {
            if (line.Trim() == "")
                count++;
        }

        return count;
    }
}

private int CountCommentLines(IWpfTextView view)
{
    string code = view.TextSnapshot.GetText();
    int count = 0;

    using (StringReader reader = new StringReader(code))
    {
        string line;

        while ((line = reader.ReadLine()) != null)
        {
            if (line.TrimStart().StartsWith("//"))
                count++;
        }

        return count;
    }
}
```

We are almost done. The final piece that we need to change from the template code is to rewrite a piece of the `OnSizeChange` event handler. This was wired to position and display the WPF Image control originally used by the template. Instead, we want this code to position and place our WPF user control. Change the code within `OnSizeChange` to this:

```
public void onSizeChange()
      {
            //clear the adornment layer of previous adornments
            _adornmentLayer.RemoveAllAdornments();

            //Place the image in the top right hand corner of the Viewport
            Canvas.SetLeft(_displayControl,
                _view.ViewportRight - _displayControl.ActualWidth);
            Canvas.SetTop(_displayControl,
                _view.ViewportTop + _displayControl.ActualHeight);

            //add the image to the adornment layer and make it relative to the
            //viewport
            _adornmentLayer.AddAdornment(
                AdornmentPositioningBehavior.ViewportRelative,
                null, null, _displayControl, null);
      }
```

Now the control is positioned and is in the adornment view layer. If you run the project and then open a code file from within the IDE instance that is launched, you should immediately see the fruits of your labor in the upper-right corner of the editor.

There is still one problem with this implementation. Although the code stats are displayed correctly, they aren't updated when we change the text within the editor. To fix this, we need to react to the adornment layer's IWpfTextView LayoutChanged event. We can hook this event inside of our CodeMetricAdornment constructor like this:

```
_view.LayoutChanged += this.OnLayoutChanged;
```

And then, we create the event handler that updates our counts:

```
private void OnLayoutChanged(object sender, TextViewLayoutChangedEventArgs e)
{
    _displayControl.LinesOfCode = CountLOC(_view);
    _displayControl.CommentLines = CountCommentLines(_view);
    _displayControl.WhitespaceLines = CountWhitespaceLines(_view);
}
```

We could also make our WPF user control more compelling to look at by tweaking the XAML to add things like a background gradient, text coloring, and so on.

Figure 15.9 shows the final product, and Listing 15.1 contains the adornment class code. The full source listing for this project is available at this book's website.

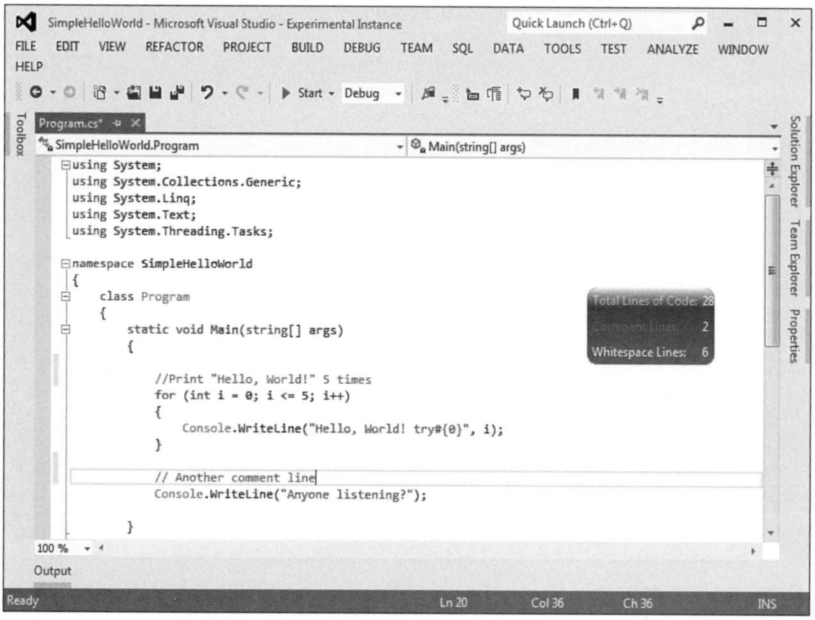

FIGURE 15.9   A simple code metric adornment.

LISTING 15.1   The CodeMetricAdornment Class

```
using System.IO;
using System.Windows.Controls;
using System.Windows.Media;
using Microsoft.VisualStudio.Text.Editor;

namespace CodeMetricAdornment
{
    /// <summary>
    /// Adornment class that draws a square box in the top-right corner of
    /// the viewport
    /// </summary>
    class CodeMetricAdornment
    {
        private IWpfTextView _view;
        private IAdornmentLayer _adornmentLayer;
        private CodeMetricDisplayControl _displayControl =
            new CodeMetricDisplayControl();
```

```csharp
public CodeMetricAdornment(IWpfTextView view)
{
    _view = view;

    _displayControl.LinesOfCode = CountLOC(view);
    _displayControl.CommentLines = CountCommentLines(view);
    _displayControl.WhitespaceLines = CountWhitespaceLines(view);

    _adornmentLayer = view.GetAdornmentLayer("CodeMetricAdornment");

    _view.LayoutChanged += this.OnLayoutChanged;
    _view.ViewportHeightChanged += delegate { this.onSizeChange(); };
    _view.ViewportWidthChanged += delegate { this.onSizeChange(); };
}

public void onSizeChange()
{
    //clear the adornment layer of previous adornments
    _adornmentLayer.RemoveAllAdornments();

    int buffer = 50;

    //Place the image in the top-right corner of the Viewport
    Canvas.SetLeft(_displayControl,
        _view.ViewportRight - (_displayControl.ActualWidth
        + buffer));
    Canvas.SetTop(_displayControl,
        _view.ViewportTop + (_displayControl.ActualHeight
        + buffer));

    _adornmentLayer.AddAdornment(
        AdornmentPositioningBehavior.ViewportRelative,
        null, null, _displayControl, null);
}

private void OnLayoutChanged(object sender, TextViewLayoutChangedEventArgs e)
{
    _displayControl.LinesOfCode = CountLOC(_view);
    _displayControl.CommentLines = CountCommentLines(_view);
    _displayControl.WhitespaceLines = CountWhitespaceLines(_view);
}
```

```csharp
private int CountLOC(IWpfTextView view)
{
    string code = view.TextSnapshot.GetText();

    int count = 1;
    int start = 0;
    while ((start = code.IndexOf('\n', start)) != -1)
    {
        count++;
        start++;
    }

    return count;

}

private int CountWhitespaceLines(IWpfTextView view)
{
    string code = view.TextSnapshot.GetText();
    int count = 0;

    using (StringReader reader = new StringReader(code))
    {
        string line;

        while ((line = reader.ReadLine()) != null)
        {
            if (line.Trim() == "")
                count++;
        }

        return count;

    }
}

private int CountCommentLines(IWpfTextView view)
{
    string code = view.TextSnapshot.GetText();
    int count = 0;

    using (StringReader reader = new StringReader(code))
    {
        string line;
```

```
            while ((line = reader.ReadLine()) != null)
            {
                if (line.TrimStart().StartsWith("//"))
                    count++;
            }

            return count;

        }
    }
}
}
```

Summary

This chapter covered a new .NET library, the Managed Execution Framework, and how
you can use it to write extensions for the Visual Studio editor. You learned the overall
architecture of MEF itself, including its extension discovery mechanisms and the core
concepts of parts and imports/exports.

This chapter also examined all the specific Visual Studio 2012 editor extension points and
outlined the value that the Visual Studio SDK provides with its prestocked set of extension
templates that target those editor extension points.

This chapter also provided a walkthrough of the creation of an editor extension that
exploits the editor's adornment layer to display a running total of three different code
metrics, all through the use of a WPF-based user control.

CHAPTER 16

Creating ASP.NET Form-Based Applications

Visual Studio 2012 gives developers the flexibility of building websites using standard ASP.NET web forms, web pages with Razor syntax, or using the ASP.NET MVC (Model-View-Controller) framework. Those used to the traditional ASP.NET page life cycle, viewstate, and web controls that generate HTML will want to leverage standard ASP.NET web forms. ASP.NET web pages with Razor syntax provides developers a fast, simple model that combines markup and server-side code with full control over the HTML output of the page. The ASP.NET MVC framework gives developers a pattern for developing lightly coupled objects, highly testable code, and simple markup.

These three models for building web application are very different. We have therefore split them across two chapters. This chapter focuses primarily on web form applications. We also cover building Razor sites and some other form technologies. Chapter 17, "Building Websites with Razor and ASP.NET MVC," is targeted at developers looking to learn more about building sites using ASP.NET MVC.

The chapter starts by covering the basics of defining Visual Studio web projects and creating simple web forms. From there we move on to more advanced topics and demonstrate how you might build a cohesive user interface for your ASP.NET application that includes master pages, themes, Web Parts, and data binding. We then cover the major controls built in to ASP.NET. We finish the chapter by discussing more advanced web form topics such as ASP.NET core services, AJAX, and other form-based technologies.

> **NOTE**
>
> ASP.NET is a huge topic. We are not able to dig in on its every aspect. Instead, we concentrate on areas where you can leverage Visual Studio to increase your productivity in building web-based user interfaces (UIs). We expect that as you build your ASP.NET interface, you will discover places that require further exploration. To that end, we point out some of them as we move through the chapter. Some examples include membership, user profiles, caching, website administration, and cross-page posting.

The Basics of an ASP.NET Website

Websites in Visual Studio start with a website project. The website project represents a connection between Visual Studio, the development version of your website (see Chapter 4, "Solutions and Projects," for more information), and a web server, be it local or otherwise. What is meant by *website*, however, continues to evolve and expand.

Simple Hypertext Markup Language (HTML) sites with just text, hyperlinks, and a few images are rarely created anymore or even discussed seriously as websites. Instead, .NET has pushed the definition of website well beyond the original ASP (active server pages) model that combined HTML with some server-side script. Nowadays, a website means user-interactive web forms; compiled code that links those web forms to a middle tier; master pages, styles, and themes that control the look of a site; configuration for such things as security, membership, and caching; database connectivity and data binding; and so on. The Visual Studio 2012 tools bring these concepts together to enable you to create rich, modern websites that offer an ever-higher degree of user interaction. In the following sections, we examine the makeup of the modern website and discuss how you create and configure them using Visual Studio.

> **NOTE**
>
> Visual Studio 2012 now has full support for HTML 5 and Cascading Style Sheets (CSS) 3. These revisions to the standards allow greater features through simple markup and styles. Of course, the target browser needs to support HTML 5/CSS 3 to really take advantage of many of these new items.

Creating a New Website or Web Application

Visual Studio enables you to create both websites and web application projects. Both are represented by project templates that define default directories, configuration, web forms, and other related files and settings. Websites and web application projects are very similar in Visual Studio 2012. Both are defined by a project file and nested in a solution. Both allow you to control properties and manage external references. A website works well for developers who typically deploy their site as a set of files. A web application project should be used when you want to deploy compiled code and need specialized control over compilation and output assemblies. Websites are the preferred option for the majority of web developers. This chapter focuses on website templates.

You create a new website using the New Web Site dialog box (File, New, Web Site). The New Web Site dialog box differs somewhat from the standard new project dialog box. Figure 16.1 shows an example. Notice that on the left side of the dialog box you are first asked to select a default language for your site (Visual Basic or Visual C#). You also select a website template, .NET Framework version, file location, and give your site a name.

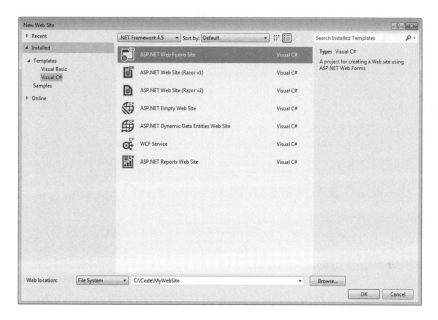

FIGURE 16.1   When you create a new website, you select both a language and a website template.

Selecting a Visual Studio Website Template

Visual Studio installs a number of ASP.NET website templates by default. You pick a template based on your specific needs. However, most sites that use ASP.NET web forms are built with the standard template, ASP.NET Web Forms Site. The following list provides an overview of many of the ASP.NET website templates:

▶ **ASP.NET Web Forms Site**—Represents the standard ASP.NET website and includes a directory for storing data (App_Data), a default page (Default.aspx), a configuration file (web.config), a master page (Site.master), a style sheet (Content/Site.css), a page for intercepting application events (Global.asax file), code for managing which scripts are loaded (BundleConfig.cs), and more. The template also includes an Account directory that contains pages for managing login and user accounts. The JQuery library is also provided by default in this template (inside the Scripts folder). Of course, additional folders and files can be added as you build out your site. This is the template most commonly used to start a new website from scratch.

▶ **ASP.NET Web Site (Razor v2)**—This template includes the same features, folders, and content items as the Web Forms template. However, these items are built using the ASP.NET Razor syntax (instead of standard ASPX). As an example, instead of Default.aspx, this template defines a Default.cshtml page. This page uses the master page defined in _SiteLayout.cshtml (instead of Site.master). The page also has its code directly embedded (instead of a separate code-behind file). See Chapter 17, "Building Websites with Razor and ASP.NET MVC," for more details on this template.

▶ **ASP.NET Empty Web Site**—Represents a website project devoid of all folders and files (except a very basic web.config file). You use this project container as a starting point. It does not presume folders and files. Instead, you explicitly add these items yourself as required.

▶ **ASP.NET Dynamic Data Entities Web Site**—This template enables you build a website that works directly with data. The site works with a data context you define (typically an Entity Framework object). There are then page and control templates that enable users to view, add, delete, filter, and edit data. These page templates make it easy for you to work in most scenarios accessing data over the web.

▶ **WCF Service**—Used to create a website that contains Windows Communication Foundation (WCF) services (see Chapter 21 for more details). The WCF Service contains the standard App_Code and App_Data folders. It also contains a specialized version of Web.config that enables you to configure the service. The service is defined by the file Service.svc. This file is markup that references Service.cs in the App_Code directory. This code file stubs out a class that implements a configurable, WCF-based service.

▶ **ASP.NET Reports Web Site**—Creates an ASP.NET Web Forms site for building web-based reports using the Microsoft Report Viewer control. Creating a site based on this template launches a wizard to walk you through configuring a data connection and your first report. Your reports are run in a web browser using the report viewer. The report viewer includes options for exporting reports as Excel and PDF.

TIP

You can find website starter kits and other templates to use as a basis for your new website. These kits do not ship with Visual Studio Professional. Rather, you can download them. Starter kits include blogs, portals, e-commerce, small business, clubs, wikis, and many more. You can find out about these sites at http://www.asp.net/downloads.

Choosing a Website Location

Visual Studio gives you a few options regarding the storage location of your website files. You can store files locally in you file system. Doing so takes advantage of the new Internet Information Services (IIS) Express web server that closely matches what you will expect when hosting with IIS. IIS Express is a lightweight version of IIS targeted to developers. It enables you to develop and test websites as they would run on IIS without all the IIS service overhead. You might instead need to work against a remote server and connect to it via FTP or HTTP. Visual Studio supports these scenarios as well. Let's look at configuring these many website location options using Visual Studio 2012.

You define the location for your website (and consequently how you want to access it) when you first create it or connect to it. Recall that in Figure 16.1, there is a drop-down list labeled "Web location" next to the Location option (bottom left). This list contains the values File System, HTTP, and FTP. Each of these locations requires you to enter the appropriate location of your website and provide the appropriate credentials to create (or open) your site. Clicking the Browse button (right of the application name text box in Figure 16.1) lets you navigate to the site's intended location. This button launches the Choose Location window. The following sections cover the various options of this dialog box.

File System   The first option you have at the top of the Choose Location window is File System, which enables you to choose any directory on your machine in which to store the contents of your website. You can use this dialog box to navigate the file system and select or create a new folder to contain your site. Figure 16.2 shows this dialog box. The Create New Folder button is in the upper-right corner (along with the Delete button).

FIGURE 16.2   You can use the Choose Location dialog box to select a location on your file system in which to store your website content.

Remember, file system websites in Visual Studio 2012 now use IIS Express. You can access IIS Express from your system tray. You can use the system tray to navigate directly to the site or launch an IIS Express admin dialog shown in Figure 16.3. Here you can see each website running on your machine and stop them if necessary.

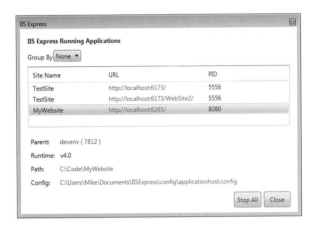

FIGURE 16.3   You can access the details of any running ASP.NET development server instance from the system tray.

Local IIS   This options enables you to configure your website to use an instance of IIS. This is equivalent of accessing your files through HTTP inside Visual Studio. You have two options here: using an actual, local IIS server you have installed (requires you run Visual Studio as an administrator); or using IIS Express. In most scenarios, running a local version of IIS on a developer's machine is less than desirable. It takes up valuable system resources and often violates internal policies by exposing an extra server to the network. This is the problem IIS Express was created to solve. If you use IIS Express, Visual Studio still stores your site locally. You can find it in your documents folder under My Web Sites.

FTP Site   Another option is to work with your site across File Transfer Protocol (FTP). The New Website dialog box enables you to indicate where on a given FTP server your site should (or does) exist. To do so, you must enter the address of the server and the port and provide appropriate credentials. All FTP constraints apply to FTP sites; this means, for example, that passwords are not secure. Figure 16.4 shows the FTP website settings. Note that sites created using FTP are still run locally using IIS Express. FTP is simply used to retrieve and store the files.

Remote Site   Finally, you can choose to communicate with a web server across Hypertext Transfer Protocol (HTTP) for working with your website. This is typically a remote web server where you are doing shared development. The development server must have FrontPage Server Extensions applied to allow this type of connectivity from Visual Studio.

Choosing a Default Programming Language

Visual Studio enables you to mix the languages you use to develop the items in your site. When you create a web form or a class file, you can determine the language in which each individual item is written. However, when you create a new site, you set a default language for the site. This default language is set in the New Web Site dialog box (recall Figure 16.1, left-side pane). Setting this value tells Visual Studio how to generate your template files. In addition, it sets the initial value for the setting that controls the default language of any new items being added to your site.

FIGURE 16.4   You can connect Visual Studio to a website on a remote server using FTP.

Figure 16.5 shows a website with mixed code. There are two web files: one with a code-behind written in VB and one with a C# code-behind. This is acceptable. For class files, however, you must have like files in each directory that contains code. Notice the App_Code directory contains a C# class file. You cannot add VB class files to this directory. If you need to mix both VB and C# class files, you have two options. First, you could consider putting your VB code into one class library project and your C# code into another. You would then add a reference from your website to these code libraries. Many web developers, however, prefer to keep their code in a single site structure. In this case, you can put VB code into one folder and C# in another. Refer again to Figure 16.5 for an example (the App_MoreCode folder). In this case, the compiler compiles code by folder; therefore, all code in a given folder must be of the same language.

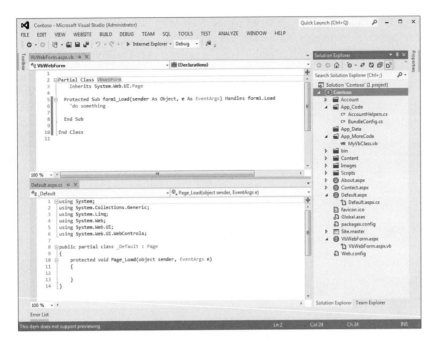

FIGURE 16.5   You can mix both C# and VB code items in the same website but must have use a single language per folder.

Understanding the Makeup of Your Website

A typical website contains a number of different files including web forms, code files, style sheets, config files, images, controls, JavaScript, and more. Keeping these many files organized and grouped together helps you find and support the items that make up your site. To this end, Visual Studio provides a number of "special" directories. The following sections provide a reference for the many directories and file types that are used to define a .NET website.

Directories   ASP.NET defines a number of folders that it uses to organize and recognize various files that make up your application. These folders have reserved names that mean something special to ASP.NET; therefore, you should use them appropriately.

You add an ASP.NET directory to your application via the context menu (right-click) for the site. Choose Add ASP.NET Folder from this menu. Figure 16.6 shows a web application with each of these special folders defined. Note that you can recognize special folders in ASP.NET as they have different icons. Table 16.1 provides details on the primary folders that make up an ASP.NET site.

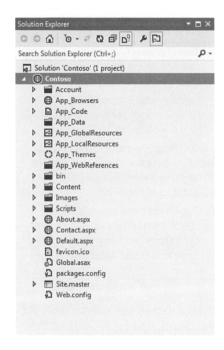

FIGURE 16.6   You can use the ASP.NET special folders to provide organization to the many files that make up your site.

TABLE 16.1   ASP.NET Directories

Directory	Description
Bin	This folder contains the compiled code (.dll files) that your application references. This might include external class libraries or controls you want to embed into your application (without embedding the source).
App_Code	This folder houses the class files that help define your application. For example, you could choose to put your business object or data access classes in this directory. All code in this directory is compiled into a single library. This includes code in any subdirectories. Therefore, all code in the directory must be of the same language.
App_Data	This directory contains data files used by your applications. This can be SQL Express files (.mdf), XML data, Excel files, and so on.
App_GlobalResources	This folder contains the resource files (.resx and .resources) that make up your application. You use resource files to abstract such things as string-based text and images from your actual application. In this way, your application reads from a resource file instead of being hard-coded with these values. This helps you support multiple language user interfaces, design-time changes, and related issues.

16

Directory	Description
App_LocalResources	This folder also contains resource files. However, these files are specific to a page or control. They are not global to the entire application scope.
App_WebReferences	This folder is used to house and maintain references to web services. The files inside the folder include web service contracts (.wsdl) and schemas (.xsd) and other related items.
App_Browsers	This folder contains browser definition files (.browser). These files are typically used for mobile application support. Each .browser file defines the various capabilities for a given browser. This helps your user interface render appropriately for a specific device.
App_Themes	This folder contains subfolders that each define a specific theme (look and feel) for your application. Each theme folder contains one or more skin (.skin) files, a style (.css) sheet, and any theme-based images. See "Creating a Common Look and Feel," later in this chapter, for more on themes.

Files   Numerous files and file types define a typical ASP.NET website. Of course, there are files that you use often, such as web forms, user controls, classes, and configuration files; and then there are those that are rarer, such as skins, master pages, resources, and site maps. Table 16.2 lists some of the more common files that might exist in any given ASP.NET web application.

TABLE 16.2   ASP.NET Files

Item Templates	File Extension	Description
Web Form	.aspx	Defines an ASP.NET web form. This is the most common ASP.NET file. See "Creating Web Pages," later in this chapter.
Web User Control, Dynamic Data Field	.ascx	Represents an ASP.NET user control. User controls enable you to define your own version or combination of controls and reuse them throughout your site. The Dynamic Data Field control is another version of the user control used for creating custom displays of data.
No item template	.asax	Creates a global application class. This enables you to define code inside events that fire when IIS starts or stops an application, an error occurs, or a user initiates or terminates a session.
Generic Handler	.ashx	A file used for creating a general, HTTP handler in your site. You can create a generic handler to receive an HTTP request, process it, and send information back in the response.
Class	.cs/.vb	Defines a class file. The extension .cs is a C# class file. The .vb extension is a class written in Visual Basic.

Item Templates	File Extension	Description
Master Page, AJAX Master Page	.master	Represents a master page. A master page is used to define common elements that might appear on multiple pages within a website. These might include menu items, navigation, headers, footers, and other related items. See "Master Pages," later in this chapter.
Web Configuration File	.config	Represents a configuration file for your web application. You use the configuration file to manage settings such as debugging and to store application-specific data (such as an encrypted connection string to a database).
Style Sheet	.css	Represents a cascading style sheet. It stores the styles of your application or theme. See "Style Sheets," later in this chapter.
ADO.NET Entity Data Model	.edmx	A data context object for working with data using the Entity Framework.
LINQ to SQL Classes	.dbml	A LINQ to SQL class file. You create such a file to provide a class file that exposes LINQ queries against a given SQL database.
Report, Report Wizard	.rdlc	Enables you to create a web-based report that leverages the Microsoft reporting technology.
Site Map	.sitemap	Enables you to create a file that defines a map of your website. Sitemaps are used for various navigation controls within ASP.NET.
WCF Service, ADO.NET Data Service, AJAX-enabled WCF Service	.svc	Represents a WCF service. The ADO.NET Data Service item is another version of a service used specifically for working with data. See Chapter 21, "Service-Oriented Applications," for more information.
Skin File	.skin	Represents a skin for one or more controls in your application. A skin is defined for an application theme. See "Themes and Skins," later in this chapter.
Jscript File, AJAX Client Library, AJAX Control Library, AJAX Client Behavior	.js	Used to create code files that contain java script. There are a number of item templates specifically for AJAX libraries. See Chapter 20, "Working with Databases."
HTML Page	.htm	A simple HTML page (no server-side processing of code).
Resource File	.resx	Used to create a resource file for storing things such as localized strings for different cultures and languages.

16

You add a new ASP.NET file to your application by right-clicking your site and selecting Add, Add New Item. Figure 16.7 shows the Add New Item dialog box. Notice that you first select a language (left side of the window). The many files that are available for selection are listed as item templates in the center. If you select a file type that belongs in a special directory, Visual Studio prompts you to put the file in that directory.

FIGURE 16.7   You can add many file types to a .NET website.

Controlling Project Properties and Options

ASP.NET applications have their own set of properties and configuration options. These properties control how an application works, gets built, works with the debugger, and so on. You access the properties for your website through the Property Pages dialog box. You can open this dialog box by right-clicking your website and selecting the Property Pages option. The following sections cover the many options of this dialog box.

References

The references in your application define the code that your application uses by reference. You add references to other projects in your solution, other .NET namespaces in the .NET Framework, third-party controls, and other .NET libraries. The code you reference is already compiled into a .dll file and exists on its own. In the case of project references, this code might get compiled each time your run the application. These .dll files might or might not be installed in the Global Assembly Cache (GAC). Figure 16.8 shows the References portion of the Property Pages dialog box.

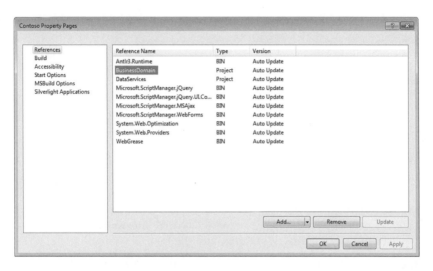

FIGURE 16.8 You can manage the code your application references using the Property Pages dialog box.

> **NOTE**
>
> Property Pages are specific to websites. Web application projects use a different window for managing properties. In addition, the references are defined by a special folder called References inside the solution hierarchy itself. Again, this chapter focuses on the website template.

Each current reference for the website is listed along with its associated reference type. Figure 16.8 shows two project references (BusinessDomain and DataServices). These references are to projects in the same solution as the website. They are automatically updated as the solution gets compiled. You could, of course, have specific .dll files you reference. These files are stored in the bin directory if they are simply local to your application. If they are global .dll files (used by more than just your application), they are stored in the GAC. From this dialog box, you can add a new reference, remove an existing reference, or refresh (update) the selected reference.

Adding a New Reference You can add references to your ASP.NET applications (as shown by the Add button in Figure 16.8). Clicking this button brings up the three reference options shown in Figure 16.9. These options include a standard reference to a .NET class library (Add Reference), a reference to an XML web service (Add Web Reference), or a reference to a WCF service (Add Service Reference). We cover the two service-type references in Chapter 21, "Service-Oriented Applications."

FIGURE 16.9   You can select the type of reference you want to add to your application.

When you add a standard reference, you are making a connection to a .dll file that exists as part of another application or another project in your solution. Establishing this reference places a copy of the compiled .dll file into your website's bin directory. The namespaces, classes, and methods inside this .dll file are available for you to code against. The compiler also checks your application against any referenced .dlls to ensure that you are not breaking type constraints, method signatures, and the like.

When you select the standard Add Reference option, Visual Studio displays the Add Reference dialog box, as shown in Figure 16.10. You can use tree on the left of the dialog box to find the specific item you want to reference. If you are looking to reference a namespace from the .NET Framework, for example, you select the Assemblies tab. This tab locates items installed in your GAC, such as those in the System or Microsoft namespace. You can also set references to COM components, set references to other projects in your solution, and browse for specific .dll files.

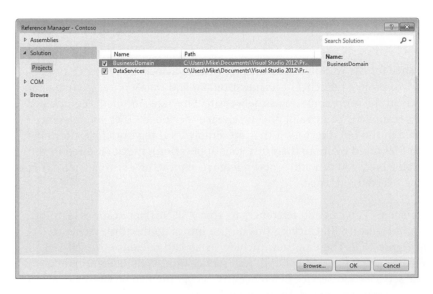

FIGURE 16.10   You use the Add Reference dialog box to reference code outside of your site.

Build

The Build page of the Property Pages dialog box enables you to control how your application is built using Visual Studio. Figure 16.11 shows the options that are available. We cover each of these options next.

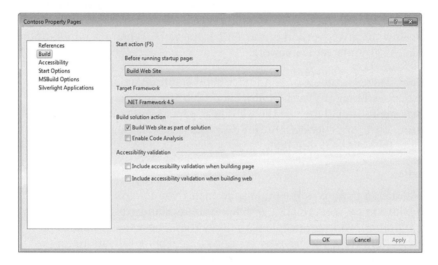

FIGURE 16.11   You can use the Build properties to control the version of the .NET Framework your site targets (among other things).

Start Action   The Start Action section of the Build page enables you to define how your application is compiled when you run it from the IDE. There are three options in this drop-down: No Build, Build Page, and Build Web Site (the default). Let's look at each of these options.

The No Build option tells the IDE to just launch the site in a browser without doing any compilation. In this instance, as pages and items are accessed in the browser, they are compiled. Instead of the errors showing in the IDE before you run the application, the errors are displayed in the browser as you find them.

The Build Page option tells the IDE to compile only the current startup page or the page you're working on. This capability is useful if you work on only one page at a time. If the IDE finds errors, they are shown in the IDE before the page launches.

Finally, the Build Web Site option, which is the default setting, tells the IDE to build the entire website and all dependent projects before launching into the browser. This capability can be helpful if you are working on a small site by yourself. However, it can also cause longer build times on larger projects.

Target Framework   The Target Framework feature enables you to indicate (and change) the version of the .NET Framework your application targets. This means you can write ASP. NET applications using Visual Studio 2012 that target .NET 2.0, 3.0, 3.5, 4.0, or 4.5. This is especially useful for those developers looking to upgrade their tools but who are restricted from upgrading their applications at present. Flipping this option compiles and checks your application against the target version of the .NET Framework. When your application runs, it calls code in the given target Framework.

Build Solution Action   There is a single option under Build Solution Action in the Build page for the professional edition of Visual Studio. Build Web Site as Part of Solution indicates whether Visual Studio should include the website as part of the solution's build. The default for this setting is true (or checked). In this case, when you choose Build Solution from the Build menu, the website is also built.

Accessibility Validation

The Accessibility Validation options in the Build page enable you to have Visual Studio check your web application for conformance with accessibility standards. These standards ensure that your application works for people with disabilities. The actual standards are covered in the next section. Here, you have two options for enabling validation: for the entire site or for just the current startup page. If these options are enabled, Visual Studio displays accessibility issues in the IDE when you run the application.

Accessibility

The Accessibility page of the Property Pages dialog box enables you to define what checks should be done relative to your site's conformance. Figure 16.12 shows the options for configuring the checks. There are three levels of checks based on two standards: the W3C's Web Content Accessibility Guidelines (WCAG) 1 and 2 and the U.S. government's standards for accessibility (Access board section 508).

TIP

Visual Studio checks only your HTML pages for accessibility standards compliance upon build. It does not check ASP.NET controls because those controls emit their own HTML. However, most, but not all, of this HTML is standards compliant. If you need to verify that the final HTML output is 100% standards compliant for accessibility, you need to know a few things. First, many of the ASP.NET controls should be safe and of no concern. There is, however, a list of controls that need to be configured properly for accessibility. These can be found in the Microsoft Developer Network (MSDN) by searching for "ASP.NET Controls and Accessibility." This also indicates those controls to stay away from.

A quick way to verify an entire ASP.NET as accessible-compliant is to run the page in a web browser, view the HTML source, copy the HTML from the page, and embed it as a separate HTML file in your solution. Visual Studio then checks to ensure that this new page is compliant on build.

For more information on building accessible applications, see "Walkthrough: Creating an Accessible Web Application" on MSDN.

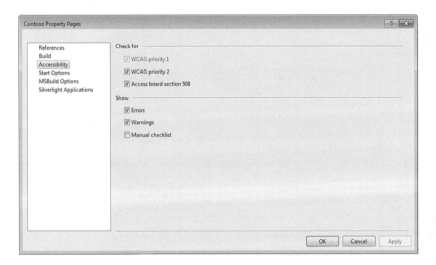

FIGURE 16.12   You can use the Accessibility options to ensure your site is checked against accessibility rules (on by default).

Start Options

The Start Options page in the Property Pages dialog box enables you to define what happens when you start (or run) your application. Figure 16.13 shows the many options available. The following sections cover each of these.

Start Action   The Start Action section of the Start Options page is useful for defining what happens when you start your application through the IDE. The first option, Use Current Page, tells Visual Studio to start the application using the current, active page in the development environment. This capability can be great for developers who work on one page at a time. The next option, Specific Page, enables you to set a startup page. This is akin to right-clicking a page and choosing Set as Start Page from the Solution Explorer. The third option, Start External Program, enables you to specify an .exe file to run (instead of the browser) when you start the application. The Start URL option enables you to send the browser to a different URL when running your application. This capability can be useful when debugging a web service. You might launch a client that uses your web service, for example. Finally, you can use the last option to tell Visual Studio to wait for a request (don't start anything). This, too, can be useful for a web service scenario.

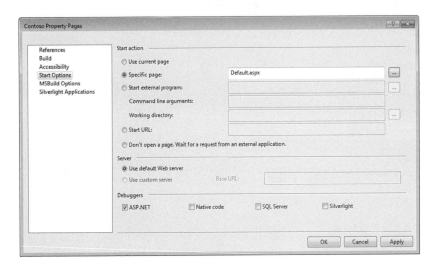

FIGURE 16.13   You use the Start Options to configure what happens when you run your application from the IDE.

Server   The Server section of the Start Options page enables you to specify a server to be launched for your application. Most applications leave this set to Use Default Web Server. This represents the file system websites. For scenarios that use IIS or FTP, you specify a URL to the actual server.

Debuggers   The Debuggers group of options on the Start Options page enables you to set the enabled debuggers used when running your application. By default, only ASP.NET is enabled. You can choose to turn off this setting. You can also add native code, SQL Server, and Silverlight debuggers to the mix.

MSBuild Options

The MsBuild Options screen in the Property Pages dialog box enables you to control precompiling of your application. These options are specific to using the MSBuild compilation tool from the command line. Figure 16.14 shows an example. From here, you can set your precompilation output folder and manage related settings.

> **NOTE**
> You can also use Publish Web Site in the IDE as an alternative to the MSBuild command-line application.

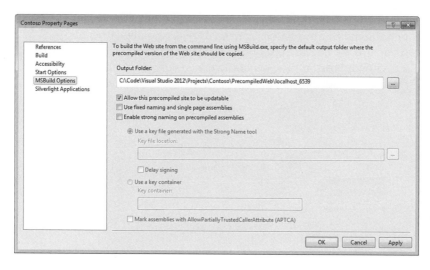

FIGURE 16.14   You can use the MSBuild Options dialog box to control precompiling options.

Silverlight Applications

The Silverlight Applications screen in the Property Pages dialog box enables you to manage settings for Silverlight applications to which your website connects. You can add a Silverlight application from here. You can then determine where the Silverlight application should copy its files (typically ClientBin).

Creating Web Pages

Web pages written using ASP.NET Web Forms make up the bulk of any given website. You create web pages to define your user interface. Web pages in ASP.NET have both a designer component and an event model. The designer piece enables you to define the controls and look of a given web page. The event model is used on the server to respond to user interaction (or events posted back to the server over HTTP). This section looks at the basics of both the web page's designer and its event model.

Adding a Web Page to Your Website

The first step to working with web pages is adding one or more to your website. To do so, you use the Add New Item dialog box and select Web Form from the item templates. Figure 16.15 shows an example of adding a CustomerEdit.aspx page to a website. Note that this figure is simply an alternate view of the same dialog box shown back in Figure 16.7.

You have a few options when adding a new web page to your site. First, you can set the page's name. It is best to use a standard naming scheme and to make sure that the name also references the page's primary function. Web page names must be unique in a given directory. A good standard is to indicate the data with which the page works followed by a user action for the page. In our example, this is CustomerEdit.aspx. The second option is the language on which the web form is based. Your website is typically either all C# or VB. However, it can be made up of a mixture of both languages. When you create a new page, the default language is chosen based on the default language for your website. However, you can use the left side of the Add New Item dialog box to choose a different language for the page.

FIGURE 16.15   You use the Add New Item dialog box to add web form pages to your site.

Next, you can indicate whether you want the code for the web page to be in a separate file. ASP.NET enables you to create a web form as a single file. This form includes both ASP markup and server-side code. In fact, you also get VB or C# IntelliSense inside the markup editor for these types of forms.

The dominant setting (and default) for most developers is code-behind (place code in separate file). Putting code in a new file enables you to manage that code independently of the UI markup. This can be a much cleaner development experience. However, some web developers prefer the simplicity of a single file model. In this case, your server-side code is placed inside a `<script/>` block.

In the case of the code-behind model, ASP.NET puts your code into what is called a *partial class*. This partial class contains only the code that you write. Code that is emitted by the tool or framework is not part of this file. Your code and the tool-emitted code are combined together during compilation. In this way, you are not burdened by code that is really not yours. Of course, the single-file model also excludes the tool-emitted code.

The final option on the Add New Item dialog box when adding a Web Form is Select master page. This setting tells the IDE that you want your new web form to use a master page for its default content and layout. We look at master pages later in this chapter.

Adding Controls to Your Web Page

You add controls to a web page by dragging them from the Visual Studio Toolbox to the web page. In the page designer, there are multiple views of your form: design, source, and split view. The design view enables you to build your form using drag and drop with a visual designer. This is similar to building a Windows or Windows Presentation Foundation (WPF) form. As you drag items onto the page, you see a visual representation of what they look like at runtime. This includes their layout with respect to one another. You can select an item on a page and use the property editor to change the look and behavior of the element.

Figure 16.16 shows a page in the design view. Notice the Toolbox on the left. This is the source of controls you can add to your page. In the center of the figure is the actual design surface. Notice that the Save Button control is selected. The properties for the Save Button are shown on the right. You can use the Properties pane to make changes to how the control looks and behaves. These changes are stored inside the markup for the page.

FIGURE 16.16   You can use the Toolbox to add controls to either the design view (shown) or the source view of your page.

You can switch from design to source view using the buttons at the bottom of the page designer (see Figure 16.16). The source view enables you to see (and edit) the markup related to a web page. Here you can still drag controls from the Toolbox onto the editor, but instead of a visual representation, you get the markup code that represents the given item. You can then use the markup editor to change the values inside the markup. This includes setting property values for controls and changing layout information. Of course, Visual Studio provides IntelliSense for doing so. Figure 16.17 shows the same page as was shown in Figure 16.16 but now in source view. Notice that the properties of the Save Button are available for edit from IntelliSense. Editing markup in source view is usually a more familiar experience for coders.

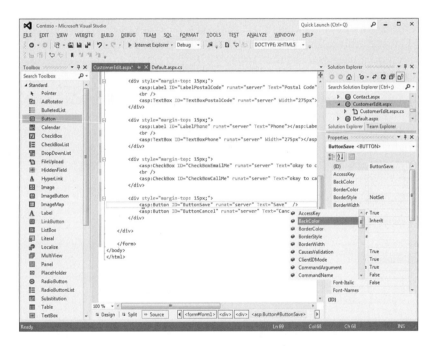

FIGURE 16.17   You can edit your page markup using source view.

The third view of your page is called split view. This gives you both markup and the visual design surface. The two try to stay in sync with one another. If you make a change in the source view, for example, the design view tries to update itself or waits for you to click it and then update. This can be useful if you do things both visually and through code (and have a big monitor). You end up doing a lot less switching back and forth between views. Figure 16.18 shows an example of the same page we've been looking at, now in split view. Notice how in both views it knows that the Save Button is selected.

TIP

You can change how Visual Studio opens your web forms by default. You can choose between viewing in source view and viewing in design view. To do so, choose Options from the Tools menu. You then select the HTML Designer node from the tree. Figure 16.19 shows an example of this window. The Start Pages In group box enables you to modify this setting.

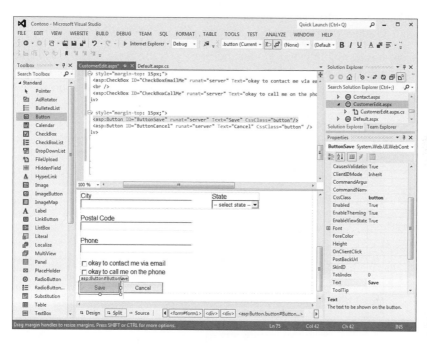

FIGURE 16.18   You use Split view to see both markup and design at the same time.

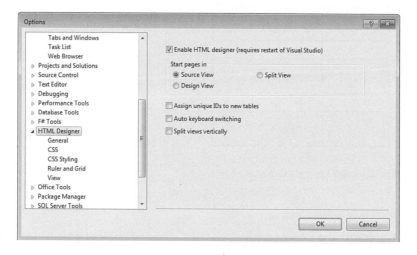

FIGURE 16.19   You can use the HTML Designer options to change how Visual Studio opens your web pages by default.

Responding to Events

When you write ASP.NET web forms, it is important to understand how the event model works. The event model represents how events are fired on the server when users make requests (or trigger actions). The ASP.NET event model differs from the standard Windows Forms event model because it must process events on the server but all user interaction happens on the client inside a web browser.

An ASP.NET web form has less of an event model and more of a life cycle. The life cycle has a series of stages through which a page goes. In each stage, there is typically one or more events that get fired. Figure 16.20 shows the life cycle stages of an ASP.NET web form.

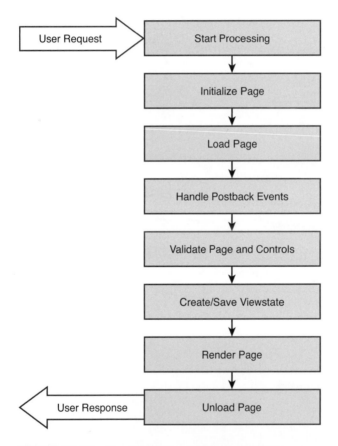

FIGURE 16.20   The ASP.NET page life cycle stages.

Each stage in Figure 16.20 is described here:

1. **User Request**—A user makes a request for a given page.

2. **Start Processing**—ASP.NET determines whether the page life cycle needs to be executed or a version of the page can be returned from cache. It also determines if the request is a postback or simply a new request.

3. **Initialize Page**—ASP.NET initializes the page and makes each control on the page available from a code perspective. However, the controls at this point are not matched to any viewstate and no postback data has been loaded.

4. **Load Page**—ASP.NET loads the page, connects controls to their viewstate information, and connects data from the postback to each control.

5. **Handle Postback Events**—If the user's request is posting back data to the page (instead of a simple request), then at this point any postback-related events are called, such as a Button control's Click event.

6. **Validate Page and Controls**—After the page has been loaded by the server, it gets validated. This means calling out to each control and ensuring that the Validation method is fired. Finally, the page's IsValid property gets set at this stage based on the results.

7. **Create/Save Viewstate**—ASP.NET begins the process of sending the response back to the user. The first thing is to create the ViewState data and embed it inside the response.

8. **Render Page**—At this stage, ASP.NET generates all the HTML for the page and writes it to an output stream.

9. **User Response**—A response is sent back to the user that made the request.

10. **Unload Page**—ASP.NET unloads the page and discards it from memory.

As a web form moves through this life cycle, a series of events are triggered. These events are where you place your code. It is important to understand this life cycle to help you understand the events, when they are fired, and what is available to you inside these events. You want to be sure to get the right code in the right event for the right job. Let's take a look at the basics of the web page event model. The following lists the key events in the page life cycle in the order in which they are fired:

1. **PreInit**—This is the first event for which you might write code. It gets raised before the initialize stage (refer to Figure 16.20). The PreInit event is useful if you are creating controls dynamically, setting a master page dynamically, or setting a page's theme dynamically.

2. **Init**—This event is called to create the controls used by the web page. It also initializes the properties of these controls. This event is typically created automatically by the IDE to set properties of controls on a given page. The init event for each control on the page is called prior to the page Init event.

3. **InitComplete**—This event is raised after the page Init event is called. It signals that view state tracking has been enabled. Any modifications to view state prior to InitComplete would be lost.

4. **PreLoad**—This event is called after the view state for the page and controls have been loaded but before the Load event.

5. **Load**—This event is called when the page is loaded and after the controls are initialized. This is a common event for web developers to use. You can use this event to determine whether a user is requesting a page or executing a postback (submitting data). You then call the appropriate code based on this information. Control Load events are also called during page load.

6. **Control Specific Event(s)**—Next, the page framework executes the event or events that are associated with the control the user used to submit the form (if any). For example, if a user clicked a Button control on your form, the Click event for the Button is called after page load.

7. **LoadComplete**—Triggered after all initialization, loading, and control-specific events have processed. You can use this event to execute any code that requires the entire page to be loaded.

8. **PreRender**—This event is called just before the final rendering of the page is sent back to the browser. You can also use this event to make changes to the page after all events are called.

9. **PreRenderComplete**—Raised after the PreRender event has processed.

10. **SaveStateComplete**—Raised after the view state and control state information has been saved for the page. If you make changes to the page or controls at this point, those changes do not persist when the page is posted back to the server. However, the changes are reflected in the response.

11. **Render**—There is no Render event. However, the page calls the render method for each control on the page at this stage. This enables the control to output the markup to be sent to the browser.

12. **Unload**—This is the last event that is called for the page (after the page is rendered). The Unload event is first called for each control on your page. It then gets called for just the page. You use this event to do cleanup. For example, you might close page-level connections or do some form of logging. You cannot, however, make any changes that affect the response to the user. That was completed in the rendering stage (refer to Figure 16.20).

These steps represent the basic event model for a page. However, there are additional events for the page. In addition, user controls have their own events that are called during the control-specific event stage. Master pages can also add default processing for all pages. Understanding the events in any given page always help when you're debugging or trying to achieve a specific result.

> **NOTE**
>
> For more information on what happens inside the ASP processing framework, see "ASP.NET Page Life Cycle Overview" on the MSDN website. This article provides additional details on the life cycle of an ASP.NET web form. For details on how IIS and the ASP.NET Framework handles your site, including application- and session-specific events, see the article "ASP.NET Application Life Cycle Overview for IIS 7.0."

Adding Page Event Handlers

There are a couple of ways to ensure that your event handlers are called by ASP. NET when a web form executes. First, you can call them automatically. If you set the AutoEventWireup page-level attribute to true (the default setting), then ASP.NET finds events that follow the Page_Event naming convention and automatically call them at their appropriate time. This approach can be convenient but requires you to recall each event's name so that you can define it appropriately.

You can also explicitly bind page events to methods in your code. In this way, you can use your own event names. You can also let Visual Studio generate the event names. You can add events to a page from the designer in a similar way you would bind events to controls: from the Properties window. However, to access a page's events, you must be in the component designer for the page. The component designer is another design view for a page. It is used to add components to the page such as event logging. You get to the component designer by right-clicking a page in Solution Explorer and choosing View Component Designer. After you have it open, you then open that page's Properties window. From there, you can select the lightning bolt icon to show all events for the page. Figure 16.21 shows an example.

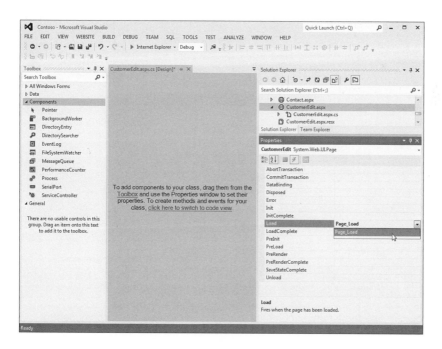

FIGURE 16.21   You can use the page's component designer to access the page events inside the Properties pane.

The right side of the figure shows the properties for the CustomerEdit.aspx page. Notice that the lightning bolt icon is selected from the Properties toolbar. This shows the events (and not the properties). You can double-click an event in this list to generate a method stub for the given event. You can also select an event from the list and then use a drop-down to choose a method already defined in your code and thus explicitly bind that method to the selected event.

Adding Control Event Handlers   You add events to controls in a similar manner. There is no component designer for a control. You simply select the control on a given page and view its properties in the Properties window. From the Properties window, you can select the lightning bolt icon to show all the events for the given control. You then double-click an event to add it to your code-behind. Of course, if you already have code written, you can use the same window to select that code and thus bind it to the selected event.

Most events you add to a control are Action events. These are events that are based on user actions (such as Button Click). There are, however, other events. These events are typically used for special purposes and control developers only. Figure 16.22 shows an example of adding an event to the Click action of the Save Button. Notice the additional events available for the Button control.

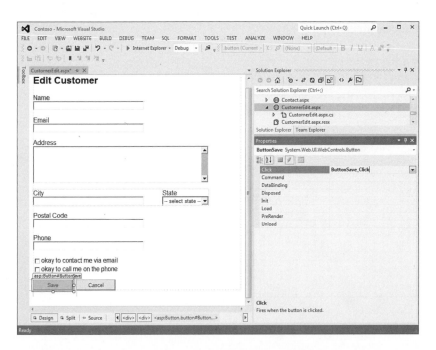

FIGURE 16.22   You can use the lightning bolt icon in the Properties pane to access control event handlers.

Designing Your User Interface

A lot goes into building a good web UI. So much so that some solid planning is typically in order before you start dragging controls onto forms. Your first step should be to consider your options, the needs of the users, and your maintenance requirements. You then put this information into some sort of design plan. Your design plan should include the following:

► Determine the type of information and user activity your site needs to support. You might make a list of the screen types in your system. For example, you might have pages that display report data, others that allow users to do data entry, still others that do searches, and so on. This helps you when deciding on the style elements required of your site.

► Decide whether you need to plan for multiple-language and culture information. This can have a big effect on how you build out the content items (such as labels, menu text, and the like) of your pages.

► Define the key areas of your site and how users navigate among them. This is often referred to as your site's taxonomy or sitemap.

► Determine what items go on all pages. This might include navigation, logos, design elements, footer information, and more. For example, you might make the key areas of your site into top-level menu items that go on all pages.

► Determine the style elements for your site. Or at least define the items that need to be stylized. As an example, you might determine that you need a consistent way to show page titles, navigation items, buttons, column headers, table data, and so on. Documenting these items enables you to plan upfront. You might also pass the list on to a designer and have the designer build out the styles for the application.

► Determine whether your site will support a high degree of user interaction. If this is the case, you should consider creating an AJAX-enabled site or consider using jQuery.

► Decide whether you will support multiple themes to enable user-configurable options. You might, for example, need to rebrand your site depending on the user accessing it. In this case, you need to think about themes. You might also need to enable user customization of layout and content. In this case, you should consider using some of the portal controls.

These and many more decisions go into planning a good web-based UI. Thinking through the items upfront pays big dividends down the road by saving you a lot of frustrating rework.

When you have your plan, Visual Studio is there to help. It enables you to create master pages for determining a common look and feel. There are controls for managing links and menus. You can support themes through skin files and style sheets. You can even allow users to participate in the customization of their layout using Web Parts. The following sections demonstrate the many features of ASP.NET Web Forms that go into creating great web UIs.

Determining Page Layout and Control Positioning

An important consideration when building your web pages is deciding how controls are placed on a page. Most modern sites are built using markup and style sheets to define layout and positioning of controls at runtime. Many older sites still relay on using table tags for layout. Each item on the page is in a table of columns and rows. Other sites place items on a page such that they do not move (absolute positioning). Of course, many sites and pages mix these concepts depending on the situation. The following list is meant to describe your layout options in more detail:

▶ **Flow layout**—If you are comfortable with the dynamic nature of a web page in a browser, you might prefer to control your positioning through flow layout. This refers to your controls moving with the flow of the page. Your controls are lined up with respect to how their neighbors are lined up. If an item moves down, for example, anything below that item also moves down in a relative fashion. This is the default setting in Visual Studio. Flow layout combined with CSS positioning is the most common method for laying out pages.

▶ **Absolute positioning**—If you are used to building Windows forms, you might be more comfortable controlling the positioning of each individual item. In this case, you drag an item onto the form and move it around relative to other items. Where you drop it is where it is positioned (and where it stays). In addition, with absolute positioning, items are positioned based on their parent container. For example, if you put a Button inside a `<div>` tag and set the position of the Button to 5 pixels from the top and 5 pixels from the left, the 5 pixels in each case are counted from the bounds of the `<div>` tag (and not the page). We recommend you shy away from this technique and only use it when you really need it. Too many times you need the page to move (or flow) based on other items on the page. This type of positioning is simply too restrictive.

▶ **Relative positioning**—This combines a flow layout with absolute positioning. With relative positioning, items are placed within the flow of a page. However, if you set an item's top and left properties, the distance defined by these properties is calculated based on the item's relative position on the page.

▶ **CSS positioning**—CSS positioning combined with flow layout is the standard for page layout as it offers the highest degree of flexibility and control. With CSS positioning, items are typically laid out on a page using flow layout. However, each item has a specific style defined either on the page or in a style sheet. Style sheets are the preferred choice so that you can reuse styles across pages. The style has positioning information defined, including margins, heights, widths, and the like, which enables you to easily change the layout of a page (or entire site) by changing the style sheet (and not the pages themselves).

You will encounter situations in which you need to mix layout techniques in a single page. For example, you could define a page that uses flow layout. Inside a given area (or `<div>` tag), you might set a panel control. This panel control might be set to allow only absolute positioning for items within the panel. You might do so to help you position an image or other controls.

Whichever path you choose, be consistent. Define your layout strategy as part of your overall site design plan. All the pages in the site should behave in a similar manner to make your maintenance easier. In addition, most pages are dependent on other page-like items (such as master pages and user controls). For this reason, you want all of these items to be laid out on a page in the same way.

Creating Forms Using Flow Layout and CSS

By default, Visual Studio is set to lay out items on your page using flow layout. That is, as you drag items from the Toolbox to the designer, the items are placed relative to one another. If you are using the most common method for controlling a page's layout (CSS positioning), flow layout works fine for your needs. Figure 16.22, presented earlier, shows a basic example of a page using flow layout. The State drop-down control leverages a little CSS behind the scenes to position it next to the City control. The following shows this markup:

```
<div style="width:450px; margin-top:15px;">
    <div id="State" style="float:right;">
        <asp:Label ID="Label5" runat="server" Text="State"></asp:Label>
        <br />
        <asp:DropDownList ID="DropDownList1" runat="server">
            <asp:ListItem>-- select state --</asp:ListItem>
        </asp:DropDownList>
    </div>
    <div id="City">
        <asp:Label ID="Label4" runat="server" Text="City"></asp:Label>
        <br />
        <asp:TextBox ID="TextBox4" runat="server" Width="275px"></asp:TextBox>
    </div>
</div>
```

In this example, there is an outer `<div>` tag that acts as a container for the two inner `<div>` tags. Each of the inner `<div>` tags represent the two control areas (State and City). The width of this outer `<div>` tag is fixed (450px) and the State `<div>` tag is set to the right (`float:right`) of the City `<div>` tag. Notice here the CSS is all contained in style attributes. We will look at creating style sheets and more on CSS later in this chapter.

Building Forms with Absolute Positioning

You might run into a situation in which you need to absolute-position an item on a page that uses flow layout. For example, suppose you want to embed your company logo on the right side of a page. We could, of course, use a table or use CSS positioning (the preferred option). However, you could also use absolute positioning. To do so, you first add the image to your site. Typically you would add it to an existing, outer `<div>` tag or a table. Next, you select the image. Then, from the Format menu, choose the Position option. This brings up the Position dialog box, shown in Figure 16.23.

16

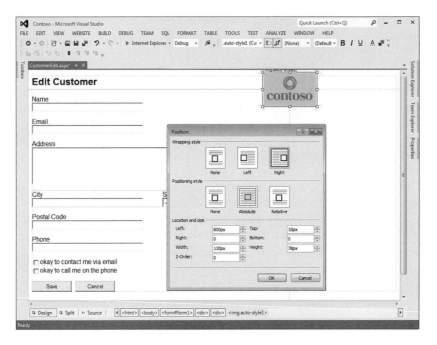

FIGURE 16.23 You can use the Position dialog box to change how a single element on a flow-layout page is positioned.

The Position dialog box enables you to indicate how a given selected item should be positioned on the page. You can see that this is similar to positioning a graphic in a Word document. You choose the wrapping style and the positioning style; in this case, the wrapping style is set to Right and the positioning style is set to Absolute. You can use the location and size information to set actual positioning. You can also use the designer to actually move the object to a new position by dragging the item around the surface.

> **TIP**
>
> The Format menu has the Set Position option. Use this for items you want to toggle between absolute and relative. After an item is set to absolute, you can drag the item to the right location.

If you intend to use absolute positioning for your entire page, you do not want to have to manually select each item and choose Position from the Format menu, which would be tedious. Instead, you can set an option that tells Visual Studio how to add controls to a page by default. You set this choice within the Options dialog box (Tools, Options). Here you navigate to the HTML Designer/CSS Styling node. Figure 16.24 shows an example. Select the last check box (Change Positioning to Absolute) to indicate that from this point forward, all controls should be added to your pages using absolute positioning.

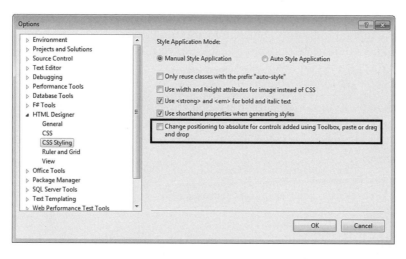

FIGURE 16.24   You can use the HTML Designer, CSS Styling options to change the default positioning for pages added to your site.

When you lay out a page using absolute positioning, all items must be put in their exact spot. For this reason, you must worry about margins and spacing issues. For example, Figure 16.25 shows the start of a page being built with absolute positioning.

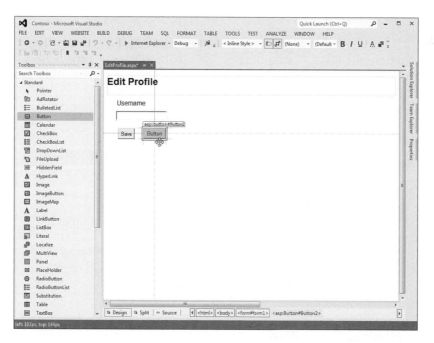

FIGURE 16.25   You can use absolute positioning to control the precise placement of controls within your page.

Here the second Button is being positioned to the right of Save and under the TextBox control. You can see the margin indicators and alignment lines. However, if additional items need to be added between the TextBox and the Button controls, each Button has to be moved and repositioned. With flow layout, the items just move or you would insert a row in the table.

When an item is absolute-positioned on a page, the designer is simply changing the item's style behind the scenes. That is, it is setting the positioning details for each item using the style tag. For example, the following code shows the markup for the TextBox items in Figure 16.25:

```
<asp:TextBox ID="TextBox1" runat="server"
  style="z-index: 1; left: 24px; top: 125px; position: absolute">
</asp:TextBox>
```

You can see here what is happening. The position attribute is set to absolute and the left and top positions are set. For this reason, items in the markup for absolute positioned pages do not typically follow in the order in which they exist on the screen. Rather, they are put into the markup in the order in which they are added to the page.

Also, notice that the code indicated something called z-index. This enables you to do layering in your output. Each item is on a layer (in this case, layer 1). Layers may overlap one another. You can change the layer in markup. Alternatively, you can use the Order option from the Format menu and choose either Bring to Front to bring the selected items to the top layer or Send to Back to push all the items to the back-most layer.

Visual Studio provides tools to help with web forms that use absolute positioning. These tools can be accessed from the Format menu or the Layout toolbar. The tools enable you to do things like make two objects the same size, align objects relative to one another, and change an items layering. Of course you might be better served setting many of these properties using a style sheet and CSS. However, Figure 16.26 shows you the options in the Layout toolbar.

TIP

If you use flow layout, you generally do not need to be concerned with the tab order of your controls (the order in which controls are accessed in the browser when a user presses the Tab key). That is because the browser tabs through the controls in the order they exist inside the page's markup. In flow layout, this order is the same order in which the controls are displayed. However, if you use absolute positioning, the controls in the markup could be in a different order than that of their display. In this case, you need to set the TabIndex property of each control to the order you want to have them accessed (1, 2, 3, and so on).

Creating a Common Look and Feel

When you create a website, you want the pages to look as if they all belong to one application. The navigation should be standard, the colors and fonts should match for like items, and sizing should be consistent. Users should not feel as though they are jumping sites simply by navigating from one page to the next. In addition, you don't want to have to manage this consistency across every single page in the site. This would be extremely tedious when you need to make a change to, for example, how all buttons in your site look.

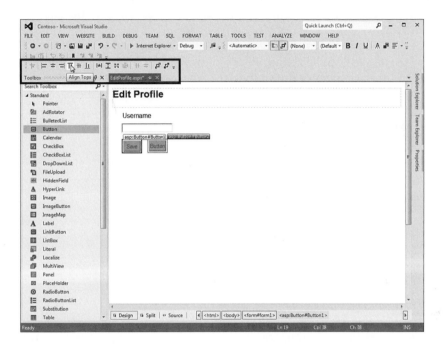

FIGURE 16.26   You use the Layout toolbar to help position and align controls on a web form.

Thankfully, you have the tools to support a consistent look across pages and make the management of it all much easier. Visual Studio provides support for building styles, managing them, and applying them to your pages. In addition, you can leverage style sheets at the site level, master pages, and themes. Let's take a look at all of these.

Styles and Style Sheets Basics

Styles and style sheets allow you to define a common look and behavior. You can then apply that common look to multiple items within your page and application. In this way, if you decide to change something, you can change it in one place and all the places that use the style will be updated.

Inline Styles   A style simply defines the look of a given item. You can create inline styles that use the style attribute for a given form element to indicate how that element looks. In the following code, there is an inline style that sets the font, font size, and color for a label control:

```
<asp:Label ID="Label1" runat="server" Text="Edit Customer"
  style="font-family: Arial; font-size: large; color: Blue">
</asp:Label>
```

Inline styles do not offer much in the way of reuse. Instead, you have to define the style for every item on every page. This is okay for the occasional, unique circumstance. However, it quickly becomes unmanageable if you are trying to keep like items on like pages looking alike. In these cases, it's best to abstract the style definition from the item by putting the style definition in a style class. In the preceding example, you might define the inline style in a class called titleText. You can then save this class either at the page level or the site level in a style sheet.

Page-Level Styles   A style class can be defined in one of two places: in the page itself or in a style sheet linked to the page. If you define a style class in the page itself, it is applicable to only that page (and not the rest of the pages in the site). Styles defined at the page level are embedded in the <head> section of the XHTML. For example, the following markup abstracts the same style discussed previously into a page-level style:

```
<head runat="server">
  <style type="text/css">
    .titleText
    {
      font-family: Arial;
      font-size: large;
      color: Blue;
    }
  </style>
</head>
```

To apply this style to the form element, you set its Class property for HTML controls or the CssClass property for ASP.NET controls. The following shows an example for the Label control discussed previously:

```
<asp:Label ID="Label1" runat="server" Text="Edit Customer"
  CssClass="titleText"></asp:Label>
```

Element Styles (Style Rules)   You can create a style rule for an HTML element. This style rule applies for all HTML elements (and their related ASP.NET counterpart) of the given type automatically. That is, you do not have to assign the style to the element; it simply picks up the style.

For example, suppose that you want to manage how hyperlinks on your site look when a user hovers the mouse pointer over them. To do so, you can define a style inside a style sheet for the anchor tag's hover (a:hover) behavior. Inside the style, you might set the color, name, and size of the font. You might also turn off underlining when a user hovers over the link. After you've defined this style, you apply it to the page. All anchor tags on the page then use the given style definition. The following code shows an example of an element style rule:

```
a:hover
{
  font-family: Tahoma;
  font-size: 10pt;
  color: #0099FF;
  text-decoration: none;
}
```

Style Sheets   A style sheet represents a file that contains a set of styles to be applied to multiple pages. In this way, you can abstract all your styles away from a single page, centralize them, and manage them as a group. Visual Studio creates a default style sheet when you define a new website. This file is called Site.css and can be found inside the Content directory. It contains definitions for many of the most common HTML elements that are stylized. This makes it a great starting point.

Inside a style sheet file, you can add HTML element styles and your own style classes. The code for these styles looks just like the code we've shown thus far.

Pages are linked to a style sheet to indicate the page should leverage these styles. A quick way to link a style sheet to a page is by dragging the style sheet from Solution Explorer to the form designer. This adds the link element to your code. You can also write this code manually. The link is added to the `<head>` section of the page, as in the following example:

```
<head runat="server">
    <link href="Content/Site.css" rel="stylesheet" type="text/css" />
</head>
```

You assign style classes to form elements as discussed previously. Of course, HTML elements you define as styles simply pick up the style without you having to make explicit assignment. The Visual Studio designer shows style rendering during the design process. This way, you can see how your application will look as you build it.

16

TIP

The CSS specification enables you to define style hierarchies. This can be a great way to manage the look of a given area within your site without having to apply many styles to individual elements. For example, you might apply a specific style to a `<div>` tag in your markup. Your style sheet might then define style hierarchies for elements within that `<div>` tag. In this way, you apply a style to only one element on your page, but all the elements within might also pickup styles from the style sheet.

As an example, suppose you want to define a style for a user input form that has controls for Label, TextBox, Button, and related elements. You could define the style using a hierarchy and then enclose the form itself inside a `<div>` tag. You then would only need to apply the style to the `<div>` tag itself. The following shows an example of a hierarchical style definition:

```
.userForm
{
  font-family: Arial; /* default style */
```

```
      font-size: 10pt;
}


.userForm input /* input item style */
{
  border-style: solid;
  border-width: 1pt;
  border-color: Gray;
  margin: 5px 0px 5px 0px;
}


.userForm span /* label style */
{
  font-weight: bold;
  padding: 5px 5px 5px 5px;
}
```

You can then apply this style to your form as in the following markup. Notice only the outer `<div/>` tag contains a style sheet definition:

```
<div class="userForm">
  <asp:Label ID="Label1" runat="server" Text="Name"></asp:Label>
  <asp:TextBox ID="TextBox1" runat="server"></asp:TextBox>
  <br />
  <asp:Button ID="Button1" runat="server" Text="Button" />
</div>
```

The Style Toolset

Thus far, we've looked at the basics of styles and style sheets. Of course, there is a lot more to creating styles, managing them, and applying them to your site. Thankfully, Visual Studio has a number of tools built-in to help us work with styles. Let's examine these tools.

Creating a Style Sheet   You can add one or more style sheets to an application through the Add New Item dialog box (refer to Figure 16.15). You can open a style sheet in the Visual Studio code editor. When you do, Visual Studio presents a Style Sheet toolbar, the CSS Outline window pane, and the actual contents of the style sheet. Figure 16.27 shows these items.

The middle pane of Figure 16.27 shows the contents of the style sheet. You can manually edit the style sheet from here. Of course, being able to edit it requires you to have a decent working understanding of CSS. Visual Studio also provides IntelliSense to help guide you.

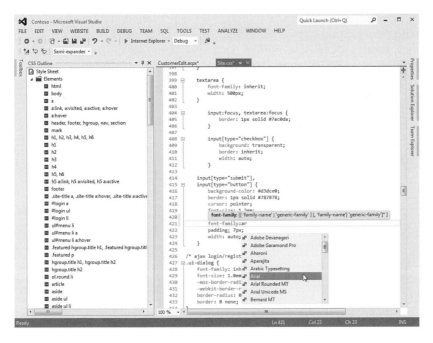

FIGURE 16.27   You can use the style sheet code editor and related tools to manage your style sheet markup.

The CSS Outline pane (left side of Figure 16.27) opens by default when you open a style sheet. You can use this pane to quickly find element styles and your custom classes. This pane simplifies the view for style sheets that are very large.

The Style Sheet toolbar (bottom toolbar in Figure 16.27) has just a few options. The first one on the left launches the Build Style Rule dialog box. You can also right-click a style inside the editor to gain access to building the style using the Modify Style dialog box. The next couple of buttons on the toolbar enable you to comment and uncomment style code in the editor. Finally, the drop-down allows you to change the layout of the XHTML in the style sheet. You have three options: Compact, Semi-Expanded, and Expanded. These options indicate if your styles are spread across a single line (Compact) or expanded across multiple lines. After you change this setting, you must right-click an open .css file and choose Format Document to change the layout of the markup.

Building a Style

You can code a style directly using the code editor or you can use the Modify Style dialog box to do so. The Modify Style dialog box provides access to key style attributes using an easy-to-use dialog box. After you build your style, the tool generates the correct markup and puts it in your style sheet file.

You can access the Modify Style dialog box by right-clicking inside an existing style, by selecting the Build Style option from the Style menu, or by clicking the Build Style option on the Style toolbar. Figure 16.28 shows an example. This figure represents the many options for controlling the font on a style. The Modify Style dialog box has many more options, such as backgrounds, tables, and borders. In addition, the Layout and Position items enable you to control how CSS positioning works.

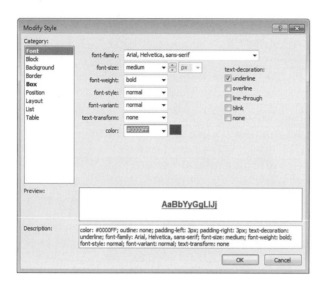

FIGURE 16.28   You can quickly build your style definition using the Modify Style dialog box.

Clicking the OK button on the Modify Style dialog box saves your changes to the style sheet. Changes are saved as they appear at the bottom of the dialog box in the Description box.

Managing Styles   Visual Studio has a Manage Styles pane that enables you to easily work with and apply styles. This pane shows the styles available for a given page, enables you to create a new style, attach a style sheet to your page, apply a style to a control, and more. This makes working with styles a fluid and fast process.

You can access the Manage Styles pane from the View menu (View, Manage Styles). This dialog is only applicable when you have a page open in Design mode. By default, the Manage Style pane loads to the left side of the IDE. Figure 16.29 shows the Manage Styles pane loaded for the EditCustomer.aspx page.

There are a number of items to note here. The first is that the pane shows all styles available for use on the page. This includes those defined on the page (not shown but available under the grouping, Current Page) and those linked to the page through a style sheet (under the grouping, Site.css). You can use these groupings to copy items that are defined at the current page level into the style sheet (and vice versa). Visual Studio moves the markup code for you. Notice, too, that you can see a preview for the style selected (at the top). You also get the style's definition by hovering over it.

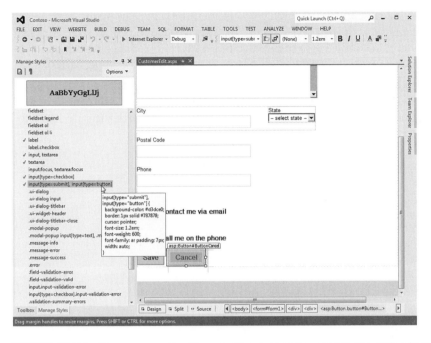

FIGURE 16.29   You can use the Manage Styles pane to manage the styles in your site and apply them to your page elements.

At the top of the Manage Styles pane is a toolbar that defines three actions. From left to right they are New Style, Attach Style Sheet, and Options. Clicking the New Style button launches the New Style dialog box. This is a version of the Modify Style dialog box discussed previously. The top of the New Style dialog box allows you to indicate the location of where you intend to define your new style (Current Page, New Style Sheet, or Existing Style Sheet).

The attach style sheet toolbar button (second from left) opens the Select Style Sheet dialog box. You use this dialog box to select an existing style sheet and attach (link) it to the page.

The Options button (top-right corner of the Manage Styles pane) enables you to filter how the styles are shown in the list. Options include categorizing styles by element, type, or order. You can also indicate that you want to see all styles, only those used on the current page, or only those used inside the items currently selected on the page.

Finally, you can right-click a style in the menu and execute one of many options. These include applying the style to the selected item in the designer and navigating to the code behind the style. You can also modify the style, delete it, or make a new style by copying the selected style.

Applying a Style   You can apply a style to a given element on a page in many ways. You have seen a couple already. In the previous section, you saw that you could select a style in the Manage Styles pane and choose the Apply Style option from the context menu. There is also a pane similar to Manage Styles called Apply Styles (View, Apply Styles).

The Apply Styles pane behaves almost exactly like the Style Manager. One difference is that you can see a visual representation of the style on the style name itself instead of at the bottom of the pane as in the Style manager (see Figure 16.30). Click the style name to apply it to your selection.

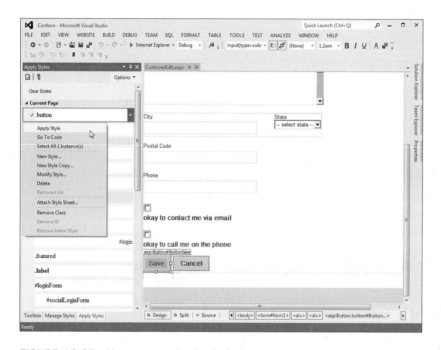

FIGURE 16.30   You can use the Apply Style option.

Another way to apply styles to your elements is in the markup itself. The good news is that both styles defined on the page and those linked as a style sheet are available inside IntelliSense. Figure 16.31 shows an example of applying the button style to an ASP.NET Button control.

Finally, you can also set an item's style inside the Property window. Simply select an item and view its properties. The property CssClass provides a drop-down of all styles available for the given element.

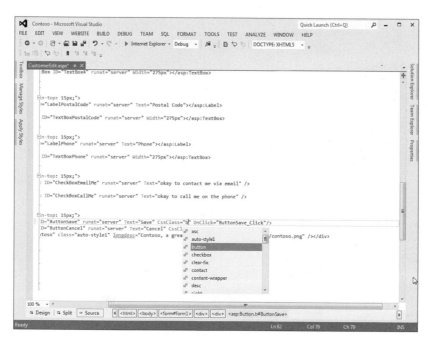

FIGURE 16.31   You can apply styles from the markup editor using IntelliSense.

Editing Styles   You can edit styles in various ways. You can right-click the code and choose Build Style to open the Modify Style dialog box. In addition, Visual Studio has the CSS Properties pane (View, CSS Properties) for editing styles. This pane enables you to see all the properties of a given style in a property editor form. Figure 16.32 illustrates this.

Notice that a Save button is selected. The CSS Properties pane then shows the applied rules and their style information for the selected item. You can edit the properties of the given style from this pane. An edit to a style here applies to wherever the style is defined. In this example, the edit is to the input element as it relates to submit and buttons. This element style rule is defined inside the Site.css style sheet file. The edit shows up immediately in the design window. It is also stored back in the .css file.

You can also use the CSS Properties pane to set and modify styles for individual items on the page. To do so, you first select an item on the page. You can then right-click inside the Applied Rules area of the CSS Properties pane and select, New Inline Style. This adds a style definition to the markup for the selected item. You can then use the CSS Properties section to set values for this specific item. The values are stored just with this item on the given page (and not in a style sheet).

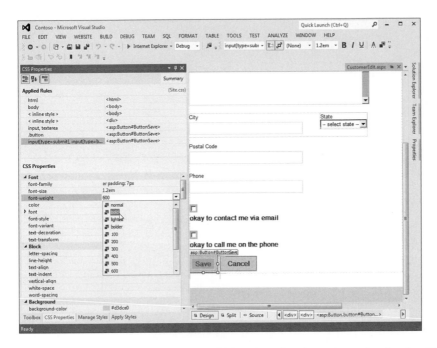

FIGURE 16.32   You can manage the CSS styles of a given element using the CSS Properties pane.

Master Pages

Master pages enable you to visually design a common look for your application in one file and then use that look in other files. This way you can centralize navigation, headers, and footers. In addition, when you derive a page from a master file, Visual Studio displays the contents of both pages at once inside the designer. This helps developers see how their page looks in the context of the overall site as they build it.

Creating a Master Page   You add a master page to your project through the Add New Item dialog box. You can have multiple master pages in your application. This capability can be especially useful if your application has more than one default layout (or look) for certain areas of the site. It is most common to have a master page that includes common navigation, common graphics, and a common footer. You can also nest master pages within one another (more on this to follow).

> **NOTE**
>
> The website template in Visual Studio 2012 includes a master page by default called Site.master. This can be a great starting point for customizing with your own details.

A master page defines the main HTML for the page. This includes the opening and closing HTML tags, head, body, and form. Inside the master page are one or more

ContentPlaceHolder controls. These controls indicate areas on the page where content pages (pages that derive from the master) may place their content.

Master pages also have their own code-behind file. This file should contain all code that relates to the workings of the master page itself. If there are working controls on the page, a menu for example, their code would go inside this code-behind file. In addition, the master page has its own set of page events (just like a standard .aspx page).

Figure 16.33 shows an example of a the standard master page that ships with Visual Studio. Notice that this master page is laid out using flow layout and CSS positioning. The selected area in the center contains a ContentPlaceHolder control with the ID MainContent) This is the only place where content pages that use the master page can add their page-specific content.

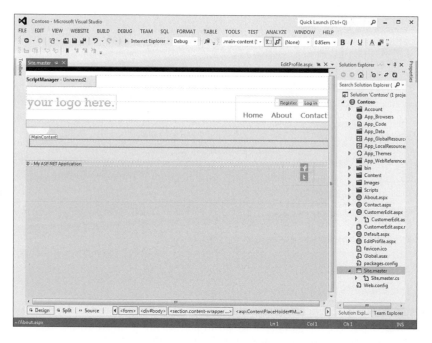

FIGURE 16.33   Use a master page to control the default look and navigation of your site.

Creating a Content Page   When a user makes a request to your ASP.NET Web Forms site, they are typically requesting a page by name such as http://www.contoso.com/customerEdit.aspx. Upon this request, ASP.NET combines the contents of the customerEdit.aspx page with any master page and returns a single response to the user.

You have the option to select a master when you add a new web form to your site. This option is titled Select Master Page and can be found at the bottom of the dialog box (refer back to Figure 16.15). When you select this option, you are presented with available master pages in your application.

When your content page opens in design view, you see the content of the master page in the background. In the foreground you see Content controls for any ContentPlaceHolder controls that were added to the master page. This is where you add controls specific to your page. This provides a separation of functionality between what belongs to your page and what belongs to the master. You work with the web form as you would any other ASP.NET web form. You add controls to the form and write event code in the code-behind file.

Figure 16.34 shows an example. This web page was created to edit a customer's profile; it is based on the application's master page. Notice that the content page has the same extension as any web form (.aspx).

> **NOTE**
>
> Control layout and positioning can be important when you work with content areas. If you have turned on absolute positioning, for example, the content placeholder acts more as a guide. Because of the nature of this layout option, the content placeholder cannot restrict you from placing your controls anywhere on the page. The flow layout option, however, has the opposite effect. Controls are allowed only inside the content areas unless otherwise marked as absolute-positioned.

> **TIP**
>
> You can use the Master object to reference the master page from the code within your content page's code-behind file. For example, suppose you have a label on the master page called LabelInstructions. You might need to set the value of this label from within each content page. You need to find the control used by the master page for the instruction text. You could then set the appropriate property on this control. The code to find the control on a master page looks like the following:
>
> ```
> Label lb = (Label)this.Master.FindControl("LabelInstructions");
> ```
>
> You could then use the variable lb to set the text on this label.

Adding Content to the `<head/>`

By default, the Visual Studio generated master page includes a ContentPlaceHolder control inside the `<head/>` area of the HTML. This enables child pages to add information to the `<head/>` tag for the page such as a style definition or JavaScript code. The following markup shows an example of this placeholder inside a master page:

```
<head runat="server">
  <asp:ContentPlaceHolder ID="HeadContent" runat="server" />
</head>
```

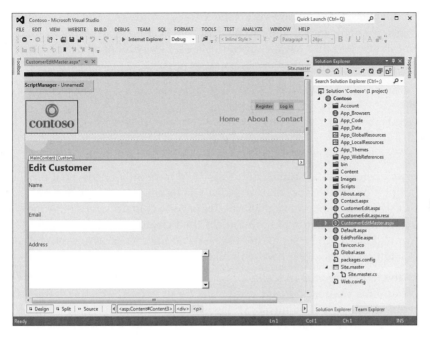

FIGURE 16.34   You add content to Content controls inside a page that uses a master page.

The page that derives from a default master page includes a Content control for the `<head/>` area of the page. For example, the following adds a `<body/>` style to the `<head/>` area of the child page:

```
<asp:Content ID="Content1" ContentPlaceHolderID="HeadContent" Runat="Server">
  <style type="text/css">
    body
    {
      font-family: Arial;
      font-size: 14pt;
    }
  </style>
</asp:Content>
```

TIP

You set the title for a page that uses a master page inside the @ Page directive. The Title attribute is used for this purpose. This ensures a `<title/>` tag is appropriately added to your page. The master page takes care of this.

One drawback for public-facing sites that used earlier versions of ASP.NET was that you could not easily set the meta tags for pages that derived from a master page. This made it difficult to add important keyword and description information used by search engines.

Thankfully, version 4.0 and later of ASP.NET adds the MetaKeywords and MetaDescription properties to the Page class. This means you can now set these values as attributes of the @ Page directive. You can also add the `<meta/>` tag to the `<head/>` section of a page or to the HeadContent Content control. The following shows an example:

```
<asp:Content ID="Content1" ContentPlaceHolderID="HeadContent" Runat="Server">
  <meta name="keywords" content="customer, shopper, edit" />
  <meta name="description" content="Used to edit a customer profile" />
</asp:Content>
```

Nesting Master Pages   Before Visual Studio 2008, you could have only one level of master page. You could not nest one inside the other and view the results in the designer. For example, a common scenario is to define a main master page to contain your site's frame, navigation, footer information, and the like. You might then create separate, submaster pages for various content types. These submaster pages would have their own, central design elements in addition to those defined by the main master page.

Visual Studio 2008 and later support this scenario. You can create an initial master page. You can then create another master page and select a master page from which it derives. In this way, you build up a master page hierarchy. Figure 16.35 shows doing just that. Note the highlighted area: Select Master Page.

FIGURE 16.35   You can use the Add New Item dialog box to create a master page that nests inside another master page.

With the new nested master page, you can define master content inside the content place-holder defined by the main master page. You then add a new content placeholder inside your nested page. Pages based on this nested master page put their content inside this area. Of course, you can go multiple levels deep with nested master pages. The designer shows your various master pages during design.

Themes and Skins

Visual Studio 2005 first introduced the concept of themes for a website. This feature enables you to define one or more specific looks for the controls that make up your application. After you do, you can switch between them based on user preference, company affiliation, or similar factors.

At first glance, it seems that themes provide nearly the same experience as style sheets. However, themes go a few steps further. First, they leverage style sheets. Each theme can have an associated style sheet. Themes can also be applied in such a way as to work with an existing style sheet or to override it (see "Applying a Theme to a Site or Page," later in this chapter). The next difference is that themes enable you to embed graphic files as part of the themes. In this way, you can switch from one set of graphics to another based on a theme's name. Themes also enable you to define skin files for your ASP.NET controls. These skin files enable you to set property values of a control that fall outside mere styles; these property values must be nonbehavioral, however. Lastly, a theme for a page can be set (and changed) at runtime. You can modify a property of the Page object to do so, which enables you to quickly switch your site's look.

> **NOTE**
>
> Unlike style sheets, only one theme can apply to a site at any given time.

16

Creating a Theme   Themes are created inside the App_Themes folder. Each theme gets its own theme folder. The name of the theme is the name of the folder (which must be unique). This ensures that no confusion occurs when applying a theme. You apply a theme to a page or your site using the folder's name.

For example, suppose that you are building an application to manage customer details and orders. Assume that this application is accessed by different companies. Therefore, company A would manage its customers, and company B would manage its customers. In this scenario, the site owner might define a different theme for each company. Perhaps the theme is based on each company's colors, fonts, and graphics.

To create a theme, you typically follow a standard set of steps:

1. You must first create the App_Theme directory through the context menu. Right-click your website and choose Add ASP.NET Folder and then Theme. Alternatively, you might add a skin file to your application through the Add New Item dialog box and then Visual Studio creates the App_Theme directory automatically for you to house the skin file. Remember to give your theme a name.

2. When you have the App_Theme directory, you can right-click it to add a new theme folder, which you can find under the Add ASP.NET Folder menu. You should name the theme folder with the name of your theme.

3. Next, you add the files that make up your theme. These files typically include a style sheet, any images or resources, and a skin file.

Figure 16.36 shows the folder and file structure based on the example we discussed here. There are three themes: one called Contoso (company A), one called Fabrikam (company B), and a noncompany theme (MainTheme).

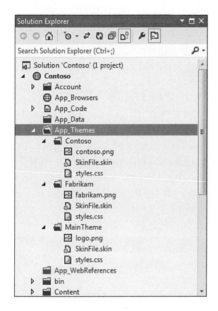

FIGURE 16.36   You add themes to the App_Themes directory for your site.

Creating a Skin File   We have already discussed style sheets. What we need to look at now is defining a skin file. You can have one or more skin files in your theme. You might want to create a new skin file for each control you intend to skin. Alternatively, you might want to define a single skin file for your entire theme. The choice is yours.

Inside the skin file are control skin definitions called skins. You declare each skin just as you would write the markup for a given control on a web page. The syntax is similar. However, you omit the property assignments for the control that do not pertain to the skin (look and feel).

There are two types of skin definitions: named skins and unnamed skins. A named skin is created by using the attribute SkinId. This enables you to define a unique name for the skin declaration. In this case, only controls in your site with this same SkinId are affected by the skin declaration. On the other hand, unnamed skins apply to all controls of a similar type. For example, if you want all your Button controls to look a similar way, you create an unnamed skin for the Button control. When you apply the skin to a page, all buttons pick up this look. Let's look at an example.

For this example, say you want to define a few skins to define your theme. You define named skins for the customer logo on the master page and the title labels on each screen. You then create unnamed skins for Label, TextBox, Button, and GridView controls.

Listing 16.1 shows the sample skin file. At the top are the named skins. Notice the use of the SkinId attribute. Again, this attribute is used when the skin is applied to specific instances of these types of controls (image and label in this case). Below this are the skins that apply to standard controls. There is one for all Button, Label, TextBox, and GridView controls. Notice that the GridView definition includes definitions for the many parts of the control. You nest these definitions within the GridView definition as you would on any ASP.NET page.

You also need a similar file for company B (Fabrikam). To create it, you copy and paste this file to that company's directory. You then make minor edits to the image skin and the fonts and colors of the other skin definitions. We next look at applying these skins to the pages in the site.

LISTING 16.1   The Contoso Skin File

```
<%-- named skins --%>
<asp:Image runat="server" SkinID="CustomerLogo"
 ImageUrl="~/App_Themes/Contoso/contoso.png"/>


<asp:Label runat="server" SkinID="TitleLabel"
 Font-Names="Arial Black"
 Font-Size="X-Large" />


<%-- default, control skins --%>
<asp:Button runat="server" Width="80px" Height="24px"
 BackColor="#FFFFFF" ForeColor="MidnightBlue"
 Font-Name="Tahoma" Font-Size="10pt"
 BorderColor="#003399" BorderStyle="Solid" />


<asp:Label runat="server" ForeColor="MidnightBlue"
 Font-Names="Arial" Font-Size="Small" />


<asp:TextBox runat="server" Width="265px" BackColor="White"
 BorderColor="MidnightBlue" BorderStyle="Solid" BorderWidth="1px"
 Font-Names="Arial" Font-Size="Small" />


<asp:GridView runat="server" CellPadding="4" ForeColor="#333333" GridLines="None">
 <FooterStyle BackColor="#5D7B9D" Font-Bold="True" ForeColor="White" />
 <RowStyle BackColor="#F7F6F3" ForeColor="#333333" />
 <EditRowStyle BackColor="#999999" />
 <SelectedRowStyle BackColor="#E2DED6" Font-Bold="True" ForeColor="#333333" />
 <PagerStyle BackColor="#284775" ForeColor="White" HorizontalAlign="Center" />
```

```
<HeaderStyle BackColor="#5D7B9D" Font-Bold="True" ForeColor="White" />
<AlternatingRowStyle BackColor="White" ForeColor="#284775" />
```

```
</asp:GridView>
```

TIP

There is not much tool support for defining skin declarations. You are forced to manually enter this markup. However, a common shortcut can be to create a page that includes each control in the theme. You then use the designer to edit the controls on the page. Finally, you copy this markup from the page to the skin declaration and then delete any unwanted declaration code (including the ID tag).

Applying a Theme to a Site or Page

You can apply a theme in a few different ways. Each is meant to provide a different level of control. For example, you can set a global theme for an entire server. You can configure a theme for just one website. You can also choose to configure a theme at the individual page level. Finally, you can apply a single skin to a single control. You can see that these levels go from the very macro (server) to the granular (control). Most websites fall somewhere in the middle, like applying a theme at the page or site level.

You apply a theme at the page level by using the @ Page directive inside the page's markup. You have a couple of options here. You can decide that your theme should always trump all control settings. That is, if a developer explicitly sets a control value and that value is overridden by the theme, then the theme takes precedence. This type of declaration looks like the following:

```
<%@ Page Theme="Contoso" %>
```

Alternatively, you can set what is called a StyleSheetTheme at the page level. This indicates that the theme applies only where controls do not have explicit overriding values. In the previous declaration, the theme overrides local control settings. Using the StyleSheetTheme, you can set the theme to apply only to control settings that are not explicitly set. That is, if the control has a value for a given attribute, that value is used. If it does not, the theme's value is used. You set this type of theme for the page as shown here:

```
<%@ Page StylesheetTheme="Contoso" %>
```

You can define the theme for an entire website through the configuration file. This enables you to set a theme and then change it without recompiling your code. To do so, you add the Theme or StylesheetTheme (see the preceding example) attributes to the pages element inside the <system.web> node. The following is an example:

```
<system.web>
  <pages theme="Contoso" />
</system.web>
```

To define just the style sheet theme, use the following:

```
<system.web>
  <pages stylesheetTheme="Contoso" />
</system.web>
```

You can also set a theme inside your code. This capability can be useful if you are allowing users to choose their theme or you are dynamically setting a theme based on some user information. Recall the example with two companies: company A and company B. Remember, a theme file was defined for each. If you determine within your code that a member of company A (Contoso), for example, has logged in, then you set the theme this way:

```
Page.Theme = "Contoso"
```

TIP

You can make changes to a theme file or skin without recompiling your site. These changes are applied on the next browser refresh.

To set a theme for a single control, you use the SkinID attribute of the control. This ID can be set to reference a particular skin inside a skin file. The skin definition has the same skin ID as the one used inside the markup. You can set the skin ID from the markup or by using the Properties window for a given control open in the designer. The Properties window provides a drop-down list of skins that are available for the given control type. For example, to create an image control that picks up the skin definition, you define this control as follows; in this case, the image control is inside the site.master page:

```
<asp:Image ID="ImageLogo" SkinID="CustomerLogo" runat="server" />
```

You can also set the skin ID programmatically. The following is an example:

```
ImageLogo.SkinId = "CustomerLogo"
```

NOTE

One drawback of using themes is that you cannot see them applied to your page in the designer. Instead, you see only styles applied inline, at the page level, or through a linked style sheet. To see your content with the theme applied, you must run your page in a browser.

Creating a User-Configurable UI

ASP.NET provides support for creating a user interface that can be configured and personalized by each individual user of a site. For example, if you have ever worked with Microsoft Office SharePoint Server or visited sites like MSN.com, you might have noticed that blocks of functionality define a given page. These blocks can be removed, added, moved around, and configured by users. To enable this functionality, the blocks all must work together as part of a portal framework. ASP.NET has just such a framework built in to the product.

The following sections provide an overview of creating a configurable UI using the Web Part controls. We walk through the basics of building a Web Part page that enables users to monitor customers in a customer management application. We cover the many basics of Web Parts. We are not, however, able to cover everything. Web Parts is a big topic. This section should get you started in the right direction.

> **NOTE**
>
> The Web Part controls built in to Visual Studio also rely on the personalization features of ASP.NET. For this reason, they require you to run a version of the ASPNETDB database, which is installed for you when you run your first Web Part page. The database, by default, is a SQL Express database and requires SQL Express on your machine.

Working with the Web Part Controls

ASP.NET includes many Web Part controls and classes; the Visual Studio Toolbox alone defines 13 Web Part controls (see Figure 16.37). In addition, the `System.Web.UI.WebControls.WebParts` namespace contains nearly 100 classes. These controls and classes work together to manage the structure of a Web Part page, its personalization and configuration, and the presentation itself.

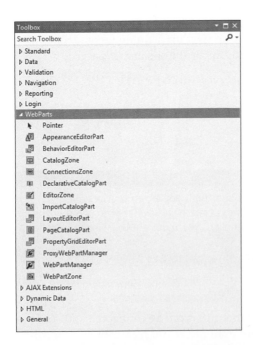

FIGURE 16.37   You use the many Web Part controls to provide web pages that allow for user customization.

When you create a basic Web Part page, you typically work with three types of controls: the WebPartManager, WebPartZone, and presentation controls themselves. The first control, WebPartManager, is actually required of all Web Part pages. It is the control responsible for managing the Web Parts on the page. You must define this control on each Web Part page and can define only one per page. The WebPartManager is responsible for tracking the controls and their zones throughout the page. It also manages the state that a page might be in, such as view or edit mode.

The second control, WebPartZone, enables you to manage the layout or "zones" of your page. A zone represents an area of the page where controls or features can be placed. To understand zones, you can think of your page in terms of horizontal and vertical content zones. For example, you might have a zone at the top of your page that presents the header for the application. Beneath this, you might have two vertical zones. The leftmost zone might be used for links and navigational controls. The middle zone might contain content Web Parts. Finally, you might have another zone at the bottom of the page to manage footer-type content.

Figure 16.38 shows an example of a Web Part page broken into zones. Of course, you can define any number of zones and lay them out as you like. This is simply one example.

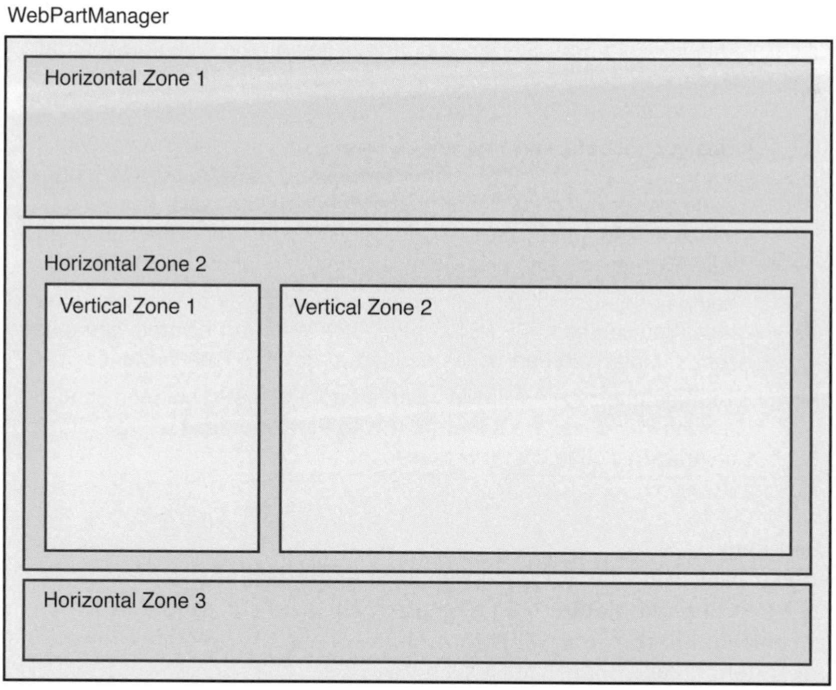

WebPartManager

FIGURE 16.38   You define multiple zones for a Web Part page.

> **NOTE**
>
> Zones also have associated styles. Each zone provides a common UI for controls within the zone. That is, they define a header, title, border, button style, and so on. This is known as the *chrome* for the controls in a given zone.

Last, you put controls into each zone of the Web Part page. These controls can be any .NET control that you want to be managed by the zone. You can also create your own user controls and Web Parts that can be placed in these zones. The advantage of the latter is that you can provide configuration capabilities for Web Parts. This enables users to edit a given Web Part's properties from within the web browser (similar to how Microsoft's SharePoint product works).

Table 16.3 provides a brief reference to the primary controls that are used to manage a Web Part page. Each of these controls can be found on the Visual Studio Toolbox (refer to Figure 16.37). These controls are all zone controls (except the manager control). As such, they constrain what type of control should be added to the given zone.

TABLE 16.3   The Web Part Zone Controls

Control	Description
WebPartManager	This control tracks the zones on the page and the Web Part controls that are in those zones. Each Web Part page requires one (and only one) instance of this control.
CatalogZone	This control defines a zone that contains one or more CatalogPart controls. The CatalogPart control provides a list of Web Parts that are available for the page. When a user is editing the page, this zone is enabled. Users then use the CatalogPart control to select one or more Web Part objects and drag them into WebPartZones.
WebPartZone	You use this control for defining the primary zones of your user interface. You can add ASP.NET controls and Web Part controls into these zones. Most Web Part pages define two or more WebPartZones.
EditorZone	You use this zone for providing an area for users to edit and configure a given Web Part. The editor for a Web Part is defined as an EditorPart control. This zone contains these types of controls.

Creating a Web Part Page

You create a Web Part page using any standard web form (.aspx). For the following example, create a form titled MonitorCustomer.aspx. The next step is to drag a WebPartManager control onto this form. This control has no visual appearance on the form. Instead, it is simply necessary to create a Web Part page.

> **TIP**
>
> Inside Visual Studio's form designer, you can decide to show or hide controls that have no visual appearance. To do so, you use the View menu, Visual Aids submenu, and check or uncheck the option ASP.NET Non-Visual Controls. Nonvisual controls show up as gray boxes inside the designer. The box typically contains a control's name and ID.

Defining Zones   Next, you add the zones to the page. Recall that the zones define where your Web Parts can exist and how they look and are sized. You can lay out your zones inside a table, use absolute positioning to place zones in specific areas, or use relative positioning. If you allow users to hide or close the controls in a zone, you might consider a table or relative positioning. If your zones are static, however, you should use absolute positioning.

In our example, we use an HTML table. First, create three rows: the top for the page title, the middle to house Web Parts, and the bottom for a footer. Inside the middle row, define a new HTML table with three columns.

Each column contains a zone for the page. The left zone contains Web Parts related to customers, the middle zone contains information related to orders and statistics, and the rightmost zone allows users to modify the Web Parts displayed on the page. At this point, your form should look something like the one defined in Figure 16.39. Note that the page is shown without the theme definition applied.

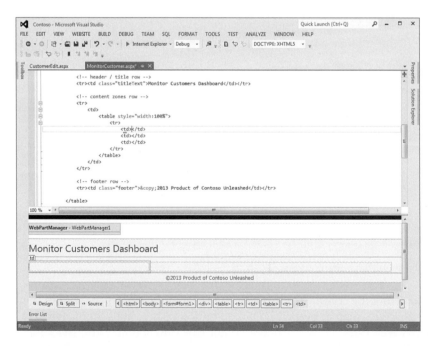

FIGURE 16.39   You can use an HTML table to define the layout of a Web Part page. (You could also use `<div>` tags and CSS.)

Next you lay out the web part zones inside the center row's HTML table. You can follow these steps to lay out the zones:

1. Drag a WebPartZone control from the Toolbox into the first column of the table.

2. Set the HeaderText property of the first control to **Customer Links**. This enables people editing the page to see a zone name (and your intentions for the zone).

3. Set the first control's ID property to WebPartZoneCustomerLinks.

4. Repeat steps 1 to 3 for the middle column in the row. This time, call the Web Part zone **Customer Statistics**. This takes the most screen area and enables users of this screen to find orders and view stats.

5. Add a CatalogZone control to the rightmost column of the middle row. This Web Part enables users to customize what they see on the screen.

At this point, your Web Part page should look something like what's shown in Figure 16.40.

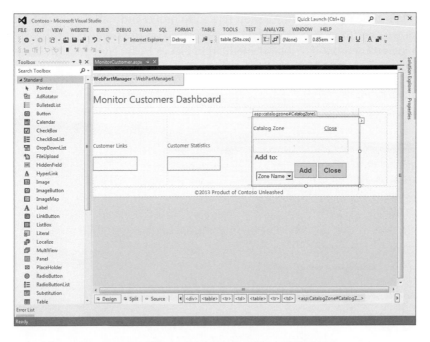

FIGURE 16.40   The Web Part zone controls added to the page.

The next step is to define the chrome for the Web Parts that are placed in the zones. Chrome refers to the styles such as header, links, and buttons. There are a lot of styles for a given zone and its Web Parts. These include styles for when there is an error, styles for when things are inactive, and many more. These styles can be configured through numerous properties of the zone. You can also use the smart tag-associated Auto Format to customize the look of the given zone. Figure 16.41 shows an example of the AutoFormat dialog box. On the left are possible formats. On the right is a preview showing how the Web Parts in the zone look. This preview is based on actual content for the zone.

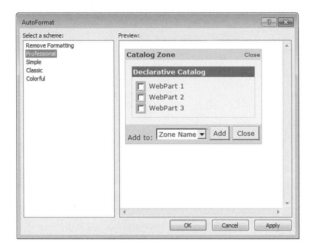

FIGURE 16.41   You can use the AutoFormat dialog box to set many of the formatting properties of a zone control simultaneously.

Adding Web Parts to Zones

Now you're ready to add Web Parts to the zones you have defined. There are a few ways to go about this. You can create actual controls that implement the WebPart class. This method allows the most flexibility for creating Web Parts, but it also happens to be the most involved method. It also enables you to create user configuration for your Web Parts. This configuration is shown when a user edits a given Web Part. Of course, it is the recommended approach for those building reusable components across a large portal.

Alternatively, a quick way to create Web Parts is by defining a user control or simply by using a standard ASP.NET control. For instance, when you drag a control such as a Label onto the form, ASP.NET defines a Web Part around the given control. This makes for an easy way to create Web Parts.

Let's look at an example of this simplified technique for creating a Web Part. The following steps you through creating a Customer Links Web Part. This Web Part provides a series of links used to manage a customer. The following steps outline the process for creating this Web Part:

1. Drag an ASP Label control inside the WebPartZone control for customer links.

2. This label is automatically turned into a WebPart control. You can see this in the markup for the page. The `<ZoneTemplate>` element is added inside the `<asp:WebPartZone>` node. Inside this goes the Label control you added to the form.

3. Set a title for the Web Part by adding the title attribute to the Label control. This attribute is picked up by ASP and applied to the Web Part.

4. Add a few links within the confines of the `<asp:Label>` declaration. The final markup looks something like Listing 16.2. Here we omitted the style information that would normally go inside the Web Part zone; this omission is for the sake of clarity.

LISTING 16.2   The Customer Links Web Part

```
<asp:WebPartZone ID="WebPartZoneCustomerLinks" runat="server">
  <ZoneTemplate>
    <asp:Label title="Customer Links" ID="Label1" runat="server" Text="Label">
      <a href="FindCustomer.aspx">Find Customer</a><br />
      <a href="FindOrder.aspx">Find Order</a><br />
      <a href="CustomerDiscounts.aspx">Customer Discounts</a><br />
    </asp:Label>
  </ZoneTemplate>
</asp:WebPartZone>
```

Repeat this method for a few more Web Parts. For the example, you might create additional label-based Web Parts inside the `<ZoneTemplate/>` area of Customer Links. Some Web Parts might include Active Shoppers, Help, and a page Edit Mode indicator. In the Customer Statistics area, you might add Web Parts for Find Orders and Top Products to round out the dashboard. You can try creating a couple of these as user controls. (For more information on user controls, skip ahead to the "Working with the ASP.NET Controls" section later in this chapter.) Also, try building out one or two of these Web Parts as tables nested inside a Label control. Figure 16.42 shows what your page might now look like inside the designer.

Enabling Users to Configure the Page   Many options are available for enabling users to customize the look and behavior of Web Parts. You can create editors for your controls that allow for full configuration on a per-control basis. You might have Web Parts that can connect (or talk to) other Web Parts. They typically require some sort of configuration. You might allow users to pick from a catalog of controls in order to determine which controls they would like to see on the page. It is also common to allow users to minimize, close, and move your controls from zone to zone. Here we look at a couple of these options.

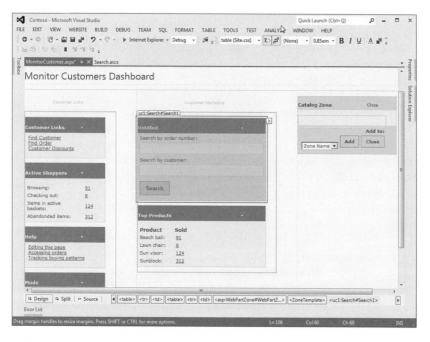

FIGURE 16.42   You can create any number of Web Parts inside the WebPartZone control's ZoneTemplate markup section.

First, let's configure our Web Part page to allow users to add Web Parts to the page as they see fit. In this way, users can determine which Web Parts they want to see on the page and where they want to see them. To modify the Web Part page to allow for this level of user customization, complete the following steps:

1. We start with a Web Part page that includes two label-based Web Parts: Customer Links and Help. The site also contains three user controls: Find Orders, Active Shoppers, and Top Products. It is these last three that we are going to turn into user-optional Web Parts. A user is able to add and remove these items from the page.

2. You use the CatalogZone Web Part to enable the management of a group (or catalog) of Web Parts. When the page was first laid out, we added this Web Part to the right-most zone. If you do not have it, add it.

3. Next, inside the CatalogZone Web Part add a DeclarativeCatalogPart. The control indicates that you declare all Web Parts that are managed in the zone. There are similar Web Parts such as PageCatalogPart, which manages all Web Parts on the page.

4. The next step is to declare the Web Parts that are managed inside the catalog by putting each user control's (or Web Part's) definition inside the DeclarativeCatalogPart section. Note you also need to add the tag <WebPartsTemplate/>. Your markup should look like the following:

```
<asp:CatalogZone ID="CatalogZone1" runat="server"
  HeaderText="Manage Web Parts">
  <ZoneTemplate>
    <asp:DeclarativeCatalogPart ID="DeclarativeCatalogPart1"
      runat="server" Title="Select a Web Part">
      <WebPartsTemplate>
      <ucl:FindOrders ID="FindOrders1" runat="server" Title="Find Orders" />
      <ucl:ActiveShoppers ID="ActiveShoppers1" runat="server"
        Title="Active Shoppers" />
      <ucl:TopProducts ID="TopProducts1" runat="server" Title="Top Products" />
      </WebPartsTemplate>
    </asp:DeclarativeCatalogPart>
  </ZoneTemplate>
</asp:CatalogZone>
```

5. The final step is to allow the user to enable editing to turn this catalog on. We will use a LinkButton control to do so. Add a LinkButton control to the bottom right of the page. Create an event handler for the LinkButton control's Click event. Inside this event handler, you need to toggle the display state of the page between Browse (normal view) and Catalog (user Web Part selection view). The following code does just that:

```
protected void LinkButtonChangeContent_Click(object sender, EventArgs e) {
  if (LinkButtonChangeContent.Text == "Change Content") {
    WebPartManager1.DisplayMode =
      WebPartManager1.SupportedDisplayModes["Catalog"];
    LinkButtonChangeContent.Text = "Finished";
  } else {
    WebPartManager1.DisplayMode =
      WebPartManager1.SupportedDisplayModes["Browse"];
    LinkButtonChangeContent.Text = "Change Content";
  }
}
```

The final step is to enable authentication for your site. Recall that personalization (changing the page content and layout) requires that the user be logged in to the site. This way, the personalization information is persisted for the logged-in user. Authentication can be set up using the ASP.NET Configuration pages accessible from the Website menu in Visual Studio. From these pages, you need to deny access to anonymous users and then add yourself as a user. See "Configuring User Authentication" later in this chapter if you are unfamiliar with this step. Also, you need a page that allows you to log in to the site. Thankfully, these pages are part of the default website template and are found in the Account folder (Login.aspx). See "The Login Controls" later in this chapter for more details.

You should now be able to run the application, log in, and select which of the three Web Parts you want to use. Figure 16.43 shows the page running in the browser. The user has clicked the Change Content LinkButton on the right to bring up the Manage Web Parts CatalogZone control. The user can select a Web Part from the list and indicate to which zone on the page it should be added. Notice, too, that the Top Products Web Part has already been added to the page by the user. Finally, users can choose to add multiple versions of the same Web Part to the page if they like.

FIGURE 16.43   Users can use the CatalogZone editor to add Web Parts to predefined zones on the page.

Another common user customization is to allow for the moving of Web Parts between the zones and above and below one another. When the user is in the catalog mode, as in Figure 16.43, this feature is enabled by default. A user can select a Web Part and move it between zones and above and below other Web Parts. However, sometimes you want to allow users to move items between zones but require another level of trust before you let them use the catalog to add and remove Web Parts from the page. In this case, you need to provide layout editing independent of content editing.

To provide layout editing independent of content editing, you need to add another control that is explicitly for editing layout independent of content selection, as follows:

1. Add an EditorZone control to the page. Adding this control creates a zone where you can put EditorParts. It is typical for you to show this zone when your page is in edit mode. In the example, assume that you are using the zone but do not intend to display it to users.

2. Add the LayoutEditorPart control to the EditorZone you just created. This control should sit inside a `<ZoneTemplate>` tag. This Web Part allows for the page's layout to be edit-enabled.

3. Create a LinkButton control for allowing a user to turn on edit mode for the page. Label this control **Edit Layout**. The design of your form should look something like that shown in Figure 16.44.

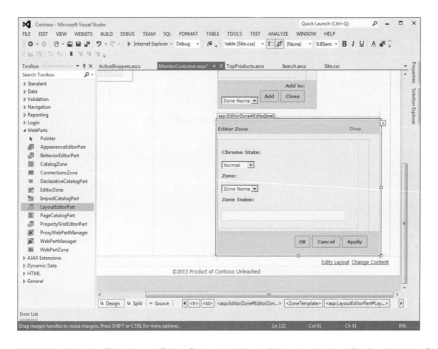

FIGURE 16.44   The LayoutEditorPart control enables users to edit the layout of the page.

4. Next you need to write some code for the LinkButton's Click event. This code is similar to the code for the change content LinkButton example. The following is an example:

```
protected void LinkButtonEditPage_Click(object sender, EventArgs e) {
  if (LinkButtonEditPage.Text == "Edit Layout") {
    WebPartManager1.DisplayMode =
      WebPartManager1.SupportedDisplayModes["Edit"];
    LinkButtonEditPage.Text = "Finish Edit";
  } else {
    WebPartManager1.DisplayMode =
      WebPartManager1.SupportedDisplayModes["Browse"];
    LinkButtonEditPage.Text = "Edit Layout";
  }
}
```

You can now run the page and view the results. When you click the Edit Layout LinkButton, the page goes into edit mode (but not content selection). Here a user can move controls between zones, rearrange them, and toggle their close versus open state. Figure 16.45 shows this in action.

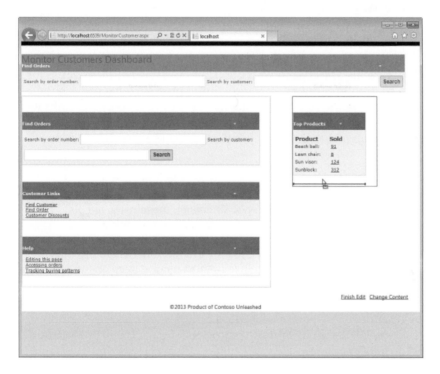

FIGURE 16.45   You can use the LayoutEditorPart control to enable users to work just with the layout of the page (and not the content displayed).

TIP

Web Part personalization is persisted from session to session. If users (or developers) close controls, you need to give them a way to get them back. You can write some code to reset personalization for a page. You might give the user a reset link, for example. Inside the event for this link, you add code that resembles the following line:

```
WebPartManagerMain.Personalization.ResetPersonalizationState()
```

This removes any personalization settings and returns you to the defaults.

Working with the ASP.NET Controls

This chapter has already covered a few of the ASP.NET controls, such as WebPart, Label, and Button. Our intent for the following sections is to provide broad coverage of the many other controls in ASP.NET. This includes the standard controls as well as controls for validation, login, navigation, and data. We also spend some time discussing user-defined controls.

An Overview of the ASP.NET Controls

Controls render your user interface to the user's browser. ASP.NET controls are considered server controls. Server controls have a few basic tenants. They exist at design time (on the Toolbox), and you can manipulate their layouts and properties. They also have associated classes in the .NET Framework. The code in your site creates instances of these classes for manipulating a given control. In addition, all server control processing happens on the web server. That is, the code of the control executes (along with your code) and emits its HTML to be sent to the user's browser. When the user posts the page back to the server, ASP.NET rebuilds the controls and then reprocesses them to build a response back to the user.

NOTE

ASP.NET also supports the standard HTML controls. By default, these items are not available to your code running on the server. However, you can add the attribute `runat="server"` to any of these controls. This enables you to work with them in your code-behind class. In general, if you do not think you will ever need access to a control on the server, it's wise to simply use the HTML controls (without running them on the server).

The ASP.NET Control Features

The ASP.NET server controls are a set of abstract controls that render their UIs in many different forms back to a user's browser. They can emit HTML and JavaScript. They store state between requests, and some work with databases. The following list outlines some of the key features found inside the ASP.NET control model:

▶ **XHTML compliance**—The ASP.NET controls are sent to the user's browser as standard HTML. All controls generate XHTML 1.1-compliant markup. This ensures that there are fewer surprises when your pages are being viewed in a web browser.

▶ **Browser detection and adaptive rendering**—The ASP.NET controls can also adapt their markup output based on the requesting browser. Therefore, they can be both XHTML compliant and browser specific. This feature works by default for ASP.NET controls. This can save a lot of time because you don't have to try to code around the various browser types. (See the note at the end of this section.)

▶ **Event model**—All the ASP.NET controls have the same server-side event model. You can write code to be called when a user triggers an event on the page, such as pulling down a drop-down or clicking a Button control.

▶ **Client event model**—The set of ASP.NET controls can participate in client-side events. That is, you can work to emit JavaScript as part of the control's rendering and call that JavaScript as part of the client's (browser's) event model.

▶ **State maintenance**—ASP.NET controls (including the HTML controls) automatically maintain state between round trips to the server. For example, suppose that a user enters a value into a text box and posts the page to the server. If you send the response back to the user, the user's entry is still maintained inside the control. This saves you from having to code this feature into your pages when doing operations such as validation processing on the server.

▶ **Data binding**—Many of the ASP.NET controls can be bound to data in your application. The data-binding model enables you to bind to many data sources such as a database, a business object, XML, and so on. In most scenarios, the binding requires little coding on your part.

▶ **Template-based layout**—Some of the ASP.NET controls provide templates to enable developers to define the control's layout. For example, you can use the ListView control to create a template that defines how the control renders when a user is editing data versus displaying it.

▶ **Skins and style support**—We have already described how themes and style sheets can be used to change the look of a site. Each ASP.NET control has support for both skins and CSS styles.

▶ **Data entry**—ASP.NET controls support layout that makes data entry easier. You can, for example, define a tab order for the controls on a page; you can set the focus to a given control; you can even assign a hotkey (or access key) to a given control. All of this is done through properties on the control. The controls themselves generate JavaScript on the client to enable these features.

▶ **Validation**—There are validation controls built into ASP.NET. The server controls work with these validation controls and ASP.NET to provide a cohesive validation model for your pages. For example, you can group a set of validation controls and manage validation at the group level (think sections of your page).

This list represents some of the basic features of the ASP.NET control set. In addition, each control has its own set of features. Experiment with each control to determine what works best for your situation. In the following sections, we discuss many of these controls.

The ASP.NET Standard Controls

There is a large set of what are called Standard controls in ASP.NET. These appear on the Toolbox in the Standard group (see Figure 16.46). Most pages you build draw heavily from this list. It includes Label, TextBox, Button, CheckBox, RadioButton, Calendar, and many more controls.

At design time, you drag one of these controls from the Toolbox onto the designer. You can then work with the control using the Properties dialog box. Each control has a host of properties for controlling appearance, behavior, accessibility, and more. You access these properties by right-clicking them in the designer and choosing Properties. You can also manage events for a given control using the lightning-bolt icon on the Properties pane toolbar.

FIGURE 16.46   You use the Standard ASP.NET controls for most data-entry scenarios.

There are many Standard controls. Table 16.4 describes a number of these.

TABLE 16.4   The Standard Controls

Control	Description
Button	Use the Button control when you expect a user to trigger an action on the page such as save, reset, or cancel. There are also the LinkButton and ImageButton controls. LinkButton behaves like a Button but looks like a hyperlink. ImageButton is similar: It behaves like a Button, but you set an image to define its look.
Calendar	Use this control when you need to allow a user to see a set of dates and select one. Use the SelectionMode property to allow a user to select a day, a week, or a month.
CheckBox	Use this control when you want to allow a user to set a setting (yes or no, on or off). Again, there is an HTML equivalent if you do not need server-side processing.
DropDownList	Use this control to provide a list of options from which a user can select. You can bind the list to data. You can also respond to a user selecting an item from the list. If you have a lot of options from which a user might need to choose, consider the List box control. There is also the CheckBoxList control for a list of multiselect items and the RadioButtonList for a list of mutually exclusive items.

Control	Description
FileUpload	Use this control to enable users to push files from their local machines or networks up to your web server.
Image	Use this control when you need to populate an image on your page dynamically (using the ImageUrl property). Static images can use the HTML `<img />` tag. There is also an ImageMap control that enables you to define sections of an image from which you can respond differently to user interaction.
Label	Use this control to provide text-based information to a user. You need a Label control only if you intend the text to be dynamic (set at runtime). If you have static text, you can typically just type it into the page using standard HTML formatting.
ListBox	Use this control when you want to allow a user to select one or more options from a set list. You can also data bind to this control.
Literal	You use the Literal control to write out HTML to the page. You typically use this control to build up markup dynamically in your code and add it to the page's rendering.
MultiView	Use this control when you want to provide multiple views to a user based on the user's selection or the state of the system. For example, you might implement a read-only view and an edit view of the same data. Each view requires that you drag a View control onto the multiview. You then add the controls you want to display for the given view to this View control. You can get similar results with multiple Panel controls. However, the MultiView control provides additional management features for you.
Panel	Use this control as a container for other controls. It is especially useful when adding controls to a page programmatically. In this case, you can call the `Panel.Controls.Add` method to do so.
RadioButton	Use this control to provide a user with a group of items from which they may select only one. Use the GroupName property to group a set of RadioButton controls that need to work together.
Table	Use the Table control to build out tables dynamically in your code. If your tables are static, consider the HTML table control.
TextBox	Use this control to allow a user to enter text-based data on your page. The TextBox control has the property TextMode. Use this property to indicate that the user's entry is a single line (default), multiple lines, or a password.
Wizard	The Wizard control is similar to the MultiView control. However, it provides the additional capabilities needed for a wizard moving from step to step (or view to view) and back again.
XML	Use this control to display XML information. You can set the XML data using the DocumentSource property. You can also provide a transform file (XSLT) that defines formatting for the XML. You set the TransformSource property to your .xslt file.

16

Validation Controls

A set of validation server controls is provided with ASP.NET. These controls enable you to indicate how user input should be validated for a page before the page is processed. In this way, you can ensure that a user has entered data in all the required fields and validate that this data meets your application's constraints.

Controls are always validated on the server and prevent an ASP page from processing if validation fails (see Figure 16.20 and the page life cycle discussed previously). The controls can emit JavaScript to be run on the client, too. (The EnableClientScript property is set to `True` by default.) In this way, a user is notified of any page-level validation errors before having to submit the page to the server.

To use the validation controls, you drag them onto your form like any other control. You want to place them near the control they validate because they provide textual clues to the user as to what is wrong with the page. A standard process is to put the validation control to the right of the control it validates. You then set the ControlToValidate property of the validation control to another control on your form (the one you want to validate).

You then typically set the Text and ErrorMessage properties of the validation control. The Text property indicates the text that should be displayed by the validation control if the validation fails. The ErrorMessage property indicates the error message that should be displayed to the user inside a ValidationSummary control for the page. The ValidationSummary groups all error messages for a user in a single area.

For example, take a look at Figure 16.47. Here you can see the validation control group in the Toolbox to the left. The page has a ValidationSummary control at the top (under Edit Customer). You can also see the Name TextBox has an associated validation control. The validation control is selected, and its properties are shown to the right. This is a RequiredFiledValidator control. With it, you can indicate a given field (in this case TextBoxName) is required to have data on submit.

Table 16.5 describes validation controls provided in ASP.NET.

TABLE 16.5   The Standard Controls

Control	Description
RequiredFieldValidator	Use this control for required fields on your page. You might combine a required field validation control with another control listed here.
RangeValidator	Use this control to validate whether a user's input is between a specified range. Use the Type property to indicate what type of range to validate, such as string, integer, double, date, or currency.

Control	Description
RegularExpressionValidator	Use this control to validate the pattern of the user's entry. You set the ValidationExpression property to a valid regular expression to do so. In addition, there are built-in regular expressions in Visual Studio. Clicking the ellipsis button in this property enables you to set standard regular expressions for such things as postal codes, email addresses, and phone numbers.
CompareValidator	Use this control to compare the user's input and validate based on this comparison. You can compare the input of the control being validated to a static value, another control, or a data type. Comparing to a data type allows you to ensure that the user has entered a valid value that can be converted to a given data type. Use the Type property to set this comparison.
CustomValidator	Use this control to write your own custom validation controls. You can write server-side validation and emit JavaScript to validate on the client.
ValidationSummary	Use this control to provide a summary of any validation errors raised by the page. The validation control's ErrorMessage property value ends up in the summary for each validation control that fails on the page.

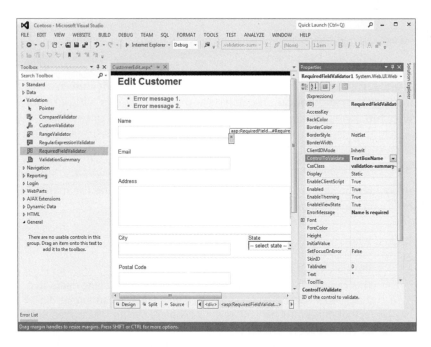

FIGURE 16.47   Use the ASP.NET validation server controls to ensure data is entered correctly for your forms.

The Login Controls

ASP.NET has a built-in set of login controls meant to provide a complete low-code (sometimes no-code) solution for managing and authenticating users. Figure 16.48 shows a list of all these controls in the Toolbox.

FIGURE 16.48   You can use the Login control to provide users a means to authenticate against your site.

By default, the Login control use what is called *ASP.NET membership*. This feature enables these controls to work with an authentication database and related features without your writing code. Membership allows for the creation of users and groups and the management of user data (including passwords). The membership services inside ASP.NET can work with a SQL Express database, SQL Server, or Active Directory. You can also write your own custom provider that can be plugged into the model.

We look at configuring membership later in this chapter. First, let's examine the many login controls. Table 16.6 provides a brief overview of these controls.

TABLE 16.6   The Login Controls

Control	Description
Login	This control provides the primary interface for challenging users for their credentials (usernames and passwords). You can format the look of the control as well as display other links and messages such as authentication errors.
	The control is set up to work with ASP.NET membership by default. If you configure it, you do not need to write code. However, if you want to write your own code, you can use the Authenticate event to write your custom scheme.

Control	Description
LoginView	This control enables you to define two views of information: a view for users who are logged in to your application and a view for anonymous users. You add controls to each view to define what users see based on their current status.
PasswordRecovery	This control is used for users to recover their passwords. Typically, you configure this control to email users their passwords. However, there are additional options as well.
LoginStatus	This control shows the authentication status of the current user. Users are either logged in or not. If they are, the control enables them to log out. If they are not logged in, the control gives them the opportunity to do so.
LoginName	This control displays the username of the currently logged-in user.
CreateUserWizard	This control enables users to create their own accounts or helps in password recovery. Users can request an account (and fill in their details) with this control.
ChangePassword	This control enables users to enter their current passwords and new passwords. The control can then validate the passwords and make the change if successful.

Configuring User Authentication

You can create a login page (or control) by dropping the Login control directly on a form. However, the ASP.NET Web Site template generates a login page (among other account related pages) for you. You can find this page in the Account directory of your site. You can open this page and make changes to your site security as necessary. Figure 16.49 shows an example.

Notice that the Login control provides access to the Administer Website link. This link takes you to the Web Site Administration Tool (WSAT) for your site, where you can begin to define how authentication and authorization should work for your site.

> **NOTE**
>
> By default, user data is sent to the server from the client as plain text. Therefore, you should enable Secure Sockets Layer (SSL) and Hypertext Transfer Protocol Secure (HTTPS) for securing your site.

The WSAT is a web-based tool that enables you to configure your site, including security. Figure 16.50 shows the Security tab for the tool. You can use the tool to define users' roles and access rules; you can also define application configuration (turn on tracing, for example) and select an administration provider. The default administration provider is configured for SQL Express (ASPNETDB.MDF). This is the place where the configuration data (such as users) for your site is stored.

16

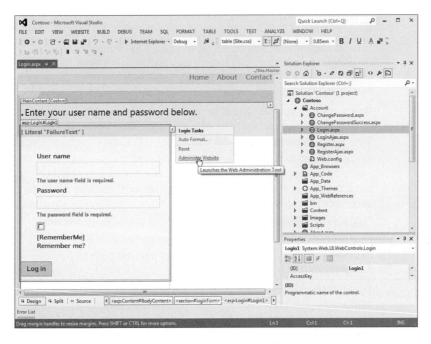

FIGURE 16.49   You can use the Login control to configure how users authenticate to your site.

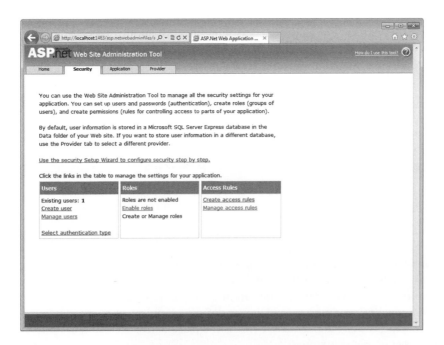

FIGURE 16.50   You use the WSAT tool to configure users and security for your site.

You can use the WSAT to change your authenticate type for your site by clicking the link and selecting the authentication type. Your options are Windows security (Active Directory on a local network) and Internet security (forms-based authentication). The former is best when working in a local area network (LAN) environment. The latter is required for most public-facing secure sites. After you configure your security model to that of Internet, ASP.NET switches you over to using the membership database for user storage.

You can use the Security tab, shown in Figure 16.50, to configure the users, roles, and access for this database. Notice the three groups at the bottom of the screen: Users, Roles, and Access Rules. These groups provide links for managing the accounts in your system. Your Login control automatically respects the information configured here. In addition, the WSAT updates your web.config file accordingly.

Site Navigation Controls

It can be easy to become lost in a lot of websites out there. If you do not provide good user navigation, chances are that users will complain (or stop visiting). ASP.NET provides a few controls to help deal with defining and controlling navigation, including the following:

▶ **Menu**—You can use this control to create menus for your web page with Visual Studio. The menus support submenus and fly-out menus. You can even bind your menus to an XML data source.

▶ **SiteMapPath**—This control enables you to leave cookie crumbs as users navigate your site. That is, you can tell them where they came from and where they are. When you do, users can use this list to jump backward to a place they just were.

▶ **TreeView**—This control could always show hierarchical data. However, it can also be bound to an XML representation of your site called a site map. In this way, you can quickly define a navigation structure for your site that is updated in a single place.

Using the SiteMapPath Control

Recall that the SiteMapPath control is used to orient users in your site. You control this orientation definition through the use of a .sitemap file. You add this file to your site through the Add New Item dialog box. Inside it, you define the logical hierarchy of your site by nesting pages inside <siteMapNode> elements.

For example, if users start at a home page, the home page is your outermost node. As a user navigates into your site, you create nested nodes. Listing 16.3 shows a simple example that includes a three-tier definition: Home, Find Customer, Edit Customer. This makes a logical progression through the sample site.

LISTING 16.3   A .sitemap File

```
<siteMap xmlns="http://schemas.microsoft.com/AspNet/SiteMap-File-1.0" >
  <siteMapNode url="Default.aspx" title="Home"  description="">
    <siteMapNode url="CustomerFind.aspx" title="Find Customer"
```

```
      description="">
      <siteMapNode url="CustomerEdit.aspx" title="Edit Customer"
        description="" />
    </siteMapNode>
  </siteMapNode>
</siteMap>
```

Figure 16.51 shows the results users see in their browsers. In this case, the SiteMapPath control was added to the page. However, if you use a master page, you could add the SiteMapPath to that so that it appears throughout the site. The control automatically picks up the content of the Web.sitemap file.

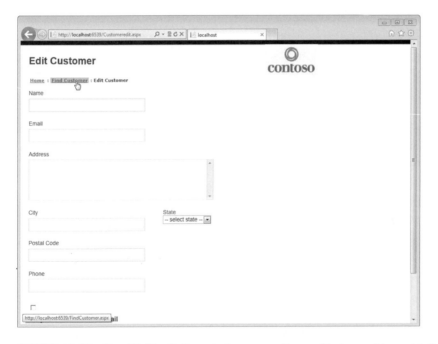

FIGURE 16.51   The SiteMapPath control uses a .sitemap file to provide navigation for users.

Data Controls

ASP.NET has a full set of controls that you can use for working with, displaying, and binding to data. These controls are meant to work with little to no additional code. Instead of writing code, you should be able to configure the controls to behave as you want. Figure 16.52 shows a list of all the data controls in the Toolbox.

FIGURE 16.52   You use the Data controls in ASP.NET to allow users to work with data inside your website.

Table 16.7 briefly describes each of these controls.

TABLE 16.7   The Data Controls

Control	Description
AccessDataSource, EntityDataSource, LinqDataSource, ObjectDataSource, SiteMapDataSource, SqlDataSource, XmlDataSource	Several data source controls are available in ASP.NET. These sources can be configured to work with the source data and execute select, update, new, and delete methods. You use a data source control to bind to other controls (such as a GridView). The ASP.NET data source controls allow access to SQL Server data, Microsoft Access data, data contained in objects, XML data, data defined as a .sitemap file, and LINQ data.
Chart	The Chart control enables you to create web pages that display data in a chart format. You can bind data to the control, display different types of charts, and allow for user interaction using AJAX.
DataList	You use this control when you want to control how your data is displayed and formatted. You can use this control with templates to gain control over when and how your data is displayed.
DataPager	This control allows you to manage the paging of data and the UI associated with that paging. You can use this control by itself or embed it as part of another control.

16

Control	Description
DetailsView	This control lets you display a single row of data (or row detail). You can display this row as an editable set of fields inside a table. The DetailsView control can be used in conjunction with the GridView control to obtain a master-detail editing structure.
FormView	This control offers the same features as the DetailsView control with the added benefit of being able to define the templates that make up the display of a given row.
GridView	This control is for binding to and working with tabular data. The control works with multiple data sources. It also allows sorting, paging, edit, add, and delete features.
ListView	This control simplifies the display of repeating data. The ListView control is driven based on user templates. In this way, you can configure how you want your UI to behave during operations such as view, edit, add, and delete. In addition, the ListView supports sorting, paging, and, of course, data binding.
QueryExtender	This control enables you to define filters for data returned by from a data source.
Repeater	This control is a container for repeating data. You use the Repeater control with a template to indicate how the contents of the repeated data should be displayed. This ListView control can be a better alternative to Repeater.

NOTE

We cover ways to work with data and databases in Chapter 20, "Working with Databases." See the section "Data Binding with Web Controls" in that chapter.

User Controls

If you still can't find the perfect control, Visual Studio provides you with the framework to create your own controls. You can take the simple approach and define a user control. A user control works a lot like a web page. You can use the designer to lay it out. It also has a code-behind and the same event model as a web page. You can create a user control and then drop it on pages across your site.

Creating a User Control

You add a user control to your project from the Add New Items dialog box. You select the Web User Control template (refer back to Figure 16.15). User controls have the extension .ascx. You define the look of your control as you would a web page. You can use the designer to drag other form elements to the page from the Toolbox. In this way, user controls are composed of one or more existing ASP.NET controls.

TIP

Visual Studio 2012 has a new feature that enables you to extract markup on a given page directly to a new user control. To use it, just highlight the markup on your web form that you want to turn into a reusable user control, right-click, and choose Extract to User Control. This creates a new user control file (.ascx), puts the highlighted markup in this file, registers your new user control on your original page, and replaces your extracted code with a call to the user control.

For example, recall the user controls discussed in the "Creating a User-Configurable UI" section. These controls could be added to a web page and used as Web Parts. Of course, you do not need to create a Web Part page to make use of a user control. You can put a user control on any ASP.NET page. Consider a control that enables a user to monitor product sales for a site similar to the one created in that section. You might define this control to allow a default set of common products as well as enable users to add their own products to the list. You can abstract this code into its own file and use it across pages.

Figure 16.53 shows an example. Here you see an .ascx user control with a SqlDataSource and GridView control. There are also controls to enable a user to type a product and add it to the monitored product list (the GridView).

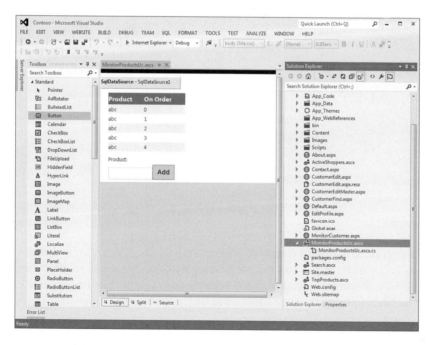

FIGURE 16.53   You can create a user control file to enable code reuse across the pages of your website.

Notice in the Solution Explorer the user control has a code-behind file. You can add a
Page_Load event here to initialize the control. You can also add a Button Click event to
handle what happens when the user clicks the Add Button control.

Adding a User Control to a Web Page

You can add a user control to a web page by dragging it from Solution Explorer onto the
web form designer. Unfortunately, user controls do not have Toolbox support. However,
they do have visual design support, as shown in Figure 16.54. In this example, the user
control, MonitorProductsUc.aspx, has been added to a web form (ProductDashboard.aspx),
which uses a master page (Site.master).

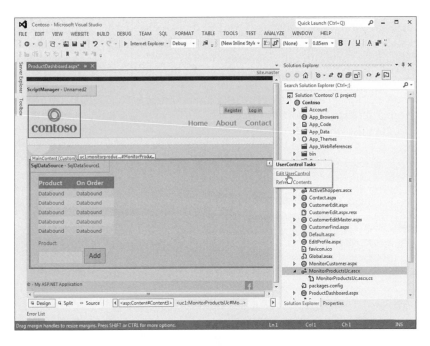

FIGURE 16.54   You can add a user control to a page by dragging it from the Solution Explorer
to the web form designer.

You work with a user control added to your web page as a single control (and not with its
constituent controls). The user control can expose properties like other controls. However,
if you need to work with the inner workings of the user control, such as positioning individual elements, you have to open the user control file in the designer.

Of course, you can add a control directly with markup, too. However, adding a control is
just a little easier using the designer. When using markup, you need to first register the
control with the page. This is done using the @ Register tag. You want to place these tags
under the @ Page directive. The @ Register tag should include the file for the user control

(the src attribute), the name used for the user control type (tagname attribute), and the prefix used to help identify the tag (tagprefix). The following shows an example:

```
<%@ Register src="MonitorProductsUc.ascx" tagname="MonitorProductsUc"
  tagprefix="uc1" %>
```

After registering the control, you can reference the control using standard markup. The following code shows an example of the control registered above:

```
<uc1:MonitorProductsUc ID="MonitorProductsUc1" runat="server" />
```

> **NOTE**
>
> We have just scratched the surface of writing your own controls in ASP.NET. For instance, one drawback of a user control is that it is site specific. That is, you cannot install it and use it across sites. You can, of course, copy and paste the file, but then you run into versioning issues. Another limitation is that you cannot provide Toolbox and full design-time support (Properties window, smart tags, and so on) for user controls. If you want to provide both design-time support and installation, you can create a *custom control*. Custom controls follow the same framework as the existing ASP.NET controls. You can even subclass and extend an existing control and turn it into your own custom version.

Building a Richer UI with ASP.NET AJAX

ASP.NET Web Forms enables you to create richer user experiences in the browser using AJAX (Asynchronous JavaScript and XML). AJAX combines JavaScript that runs in a user's browser with code running on your web server. JavaScript is a standard (ECMAScript) and therefore part of all modern browsers (IE, Firefox, Chrome, Safari) running on all platforms (Windows, Mac, and so on). Therefore, the web applications you build with it work cross-platform, cross-browser. AJAX leverages this JavaScript to call your server code asynchronously. This allows your web page and controls to update without your entire page having to update. This gives the user a much richer experience when working with your page.

The AJAX tools available to Visual Studio developers include a set of base controls known as the AJAX Extensions controls, the Microsoft AJAX code library, and access to a community-supported toolkit called the AJAX Control Toolkit. Each tool helps you better work with client-side JavaScript that adds interactivity to your user interface. This interactivity might include modal dialog boxes, progress notification, partial-page updates, and much more.

The AJAX technology also enables you to continue to leverage the investments you've made in ASP.NET Web Forms development. The AJAX extensions work with the same ASP.NET control set you are used to. AJAX is simply an addition to these controls.

NOTE

Many ASP.NET Web Forms controls have been using JavaScript on the client to provide better user interaction for a long time now. These include the validation controls for doing client-side validation, the Web Part controls for doing drag and drop of Web Parts across zones, the menu control, the TreeView control to open and view nodes, the calendar control, and more.

The ASP.NET AJAX Extensions

The controls grouped in the Toolbox under ASP.NET AJAX extensions are a set of five basic controls that serve one primary purpose: partial-page updates. Partial-page updates provide users a better experience when working with your website. Most web pages require a full refresh after the user has either requested or posted data to the server. This refresh of the page makes your entire page reload, which takes time and seems less than responsive to users (especially for large pages). A partial-page update submits only a portion of the page to the server for processing. In addition, the response returned from the server can be updated inside a portion of the page. This eliminates the refresh and makes your application more interactive for users. The ASP.NET AJAX Extensions controls work together to enable portions of a page to submit and then update independently.

The ASP.NET AJAX controls are used like any other ASP.NET control. You can drag a control from the Toolbox onto your form. You can then work with the control from the Properties window inside Visual Studio, inside your page's markup, and in your code file. Figure 16.55 shows you the list of AJAX controls available inside the Visual Studio Toolbox.

FIGURE 16.55   You access the AJAX controls from the Visual Studio Toolbox.

Notice the ScriptManager control in the Toolbox. This control is required on all pages that leverage the AJAX extensions for partial-page update. You can only have one instance of this control on your page. It is responsible for adding the Microsoft AJAX library to your page. This library is used in the asynchronous calling to and from the server during the partial-page update process.

Table 16.8 provides a list of all the AJAX Extensions controls shown in Figure 16.55. This list provides a quick-reference description of each control. You will learn more about these controls in the coming sections.

TABLE 16.8   ASP.NET AJAX Controls

Control	Description
ScriptManager	All AJAX pages you write using the standard AJAX controls listed here require a single ScriptManager control on the page. It is used by ASP.NET to manage the other AJAX controls on the page to and handle partial-page rendering, globalization, localization, and more.
ScriptManagerProxy	A page may only contain a single ScriptManager control. You might have defined a master page that contains a ScriptManager control. In this case, a page that uses the master can take advantage of partial-page updates. However, if the child page needs to add additional script files, it can use the ScriptManagerProxy control to do so. The ScriptManagerProxy may also be used with user controls that might be placed on a page that already defines a ScriptManager control.
UpdatePanel	Use an UpdatePanel when you want to group items for partial-page update. Items inside an UpdatePanel that execute a postback to the server do so only for the panel (and not the rest of the page). In this way, you get an easy model for updating only portions of your page from the server without executing a full-page refresh in the browser.
UpdateProgress	The UpdateProgress control enables you to provide the user with status information as a partial-page update is processing on the server. The UpdateProgress is used in conjunction with the UpdatePanel control. When a partial-page postback is started, progress indication is made to the user. When the postback is complete, the user is again notified.
Timer	The Timer control provides a client-side timer that lets you postback the contents of an UpdatePanel at set intervals. In this way, you can trigger partial-page updates on a periodic basis.

16

Creating a Page That Supports Partial Update

You will find that the process of creating a page using the AJAX Extensions controls is very similar to creating standard pages. There are just a few things you need to worry about. This section walks you through an example of creating an ASP.NET web form that supports partial-page update. You then build on this example to provide notification of server progress to the user's browser.

Partial-Page Update

A partial-page update posts only a portion of the page to the server; the server processes it and then updates only that portion in the user's browser. This cuts down on overhead, increases speed, and decreases server processing; users also end up with a better experience. Only the section of the page with which they are working is updated. The page does not refresh and reload. This experience seems natural and faster to most users.

In this walkthrough example, you create a web page that enables users to search for customer orders. We use the Northwind database as the source database. We then build the page such that when results are displayed a user can page through them. When they do, the data pages are implemented as partial-page updates. This ensures that users do not feel as though they are performing a new search every time they select a new page of data.

To get started, you create an ASP.NET Web Forms site. This site already supports ASP.NET AJAX; you do not need to do anything special. To create the partial-page update example, follow these steps:

1. Create a new ASP.NET Web Forms site in Visual Studio (File, New, Web Site).

2. The ASP.NET Web Forms Site template uses a master page (Site.master). Open this page to view its markup. Notice that by default this template already defines a ScriptManager control. Microsoft has made changes to how it manages scripts in Visual Studio 2012. You can see here that you explicitly indicate the scripts you want loaded for your website. In addition, these scripts can all be accessed from within the Scripts folder in Solution Explorer. Figure 16.56 shows an example of both the markup and the script files. You do not need to change anything here. Just close the master page.

3. Open the Default.aspx page. You turn this page into a form that enables users to search for customers in the database. Their search and subsequent data paging is done as partial-page updates. The next step is to lay out a portion of the page. Add a page title, some instructions, a TextBox for users to enter a portion of a customer's name, a Find Button, and a Label for the search results. Your page should look similar to Figure 16.57. Notice that the ScriptManager control from the master page displays in the designer.

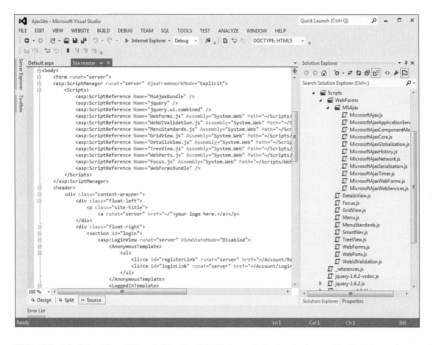

FIGURE 16.56   The Visual Studio 2012 template includes a ScriptManager control by default and loads many script files, including those required by AJAX.

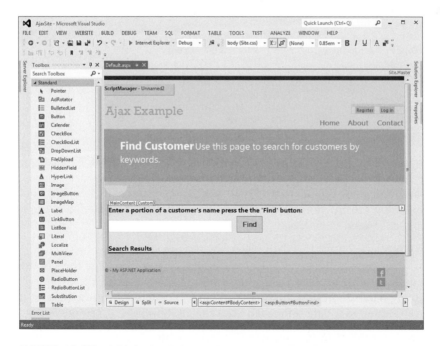

FIGURE 16.57   Add the basic layout items to your Find Customer page.

4. Add to the page an UpdatePanel from the AJAX Extensions control group in the Toolbox; place it under the Search Results label. The UpdatePanel contains the portion of the page you want to partially update. The items placed inside the UpdatePanel are posted back to the server independently of the rest of the page and thus update independently. The user does not see a full page refresh when executing a find. The markup for your main content area should look similar to the following:

```
<asp:Content runat="server" ID="BodyContent"
  ContentPlaceHolderID="MainContent">
  <h3>Enter a portion of a customer's name press the 'Find' button:</h3>
  <asp:TextBox ID="TextBoxSearchText" runat="server"></asp:TextBox>  
  <asp:Button ID="ButtonFind" runat="server" Text="Find" />

  <div style="border-bottom: thin solid #000;">
    <h3>Search Results</h3>
  </div>

  <asp:UpdatePanel ID="UpdatePanelResults" runat="server"></asp:UpdatePanel>

</asp:Content>
```

5. Configure a GridView control to access some data. To do so, drag a GridView control from the Data controls group in the Toolbox. Put the GridView inside the UpdatePanel. You can use source or split view to verify that the control made it inside the UpdatePanel. The following shows an example of what the UpdatePanel markup should look like:

```
<asp:UpdatePanel ID="UpdatePanelResults" runat="server">
  <ContentTemplate>
    <asp:GridView ID="GridViewResults" runat="server">
    </asp:GridView>
  </ContentTemplate>
</asp:UpdatePanel>
```

6. Add the Northwnd.mdf file to your project. You can get this from the download code for this book or by searching for it on Microsoft.com. If you do the latter, you will likely have to upgrade the file to work with the 2012 edition of SQL Server. You can find walkthrough instructions on MSDN for this procedure. Add the file to the project's App_Data folder.

7. Connect the GridView control to a data source. In design view for your page, click the SmartTag (the arrow in the upper right) of the GridView control. Use the Choose Data Source option and select New Data Source. Follow along through the wizard. First, select a SQL database in the Choose Data Source Type screen. You can use SqlDataSourceNwd for your data source ID. Click the OK button to continue.

On the Choose Your Data Connection screen, select northwnd.mdf from the drop-down. Click the Next button and save your connection as **ConnectionStringNwd**.

When you get to the Configure the Select Statement step, select the Specify a Custom SQL Statement or Stored Procedure RadioButton. Click the Next button to continue. You can use the Query Builder tool to build a SQL statement that joins the Customers and Orders tables. The following code provides an example. Notice that the WHERE clause uses the parameter @cust along with the LIKE keyword to define a user-specified value for the search:

```
SELECT Customers.ContactName, Customers.CompanyName, Customers.Phone,
       Orders.OrderDate, Orders.RequiredDate, Orders.ShippedDate,
       Orders.ShipAddress, Orders.ShipCity, Orders.ShipVia,
       Orders.Freight, Orders.OrderID
FROM Orders INNER JOIN Customers ON Orders.CustomerID =
                      Customers.CustomerID
WHERE (Customers.ContactName LIKE @cust + '%')
ORDER BY Customers.ContactName, Orders.OrderDate
```

After defining the query, click the Next button on the wizard. You should now be on the Define Parameters page. Here you can define the source of the parameter you created in the prior SQL statement. In this example, you set the parameter value from your code-behind. Therefore, configure your parameter as None. Figure 16.58 shows an example.

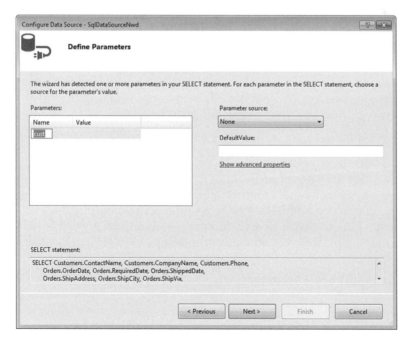

FIGURE 16.58   Use the Define Parameters screen to either link your SQL statement's parameters to your ASP.NET form or indicate no parameter source and thus use code to set the parameter value.

8. Double-click the Find Button in the designer to generate an event handler in the code-behind file. Add code to set the data source parameter's DefaultValue property to the user's input from the text box. The following code shows an example:

```
protected void ButtonFind_Click(object sender, EventArgs e)
{
  SqlDataSourceNwd.SelectParameters["cust"].DefaultValue =
    TextBoxSearchText.Text;
}
```

9. Configure paging for the GridView control. You can do so from the SmartTag in design view; check the EnablePaging check box.

10. As an optional step, you can make the GridView display a bit better. From the quick actions smart tag, choose AutoFormat to apply a format to the grid. You can also use the Edit Columns link to bring up the column editor. Here you can change the column header text for each column, change the column order, and set formatting options for date values and currency.

You now have a customer search page that displays customer and order results to a user based on what she's entered. When the user clicks one of the paging links at the bottom of the grid, the page partially updates. This is the result of the GridView being placed inside the UpdatePanel. Run the application and enter a couple of letters in the Find Customer text box field and click the Find Button. In Figure 16.59, we've done just that. When you select a page link at the bottom of the page, the grid updates as a partial-page refresh.

Notice that when you run the page clicking the Find Button does a full-page refresh and paging does only a partial page-refresh. You can actually include the Find operation as a partial page refresh. To do so, complete these two steps:

1. Move the TextBox and Button controls into the ContentTemplate area of the UpdatePanel control.

2. From design view, select the UpdatePanel control inside the Properties window. Click the ellipsis button next to the Triggers property to launch the UpdatePanelTrigger Collection Editor. Add an item to this collection using the editor. Configure this item to trigger an async postback when the Click event is raised from the Find Button. Figure 16.60 shows an example.

Run the page again. Notice that both the find process and the data paging result in partial-page updates.

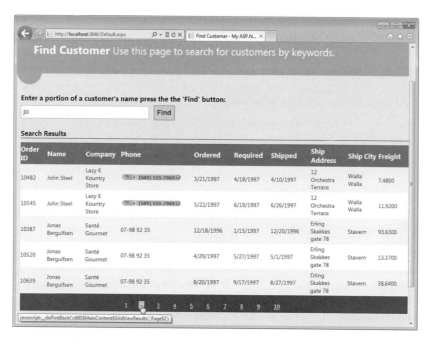

FIGURE 16.59   Your page does a partial-page refresh as users page through the data.

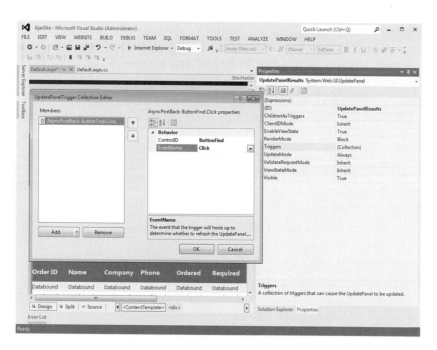

FIGURE 16.60   You can add a trigger to indicate a specific control will fire a partial-page update.

Show Server Progress to the User

Users feel more comfortable when they receive immediate feedback after clicking somewhere on a web page and initiating an action. Of course, many server operations can take many seconds and longer. A better experience is to let the user know you are working on his request when either retrieving pages that have long operations (more than a second or so) or working across an occasionally slow network.

The ASP.NET Update progress control enables you to do just that. When a user clicks to execute a partial-page update, you can put up a wait notification or an animated .gif image. Then, when the page has finished, the wait notification disappears and a portion of the page updates. Let's look at building this in to the Find Customer sample page.

In the preceding example, you implemented a partial-page update for finding a customer and paging through a GridView. In this example, you provide users with a progress indicator during the find process and the paging. To get started, you use the page created in the earlier walkthrough. To implement progress notification, follow these steps:

1. Drag an UpdateProgress control to the page. Place the control under the GridView control but outside the UpdatePanel control. In this example, we show the progress indicator below the data pager. In this way, the user sees a progress indicator in the same area where his attention is focused.

   You can place an UpdateProgress control anywhere on the page, but not inside the UpdatePanel itself. When the partial-page postback triggers, code on the client immediately kicks off the progress notification.

2. Set a few properties on the UpdateProgress control for the page. You need to set the AssociatedUpdatePanelID property of the UpdateProgress control to the UpdatePanel control on the page. In this way, the two are linked. Because a given page might have multiple update controls, setting this property is required.

   You can also set the DisplayAfter property to the number of milliseconds the client should wait before display notification. In this example, set the value low; 250 is a quarter of a second.

3. Define the message that is displayed to the user while he waits. You can put any HTML or markup inside the UpdateProgress control. You do so by dragging items onto the control in design view. In source view, you must create a ProgressTemplate node to house your markup.

   In the example, you can put the text "Please wait...." Also, if you have an animated .gif file that cycles back and forth or in a circle, you can add it here. The UpdateProgress markup should look something like the following:

```
<asp:UpdateProgress ID="UpdateProgress1" runat="server"
  AssociatedUpdatePanelID="UpdatePanelResults"
  DisplayAfter="250" DynamicLayout="true">
  <ProgressTemplate>
   <div>Please wait ... <img src="Content/rotation.gif" /></div>
  </ProgressTemplate>
</asp:UpdateProgress>
```

4. Optional. If you are running this example locally, you might not see much in the way of wait time. Therefore, you might introduce a wait time just to see it work. Of course, you would never do such a thing in a real application. To add a wait time, add code in the PageIndexChanged event of the GridView control to put the executing thread to sleep. The following code introduces a 4-second delay:

```
protected void GridView1_PageIndexChanged(object sender, EventArgs e) {
  System.Threading.Thread.Sleep(4000);
}
```

You should now be able to run the application. If you added the find operation to the UpdatePanel, you should see the wait notification twice, after you click the Find Button and again when the user pages through data. Figure 16.61 shows the page in action.

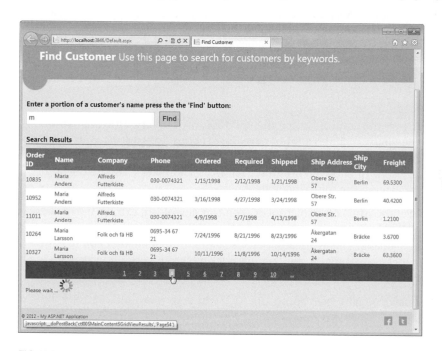

FIGURE 16.61   You can use the UpdateProgress control to show user information while waiting for a partial-page update to complete.

The ASP.NET AJAX Library/Control Toolkit

Microsoft worked with the development community to introduce an early version of AJAX inside of Visual Studio in the 2003/2005 versions. This support was referred to as ATLAS. From these early beginnings grew the AJAX Control Toolkit. Arguably, this toolkit represents one of the most successful open-source projects worked on jointly by a big company and the development community. This toolkit continues to evolve. The latest version has grown and is now called the AJAX Control Toolkit. The library provides developer support for building AJAX controls, doing data binding, and it works with jQuery. The library also includes new versions of the toolkit controls.

The AJAX Control Toolkit is a set of AJAX-based custom controls that provide many dynamic user activities inside the browser. The toolkit supports all modern browsers and has deep backward compatibility for older browsers. There are controls for all sorts of features, including autocomplete as a user types, masked edit text boxes, password strength verification, modal pop-up dialog boxes, and many more. You can download the collection of controls either as full source or as a binary version. You can then leverage these controls inside your application.

> **NOTE**
>
> We discuss the ASP.NET AJAX library and Control Toolkit here because it has become a part of the ASP.NET Web Forms developer's world. You can find tutorials and discussions on Microsoft's site: http://www.asp.net/ajaxlibrary/. You can get the source code or download the latest version from http://ajaxcontroltoolkit.codeplex.com/.

Getting Started

Here we primarily cover the controls inside the ASP.NET AJAX library. However, you should note that the library includes a lot of developer support for creating your own AJAX functionality. The latest version targets the .NET Framework 4.0 or later. You can download the source code or choose a no-source release version. Let's assume the latter because we are not covering the source code here.

The first step is to get the AJAX Control Toolkit. You can download, extract, and manually install the toolkit. A much simpler way to add the toolkit to your project is through the NuGet Package Manager. This is a feature of Visual Studio that enables you to easily download, install, upgrade, configure, and remove packages from your projects. Let's look at using NuGet to add the AJAX Control Toolkit to an existing project.

Start by creating a new ASP.NET Web Forms site with which to work. Alternatively, if you've created one for the previous walkthrough, you can use it.

Next, right-click your project in Solution Explorer and choose the Manage NuGet Packages option. This launches the UI for managing packages. (There is also a console for doing the same.) Enter **AjaxControlToolkit** in the Search box and press Enter. This should find and display the toolkit for installation. Figure 16.62 shows an example.

Click the Install button. This will download and install the toolkit for you. You can then click the Close button on the dialog. That's it; the toolkit is installed. To prove it, navigate to your site's Bin directory and notice the additional folders and the AjaxControlToolkit.dll file.

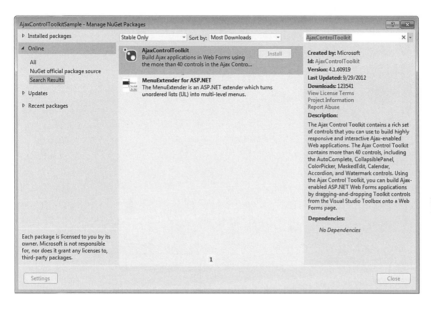

FIGURE 16.62   You can use the NuGet package manager to add the AJAX Control Toolkit to your project.

You will want to add the controls to your Toolbox to make them easier to add to pages. To do so, right-click the Toolbox and choose Add Tab; this will give you a new Toolbox group. Name this tab **Ajax Control Toolkit** or something similar. Next, right-click the area inside your new Toolbox group and select Choose Items. In the Choose Toolbox Items dialog, make sure you are on the .NET Framework Components tab. Click the Browse button and navigate to your site's Bin directory. Select the file AjaxControlToolkit. dll and click the Open button. Close the Choose Toolbox Items dialog by clicking OK. You should be notified of the files added to the Toolbox. Close this notification window. The AJAX controls are now added to your Toolbox pane. You can open a web page to confirm. Figure 16.63 shows an example. Note that there are many controls listed here (more than we can even show). Most of them provide a specific-enough feature that you can understand them by name.

The Controls in the AJAX Control Toolkit

The controls inside the AJAX Control Toolkit have full design-time support. They can be worked with from the Toolbox and dragged onto your forms for use. Of course, it's important to know how you can leverage each control for your specific purpose.

Table 16.9 provides a high-level overview of a sampling of the many controls in the toolkit. Remember, these controls execute the vast majority of their functionality on the client. This gives the user a more interactive experience. Use the list in Table 16.9 as a reference and starting point when building these features in to your applications.

16

FIGURE 16.63   You can add the AJAX controls to the Toolbox for use on your web forms.

TABLE 16.9   ASP.NET AJAX Control Toolkit Controls

Control	Description
Accordion	Use the Accordion control to display several sections of information (or panes) that have a title and content. However, only one of the Accordion sections is open at a given time. As one opens, the currently open one closes, giving an accordion-like effect for a user.
AjaxFileUpload	Use the AjaxFileUpload control to upload multiple file to your server asynchronously. With HTML 5 browsers, the control will show progress to the user.
AlwaysVisibleControlExtender	Use the AlwaysVisible control to float content on top of a web page that should always remain visible to the user. If the user scrolls the page, the AlwaysVisible content remains on top (and visible).

Control	Description
AutoCompleteExtender	The AutoCompleteExtender control can respond to users' typing and provide them with options that they might be trying to type. It does so by attaching to a TextBox control and providing a pop-up panel with a list box. You populate the list box based on the user's typing as processed on the server. You might, for example, look up customer names as a user is entering an order.
BalloonPopup	The BalloonPopup control is used to display a popup that can contain any markup. By default, the popup looks like a cartoon balloon.
CalendarExtender	Use the CalendarExtender control to attach a calendar picker to any ASP.NET text box. The control enables a user to browse a calendar and select a date for populating a text box. The calendar control shows up when the user sets focus to the text box or clicks a button. When the user has selected the date, the calendar disappears.
CascadingDropDown	Use CascadingDropDown to populate a series of DropDownList controls based on a user's selection.
CollapsiblePanelExtender	The CollapsiblePanelExtender enables you to easily define a panel on your form that the user can open and close. The panel has a title bar that includes the expand and collapse button.
ColorPicker	Use ColorPicker to allow a user to select a color.
ConfirmButtonExtender	The ConfirmButtonExtender control is another pop-up type control. Use it when you want to define a button whose action requires a confirmation by the user (see an example later in this chapter).
FilteredTextBoxExtender	The FilteredTextBoxExtender control enables you to indicate the type of data a user can enter into a given text box. You might, for example, restrict entry to only numeric characters, only letters, only lowercase letters, and so on.
HTMLEditor	The HTMLEditor control allows users to create and edit their own HTML content. It includes toolbars for doing so and a preview of what the results will look like.

16

Control	Description
HoverMenuExtender	The HoverMenuExtender control provides users with a small menu of actions based on where they hover their cursors on the page. You might, for instance, provide a menu for edit, delete, and modify when a user selects a given item in a list. You attach a HoverMenuExtender to a given control on the page. In this way, you can get the context of where the user was when she selected an action.
ListSearchExtender	ListSearchExtender enables a user to type a letter in a ListBox or DropDownList and immediately select the first item in the list that starts with that letter.
MaskedEditExtender	The MaskedEditExtender control attaches to an ASP.NET text box and is used to both provide users with assistance when entering data and restrict the type of data they enter. For example, a user might need to enter a phone number in a certain format, such as area code-exchange-number. The MaskedEditExtender can enforce this format.
ModalPopupExtender	The ModalPopupExtender control enables you to create a window that pops up based on user action. This window is be modal on your page. That is, the page is disabled and the user has to respond to the dialog box to continue. This control is great for confirming a user's request and allowing for complex data-entry scenarios where another form is required.
PasswordStrength	The PasswordStrength control attaches to a TextBox control and indicates visually to the user the strength of the password as the user enters it. You can use the control to set minimum password lengths, require nonalphanumeric characters, and more.
PopupControlExtender	Use PopupControl to open (and close) a pop-up window that displays additional content to a user.
ReorderList	The ReorderList control creates a data-bound list of items that a user can reorder inside the browser. Users select an item and move it above and below other items (without accessing the server, of course). New items can also be added to the list by users.
Seadragon	The Seadragon control is used for viewing deep zoom images.

Control	Description
SliderExtender	The SliderExtender control works with an ASP.NET text box to capture user input. A user slides a graphical element up and down or left and right across a range. The text box is updated as the user moves the slider.
SlideShowExtender	The SlideShow control is a set of buttons that enables a user to cycle through a set of images on your form. You can also set the control to automatically transition between slides on a timed interval.
TabContainer	The TabContainer control enables you to group areas of functionality for a page into logical tabs. A user can then click each tab and see the given functionality without refreshing from the server. Each TabContainer contains a TabPanel control. You place your ASP.NET controls onto the TabPanel control.
TextBoxWatermarkExtender	The TextBoxWatermark control extends the TextBox control to include a faded message when the TextBox is empty. When a user sets focus to the control, the message disappears.
Twitter	The Twitter control allows you to display tweets from a Twitter account.

16

Using the Toolkit Controls on a Page

Notice that many of the controls in Table 16.9 include the Extender suffix. This indicates that the control extends an existing ASP.NET Web Forms control. Or, put a better way, the control works with another control to provide its functionality. For example, a CalendarExtender works with a TextBox control. Those controls in the library without this suffix exist as their own standalone control.

The AJAX Control Toolkit makes it easy to work with the controls, and even easier to work with the extender controls. To add an extender control to an ASP.NET control, you can use a smart tag action on the given web form control. To add a basic user confirmation pop-up window to a Button control, for example, follow these steps:

1. Create a new .aspx page for the sample; name this page **ConfirmationSample.aspx**.

2. Add a TookitScriptManager control from the AJAX control library to your page. This control works like the ScriptManager control. It provides the correct libraries for the AJAX controls to operate. Make sure you add this inside the page's form tag. You can verify inside Source view for the page.

3. Add an ASP.NET Button control to the page from the Standard group on the Toolbox. Set the ID to **ButtonSave** and set the Text property to **Save**.

4. From Design view, double-click the Button control to add an event handler in the code-behind file. In the event handler, you might set the Text property of the Button to something different just to confirm that user cancellation is working. The following is an example:

```
protected void ButtonSave_Click(object sender, EventArgs e) {
  ButtonSave.Text = "Saved";
}
```

5. In Design view for your form, select the Button and its smart tag. Notice that there is an option for Add Extender. This option is added to Visual Studio by the AJAX Control Toolkit. Figure 16.64 shows an example. Select the option.

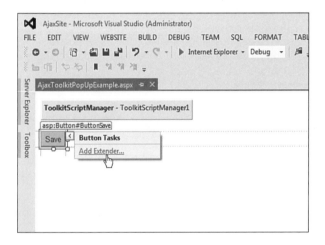

FIGURE 16.64   You use the Add Extender option to apply an AJAX extender control to an ASP.NET server control.

6. You should now be presented with the Choose an Extender dialog box (see Figure 16.65). Here you see all the extender controls. Select ConfirmButtonExtender. Notice that the ID is automatically set for the control based on the control you are extending. Click the OK button to continue.

7. The extender control you just added to your page has no visual representation because it simply extends the Button control. Therefore, you need to either find it in the Properties window (recall that it is named ButtonSave_ConfirmButtonExtender) or switch to split or source view. From either place, set the ConfirmText property to a message that confirms the user's operation such as "Are you sure you wish to save?". You may also notice in Source view that the extender control's TargetControlID attribute was automatically set to the ID of the control being extended (in this case, ButtonSave).

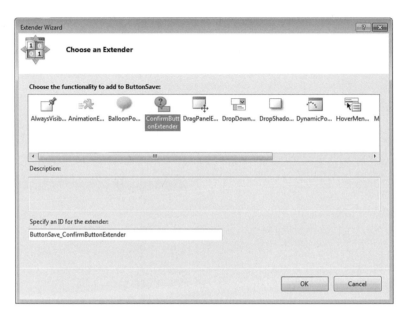

FIGURE 16.65   The Extender Wizard dialog box enables you to choose an extender control to apply to a standard ASP.NET control.

8. Finally, run your application. You should see your form display as you would expect. Click the Save button and you are presented with a confirmation dialog box, as shown in Figure 16.66. Click Cancel to cancel the postback. Click OK to complete the postback on the server.

We've covered the AJAX basics that are built in to Visual Studio and those that are available in the ASP.NET AJAX library and Control Toolkit. Our primary focus is on helping you use the AJAX controls to build better user experiences. Of course, there is more out there for those of you looking to build your own AJAX controls (including both the Microsoft AJAX library and the ASP.NET AJAX library). Both libraries make building AJAX extensions into your controls easier. The Microsoft AJAX library provides an object-oriented structure for those looking to build more JavaScript in to their controls and pages. Visual Studio 2012 also has great support for debugging your client scripts.

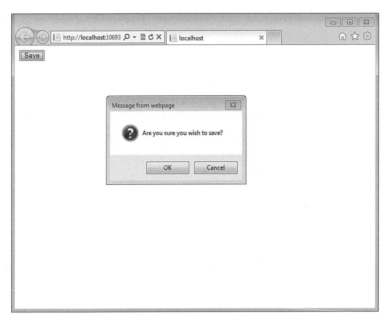

FIGURE 16.66   The ConfirmButtonExtender control in action.

Summary

This chapter described how to create a ASP.NET Web Forms site. In addition, you learned how to leverage the features of ASP.NET to create a consistent (sometimes configurable) user interface. The chapter also covered the many controls in ASP.NET. Some key points in this chapter include the following:

▶ You can create a website using a local built-in server. You can also create your site on a remote server using HTTP (and IIS) or FTP.

▶ The website project property pages enable you to set what happens when you start your application from Visual Studio (among other things).

▶ You can create themes to switch the look and feel of your site without writing code or recompiling. The themes contain style sheets, images, and skin files.

▶ Web Parts enable you to define a user-configurable user interface. You lay out this interface with zones and place Web Parts inside these zones.

▶ ASP.NET ships with login controls, membership, and WSAT to help you manage the authentication of users on your site.

▶ Data controls inside ASP.NET make data binding, editing, and updating easier (often requiring no code). The new Chart control enables you to create graphical representations of data.

▶ You can create a user control to abstract reusable code into its own file and leverage it across pages. A custom control, although more difficult to create, can provide installation and a better design-time experience for developers.

▶ You can use the AJAX extensions in Visual Studio to do asynchronous partial-page updates. This gives the user a much richer experience when working with your page.

▶ The AJAX Control Toolkit is more than 40 controls that help you add richer interactivity to your web forms.

16

Building Websites with Razor and ASP.NET MVC

ASP.NET MVC (Model-View-Controller) and the Razor syntax offer ASP.NET developers a compelling alternative to traditional web forms. The ASP.NET Web Forms template has been around for a long while and offers developers ease of use, a strong set of controls, and a rich framework to extend (see Chapter 16, "Creating ASP.NET Form-Based Applications"). However, web forms tend to abstract the basic HTML and JavaScript from the developer, leaving us to work with controls that do much of the work for us. In addition, Web forms combine UI code with presentation, making it very difficult to test your user interface (UI) code or to get good reuse of many of your UI methods. ASP.NET MVC and Razor were created as an alternative to get developers back in control of their HTML and JavaScript and to simplify their UI code into separate methods that can easily be tested.

This chapter starts by covering building applications with the Razor engine. This is a simple model for creating basic websites that combine code and HTML inside the same page. We then cover the more powerful ASP.NET MVC model (which can also leverage Razor).

Building ASP.NET Web Pages with Razor

Microsoft first introduced the Razor syntax as a means to simplify the code inside ASP.NET MVC pages (more on these shortly). This syntax has now been extended for use on its own. The ASP.NET Web Pages with Razor syntax gives developers a very simple, easy-to-learn model for creating web pages. Recall from Chapter 16 that ASP.NET Web Forms is largely based on controls that render their HTML and JavaScript to the browser at runtime. This is very feature-rich but also carries with it a steep learning curve and some very heavyweight pages. Web Pages with Razor eliminates these controls in favor of just HTML (including HTML 5). You can still add server-side code to your page to affect how the HTML is written to the browser and to respond to user requests. The results are web pages that are easier to understand, a technology that is faster to learn, and a very lightweight processing engine.

Creating a Razor Website

You create an ASP.NET Razor website using the File menu: File, New Web Site. Inside the new Web Site dialog, you select the ASP.NET Web Site (Razor v2) template. Figure 17.1 shows an example. Note that there is also a Razor v1 template. Visual Studio 2012 developers will want to use the v2 template.

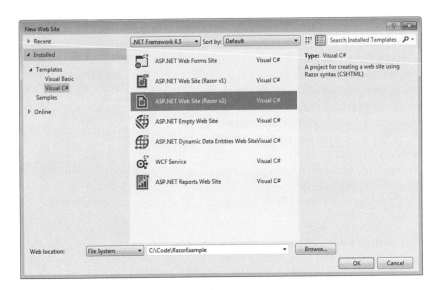

FIGURE 17.1   You use the File, New Website menu to create a new site based on Razor.

The template provides a great starting point. In fact, for 2012, Microsoft has provided the same set of features for all their website templates. This means the account pages, master pages, look and feel, and so on offer the same set of features for Razor, ASP.NET Web Forms, and ASP.NET. Figure 17.2 shows the Razor site template inside Solution Explorer.

The structure of the site should be very familiar to that of Web Forms and MVC. There is a bin folder for compiled code. The Content folder holds style sheets and theme content (see Chapter 16). The Scripts folder is used for JavaScript files. The App_Data folder is a special folder where you store data files for your website. There is also a Web.config file for handling site configuration information.

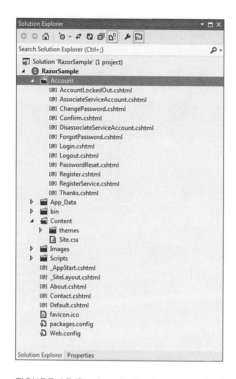

FIGURE 17.2   A website that uses the Razor template has the same set of features as other ASP.NET website templates.

Notice the site template shown in Figure 17.2 also includes a number of files with the .cshtml extension. These are Razor web pages. The cs stands for C#. (Note that VB pages are .vbhtml.) The html indicates these pages include HTML markup along with code.

You can run your newly created site without modification. To do so, you press the Play (green arrow) button on Visual Studio toolbar. This brings up the site as shown in Figure 17.3. Notice that the site is already somewhat robust. It includes a nice look and feel for you to edit, pages for handling user registration and login, and more.

TIP

Visual Studio 2012 now has the browser select feature available for when you run (or debug) your applications. This allows you to set a default browser when building and debugging your websites. You can also easily switch between browsers to check compatibility and usage. Figure 17.4 shows an example.

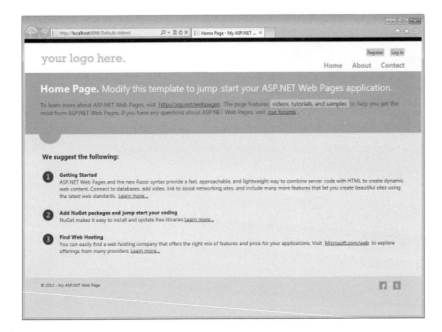

FIGURE 17.3   The Razor website template looks good out of the box.

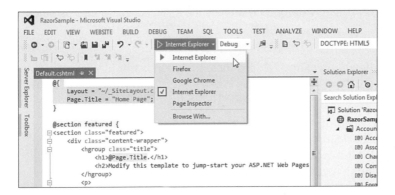

FIGURE 17.4   You can now select different installed browsers when running your ASP.NET applications (regardless of how they are built).

NOTE

If you click around your new site, you will notice you can actually register as a user, login, change your password, and so on. These features were prebuilt in the template. They use the StarterSite.sdf database that gets installed in your App_Data directory upon first use. Here you will find tables for UserProfile, Membership, and Roles. Like a Web Forms site, you can use the WSAT tool (Website menu, ASP.NET Configuration) to define security for your site. Refer back to Chapter 16 for more on using this tool.

A Look at the Razor Syntax

The Razor syntax refers to how you write code mixed inside your page. Remember, this code is meant to run on the server. The Razor syntax strives to make it easy to embed code throughout your page. If you have done this in earlier versions of ASP, you will recall things like brackets and percent signs (<% ... %>) to indicate code start and end blocks. These statements were painful to write and hard to read. Razor makes it much easier.

Razor uses the at sign, @, to indicate an inline expression of code. Typically, this is all you need to tell the engine that you intend it to process some code on your page. If you have just a single line of code, you can embed it right within your HTML. The code and markup shows an example. Here you can see markup (the div and p tags) combined with the code as written with the @ character. Notice, too, that the engine knows when you are done with code and on to text, as in – My ASP.NET Web Page:

```
<div class="float-left">
  <p>&copy; @DateTime.Now.Year - My ASP.NET Web Page</p>
</div>
```

> **NOTE**
>
> Note that in the example, @DateTime.Now.Year, we are using the Razor syntax to indicate the year should be written to the page. ASP.NET makes sure to HTML encode this output before displaying it to the user. This protects you from inadvertently sending HTML or script to the page from an object. Of course, if this is your intent, you can use @Html.Raw to send unencoded content to the browser.

If you have code that runs across multiple lines, you can use brackets, {}. (VB developers can go without the brackets and simply use things like End If and Next.) You can, of course, still mix markup with this code. Consider the following markup and code. Notice the code starts with the call to @if. This if statement is defined inside the brackets. However, the brackets contain markup and more code (in the case of the call to @WebSecurity.CurrentUserName). The Razor engine can parse all of this just fine. This leaves developers free to easily express code and markup on the same page:

```
<section id="login">
  @if (WebSecurity.IsAuthenticated) {
    <p>
      Hello, <a class="username" href="~/Account/ChangePassword"
        title="Change password">@WebSecurity.CurrentUserName</a>!
      <a href="~/Account/Logout">Logout</a>
    </p>
  } else {
    <ul>
      <li><a href="~/Account/Register">Register</a></li>
      <li><a href="~/Account/Login">Log in</a></li>
    </ul>
  }
</section>
```

17

For longer sections of code, you can declare the @ character followed directly by a bracket. In this case, you are telling the engine to expect a fair amount of code here. An example might look as follows. Here there are two lines of code. The first sets the layout for the page (more on this to come), and the second sets the page's title. You could also declare variables to be used later in your page, run other code, create loops; pretty much anything you can write in C# or VB can be added to your web page using the Razor syntax:

```
@{
    Layout = "~/_SiteLayout.cshtml";
    Page.Title = "Home Page";
}
```

Notice that in the previous examples, all the code and markup combinations include markup inside of HTML tags (like `<p>` and `<ul>`). This makes it easy for the Razor engine to distinguish between what is code and what is markup. Sometimes, however, you might want to output text to the page from within your code that is not surrounded by tags. In this case, you need to use the at sign with a colon, also called the @: operator. The following code shows an example:

```
@if (WebSecurity.IsAuthenticated) {
  @: Current time: <br /> @DateTime.Now
}
```

Building a Razor Page

A Razor page is self-contained. It includes all the server-side code for the page as well as all the markup. If you want to extract code and markup, you should consider ASP.NET MVC (or even Web Forms). This construct makes the pages easy to build and easy to understand.

You can add a new page to your Razor site by right-clicking your project in Solution Explorer and choosing Add, Add New Item. This brings up the dialog shown in Figure 17.5. Notice that multiple page templates are available to you. For most web pages, you will choose the Content Page template. This allows you to define content to be used on a master layout page (more on this in a moment). You can also use the Web Page template if you are not using a master layout page.

The Web Page template defines a completely new web page. This includes the full markup, like the `<html>`, `<head>`, `<body>`, and `<form>` tags. You use this template if your page does not contain content that is used across other pages. This is, of course, rare. In most circumstances, you have a standard header, navigation, footer, and so on. In this case, you define a master layout page and then use the Content Page template. Let's take a look at the master layout page before digging into the Content Page template.

FIGURE 17.5   Multiple Razor Web Page templates available to you.

The Razor Layout (Master) Page

Recall from Chapter 16 that a web form master page contains site-specific content that applies across multiple pages. A master page is usually used for defining a common site header, navigation, footer information, and setting any site-wide elements. Razor pages have a similar concept called Layout. Notice the layout template shown back in Figure 17.5.

You use a Layout page in Razor as you would a master page. The Layout page contains the page's <html>, <head>, <body>, and related tags. It also links to a common style sheet and script files. The layout page is then combined with a content page at runtime to render a full set of HTML to the browser.

The Razor template defines a common layout page called _SiteLayout.cshtml. Note that the underscore used in the name of a page is a common way to indicate the page is shared (and not accessed directly by a user). The layout page contains basic markup for defining the overall layout of the page, the header, the footer, and more. In addition, the layout page uses Razor object calls to define sections that are replaced by content sections from content pages when the page is rendered.

As an example, the following code from the default _SiteLayout page uses the @ RenderSection call to indicate this is the location on the page that the section defined as "featured" inside your content page should be rendered. Notice, too, the call to @ RenderBody(). This call indicates that any markup in your content page not inside a section should be placed here. Of course, you can define your own sections, move them around as necessary, and generally customize the layout of the page to fit any need:

```
<div id="body">
  @RenderSection("featured", required: false)
  <section class="content-wrapper main-content clear-fix">
    @RenderBody()
  </section>
</div>
```

> **NOTE**
>
> The _SiteLayout page renders a special section called Scripts. You can use this section in
> your content pages to define links to script files that are page specific.

The Razor Content Page

You have already seen how to add a new Content page to your site (see Figure 17.5).
This page uses a layout page to get its overall look and feel. The link to the layout page
is defined at the top of the page using the Layout property of WebPageBase. The content
for the page is then defined anywhere inside the page. Content can be added to a specific
section using the <section> tag. Other content on the page will be added to the
@RenderBody area of the layout page. The following markup shows an example:

```
@{
  Layout = "~/_SiteLayout.cshtml";
  Page.Title = "Sample Page";
}

@section featured {
  <section class="featured">
    <div class="content-wrapper">
      <hgroup class="title">
        <h1>@Page.Title.</h1>
      </hgroup>
      <p>A sample Razor page.</p>
    </div>
  </section>
}

<form method="post">
  <fieldset>

  </fieldset>
</form>
```

Notice the top of the page makes the call to Layout to set the layout master page. The
next bit of markup uses @section to ensure this markup ends up inside the

`@RenderSection("featured")` areas on the layout page. Finally, the `<form>` tag is the start of markup that will end up where the `@RenderBody()` exists inside the layout page.

TIP

Defining areas of your page, or sections, also allows you to apply specific styling to that section. If you examine the default template for Razor sites, you will notice that the Site.css defines special styling for featured content. You will see a `section` class and `section.feature` styles too. See Chapter 16 for more on working with style sheets.

The `@Html` Helper

ASP.NET Razor pages allow developers to create standard HTML and have fine control of that HTML. The markup you write is not abstracted and generated by controls. For example, if you were creating a page that does conversion of Fahrenheit to Celsius, you might add an `<input>` element as follows:

```
<input type="text" id="fahrenheitTemp" name="fahrenheitTemp" />
```

Writing this HTML gives you fine control and makes the page very easy to read. However, it can be a lot of repetitive HTML for larger forms. Therefore, Razor gives you a helper class called `@Html`. This class helps generate basic, standard HTML for things such as text boxes, password fields, text areas, drop-down lists, and more. It can really make writing your markup easier. For example, the previous input element could be defined with the following call to `@Html`:

```
@Html.TextBox("fahrenheitTemp")
```

This same method also gives you fine control over your HTML. You can use one of the overrides to set the initial value and to set additional HTML attributes on the control. For example, the following adds a style attribute definition to the `<input>` tag when rendered to the browser:

```
@Html.TextBox("fahrenheitTemp", null, new { style = "color: red;" })
```

We use this example in the coming sections to discuss input validation and postbacks. Figure 17.6 shows the full markup for this content page.

TIP

You can build your own Razor helpers. You create these helpers to make writing markup easier for you or your team of developers. In fact, there is a template for doing so called Helper (refer back to Figure 17.5). The Helper can contain both code and markup. It will show up in intelliSense and work the same way as `@Html` to generate markup for you.

17

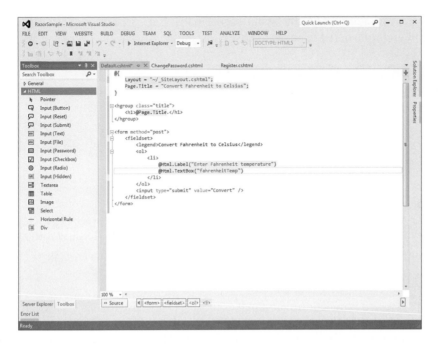

FIGURE 17.6   The markup for the Fahrenheit to Celsius converter page.

User Input Validation

Pages written using the Razor syntax can take advantage of both client-side and server-side validation. This validation is actually provided by the jquery.validate script files included with the project. With it, you can define required fields, set field rules, generate messages on the client before the form posts to the server, and revalidate the form back on the server against your validation rules.

To get started with Razor validation, you need to add the validation scripts to your page. Recall that the layout master page defined a section called Scripts for adding script files to the page. You can use that section to add the validation scripts. Note that if you intend to use these throughout your site, you might add them directly to the layout page. The following shows the markup required to add the two validation scripts to your page:

```
@section Scripts {
    <script src="~/Scripts/jquery.validate.min.js"></script>
    <script src="~/Scripts/jquery.validate.unobtrusive.min.js"></script>
}
```

The next step is to create your validation rules. In this case, we do not have a data model and therefore cannot rely on simple data annotations for defining our rules against our model (see the MVC example later in this chapter). Instead, we need to create our rules explicitly. You do so in a code section for the page. You can use the Validation helper class to create these rules. The following code shows an example. Here we create a required field validator. Next, we add a custom validation rule that indicates the Fahrenheit input must be of type Integer:

```
@{
  Layout = "~/_SiteLayout.cshtml";
  Page.Title = "Convert Fahrenheit to Celsius";

  // Setup validation
  Validation.RequireField("fahrenheitTemp", "The Fahrenheit field is required.");
  Validation.Add("fahrenheitTemp",
    Validator.Integer("Fahrenheit field must be an integer."));
}
```

We now use the @Html helper to add the validation message to the right spot on the page. Figure 17.7 shows the full markup and code for the page. Notice, too, that we added a call to @Html.ValidationSummary. This will show a message to the user should the form postback to the server and result in errors that are not field validation related (excludeFieldErrors: true).

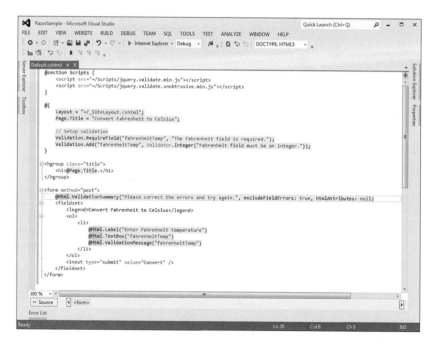

FIGURE 17.7   The validation code added to the markup for the page.

Running the page at this point results in the required field validation firing client side. That is, the page will not post back to the server unless the user enters data in the Fahrenheit field. However, the Integer rule does not fire on the client. Instead, the page has to post back and then deal with this validation. Let's look at handling the postback.

Handling Page Posts

Like any web page, postback occurs when the user clicks a Submit button on a form. In most cases, you will want to trap this occurrence and run some specific code to deal with the post. The example with which we have been working will calculate Celsius from the user's input and return the result.

To get started, we declare a variable called `fTemp` to initialize the value of the Fahrenheit form field (in this case, to empty string). This same variable will be used to redisplay the value in the text box should the form fail server-side validation. We do so by adding the variable to the `@Html.TextBox` call in the markup. This sets the value for the Fahrenheit text box both on request and as part of the post response. You can see both these lines of this code inside Listing 17.1, which shows the full, complete page.

The next step is to add code for `IsPost`. This is an `if` statement that runs code if the page is a posts back to the server. The first check here is to see whether the page is valid (`Validation.IsValid`). If not, no processing happens and the page is returned to the user. An example of this might be if the user enters a non-numeric value in the text box. This validator fires server side and therefore results in an error that must be shown to the user. This example is shown in Figure 17.8.

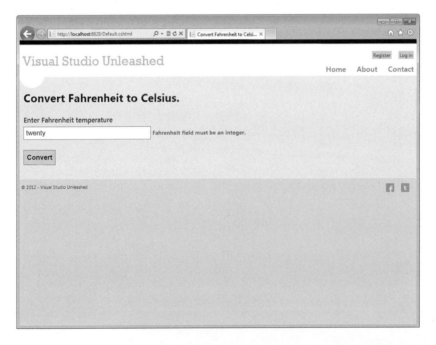

FIGURE 17.8   The server-side validation has fired and the results are shown to the user.

If the user enters good data (a numeric value), we convert it to Celsius and set the flag `isSuccess` to `true`. You can see from Listing 17.1 that we have added an `if` statement to the markup to show the results if this flag is set to `true`. Figure 17.9 shows the fully working example. You can also download this code from the book's website.

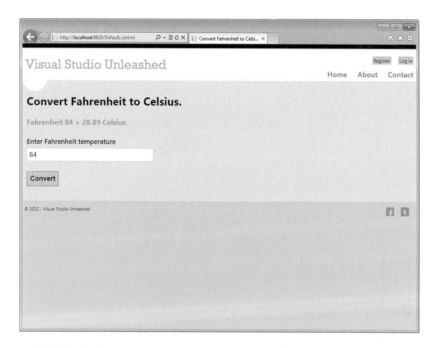

FIGURE 17.9　The complete working temperature calculator example.

LISTING 17.1　The Full Markup and Code for the Fahrenheit to Celsius Converter Page

```
@section Scripts {
  <script src="~/Scripts/jquery.validate.min.js"></script>
  <script src="~/Scripts/jquery.validate.unobtrusive.min.js"></script>
}

@{
  Layout = "~/_SiteLayout.cshtml";
  Page.Title = "Convert Fahrenheit to Celsius";

  //init form variables
  var fTemp = "";
  decimal cTemp = 0;
  bool isSuccess = false;

  //setup validation
  Validation.RequireField("fahrenheitTemp",
    "The Fahrenheit field is required.");
```

```
  Validation.Add("fahrenheitTemp",
    Validator.Integer("Fahrenheit field must be an integer."));

  //if POST request then validate and process
  if (IsPost) {
    fTemp = Request["fahrenheitTemp"];

    //check for validation before processing
    if (Validation.IsValid())
    {
      //convert temperature to C
      cTemp = (int.Parse(fTemp) - 32) * ((decimal)5 / (decimal)9);
      isSuccess = true;
    }
  }

}

<hgroup class="title">
  <h1>@Page.Title.</h1>
</hgroup>

@if (isSuccess) {
  <p class="message-success">
    @String.Format("Fahrenheit {0} = {1} Celsius", fTemp, cTemp.ToString("#.##"))
  </p>
}

<form method="post">
  @Html.ValidationSummary("Please correct the errors and try again.",
    excludeFieldErrors: true, htmlAttributes: null)
  <fieldset>
    <legend>Convert Fahrenheit to Celsius</legend>
    <ol>
      <li>
        @Html.Label("Enter Fahrenheit temperature")
        @Html.TextBox("fahrenheitTemp", fTemp)
        @Html.ValidationMessage("fahrenheitTemp")
      </li>
    </ol>
    <input type="submit" value="Convert" />
  </fieldset>
</form>
```

There is much more you can do with Razor Web Pages. You can use Razor with jQuery and other JavaScript libraries to create rich UIs. You can write data-driven applications with Razor; you can combine HTML 5 and CSS 3 effects with Razor. In fact, there is not much you can't do with Razor when it comes to web programming.

NOTE

This section introduced the Razor syntax. This syntax is also used by ASP.NET MVC. at the next section provides a longer example of building a data-driven form with ASP.NET MVC and the Razor syntax. This form could have also been built using just Razor following the techniques outlined earlier.

Creating ASP.NET MVC Websites

The ASP.NET MVC template leverages the MVC design pattern to separate the various elements of your application into their own parts. This separation helps to increases opportunities for code reuse, makes your code more understandable, and supports test-driven development. However, it can take a little bit of time for web developers to adjust to this pattern. This section introduces the MVC pattern and walks through using it with Visual Studio.

Understanding the MVC Pattern

The ASP.NET MVC application template works to separate your code and markup into three distinct layers: the model represents your data and data access code, the view is how you render data to the user and request their input, and the controller is where you write UI logic to handle user requests and combine data with the right view when responding to users. Putting code into layers has been a good practice for many years. The ASP.NET MVC framework, however, requires this separation. Figure 17.10 shows an illustration of the ASP.NET MVC implementation.

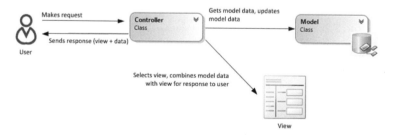

FIGURE 17.10   An ASP.NET MVC application abstracts the model (data) from the view (user interface markup), and the controller (code to connect the model and view).

The following provides additional details the three layers of ASP.NET MVC:

▶ **Model**—A model represents the code that is used for managing the data in your application. Model state is referred to as the actual data stored in a relational database (or similar). You can think of a model object in a similar way to domain objects in other architectures. As an example, you might create a `Customer` object that is used to represent a customer in your application. The attributes of a customer might exist inside a database. The `Customer` object in MVC would know how to work with a database to persist its state. It would also contain any business rules surrounding a customer. Of course, you might still implement a data access layer for your application and allow model objects to leverage that layer. A common scenario for ASP.NET MVC sites is to leverage the Entity Framework for creating the model. We will look at such an example later in this chapter. You may also refer to Chapter 20, "Working with Databases," for more information about working with databases.

The ASP.NET MVC framework does not require a model. If you do not have (or need) domain objects, you might not write a lot of code in the model. For example, if you rely on `DataSet` objects to work with the data in your database, you might access these `DataSet` objects directly from the controller and then pass them to the view. In this case, the `DataSet` objects themselves act like the model. In the same way, you may display a view of information that is wholly contained within the view (and does not rely on a model). In this case, you would process a request with a controller and display the results in a view without ever instantiating a model object.

▶ **View**—A view displays data to a user for their consumption and interaction. Views are the user interface markup in your site. A view uses data provided by the model as its source information. This data is sent to it from the controller. For example, a controller might send the `Customer` data to a customer edit view. That page might present the `Customer` data for edit using basic HTML controls like input, select, and others.

▶ **Controller**—A controller is code you write to handle the user interaction and events inside an MVC application (often called input logic). Requests to your site are routed to a controller class via a routing engine. Your controller code knows how to handle a user's request, work with the model, and connect results to the right view. For example, when a page to edit customer details is requested, the controller works with the model to get the customer details, select the appropriate view, and provide the model data to that view. When the user clicks the Save button, the controller again takes over to move the data back into the model (and the model moves it to the database). The controller then sends the results (as another view) back to the user.

The Execution Model of an ASP.NET MVC Request

An application written using the ASP.NET MVC framework has a different processing model than that of a ASP.NET web form or even a Razor web page. One of the biggest differences is how user requests are mapped to your pages For example, web developers are used to creating a page like EditCustomer.aspx (or .cshtml) and then requesting that page from a browser's URL, as in http://www.mydomain.com/EditCustomer.aspx. With MVC, however, the request gets routed through a routing engine to a method on your controller class.

Your controller method then processes the request. It understands the user's action, works with the model, and selects the appropriate view to display back to the user. The view generates the HTML to be sent back to the user's browser for rendering. The following provides an overview of the ASP.NET MVC processing model:

1. A user requests a URL. This request is passed from ISS to the `UrlRoutingModule` class. This is an HTTP module that serves as the front controller for routing requests.

2. The `UrlRoutingModule` parses the request and performs route selection, ultimately using the `MvcRouteHandler` class to select one of the controller objects in your site to receive the request. You manage which of your controller objects receives the request using the Global.asax file's `Application_Start` method.

> **NOTE**
>
> If no route is found, the request passes to ASP.NET. This enables you to mix both MVC and standard ASP.NET code in a single site.

3. After a controller class is identified, the MVC framework creates an instance of the controller and calls its `Execute` method.

4. An action method inside your controller is identified based on the request details. This action method is then called by the MVC framework. An action method is a method you write in your controller to handle the request and connect the model with the view.

5. An action method takes user input from the request (view), connects that information to the model, and then passes any response back as a specific MVC return type. The most common return type is `ViewResult`. It contains results to be passed to a view for display back to the user. Other return types include `ActionResult`, `RedirectToRouteResult`, `RedirectResult`, `ContentResult`, `JsonResult`, `FileResult`, and `EmptyResult`.

This processing model is much different than the standard ASP.NET Web Forms. Notice that it does not rely on page requests and page postbacks but routes all requests through central controller classes. Also gone from Web Forms is the page life cycle event and the view state. This means ASP.NET Web Forms controls that rely on postbacks and view state do not work with MVC. This includes `GridView`, `Repeater`, and `DataList`. This tradeoff does come with a few benefits. We discuss these next.

> **NOTE**
>
> Traditional web forms and ASP.NET MVC can coexist; neither excludes the other. If you build on ASP.NET MVC, there still might be many times you create a standard ASP.NET page for certain scenarios such as simple data binding and display or to make use of a specific control.

Creating an MVC Project

You create an ASP.NET MVC application using the Visual Studio template ASP.NET MVC 4 Web Application. This is an application template and not a website template. An application template assumes you will have multiple projects in the same solution and uses a different configuration model. You can access this application template from the Add New Project dialog box (menu option File, New, Project). Figure 17.11 shows an example of creating a site based on this template.

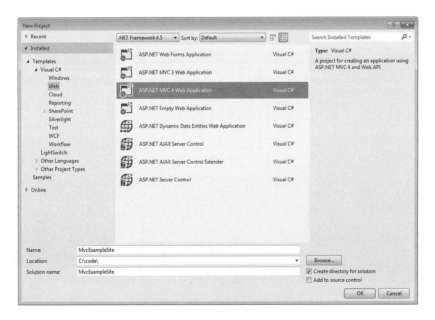

FIGURE 17.11   You create an ASP.NET MVC project using the related project template.

Multiple MVC templates are available to you in Visual Studio. When you select the ASP.NET Web Application template, Visual Studio prompts you to select a more specific template. These templates are shown in Figure 17.12. The most common templates here are Internet and Intranet. These templates include the membership and account management pieces as shown in previous web template discussions. The Internet template uses forms authentication, and the Intranet uses Windows authentication. Other templates include a Mobile template for writing mobile websites and the Web API for creating basic web services (more on this in Chapter 21, "Service-Oriented Applications").

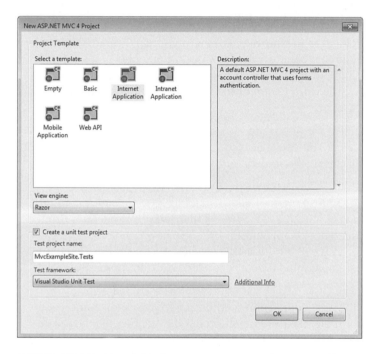

FIGURE 17.12   Visual Studio prompts you to select a specific MVC template as well as define a related unit testing project.

Notice, too, in Figure 17.12 that Visual Studio gives you the option here to create a related unit test project for your MVC site. Recall that one of the advantages of ASP.NET MVC is that you can more easily unit test your web UI logic (controllers). Therefore, we suggest you select this option and allow Visual Studio to create a test project that references your web application. We are not going to re-cover unit testing in this chapter. For more information, refer to Chapter 9, "Testing Code."

The ASP.NET MVC template organizes your code into a different structure. This structure is based on folders that contain models, views, and controllers. Figure 17.13 shows an example inside the Solution Explorer. Notice that each of the MVC layers has a separate folder. The following provides more details on each of the key folders inside an ASP.NET MVC site:

▶ **Models**—Use the Models folder for class files that define your business logic and work with your database. For example, you might write a `Customer.cs` class and store it here. You might also define an Entity Framework model (.edmx) and store it here. You are not bound to this folder. You can create your model as a separate class library (.dll) and reference it from your website.

▶ **Controllers**—Use this folder for all controller classes in your application. Controller classes contain action code that connects user actions to the model and selects the appropriate response (typically a view). The ASP.NET MVC framework uses the convention of appending the word *Controller* to the end of each controller class, such as `AccountController.cs`.

▶ **Views**—Use the Views folder for files related to your user interface. Files here can include site-specific content. This folder also contains site-wide content. The site-wide content is stored in the Shared folder and typically includes the master layout page (_Layout.cshtml) and partial views that work like user controls.

Notice that in Figure 17.13, there are multiple view folders: Home and Account. The standard convention for ASP.NET MVC sites is that each controller has its own corresponding view folder. For example, notice the `AccountController.cs` class has a corresponding Views\Account folder. This is where the ASP.NET MVC framework looks when trying to determine the view you are returning from a controller method.

Another convention is to name your action methods in your controller and your views the same. As an example, the `Account` controller has the method, `Register`. There is a corresponding `Register.cshtml` view inside the Account view folder. In this way, the MVC framework will try to map requests to http://www.mydomain.com/account/register to the `Account` controller's `Register` method. When you return a view from this method, it will actually look first for a view in the Accounts folder with the same name as the method (Register) unless, of course, you specify otherwise.

The remaining files inside the site template are similar to other websites you build in ASP.NET. For example, the Scripts folder is used to house your script files such as jQuery. The Content folder is where you place style sheets and images. There is also an App_Data directory to store data if required and a Web.config file to manage site configuration.

FIGURE 17.13 The ASP.NET MVC application template structures your site into different folders for the models, views, and controllers.

An ASP.NET MVC Page in Action

Let's take a look at HomeController.cs class and related views that the site template generated. This will give you a feel for how an ASP.NET MVC request gets processed. The HomeController has three methods: Index, About, and Contact. None of these methods actually rely on a model, so no model is required in this example. Each method returns an ActionResult. The ActionResult class is actually the base class for all MVC return results. Your controller methods must return a result to the MVC framework to tell it what to do next. In this case, we are returning a ViewResult (which derives from ActionResult). Listing 17.2 shows the code.

LISTING 17.2 The HomeController.cs Class and Related Action Methods

```
using System;
using System.Collections.Generic;
using System.Linq;
using System.Web;
using System.Web.Mvc;

namespace MvcExampleSite.Controllers
{
    public class HomeController : Controller
    {
```

```
   public ActionResult Index()
   {
     ViewBag.Message = "Modify this template to kick-start your ASP.NET MVC
⇒application.";

     return View();
   }

   public ActionResult About()
   {
     ViewBag.Message = "Your app description page.";

     return View();
   }

   public ActionResult Contact()
   {
     ViewBag.Message = "Your contact page.";

     return View();
   }
  }
}
```

Notice that these action methods do not indicate the ViewResult they return. They could. However, in this case, the developer relies on ASP.NET MVC convention. Therefore, a call to the Index method (routed by MVC from the URL http://www.mydomain.com/index) will return the Index view stored in the Home (take from the name of the controller) folder. Notice that this method also has a call to ViewBag.Message. This is a simple means of sending view data from the controller into the view.

The actual Index.cshtml view is shown in Listing 17.3 (minus a lot of the basic HTML and text). Notice that it looks just like a Razor web page as discussed previously (and works like one too). The page works with the _Layout.cshtml for its master layout page. Notice this is not explicitly defined here as it would be in a Razor web page. You can explicitly define it; however, MVC give us the _VewStart.cshtml page to indicate a default layout page for the site. Notice, too, that the use of sections for rendering content to sections on the master page. Again, this is just like the Razor example discussed previously. Finally, notice the @ViewBag.Message is used to show the view data from the controller to the user.

LISTING 17.3   The HomeController.cs Class and Related Action Methods

```
@{
   ViewBag.Title = "Home Page";
}

@section featured {
```

```
<section class="featured">
  <div class="content-wrapper">
    <hgroup class="title">
      <h1>@ViewBag.Title.</h1>
      <h2>@ViewBag.Message</h2>
    </hgroup>
    <p>
      ...
    </p>
  </div>
</section>
}
<h3> </h3>
<ol class="round">
  ...
</ol>
```

NOTE

You do not have to use the Razor syntax with ASP.NET MVC. You can instead use the older syntax standards. This is actually an option when you create a new site. Refer back to Figure 17.12; notice the View Engine option.

You run the application like you would any other website. Just click the Play button on the toolbar. You can see the request and the result in Figure 17.14.

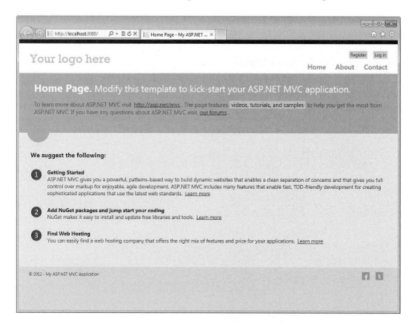

FIGURE 17.14   The Index (home) view running in a browser.

Adding Features to an ASP.NET MVC Application

Visual Studio provides a lot of assistance for defining models, controllers, and views. This section walks through an example of using the ASP.NET MVC tools to create functionality that enables a user to view customers in a list, select a customer, edit the customer's details, insert new customer, and delete an existing customer.

Creating the Model

Recall that a model is the code used to interact with the data in your application. If you work with a database, this code typically returns lists of data and single records. It also lets users act on that data (add, update, and delete). If you already have a set of classes for working with your database and expressing your business logic, you can use them for your model. If you don't have these classes, you need to create them.

In this example, imagine you have a database that contains a Customers table. (In this case, we leverage the Northwind database for simplicity.) You could write a custom class to express the properties and validation rules of a `Customer` object. You might also write functionality to get a list of customers, read a single customer, and update a customer in the database, and more. Alternatively, you can leverage the Entity Framework to create your model for you. This saves you from writing the model from scratch. In this example, you use the code-first version of the Entity Framework. (See Chapter 20 for more details on working with databases.)

With code-first, you write very little code and you do not have a bunch of generated code in your solution. Instead, you write POCO (plain old C# objects) classes to represent your model. These classes simply define objects, properties, and business rules. The database access is taken care of for you. In this case, you create a `Customer.cs` class and add it to the site's Models folder. Listing 17.4 shows an example.

LISTING 17.4   The `Customer.cs` POCO Model Class

```
using System;
using System.Collections.Generic;
using System.Linq;
using System.Web;
using System.ComponentModel.DataAnnotations;

namespace MvcExampleSite.Models
{
  public class Customer
  {
    [StringLength(5, MinimumLength=5,
      ErrorMessage="Customer ID must be 5 characters long.")]
    public string CustomerID { get; set; }

    [Required(ErrorMessage="Company name is required.")]
    public string CompanyName { get; set; }
```

```
    [StringLength(10, MinimumLength=5,
      ErrorMessage="Postal codes must be at least 5 digits (and no more than 10)")]
    public string PostalCode { get; set; }

    public string ContactName { get; set; }
    public string ContactTitle { get; set; }
    public string Address { get; set; }
    public string City { get; set; }
    public string Region { get; set; }
    public string Country { get; set; }
    public string Phone { get; set; }
    public string Fax { get; set; }
  }
}
```

Notice that Listing 17.4 simply defines a class called `Customer`. This class has a series of properties that happen to have a one-to-one match on the Customers table in the database. This naming convention will help us later when we connect our model to a data context. Notice also the use of `System.ComponentModel.DataAnnotations`. This library allows us to define business rules for the properties on our objects. A couple examples here are the `StringLength` and `Required` annotations on the various properties of `Customer`. As with Razor Web Pages, the ASP.NET MVC framework is designed to pick up on these annotations and use them inside of page validation.

The next step with Entity Framework code is to create a class that derives from `DbContext`. In this case, we name the class **NwdContext** and store it in the Models folder too. This class file defines database context collections you intend to work with. It defines each collection as a `DbSet` object. Listing 17.5 shows the `NwdContext.cs` class.

LISTING 17.5   The `NwdContext.cs` Data Context Class

```
using System;
using System.Collections.Generic;
using System.Data.Entity;
using System.Linq;
using System.Web;

namespace MvcExampleSite.Models
{
  public class NwdContext : DbContext
  {
    public DbSet<Customer> Customers { get; set; }
  }
}
```

17

NOTE

If you are coding along with this example, be sure to grab a copy of the Northwind database and copy it to your App_Data directory. You can get it from the source code for this book. This includes a SQL 2012 edition.

Finally, you need to add a data connection string to the Web.config file. This sets connectivity to your database (or data file). You can name this connection string the same as your data context class. This is how the Entity Framework will look for the connection. The following markup shows an example:

```
<connectionStrings>
  <add name="NwdContext" providerName="System.Data.SqlClient"
    connectionString=
    "Data Source=(LocalDb)\v11.0;AttachDBFilename=|DataDirectory|Nwd2012.mdf" />
</connectionStrings>
```

TIP

Not all your models will align this directly to your web pages. Many times, you will have a page that needs to use multiple model classes or needs page-specific properties that have little to do with your model. In this case, you create what are called view models. These are view-specific versions of your model. Typically, developers store view models in their own folder called ViewModels. You create a view model by simply defining a class file. This class usually contains properties for your view-specific model. These properties often extend one or more existing models from your regular model classes.

Creating a Controller

The tooling inside Visual Studio 2012 makes it remarkably easy to create controllers and basic views derived from a model. To get stared, you can right-click the Controllers folder in Solution Explorer and choose Add, Controller. This brings up the Add Controller dialog box shown in Figure 17.15.

You have many options here. First, you specify a name for your controller using the naming standard, [FeatureArea]Controller (in this example, CustomerController). Of course, this serves as your classname. Next you select a scaffolding template. The template you choose can generate a lot of the basic code and pages (or scaffolding) found on most websites. In this example, you choose the MVC using the Entity Framework option. This template has the ability to create controller code for listing and editing data records. The next step is to choose a model class file. In this case, you choose the Customer class created earlier. You also need to select the data context class with which the controller will work. Remember, with Entity Framework code first, the data context class acts as the data access layer for the model. The final drop-down on this dialog is for views. You can choose to not have views created as part of creating a controller or you can have basic views for list (index), create, edit, delete, and details generated for you. In this example, you choose the last option.

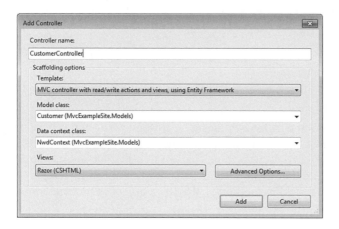

FIGURE 17.15   You add a new controller to an ASP.NET MVC project using the Add Controller dialog box.

The Add Controller dialog shown in Figure 17.15 generates a `CustomerController.cs` class in the Controllers folder. It also creates a Customer folder in the Views folder. Inside this folder, it creates a number of views (more on these in a moment). Each method in the `Customer` controller class is an action method designed to respond to a specific user action, work with the model, and return a view. The class file first declares a variable at the class level for working with the data context. This code is shown here:

```
namespace MvcExampleSite.Controllers
{
  public class CustomerController : Controller
  {
    private NwdContext db = new NwdContext();
...
```

The controller then defines a series of action methods that respond to user requests. Recall that the MVC framework uses the convention of action method name maps to view name. Therefore, the following action methods (and related views) were created: `Index`, `Details`, `Create`, `Edit`, `Delete`, and `DeleteConfirm`. Let's examine of few of these methods.

Returning a List of Customers

The `Index` action method returns a list of customers from the model and passes it to view page called `Index.cshtml`. This method returns an `ActionResult` object. This is common for most of your action methods (see the "ActionResult Objects" section for more action method return types) and indicates the result should be an action. One such action is to create a view. Therefore, the code returns a view object. The view object is not named because you can rely on the framework to look for a view called Index in the Views/Customer folder. Finally, you pass the model data to the view (in this case, a list of customers). The view is strongly typed and will be expecting this list, as you will see in a moment. The following code shows this action method:

```
public ActionResult Index()
{
  return View(db.Customers.ToList());
}
```

Returning a Single Customer

The Details action method returns a detailed view of a single customer. The code is shown here. Notice the method takes an id as a parameter. This is the customer ID. This id is passed to the action method again as convention as part of the URL. A user may make this request as http://www.mydomain.com/customer/details/ALFKI. In this case, the text ALFKI is passed to the Details action method as the id parameter. You could also write this request using a query string, as in http://localhost:3080/customer/Details?id=ALFKI:

```
public ActionResult Details(string id = null)
{
  Customer customer = db.Customers.Find(id);
  if (customer == null)
  {
    return HttpNotFound();
  }
    return View(customer);
  }
}
```

The code then looks for a customer using the Entity Framework model. If found, it returns the Details view. If not, it returns the HttpNotFound error, which results in a HTTP 404 error page.

The Edit action method works the same way. It takes an id parameter, searches for a customer, and if found, returns the Edit view.

Editing and Creating Customers

You have seen how to create simple action methods that return views. These action methods are called as part of HTTP GET requests. The Customer controller class defines such methods for Create and Edit. However, after the user fills out the form, another action method is required to handle the update to the model. The convention is to define these action methods with the same name as their corresponding request action method. The difference is that these action methods include the attribute HttpPost to indicate the method should be called as part of an HTTP POST request. These action methods also take different parameters. The Create and Edit methods, for example, take a Customer object. The following code shows an example of both methods:

```
[HttpPost]
public ActionResult Create(Customer customer)
{
```

```
  if (ModelState.IsValid)
  {
    db.Customers.Add(customer);
    db.SaveChanges();
    return RedirectToAction("Index");
  }

  return View(customer);
}


[HttpPost]
public ActionResult Edit(Customer customer)
{
  if (ModelState.IsValid)
  {
    db.Entry(customer).State = EntityState.Modified;
    db.SaveChanges();
    return RedirectToAction("Index");
  }
  return View(customer);
}
```

Notice that both the `Create` and `Edit` action method first check to ensure the `ModelState` is valid. This checks for any business or validation rules in your model. If the model is not valid, the corresponding page is returned with the same object and the errors should be displayed to the user. If all is well with the model, the `Create` method adds the `Customer` object to the model; the `Edit` method indicates the model record needs to be updated. Both then saves changes and returns the action object `RedirectToAction` to redirect the user to the customer listing (Index) page.

The `ActionResult` Objects

The examples shown thus far have all returned ActionResult objects from action methods on the controller. This is the base class for all action results. Action result objects represent specific commands the framework will perform on behalf of your action methods. The MVC framework defines additional objects that derive from ActionResult for specific purposes. Many of these are listed here:

▶ **ContentResult**—Used to return a custom content type as the result of the action method. This is an HTTP content type, such as text/plain.

▶ **EmptyResult**—Used to return nothing (void) as the result.

▶ **FileResult**—Used to send binary output as the response.

▶ **HttpUnauthorizedResult**—Used to send unauthorized HTTP request results .

▶ **JavaScriptResult**—Used to return JavaScript code that will be executed in the user's browser.

▶ **JsonResult**—Used to return a message formatted as JSON.

▶ **RedirectResult**—Used to redirect to another URI.

▶ **RedirectToRouteResult (RedirectToAction, RedirectToRoute)**—Used to redirect to another action method.

▶ **PartialViewResult**—Used to send a section of a partial view (portion of HTML) to be rendered inside another view.

▶ **ViewResult (View)**—Used to return a web page from an action method.

Creating Views

You create views using either .aspx or Razor syntax. In this example, we assume the Razor syntax. A Razor view works the same way as was described in the first section of this chapter, "Building ASP.NET Web Pages with Razor." This means it uses the @Html helpers for creating forms and defining validation. It also relies on very simple HTML markup. The big differences is that the page relies on the controller action methods for storing all its logic (rather than embedding this code directly in the page). The other big difference is that views can be (they do not have to be) strongly typed.

A strongly typed view is one that is designed to work with an object from your model (or view model, as discussed later in this chapter). You create a strongly typed view by adding the @model definition at the top of your page. When creating the controller for this example, recall that we generated a number of views too. Each of these are strongly typed. For example, the following line of code is atop the Edit.cshtml view inside the Customers folder:

```
@model MvcExampleSite.Models.Customer
```

This definition indicates to the MVC framework that this page expects a Customer object when it is built. It will also post this same customer object back to your POST action method when a user clicks a Submit button. You can use this model declaration inside your markup and with the @Html helper classes. For example, the following markup shows creating a label, text box, and validation message for the CompanyName field from the model:

```
<div class="editor-label">
  @Html.LabelFor(model => model.CompanyName)
</div>
<div class="editor-field">
  @Html.EditorFor(model => model.CompanyName)
  @Html.ValidationMessageFor(model => model.CompanyName)
</div>
```

You can run this page and see the results of controller, model, and view working together. When you navigate to http://www.mydomain.com/customer/, you will get the Index page that shows a list of customers. Clicking the Edit link next to a customer will take you to the edit page for the selected customer, as shown in Figure 17.16. If you make a change here and click the Save button, the page will send a post request to the `Edit` action method and update the model accordingly.

FIGURE 17.16   The controller, model, and view all working together to edit a customer.

Thus far, we have looked at the views generated when creating a controller. Visual Studio gives you similar tooling when just adding views (and not as part of creating a controller). To do so, you can right-click a folder in the Views folder and choose Add, View. This brings up the Add View dialog shown in Figure 17.17.

The Add View dialog allows you to create both basic view pages and strongly typed views. Notice, too, that you can create scaffolding (generated page markup) for your strongly typed views. In this case, we are creating a view for assigning a customer website credentials. It will use the Customer model, but we will have to create the appropriate view markup. Also, notice that you can define a separate master layout page with this dialog or use the default.

TIP: CREATING PARTIAL VIEWS

Figure 17.17 also shows a Create as Partial View check box. A partial view is just markup that does not represent a full web page. Instead, the markup should be used inside another, full page. This markup is often reused across multiple pages in your site. Partial views can also be strongly typed and returned as their own action methods (`PartialViewResult`).

FIGURE 17.17   Use the Add View dialog to create new views.

Summary

This chapter started by showing you how to use ASP.NET Razor Web Pages to quickly create sites that leverage basic HTML, CSS, and both server- and client-side script to quickly create power web pages. The second half of the chapter focused on using Razor and ASP.NET MVC to create websites. This pattern allows you to abstract your UI code into testable classes called controllers. Your markup code is abstracted into views, and your domain layer and data is represented by basic class objects.

Visual Studio provides tooling that makes adding ASP.NET MVC features straightforward. It can generate your models and data access code through the Entity Framework. It can create strongly typed views using the Add View dialog. It can even generate controller action methods using the Add Controller dialog.

CHAPTER 18

Building Windows Forms Applications

One of the core goals for Visual Studio is enabling rapid Windows Forms construction. Using the Windows Forms Designer, the Controls Toolbox, and the various common controls provided by the .NET Framework, this chapter serves as your guide to the drag-and-drop creation of rich form-based applications. Specifically, we look at how best to leverage the built-in capabilities of the Forms Designer and the Visual Studio project system to quickly build a baseline form from scratch.

We don't worry about the code behind the form at this point; instead, the focus is on the user interface and Visual Studio's inherent rapid application development (or RAD) capabilities with the Windows Forms Designer. In other words, we focus on the design-time capabilities of the IDE as opposed to the runtime capabilities of the form and control classes.

The Basics of Form Design

Designing the appropriate user interface for a Windows application is still part art and part science. In the Windows Forms world, a user interface is a collection of images, controls, and window elements that all work in synergy. Users absorb information through the user interface (UI) and also use it as the primary vehicle for interacting with the application.

The task in front of any developer when creating a user interface is primarily one of balance: balancing simplicity of design with the features that the application is required to implement. Also thrown in the mix is the concept of standards, both formal and experiential.

> **NOTE**
>
> Although we use the term *developer* in this chapter, much of the UI design and layout process is actually squarely in the camp of the *designer*. Although many development teams don't have the luxury of employing a full-time UI designer (developers handle this area on many teams), this is rapidly becoming a key competitive differentiator as software development firms look to distinguish their applications and rise above their competitors at the "look and feel" level.

Considering the End User

You can't start the design process unless you understand how the application will be used and who its intended audience is. Even applications that surface similar feature sets might need to provide significantly different user experiences. An application designed to store medical information might have the same data points and functions but would likely have a different persona if it was designed for the ordinary consumer as opposed to a physician or registered nurse.

Use cases and actual usability labs are both great tools for understanding user expectations, and they provide great data points for preserving that function versus simplicity of design balance.

Location and Culture

Location and culture figure into the equation as well. The typical form application used in the United States caters to this culture's expectations by anticipating left-to-right, top-to-bottom reading habits. In this environment, the most important elements of the UI are typically placed in the most prominent position: top and left in the form. Other cultures require this strategy to change based on right-to-left and even bottom-to-top reading traits.

Most controls in Visual Studio directly support right-to-left languages through a `RightToLeft` property. By setting this property to an appropriate `RightToLeft` enum value, you can indicate whether the control's text should appear left to right or right to left, or should be based on the setting carried on the parent control. Even the `Form` class supports this property.

Beyond the `RightToLeft` property, certain controls also expose a `RightToLeftLayout` property. Setting this Boolean property actually affects the overall layout within the control. As an example, setting `RightToLeftLayout` to `True` for a `Form` instance causes the form to mirror its content.

> **TIP**
>
> Search for "Best Practices for Developing World-Ready Applications" in the Microsoft Developer Network (MSDN) for more detailed information on how to design an application for an international audience.

In addition, simple things such as the space allocated for a given control are affected by language targets. A string presented in U.S. English might require drastically more space when translated into Farsi. Again, many controls support properties designed to overcome this design issue; setting the `AutoSize` property on a control to `True` automatically extends the client area of the control based on its contained text.

Understanding the Role of UI Standards

Applications must also strive to adhere to any relevant standards associated with their look and feel. Some standards are documented for you by the platform "owner." Microsoft, for example, has a set of UI design guidelines documented within MSDN. The book *Microsoft Windows User Experience*, published by Microsoft Press, is included in its entirety within MSDN. By tackling topics such as data-centered design, input basics, and design of graphic images, this book provides a structured baseline of UI design collateral for Windows application developers.

Design guidelines and UI standards are often specific to a given platform. The current look and feel expected from a Windows application trace primarily back to the "new" design that debuted with Windows 95. Windows XP further refined those expectations. Windows Vista and Windows 7 offered a new set of design principals and now, Windows 8 offers the most radical set of changes in recent history with its focus on the touch experience and Metro-style applications.

Visual Studio surfaces some of these design guidelines and standards to make it easy to develop conforming interfaces. For instance, default button heights match the recommended standard, and Visual Studio assists developers with standard control positioning relative to neighboring controls by displaying snaplines as you move controls on the form surface. We cover this topic more fully later in this chapter.

De Facto Standards

Sometimes the influence of a particular application or suite of applications is felt heavily in the UI design realm. One example here is Microsoft Outlook. Various applications now in the wild mimic, for instance, the structure and layout of Microsoft Outlook even though they are not, per se, email applications. The Microsoft Outlook designers struck a vein of usability when they designed its primary form, and now other companies and developers have leveraged those themes in their own applications. A similar comment can be made about the visual appearance of the "ribbon" toolbar that debuted with Microsoft Office 2007.

Although there are limits, Visual Studio enables developers to achieve the same high-fidelity UIs used in Microsoft Office and other popular applications. In fact, if you look at the official Windows Forms website, you see demo applications written with Visual Studio showcasing how you can develop replicas of the Microsoft Outlook, Quicken, or even Microsoft Money facades. (Visit the Downloads page at http://www.windowsclient.net.)

Planning the User Interface

Before you embark on the design process in Visual Studio, it is probably a decent idea to first draft a mock-up of the form's general landscape. This can be a simple pen and paper sketch; what we are looking for is a simple, rough blueprint for the application.

As a sample scenario, consider a Windows Forms application written for Contoso customer service representatives. The application needs to expose a hierarchical list of orders placed with Contoso, and it should enable the reps to search on orders and edit data.

Preliminary Design

A few basic components have been established as de facto standards for a Windows form: Menus, toolbars, and status bars are all standard fare and can certainly be leveraged within this fictional order application.

Beyond those staples, you know that you need to list orders on the screen and also provide for a region that shows order details. By borrowing liberally from an existing layout theme à la Microsoft Outlook, you might arrive at a tentative form layout plan like the one shown in Figure 18.1.

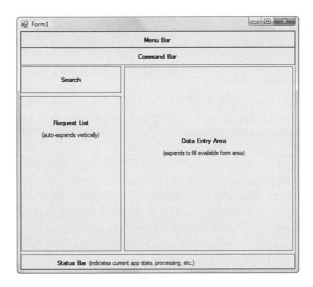

FIGURE 18.1   An initial layout plan.

It is important to pay some attention to the concept of resizing: How do the form's constituent controls respond relative to one another when a user resizes the form? What if a control element is resized because of a language change or a change in the underlying data? By fleshing out some of the resizing design intent now, you can save a mountain of work later. The prototype sketch in Figure 18.1 includes some simple text to remind you how to accommodate the different form regions during resizing.

Creating a Form

Although there are many different ways of approaching form design, the starting point for all of them within Visual Studio is the Windows Forms Application project template. From the New Project dialog box, select this template, give the project an appropriate name, and click OK (see Figure 18.2).

FIGURE 18.2   Creating a new Windows Forms project.

The Windows Forms Application Project Type

Windows Forms Application projects consist of a default form class and, in the case of C#, a default static `Program` class. After creating the project, you are immediately presented with a blank, default form opened in the Windows Forms Designer. For a refresher on the basic capabilities and components of the Windows Forms Designer, see Chapter 6, "Introducing the Editors and Designers."

Setting the Startup Form

Although the default project creates only a single form, you can, of course, add multiple forms at any time. This then raises the question of how to indicate at design time which form you initially want displayed at runtime (if any). There are two methods:

▶ For Visual Basic projects, the startup form is set using the Project Properties dialog box. The Startup Object drop-down in this dialog box contains a list of all valid form objects. You simply select the form you want launched on startup, and you're all set.

▶ For Visual C# projects, a slightly more complex approach is needed. The notion of a C# startup object is simply any class that implements a `Main()` method. Within the body of the `Main` method, you need to place a line of code that passes in a form instance to the `Application.Run` method, like this: `Application.Run(new OrderForm()`). Assuming that you have a class that implements `Main` and code that calls `Application.Run` in that `Main` method, you can then select the specific startup object via the Project Properties dialog box. The `Program` class, which is created for you during the project creation process, already implements the `Main` method, and by default runs the default form (Form1) on startup.

Inheriting Another Form's Appearance

If your form looks similar to another form that you have already developed, you have the option of visually inheriting that other form's appearance. Visual Studio provides an Inherited Form project item template to help you along this path.

To create a form that visually inherits another, select Project, Add New Item. In the Add New Item dialog box, select the Inherited Form item type (located under Visual C# Items, under the Windows Forms category). The Inheritance Picker dialog box then lists the available forms within the current project that you can inherit from. Note that you also have the option of manually browsing to an existing assembly if you want to inherit from a form that doesn't appear in the list. After you select the base form, Visual Studio creates the new form class; its code already reflects the base class derivation.

Form Properties and Events

A form is like any other control: You can use the Properties window in the IDE to control its various properties. Although we don't touch on all of them here, you should consider a few key properties as you begin your form design process.

Startup Location

You use the form's `StartPosition` property to place the form's window on the screen when it is first displayed. This property accepts a `FormStartPosition` enumeration value; the possible settings are documented in Table 18.1.

TABLE 18.1   `FormStartPosition` Enumeration Values

Value	Description
CenterParent	Centers the form within its parent form.
CenterScreen	Centers the form within the current display screen.
Manual	The form positions itself according to the `Form.Location` property value.
WindowsDefaultBounds	Positions the form at the Windows default location; the forms bounds are determined by the Windows default as well.
WindowsDefaultLocation	Positions the form at the Windows default location; the form's size is determined by the `Form.Size` property. (This is the default setting.)

Appearance

Given our discussion on the priority of UI design, it should come as no surprise that the appearance of the form is an important part of the overall application's user experience. For the most part, the default appearance property values are sufficient for the typical application. You should set the `ForeColor` and `BackColor` properties according to the color scheme identified for your application. Note that when you add controls to the form, most of them have their own individual `ForeColor` values set to mimic that of the form.

Some properties enable you to implement a more extravagant user interface. The `Opacity` property enables you to implement transparent or semitransparent forms. This capability might be useful for situations in which users want to see a portion of the screen that actually sits behind the form's window. In addition to the `Opacity` property, you use the `Form.BackgroundImage` property to set an image as the form's background. This property is best used to display subtle color gradients or graphics not possible with just the `BackColor` property.

In keeping with our goal of rapidly crafting the form, most of the activities within the designer described in this chapter consist of tweaking the form's properties and adding controls from the Toolbox to the form.

Form Events

Forms inherit the same event-driven architecture as other controls do. Certain public events defined on the `Form` class are useful as injection points across the continuum of a form's life.

Figure 18.3 shows the various stages (and corresponding events) from form inception to close. To react to a form event, you first need to create an event handler.

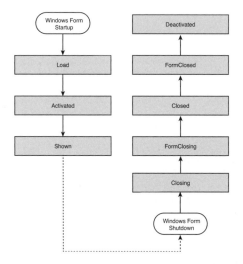

FIGURE 18.3   The events in the life of a Windows form.

Creating an Event Handler   Visual Studio's Properties window provides a speedy mechanism for defining an event handler. First, select the form of interest. Then click the Events button in the Properties window's toolbar. The window now shows a list of every event defined on the form. Double-clicking the event creates a blank event handler routine and opens it in the code editor for you. The event handler has the correct arguments list and follows established standards for event handler naming (typically, object_eventname).

> **NOTE**
>
> The form needs to be opened in the IDE before the events can be accessed in the properties window. If the form is selected in the solution explorer, but not opened in the IDE, you can still edit the form properties but you won't be able to access the events in this fashion.

Figure 18.4 depicts the form events within the Properties window.

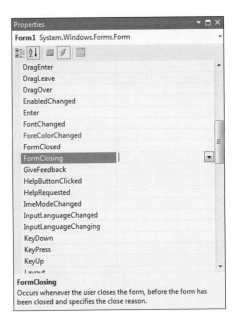

FIGURE 18.4   Accessing Form events in the Properties window.

With the form in place, you can start placing controls onto its surface.

Adding Controls and Components

When you are building a form-based application, the user interface design really involves three separate tools within Visual Studio: the Forms Designer tool, which provides the canvas for the form; the Toolbox, which contains the controls to be placed onto the canvas; and the property browser, which is used to affect the form and its child controls, appearance, and behavior. This triad of IDE tools provides the key to rapid form construction with Visual Studio, especially as it relates to building a form's content.

The term *control* technically refers to any .NET object that implements the `Control` class. In practice, we use the term to refer to the visual controls hosted by a form. This is in contrast to a component, which has many of the same characteristics of a control but doesn't expose a visual interface. A button is an example of a control; a timer is an example of a component.

Controls and components alike live in the Toolbox window (see additional coverage of the Toolbox in Chapter 6). Adding either a control or a component to a form is as easy as dragging its likeness from the Toolbox and dropping it onto the form's surface.

After you place a control on a form, the Windows Forms Designer paints the control onto the form to give you a WYSIWYG view of how the form will look at runtime. As noted in Chapter 6, components are handled in a slightly different fashion. The Forms Designer has a special region called the component tray; any components placed onto the form are represented here. This enables you to interact in a point-and-click fashion with the component as you would with a control but doesn't place a representation onto the form itself because a component has no visual aspect to it.

Figure 18.5 highlights the component tray area of the Windows Forms Designer.

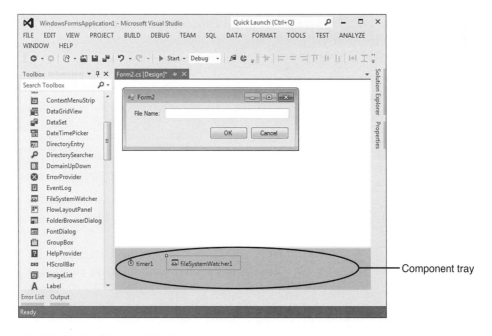

FIGURE 18.5   The component tray.

TIP

The Toolbox is customizable: You can add or remove controls from the Toolbox within any of the Toolbox tabs. Right-click anywhere in the interior of the Toolbox window and select Choose Items to launch the Choose Toolbox Items dialog box; from here, you can select or deselect the Toolbox control population. If a control doesn't show up in the .NET Framework Components tab or the COM Components tab of the dialog box, you can browse to the control's assembly and add it directly.

Control Layout and Positioning

When a few controls are on a form, the Windows Forms Designer can help automate some of the more common layout tasks, such as aligning a group of controls vertically to one another. Again, refer to Chapter 6 to see how you can leverage these productivity tools. But these layout functions, although nice from a design perspective, do nothing for you at runtime.

As previously noted, a control's runtime behavior within its parent form is an important area that needs attention if you are to implement your form according to your design intent. That is, you not only want controls to look a certain way, but also want them to act a certain way when the form is resized.

The simplest way to underscore the issue presented during a form resize is to look at a few figures. Figure 18.6 shows the simplest of forms: a label, a text box, and OK and Cancel buttons. The controls on the form have been carefully placed to maintain equal spacing; the controls are nicely aligned in the vertical and horizontal planes; and, in short, this form looks just like the developer intended it to look.

FIGURE 18.6   Controls aligned on a form.

But then a user becomes involved. Figure 18.7 shows the results of resizing the form horizontally and vertically.

This appearance is clearly not what was intended; the nice clean design of the form has failed to keep up with the form's size. Perhaps the user resized the form in an attempt to get more room to type in the text box. Or perhaps the user tiled this application's window with other applications, causing its size to change. Whatever the reason, it is clear that further intervention by the developer is needed to keep the design "valid," regardless of the size of the form.

FIGURE 18.7   Form resize effects on design.

Just by viewing the before and after figures, you can decide on a strategy and answer the question "What should happen when a user resizes the form?" Figure 18.8 is a snapshot of the ideal; the text box has "kept pace" with the resize by horizontally extending or shrinking its width. The command buttons have kept their alignment with one another and with the text box, but they have not altered their overall dimensions. Plus, the label has stayed in its original location.

FIGURE 18.8   Reacting to a form resize.

Every form object has a resize event that fires whenever the form boundary size changes (most commonly as the result of a user dragging the form's border to increase or decrease the size of the form). Because every control has positioning properties such as `Top`, `Left`, `Height`, and `Width`, you could implement a brute-force approach to achieving the form shown in Figure 18.8. By writing several lines of code for each control, you can manually move or redimension the controls in response to the form size and the position of the other controls. But this approach is tedious at best and results in brittle code that has to be touched every time the layout and placement of controls are tweaked.

Thankfully, the Visual Studio Windows Forms Designer, in conjunction with some standard control properties, enables you to take all the common resize optimizations into

18

account during the layout of the form. By anchoring and docking your controls, you can dictate their position relative to one another and to their position within the borders of the form.

Anchoring

Anchoring, as its name implies, is the concept of forcing a control's left, top, right, or bottom border to maintain a static, anchored position within the borders of the form. For instance, anchoring a label control to the top and left of a form (this is the default) causes the label to maintain its exact position regardless of how the form is resized. Each control's Anchor property can be set to any combination of Top, Left, Bottom, and Right. The control's property browser provides a convenient property editor widget, shown in Figure 18.9, which graphically indicates the sides of the control that are anchored.

FIGURE 18.9   Setting the Anchor property.

Anchoring opposite sides of a control has an interesting effect. Because each side must maintain its position relative to the sides of the form, the control itself stretches either vertically or horizontally depending on whether the Top and Bottom or Right and Left anchors have been set. In fact, this is the exact behavior you want with the text box: You want its width and height to adjust whenever the form is resized. By anchoring all sides of the control, you get the behavior shown with the TextBox control in Figure 18.8; the control has automatically adjusted its dimensions (by stretching both horizontally and vertically) with no code required from the developer.

> **NOTE**
>
> By default, controls are typically anchored on their top and left sides. You might be wondering what happens if no anchors are specified at all. In that case, the control maintains its exact position regardless of form resize actions. This is, in effect, the same behavior as top and left anchors would have because forms have their top leftmost points as their "origin."

Anchoring also solves the positioning problem with the OK and Cancel buttons. If you change their Anchor properties to Bottom, Right, they anchor themselves to the bottom right of the form, which is consistent with their recommended placement on a form. Because you aren't anchoring opposing sides of the control, you aren't forcing the buttons to resize; they are merely repositioned to keep station with the right and bottom edge of the form. Contrast this with the anchoring performed for the text box: Because you anchored all sides, you are not only keeping a uniform border between the edge of the text box and the form but also causing the text box to stretch itself in both dimensions.

Docking

For the simple form in Figure 18.8, you can implement most of your layout logic using the Anchor property. But if you refer to the overall plan for the CSR screen (see Figure 18.1), you can see that you have some positioning needs that would be cumbersome to solve using anchors. For instance, the data entry region of the form should automatically expand vertically and horizontally to fill any space left between the list of requests, the status bar, and the command bar. This is where the concept of docking comes to the rescue. Docking is used either to stick a control to a neighboring control's edge or the form's edge, or to force a control to fill all the available space not taken by other controls.

As with the Anchor property, the property browser provides a graphical tool to set a control's Dock property (shown in Figure 18.10).

Control Auto Scaling

The Windows Forms engine supports the capability to dynamically adjust a control's dimensions to preserve its original design proportions. This capability is useful if the form or control is displayed at runtime on a system with different display characteristics (resolution, DPI, and so on) than the system the form or control was designed on.

A simple example of this occurs when an application that uses a reasonable 9pt. font during design becomes almost unusable when displayed on a system whose default font size is larger. Because many UI elements auto-adjust based on the font of their displayed text (such as window title bars and menus), this can affect nearly every visual aspect of a form application.

Container controls (for example, those deriving from the ContainerControl class, including the Form class and UserControl among others) starting with .NET 2.0 support two properties that enable them to counter these issues automatically without a lot of developer intervention: AutoScale and AutoScaleDimensions. AutoScaleMode specifies an enumeration value indicating what the scaling process should use as its base reference (DPI or resolution). Table 18.2 shows the possible AutoScaleMode values.

18

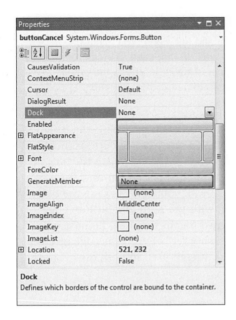

FIGURE 18.10   Setting the Dock property.

TABLE 18.2   `AutoScaleMode` Enumeration Values

Value	Description
Dpi	Scale relative to the resolution (96 DPI, 120 DPI, and so on)
Font	Scale relative to the dimensions of the font being used
Inherit	Scale according to the base class `AutoScaleMode` value
None	No automatic scaling is performed

`AutoScaleDimensions` sets the dimensions (via a `SizeF` structure) that the control was originally designed to. This could refer to a font size or the DPI.

Using Containers

Containers are .NET controls designed to hold other controls. You can use containers in conjunction with the Anchor and Dock control properties to create intricate design scenarios. Although there are various container controls, the ones most applicable to control layout are the `FlowLayoutPanel`, `TableLayoutPanel`, and `SplitContainer` classes.

Both the `TableLayoutPanel` and the `FlowLayoutPanel` classes derive from the more generic `Panel` class. The `Panel` class provides high-level capabilities for grouping controls. This is beneficial from a placement perspective because you can aggregate a bunch of controls into one group by positioning them within a panel. This way, you can act on them as a group; for instance, disabling a panel control disables all of its child controls. The `TableLayoutPanel` and `FlowLayoutPanel` build on that functionality by also providing the capability to dynamically affect the positioning of their child controls.

The `TableLayoutPanel`

Consider a series of labels and text boxes for entering address information. They are typically arrayed in a column-and-row fashion. The `TableLayoutPanel` is ideal for implementing this behavior because it automatically forces the column and row assignment that you make for each of the controls. Figure 18.11 shows a series of label and text box controls embedded within a `TableLayoutPanel`. Notice that resizing the form (and thus the panel, which is docked to fill the form interior) causes the panel's controls to auto-adjust their alignment.

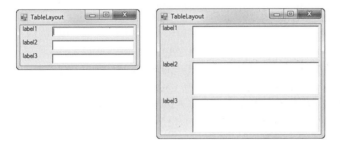

FIGURE 18.11   The `TableLayoutPanel`.

If an item within one of the cells extends beyond the cell's boundaries, it automatically overflows within the cell. This provides you with the same layout capabilities that HTML provides for web browser-based interfaces.

NOTE

When a control is added to a `TableLayoutPanel`, it is decorated with five additional properties: `Cell`, `Column`, `Row`, `ColumnSpan`, and `RowSpan`. These properties can be used to change the control's row/column position within the layout panel at runtime. The `ColumnSpan` and `RowSpan` properties are used the same way as their namesakes in the HTML world. In .NET, controls that imbue other controls with additional properties are called *extender providers*.

The `FlowLayoutPanel`

The `FlowLayoutPanel` has a simpler layout algorithm: Items are ordered either vertically or horizontally by wrapping control sets across rows or columns as needed. The two screens shown in Figure 18.12 illustrate the effect of resizing a flow layout panel containing a series of radio buttons.

FIGURE 18.12   The `FlowLayoutPanel`.

The `SplitContainer`

The `SplitContainer` control is a much enhanced alternative to the original `Splitter` control that was first included with .NET 1.0/1.1/Visual Studio 2003. This control represents the marriage of two panels and a splitter; the splitter separates the two panels either horizontally or vertically and enables a user to manually adjust the space (in the horizontal or vertical) that each panel consumes within the overall container.

Figure 18.13 shows the versatility of this control; two split containers, one embedded within a panel hosted by the other, are used to provide both vertical and horizontal resizing capabilities for the panels on a form. (Panel 2 isn't visible because it is the panel functioning as the container for the split container with panels 3 and 4.) By dragging the split line to the right of panel 1, you can increase or decrease the horizontal real estate it occupies on the form. The same is true for the split line between panel 3 and panel 4; dragging this adjusts the ratio of space that both panels vertically occupy in relation to one another.

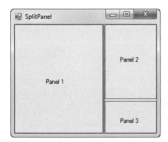 

FIGURE 18.13   Resizing with the `SplitContainer`: a horizontal `SplitContainer` embedded in a vertical `SplitContainer`.

The `ToolStripContainer`

Many applications support the capability to drag and dock a toolbar, menu, and the like to any side of a form: top, bottom, left, or right. Visual Studio itself is an example of just such an application. By grabbing and dragging a Visual Studio toolbar, you can reposition it, for example, to the left side of the form. The `ToolStripContainer` control enables this functionality in your applications as well; it is a combination of four panels, each positioned on the four different edges of the containing form. These panels are used to host

`ToolStrip` controls (more on these in a bit) and (at runtime) enable users to move tool strips within and between the four panels.

> **NOTE**
>
> Although the `ToolStripContainer` provides a convenient vehicle for snapping tool strips to the sides of a form, there is unfortunately no built-in support for "floating" tool strips.

The design experience is simple: You can shuffle controls around to the four different panels depending on where you want them positioned within the parent form. Figure 18.14 shows a `ToolStripContainer` in design mode. The smart tag offers up control over the visibility of the top, left, right, and bottom panels. Each panel is hidden by default. You can click any of the arrows on the sides of the container to expand the corresponding panel and give you room to place tool strips within the panel.

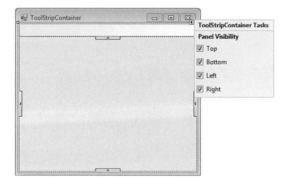

FIGURE 18.14 `ToolStripContainer` in design mode.

Although it is convenient to be able to place items in a `ToolStripContainer` within the designer, the real benefit that you get from the control is the automatic support for dragging and dropping between panels at runtime. This means that, without writing a single line of layout or positioning code, you have enabled functionality that enables users to place their menus or toolbars wherever they want within the form. Figure 18.15 shows a toolbar, hosted in a `ToolStripContainer`, which has been redocked from the top panel to the left panel at runtime.

Multiple `ToolStrip` controls can also be stacked within any of the given panels in the `ToolStripContainer`. Figure 18.16 shows multiple command bars stacked within the rightmost panel. As noted later in the chapter, a control's z-order dictates its place within the stack.

> **NOTE**
>
> The sharing of space (vertically or horizontally) within a tool strip container is sometimes referred to as *rafting*. The tool strip controls are free to float anywhere within the panel.

FIGURE 18.15   A toolbar positioned at runtime within a `ToolStripContainer`.

FIGURE 18.16   Multiple toolbars stacked within the same panel.

A few other intricacies are involved with form/control layout and positioning, but we have now covered the basics. With these concepts in hand and a general design for your form, you can start using the Windows Forms Designer.

Control Appearance and Behavior

A control's appearance is set via the same set of basic properties used to control form appearance: Items such as `ForeColor`, `BackColor`, and `Font` all make an appearance on most controls.

Visual Styles

One item of interest is the capability for a control to automatically alter its appearance to conform to the currently selected "Desktop Theme" if it's running on Windows XP, Windows Vista, or Windows 7. This capability is enabled by a call to the `Application.Enable VisualStyles` method. This line of code is automatically included for you by default as the first line in the `Main` method. This location is ideal because it must be called before the controls in the application are actually created. If you remove the call, you can easily compare the appearance with and without the effects enabled. Figure 18.17 shows a form without visual styles enabled (left) alongside one with visual styles enabled (right).

FIGURE 18.17   The effects of `Application.EnableVisualStyles`.

Tab Order

By default, the order in which the controls on a form receive focus (tab order) is the same as the order in which they were placed on the form. To explicitly set the tab order for all the controls on a form, the IDE has a tab order selection mode.

To enter tab order selection mode, select View, Tab Order from the menu. The Windows Forms Designer annotates every control on the form with a number. This number represents that control's position within the overall tab order for the form. To set the tab order that you want, click sequentially on the controls; their tab order numbers automatically change as you click.

ToolTips

ToolTips are small "balloons" that display text as a user moves his or her cursor over a control. Typically, they are used to provide helpful hints or descriptions of a control's purpose, action, and so on. ToolTips are implemented with the `ToolTip` class and can be assigned to controls at design time.

The `ToolTip` class is an example of an extender provider (see the previous note on extender providers in our discussion on the `TableLayoutPanel` control). When you add a ToolTip component to a form, every control on the form now implements a ToolTip property that is used to assign a ToolTip to that specific control.

For illustration, if you wanted to add a ToolTip to a ToolStrip button, you would first drag the ToolTip component over to the form from the Toolbox. You would then select the ToolStrip button that you want to add the ToolTip to, and you would set its `ToolTip` property to reference the ToolTip instance on your form.

Working with ToolStrip Controls

Many of the standard, core visual elements of a form are realized with ToolStrip controls. A ToolStrip control functions as a container for other controls that derive from ToolStripItem. It can host various types of controls: buttons, combo boxes, labels, separators, text boxes, and even progress bars. The `ToolStrip` class itself is used to directly implement toolbars on a form and also functions as a base class for the StatusStrip control and the MenuStrip control.

ToolStrip controls come with an impressive list of built-in capabilities. They intrinsically support, for example, dragging an item from one tool strip to another, dynamically reordering and truncating items in the tool strip as users resize the strip or its parent form, and fully supporting different OS themes and rendering schemes.

All the different flavors of the ToolStrip control have some common traits:

▶ A design-time smart tag provides quick and easy access to common commands.

▶ In-place editing of child controls is supported. (For example, a point-and-click interface is offered for adding, removing, and altering items within the ToolStrip, StatusStrip, or MenuStrip.)

▶ An Items Collection Editor dialog box enables you to gain more fine control over child control properties and also enables add/reorder/remove actions against the child controls.

▶ Tool strips support a pluggable rendering model; you can change the visual renderer of a tool strip to a canned rendering object or to a custom object to obtain absolute control over the appearance of the tool strip.

From the initial form design, you know that you need menus, toolbars, and status bars, so the ToolStrip control and its descendants play a crucial role.

Creating a Menu

MenuStrip controls enable you to visually construct a form's main menu system. Dragging and dropping this control from the Toolbox onto the blank form automatically docks the menu strip to the top of the form (see Figure 18.18).

After you place this control on the form, selecting the MenuStrip control activates the smart tag glyph. (Smart tags are covered in Chapter 8, "Working with Visual Studio's Productivity Aids.") Clicking the smart tag enables you to quickly do three things:

▶ Automatically insert standard items onto the menu

▶ Change the menu's RenderMode, Dock, and GripStyle properties

▶ Edit the menu items

Leveraging the capability to automatically equip a menu strip with a standard set of menus shaves a few minutes of design time off the manual approach. Figure 18.19 shows the result.

Not only has the designer inserted the standard File, Edit, Tools, and Help top-level menu items, but it also has inserted subitems below each menu. Table 18.3 indicates the exact menu structure that results from using the menu's Insert Standard Items feature.

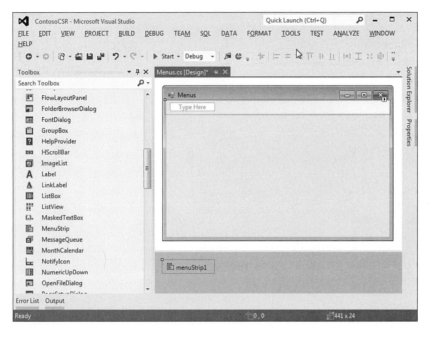

FIGURE 18.18   A menu positioned on the form.

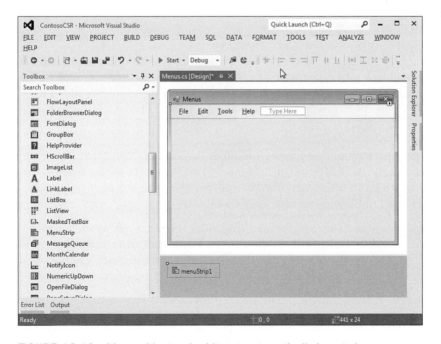

FIGURE 18.19   Menu with standard items automatically inserted.

TABLE 18.3   Standard Menu Items

Main Menu	Menu Items
File	New
	Open
	Save
	Save As
	Print
	Print Preview
	Exit
Edit	Undo
	Redo
	Cut
	Copy
	Paste
	Select All
Tools	Customize
	Options
Help	Contents
	Index
	Search
	About

If you want to manually add menu items into the menu strip, you can use the placeholder block within the menu strip labeled with the text "Type Here." Every time you type in the placeholder block, additional placeholders become visible, and a menu item is added to the menu strip (see Figure 18.20).

Creating a Toolbar

The next item up for inclusion on the form is a toolbar. Toolbars in .NET 2.0 and later are implemented directly with ToolStrip controls. As mentioned before, ToolStrip controls can host various child controls; each inherits from the `ToolStripItem` base class. Figure 18.21 shows the controls that can be implemented inside a tool strip.

In fact, the interactive layout features of the tool strip work the same way as the menu strip: Dragging the control onto the form will result in a blank ToolStrip control docked to the top of the form just under the existing menu control, and you can quickly add a roster of standard items to the tool strip by using its smart tag and selecting Insert Standard Items.

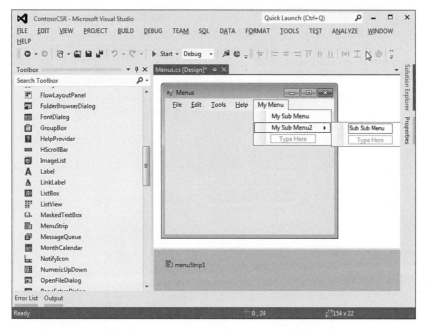

FIGURE 18.20   Manually adding menu items.

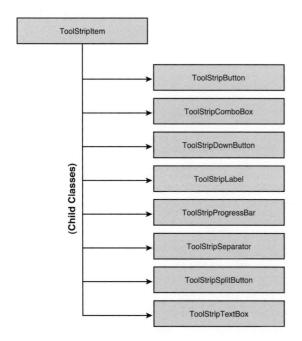

FIGURE 18.21   Classes inheriting from `ToolStripItem`.

NOTE

Controls use the concept of *z-order* to determine their "depth" on the form. If two controls occupy the same space on a form, the control's individual z-order determines which of the two controls is on top and which is on the bottom. You control this layering in the IDE by right-clicking a control and using the Send to Back and Bring to Front menu commands.

Z-order plays an important role in the placement of docked controls. Docked controls are arrayed in increasing order of their z index on the form. For instance, if you select the ToolStrip and issue the Send to Back command, the order of the MenuStrip and ToolStrip containers is altered to place the ToolStrip first (at the top of the form) and the MenuStrip second (just below the ToolStrip instance).

Figure 18.22 shows the in-progress form with the added ToolStrip control.

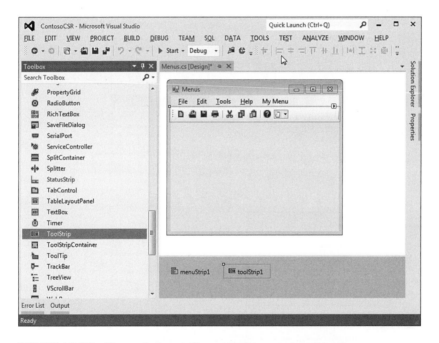

FIGURE 18.22   The main form with a complete menu and toolbar.

If you want to enable users to drag and drop the toolbar or menu onto one of the form's four sides, you use the ToolStripContainer. In fact, there is a shortcut option here: You can take any of the ToolStrip controls currently on the form and add them to a ToolStripContainer with just a couple clicks of the mouse. One of the items available via a tool strip's smart tag is the command Embed in a ToolStripContainer. If you issue this command against the toolbar that you just added to the sample form, Visual Studio does two things for you: It adds a ToolStripContainer to the form, and it places the selected ToolStrip into the container, specifically, in the top panel of the ToolStripContainer.

Creating a Status Bar

Status bars provide the user feedback on an application's current status, progress within an action, details in context with an object selected on a form, and so on. The StatusStrip control provides this functionality in starting with .NET 2.0/Visual Studio 2005, and it supplants the StatusBar control found in earlier versions.

As with the other ToolStrip descendants, the StatusStrip control functions as a container; its capability to host labels in addition to progress bars, drop-downs, and split buttons makes it a much more powerful control than the StatusBar.

Figure 18.23 shows the fictional Contoso CSR form with a StatusStrip docked at the bottom of the form. In design mode, you see a drop-down button that holds a selection for each of the four supported child controls. For the purposes of this demonstration prototype, add a label control to report general application status and an additional label and progress bar to be used if you run into any long-running retrieval or edit operations.

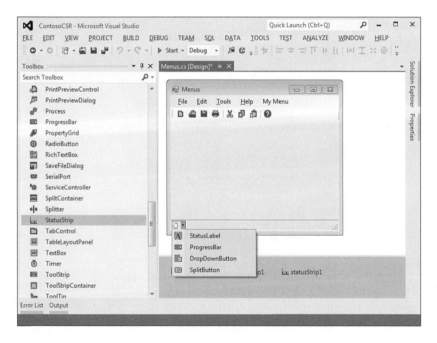

FIGURE 18.23   StatusStrip in design mode.

By default, child controls are added in a left-to-right flow layout pattern within the StatusStrip pattern. With just six clicks (two per item), you can add these controls to the strip. The in-place editing capabilities are great for quickly building out the look and feel of the strip; for greater control of the strip's child controls, you can use the Items Collection Editor dialog box.

TIP

By right-clicking any of the StatusStrip child controls and selecting Convert To, you can quickly change the type of the control. For instance, if you have a label control currently on the strip but you really want a drop-down button, you right-click the label and select Convert To, DropDownButton. This saves you the hassle of deleting the control and adding a new one.

Editing the StatusStrip Items   You use the StatusStrip's smart tag and select Edit Items to launch the Items Collection Editor dialog box. The editor provides direct access to all the hosted control's properties and also enables you to edit, delete, and reorder items within the status strip (see Figure 18.24).

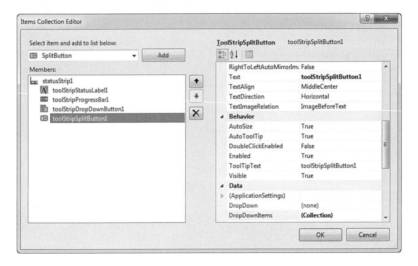

FIGURE 18.24   The StatusStrip Items Collection Editor.

By tweaking some properties here, you can improve the layout and appearance of your items. Figure 18.25 shows the default layout of the controls you added; ideally, you want the progress bar and its label control to sit at the far right of the status strip and the status label to sit at the far left to consume any remaining space.

FIGURE 18.25   Default positioning of the StatusStrip items.

To make this happen, you need to set the Spring property to True for the leftmost label. This will cause the label to expand and contract to fill the available space on the status strip. Next, set its TextAlignment property to situate the text to the left of the label region and change the Text property to something more appropriate.

Figure 18.26 shows the fruits of our labor.

FIGURE 18.26   The final StatusStrip look and feel.

Displaying Data

So far, we have only touched on form elements that provide the basic framework user navigation, status, commands, and so on. However, the capability to access, display, and edit data from an underlying data store (relational or otherwise) is the real value of an application such as the fictional Contoso CSR application. We touch on the details of working with databases in the next chapter; here, we describe some of the basic controls used to display data in a form.

Hierarchical Data

The TreeView control is ideal for presenting data with hierarchical relationships and is thus a good candidate for housing the list of order records (which can be grouped by different criteria). First, add a SplitContainer control to partition the leftover interior space in the form into two discrete panels. Yet another panel houses the search function for orders; this is docked to the top of the left split panel. A TreeView dock fills the remainder of this leftmost panel, and the right panel houses the data fields (text boxes, labels, radio buttons, and so on) for an individual CSR record.

TreeView controls present data as a list of nodes; each node can serve as a parent for additional nodes. Typically, with applications that front a database, you build the contents of the TreeView by binding to a resultset from the database, or by programmatically looping through the resultset and adding to the TreeView's node list through its application programming interface (API). But you also have control over the TreeView content in the designer by launching the TreeNode Editor.

The TreeNode Editor   The TreeNode Editor (see Figure 18.27) is a dialog box that acts much the same as the Items Collection Editor examined previously. It enables you to add, edit, and remove items from the TreeView control. You launch the editor dialog box by selecting Edit Nodes from the TreeView's smart tag.

Using the Add Root and Add Child buttons, you can insert new nodes into the tree's data structure at any given nesting level. Figure 18.27 shows manually inserted nodes with test data so that you can get an idea of what the order list would look like using the company as a parent node and order instances as child nodes under the corresponding company. Each item, or node, in the TreeView consists of two parts: an image and text. The image is optional; if you want to attach an icon to a node, you start by first assigning an ImageList control to the TreeView control.

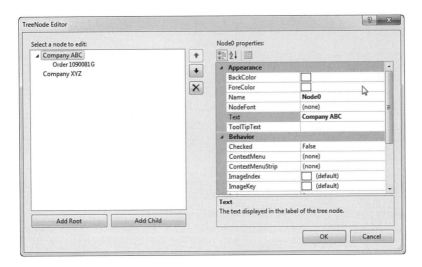

FIGURE 18.27   Using the designer to edit nodes in the TreeView control.

Using an ImageList   ImageList controls function as an image provider for other controls. They maintain a collection of Image objects that are referenced by their ordinal position or key within the collection. Any control that provides an ImageList property can reference an ImageList component and use its images. ListView, ToolStrip, and TreeView are some examples of controls that can leverage the ImageList component.

NOTE

Visual Studio ships with a large library of images that you can use with the TreeView or any other control that requires these types of standard graphics such as toolbars and menus. By default, the image files are placed in a zipped file located at C:\Program Files\ Microsoft Visual Studio 11.0\Common7\VS2012ImageLibrary.

An ImageList doesn't have a visual presence on a form; in other words, you can't see the ImageList itself. Its sole use is as a behind-the-scenes component that feeds images to other controls. Dropping an ImageList onto the designer puts an instance of the component in the component tray. You can then use the Images Collection Editor dialog box to add, edit, and remove the images hosted by the component. Changing the images associated with the image list automatically changes the images used by any controls referencing the ImageList.

Figure 18.28 shows a few images added within the Images Collection Editor. To enable the TreeView to use these images, you have to do two things:

1. Assign the TreeView.ImageList property to point to the instance of the ImageList component (in this case, ImageList1).

2. Set the image associated with a node either programmatically or via the TreeNode Editor dialog box.

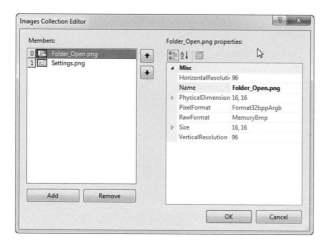

FIGURE 18.28   The Images Collection Editor.

With the ImageList component in place and the TreeView dropped in the SplitContainer's left panel, the form is almost there from a design perspective. The remaining piece is the series of fields that display the data for a record selected in the TreeView control.

You could add this piece by just dragging a bunch of text boxes and labels over into a TableLayoutPanel and then docking the whole mess in the open SplitContainer panel. But because you really want to treat this as one cohesive unit to simplify positioning, eventual data binding, and so on, you instead create a user control for displaying a CSR record.

Tabular Data

The DataGridView control is the premium Visual Studio control for displaying data in a tabular format. It provides a row/column format for displaying data from a wide variety of data sources. Figure 18.29 shows a DataGridView with its smart tag menu opened; the smart tag menu provides fast access to the column properties of the grid control and also enables you to directly bind the DataGridView to a data source.

Data Sources   The DataGridView control supports various possible data sources. For instance, scenarios such as displaying name/value pairs from a collection are supported, in addition to mainstream support for datasets returned from a relational data store. If you select a data source for the grid, a column is added to the grid for every column that appears in the data source, and the row data is automatically provided inside the DataGridView control.

Data can be displayed in the grid control in an "unbound" mode as well; using the grid's row/column API, you can programmatically define the structure of the grid and add data to it at runtime.

18

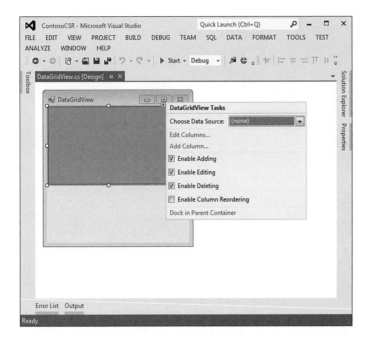

FIGURE 18.29   Configuring a DataGridView control with its smart tag.

Cell Types   Each individual cell in a DataGridView functions as if it is an embedded control. Each cell can express the underlying data that it contains in various ways; check boxes, drop-downs, links, buttons, and text boxes are all supported cell types. In addition to the data visualization possibilities, each cell also has its own set of events that can be hooked within your code. For example, you can hook the mouse enter and leave events for a specific cell.

We cover this control in depth in Chapter 20, "Working with Databases."

Creating Your Own Controls

If none of the stock .NET controls meets your specific needs, you can create your own controls for use on a Windows Form in three ways:

▶ You can subclass an existing control and modify or extend its behavior and appearance.

▶ You can create a user control by compositing together two or more existing controls.

▶ You can create a custom control from scratch, implementing your own visuals and behavior.

Subclassing an Existing Control

Subclassing an existing control is the best approach if your needs are only slightly different from one of the standard .NET Framework controls. By inheriting from an existing control class, you are riding on top of its behavior and appearance; it's up to you to then add the specialized code to your new control class.

For example, suppose that you want a text box that turns red anytime a numeric (that is, nonalphabetic) character is entered. This is easy to do with just a few lines of code sitting in the TextBox control's TextChanged event, but consolidating this behavior into its own class provides a reuse factor.

You start by adding a new user control to the project. User controls actually inherit from the UserControl class; because you want to inherit from the TextBox class, you need to change the class definition by using the code editor. After you do that, you can place the new component on a form and use its functionality.

Working with an Inherited Control

Because TextBox already has a UI, you don't need to do anything with regard to the appearance of the control. In fact, it works just like any other text box control within the Windows Forms Designer (see Figure 18.30).

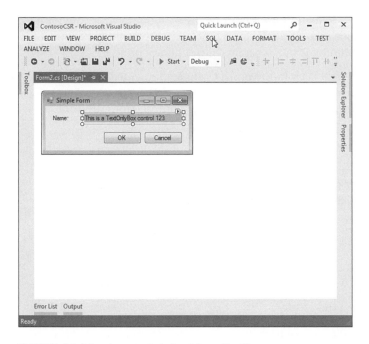

FIGURE 18.30   A control derived from TextBox.

The Properties window for the control behaves as expected, and double-clicking the control immediately takes you to an open code editor window. In short, the design-time experience remains fully functional and requires no effort on the part of the developer.

Designing a User Control

A user control is technically the same as any other class that you author as a developer. Because a user control has a visual aspect to it, Visual Studio provides a designer, just as with Windows Forms, to help in the drag-and-drop creation of the control.

User controls are composite controls; that is, they are constructed from one or more existing .NET controls. As with a derived control, their user interfaces inherit from the native controls they are composed of, making them simple to build and use in the designer.

There are two approaches to the user control creation process: You can create a separate Windows Control Library project, or you can simply add a user control class to an existing Windows Forms project.

Creating a separate project enables the user control to live in its own assembly. If it is a separate assembly, you can treat the user control as the quintessential black box, giving you greater flexibility from a source control perspective and enabling you to share the control among multiple projects. For production scenarios, this is clearly the best route. However, for simple prototyping work, as you are doing here with the CSR form application, the ease and simplicity of just adding a new class to the existing project make this approach preferable to using the separate project approach. The class lives inside the same namespace as the form class.

If you were ever in a position to transition from prototyping to actual production development, nothing would preclude you from refactoring the control by simply copying the user control class file and embedding it in a separate control library project.

As soon as you add the user control class to the project, you are presented with the User Control Designer. The designer works in exactly the same way as the Windows Forms Designer; to build the user control, you drag components or controls from the Toolbox onto its surface.

Adding Controls

Obviously, the controls that you use to build your composite control entirely depend on how you envision the control's functionality. As an example, to create an order display control, you need to think about the underlying data structure of an order. An order record might contain the following:

- ▶ An order number
- ▶ A series of dates that capture the date the order was placed, date the order was shipped, and so on
- ▶ A list of items included on the order
- ▶ Billing information and shipping address
- ▶ Miscellaneous comments

Because this is a lot of information to try to cram onto one screen, you can turn to the TabControl. A tab control is another general-purpose container control that enables you to organize content across several pages that are accessed via tabs. Within each tab, you can leverage the TableLayoutPanel and implement most of the order fields with simple label and text box pairs.

As mentioned earlier, the whole process of getting these controls into the user control works identically to the Windows Forms Designer: You drag and drop the controls from the Toolbox onto the user control design surface. Figure 18.31 shows the OrderDisplay user control with its user interface completed.

FIGURE 18.31   Designing a user control.

Embedding the User Control

Now that you have a completed design for your user control, the only remaining step is to embed the control into your primary form. If you compile the project, Visual Studio automatically recognizes the user control class and include an entry for the control in the Toolbox. From there, you are just a drag and drop away from implementing the OrderDisplay control.

In Figure 18.32, you can see the OrderDisplay item in the Toolbox and the results of dragging it onto the form surface.

Creating a Custom Control

Custom controls represent the ultimate in extensibility because they are built from scratch. As a result, they are relatively hard to develop because they require you to worry not only about functionality but also about every single aspect of the control's visual appearance. Because the physical user interface of the custom control needs to be drawn 100% by custom code, a steep learning curve is associated with authoring a custom control.

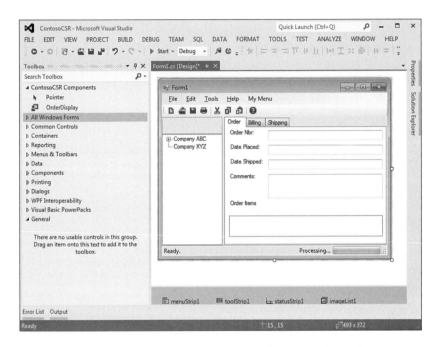

FIGURE 18.32   A user control displayed in the Toolbox and on a form.

Because much of the work that goes into creating a custom control is at the code level, we won't try to tackle this subject with any useful degree of detail in this book. You should note, however, that the process starts the same way as with other control options: Visual Studio has a custom control project item template; adding this to your project gives you a baseline of code to start with. From there, it's up to you.

NOTE

The OnPaint event is where you place the code to draw your control's user interface. Although so-called "owner draw" controls can involve complex drawing code, the good news is that the Windows Forms Designer leverages whatever code you place in the OnPaint event to render the control at design time. This means that you can still rely on the Windows Forms Designer to provide you with a WYSIWYG experience even with custom controls.

Summary

This chapter described the various design-time capabilities of the Windows Forms Designer tool. Windows Forms are a powerful presentation layer technology, and Visual Studio 2012 provides an array of tools for quickly building impressive, rich user interfaces based on this technology.

The role of the Windows Forms Designer, the Toolbox, and the Properties window were introduced in the context of delivering a modern, well-thought-out, standards-based user interface for a .NET Windows application. Using the tools documented here, you can wring the most out of your WinForm development experience.

18

Creating Richer, Smarter User Interfaces

With .NET 3.0, Microsoft delivered a brand-new set of technologies for powering the presentation layer in your applications: the Windows Presentation Foundation (WPF). WPF was designed from the ground up to leverage the strengths of both the Windows Forms development world and the web forms development world. At the same time, WPF attempts to overcome many of the obstacles that developers face when trying to build rich, compelling user interfaces that involve media and highly customized user interfaces and that exploit all the horsepower available in modern CPUs and graphics processors.

WPF is intended to be a unifying platform with built-in, first-class support for data binding, audio, video, and both 2D and 3D graphics. Because WPF likely represents a significant learning curve for both new and experienced developers, we spend some time up front in this chapter discussing the basics before diving into the real target: how to use the Visual Studio WPF Designer tool (previously known by its code name Cider) to build high-octane user interfaces for your Windows applications.

The Windows Presentation Foundation Platform

As a relatively new presentation layer framework, WPF brings a lot of new concepts and new coding territory with it (and can represent a fairly significant learning curve for developers). But let's take a brief look at the overall architecture of the WPF platform, and then dissect the programming model.

Physically, WPF is implemented with a series of three dynamic link libraries (DLLs):

▶ WindowsBase.dll

▶ PresentationFramework.dll

▶ PresentationCore.dll

Every presentation layer framework has to eventually paint pixels onto a screen, and WPF is no different. Implemented within its binaries is a composition and rendering engine, which talks to your hardware through DirectX. In addition to the rendering layers, there is also obviously a rich programming model that is implemented with deep support for things such as layout, containership (the capability for one element to contain another), and events/message dispatches. In short, it does all the heavy lifting to ensure that some very complicated user interface scenarios can be rendered on the screen with enough performance to appeal to a wide range of solution scenarios.

Figure 19.1 shows the logical architecture of the various WPF components. The actual rendering "engine" is contained within the Media Integration Layer component; `PresentationCore` handles interop with the Media Integration Layer, and `PresentationFramework` contains all the other magic necessary to make WPF successful as an end-to-end platform such as layout, data binding, and event notifications.

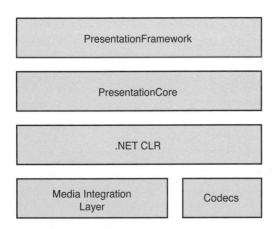

FIGURE 19.1   WPF logical architecture.

NOTE

Most of WPF itself is implemented in managed .NET code. The exception is the Media Integration Layer. When it comes to rendering the user interface (UI) to the screen, WPF needs to optimize for performance over nearly all other concerns, and therefore the Media Integration Layer is implemented as native code.

All of these WPF components work in concert to deliver an impressive laundry list of improvements to the state of the art with regard to presentation layer design, construction, and runtime support with .NET. Here is a small sample:

▶ **Media**—WPF supports 2D and 3D graphics, as well as WMV, MPEG, and AVI video.

▶ **Data binding**—WPF was built from the start to fully support the entire spectrum of data binding scenarios, up to and including LINQ and the Entity Framework.

▶ **Windows Forms Interoperability**—WPF applications can host WinForms components and vice versa. This is comforting because it means developers won't need to abandon the hard-won knowledge that comes with programming WinForms for many years.

▶ **Document Support**—WPF has several native constructs for building document-centric applications. For instance, there is a `DocumentReader` class for displaying fixed-format documents, and a `FlowDocumentReader` class for displaying documents with a dynamic layout. Think of a newspaper article, for instance, that automatically repaginates while remaining true to the column structure.

▶ **Animation**—Developers can create storyboard-based animations, and specify animation triggers and timers.

▶ **Control "look and feel"**—Controls in WPF have their appearance controlled by a template, which developers can replace or change to fully customize nearly every aspect of a control's "chrome."

▶ **Text**—There is rich typography support in WPF. Developers can manipulate a slew of font attributes (kerning; effects such as glow, drop-shadows, and motion blur; auto line spacing; and so on), and WPF developers can choose to have text rendered using ClearType technology or via two additional rendering modes introduced in WPF 4: aliased and grayscale.

During the initial beta cycles, Microsoft produced a series of prototype applications to showcase the new technologies in .NET 3.0, including WPF. Figure 19.2 shows a screenshot from the healthcare prototype. Although a static shot in black and white doesn't do the application much justice, you can get a good sense for the possibilities: The UI for this application would have been extremely difficult to implement using Windows Forms technology.

For the most part, developers are free to not worry so much about the low-level architectural details of WPF; the programming model (and the tools which help us leverage that model) is where most developers will focus their energies.

Programming Model

The WPF class library consists of approximately 1,600 public types and more than 3,500 classes. As such, it has a considerably larger application programming interface (API) surface than either ASP.NET or Windows Forms. As you would expect from a .NET class library, all of these classes can trace their ancestry back to `System.Object`. In addition, most WPF classes are based on so-called base elements: the `UIElement`, `FrameworkElement`, `ContentElement`, and `FrameworkContentElement` classes. These classes are responsible for basic item presentation and layout capabilities and are contained within the `System.Windows` namespace.

FIGURE 19.2   An early, WPF-based, healthcare prototype.

In addition to these four base element classes, a few other important base classes drive a lot of the functionality found in WPF:

▶ **Visual**—This class is the core rendering unit within WPF; `UIElement` inherits from Visual as do the higher-level classes such as `Button`.

▶ **DispatcherObject**—This class implements the WPF threading model.

▶ **Control**—This is the base class for controls in WPF.

▶ **Application**—The `Application` class encapsulates all WPF applications; it provides application lifetime services, including the basic concepts of `Run` (to start an application) and `Exit` (to quit an application).

As you would expect, the WPF class library also provides all the major controls that you would typically find in a Windows application such as buttons, labels, list boxes, and text boxes.

The following snippet shows a WPF Button control being instantiated, and the text Push Me is assigned to the button. Note that the control constructs are all familiar but that the actual object model is slightly different; the `Button` object in WPF does not have a `.Text` property as we would expect from an ASP.NET or WinForms button. Instead, it exposes a `.Content` property:

```
System.Windows.Controls.Button btn = new Button();
btn.Content = "Push Me";
```

Besides procedural code like that shown here, WPF enables us to create and manipulate objects in a declarative fashion using a markup syntax called Extensible Application Markup Language (XAML).

Extensible Application Markup Language

Extensible Application Markup Language, or XAML, is an XML dialect that can be used to describe the structure of a WPF application's presentation layer (for example, control instantiation, appearance, and layout).

XAML is a new "language," and is the principal way in which the various WPF tools create objects and set properties in a declarative fashion. As such, it is tempting to compare XAML to HTML: It certainly fills a similar role in that XAML and HTML are both declarative ways to describe objects. But XAML is actually tightly coupled to the .NET Framework. In fact, XAML is really a generic way to create and manipulate .NET objects. WPF tools, such as the WPF Designer in Visual Studio, happen to leverage XAML, but strictly speaking, XAML is not a part of WPF. You can write an entire XAML application, for instance, using only the managed code language of your choice. Because XAML, as a programming model, brings several important advancements to the scene, it is heavily leveraged by all the Microsoft and non-Microsoft tools in the WPF world, and beyond. For instance, it is also used by Windows Workflow Foundation to describe workflows. It is also one of the ways that you can create Metro-style applications in Windows 8.

Just as we did previously, let's create a `Button` object and assign some text to the button; but this time, let's do all the work with XAML:

```
<Button Content="Push Me"></Button>
```

Alternatively, we could write this code like this:

```
<Button>Push Me</Button>
```

19

NOTE

XAML functionality is a subset of what is possible in .NET code. Or, to put it another way, anything you can do in XAML you can do in code, but not everything done in code can be done in XAML.

In a typical WPF application, XAML coexists with managed code through the same partial class paradigm introduced with ASP.NET. In other words, we may have a MainForm.xaml file with the look and feel of a window, and a MainForm.xaml.vb (or .cs) file that contains code that reacts to a user's input on that form. We see more of this in action a little later in this chapter when we take a close look at the WPF Designer.

If XAML isn't necessary to create a WPF application, why is it desired? Given the fact that you can accomplish the necessary tasks to create UI objects in XAML or in managed code, why is XAML even in the picture? There are a few areas where the declarative syntax becomes tremendously important.

Syntax Simplicity   As is true with all XML-based languages, XAML is relatively easy for applications to parse and understand. Several developers have used this to their advantage and delivered lightweight tools for WPF development such as XAMLPad. This has also enabled tool vendors, including Microsoft, to rapidly release products into the market that understand XAML. Adobe Illustrator, for example, has a XAML plug-in that enables you to emit XAML, and of course Microsoft has not one but two design tools that read and write XAML: Expression Design and Expression Blend.

The boundary between XAML and code also turns out to be a nice dividing line between appearance and behavior. In this scenario, XAML is used to create the UI objects and the general look and feel of the application, while procedural code is used to implement the business logic and to react to a user's input. This leads us directly to the other important advantage of XAML: collaboration.

Collaboration   If we separate appearance and behavior, we can also reap the benefits of improved collaboration among project team members (specifically, collaboration between designers and developers). Before WPF, designers would rely on "flat" bitmaps created with drawing programs, or would even rely on applications such as PowerPoint to mock up the user experience for an application. When that design is eventually handed off to the developer for implementation, there is an inherent disconnect: Programming tools don't understand 2D bitmaps or PowerPoint storyboards. They understand code and objects. And in the reverse direction, we have the same problem: Tools made for designers don't understand managed code. A developer can't implement a form in Visual Basic, for example, and hand it back to a designer for review and tweaking.

So, developers are forced to re-create, as best they can, the vision delivered from the design team. This is a decidedly second-rate way to design and build applications. But with XAML, this situation changes dramatically. Because designers can now use tools that express their design in XAML (such as Microsoft Expression Blend), the developer can simply open that XAML file and provide the coding "goop" necessary to flesh out the desired features. In the process, we have 100% preserved the fidelity of the designers' original vision because the developer's tools are talking the same language. We also have full collaboration in the other direction: Changes that a developer makes to the designer's XAML can be instantly reviewed and tweaked within the designer's tools. This simple concept—the sharing of a codebase and language between design and development roles and tools—proves to be a powerful argument for leveraging XAML in your applications.

Now that we have covered the basics of WPF, let's see how we can start writing WPF applications using Visual Studio.

Introducing the WPF Designer

We first introduced the WPF Designer in Chapter 6, "Introducing the Editors and Designers." Let's recap the basics and then move on to a more involved discussion of the WPF designer.

The WPF Designer is the tool in Visual Studio that provides the WYSIWYG design surface for building WPF windows. In many ways, it behaves just like the designers we use for web forms and Windows forms. But it is in fact a brand-new tool, with some subtle differences over its IDE brethren. To see the designer in action, let's create a new project in Visual Studio. The project template we want to select is WPF Application, and it is located in the Windows category on the New Project dialog box (see Figure 19.3).

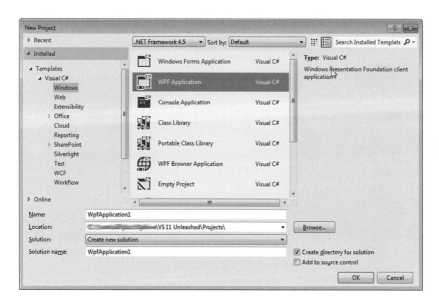

FIGURE 19.3   Creating a new WPF application.

This template takes care of adding the necessary WPF namespaces for us; the project also includes a file that implements the default window for the application: MainWindow.xaml. Double-clicking the Window1.xaml file launches the designer, which is shown in Figure 19.4.

XAML and Design Panes

The WPF Designer offers two different views: the visual representation of the window, and the XAML that implements the window. You can make changes to the window and its controls by either editing the XAML or changing elements on the design surface. Either way, the designer keeps both panes in sync.

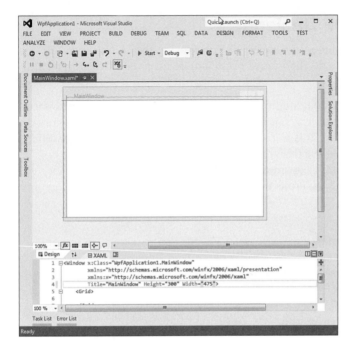

FIGURE 19.4   The WPF Designer.

You can configure the position and layout of the XAML and design panes in the following ways:

▶ The Swap button swaps the positions of the XAML and design panes with one another.

▶ The Vertical Split button tiles the panes vertically.

▶ The Horizontal Split button tiles the panes horizontally.

▶ The Collapse/Expand Pane button minimizes or restores the bottom or leftmost pane (depending on the view mode you are in).

Figure 19.5 shows the location of these pane management buttons on the designer.

TIP

If you are lucky enough to have a multimonitor setup, the vertical split view is particularly helpful because you can display your XAML code on one screen and your visual design surface on another.

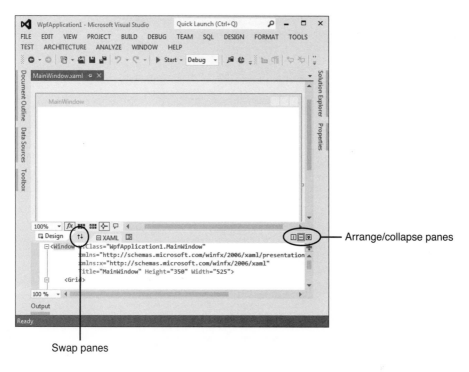

FIGURE 19.5   Controls for configuring the XAML and designer panes.

We interact with the designer in the same way we interact with other design surfaces or code editors: Controls can be placed on the design pane from the Toolbox and then manipulated, and we can use the XAML pane to handcraft or alter XAML (with complete IntelliSense and formatting).

For the most part, control placement and positioning works the same as it does in the Windows Forms designer. There are a few minor exceptions: The WPF Designer has some unique visualizations for displaying snap lines and control sizing (see Figure 19.6).

The Property Window
As expected, when you have a control selected in the designer, you can manipulate its attributes using the Properties window. The WPF Properties window has some significant differences over its Windows Forms sibling. It supports two unique ways for locating control properties: Besides the categorized and alphabetic display modes, you can group and sort properties by source. This is great for quickly looking at those properties, for instance, that have their value set explicitly in XAML or that have values that are currently being inherited down from a style. The WPF Properties window also enables you to search for properties of the control by typing in a search box. As you type, the window automatically filters the property list to just those that match your search criteria. Figure 19.7 shows an image of the Properties window.

19

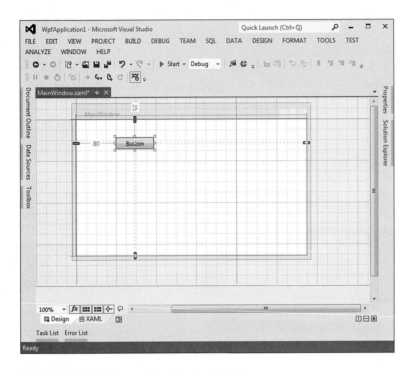

FIGURE 19.6   Sizing and positioning indicators.

FIGURE 19.7   The WPF Designer property window.

The Zoom Control

One additional item is present with the WPF designer: a zoom control. Perched in the small toolbar at the bottom of the design page, this drop-down can be used to zoom in or out on the current window from 3% to 6400% of the window's actual size. Figure 19.8 shows the magnification control, and Figure 19.9 shows our Push Me button (and container window) at 8x magnification.

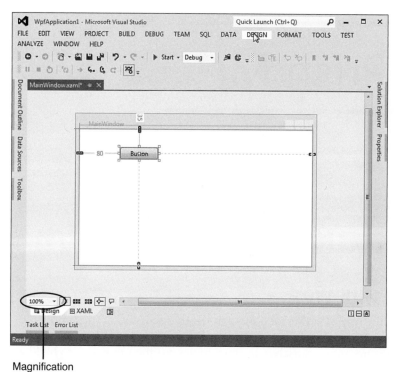

Magnification

FIGURE 19.8   The zoom slider.

TIP

The zoom control is particularly useful when you have a complex form layout with a lot of snap lines and nested/layered controls amassed in a certain area. By zooming in on the area, you can get a crisp view of where things are positioned, and it becomes much easier to select or position the control you want instead of one of its neighbors. By zooming out, you can get a thumbnail look at your window to see how your overall look and feel is shaping up.

The XAML pane also has a zoom control; this can prove useful when you want to zoom out to quickly drill through lines or code or zoom in for readability or presentation purposes.

19

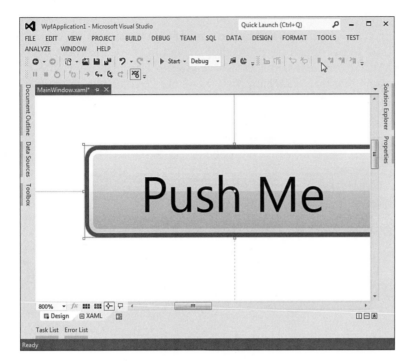

FIGURE 19.9   A button at 800% magnification.

Programming with WPF

With the basics out of the way, it's time for a more in-depth discussion of the various controls and technologies that you typically encounter when creating a WPF-powered application. After firmly grounding ourselves in these topics, we then move on to build a simple application, end to end, using the WPF Designer.

Layout

Because software needs to present controls and data on a screen for visual consumption by users, the layout (or how things are arranged onscreen) becomes an important design feature. Good layout systems not only have to enable developers to structure controls in a coherent fashion, but also need to be robust in terms of how they handle things such as window resizing and flow.

In WPF, layout is exercised through a set of container controls called panels. Each panel is uniquely suited for a specific layout scenario, and the capability to combine them with one another means that the layout system in WPF can handle a large number of different control organization scenarios. The key point to understand with panels is that, as containers, they are responsible for the positioning (and in some cases, the sizing) of all the controls placed within. This means that the individual child controls themselves don't need to be aware of the specific layout system they are participating in, which greatly simplifies the code and architecture.

Table 19.1 lists the available layout panel controls.

TABLE 19.1   The WPF Layout Panels

Class	Description
Canvas	A container control with no built-in layout logic
DockPanel	Panel that enables docking of its child elements
Grid	A container control that allows child objects to be positioned within columns and rows
StackPanel	A container control that implements horizontal and vertical stacking behavior for its child controls
WrapPanel	Panel that will automatically wrap elements to a new row as needed

Let's examine these controls, and their subtypes, one by one.

The Canvas Control

The Canvas control is unique among all the layout controls because it is the only one that actually performs no layout at all. It is functionally similar to the GroupBox control that you might have used with a Windows Forms project: Child objects that are placed within a Canvas control are placed using coordinates relative to the canvas itself. No automatic resizing, flow layout, or positioning is done on behalf of the child controls by the canvas. If any such logic is needed, you need to implement it yourself. This highlights the purpose of the Canvas control: providing the developer with the absolute control to position things as you want them positioned.

In Figure 19.10, we have a Canvas control with four buttons in a unique arrangement. They are all positioned relative to the sides of the Canvas container.

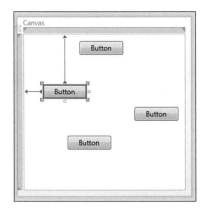

FIGURE 19.10   Buttons positioned within a Canvas control.

19

Here is the XAML:

```
<Window x:Class="ContosoAvalon.Canvas"
    xmlns="http://schemas.microsoft.com/winfx/2006/xaml/presentation"
    xmlns:x="http://schemas.microsoft.com/winfx/2006/xaml"
    Title="Canvas" Height="300" Width="300">
    <Canvas>
      <Button Canvas.Left="102" Canvas.Top="11" Height="23" Name="button1"
        Width="75">Button</Button>
      <Button Canvas.Left="47" Canvas.Top="38" Height="23" Name="button2"
        Width="75">Button</Button>
      <Button Canvas.Right="46" Canvas.Top="38" Height="23" Name="button3"
        Width="75">Button</Button>
      <Button Canvas.Left="102" Canvas.Top="99" Height="23" Name="button4"
        Width="75">Button</Button>
    </Canvas>
</Window>
```

Note that we have provided coordinates that are relative to a specified side of the canvas. If we resize the window, the buttons move accordingly. Unless you absolutely need to manually specify control positions (as may be the case, for instance, if you are arranging controls in a nonstandard way or using controls to "draw" something in a window), it is recommended that you use one of the other panels that automatically perform the layout you need.

The DockPanel Control

Modern lines of business applications typically use some kind of docking arrangement for their controls: Toolbars may be docked at the top or sides of the window, a status bar may be docked at the bottom, and so forth. The DockPanel in WPF provides the capability to dock controls to one of the four sides of a window.

If we need to create a window with a toolbar docked to the top and the left side of the window, with the remainder of the screen occupied by a canvas, we do the following:

```
<Window x:Class="ContosoAvalon.DockPanel"
    xmlns="http://schemas.microsoft.com/winfx/2006/xaml/presentation"
    xmlns:x="http://schemas.microsoft.com/winfx/2006/xaml"
    Title="DockPanel" Height="300" Width="300">
    <DockPanel Name="dockPanel1">
        <ToolBar DockPanel.Dock="Top">
            <Button BorderBrush="Black">Button1</Button>
        </ToolBar>
        <ToolBar DockPanel.Dock="Left" MaxWidth="75">
            <Button BorderBrush="Black">Button2</Button>
        </ToolBar>
        <Canvas>
            <TextBlock>Canvas</TextBlock>
```

```
        </Canvas>
    </DockPanel>
</Window>
```

With the DockPanel, you can place more than one element in a certain dock position. Figure 19.11 shows six regions docked in a window: three of them are docked to the left, and three of them are docked to the top.

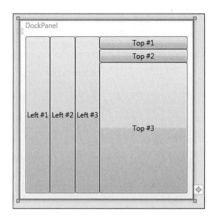

FIGURE 19.11   Docking controls within a DockPanel.

And here is the matching XAML:

```
<Window x:Class="ContosoAvalon.DockPanel"
    xmlns="http://schemas.microsoft.com/winfx/2006/xaml/presentation"
    xmlns:x="http://schemas.microsoft.com/winfx/2006/xaml"
    Title="DockPanel" Height="300" Width="300">
    <DockPanel Name="dockPanel1">
        <Button DockPanel.Dock="Left">Left #1</Button>
        <Button DockPanel.Dock="Left">Left #2</Button>
        <Button DockPanel.Dock="Left">Left #3</Button>
        <Button DockPanel.Dock="Top">Top #1</Button>
        <Button DockPanel.Dock="Top">Top #2</Button>
        <Button DockPanel.Dock="Top">Top #3</Button>
    </DockPanel>
</Window>
```

All the elements within a DockPanel are resized such that they stay docked in their designated position, and they entirely "fill" the window edge that they are docked to.

The Grid Control
The Grid panel is used for row and column arrangements, similar to an HTML table or to the TableLayoutPanel control in WinForms.

One common use for the Grid control is with dialog boxes or data-entry forms where labels and values exist side by side and row by row; we can use the columns in the grid to align items horizontally, and the rows to align items vertically.

Columns are created in a grid through the use of the `Grid.ColumnDefinitions` element. For example, this XAML snippet would create a grid with three columns:

```
<Grid>
    <Grid.ColumnDefinitions>
        <ColumnDefinition></ColumnDefinition>
        <ColumnDefinition></ColumnDefinition>
        <ColumnDefinition></ColumnDefinition>
    </Grid.ColumnDefinitions>
</Grid>
```

In a similar fashion, the `Grid.RowDefinitions` element defines the rows within a grid:

```
<Grid>
    <Grid.RowDefinitions>
        <RowDefinition></RowDefinition>
        <RowDefinition></RowDefinition>
        <RowDefinition></RowDefinition>
    </Grid.RowDefinitions>
</Grid>
```

The WPF Designer also has interactive features that allow for row and column addition, deletion, and sizing. Figure 19.12 shows a two-column, six-row grid placed in a window. Note that the designer shows the grid lines demarcating the rows and columns, and that there is a shaded border area to the top and to the left of the Grid control. Not only does this border area show us the current size (width or height) of a column or row, but we also can use this border area to create new rows or columns by just clicking where we want to place the new element. We can also drag the row or column lines to increase or decrease the size of the row or column.

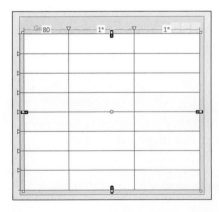

FIGURE 19.12   Working with a Grid control in the designer.

The dialog box shown in Figure 19.13 is easily achieved using a Grid panel; the XAML is shown in Listing 19.1. Arguably, the Grid control is the most flexible and relevant of the panel controls for almost all layout scenarios. For this reason, when you add a new window project item to a WPF project, the window by default already contains a Grid control.

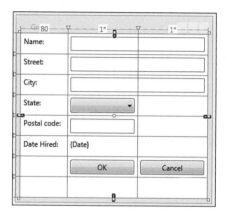

FIGURE 19.13   Implementing a dialog box using the rows and columns of a Grid control.

LISTING 19.1   Implementing a Dialog Box with a Grid Panel

```xaml
<Window x:Class="ContosoAvalon.Grid"
    xmlns="http://schemas.microsoft.com/winfx/2006/xaml/presentation"
    xmlns:x="http://schemas.microsoft.com/winfx/2006/xaml"
    Title="Grid" Height="300" Width="300">
    <Grid>
        <Grid.ColumnDefinitions>
            <ColumnDefinition Width="80"></ColumnDefinition>
            <ColumnDefinition Width="*"></ColumnDefinition>
            <ColumnDefinition Width="*"></ColumnDefinition>
        </Grid.ColumnDefinitions>
        <Grid.RowDefinitions>
            <RowDefinition></RowDefinition>
            <RowDefinition></RowDefinition>
            <RowDefinition></RowDefinition>
            <RowDefinition></RowDefinition>
            <RowDefinition></RowDefinition>
            <RowDefinition></RowDefinition>
            <RowDefinition></RowDefinition>
            <RowDefinition></RowDefinition>
        </Grid.RowDefinitions>
```

```
<Label Grid.Column="0" Grid.Row="0">Name:</Label>
<Label Grid.Column="0" Grid.Row="1">Street:</Label>
<Label Grid.Column="0" Grid.Row="2">City:</Label>
<Label Grid.Column="0" Grid.Row="3">State:</Label>
<Label Grid.Column="0" Grid.Row="4">Postal code:</Label>
<Label Grid.Column="0" Grid.Row="5">Date Hired:</Label>

<TextBox Margin="5,5" BorderBrush="Gray" Grid.Column="1" Grid.Row="0"
Grid.ColumnSpan="2"></TextBox>
<TextBox Margin="5,5" BorderBrush="Gray" Grid.Column="1" Grid.Row="1"
Grid.ColumnSpan="2"></TextBox>
<TextBox Margin="5,5" BorderBrush="Gray" Grid.Column="1" Grid.Row="2"
Grid.ColumnSpan="2"></TextBox>
<ComboBox Margin="5,5" Grid.Column="1" Grid.Row="3"></ComboBox>
<TextBox Margin="5,5" BorderBrush="Gray" Grid.Column="1" Grid.Row="4">
</TextBox>
<Label Grid.Column="1" Grid.Row="5">{Date}</Label>

<Button Margin="5,5" Grid.Column="1" Grid.Row="6">OK</Button>
<Button Margin="5,5" Grid.Column="2" Grid.Row="6">Cancel</Button>
    </Grid>
</Window>
```

There are three things to note in this XAML:

▶ We have used the concept of column spanning to get our controls to line up the way we want.

▶ We are using the Margin property on the child elements to give each label, text box, and so on some room. Without a margin specified, each control automatically fills the bounds of the cell it resides in, meaning that we have absolutely no border or gap between the controls (either horizontally or vertically).

▶ In the grid's column definitions, we use an asterisk to denote a proportional size. In other words, the second and third columns equally share whatever space is left over after the first column has been rendered. We can adjust the proportion "ratio" by including a number as well (for example, ColumnDefinition.Width="2*"). We cover the details on grid sizing later in this chapter when we build a sample application.

The StackPanel Control

StackPanel controls implement a vertical or horizontal stack layout for their child elements. Compared with the Grid control, this is a simple panel that supports very little tweaking: You can select to stack children horizontally or vertically using the Orientation property, and after that the panel takes care of everything else. Each element within the StackPanel is resized/scaled to fit within the height (if stacked vertically) or width (if stacked horizontally) of the panel. Owing to the control's simplicity, the XAML is straightforward as well. Here, we are vertically stacking several check boxes, labels, a button, and a text box (see Figure 19.14):

```
<StackPanel>
  <Label>Format Options:</Label>
  <CheckBox Margin="4" Height="16" Name="checkBox1">Perform Fast Format</CheckBox>
  <CheckBox Margin="4" Height="16" Name="checkBox2">Verify After Format</CheckBox>
  <CheckBox Margin="4" Height="16" Name="checkBox3">Enable Large Partition
   Support</CheckBox>
  <Label>Drive Label:</Label>
  <TextBox Margin="10,0" BorderBrush="Gray" Height="23" Name="comboBox2" />
  <Button Margin="80,20" Height="23" Name="button1" >Format</Button>
</StackPanel>
```

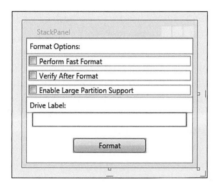

FIGURE 19.14   The StackPanel in action.

Another similar panel is the WrapPanel: This is essentially a StackPanel with additional behavior to wrap its children into additional rows or columns if there isn't enough room to display them within the bounds of the panel. See Figure 19.15 to see how the WrapPanel has auto-adjusted a series of buttons when its Window is sized smaller.

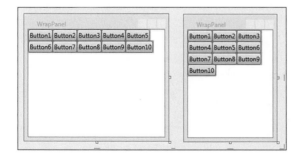

FIGURE 19.15   The WrapPanel.

Styles and Templates

The capability to customize the look of a control in WPF, without losing any of its built-in functionality, is one of the huge advantages that WPF brings to the development scene. Consider the two slider controls in Figure 19.16: The top is the default style, and the bottom represents a restyled slider. Functionality is identical. We have simply changed the appearance of the control.

FIGURE 19.16   The standard slider (top) and a restyled slider (bottom).

Style is an actual class (in the System.Windows namespace) that is used in association with a control; it groups property values together to enable you, as a developer, to set them once and have them applied to controls en masse instead of having to set them individually on each control instance. Suppose, for instance, that your application uses a nice grayscale gradient for its button backgrounds. In addition, each button has a white border and renders its text with the Segoe UI font. We can manipulate each of these aspects using Button properties; but it would quickly become laborious to do this on every single button. A Style enables us to set all of these properties once and then refer each Button control to these properties by assigning the style to the button.

Here is the Style defined within a window in XAML:

```
<Window.Resources>
    <Style x:Key="GradientButton" TargetType="Button">
        <Setter Property="Margin" Value="2"/>
        <Setter Property="BorderBrush" Value="White" />
        <Setter Property="FontFamily" Value="Segoe UI"/>
        <Setter Property="FontSize" Value="12px"/>
        <Setter Property="FontWeight" Value="Bold"/>
        <Setter Property="Foreground" Value="White" />
        <Setter Property="Background" >
            <Setter.Value>
                <LinearGradientBrush StartPoint="0,0" EndPoint="0,1" >
                    <GradientStop Color="Gray" Offset="0.2"/>
                    <GradientStop Color="DarkGray" Offset="0.85"/>
                    <GradientStop Color="Gray" Offset="1"/>
                </LinearGradientBrush>
            </Setter.Value>
        </Setter>
    </Style>
</Window.Resources>
```

To assign this style to any button within the window, it is as simple as this:

```
<Button Style="{StaticResource GradientButton}" Height="38" Name="button1"
Width="100">OK</Button>
```

This works very well for simplifying property sets. But what happens when we want to customize an attribute that isn't surfaced as a property? To continue with our Button control, what if we wanted an oval shape rather the standard rectangle? Because the Button class doesn't expose a property that we can use to change the background shape, we appear to be out of luck.

Enter the concept of templates. Templates enable you to completely replace the visual tree of any control giving you full control over every aspect of the control's user interface. A visual tree in WPF is the hierarchy of controls inheriting from the Visual class that provide a control's final rendered appearance. A good overview of WPF visual trees and logical trees can be found at http://www.msdn.microsoft.com. Search for the article "Trees in WPF."

> **NOTE**
>
> Earlier we mentioned that controls in WPF were "lookless"; templates are evidence of that fact. The functionality of a control exists separately from its visual tree. The default look for all the controls is provided through a series of templates, one per each Windows theme. This means that WPF controls can automatically participate in whatever OS theme you are running.

Templates are created via the ControlTemplate class. Within this class (or element, if you are implementing the template in XAML), you need to draw the visuals that represent the button. The Rectangle class in WPF can be used to draw our basic background shape. By tweaking the RadiusX and RadiusY properties, we can soften the normal 90-degree corners into the desired elliptical shape:

```
<Rectangle RadiusX="25" RadiusY="25" Width="100" Height="50"
Stroke="Black" StrokeThickness="1" />
```

We can also add some more compelling visual aspects such as a gradient fill to the button:

```
<Rectangle.Fill>
   <LinearGradientBrush>
      <LinearGradientBrush.GradientStops>
         <GradientStop Offset="0" Color="Gray" />
         <GradientStop Offset="1" Color="LightGray" />
      </LinearGradientBrush.GradientStops>
   </LinearGradientBrush>
</Rectangle.Fill>
```

TIP

To test the look and feel so far, type your "shape" XAML into the XAML editor, and tweak it as desired. After you are satisfied, you can copy and paste the XAML into the template. A better tool for designing user interfaces is Microsoft Expression Blend, but handcrafting the XAML or relying on Visual Studio's designer should be sufficient for simple design scenarios.

The text within the button is easily rendered using a `TextBlock` object:

```
<TextBlock Canvas.Top="5" Height="40" Width="100" FontSize="20"
TextAlignment="Center">OK</TextBlock>
```

After we are happy with the look and feel, we can "template-ize" this appearance by nesting everything within a `ControlTemplate` element. Because we need to refer to this template later, we provide a key/name:

```
<ControlTemplate x:Key="OvalButtonTemplate">
```

And finally, we embed the whole thing as a resource. A resource is simply a .NET object (written in XAML or code) that is meant to be shared across other objects. In this specific case, we want to be able to use this template with any button we want. Resources can be declared at any level within a WPF project: We can declare resources that belong to the overall window, or to any element within the window (such as a Grid panel), or we can store all of our resources in something known as a `ResourceDictionary` and allow them to be referenced from any class in our project. For this example, we stick to a simple resource defined in our parent window. (For reference, this is the `Window.Resources` element that you see in the following code.)

Listing 19.2 pulls this all together, and Figure 19.17 shows the resulting button.

LISTING 19.2   Replacing a Button's Template

```
<Window x:Class="ContosoAvalon.CustomLook"
    xmlns="http://schemas.microsoft.com/winfx/2006/xaml/presentation"
    xmlns:x="http://schemas.microsoft.com/winfx/2006/xaml"
    Title="CustomLook" Height="300" Width="300"
    Background="#F8F8F8">
  <Window.Resources>
    <ControlTemplate x:Key="OvalButtonTemplate">
      <Canvas Width="100" Height="25" Margin="2">
        <Rectangle x:Name="BaseRectangle" Canvas.Top="0" RadiusX="25"
          RadiusY="25" Width="100" Height="40" Stroke="DarkGray"
          StrokeThickness="1">
          <Rectangle.Fill>
            <LinearGradientBrush>
              <LinearGradientBrush.GradientStops>
                <GradientStop Offset="0" Color="Gray" />
```

```
                    <GradientStop Offset="1" Color="LightGray" />
                </LinearGradientBrush.GradientStops>
            </LinearGradientBrush>
          </Rectangle.Fill>
        </Rectangle>
        <TextBlock Canvas.Top="5" Height="40" Width="100" FontSize="20"
         TextAlignment="Center">OK</TextBlock>
      </Canvas>
    </ControlTemplate>
  </Window.Resources>
  <Canvas>
  <Button Canvas.Left="49" Canvas.Top="44" Height="38" Name="button1"
   Width="93" Template="{StaticResource OvalButtonTemplate}" />
  </Canvas>
</Window>
```

FIGURE 19.17   A custom button template.

Data Binding

Data binding, in its purest sense, is the capability of a control to be wired to a data source such that the control (a) displays certain items from that data source and (b) is kept in sync with the data source. After the connection is made, the runtime handles all the work necessary to make this happen. It doesn't really matter where or how the data is stored: It could be a file system, a custom collection of objects, a database object, and so on.

So, let's look briefly at how we can establish a data binding connection using WPF. The key class here is the System.Windows.Data.Binding class. This is the mediator in charge of linking a control with a data source. To successfully declare a binding, we need to know three things:

▶ What UI control property do we want to bind?

▶ What data source do we want to bind to?

▶ And, within the data source, what specific element or property or such holds the data we are interested in?

We can bind to either single objects (such as binding a string property on an object to a text box), or to collections of objects (such as binding a List<> collection to a list box). Either way, the mechanics remain the same:

```
Binding binding = new Binding();
binding.Source = _stringList;

listBox1.SetBinding(ListBox.ItemsSourceProperty, binding);
```

The preceding code snippet creates a `Binding` object, sets the source of the `Binding` object to our `List<string>` collection, and then calls `SetBinding` on our control (a list box), passing in the exact property on the control we want to bind to our data source, and the `Binding` object instance.

We can also assign data sources into a special object called the data context. Every `FrameworkElement` object, and those that derive from that class, implement their own `DataContext` instance. You can think of this as a global area where controls can go to get their data when participating in a data binding arrangement.

This ends up simplifying our data binding code quite a bit. We can set the context in our Window constructor like this:

```
this.DataContext = _stringList;
```

Now, we just point our `ListBox` to this data context using a tag within the `ListBox`'s XAML element:

```
<ListBox Name="listBox1" ItemsSource="{Binding}" />
```

The `Binding` object in this case automatically hunts for objects stashed within a data context somewhere within the object tree. When it finds one, it automatically binds the objects.

This works great for our simple `List<string>` example, but what if we are trying to bind a collection of custom objects to the list box? If we have a simple `Employee` class with a `Name` property and a `PhoneNbr` property, how could we bind to a collection of those objects and show the employee name? Our process would actually remain the same. If we create an `Employee` class, and then create a `List<Employee>` collection, all of this code still works. But there is a problem: Figure 19.18 highlights an issue we have to solve.

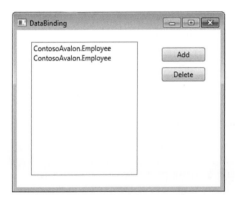

FIGURE 19.18   Binding a `ListBox` to a collection of custom objects.

We haven't yet told the binding engine how exactly we want our data to be represented within the list box. By default, the binding process simply calls `ToString` on every object.

One quick remedy is to simply override the `ToString` method:

```
public override string ToString()
{
    return _name;
}
```

This corrects the problem in this instance. But a more robust approach involves the use of a `DataTemplate`. We cover that approach a little later, in the section "Building a Simple Image Viewer Application."

Routed Events

The standard way that .NET classes and controls raise and handle events is essentially the way that you perform these tasks in WPF. But the WPF libraries bring an important improvement to standard events. We call these routed events.

Consider a simple scenario: You have a Button control that consists of a background image and some text (see Figure 19.19). If you recall from our discussion of a controls template and visual tree, this means we actually have a few discrete elements that make up the button: a `TextBlock`, an `Image`, and the basic frame and background of the button.

FIGURE 19.19   A button with multiple elements.

These are separate objects/elements unto themselves. So the event situation becomes a little complex. It isn't enough to react to a click the button background; we also have to react to a click the button's text or the button's image. This is where routed events come into play. Routed events are capable of calling event handlers up or down the entire visual tree. This means we are free to implement an event handler at the `Button` level, and be confident that a click on the button's image or text will bubble up until it finds our event handler.

Routed events in WPF are broken down into three categories: bubbling events, tunneling events, and direct events:

> ▶ **Bubbling events**—These events travel up the visual tree starting at the initial receiving element.

> ▶ **Tunneling events**—These events start at the top of the control's visual tree and move down until they reach the receiving element.

> ▶ **Direct event**—These are the equivalent of "standard" .NET events: Only the event handler for the receiving element is called.

Events themselves, like nearly everything else in WPF, can be declared in XAML or in code. Here we have a Button control with a `MouseEnter` event defined:

```
<Button MouseEnter="button1_MouseEnter" Height="23" Name="button1"
Width="75">OK</Button>
```

The event handler itself, in C#, looks like any other .NET event handler:

```
private void button1_MouseEnter(object sender, MouseEventArgs e)
{
    MessageBox.Show("MouseEnter on button1");
}
```

We have only scratched the surface on many of the basic programming concepts within WPF, but you should now be armed with enough knowledge to be productive writing a simple WPF application. Let's do just that, using the tools available to us in Visual Studio.

Building a Simple Image Viewer Application

To illustrate the role that Visual Studio plays in WPF application development, let's build a sample application from scratch. In the tradition of "experience first," let's select something that can benefit from WPF's strong suits, namely visualizations and robust control layouts and templating.

Consider an image viewer application. We can use this application to view a list of image thumbnails and, after selecting a thumbnail, can view the image itself and even make changes to the image.

We target the rough design shown in Figure 19.20.

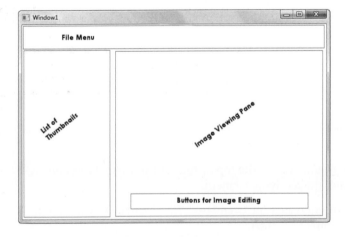

FIGURE 19.20   A sketch of an image viewer UI.

Here are our base requirements:

▶ When the application loads, it parses the images contained in the specified folder.

▶ Every image is listed in a list box; the list box shows image thumbnails and no text.

▶ When the user clicks one of the items in the list box, the image viewing area is populated with the selected image.

▶ The user can then choose to manipulate the image: a black-and-white effect can be applied, the image can be rotated clockwise or counterclockwise, the image can be flipped, and it can be mirrored.

▶ In general, we try to use WPF's capabilities when possible to make the application more visually compelling; a standard battleship gray application is not what we are looking for here.

Starting the Layout

After creating a new WPF project, we double-click the MainWindow.xaml file and start designing our user interface. To start, a `Grid` panel and some nested `StackPanel` or `WrapPanel` containers provide the initial layout. Referring to the sketch design (see Figure 19.20), one can envision a `Grid` with two rows and two columns to start. The top row holds the Menu control (which should span both columns), and the bottom row hold the list box of images in the left column, and another parent control in the right column which display the image and the editing buttons.

To get started on this layout, we can use the grid control that has been automatically placed on our window during project creation. We could use the XAML pane for our window to quickly enter some XAML tags for the right elements, but let's see how quickly the WPF Designer enables us to create a layout without typing anything. Select the grid within the designer; you can do this by either clicking within the designer or clicking within the `<Grid>` element in the XAML pane. With the grid control selected, notice two shaded border areas to the top and to the left side of the grid control. These are known as grid rails. The grid rails enable you to quickly create columns and rows within the grid. If you move the mouse cursor over one of the grid rails, the cursor changes to cross-hairs. A grid splitter also appears; this visually indicates where the exact column or row divider is positioned within the grid. By clicking within the top grid rail, you can add a column; clicking in the left grid rail adds a row. Figure 19.21 shows an example of a grid selected in the designer, with the grid rails visible to the top and to the left of the grid.

For this project, move your cursor over the top grid rail and move the resulting column splitter so that it is approximately one-third of the way through the Grid's width. Now, click within the rail to create the two columns. Note that the designer shows us the exact width, in pixels, for each column (see Figure 19.22).

Now, do the same within the left grid rail. Position the row splitter so that the top row has a height of about 30 pixels. Don't worry about getting this exact; we tweak the sizing a little later.

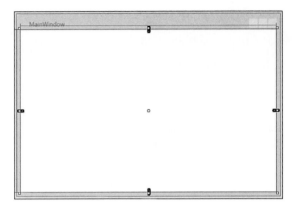

FIGURE 19.21   Grid with grid rails visible to the top and left.

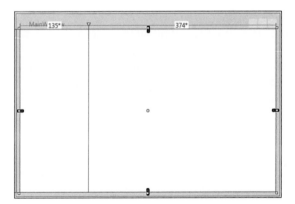

FIGURE 19.22   Sizing columns within a grid.

Add the List of Images

Drag a ListBox into the first column, second row. Initially, this list box has a height, width, and margin value set for it. Because we want this control to resize itself based on the size of the column and row that it sits within, we need to change these properties. Make sure the list box is selected within the designer, and then delete any values within the Height and Width properties. You should also set the VerticalAlignment and HorizontalAlignment properties to Stretch. And finally, set the Margin property to 5.

You should now have a design surface that looks something like the window in Figure 19.23.

Add the Top Menu

The top Menu control in our application will be used to open a folder selection dialog box. Drag a Menu control into the first column and first row. This control needs to span both of the columns in our grid, so resize it within the designer so that it crosses the border between column one and column two. We can now make adjustments similar to those we made for our list box: Using the property window, remove any Height value, and set the Width to Auto. Set the HorizontalAlignment and VerticalAlignment properties to Stretch, and set the Margin to 5.

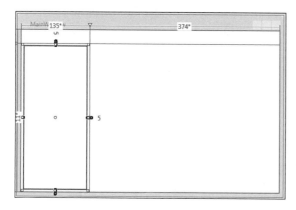

FIGURE 19.23   Our UI in progress.

We know we need to provide folder selection capabilities, so we title a main menu item as Folder, and include a subitem under that titled Open. To implement this design, use the property window and edit the Items property; a collection editor dialog box opens that enables us to add the Folder menu items. Via the Header property, we need to specify the text that is displayed for the menu (see Figure 19.24) and also the name: **FolderOpenMenuItem**.

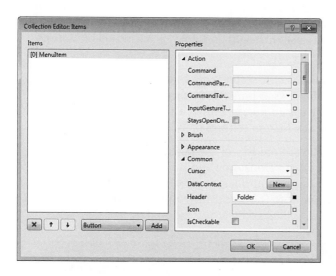

FIGURE 19.24   Creating a MenuItem.

After the Folder menu item has been created, select it and use the property window to edit its Items collection to add the final Open menu item. For this menu item, we also want to specify an event handler for its Click event. Make sure you have the Events tab selected in the property window, and then enter **FolderOpenMenuItem_Click** in the Click event (see Figure 19.25). Visual Studio automatically creates a stub for the event handler, and opens it within the code editor for you. Because we aren't ready to implement this event yet, you can simply click back to the WPF Designer within the IDE.

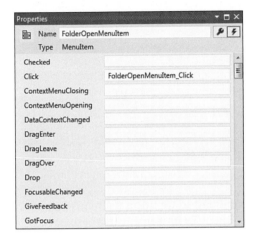

FIGURE 19.25   Wiring the Click event for our Open MenuItem.

Add the Image Viewer

The main screen area for this application is the image viewer and its associated command buttons. This consists of a grid with two rows: the top row holds an Image control, and grows as we resize. The bottom row is a static height and holds a StackPanel of buttons oriented horizontally.

Drag a Grid control from the Toolbox into the second row and second column of our original parent grid. You configure the rows as indicated the same way you did for the root grid. For the image view box, we use an Image control. Drag one into the top row of the new grid and, as before, remove any Margin settings or Width/Height values.

And finally, drag a StackPanel into the bottom row of the new grid, remove any Margin settings, and set its Orientation property to Horizontal and the HorizontalAlignment property to Center. This panel is where we place our image manipulation buttons, which you can add now as well. Drag four buttons into the StackPanel, and adjust their margins and height/width until you get the workable look and feel you are after.

NOTE

While building this app, we have mostly relied on the WPF Designer's property window to tweak our control properties. But because the XAML code editor supports IntelliSense, and because XAML is fairly readable, you might find it faster and more productive to make the changes directly within the XAML. The bottom line here is that the IDE enables you to choose how you are most productive.

Grid Sizing Details

With all of our grids, columns, and rows now in place, we can think about how we want to handle sizing. In other words, how do we want our columns and rows to resize themselves if a user happens to resize the parent window? To configure the grid correctly, we need to understand the concepts of fixed, auto, and proportional sizing.

Proportional sizing, also sometimes referred to as *star sizing*, is used to apportion row height or column width as a proportion of all available space. XAML-wise, proportional sizing is expressed with an asterisk inside of the `Row.Height` or `Column.Width` properties. With star sizing, you indicate the proportional "weight" that you want the column to occupy. For instance, for a grid with two columns, if we specified a width on both columns of `".5*"`, we would end up with both columns taking up half of the available space (width-wise) of the grid. Figure 19.22 shows some example column sizes using proportional sizing. If we just specify an asterisk with no weight (for example, Width="*"), we are instructing that column to take all the remaining space.

Auto sizing causes the row height or width to grow or shrink as necessary to exactly fit whatever is currently placed within the row or column. So, a row that is auto sized would be as tall as the tallest control it hosts. Note that in addition to the control height, other things can affect the space reserved for a control such as margins and padding.

And finally, *fixed sizing* works exactly like you think it would. You specify a width or height in pixels, and the column or row snaps to that dimension regardless of how the grid's parent control or window is sized.

With these details exposed, we can formulate a strategy for our layout. Figure 19.26 shows a revised sketch indicating our sizing scheme.

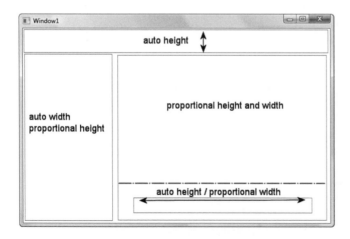

FIGURE 19.26   UI sketch with resizing notes.

The WPF Designer provides a way to directly indicate the sizing type for each row and column. Using the grid rails again, hover the mouse over the rail space for a column. A small toolbar pops up directly above the rail with three buttons. These three buttons correspond to the three sizing modes. Go ahead and cycle through all of the rows and columns in the designer, setting the height and width properties using the designer toolbar.

Here is a look at the current XAML with all of the basic elements in place:

```
<Grid>
        <Grid.RowDefinitions>
            <RowDefinition Height="Auto" />
            <RowDefinition Height="*" />
        </Grid.RowDefinitions>
        <Grid.ColumnDefinitions>
            <ColumnDefinition Width="Auto" />
            <ColumnDefinition Width="*" />
        </Grid.ColumnDefinitions>
        <ListBox Grid.Row="1" HorizontalAlignment="Stretch"
         Margin="5" Name="listBox1" VerticalAlignment="Stretch"
         ItemsSource="{Binding}"
         Width="175" />
        <Menu Grid.ColumnSpan="2" HorizontalAlignment="Stretch"
         Margin="0" Name="menu1" VerticalAlignment="Stretch">
            <MenuItem Header="_Folder" VerticalAlignment="Center">
                <MenuItem x:Name="OpenMenuItem" Header="_Open"
                 Click="FolderOpenMenuItem_Click"
                 VerticalAlignment="Center">
                </MenuItem>
            </MenuItem>
        </Menu>
        <Grid Grid.Row="1" Grid.Column="1">
            <Grid.RowDefinitions>
                <RowDefinition Height="*" />
                <RowDefinition Height="Auto" />
            </Grid.RowDefinitions>
            <Image Grid.Row="0" Name="image1" Stretch="UniformToFill"
             Margin="5" VerticalAlignment="Center"
             HorizontalAlignment="Center" />
            <StackPanel Grid.Row="1" Orientation="Horizontal"
             HorizontalAlignment="Center" >
                <Button Width="50" Height="50" Margin="10">
                 Button</Button>
                <Button Width="50" Height="50" Margin="10">
                 Button</Button>
                <Button Width="50" Height="50" Margin="10">
                 Button</Button>
```

```
            <Button Width="50" Height="50" Margin="10">
                Button</Button>
          </StackPanel>
        </Grid>
      </Grid>
```

Storing the Images

With the UI elements in place, we can move on to the data binding issues. (We come back later and give the UI more polish.) The first task is to store the files in a collection of some sort. It turns out that there is a class in the `System.Windows.Media.Imaging` namespace that is suitable for our needs: `BitmapSource`. For a collection, a `List<BitmapSource>` object should work for the moment, but we need some way to populate the list. So, let's create a wrapper class that both loads the list and exposes it as a property. Add a new class to the project with the following code:

```
public class DirectoryImageList
{
   private string _path;
   private List<BitmapSource> _images = new List<BitmapSource>();

   public DirectoryImageList(string path)
   {
      _path = path;
      LoadImages();

   }

   public List<BitmapSource> Images
   {
      get { return _images; }
      set { _images = value; }
   }

   public string Path
   {
      get { return _path; }
      set
      {
         _path = value;
         LoadImages();
      }
   }

   private void LoadImages()
   {
```

19

```
        _images.Clear();
        BitmapImage img;

        foreach (string file in Directory.GetFiles(_path))
        {
            try
            {
                img = new BitmapImage(new Uri(file));

                _images.Add(img);
            }
            catch
            {
                // empty catch; ignore any files that won't load as
                // an image...
            }
        }
    }
}
```

The LoadImages method in the preceding code is where most of the important logic is found; it enumerates the files within a given directory and attempts to load them into a BitmapImage object. If it succeeds, we know that this is an image file. If it doesn't, we just ignore the resulting exception and keep on going.

Back in our MainWindow class, we need to create some private fields to hold an instance of this new class, and to hold the currently selected path. This is something we let the user change through a common dialog box launched from the Folder, Open menu item.

Here are the fields:

```
private DirectoryImageList _imgList;
private string _path =
    Environment.GetFolderPath
            (Environment.SpecialFolder.MyPictures);
```

Note that we have defaulted our path to the Pictures folder. To load up the list object, we write a ResetList method in our MainWindow class:

```
private void ResetList()
{
    _imgList = new DirectoryImageList(_path);
}
```

Referring to our earlier discussion on data binding, we round things off by adding a few lines of code to the Window1 constructor: an initial call to ResetList, and a call to assign the data context to the Images property from the DirectoryImageList instance:

```
public MainWindow()
{
    InitializeComponent();
    ResetList();
    this.DataContext = _imgList.Images;
}
```

If we run the application now, we see a familiar sight (as in Figure 19.27): The data binding is working but isn't quite the presentation format we want.

FIGURE 19.27   Initial data binding results.

Binding to the Images

Because our earlier trick of overriding ToString won't give us the right data presentation (an image, after all, is not a string), we need to turn to data templates. The DataTemplate class is used to tell a control specifically how you want its data to be displayed. By using a data template within the visual tree of the control, you have complete freedom to present the bound data in any fashion you want.

For this application, we are looking for images in the ListBox. This turns out to be quite easy. Create a Window1.Resources element in XAML, and create a DataTemplate that sets up the exact visualization we need:

```
<Window.Resources>
    <DataTemplate x:Key="ImageDataTemplate">
        <Image Source="{Binding UriSource.LocalPath}" Width="125"
          Height="125" />
    </DataTemplate>
</Window.Resources>
```

Then assign the `DataTemplate` to the `ListBox`:

```
<ListBox Grid.Row="1" Name="listBox1" ItemsSource="{Binding}"
 ItemTemplate="{StaticResource ImageDataTemplate}"/>
```

In our data template, the `Image` element is expecting a source URI for each image. So we use the `UriSource.LocalPath` that is provided on the `BitmapSource` object. If you now rerun the application, you should immediately see that our `ListBox` is now displaying thumbnail-sized images (125x125) for every picture it finds in our local pictures directory.

We aren't done yet; clicking a thumbnail in the list box should cause the central `Image` control to display the indicated picture. By creating a `SelectionChanged` event handler and wiring it to the `ListBox`, we can update our `Image.Source` property accordingly.

The event is declared as expected within the `ListBox` XAML element:

```
<ListBox SelectionChanged="listBox1_SelectionChanged" Grid.Row="1"
 Name="listBox1" ItemsSource="{Binding}"
 ItemTemplate="{StaticResource ImageDataTemplate}"/>
```

And for the event handler, we cast the `SelectedItem` from the `ListBox` to its native `BitmapSource` representation and assign it to our image control:

```
private void listBox1_SelectionChanged(object sender,
    SelectionChangedEventArgs e)
{
    image1.Source = (BitmapSource)((sender as ListBox).SelectedItem);
}
```

Button Event Handlers and Image Effects

With the images successfully loaded into the list box, and displayed in the central `Image` control, we can turn our attention to our four image editing/effects features:

- ▶ Black and white filter
- ▶ Image blur
- ▶ Rotate
- ▶ Flip

Because these four functions are controlled by the four buttons, we need to add some appropriate button images and events; we don't cover the button stylings here because they involve external graphics resources, but you can see how they turn out in the final screenshot (at the end of this chapter) or by downloading the source from this book's website.

The code for the events, however, is fair game. First, here are the XAML event declarations on each button:

```
<Button Click="buttonBandW_Click" Margin="20,0,0,0" Height="23"
 Name="buttonBandW" Width="30"/>

<Button Click="buttonBlur_Click" Margin="20,0,0,0" Height="23"
 Name="buttonBlur" Width="30"/>

<Button Click="buttonRotate_Click"  Margin="20,0,0,0" Height="23"
 Name="buttonRotate" Width="30"/>

<Button Click="buttonFlip_Click" Margin="20,0,20,0" Height="23"
Name="buttonFlip" Width="30"/>
```

Notice as you type these click events into the XAML pane that the XAML editor inter-
venes with IntelliSense pop-ups that not only complete our `Click` declaration but also
create the corresponding event handler in our code-behind class!

Changing the image to grayscale is accomplished via the class `FormatConvertedBitmap`,
which allows you to specify the color depth and format of your palette:

```
private void buttonBandW_Click
    (object sender, RoutedEventArgs e)
{
    BitmapSource img = (BitmapSource)image1.Source;
    image1.Source =
        new FormatConvertedBitmap
            (img, PixelFormats.Gray16,
            BitmapPalettes.Gray256, 1.0);
}
```

To perform the image manipulations, we use something known as a transform: the manipulation of a 2D surface to rotate, skew, or otherwise change the current appearance of the
surface. We can handle our rotation feature directly with `RotateTransform` like this:

```
private void buttonRotate_Click(object sender, RoutedEventArgs e)
{
    CachedBitmap cache = new CachedBitmap((BitmapSource)image1.Source,
        BitmapCreateOptions.None, BitmapCacheOption.OnLoad);
    image1.Source = new TransformedBitmap(cache, new RotateTransform(90));
}
```

Our flip action ends up being just as easy, but uses a `ScaleTransform` instead:

```
private void buttonFlip_Click(object sender, RoutedEventArgs e)
{
    CachedBitmap cache = new CachedBitmap((BitmapSource)image1.Source,
        BitmapCreateOptions.None, BitmapCacheOption.OnLoad);
```

19

```
    ScaleTransform scale = new ScaleTransform(-1, -1, image1.Source.Width / 2,
        image1.Source.Height / 2);
    image1.Source = new TransformedBitmap(cache, scale);
}
```

The image blurring action is provided through a different mechanism known as an effect. By creating a new `BlurBitmapEffect` instance and assigning that to our image control, WPF apply the appropriate algorithm to the bitmap to blur the picture:

```
image1.Effect = new BlurEffect();
```

Path Selection with a Common Dialog Box

The last item on our to-do list is allowing the user to change the path of the picture files. WPF itself doesn't have any built-in dialog box classes to manage this, but the `System.Windows.Forms` namespace has just what we need: the `FolderBrowserDialog` class. This is launched from within the event handler for our `FolderOpenMenuItem Click` event:

```
private void FolderOpenMenuItem_Click(object sender, RoutedEventArgs e)
{
    SetPath();
}

private void SetPath()
{
    FolderBrowserDialog dlg = new FolderBrowserDialog();
    dlg.ShowDialog();
    _path = dlg.SelectedPath;
    ResetList();
}
```

When a user selects a folder, we update our internal field appropriately, reload the `DirectoryImageList` class with the new path, and then reset our window's `DataContext` property to reflect the change. This is a perfect example of how seamless it is to use other .NET technologies and class libraries from within WPF. By adding the appropriate namespace and reference to our project, we just instantiate this class like any other class in our solution.

TIP

Because there are a fair number of controls that share the same name between WPF and WinForms (the ListBox control is one example), if you find yourself using classes from the `System.Windows.Controls` and the `System.Windows.Forms` libraries, you inevitably need to fully qualify some of your object names to avoid operating against the wrong class.

And with that, the application is functionally complete. For reference, we have provided the current state of the XAML and the code-behind listings in Listing 19.3 and Listing

19.4, respectively. If you really want to dissect this application, however, you should download the source code from this book's website. This enables you to see the improvements made with graphics resources and general look and feel, producing the final polished version shown in Figure 19.28.

FIGURE 19.28   After the finishing touches.

LISTING 19.3   The Image Viewer XAML Code

```xaml
<Window x:Class="WpfImageViewer.MainWindow"
        xmlns="http://schemas.microsoft.com/winfx/2006/xaml/presentation"
        xmlns:x="http://schemas.microsoft.com/winfx/2006/xaml"
        Title="Image Viewer Sample Application"
        Height="400" Width="550"
        Background="{DynamicResource BackgroundGradientBrush}">

    <Window.Resources>
        <DataTemplate x:Key="ImageDataTemplate">
            <Image Source="{Binding UriSource.LocalPath}"
                   Width="125" Height="125" />
        </DataTemplate>
    </Window.Resources>

    <Grid>
        <Grid.RowDefinitions>
```

```xml
                <RowDefinition Height="Auto" />
                <RowDefinition Height="*" />
            </Grid.RowDefinitions>
            <Grid.ColumnDefinitions>
                <ColumnDefinition Width="Auto" />
                <ColumnDefinition Width="*" />
            </Grid.ColumnDefinitions>
            <ListBox Grid.Row="1"
                     HorizontalAlignment="Stretch"
                     Margin="5" Name="listBox1"
                     VerticalAlignment="Stretch"
                     Width="175"
                     ItemsSource="{Binding}"
                     ItemTemplate="{StaticResource ImageDataTemplate}"
                     SelectionChanged="listBox1_SelectionChanged" />
            <Menu Grid.ColumnSpan="2"
                  Background="{DynamicResource MenuBackgroundGradientBrush}"
                  HorizontalAlignment="Stretch"
                  Margin="0"
                  Name="menu1"
                  VerticalAlignment="Stretch">
                <MenuItem Header="_Folder"
                          VerticalAlignment="Center">
                    <MenuItem x:Name="OpenMenuItem"
                              Header="_Open"
                              Click="FolderOpenMenuItem_Click"
                              VerticalAlignment="Center">
                    </MenuItem>
                </MenuItem>
            </Menu>
            <Grid Grid.Row="1" Grid.Column="1">
                <Grid.RowDefinitions>
                    <RowDefinition Height="*" />
                    <RowDefinition Height="Auto" />
                </Grid.RowDefinitions>
                <Image Grid.Row="0"
                       Name="image1"
                       Stretch="UniformToFill"
                       Margin="5"
                       VerticalAlignment="Center"
                       HorizontalAlignment="Center" />
                <StackPanel Grid.Row="1" Orientation="Horizontal"
                            HorizontalAlignment="Center" >
                    <Button Name="buttonBandW"
                            Style="{DynamicResource BWImageButtonStyle}"
                            Click="buttonBandW_Click"
```

```
                    Width="50"
                    Height="50"
                    Margin="10" />
            <Button Name="buttonBlur"
                    Style="{DynamicResource BlurImageButtonStyle}"
                    Click="buttonBlur_Click"
                    Width="50"
                    Height="50"
                    Margin="10" />
            <Button Name="buttonRotate"
                    Style="{DynamicResource RotateImageButtonStyle}"
                    Click="buttonRotate_Click"
                    Width="50"
                    Height="50"
                    Margin="10" />
            <Button Name="buttonFlip"
                    Style="{DynamicResource FlipImageButtonStyle}"
                    Click="buttonFlip_Click"
                    Width="50"
                    Height="50"
                    Margin="10" />
        </StackPanel>
    </Grid>
  </Grid>
</Window>
```

LISTING 19.4   The Image Viewer Code Behind C#

```
using System;
using System.Collections.Generic;
using System.Linq;
using System.Text;
using System.Windows;
using System.Windows.Controls;
using System.Windows.Data;
using System.Windows.Documents;
using System.Windows.Input;
using System.Windows.Media;
using System.Windows.Media.Effects;
using System.Windows.Media.Imaging;
using System.Windows.Navigation;
using System.Windows.Shapes;
```

19

```csharp
namespace WpfImageViewer
{
    /// <summary>
    /// Interaction logic for MainWindow.xaml
    /// </summary>
    public partial class MainWindow : Window
    {
        #region Private fields

        private DirectoryImageList _imgList;
        private string _path =
            Environment.GetFolderPath(
            Environment.SpecialFolder.MyPictures);

        #endregion

        #region Ctor

        public MainWindow()
        {
            InitializeComponent();
            ResetList();
            this.DataContext = _imgList.Images;
        }

        #endregion

        #region Event handlers and delegates

        private void FolderOpenMenuItem_Click
            (object sender, RoutedEventArgs e)
        {
            SetPath();
        }

        private void listBox1_SelectionChanged
            (object sender, SelectionChangedEventArgs e)
        {
            this.image1.Source = (BitmapSource)
                        ((sender as ListBox).SelectedItem);
            this.image1.Effect = null;
        }

        private void buttonBandW_Click
            (object sender, RoutedEventArgs e)
        {
            BitmapSource img = (BitmapSource)image1.Source;
```

```
        image1.Source =
            new FormatConvertedBitmap
                (img, PixelFormats.Gray16,
                BitmapPalettes.Gray256, 1.0);
    }

    private void buttonBlur_Click
        (object sender, RoutedEventArgs e)
    {
        if (image1.Effect != null)
        {
            // if blur is current effect, remove
            image1.Effect = null;
        }
        else
        {
            // otherwise, add the blur effect to the image
            image1.Effect = new BlurEffect();
        }
    }

    private void buttonRotate_Click
        (object sender, RoutedEventArgs e)
    {
        CachedBitmap cache =
            new CachedBitmap((BitmapSource)image1.Source,
                BitmapCreateOptions.None,
                BitmapCacheOption.OnLoad);
        image1.Source =
            new TransformedBitmap(cache,
                new RotateTransform(90));


    }

    private void buttonFlip_Click
        (object sender, RoutedEventArgs e)
    {
        CachedBitmap cache =
            new CachedBitmap((BitmapSource)image1.Source,
                BitmapCreateOptions.None,
                BitmapCacheOption.OnLoad);
        ScaleTransform scale =
            new ScaleTransform(-1, -1, image1.Source.Width / 2,
                image1.Source.Height / 2);
        image1.Source =
            new TransformedBitmap(cache, scale);
    }
```

19

```csharp
#endregion

#region Implementation

private void SetPath()
{
    System.Windows.Forms.FolderBrowserDialog dlg =
        new System.Windows.Forms.FolderBrowserDialog();
    dlg.ShowDialog();
    _path = dlg.SelectedPath;
    ResetList();
}

private void ResetList()
{
    if (IsValidPath(_path))
    {
        _imgList = new DirectoryImageList(_path);
    }

    this.DataContext = _imgList.Images;

}

private bool IsValidPath(string path)
{

    try
    {
        string folder =
            System.IO.Path.GetFullPath(path);
        return true;
    }
    catch
    {
        return false;
    }
}

#endregion


    }


}
```

Summary

In this chapter, you had a brief introduction to the Windows Presentation Foundation. We investigated the overall framework architecture and its programming model, including the new concept of using declarative markup to design and lay out a WPF client application's user interface. And you saw how the Visual Studio WPF Designer can be used to quickly craft compelling user interfaces using the same development processes you use when building Windows Forms or even ASP.NET applications.

We spent some time discussing the basics of control layout (a central theme in WPF) and covering the first-class data binding support that WPF enjoys.

As mentioned, developers trying to learn WPF and XAML-based development in general will find that it is both a broad and deep subject. It is highly recommended that you spend some time with Microsoft Developer Network (MSDN) resources (such as the WPF developer center at www.msdn.microsoft.com/wpf) and then revisit this chapter to get a full sense of the skills and knowledge required to come up to speed on WPF development. Spending time with the design tools is also highly recommended; free trials are available. See www.microsoft.com/expression for more information.

CHAPTER 20

Working with Databases

This chapter is all about how you can manage databases and build data-aware applications using Visual Studio and SQL Server.

Six different Visual Studio tools enable you to interact with a database and assist with building applications that leverage data from a database:

▶ Solution Explorer

▶ Server Explorer

▶ SQL Server Object Explorer

▶ Database Diagram Designer

▶ Table Designer

▶ Query and View Designer

Collectively, they are referred to as the SQL Server Data Tools (SSDT). You first came across a few of these tools in Chapter 5, "Browsers and Explorers." Now this chapter explores how developers use these tools to create database solutions.

Project templates for database maintenance are also provided as a part of the SQL Server Data Tools.

We start by examining how to build databases and database objects with the SSDT. From there, we can cover the specifics of creating data-aware applications with data-bound controls.

NOTE

At the time of this writing, Microsoft SQL Server 2012 and the SQL Server Data Tools for Visual Studio 2012 were newly released. There are many features areas where functionality has actually been degraded in moving from SQL Server 2008 to SQL Server 2012. For example, there is no query designer available for SQL Server 2012 databases, nor is there the ability to create database diagrams. Although Microsoft may add these features in at a later date, we have chosen in this chapter to focus on SQL Server 2008 databases as a result.

Regardless of the what the future roadmap holds in store for SSDT and SQL Server 2012, you can still access most of the functionality and tools described in this chapter by using the SQL Server Management Studio instead of Visual Studio 2012.

Creating Tables and Relationships

The primary entities in any database are its tables. Tables are composed of a structure and data. Server Explorer and the new SQL Server Object Explorer are the Visual Studio instruments used to define or edit the structure or data of any table within a connected database. In fact, using either Explorer, it is possible to create a new SQL Server database instance from scratch. Since the functionality between these explorer windows is nearly identical, we won't bother to illustrate every detail here within the context of both explorers. The SQL Server Object Explorer (launched from the View menu, or by clicking the SQL Server Object Explorer button in the Server Explorer command bar) looks much more like the management console that ships with SQL Server itself, and may be preferable to some people. Other than that, it will largely be a matter of preference in terms of which tool you use. For a quick side-by-side comparison of the two windows, see Figure 20.1.

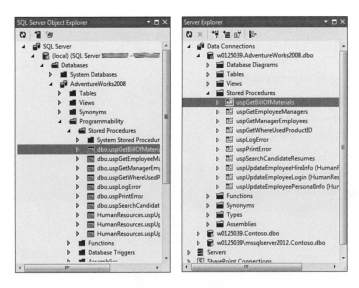

FIGURE 20.1   The Server Explorer versus the SQL Server Object Explorer.

We focus here on using the Server Explorer because most Visual Studio users are already familiar with the tool.

Creating a New SQL Server Database

Data connections are physical connections to a database. In Server Explorer, the Data Connections node has a list of every established database connection. To start the database creation process, right-click the Data Connections node and select the Create New SQL Server Database option. In the resulting dialog box (see Figure 20.2), you need to provide a server name, login credentials, and a name for the new database.

FIGURE 20.2   Creating a new SQL Server database.

This immediately creates the indicated database and adds a connection to the new database under the Data Connections node. Figure 20.3 shows the newly created Contoso database added to the list of connections.

FIGURE 20.3   The new database added to the data connections.

Connecting to an Existing Database

Of course, you can also establish a connection to an existing database. Again, you right-click the Data Connections node; this time, though, you select the Add Connection option. The Add Connection dialog box (see Figure 20.4) is similar to the new database dialog box. You specify a data source, server name, login credentials, and database name/database filename to connect to the database.

FIGURE 20.4   Connecting to an existing database.

Under each connection are folders for the following classes of database objects:

▶ Database diagrams (not available with SQL Server 2012)

▶ Tables

▶ Views

▶ Stored procedures

▶ Functions

▶ Synonyms

▶ Types

▶ Assemblies

These folders are the launching point for creating corresponding objects within the database.

Defining Tables

The table designer is the SQL Server Data Tool you use to define or edit the definition for a table. Using the Server Explorer window, right-click the Tables folder under an existing connection and select Add New Table. The table designer opens in the main document pane of the IDE. There are two different versions of this designer. A SQL Server 2012 designer, which is new with Visual Studio 2012, is used when you are accessing a SQL Server 2012 data source. Otherwise, the earlier table designer is used. We cover the new table designer after we tackle the basics with the original.

The designer is implemented in a tabular format; you add a row in the designer for every column you want to define in the table. For each table column, you specify a name, data type, and nullability. In addition to the tabular designer interface, a Properties window is present that provides complete access to all the different properties for any given column in a table (see Figure 20.5).

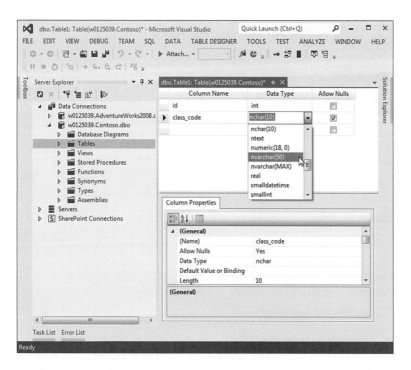

FIGURE 20.5   Defining a table.

In addition to the basics, the table designer enables you to define a column, or group of columns, as part of the primary key for the table, or as part of an index.

Setting a Primary Key

With the table designer active in the IDE, a new table designer top-level menu item is available. You can use this menu, or the shortcut menu displayed whenever you right-click within the table designer, to access a list of useful actions. For instance, to create a primary key for the table, you select the column or columns that constitute the key and then select Set Primary Key from the designer's menu. A key icon indicates any primary keys defined in the table.

Creating Indexes, Foreign Keys, and Check Constraints

Indexes, foreign keys, and check constraints are all created using the same interface and process: Select the appropriate action from the Table Designer menu; use the settings dialog box to first add the index, key, or constraint; and then set its properties in the property grid. For example, to create an index across one or more columns in the table, select the Indexes/Keys item from the Table Designer menu. In the Indexes/Keys dialog box (see Figure 20.6), you can add a new index and then set its properties in the property grid.

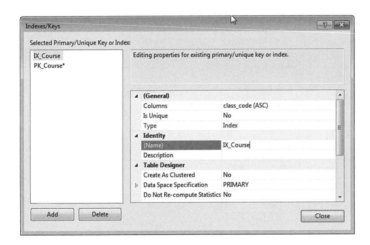

FIGURE 20.6   Creating an index.

Column population for the index is controlled with the index's Columns property; a separate Index Columns dialog box (see Figure 20.7) enables you to change the column membership and specify the sort order for each column.

Using the SQL Server 2012 Table Designer

As mentioned, there is a different and improved designer used for SQL Server 2012 databases. Figure 20.8 shows a table under construction using the new designer. Compare and contrast this with Figure 20.5. The first thing to point out is that you can do all of the same things with this designer as you can with the prior: You can create define columns, set keys, and create indexes, foreign keys, and check constraints. The way that you do it is slightly different, but the functionality is the same.

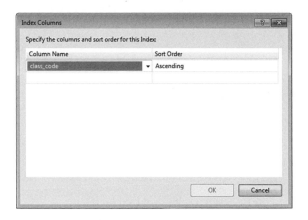

FIGURE 20.7   Specifying columns within an index.

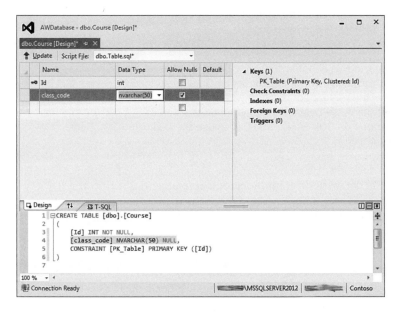

FIGURE 20.8   Designing a table against SQL Server 2012.

The major difference with this new designer is the introduction of the split script pane/ design pane surfaces. The design pane also provides another way to view and edit keys, indexes, and triggers for your table.

Just as with Hypertext Markup Language (HTML) or Windows Presentation Foundation (WPF) development, you have the option of creating your table by typing the actual SQL schema script into the script pane or by visually manipulating things within the design pane. The two are automatically kept in sync. Therefore, we could create our table's columns and set the primary key by filling out the grid in the design pane or we could move down to the script pane and type:

```
CREATE TABLE [dbo].[Course]
(
    [Id] INT NOT NULL,
    [class_code] NVARCHAR(50) NULL,
    CONSTRAINT [PK_Course] PRIMARY KEY ([Id])
)
```

Using the Database Diagram Designer

The table designer and dialog boxes enable you to define tables and table-related constructs on a table-by-table basis. The database diagram designer provides the same functionality in a more visual format. It enables you to build a diagram of the whole database showing tables, table columns, keys, and table relationships, and also enables you to create each of these items from within the diagram designer tool.

> **NOTE**
>
> As mentioned at the start of this chapter, there are many features of the SSDT designers that are not currently available with the SQL Server Data Tools for SQL Server 2012. Database diagrams, and their attendant designer, are one such example. Although you can still create and edit database diagrams against prior versions of SQL Server, the only way to create/edit diagrams on SQL Server 2012 is to use the dedicated SQL Server Management Studio application.

Like the table designer, the database diagram designer is implemented within the IDE's document pane. It has its own menu and toolbar associated with it; you can access many of the commands on the menu/toolbar through the designer's shortcut menu by right-clicking anywhere within the designer.

> **TIP**
>
> Within a diagram, you can change the view style on a per-table basis. Right-click the table and select one of the available Table views: Standard (shows column name, data type, and allow nulls), Column Names, Keys, Name Only, and Custom (you select the data you want to display). The Name Only view is particularly useful if you want to see an entire database diagram to get a sense of the relationships without necessarily caring about the table details themselves.

Creating a Database Diagram

To create a database diagram, right-click the Database Diagrams node in the Server Explorer window and select Add New Diagram. A blank diagram opens, and the designer immediately displays a dialog box for adding tables to the diagram (see Figure 20.9).

FIGURE 20.9   Adding tables to a diagram.

After you've added a few tables, the diagram shows a graphical representation of the tables' columns and any relationships that the tables participate in. The diagram is fully interactive; you can directly edit column definitions, keys, relationships, and so on.

TIP

Here is a quick shortcut for adding groups of related tables: Add a table to the diagram, select it, and click the Add Related Tables button in the designer's toolbar. This automatically adds to the diagram any table in the database that has a current relationship with the selected table.

Modifying Table Definitions

Tables can be edited "inline" within the diagram. To change column details, you click within the table and then enter column name information or change the data type and nullability rules. To add a column, just fill out a new row within the table representation in the diagram.

Building Table Relationships

Table relationships are easy to define within a diagram: Just drag and drop the primary key column from one table to the foreign key column on another table to automatically display the Foreign Key Relationship dialog box (see Figure 20.10). This dialog box captures the general relationship information; note the text in the dialog box that clearly states that we are editing a new relationship. Because the relationship is new, we need to define the table columns that participate in the relationship.

Clicking the Tables and Columns Specification property launches a second dialog box (see Figure 20.11). Here, we establish a common one-to-many relationship between a category table and a product table. The product table has a category ID column that is foreign-keyed to the primary key on the category table. After committing the column assignments, you complete the relationship by changing any properties (if needed) on the relationship itself in the Foreign Key Relationship dialog box and then clicking OK.

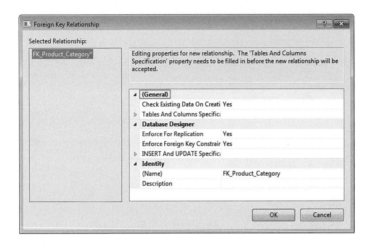

FIGURE 20.10   Creating a foreign key.

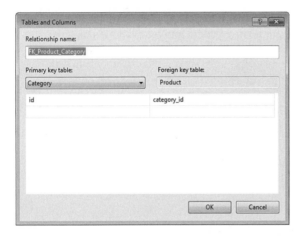

FIGURE 20.11   Establishing foreign key column assignments.

Relationships are depicted within the diagram as a line between the two tables. The line indicates the direction of the relationship by showing a key on the primary key side and an infinity symbol on the foreign key side (or the "many" side) of the relationship. Figure 20.12 illustrates tables with one-to-many relationships as they appear within the database diagram designer.

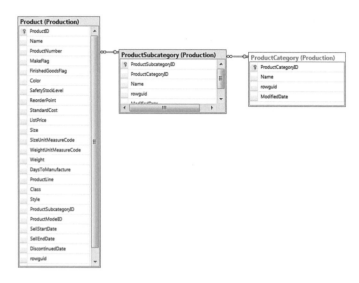

FIGURE 20.12   Table relationships in the database diagram designer.

By default, relationships enforce referential integrity. That is, they prevent any action (insert, update, delete) that would result in a mismatch of keys between the two related tables. This includes inserting a foreign key (FK) value when it doesn't exist as a primary key (PK) in the related table, changing a PK value that is referenced as a FK value, and so on.

You can control whether a relationship enforces referential integrity through the Enforce Foreign Key Constraint setting in the Foreign Key Relationship dialog box. Relationships that do not enforce referential integrity are depicted as banded lines instead of solid lines within the diagram designer. You should also note that the diagram designer shows only relationships that have been explicitly defined through the process covered in the preceding paragraphs. Just having similarly named foreign keys and primary keys does not automatically create a relationship for you.

In addition to one-to-many relationships, you can model one-to-one, many-to-many, and reflexive relationships using the database diagram designer.

One-to-One Relationships   You build a one-to-one relationship in the same way you create a one-to-many relationship. The difference is this: One-to-one relationships are between two primary keys instead of a primary and a foreign key. If you drag a primary key column from one table to a primary key column on another table, this automatically creates a one-to-one association. These relationships are depicted with a key icon on both ends of the relationship line.

20

Many-to-Many Relationships   You create a many-to-many relationship with the help of a junction table. If you had to model a many-to-many association between an order table and an item table (an order can have many items, and an item can belong to many orders), you would first add a third table to the database to hold the foreign keys of this relationship.

After adding the junction table, you then establish a one-to-many relationship between the `order` and `orderitem` tables, and between the `item` and `orderitem` tables. The last step is to define the multicolumn primary key on the junction table. Figure 20.13 shows the results in the diagram.

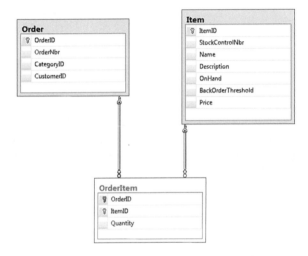

FIGURE 20.13   A many-to-many relationship.

Reflexive Relationships   A reflexive relationship is a relationship between a table and itself. A typical example used to illustrate reflexive relationship is that of a part table that relates back to itself to represent the fact that a part could be made up of other parts. In this case, the part table might carry a `parent_part_id` field that is meant to be a foreign key related to the employee table's primary key.

To create a reflexive relationship, select the primary key column and drag it back onto the same table. The configuration of the key associations and the relationship values is the same as with any other relationship. Figure 20.14 shows a diagram of a reflexive relationship.

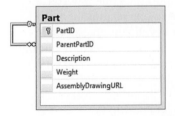

FIGURE 20.14   A reflexive relationship.

Working with SQL Statements

There is full support within the SQL Server Data Tools set for crafting and executing SQL statements against a connected database. This includes support for compiling SQL statements as stored procedures, creating views and triggers, and writing user-defined functions.

Writing a Query

The primary tool that facilitates the development of SQL statements is the query/view designer, which is a graphical tool that enables you to build queries with a point-and-click interface. After a query is constructed, this tool also enables you to view and interact with any results returned as a result of executing the query.

Now you're ready to put this tool through its paces.

Creating a new select query against a table is as simple as selecting the database in Server Explorer and then, under the SQL menu, selecting New Query. An initial prompt gathers a list of the tables, views, functions, and synonyms to use as the target of the query (see Figure 20.15).

FIGURE 20.15   Adding tables to the query.

After you have selected the objects you want the query to target, the query designer opens. As Figure 20.16 illustrates, the designer has four panes:

▶ **Criteria pane**—This pane enables you to select, via a point-and-click diagram, the data columns to include in the select statement, sorting, and alias names.

▶ **Diagram pane**—This pane is similar to the diagram in the database diagram designer; it graphically depicts the database object relationships. This makes creating joins a simple action of using existing relationships or creating new ones right within this tool.

▶ **Results pane**—After the query is executed, this pane holds any data returned as a result. Note that this pane is equipped with navigation controls to enable you to page through large resultsets.

▶ **SQL pane**—The SQL pane holds the actual SQL syntax used to implement the query. You can alter the statement manually by typing directly into this pane, or you can leverage the designer and let it write the SQL for you based on what you have entered in the diagram and criteria panes.

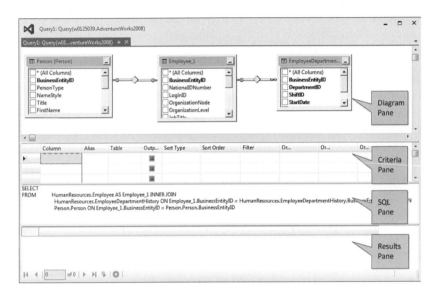

FIGURE 20.16   The query/view designer.

You can show or hide any of these panes at will. Right-click anywhere in the designer and select the Pane fly-out menu to select or deselect the visible panes.

Fine-Tuning the SQL Statement

To flesh out the `select` statement, you can indicate which columns from which tables you want returned by placing a check next to the column in the diagram pane. You use the criteria pane to specify a sort order, provide alias names for the return columns, and establish a filter for the resultset. As you select these different options, the designer turns them into SQL, visible in the SQL pane.

NOTE

We are using the AdventureWorks sample database in a SQL Server 2008 R2 instance for most of this chapter. If you want to follow along, you can download a copy of this database and others by visiting http://MSFTDBProdSamples.codeplex.com/. AdventureWorks is also the sample database used by the SQL Server 2008 Books Online help collection.

Figure 20.17 shows the completed "Employee" query, with results visible in the bottom pane.

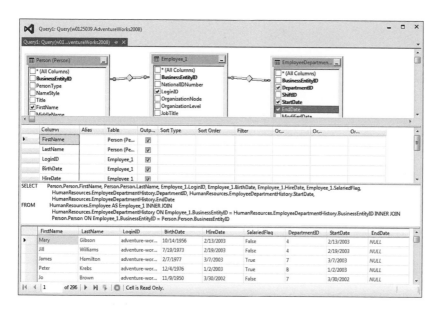

FIGURE 20.17   Querying for employee information in the AdventureWorks database.

Specifying Joins and Join Types

When you add multiple related tables to the query designer, the designer uses their key relationships to automatically build a JOIN clause for the query. You also have the option to create joins on table columns that don't have an existing relationship. You do this the same way that you specify relationships in the database diagram designer: You select and drag the column from one table to another within the diagram pane. The columns to be joined must be of compatible data types; you can't join, for instance, a varchar column with an integer column.

Joins are created using a comparison operator. By default, this is the equal operator; in other words, return rows where the column values are equal across the join. But you have control over the actual comparison operation used in the join. For example, perhaps you want the resultset to include rows based on a join where the values in Table A are greater than the values in Table B on the joined columns. You can right-click the join relationship line in the diagram pane and select Properties to see the properties for the join; clicking the ellipsis button in the Join Condition and Type property reveals the Join dialog box, shown in Figure 20.18.

Other Query Types

By default, creating queries from the Server Explorer results in a select query. But the query designer is equally adept at building other query types. If you want, for instance,

20

an insert query, you can change the type of the query loaded in the designer by selecting Query Design, Change Type.

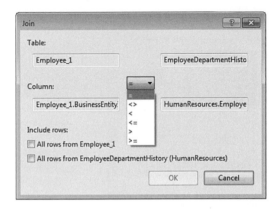

FIGURE 20.18   Setting the join type and operator.

Table 20.1 shows the different query types supported by the designer.

TABLE 20.1   Supported Query Types

Query Type	Comments
Select	Returns data from one or more tables or views; a SQL SELECT statement
Insert Results	Inserts new rows into a table by copying them from another table; a SQL INSERT INTO ... SELECT statement
Insert Values	Inserts a new row into a table using the values and column targets specified; a SQL INSERT INTO ... VALUES statement
Update	Updates the value of existing rows or columns in a table; a SQL UPDATE ... SET statement
Delete	Deletes one or more rows from a table; a SQL DELETE statement
Make Table	Creates a new table and inserts rows into the new table by using the results of a select query; a SQL SELECT ... INTO statement

TIP

If you just want to quickly see the data contents of any given table, you can right-click the table within the Server Explorer and then select Show Table Data. This initiates a new query/view designer with a SELECT * statement for the given table. By default, only the results pane is visible. This functionality is ideal for testing scenarios in which you need to quickly edit data in the database or observe the effects of SQL statements on a table.

Creating Views

Views are virtual tables. They look and act just like tables in the database but are, in reality, `select` statements that are stored in the database. When you look at the content of a view, you are actually looking at the resultset for a select statement.

Because views are implemented as select statements, you create them using the query/view designer tool. In Server Explorer, right-click the Views folder under the database where you want to create the view. From there, you build the `select` statement just as you would for any other SQL statement.

Saving the view refreshes the database's copy of the view's `select` statement.

Developing Stored Procedures

A stored procedure is a SQL statement (or series of statements) stored in a database and compiled. With SQL Server, stored procedures consist of Transact-SQL (T-SQL) code and have the capability to involve many coding constructs not typically found in ad hoc queries. For instance, you can implement error-handling routines within a stored procedure and even call into operating-system functions with so-called extended stored procedures.

For a given database, right-click the stored procedures folder in Server Explorer and select Add New Stored Procedure. A template for a stored procedure opens in the SQL Editor. The SQL Editor is a close sibling to Visual Studio's Code Editor; although it doesn't have IntelliSense, it does support syntax coloring, breakpoints, and the more general text-editing features (cut-copy-paste, word wrapping, and so on).

Figure 20.19 shows the beginnings of a stored procedure in the SQL Editor window.

With the template loaded into the SQL Editor, writing a stored procedure involves typing in the lines of code and SQL that perform the required actions. But stored procedure developers haven't been left out in the cold with regard to productivity in Visual Studio. You can leverage the power of the query/view designer to write portions of your stored procedure for you.

Using the SQL Editor with the Query/View Designer

As you build the body of the procedure, the editor window highlights and boxes in certain parts of the procedure. These boxed-in areas represent SQL statements that you can edit using the query designer. Consider the stored procedure featured in Figure 20.20.

This procedure, from the AdventureWorks database, essentially consists of an update and an insert command. Both of these commands are contained within a blue-bordered box in the SQL Editor window. This is the editor's way of indicating that it has recognized a SQL statement within the procedure that can be designed using the query/view designer. If you right-click within the boxed-in area, the shortcut menu includes an option titled Design SQL Block. If you select this option, the query/view designer opens in a separate dialog box. Figure 20.21 shows the first of the two statements as they appear in the query/view designer.

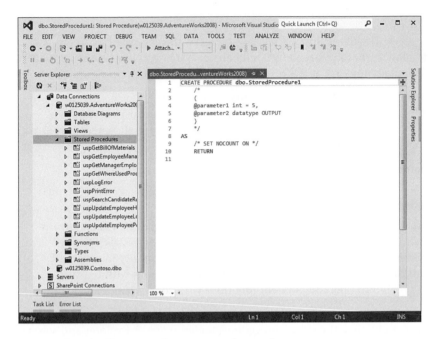

FIGURE 20.19   The start of a new stored procedure.

FIGURE 20.20   SQL statements in a stored procedure.

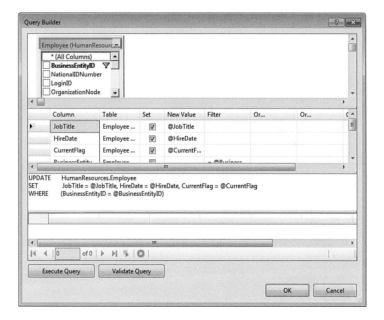

FIGURE 20.21   Designing a query for a stored procedure.

Using the same process outlined before for writing queries, you can construct the SQL within the relative luxury of the query designer's drag-and-drop interface. Clicking OK on the designer dialog box will saves the query back into the stored procedure, updating the code in the editor window.

Notice that the query designer fully supports the use of parameters. When you fill in the parameter names in the New Value column (see the criteria pane in Figure 20.21), the designer is able to construct the appropriate SQL.

> **NOTE**
>
> The capability to create and edit stored procedures is supported only in Microsoft SQL Server. You cannot use the Visual Studio tools to create a procedure in, say, an Oracle database.

The query designer can also be pressed into play for inserting new blocks of SQL into a stored procedure (as opposed to editing existing SQL statements). First, in the SQL Editor window, right-click the line within the procedure where you want to place the new query. From the pop-up menu, select Insert SQL. You can now use the query/view designer to craft the appropriate SQL. After you close out the dialog box by clicking OK, the new SQL is inserted into the procedure and can be saved into the database.

Debugging Stored Procedures

In addition to coding stored procedures, you can leverage the Server Explorer tool to help you debug them. With the stored procedure open in the SQL Editor window, set a breakpoint in the procedure by clicking in the Indicator Margin. (For more details on the indicator margin and general editor properties, see Chapter 6, "Introducing the Editors and Designers.") With a breakpoint in place, right-click the stored procedure's name in the Server Explorer tree and select Execute (see Figure 20.22).

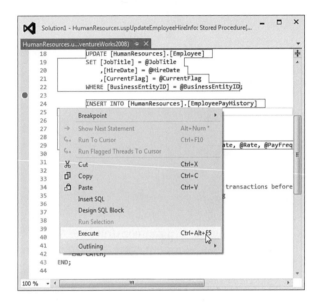

FIGURE 20.22   Executing a stored procedure with a breakpoint.

The SQL Debugger is also parameter friendly. If the stored procedure uses any parameters, the debugger shows a dialog box to capture values for the parameters (see Figure 20.23).

You can quickly cycle through the list of parameters, supplying appropriate values. After you click OK, the stored procedure is executed. If you have set a breakpoint, execution pauses on the breakpoint. (A yellow arrow indicates the current line of execution within the editor, just the same as with the code editor window.) With execution stopped, you can use the Locals and Watch windows to debug the procedure's code. See Chapter 11, "Debugging Code," for a more thorough treatment of the Locals and Watch windows as debugging tools in Visual Studio.

The Debug menu is used to control execution and flow. If you select Continue, the procedure continues running up to the next breakpoint (if present).

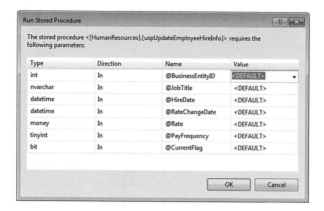

FIGURE 20.23   Entering parameter values in the SQL Debugger.

Creating Triggers

Triggers are a type of stored procedure designed to run when the data in a table or view is modified. Triggers are attached to an individual table; when a query (an update, insert, or delete query) affects data in the table, the trigger executes.

Because a trigger is really a stored procedure with a controlled execution time (hence the name trigger), it can have quite complex SQL statements and flow execution logic.

To create a trigger, use Server Explorer and locate the table to which the trigger is to be attached. Right-click the table name, select Add New Trigger, and then use the SQL Editor to write the SQL for the trigger. When the trigger is saved to the database, it shows up under its related table in Server Explorer (alongside the columns in the table). Figure 20.24 shows a simple trigger designed to raise an error if an update statement changes the Availability column in the Location table.

Creating User-Defined Functions

User-defined functions are bodies of code/SQL designed to be reusable across a variety of possible consumers: stored procedures, applications, or even other functions. In that respect, they are no different from functions written in C# or Visual Basic. They are routines that can accept parameters and return a value. User-defined functions return scalar values (for example, a single value) or a resultset containing rows and columns of data.

One example of a user-defined function might be one that accepts a date and then determines whether the day is a weekday or weekend. Stored procedures or other functions in the database can then use the function as part of their processing.

20

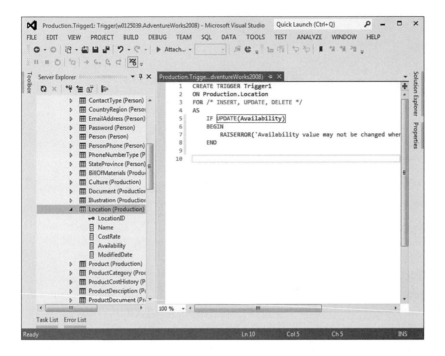

FIGURE 20.24   Creating a trigger.

Because user-defined functions are T-SQL statements with a format similar to stored procedures, the SQL Editor again is the primary tool for writing them. For each data connection visible in Server Explorer, a Functions folder contains any existing functions. To create a new function, you can right-click this folder, select Add New, and then select the type of function to create. There are three options:

▶ **Inline Function**—Returns values as a resultset; the resultset is built from the results of a SELECT query.

▶ **Table-Valued Function**—Returns values as a resultset; the resultset is built by programmatically creating a table within the function and then populating the table using INSERT INTO queries.

▶ **Scalar-Valued Function**—Returns a single value.

After selecting the appropriate function type, template code for the function is delivered inside a new SQL Editor window. Feel free to use the query/view designer to construct any required lines of SQL within the function.

For the specifics on how to write a function and put it to best use within the database, consult your database's documentation.

Using Database Projects

Up to this point, we have discussed the use of the Visual Database Tools outside the context of a Visual Studio solution/project. Now let's investigate the role of the Database project type. Database projects in Visual Studio are used to manage the development and deployment of databases. They essentially represent an offline version of a database. It mirrors a database through a set of SQL files that contain the schema and object definitions for things such as tables, indexes, and stored procedures. With database projects, Visual Studio enables an end-to-end database development workflow that typically goes something like this:

▶ The DBA, who is typically the only person on a project team with access to the production database, uses VSTS Database Edition to create an initial database project and reverse engineer a production database into that project.

▶ The DBA is also typically responsible for generating test data sets for use in nonproduction databases.

▶ From there, the database developer gets involved. The database developer works within the confines of the database project to write the database code, changes schema items as needed to implement the required functionality, and writes unit tests that validate those changes.

▶ When done with a set of changes, the database developer checks the schema changes into the Team Foundation Server source control system.

▶ The DBA is then re-injected into the process. The DBA reviews the changes, compares the changes to the schema and data already in production, builds a deployment package containing those changes, and then oversees the deployment of those changes in a moderated way into production.

> **NOTE**
>
> Scripts are nothing more than SQL statements stored in a file. They are useful because they can be executed in batch to do such things as create tables in a brand-new database or add a canned set of stored procedures to a database. Because they are merely files, they can be transferred from computer to computer, enabling you to duplicate database structures across machines with ease.

The SQL scripts in the database project can create many of the database objects that we have already discussed: tables, views, triggers, stored procedures, and so on. Queries developed using the query/view designer can also be directly saved into a database project. In short, you use the Visual Database Tools in conjunction with a database project to create and save SQL scripts and queries.

Creating a Database Project

Database projects use the same project template system and "new project" process as all other Visual Studio project types. This means that we launch the creation process by selecting File, New, and then selecting one of the templates located in the Other Languages/SQL Server category on the New Project dialog box (see Figure 20.25).

> **NOTE**
>
> If you are coming to Visual Studio 2012 as a prior user of Visual Studio 2010 or earlier, note the fundamental changes that have taken place with regard to the database tools. There is no longer a wizard that is launched when you create a new database project, and the number of project templates has shrunk to just the single SQL Server Database Project that comes in the currently shipping version of the SQL Server Data Tools.

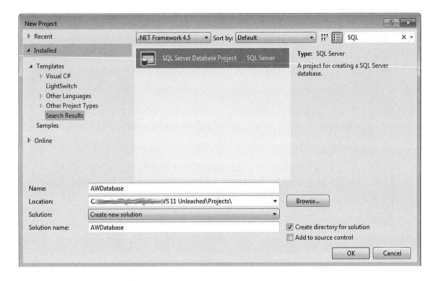

FIGURE 20.25   Selecting the database project template.

> **NOTE**
>
> To be able to parse and validate the objects within a database project, Visual Studio needs to communicate with a local instance of SQL Server: This can be the Express Edition, Developer Edition, or Enterprise Edition of the particular database version you are targeting. If you do not have a local instance of SQL Server running, you see a dialog box at the start of the new project process prompting you to supply the path to a valid SQL Server local instance.

Importing a Database

After the project has been created, we are left with a rather sparse and empty solution tree (see Figure 20.26). We have two basic options at this point. We can create items within the project and configure the properties of the database by right-clicking the project name and running the properties dialog, or we can import an existing database, thus pulling in all of its attendant information into the project. Most database developers will want to build their initial project from an existing database. This preserves the concept of a production database being the "one version of the truth." This is a recognition of the fact that we really want our test and development database environments to mirror the production environment in terms of structure. By reverse engineering a database into its component objects, Visual Studio enables us to create copies of a database, and that, in turn, enables developers to work in their own private sandboxes without worrying about affecting the production data store.

FIGURE 20.26   The initial empty database project structure.

Let's import a database. Right-click the project, select Import, and then select Database. This launches the import window.

The import tool (see Figure 20.27) captures the database connection to use (effectively answering the question "Which database should be imported?") and the various items to be imported.

At the bottom of the screen is a drop-down labeled Folder structure; the value set here dictates exactly how Visual Studio structures the project around the imported items. There are two approaches: organizing by object type and organizing by schema. For the object type approach, Visual Studio creates a schema objects folder with subfolders for your database objects such as tables and stored procedures. This is very similar to the way that the Server Explorer represents a database in its tree view. The schema approach will group your project objects by the schema type that they belong to. And there is also a hybrid approach, Schema/ObjectType, which will first organize by schema and then, within each schema folder, by object type. For most database implementations, the object type setting is the most useful. The exception is those cases where the database itself has multiple schemas. In those scenarios, the hybrid Schema/ObjectType option will likely be best. Because our sample AdventureWorks database contains multiple schemas, this is the option we will select.

Click the Start button to start the import. A status dialog will detail the progress of the import (see Figure 20.28).

20

FIGURE 20.27   Importing a database.

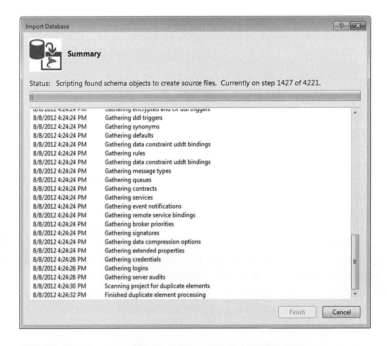

FIGURE 20.28   Importing the AdventureWorks database.

At its conclusion, project items (which correspond to all of the database schema items) will now exist in the project (see Figure 20.29). Note that each object in the database (be it a table, a stored procedure, an index, a key, or a constraint) is represented by a single .sql file. In addition to the schema files, we also have folders for holding data generation plans (more on these in a bit), and pre- and post-deployment scripts. Scripts placed into the pre- and post- folders are executed just before, or immediately after, deployment.

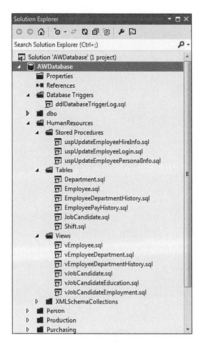

FIGURE 20.29   A fully populated database project tree.

Changing the Database

With a fully populated database project, you can now make any desired changes by opening any of the generated .sql files and editing the file. This works the same way that object editing works using the Server Explorer or the SQL Server Object Explorer: You can edit the raw SQL commands using the SQL editor or, if you opened a table's .sql file for instance, you can edit the table definition by using the designer or the SQL editor.

You can control a number of database and server options via the database project. These are all accessed via the project properties dialog. These would rarely need to be changed by a developer (they are more likely to be within the database administrator's scope of work), but let's briefly cover what is available. First, launch the dialog by right-clicking the project (in our example, the project is AWDatabase), and then select Properties. The project settings page (see Figure 20.30) is where you can set the target deployment platform (in other words, the version of SQL Server) and general scripting options. This is also where you can set more fine-grained database options via the Database Settings button.

20

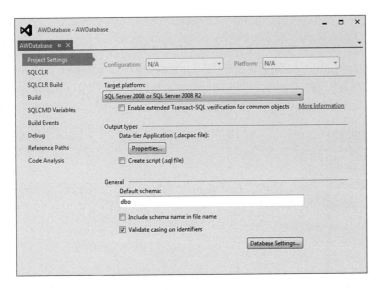

FIGURE 20.30   Database project properties.

Database Settings

Clicking the Database Settings button launches a dialog where you can set things like collation, filegroup, transaction, cursor, and text search options. Figure 20.31 shows the Operational tab of this dialog for a SQL Server 2008 database.

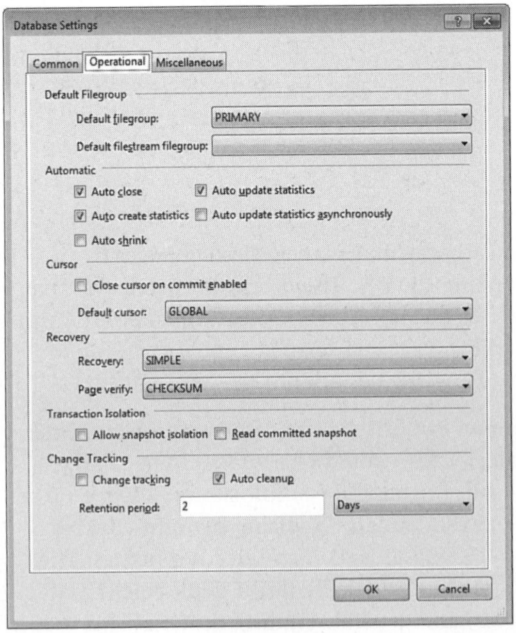

FIGURE 20.31   Setting database options.

Building and Deploying

The final item we haven't covered is the actual act of updating a schema in a database with the schema in a database project. You use the familiar build-and-deploy paradigm leveraged by other Visual Studio project types. In the context of a database project, the build process parses all the SQL files and identifies any files that have SQL syntax errors. If the build is clean, you can now publish the database by right-clicking the project within Solution Explorer and selecting Publish (see Figure 20.32). This actually updates the target database with the schema (or creates a new database if the target database doesn't exist).

FIGURE 20.32   Publishing a database.

> **NOTE**
>
> You don't have to use Visual Studio to do the actual schema deployment to the server. By building the database project, you are generating a SQL script file with all the necessary SQL commands. You can execute that script file from within any tool that understands T-SQL (including SQL Enterprise Manager itself). This is useful in situations in which the actual schema change is implemented by someone in the DBA role, who might or might not have Visual Studio installed, or who might have a specific tool that he or she is required to use for schema propagation.

A Note on Data Tier Applications

Another way to manage database development projects using Visual Studio is through a new concept introduced with SQL Server 2008 R2: data tier applications, also referred to as DACs.

The concept of a DAC isn't that much different than the database project we have been discussing: It is meant to expose all of the database objects from a particular database in an "offline" fashion so that developers and DBAs can make and test changes against a database right from within the IDE. The key difference is in the approach: data tier application projects "compile" down to a .dacpac file. This file is a single unit of deployment, which contains all the necessary database objects required by a given application: stored procedures, tables, server-side objects, management policies, and even user logins. A DAC does not contain any data.

The intent is to enable developers to work more in a declarative world (that is, we need to make these changes to a database for our application), instead of the current procedural world (that is, we need to execute these statements and scripts in this order against this database to run our application).

These project types are only supported with SQL Server 2008 R2 (and now, SQL Server 2012 which, at the time of this writing, has not yet been released) and are not compatible with any other versions of SQL Server. Given the unreleased state of the technology, we leave this topic without investigating the specifics here. You should know that the data tier application project looks and feels identical to the database project from within the IDE.

Creating Database Objects in Managed Code

Database objects are commonly implemented using some dialect of the SQL language. This is true with SQL Server, as well, and as we have just reviewed, the Visual Studio database project allows you to craft your database objects using SQL. But using that same project, you can also design database objects using C#.

SQL Server 2005 introduced the capability of authoring SQL objects in managed code. So, instead of using Transact SQL, you can actually write your stored procedures, queries, views, and so on using C#. These are run under the auspices of SQL Server's very own version of the .NET Common Language Runtime (CLR).

The SQL Server CLR supports objects a variety of object types that can be written in C#:

▶ Stored procedures

▶ Triggers

▶ Aggregates

▶ User-defined functions

▶ User-defined types

The following sections look at how to go about creating a straightforward stored procedure using C# instead of T-SQL.

Creating a Stored Procedure in C#

First, add a stored procedure item to your database project by right-clicking the project and selecting Add, New Item. From the new item dialog, you select the SQL CLR C# category, and then the SQL CLR C# Stored Procedure project item, as shown in Figure 20.33. Let's name the stored procedure **UpdateEmployeeLogin**.

FIGURE 20.33   Adding a C# stored procedure.

A new class is added to the project. Listing 20.1 shows the base code that shows up within the new class file. You can add your custom code to the static void routine UpdateEmployeeLogin.

LISTING 20.1   The Start of a Managed Code Stored Procedure

```
using System;
using System.Data;
using System.Data.SqlClient;
using System.Data.SqlTypes;
using Microsoft.SqlServer.Server;


public partial class StoredProcedures
{
```

20

```
[Microsoft.SqlServer.Server.SqlProcedure]
public static void UpdateEmployeeLogin()
{
    // Put your code here
}
}
```

Managed code objects in SQL Server all leverage the .NET Framework data classes (that is, ADO.NET) to do their work. This means that stored procedures you write will instantiate and use classes such as SqlConnection and SqlCommand. The code you write is identical to data access code that you would write from within any other .NET project type: class libraries, web projects, and Windows Forms projects. Because the common denominator is the use of ADO.NET classes, developers don't need to learn another language (such as T-SQL) to perform work in the database.

> **NOTE**
>
> It's beyond the scope of this chapter to cover the relative merits or disadvantages of writing your database objects in managed code as opposed to T-SQL. Check out the whitepaper available on Microsoft Developer Network (MSDN) titled "Using CLR Integration in SQL Server 2005." Although fairly old (it was written in November 2004), it is a great treatment of this subject and is highly recommended reading.

Listing 20.2 shows a fleshed-out C# routine that updates the AdventureWorks Employee table with login information. None of this code is complicated, and it can be easily understood (and written) by anyone with C# data access experience.

LISTING 20.2   Managed Code for Updating Employee Login Values

```
using System;
using System.Data;
using System.Data.SqlClient;
using System.Data.SqlTypes;
using Microsoft.SqlServer.Server;


public partial class StoredProcedures
{
    [Microsoft.SqlServer.Server.SqlProcedure]
    public static void UpdateEmployeeLogin(SqlInt32 employeeId,
    SqlInt32 managerId, SqlString loginId, SqlString title,
    SqlDateTime hireDate, SqlBoolean currentFlag)
    {
        using (SqlConnection conn =
            new SqlConnection("context connection=true"))
        {
```

```
        SqlCommand UpdateEmployeeLoginCommand =
          new SqlCommand();

        UpdateEmployeeLoginCommand.CommandText =
            "update HumanResources.Employee SET ManagerId = " +
          managerId.ToString() +
            ", LoginId = '" + loginId.ToString() + "'" +
            ", Title = '" + title.ToString() + "'" +
            ", HireDate = '" + hireDate.ToString() + "'" +
            ", CurrentFlag = " + currentFlag.ToString() +
            " WHERE EmployeeId = " + employeeId.ToString();

        UpdateEmployeeLoginCommand.Connection = conn;

        conn.Open();
        UpdateEmployeeLoginCommand.ExecuteNonQuery();
        conn.Close();

    }
  }
};
```

One line of code, however, deserves a more detailed explanation. The `SqlConnection` object is created like this:

```
SqlConnection conn = new SqlConnection("context connection=true")
```

The connection string `"context connection=true"` tells the data provider engine that the connection should be created in the same context as the calling application. Because this routine is running inside a database, that means you are connecting to the host database and run using the context (transactional and otherwise) of the calling application. Because you are piggybacking on the context of the database that the routine is running in, you don't need to hard-code a full SQL connection string here.

For comparison purposes, Listing 20.3 shows the same update query implemented in T-SQL.

LISTING 20.3   T-SQL for Updating Employee Login Values

```
ALTER PROCEDURE [HumanResources].[uspUpdateEmployeeLogin]
    @EmployeeID [int],
    @ManagerID [int],
    @LoginID [nvarchar](256),
    @Title [nvarchar](50),
    @HireDate [datetime],
    @CurrentFlag [dbo].[Flag]
```

20

```
WITH EXECUTE AS CALLER
AS
BEGIN
    SET NOCOUNT ON;

    BEGIN TRY
        UPDATE [HumanResources].[Employee]
        SET [ManagerID] = @ManagerID
            ,[LoginID] = @LoginID
            ,[Title] = @Title
            ,[HireDate] = @HireDate
            ,[CurrentFlag] = @CurrentFlag
        WHERE [EmployeeID] = @EmployeeID;
    END TRY
    BEGIN CATCH
        EXECUTE [dbo].[uspLogError];
    END CATCH;
END;
```

Building and Deploying the Stored Procedure

When you build your SQL Server project, the typical compilation process takes place. Assuming that your code will build, you can now deploy the resulting assembly to the database as we have already seen by using the Publish command on the project.

After the assembly has been deployed, you can test it by calling it from an application or from a query window. For detailed information on how to call managed assemblies and write them, consult the SQL Server Books Online.

Binding Controls to Data

You have now seen all the various ways you can use Visual Studio to create and manage databases. The following sections look at the tools available for consuming data within Windows forms, WPF, or web applications.

An Introduction to Data Binding

There is a common problem and solution pattern at hand with applications that front databases. Typically, data has to be fetched from the database into the application, and the application's user interface has to be updated to display the data in an appropriate manner. For large data sets, the concept of paging comes into play. Because it is inefficient to load in, say, a 100MB data set, a paging mechanism needs to be pressed into action to enable the user to move forward and back through the data "stream." After the data has safely made it into the application's UI, the application-to-database flow needs to be handled. For any pieces of data that have been changed, those changes have to be reconciled and committed back into the database.

Data binding is the term given to the implementation of a design pattern that handles all facets of this round trip of data from a data structure, into an application's controls, and back again (see Figure 20.34). Although the data structure is most commonly a database, it could be any sort of container object that holds data, such as an array or a collection. .NET further stratifies the concepts of data binding into simple data binding and complex data binding. Both of these terms refer to a control's intrinsic capabilities in the larger context of the data-binding process.

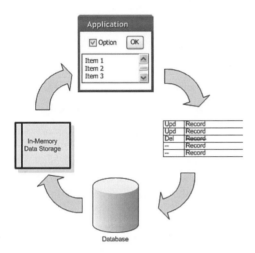

FIGURE 20.34   The data-binding process.

Simple Data Binding

Simple data binding is the capability for a control to bind to and display a single data element within a larger data set. A `TextBox` control is a great example of a control commonly used in simple data-binding scenarios. You might use a `TextBox`, for example, to display the last name of an employee as it is stored within the employee table of a database.

Support for simple data binding is widespread throughout both the Windows and web forms controls. When you use the built-in capabilities of the Windows and Web Forms Designer, it is trivial to add a group of controls to a form and simple-bind them to a data set (more on this in a bit).

Complex Data Binding

The term *complex data binding* refers to the capability of a control to display multiple data elements at one time. You can think of this as a "multirow" capability. If a control can be leveraged to view multiple rows of data at one time, it supports complex data binding.

The `DataGridView` control (for Windows forms) and `DataGrid` control (for web forms) are premier examples of controls that were purpose-built to handle tabular (multirow and multicolumn) data.

20

Although the internals necessary to implement data binding are messy, complex, and hard to understand, for the most part the Visual Studio tools have abstracted the cost of implementing data binding out to a nice and easy drag-and-drop model. Now let's look at how to rapidly build out support for round-trip data binding.

Autogenerating Bound Windows Forms Controls

Although there are various ways to approach and implement data-bound controls with Visual Studio, they all involve the same basic two steps:

1. Establish a data source.

2. Map the data-source members to controls or control properties.

From there, the Visual Studio Form Designers can generate the correct controls and place them on the form. All the data-binding code is handled for you; all you need to worry about is the layout, positioning, and UI aspects of the controls.

As you might imagine, your form might have controls that use simple data binding or complex data binding or a mix of both. Now you're ready to look at the steps involved with creating a series of controls that leverage both simple and complex data binding to display information from the AdventureWorks Employee table. In this scenario, you work with the Windows Forms Designer. The ASP.NET Web Forms Designer works in a similar fashion, and you have a chance to investigate drag-and-drop approaches for data binding in the web environment in just a bit. As we have already established, the first step is selecting a data source.

Selecting a Data Source

In Visual Studio, make sure you are working inside a Windows Application project and use the Data Sources window to select a data source. If this window isn't already visible, select View, Other Windows, Data Sources. If your current project doesn't have any defined data sources, you need to create one. Click the Add New Data Source button in the toolbar of the window to start the Data Source Configuration Wizard. On the first page of this wizard (see Figure 20.35), select the type of the data source. There are four options here:

▶ **Database**—The data source resides as a table within a relational database.

▶ **Service**—The data source is a web service that returns the data to be bound to the form controls.

▶ **Object**—The data source is an object that provides the data. (This is useful in scenarios in which a business object from another layer of the application is responsible for delivering the data to the form.)

▶ **SharePoint**—The data source is an object that is hosted within a SharePoint site.

Because the concepts of data binding are most easily understood within the context of a database, we use the database data-source type as the underpinning for our walkthroughs in this chapter.

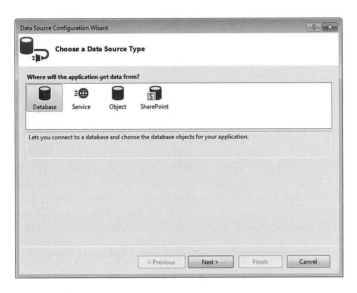

FIGURE 20.35   Choosing the data-source type.

If you have selected the database data-source type, the second page of the wizard focuses on selecting the type of data model you use. Prior versions of Visual Studio simply enabled you to model your data using data sets. Visual Studio now also enables you to build an Entity Data Model, and use that as a data source for your binding. Entity Data Models are a feature of the Entity Framework, which we discuss later in this chapter. Regardless of the model you select, you need to indicate where the model gets its data (via connection string, and so on) and what data should be pulled into the model from the source database.

Select DataSet, and then click through the next two pages of the wizard, which will capture the connection and connection string to use. The final page of the wizard, shown in Figure 20.36, enables you to select which of the objects in the database should be used for the source data. You can select from any of the data elements present in any of the various tables, views, stored procedures, or user-defined functions in the database. For the purposes of this example, we have selected a DataSet model that pulls its data from the AdventureWorks database, and we have selected a few employee table data columns that are of interest: BusinessEntityID, LoginID, HireDate, rowguid, BirthDate, SalariedFlag, VacationHours, SickLeaveHours, and CurrentFlag.

At the conclusion of the wizard, your selected data source is visible in the Data Sources window (see Figure 20.37).

20

NOTE

If you have chosen to use a DataSet as your data model, behind the scenes Visual Studio is really just using the data-source information collected in the Data Source Configuration Wizard to create a typed data set. This data set is then stored as a project item in the current project.

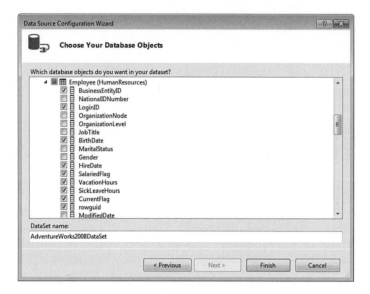

FIGURE 20.36   Selecting the data source objects.

FIGURE 20.37   The Data Sources window.

With the data source in place, you're ready to move on to the next step: mapping the data-source elements to controls on your form.

Mapping Data Sources to Controls

The really quick and easy way to create your data-bound controls is to let Visual Studio do it for you. From the Data Sources window, click the drop-down button on the data-source name to reveal a menu (see Figure 20.38).

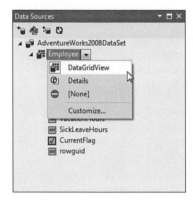

FIGURE 20.38   Changing the data table mapping.

This menu enables you to set the control generation parameters and really answers the question of which controls you want generated based on the table in the data source. By setting this to DataGridView, you can generate a `DataGridView` control for viewing and editing your data source. The Details setting enables you to generate a series of simple data-bound controls for viewing or editing data in the data source.

For this example, select Details, and then drag and drop the data source itself from the Data Sources window and onto a blank form.

Figure 20.39 shows the results. In just two short steps, Visual Studio has done all of the following for you:

▶ Autogenerated a set of `Label`, `TextBox`, and `DataTimePicker` controls

▶ Autogenerated a tool strip with controls for navigating among records in the data source, saving changes made to a record, deleting a record, and inserting a new record

▶ Created all the necessary code behind the scenes to establish a connection to the data source, read from the data source, and commit changes to the data source

You have essentially created an entire data-enabled application from scratch with absolutely no coding on your part.

The approach of using simple data binding might not fit into the user interface design, so you always have the option of working in the complex data-binding world and using the `DataGridView` as an alternative. Figure 20.40 shows the results of autogenerating a DataGridView instance `using` this same process.

20

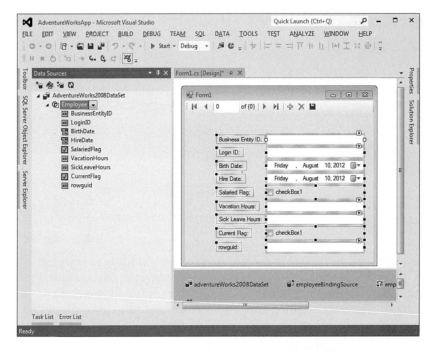

FIGURE 20.39   Autogenerated controls: viewing employee data.

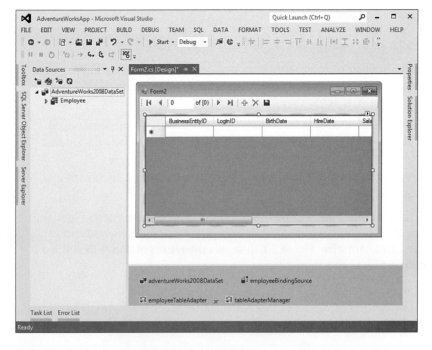

FIGURE 20.40   An autogenerated DataGridView.

Customizing Data-Source Mappings   Refer again to Figure 20.37 and look at the individual data elements that show up under the Employee data source. Each of these is displayed with a name and an icon. The name is, of course, the name of the data element as defined in the database. The icon represents the default mapping of that data type to a .NET control. For example, the Title field maps to a `TextBox` control, and the BirthDate field maps to a `DataTimePicker` control. Visual Studio actually attempts to provide the best control for any given data type. But feel free to manually indicate the specific control you want used. If you want to display the value of the Employee ID column in a label instead of a text box (in recognition of the fact that you cannot edit this value), it would be easy enough to change this before generating the controls by selecting the EmployeeID column in the Data Sources window and then clicking the drop-down arrow to select Label instead of TextBox.

In addition to changing the control to data type mapping on an individual level, you can affect the general default mappings that are in place by selecting the Customize option from that same drop-down menu. The Visual Studio Options dialog box opens with the Windows Forms Designer page selected. Using the settings there (see Figure 20.41), you can specify the default control type that you want to apply for each recognized data type.

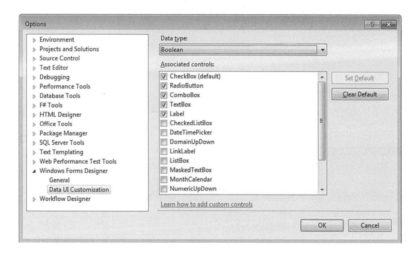

FIGURE 20.41   Customizing the UI representation for different data types.

Editing Typed Data Sets

There is a designer provided solely for editing (and creating) typed datasets within Visual Studio: the data set designer. This designer launches automatically when you open a DataSet project item such as the AdventureWorksEmployeeDataSet.xsd file that we just created when investigating data binding.

NOTE

Typed `DataSet` objects can be huge productivity enhancers over a normal dataset: Instead of using indexes into collections, you can reference tables and columns by their actual names. In addition, IntelliSense works with typed `DataSet` members, making coding against large data hierarchies much easier.

The data set designer can be used to easily tweak data sets by changing any of the various constituent parts, including the queries used to populate the data set. Figure 20.42 shows the previously created AdventureWorksEmployeeDataSet open in the data set designer.

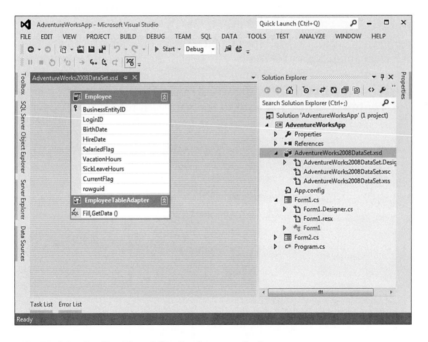

FIGURE 20.42   The Visual Studio data set designer.

Note that each piece of the data set is visually represented here, and we can interact with those pieces to effect changes. For instance, if we want to alter the query we originally constructed using the Data Set Configuration Wizard, we right-click the Employee table on the design surface and select Configure to relaunch the query editor.

In the scenario we have been discussing, we are wiring the dataset directly to the results from a SQL query, but we can also use the data set designer to create "unbound" new datasets. Adding a DataSet project item to our project enables us to start with a blank slate, adding tables, queries, and so on to the dataset to satisfy any storage requirements (or data retrieval requirements) that our application might have. This is especially useful for applications that read and write data but don't necessarily interact with a database. These dataset files can be used as simple file storage that you can easily bind later to a relational database.

Manually Binding Windows Forms Controls

In many situations, you don't want Visual Studio to create your data-bound controls for you, or you might need to bind existing controls to a data source. Data binding in these cases is just as simple and starts with the same step: creating or selecting a data source. Some controls, such as the `DataGridView`, have smart tag options for selecting a data source. Others don't have intrinsic data dialog boxes associated with them but can be bound to data just as easily by working, again, with the Data Sources window.

Binding the `DataGridView`

Grab a DataGridView from the Toolbox and drag it onto the form's surface. After you've created the control, `select` its smart tag glyph and use the drop-down at the top of the task list to select the data source to bind to (see Figure 20.43).

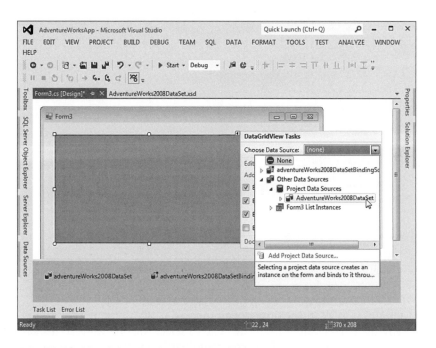

FIGURE 20.43   Selecting the control's data source.

With a data source selected, you have again managed to develop a fully functional application with two-way database access. All the code to handle the population of the grid and to handle committing changes back to the database has been written for you.

Customizing Cell Edits   The power of the `DataGridView` lies in its capability to both quickly bind to and display data in a tabular format and also to provide a highly customized editing experience. As one small example of what is possible in terms of cell editing, follow through with the Employee table example. When you auto-generated form controls to handle Employee table edits, you ended up with `DateTimePicker` controls to accommodate the date- and time-based data in the table. With the `DataGridView`, the cell editing experience is a simple text box experience: Each cell contains text, and you can edit the text and save it to the database. But you can provide a more tailored editing experience. You can use various stock controls (such as the `DataGridViewButtonColumn`, `DataGridViewComboBoxColumn`, and others that inherit from `DataGridViewColumn`; see Chapter 18, "Building Windows Forms Applications") to display data within the columns of the grid.

For example, you can use the `DataGridViewComboBoxColumn` class to provide a drop-down edit for the Gender column in the grid. To do this, you first need to change the default column type. Select the grid control, open the smart tag glyph, and select the Edit Columns action. In the Edit Columns dialog box, find the column for the employee gender data and change its column type to DataGridViewComboBoxColumn (see Figure 20.44).

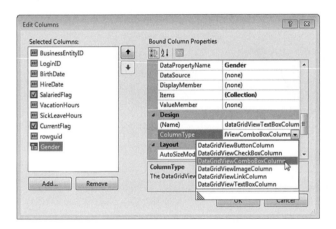

FIGURE 20.44   Changing the column type.

With the column type changed, you now need to specify how the grid should retrieve the list of possible values to display in the drop-down; the grid is smart enough to already know to use the underlying gender values from the table to select the one value to display in the grid. To handle the list of possible values, you could hard-code them in the column (see the Items property in Figure 20.42), or you could wire up a separate query (something along the lines of `SELECT DISTINCT(Gender) FROM Employees`) and have that query provide the list of possible values. Because constructing another query or data source is easy and doesn't lead to a brittle hard-coded solution, that's the approach we investigate here. To create a query to feed the combo-box column, you can visit the Data Sources window, select the Add New Data Source action, and follow the same steps you followed before to add the original Employee data source. This time, though, select only the Gender column.

After the data source is created, right-click the data source and select Edit DataSet with Designer. We use the data set designer to modify our query appropriately. In the designer (see Figure 20.45), you can see the Fill query and TableAdapter used to populate the data set. If you click the query (that is, click the last row in the table graphic in the designer window), you can use the Properties window to directly edit the SQL for the query. By modifying this to reflect SELECT DISTINCT syntax, you can return the valid gender values for inclusion in the grid.

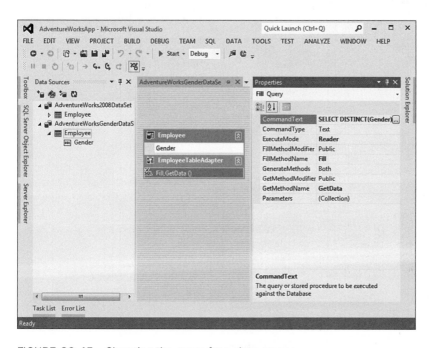

FIGURE 20.45   Changing the query for a data source.

There are two more steps needed: We need a new binding source to connect to our gender data set, and then we need to set our gender column drop-down to point to that binding source. We already have one binding source that was automatically added to our form when we added the DataGridView and connected it to a dataset. Now we need another binding source to connect to the new dataset that is retrieving the distinct gender values. From the Toolbox window, under the Data category, select the binding source component and drag it onto your form. This will add a new binding instance to the component try. Click the binding source, and in the property window set its data source to the gender data set that we just created.

Last step: Go back to the grid view control, use the smart tag to select the Edit columns option, go back to the gender column, and then set the DataSource, DisplayMember, and ValueMember properties. The DataSource will be set to the binding source we just configured (here, we have called it simply bindingSourceGender). Figure 20.46 shows the binding source property values, and Figure 20.47 shows the grid view drop-down property values, as they should look when you are done.

20

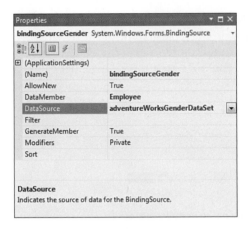

FIGURE 20.46   Configuring the binding source.

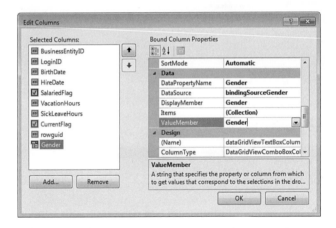

FIGURE 20.47   Connecting the drop-down column to the binding source.

And finally, Figure 20.48 shows the results. If you need to implement a cell edit control that doesn't currently exist, you can create your own by inheriting from the DataGridViewColumn base control. This employee grid could benefit from a DateTimePicker control for the date- and time-based data such as birth date and hire date.

> **NOTE**
>
> If you look in the MSDN documentation, there is a specific example of creating a DataGridViewDateTimePickerColumn control and then wiring it up within the grid. Search for "How to: Host Controls in Windows Forms DataGridView Cells."

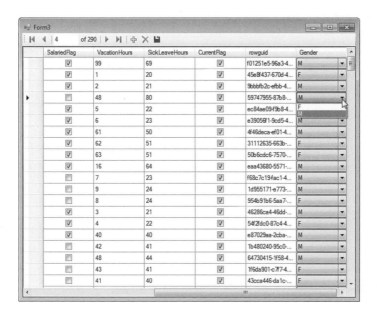

FIGURE 20.48   A data bound drop-down within a `DataGridView`.

Binding Other Controls

For other controls that don't have convenient access to binding via their smart tag, you can leverage the Data Sources window. Drag a data source from the Data Sources window and drop it onto an existing control. The designer creates a new binding source, sets it appropriately, and then makes an entry in the control's `DataBinding` collection. If you try to drag a data element onto a control that doesn't match up (for instance, dragging a character field onto a check box), the drop operation isn't allowed.

Data Binding in WPF Applications

Just as with Windows Forms applications, Visual Studio supports drag-and-drop data binding with WPF projects. The process is identical to the one we just covered for binding Windows Forms controls; we first need a data source added to our project. To change things up a bit, let's quickly build out a form that shows purchase orders and their detail line items.

First, create a new WPF project. Refer to Chapter 19 if you want to refresh your knowledge of the WPF project type and its designers/editors. Add the data sources in the same exact fashion as we did previously by using the Data Sources Wizard. From the AdventureWorks database, we select both the PurchaseOrderHeader and PurchaseOrderDetail tables to be included in our data set (which we will call AdventureWorksPurchasingDataSet).

With the data source added, we build out a simple UI: on Window1, create a two-column grid and place a list box in the left column of the grid. Name the list box **listBoxPurchaseOrders**. At this point, your workspace should look similar to the one depicted in Figure 20.49.

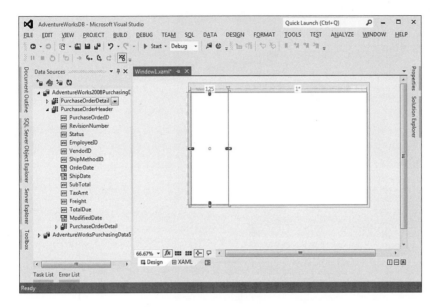

FIGURE 20.49   A UI and data sources added to a WPF project.

Now drag the PurchaseOrderID field from the PurchaseOrderHeader data source to the list box. Although nothing appears to have changed visually, the list box has actually been bound with a few lines of Extensible Application Markup Language (XAML):

▶ First, our data source has been referenced as a resource with the key `AdventureWorksPurchasingDataSet` (picking up from the name we gave the data set in the wizard).

▶ Additionally, a `CollectionViewSource` has been added with the appropriate binding path into the data set to pick up the Department table data.

▶ And finally, `DisplayMemberPath`, `ItemsSource`, and `SelectedValuePath` properties have been set on the list box itself.

Besides the XAML modifications that were made by us, a series of statements have been added to the code file, within the `Window_Loaded` event. These statements are responsible for loading the data from the database via a table adapter object.

Listing 20.4 shows the current state of our XAML.

LISTING 20.4   XAML with Visual Studio-Generated Data Binding

```
<Window x:Class="AdventureWorksUI.MainWindow"
        xmlns="http://schemas.microsoft.com/winfx/2006/xaml/presentation"
        xmlns:x="http://schemas.microsoft.com/winfx/2006/xaml"
        Title="MainWindow" Height="350" Width="525"
        xmlns:my="clr-namespace:AdventureWorksUI"
        Loaded="Window_Loaded">
```

```
<Window.Resources>
    <my:AdventureWorksPurchasingDataSet
        x:Key="AdventureWorksPurchasingDataSet" />
    <CollectionViewSource x:Key="purchaseOrderHeaderViewSource"
                          Source="{Binding Path=PurchaseOrderHeader,
        Source={StaticResource AdventureWorksPurchasingDataSet}}" />
</Window.Resources>
<Grid DataContext="{StaticResource purchaseOrderHeaderViewSource}">
    <Grid.ColumnDefinitions>
        <ColumnDefinition Width="150" />
        <ColumnDefinition Width="*" />
    </Grid.ColumnDefinitions>
    <ListBox Grid.Column="0" Margin="5"
             Name="listBoxPurchaseOrders"
             VerticalAlignment="Stretch"
             DisplayMemberPath="Name" ItemsSource="{Binding}"
             SelectedValuePath="DepartmentID"
             SelectedValue="{Binding Path=PurchaseOrderID, Mode=OneWay}" />
</Grid>
</Window>
```

If we run the application at this stage, we see that we have a list of all of the purchase order IDs displayed in our list box (see Figure 20.50).

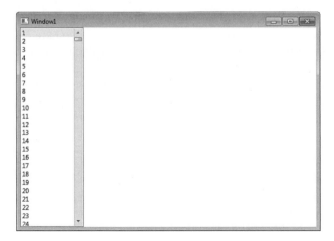

FIGURE 20.50   Data-bound purchase order headers.

Now, every time we select a purchase order ID in the list box, we want to see its line items in the right column of our window. This is another, easy drag-and-drop operation requiring no hand-coding on our part. Grab the PurchaseOrderDetail data source that sits under the PurchaseOrderHeader data source, and drag it over into the right-most column of our

WPF window. (Figure 20.51 shows this drag-and-drop operation in progress.) This has the net effect of creating a `DataGrid` control bound to the PurchaseOrderDetail rows that correspond to the currently selected `PurchaseOrderHeader` object in the list box.

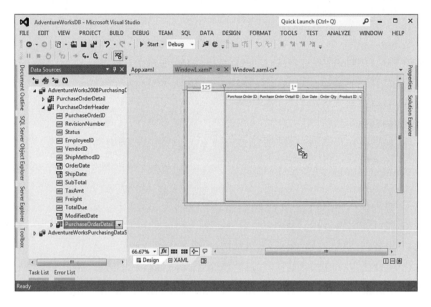

FIGURE 20.51   Adding a master-detail data source to the WPF form.

It's important that you grab the correct `PurchaseOrderDetail` object from the Data Sources window; by selecting the one that lies under the `PurchaseOrderHeader`, you are also grabbing the foreign key relationship between those two tables in the database, and that provides the context necessary for the WPF designer and editor to wire up the correct code to respond to selections in the list box and display related records in the `DataGrid`.

Figure 20.52 shows the complete app that was accomplished with absolutely no coding required!

Data Binding with Web Controls

Although the general concepts remain the same, data-binding web-based controls is a slightly different game than in the Windows Forms or WPF world. The first obvious difference is that data sources for web forms are implemented by data-source controls in the `System.Web.UI.WebControls` namespace; there is no concept of the Data Sources window with web applications. Because of this, instead of starting with a data source, you need to start with a data control and then work to attach that control to a data source.

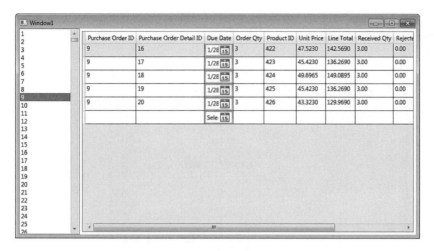

FIGURE 20.52   Master-detail data bound form in a WPF project.

Selecting a Data Control

You work with five primary controls in a web application to deliver data-bound functionality:

▶ **GridView control**—Provides a tabular presentation similar to the `DataGridView` control.

▶ **DetailsView control**—Displays a single record from a data source; with a `DetailsView` control, every column in the data source shows up as a row in the control.

▶ **FormView control**—Functions in the same way as the `DetailsView` control with the following exception: It doesn't have a built-in "default" for the way that the data is displayed. Instead, you need to provide a template to tell the control exactly how you want the data rendered onto the web page.

▶ **Repeater control**—Simply renders a list of individual items fetched from the attached data source. The specifics of how this rendering looks are all controlled via templates.

▶ **DataList control**—Displays rows of information from a data source. The display aspects are fully customizable and include header and footer elements.

For demonstration purposes, let's continue working with the AdventureWorks Employee table and see how you can implement a data-bound web page for viewing employee records.

Using the `GridView`   First, with a web project open, drag a `GridView` control from the Toolbox onto an empty web page. The first thing you notice is that the `GridView`'s smart tag menu is just as efficient as the `DataGridView`'s menu. You are directly prompted to

20

select (or create and then select) a data source as soon as you drop the control onto the web page surface (see Figure 20.53).

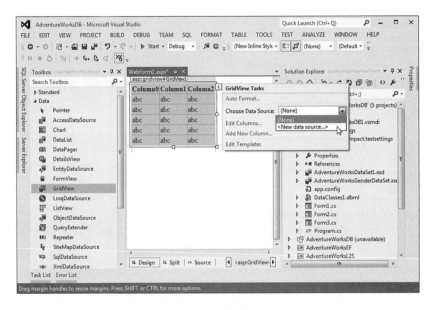

FIGURE 20.53   Selecting the GridView's data source.

Selecting the <New Data Source...> option uses a similar data-source wizard to collect information about your data source and add it to the project.

Once again, because of the data-binding support in the designer, you now have a fully functional application without writing a line of code. Figure 20.54 shows this admittedly ugly web page with live employee data.

Thankfully, you can just as easily put some window dressing on the table and make it look nice. By using the GridView's smart tag menu again, you can select the Auto Format option to apply several flavors of window dressing to the table (see Figure 20.55). And, of course, by applying a style sheet, you can really affect the look and feel of the page.

Updating Data with the GridView   Creating the web grid was easy, and no data access coding was required on your part. The GridView you currently have is great for static reporting, but what if you want to edit data within the grid just as you did earlier in the Windows forms application? The key here is a set of properties on the GridView: AutoGenerateEditButton and AutoGenerateDeleteButton. When you set these properties to True, the GridView automatically includes an Edit link and a Delete link (shown on the previous figures). The Edit link comes fully baked with rendering code so that when it is clicked, that particular row in the grid becomes editable.

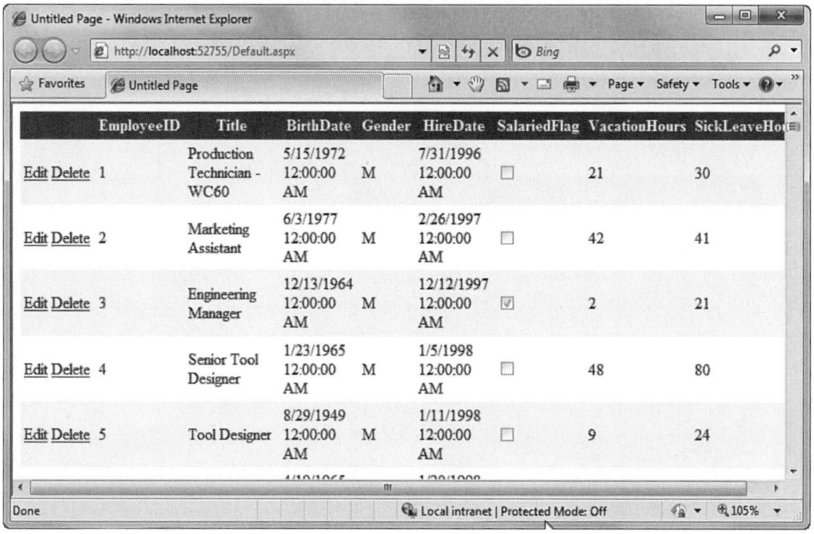

FIGURE 20.54   Live employee records in the `GridView`.

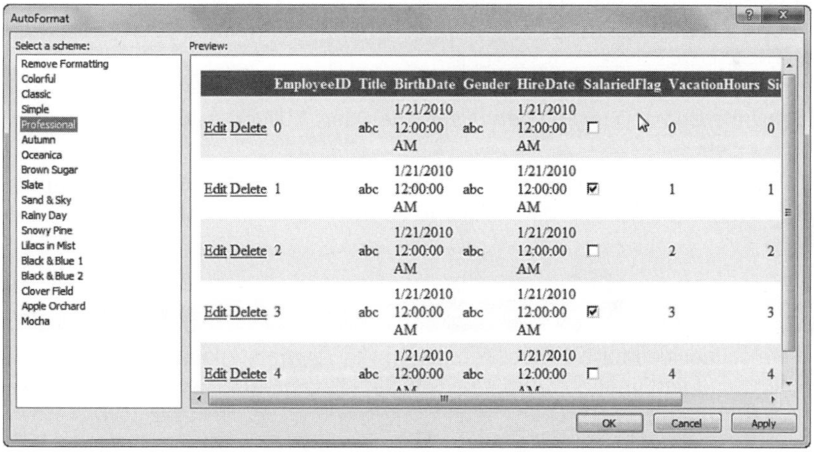

FIGURE 20.55   Autoformatting options for the `GridView` control.

After changing the data in one or more of the columns, you can click the Update link to send the data back to the database. For the update to work, however, you need to explicitly tell the data-source control (in this case, a `SqlDataSource` control) which query to use for processing updates. This is done with the `SqlDataSource.UpdateQuery` property. By specifying a parameterized UPDATE query in this property, you have fully informed the data source on how to deal with updates. You can take advantage once more of the Query

20

Builder window to write this query for you: Select the data-source control on the web form, and in the Properties window select the UpdateQuery property. This launches the Query Builder window and enables you to construct the parameterized update command (see Figure 20.56).

FIGURE 20.56   Setting the UpdateQuery property using the Query Builder dialog box.

With that last piece of the puzzle in place, you now have a fully implemented and bound grid control that pages data in from the database and commits changes back to the database.

> **NOTE**
>
> To implement delete capabilities for a record, you perform the same steps using the
> DeleteQuery property and setting the AutoGenerateDeleteButton to True.

Data-Source Controls

As mentioned, data sources are surfaced through one or more data-source controls placed onto the web form. In the GridView example, the designer actually adds a SqlDataSource control to the form for you (based on your creation of a new DB-based data source). But there is nothing preventing you from adding one or more data-source controls to a web page directly. Just drag the control from the Toolbox onto the form surface. Table 20.2 itemizes the available data-source controls.

TABLE 20.2   Data-Source Controls

Control	Description
ObjectDataSource	Exposes other classes as data sources.
SqlDataSource	Exposes a relational database as a data source. Microsoft SQL Server and Oracle databases can be accessed natively; ODBC and OLE DB access is also supported.
AccessDataSource	Exposes a Microsoft Access database as a data source.
XmlDataSource	Exposes an XML file as a data source.
SiteMapDataSource	A special-case data source that exposes an ASP.NET site map as a data source.

After configuring the data source, you can then visit any data-aware control and bind it to the source.

Object Relational Mapping

We have spent most of this chapter covering the "standard" process for creating .NET applications that read and write data that resides in a database. Although Visual Studio and the ADO.NET libraries themselves do a lot to abstract away the difficult pieces of that process, problems still remain. In fact, there is one common problem that developers writing database-driven applications face: the mismatch between an application's normal object-oriented programming model, implemented in C# or Visual Basic, and the relational programming model surfaced in databases or datasets, implemented primarily with SQL.

In the object-oriented world, we manipulate objects via methods and properties, and each object itself can be (and often is) a parent or container for other objects. The relational database world is much more straightforward: Entities are implemented as row/column-based tables, and each "cell" in a table holds simple scalar values. The core issue is that you must change programming models when dealing with an application's internal framework or the relational database used as its data store (and translating from one to the other isn't a straightforward task).

As a simple example, rows from an invoice table are easily fetched into a data set object using the various data-binding tools and classes discussed previously. But deriving a "native" Invoice object from the data set involves two-way manual translation and manipulation to get the core values to translate across this object/relational barrier. This highlights several issues: Do you abandon the data set approach and read directly from the database into your applications' objects? Do you eschew the object approach and try to use the DataSet component throughout all layers of your application? Or is a hybrid approach best, maintaining strongly typed object collections in addition to the datasets?

Ideally, application developers would be free to work with and manipulate objects within the program's object model and have those objects and changes automatically stored in the database with little or no intervention. Not only does this keep the focus on core

20

well-understood object design patterns, but it also lets the individual developer work with his core language strength without having to learn or become expert in SQL. Pursuit of this goal obviously requires some sort of standard approach, and tooling support, for mapping objects to and from their equivalents within the relational database. And this is exactly what object/relational mapping tools do.

The term *object/relational mapping* (or *O/R mapping*) refers to this general process of translating objects to and from databases. O/R mapping tools have been on the market for years now, and Microsoft has finally delivered O/R mapping support directly in the .NET Framework and in Visual Studio through two different but similar technologies: LINQ to SQL and Entity Framework. Let's briefly discuss both of these technologies, and their Visual Studio tooling, starting first with LINQ to SQL.

An Overview of LINQ

LINQ is an acronym for Language Integrated Query. It is a component of the .NET Framework 3.5 and later that adds SQL-like querying capabilities to .NET objects. Specifically, it extends the core .NET languages (Visual Basic and C#) and the runtime to try to erase the object-to-database-entity barrier. Visual Basic and C# both support new query operators that operate over objects similar to the way SQL operates over tables in a database.

For example, you could query for all approved invoice objects like this:

```
var approved =
    from invoice in invoices
    where (invoice.Approved) == true
    select invoice;

foreach (Invoice invoice in approved)
{
    // do some work here
}
```

And runtime support is introduced for physically translating objects and methods to and from their database equivalents (primarily through the use of code attributes, as you see in a moment). This is a simple example of a class method mapped to a SQL Server stored procedure:

```
[Function(Name="HR.uspDeleteEmployee")]
public int uspDeleteEmployee([Parameter(Name="EmployeeID", DbType="Int")]
                            System.Nullable<int> employeeID)
{
    IExecuteResult result = this.ExecuteMethodCall(this,
            ((MethodInfo)(MethodInfo.GetCurrentMethod())), employeeID);
    return ((int)(result.ReturnValue));
}
```

LINQ comes in several different flavors, each targeted at a specific mapping problem:

▶ **LINQ to SQL**—This enables you to map objects to database entities.

▶ **LINQ to XML**—This enables you to query XML documents and map objects to Extensible Markup Language (XML) document elements.

▶ **LINQ to Objects**—This specifically refers to the inclusion of .NET language syntax that enables queries to be written over collections of objects (as in our previous example with the approved invoices).

You need to be aware of one important fact regarding LINQ to SQL: Although the technology is fully supported by Microsoft, it has been deprecated in favor of the Entity Framework. Some developers might still prefer to use LINQ to SQL because it is a lighter weight, and simpler, ORM to implement.

NOTE

In 2007, Microsoft released a technology preview of a version of LINQ designed specifically for parallel execution. This technology, called PLINQ (for Parallel LINQ), has now been officially released as a part of .NET 4.0. In essence, PLINQ builds on the LINQ concepts by accepting any LINQ to XML or LINQ to Objects query, and executes those queries by optimizing for multiple CPU or multiple core scenarios.

If you are interested more in PLINQ or parallel programming in general, the Parallel Computing center on MSDN is a great start: http://msdn.microsoft.com/en-us/concurrency/default.aspx.

LINQ is a fairly broad and deep set of technology pieces, and covering even one in depth is beyond of the scope of this book. We do, however, dig into the primary Visual Studio tool used when writing LINQ to SQL applications: the O/R designer.

Mapping Using the O/R Designer

The first step in creating a LINQ to SQL application is typically the construction of an object model that is based on a given database definition. This is the exact function of the O/R designer. It enables you to select a database and generate an object model that maps to the database's structure. Table 20.3 shows how the database components are mapped to object components.

TABLE 20.3   Default Database to Object Mappings

Database	Application Object
Table	Class
Table Column	Class Property
Foreign Key Relationship	Association
Stored Procedure/Function	Class Method

Adding Database Entities

The O/R designer is the design surface for project items known as LINQ to SQL Classes, and so the first step in using the designer is to add a new LINQ to SQL Classes project item to a project. Figure 20.57 shows where this project item lives in the Add New Item dialog box.

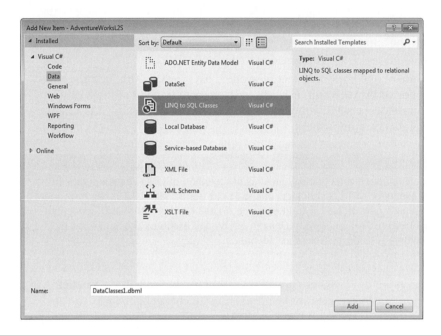

FIGURE 20.57   Adding a LINQ to SQL Classes item to an existing project.

After you've selected the LINQ to SQL Classes item and added it to the project, the O/R designer immediately launches (see Figure 20.58).

There isn't much to see yet because we haven't selected which database entities we want to represent within our object model. This involves the use of the second primary tool for performing the O/R mapping: Server Explorer.

By selecting a valid data source in Server Explorer, we can simply drag and drop a table over onto the left side (the "data class" side) of the O/R designer (see Figure 20.59).

Although nothing obvious happens after the table is dragged onto the data class pane (beyond having its visual representation in the designer), in reality potentially thousands of lines of code have been automatically generated to implement a class structure that mimics the table structure. In addition, all the attribute-based wiring has been implemented so that the LINQ engine can understand and process updates between the class object and the table's rows and columns.

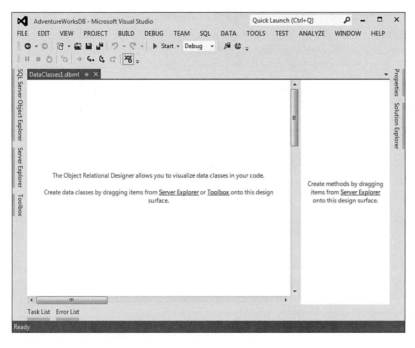

FIGURE 20.58   The LINQ to SQL O/R designer.

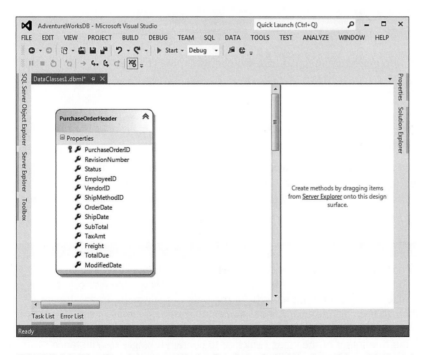

FIGURE 20.59   The AdventureWorks PurchaseOrderHeader table added to the O/R designer.

This exact process is also used to create methods within our object model. We can, for instance, drag a stored procedure over onto the right-side pane of the designer (the "methods" pane) to map a method within our object model to the stored procedure (see Figure 20.60).

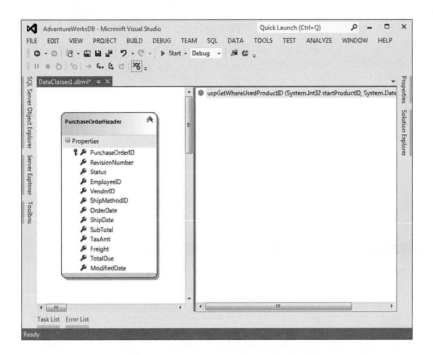

FIGURE 20.60   A stored procedure mapped as a method within the O/R designer.

LINQ Code

Let's examine exactly what has taken place behind the scenes as a result of the drag-and-drop operation between Server Explorer and the O/R designer.

For one, the connection string necessary to open a connection to the selected database is automatically stored in the app.config (or web.config) file for you. This is then leveraged by LINQ to make calls into the database when needed. In addition, a new class has been defined, in this case one named `PurchaseOrderHeader`

> **NOTE**
>
> The O/R designer actually "de-pluralizes" entity names for you automatically. Many HR databases, for instance, might choose to implement an employee table and call it "employees" because it stores the data records for more than one worker. In an attempt to further push through the object model to data model impedance mismatch, the O/R designer actually creates a class called `Employee` and *not* `Employees`; this correlates much better with the true intent of the class (which is to contain a single row/instance from the table and not the entire table).

If you look at the resulting LINQ code (in our example, by viewing the code inside of the file DataClasses1.designer.cs), you will see that LINQ marks up the object model with attributes to perform the magic linking between the objects and the database: Via the `Table` attribute, this class has been identified as a direct map to the HumanResources.Employee table.

Each column in the PurchaseOrderHeader table has also been implemented as a property on the Employee class. This snippet shows the `PurchaseOrderHeaderID` property:

```
[global::System.Data.Linq.Mapping.ColumnAttribute(Storage="_PurchaseOrderID",
AutoSync=AutoSync.OnInsert, DbType="Int NOT NULL IDENTITY", IsPrimaryKey=true,
IsDbGenerated=true)]
public int PurchaseOrderID
{
        get
        {
                return this._PurchaseOrderID;
        }
        set
        {
                if ((this._PurchaseOrderID != value))
                {
                        this.OnPurchaseOrderIDChanging(value);
                        this.SendPropertyChanging();
                        this._PurchaseOrderID = value;
                        this.SendPropertyChanged("PurchaseOrderID");
                        this.OnPurchaseOrderIDChanged();
                }
        }
}
```

Beyond the `PurchaseOrderHeader` object, there has also been code generated for the data context. Here is a snippet of the class definition created automatically for us:

```
[global::System.Data.Linq.Mapping.DatabaseAttribute(Name="AdventureWorks2008")]
public partial class DataClasses1DataContext : System.Data.Linq.DataContext
{
    private static System.Data.Linq.Mapping.MappingSource mappingSource
        = new AttributeMappingSource();
#region Extensibility Method Definitions
partial void OnCreated();
partial void InsertPurchaseOrderHeader(PurchaseOrderHeader instance);
partial void UpdatePurchaseOrderHeader(PurchaseOrderHeader instance);
partial void DeletePurchaseOrderHeader(PurchaseOrderHeader instance);
#endregion
        public DataClasses1DataContext() :
                base(global::AWL2S.Properties.Settings.Default.
```

20

```
            AdventureWorks2008ConnectionString, mappingSource)
        {
            OnCreated();
        }
        public DataClasses1DataContext(string connection) :
            base(connection, mappingSource)
        {
            OnCreated();
        }
        public DataClasses1DataContext(System.Data.IDbConnection connection) :
            base(connection, mappingSource)
        {
            OnCreated();
        }
        public DataClasses1DataContext(string connection,
            System.Data.Linq.Mapping.MappingSource mappingSource) :
            base(connection, mappingSource)
        {
            OnCreated();
        }
        public DataClasses1DataContext(System.Data.IDbConnection connection,
            System.Data.Linq.Mapping.MappingSource mappingSource) :
            base(connection, mappingSource)
        {
            OnCreated();
        }
        public System.Data.Linq.Table<PurchaseOrderHeader>
            PurchaseOrderHeaders
        {
            get
            {
                return this.GetTable<PurchaseOrderHeader>();
            }
        }
    }
}
```

You can think of DataContext as the LINQ manager: It handles the connection back to the database, manages the in-memory entities, and marshals the calls necessary for data updates and any issues that might arise from concurrency and locking conflicts. In total, more than 500 lines of functioning code were emitted to make this all work. So, how do you actually use a LINQ object within your application? Read on.

Working with LINQ Objects

The goal with LINQ, again, is simplicity; LINQ classes look and behave just like any other class in our object model. If we wanted to add a new employee to the system, we would create a new Employee object and set its properties like this:

```
Employee emp = new Employee();

emp.BirthDate = new DateTime(1965, 4, 4);
emp.Gender = 'F';
emp.LoginID = "templogin";
emp.MaritalStatus = 'M';
emp.Title = "Project Resource Manager";
...
```

To commit this new `Employee` object to the Employee table, we need to add the object to the `Employees` collection held by our data context, and then call the `SubmitChanges` method. Remember that the type is simply the default name given by the O/R designer to our data context class; we can change this to anything we want:

```
DataClasses1DataContext db = new DataClasses1DataContext();
db.Employees.InsertOnSubmit(emp);
db.SubmitChanges();
```

In a similar fashion, employees can be removed from the collection (and then from the database):

```
db.Employees.DeleteOnSubmit(emp);
db.SubmitChanges();
```

We have really just scratched the surface here with regard to the intricacies and complexities of O/R application development using LINQ; but hopefully this overview of the O/R designer can be used as a starting point for your O/R explorations in Visual Studio. Let's move on to the Entity Framework.

Working with the Entity Framework

Like LINQ to SQL, Entity Framework (or EF) is a technology that enables you to program against objects that are backed by tables within a relational database. And because they share that same overall goal, most of the concepts we covered with LINQ to SQL apply to EF-based applications as well. The notable difference with EF is the level of abstraction it provides. Whereas LINQ to SQL is a direct map of objects to database tables, EF maps database tables to an Entity Data Model (EDM). From there, you can map objects to the EDM.

Within an EF's EDM, there are actually two discrete models that are maintained by Visual Studio: the conceptual model (think application objects) and the storage model (the database that stores those application objects).

In Visual Studio, the EF models are used by adding an ADO.NET EDM item to your project. Just like our previous look at the LINQ to SQL Data Classes project item, the EF project item is located under the Data category in the Add New Item dialog box (see Figure 20.61).

20

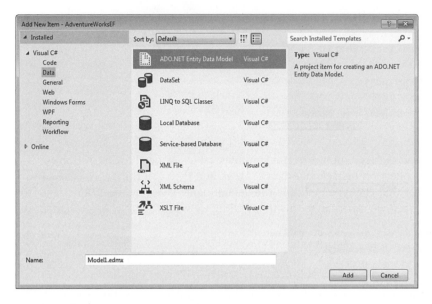

FIGURE 20.61   Adding the Entity Data Model project item.

When you add an entity model to your project, a wizard launches; this wizard gives you the option to start with an empty conceptual and storage model or create a conceptual model from an existing database (see Figure 20.62). In our case, we continue our walk-through again using the AdventureWorks database.

FIGURE 20.62   Configuring the Entity Data Model with the wizard.

Editing the Entity Data Model

After the entity model is added to your project, you can make changes to that entity model using the Entity Data Model designer. This is the visual design surface for your model. There are also two other windows displayed in conjunction with the model designer. The Model Browser provides a Solution Explorer-like view of both the conceptual model and the storage model for your entities, and the Mapping Details window shows exactly how objects in the conceptual model are mapped and linked to tables in the storage model. Figure 20.63 shows all three windows open within the IDE. Note that when we added the entity model to our project, we opted to build out the model using every existing table within the AdventureWorks database, under the Human Resources schema. Let's take a closer look at each of these windows.

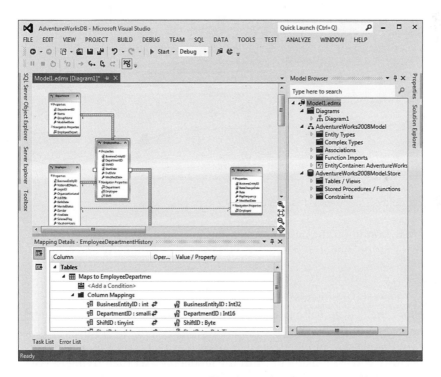

FIGURE 20.63   Editing an Entity Data Model.

The Designer   The designer shows a familiar, visual view of conceptual model. Each object is depicted, along with its properties/fields, and relationships between objects are also clearly visible. In Figure 20.64, we see the now familiar Employee to EmployeeDepartment to Department relationships. These relationships were copied directly from the database foreign key relationships. On the design window itself, there is a small set of navigation buttons set just under the vertical scroll bar (highlighted for you in Figure 20.64). Because you might be dealing with hundreds or even thousands of objects within the designer, you need a way to zoom in and out on the design surface. From top to bottom, these buttons enable you to zoom in, zoom the diagram to 100%, zoom out, and zoom the diagram so that all objects are visible at once.

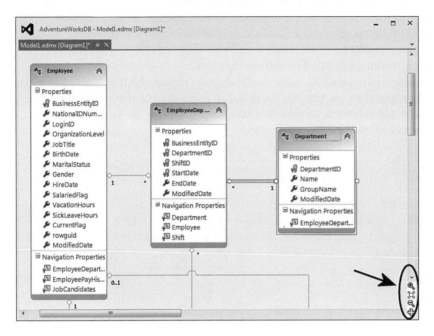

FIGURE 20.64   The Entity Data Model design surface.

Objects can be moved around on the design surface, but you can also use the designer to directly make changes to the model. For instance, you can select a property and change its name.

The Model Browser   The model browser window shows you all of the elements that are contained within both the conceptual model and within the storage model. This includes entities, tables, and relationships. You can use the model browser window to directly delete items from your models, or modify their properties. With large models, it is often easier to locate the entity you are looking for with the model browser than trying to visually find the object within the Entity Data Model designer pane.

TIP

You can immediately show any model element within the designer by right-clicking the element within the Model Browser and selecting Show in Designer.

One of the coolest things about the Model Browser window is its search functionality. By typing a search term into the search box at the top of the window, you can see every instance of that term anywhere within the model. The vertical scrollbar actually graphically depicts everywhere within the models that a search hit was found. If you examine

Figure 20.65 closely, you see the results of a search for "Employee"; 72 matches were found. Within the vertical scrollbar, you see "blocks" that represent where the match was found within the model hierarchy. Hovering over those blocks give you a ToolTip that identifies the exact name that contains the match. This enables you to very quickly jump around your search matches within large models.

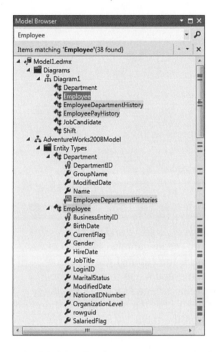

FIGURE 20.65   Searching within the Model Browser window.

The Mapping Details Window   We have discussed the idea of the conceptual model and of the storage model. But if these models lived in isolation, EF wouldn't be able to achieve its ultimate goal of linking code objects to database tables if there weren't some way of mapping between the two models. The Mapping Details window is the tool within the IDE that lets you view and edit all of the conceptual-to-storage model mappings.

Figure 20.66 shows the mapping details for Employee object. All of the mapping properties were preset for us because we chose to build out our conceptual model based on an existing database. When you select an entity with the designer, the mapping window will show an alphabetic list of all of the table columns. To the right of each column is displayed the property that the column maps to on the object.

The Mapping Details window is also used to map an object to your own, custom functions for performing inserts, updates, or deletes. Click the two icons on the top-left border of the mapping window to change between these two modes.

20

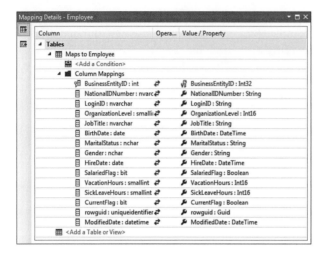

FIGURE 20.66   Mapping properties for the `Employee` object/table.

NOTE

You aren't limited to performing just a one-to-one map between objects and database tables. You could decide, for instance, that your conceptual model contains two `Employee` classes: `HourlyEmployee` and `SalariedEmployee`. You have the capability to create a function that filters the rows in the underlying Employee table and maps those rows to one or the other of these two objects. This is done quite easily in the Mapping Details window by adding a condition. Click the Add a Condition link within the window, and then specify a condition to apply against the SalariedFlag field on the table.

We have now covered the high-level overview of what the EF platform is and the tools and project items you use within Visual Studio to create EF-based projects. Now let's dig a bit deeper to see how we would use these tools to perform common EF tasks.

Querying Against the Entity Data Model

The real power of EF is the ability to perform SQL-like operations against a set of objects (for example, the objects you have defined in your entity data model) using a variety of different methods.

Because every object in EF is LINQ enabled, we could use LINQ to Entities to query for a list of salaried employees, like this:

```
using (AdventureWorksEntities entities = new AdventureWorksEntities())
{
    List<Employee> employees =
        (from e in entities.Employees
        where e.SalariedFlag == true select e).ToList();
}
```

The AdventureWorksEntities object seen on the first line of code above represents our conceptual model; LINQ provides the syntax we need to iterate over those objects within the `AdventureWorksEntities` object.

EF also supports the ability to construct queries using the `ObjectQuery` class. This class lives within the `System.Data.Objects` namespace and enables us to use standard SQL-like syntax for generating queries. Here is that same query, rewritten using the `ObjectQuery` class:

```
using (AdventureWorksEntities entities = new AdventureWorksEntities())
    {
        ObjectQuery<Employee> query =
            entities.Employees.Where("it.SalariesFlag=@flag");

        query.Parameters.Add(new ObjectParameter("flag", "True"));

        List<Employee> employees = query.ToList();

    }
```

We could even query our objects using nothing more than standard stored procedures. This would be a two-step process: First, we create a stored procedure in our underlying database (and thus our store model). Second, we map that stored procedure to a function within our model. With the function in place (here we have named it `GetSalariedEmployees`), we can call that function like this:

```
using (AdventureWorksEntities entities = new AdventureWorksEntities())
    {
        List<Employee> employees = entities.GetSalariedEmployees().ToList();
    }
```

Updating Data in the Entity Data Model

Because we are simply programming against standard .NET objects within the entity data model, updating data that resides in those objects is as simple as setting the object properties.

We can create a new employee like this:

```
Employee newEmp = new Employee();
```

And set its properties like we would for any other object:

```
newEmp.SalariedFlag = true;
newEmp.HireDate = DateTime.Today;
newEmp.Title = "HR Manager";
```

We then add the new employee to the Entity Data Model like this:

```
entities.Employees.AddObject(newEmp);
```

And finally, we would need to tell the entity model to persist these changes to the database:

```
entities.SaveChanges();
```

In a similar fashion, we can delete objects by first referencing the object we want to remove and then calling the `DeleteObject` method from our entities object. This code deletes the first employee in the Employee table:

```
Employee firstEmp = entities.Employees.First();
entities.DeleteObject(firstEmp);
```

NOTE

We have discussed how to change data within Entity Data Model, but what happens if either the database schema changes or you want changes within your conceptual model to be made at the storage level as well? If you right-click the Entity Data Model designer, you see two options that essentially sync schema of the database with the object model or vice versa: Generate Database from Model and UpdateModelFromDatabase.

As you have probably guessed by now, Entity Framework is a vast and deep ORM platform. We have really only been able to scratch the surface here. If you intend on leveraging EF inside of your applications, we wholeheartedly recommend a book dedicated to the subject such as Julia Lerman's *Programming Entity Framework* from O'Reilly.

Summary

In this chapter, you read about the broad and deep support that Visual Studio 2012 has for building and managing databases and for creating applications that access data in a database. We discussed the suite of SQL Server Data Tools, available right within the IDE, that function in synergy with one another and with the various Visual Studio designers to provide a seamless experience for writing queries, creating table structures, and crafting stored procedures. We also investigated the newfound support for writing SQL Server database procedures and functions using entirely managed code.

We spent some time discussing the basics of data binding: how it is a core problem space with many application development efforts and how the Visual Studio web, Windows Form Designers, and WPF Designers and controls provide first-class support for simple to complex data-binding scenarios. In particular, we examined the role that these Visual Studio designers play in the data-binding world by enabling developers to rapidly build forms-based applications with sophisticated data needs without writing a single line of code.

And finally, we examined the built-in support that Visual Studio provides for mapping entire object models to a database using two different technologies: LINQ2SQL and Entity Framework.

Hopefully, by exposing you to all of these great built-in tools, we have started you on the road to becoming even more efficient in leveraging Visual Studio across a range of database interactions.

CHAPTER 21

Service-Oriented Applications

Services have transformed the way we think of the Web and how we leverage it to build software. Prior to services, the Web was mostly a means to deliver cross-platform user interfaces with low deployment costs. Of course, that was a huge deal (and remains so) for both Internet and intranet applications. Services have shown a similar potential to change the way we build our applications both for the Web and across networks.

At their core, services represent an interface (or set of methods) that provide black-box-like access to shared functionality using common formats and protocols. By this definition, a service should be loosely coupled with its clients and work across boundaries. These boundaries have, for a long time, prevented the true promise of reusable application components such as services. By working across boundaries such as process, machine, language, and operating system, services can truly be leveraged by the many potential clients that an organization might have today and tomorrow.

Visual Studio 2012 and the .NET Framework 4.5 enable developers to create rich service-oriented applications. In this chapter, we cover the two primary service technologies built into Visual Studio: the new ASP.NET Web application programming interface (API) for creating Hypertext Transfer Protocol (HTTP) services and Windows Communication Foundation (WCF) technology for building services that work over the Web or a network. For each section, we discuss both creating services and writing service clients.

Service Fundamentals

A service defines a contract between a calling client and the service itself. In English, this contract states something like this: "If you send me data in this format, I will process it and return you the results in this other format." The format of this data and the communication parameters of these calls are all based on open standards. These service standards apply across technology boundaries and therefore make services attractive for exchanging data between heterogeneous environments.

To help frame the benefits of services, it can be helpful to think of them within the context of the problems they were designed to solve. For example, many large companies have multiple applications that need to access and update similar information. They might, for instance, rely on customer data records inside a customer relationship management (CRM) system, an order-processing application, a shipping tool, a financial system, and a reporting package. In this case, the customer record is duplicated per system. This means the data may be contradictory (or out-of-date) in any one system. Companies might have band-aids in place such as batch processing that tries to keep the data in sync on a daily basis. Figure 21.1 illustrates this problem example.

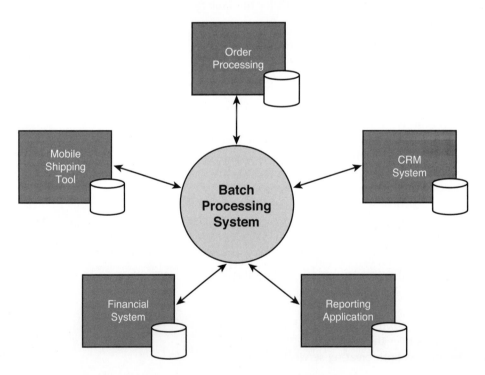

FIGURE 21.1   Heterogeneous applications often share data and have similar needs around that data. Nightly batch processing to update data across applications is not the best way to solve this dilemma.

What's worse, a company might have multiple systems that offer the same functionality (like two CRM systems). This can happen if the company has grown through acquisition and merger activities, or if each department has chosen its own technology. In fact, even if a company wrote all of these applications from scratch, you often see duplicate (or similar) code in each application for doing the same thing. This code, of course, has to be maintained and changes to it can often have unintended consequences on the other systems.

These problems are what service-oriented solutions are intended to solve. Consider that each of the applications in the earlier example might work on different servers running different code on different operating systems. They often even have different database technologies. Therefore, a reusable component that could be plugged into each application could not be easily created. Even if it did, the need to centralize this information into a common view would still exist. For example, an update to a customer record in one system needs to somehow be recorded in the other systems.

What is required to solve this problem (and problems like it) is a common shared interface into a centralized view of the data (in this case, customer data). This interface should be able to work across application boundaries such as protocols, data types, and processes. Architects recognized this problem but did not see a viable solution until the advent of the Web. With web technologies, the HTTP protocol was ubiquitous. Servers could talk to each other. Then along came the Extensible Markup Language (XML) standard for describing messages and later the more lightweight JavaScript Object Notation (JSON). With a ubiquitous protocol such as HTTP and standard message formats like XML and JSON, applications running on different platforms had a way to communicate.

Why ASP.NET Web API and WCF

ASP.NET Web API is the new standard for developing HTTP web services (replacing ASMX). This technology makes it easy to write robust services that are based on HTTP protocols that all browser and most native devices understand. Therefore, you can create these services, and they can be called from other web application, tablets, mobile phones, and PCs. This makes communicating across the Internet easier. However, communicating across the Internet is not always the most efficient means. For example, if both the client and the service exist on the same technology (or even the same machine), they can often negotiate a more efficient means to communicate (such as remoting). Service developers found themselves making the same choices they were trying to avoid. They now would have to choose between creating efficient internal services and being able to have the broad access found over the Internet. And, if they had to support both, they might have to create multiple versions of their service or at least separate proxies for accessing their service. This is the problem Microsoft solved with Windows Communication Foundation (WCF).

With WCF, you can create your service without concern for boundaries. You can then let WCF worry about running your service in the most efficient way, depending on the calling client. To manage this task, WCF introduces the concept of endpoints. Your service might have multiple endpoints (configured at design time or after deployment). Each endpoint indicates how the service might support a calling client over the web, via remoting, through Microsoft Message Queuing (MSMQ), and more. WCF enables you to focus on creating your service functionality. It worries about how to most efficiently speak with calling clients. In this way, a single WCF service can efficiently support many different client types.

Consider the example from before. The customer data is shared among the applications. Each application might be written on a different platform, and it might also exist in a different location. You can extract the customer interface into a WCF service that provides common access to shared customer data. This centralizes the data, reduces duplication, eliminates synchronization, and simplifies management. In addition, by using WCF, you can configure the service endpoints to work in the way that makes sense to the calling client. Figure 21.2 shows the example from before with centralized access of customer data in a WCF service.

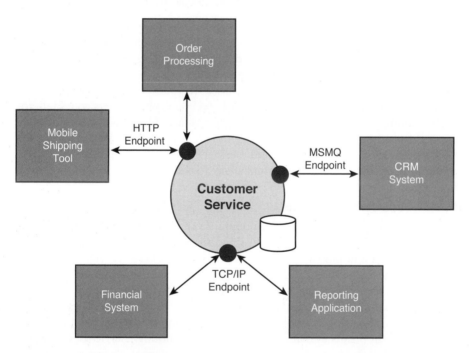

FIGURE 21.2   A centralized, service-oriented implementation of the customer data and service contract using WCF and multiple endpoints.

In the coming sections, we cover creating HTTP services using the ASP.NET Web API and creating services using WCF. Visual Studio 2012 and the .NET Framework 4.5 do a lot to abstract the intricacies or "plumbing" of building services away from everyday programming tasks. The result is a more productive development experience. You spend less time worrying about how to negotiate content types or building communications channels and more time developing real business value.

Key Web Service Terms

It can be important for developers to understand the key concepts and standard terms around web services. This knowledge ensures that you know what is happening in your application. It also helps when you are reading the .NET documentation and articles related to building web service applications. Therefore, we have put together the following glossary of key terms related to web services:

▶ **Web service**—A web service represents a cohesive set of application logic that performs actions and provides data. A web service groups this logic as methods that can be called over HTTP. Not all services are web services; only those that work over the Internet are considered web services.

▶ **Web service method (or web method)**—A web service method represents a method exposed by a web service. A web method can take parameters and return a response.

▶ **XML (Extensible Markup Language)**—XML is used to both represent and describe data in a platform-neutral manner. XML can be used to represent both simple and complex data elements and relationships. It is the XML standard that makes web services possible.

▶ **JSON (JavaScript Object Notation)**—JSON was created as a reaction to overly large XML messages. It is a lightweight data-interchange format that is human readable. It is built on simple collections of name-value pairs.

▶ **WSDL (Web Service Description Language)**—WSDL is used to describe the contents of a web service and its web methods. The WSDL provides the message data contracts that enable clients to work with a given service.

▶ **XSD (XML Schema Document)**—XSD contains a set of predefined types (string, decimal, and so on) and a standard language for describing your own complex types. An XML Schema Document (also referred to as an XSD) uses these types to describe (and restrict) the contents of an XML message.

▶ **SOAP**—SOAP is an XML-based protocol for communicating between client and web service. It is helpful to think of SOAP as representing the format of the messages as they pass over the wire. SOAP wraps XML messages (in envelopes) for communication across the Web. Most SOAP messages are sent over HTTP. However, they can also be sent with transport protocols such as Simple Mail Transfer Protocol (SMTP) and File Transfer Protocol (FTP).

▶ **HTTP (Hypertext Transfer Protocol)**—HTTP represents the communication protocol used by web services to transfer SOAP-formatted (or encoded) messages. HTTP is also the way standard web page requests (GET and POST) communicate.

▶ **UDDI (Universal Description, Discovery, and Integration)**—UDDI is used to define a registry of web services. This capability is useful for the publication of services for developers to find and consume.

21

▶ **URI (uniform resource identifier)**—URIs provide a means for locating items on the web. In most cases, URIs are URLs (uniform resource locators) that point to a given service.

▶ **DISCO (Discovery Document)**—A DISCO file provides information that links to other key elements of a web service. This includes links to XSDs, SOAP bindings, and namespaces. A program can use a DISCO file to determine how to work with a given web service.

▶ **WS-*** —This term represents the overall standards for web services.

Building HTTP Services Using the ASP.NET Web API

Nearly all devices created these days can speak HTTP. This includes computers and mobile devices running on all platforms, including Windows, iOS, Android, and more. These devices use HTTP because users want access to the Internet. In addition, HTTP is open on firewalls across nearly all networks. For this reason, HTTP web services have emerged as a default standard that is highly accessible on nearly all client devices and increases interoperability across platforms.

Microsoft has created the ASP.NET Web API model for easing the development of HTTP services. You can use the skills you learned in Chapter 17, "Building Websites with Razor and ASP.NET," regarding web development with the Model-View-Controller (MVC) design to build service-oriented websites that work with nearly all clients.

The Web API framework takes care of all the plumbing code for you. For example, it includes features like content negotiation, which allows a client and service to negotiate the right message format, including XML and JSON. Furthermore, ASP.NET Web API services are fully asynchronous and task based. They also have a very lightweight hosting model, which gives you a lot of hosting options including the cloud.

The Web API services are built on the basic nature of HTTP: GET and POST. In this way, you can send a request to a service the same way you would type a uniform resource locator (URL) into your browser. This request can pass parameters on the query string. Of course, you can get a response to the service too. You can also post data to a service, work with Secure Sockets Layer (SSL) for security, and do most of the basic web-like things you would do in any website.

Creating an ASP.NET Web API Project

You can add a ASP.NET Web API service to any ASP.NET web application. The services can be hosted on the same server and domain as another website. (Of course, there are other hosting options too.) This means you can define a Web API service inside your ASP.NET MVC sites, Razor web page sites, and web form sites. To do so, you simply right-click the website in Solution Explorer and choose Add, Add New Item. From here, you select the Web API Controller Class template. We examine this template in a moment.

Visual Studio 2012, however, provides a specific template for creating sites that are meant to host just ASP.NET Web API services. This template is accessed by creating a new ASP. NET MVC 4 website (refer back to Figure 17.11 in Chapter 17). Recall that you do so via File, New, Project and selecting the ASP.NET MVC 4 Web Application template. Doing so brings up the secondary dialog for selecting an MVC subtemplate. Here you select the Web API template. This dialog and template is shown in Figure 21.3.

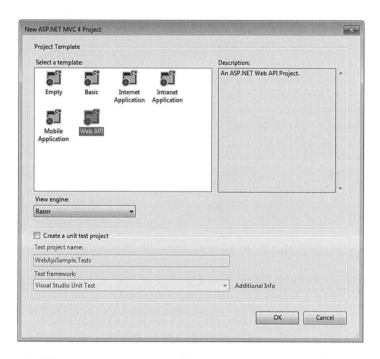

FIGURE 21.3   Select the Web API template from the available ASP.NET MVC template options.

The Web API project template is not unlike the standard ASP.NET MVC template. In fact, you can run the site and you will get a web page. The site includes a Home.cshtml page, a shared layout page, and a HomeController.cs class. These pages are not really relevant to your services but make it easier if you intend to combine web pages with web services. They also provide a start page when debugging your services.

Defining the Model

Chapter 17 presented the ASP.NET MVC application. Recall that in this pattern, there is a Model that represents your business objects and their persistence layer. The Controller is used to manage requests and response from the HTTP traffic to your site. Views, of course, allow you to render UI to the user. The ASP.NET Web API service model leverages this same pattern. You define models for your data and a controller for handling service requests and response. (There is no real UI, of course, and hence no views.)

The framework for the ASP.NET Web API handles the plumbing of turning your model objects into serialized data that can be embedded in the HTTP response message. This serialization is typically JSON or XML but can be other formats too. In this way, clients that can make a basic HTTP GET or POST request and read the response as JSON, XML, or a related format that can work with your service. In fact, a client call may indicate which format they need (called content negotiation) as part of the Accept header in the HTTP request.

For example, let's work to create a set of services for managing customer objects. To get started, you can create an EF code first model. This involves getting a copy of the Northwind database, creating a POCO object, defining a data context class, and adding a configuration setting to your project. Instead of repeating these steps here, refer back to Chapter 17, specifically the subsection "Creating the Model" under the "Adding Features to an ASP.NET MVC Application" section. This will walk you through these steps if you need them. The rest of this example assumes you have defined this model.

Creating the Services (Controller)

You can hand-code your controller service or you can use the Visual Studio tooling to help you. If you are hand-coding, you simply create a class file and make sure to inherit from the class `System.Web.Http.ApiController`. You then write methods that take parameters and return objects. Just like an MVC application, these parameters can be passed on the query string of the request and the response will be sent as the body of the HTTP response message (more on all this in a moment).

The Visual Studio tooling can generate basic services for you from your model. This makes creating these types of services very easy. To get started, you right-click the Controllers folder in Solution Explorer and choose Add, Controller. This brings up the Add Controller dialog shown in Figure 21.4. Notice there is a template defined just for the Web API and the Entity Framework. In this case, you select the template, indicate your model class, and set a data context class. This allows the template to generate a set of services in your Controller class that work directly with your model.

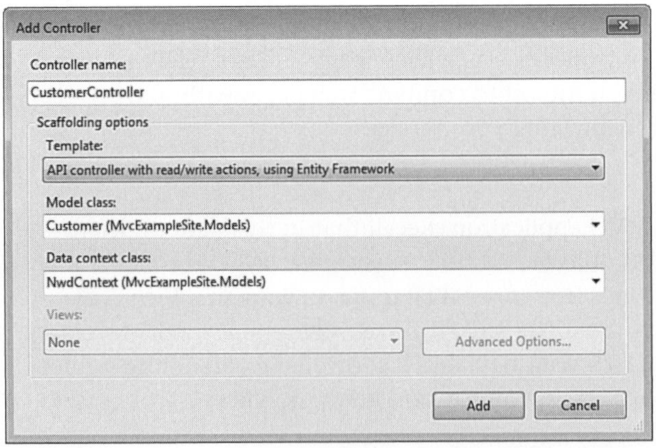

FIGURE 21.4   Select the Web API template from the available ASP.NET MVC template options.

Listing 21.1 shows the generated code. Notice the naming conventions used for the method names: Get, Put, Post, and Delete. These are all HTTP verbs that indicate the required HTTP actions. The following outlines their usages:

- ▶ **Get**—Indicates a request for data and is used to retrieve an object, as in `GetCustomer()`, or list of objects, as in `GetCustomers()`.

- ▶ **Post**—This is used to indicate an HTTP post to submit data to the service. Use this for creating a new item, as in `PostCustomer()`.

- ▶ **Put**—Used to upload data to a service. Use this to update an object, as in `PutCustomer()`.

- ▶ **Delete**—Used to indicate an item should be deleted, as in `DeleteCustomer()`.

The use of HTTP verbs makes aligns your services clearly with the HTTP specification and makes them easy to understand and work with. It also makes your code clear.

Notice, too, that those methods that do not return a business object instead return an instance of HttpResponseMessage. This class wraps an HTTP response and makes it easy for you to write HTTP responses back to the calling clients such as NotFound, BadRequest, and OK.

LISTING 21.1   The CustomerController.cs Services as Generated by the MVC Template

```
using System;
using System.Collections.Generic;
using System.Data;
using System.Data.Entity.Infrastructure;
using System.Linq;
using System.Net;
using System.Net.Http;
using System.Web;
using System.Web.Http;
using MvcExampleSite.Models;

namespace WebApiSample.Controllers
{
  public class CustomerController : ApiController
  {
    private NwdContext db = new NwdContext();

    // GET api/Customer
    public IEnumerable<Customer> GetCustomers()
    {
      return db.Customers.AsEnumerable();
    }
```

```
// GET api/Customer/5
public Customer GetCustomer(string id)
{
  Customer customer = db.Customers.Find(id);
  if (customer == null)
  {
    throw new HttpResponseException(Request.CreateResponse(HttpStatusCode.
➥NotFound));
  }

  return customer;
}

// PUT api/Customer/5
public HttpResponseMessage PutCustomer(string id, Customer customer)
{
  if (ModelState.IsValid && id == customer.CustomerID)
  {
    db.Entry(customer).State = EntityState.Modified;

    try
    {
      db.SaveChanges();
    }
    catch (DbUpdateConcurrencyException)
    {
      return Request.CreateResponse(HttpStatusCode.NotFound);
    }

    return Request.CreateResponse(HttpStatusCode.OK, customer);
  }
  else
  {
    return Request.CreateResponse(HttpStatusCode.BadRequest);
  }
}

// POST api/Customer
public HttpResponseMessage PostCustomer(Customer customer)
{
  if (ModelState.IsValid)
  {
    db.Customers.Add(customer);
    db.SaveChanges();
```

```
      HttpResponseMessage response =
        Request.CreateResponse(HttpStatusCode.Created, customer);
      response.Headers.Location = new Uri(Url.Link("DefaultApi",
        new { id = customer.CustomerID }));
      return response;
    }
    else
    {
      return Request.CreateResponse(HttpStatusCode.BadRequest);
    }
  }


  // DELETE api/Customer/5
  public HttpResponseMessage DeleteCustomer(string id)
  {
    Customer customer = db.Customers.Find(id);
    if (customer == null)
    {
      return Request.CreateResponse(HttpStatusCode.NotFound);
    }

    db.Customers.Remove(customer);

    try
    {
      db.SaveChanges();
    }
    catch (DbUpdateConcurrencyException)
    {
      return Request.CreateResponse(HttpStatusCode.NotFound);
    }

    return Request.CreateResponse(HttpStatusCode.OK, customer);
  }

  protected override void Dispose(bool disposing)
  {
    db.Dispose();
    base.Dispose(disposing);
  }
}
}
```

> **TIP**
>
> When you're building a web service, it is best to group functionality into coarse-grained interfaces. You don't want web methods that do a number of fine-grained operations such as setting properties. This chatty nature can be expensive when communicating across the Internet.
>
> Of course, this approach is also contrary to most object-oriented application designs. Therefore, the use of a proxy object to bundle operations around a business object is ideal. The business object is serialized and passed across the wire. On the other side, it can be deserialized and then worked with in an in-process manner (in which chatty calls are not expensive).

Viewing Your Web API Service in the Browser

You can run your services in a web browser and view the results. To get started, run your web application in debug mode. It will open to the home page. To invoke it, you need to enter a URI that points to the service. Recall from Listing 17.1 that the comments above each service method actually describe the URI format required to invoke the method. These URI formats, like the rest of MVC, follow a routing convention which we will discuss momentarily. In the meantime, to access the GetCustomers service you need to enter the URI, `http://localhost:xxxxx/api/customer` (where xxxxx is the random port number Internet Information Services [IIS] Express has assigned to your site). Doing so results in IE asking you if you want to open or save the JSON result as a file. The lower part of Figure 21.5 shows an example.

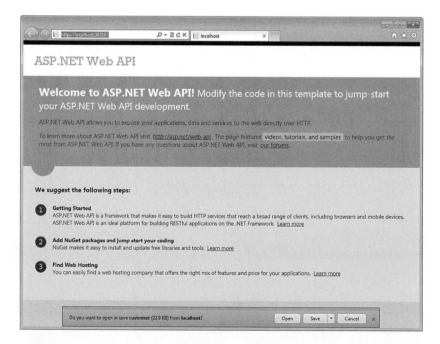

FIGURE 21.5   Your services will return a JSON formatted result to an IE request for a list of data.

Similarly, to get a single customer, you enter the URI format `/api/customer/id` where id is the OD passed into the `GetCustomer()` method. For example, a request to `http://localhost:30218/api/customer/alfki` will return the customer object from the Northwind database with the Customer ID of ALFKI. The following shows the JSON message results. Remember, these are name-value pairs to be parsed by a service client:

```
{"CustomerID":"ALFKI","CompanyName":"Alfreds Futterkiste","PostalCode":"12209",
➥"ContactName":"Maria
Anders","ContactTitle":"Sales Representative","Address":"Obere Str.
57","City":"Berlin","Country":"Germany","Phone":"030-0074321","Fax":"030-0076545"}
```

Note that the same request in Firefox and Chrome will, by default, return the message in the browser as XML.

TIP

When debugging HTTP services, it is very useful to view the HTTP request and response messages sent to and from your service. You can use the F12 tools built in to IE 9 and later to help. Within IE, press the F12 key. Then click the Network tab and click the Start Capturing button. You can now call your web service and IE will capture the messages for you. To view them, find the entry in the list and click Go to Detailed View. From there, you have tabs to view the request and response headers and bodies.

Understanding Service URIs and Routing

Service URIs work just like MVC: A request is sent to your website, that request is then parsed and processed through a routing table, and that routing table uses conventions to find your controller and the appropriate action method on your controller. The default routing table for ASP.NET Web API uses the construct `/api/{controller}/{id}`.

The `/api/` portion of the construct is a fixed indicator that this request is meant for a service. The `{controller}` portion is used to find your controller. In the example you have been creating, this is `customer` (the word *controller* is not necessary). The `{id}` portion is used to indicate a single parameter value, as in `/api/customer/alfki`.

These routes along with the client's requesting HTTP method (GET, POST, PUT, DELETE) indicate which action method gets called on your service. For example, a GET request for `/api/customer/alfki` will map to the Customer controller. It is a GET request, so it maps to a Get action method. It takes a single parameter (ALFKI), so it maps to `GetCustomer(string id)`.

As another example, if a client sends the HTTP DELETE method to `/api/customer/alfki`, the action method invoked will be `DeleteCustomer(string id)`.

TIP

If you want to customize the HTTP method used for your service or the default naming conventions are not to your liking, you can explicitly set the HTTP method on a given service. You do so by decorating the service method with one of the following attribute classes: `HttpGet`, `HttpPut`, `HttpPost`, or `HttpDelete`.

The routing for your site can actually be modified using the `RouteConfig.cs` class found in the `App_Start` directory. Here you will find code that sets up the site's routes. The following shows the `DefaultApi` route. You can modify this routing template here if you like:

```
routes.MapHttpRoute(
  name: "DefaultApi",
  routeTemplate: "api/{controller}/{id}",
  defaults: new { id = RouteParameter.Optional }
);
```

Consuming an ASP.NET Web API Service

ASP.NET Web API services can be consumed by any client capable of speaking HTTP. This means other websites as well as native client applications. In the case of a website, you can use standard HTTP GET and POST messages to work with the service. Typically, you use a helper library called jQuery to send requests and receive messages. For native clients like iOS and Windows, you use an HTTP framework class library. In Windows, this is the `System.NET.Http` namespace and the HttpClient class. This framework lets you easily make a request to an HTTP service and consume the results. The following shows both client access methods (jQuery and HttpClient).

Consume a Service Using jQuery on a Website

The jQuery library is a JavaScript library that makes the business of writing JavaScript very easy. It is a framework that wraps some complex JavaScript for client-side programming. It can really make life easy when you need to write client-side JavaScript for various tasks. (For more details on jQuery, see http://www.jQuery.com.) jQuery is also included with all Microsoft web templates in the Scripts folder.

jQuery is especially useful because it contains helper methods that allow you to make HTTP GET and POST requests. These methods are part of the jQuery AJAX (Asynchronous JavaScript) capabilities. The following are key methods here:

▶ `jQuery.get()` sends a GET request to a server and manages the results.

▶ `jQuery.post` sends data via a POST to a server and handles the response.

▶ `jQuery.getJSON()` sends a GET request and processes the results as JSON-encoded data.

Notice each of these methods are prefixed by a call to the jQuery object. The shorthand for this call is dollar sign ($), as in `$.getJSON`. The getJSON method takes a URI to the service, data that is to be sent to the service, and a callback function that gets executed when the request completes. Let's look at creating an example with the Customer service created previously:

1. First, you add a new project to your solution (right-click the solution, Add, New Project). In this case, you use an ASP.NET Web Forms client application called WebFormClient.

2. Next, you edit the Default.aspx page to create a basic form that allows a user to enter a customer ID and click a Find button. The following markup shows an example. Note that you give the input elements IDs so that they can be referenced in the JavaScript easily using jQuery. There is also a `<p>` tag with the ID of `foundCustomer` to be used to display the found customer details from the web service:

```
<%@ Page Title="Home Page" Language="C#" MasterPageFile="~/Site.Master"
  AutoEventWireup="true" CodeBehind="Default.aspx.cs"
  Inherits="WebFormClient._Default" %>

<asp:Content runat="server" ID="FeaturedContent"
  ContentPlaceHolderID="FeaturedContent">
  <section class="featured">
    <div class="content-wrapper">
      <hgroup class="title">
        <h1>Find Customer</h1>
      </hgroup>
    </div>
  </section>
</asp:Content>

<asp:Content runat="server" ID="BodyContent" ContentPlaceHolderID="MainContent">
  <div>
    <p>Enter a customer id:</p>
    <input type="text" id="customerId" size="5" />
    <input type="button" value="Find" onclick="findCustomer();" />
  </div>
  <div>
    <p id="foundCustomer"></p>
  </div>
</asp:Content>
```

3. The next step is to write the JavaScript using jQuery. In this case, we add this script to the top of our page using a `Content` control that puts our script inside the `<head>` tag of the Site.master page.

The code itself defines a function called `findCustomer()`. Here we use the jQuery selector `$('#customerId')` to pull the value of the text box on our form. We then concatenate this value to the URI on the call to `$.getJSON`.

The results are passed into a function where we use the parsed data object to concatenate some values and put the results into the `foundCustomer` `<p>` tag on our page. The following code shows an example:

```
<asp:Content ContentPlaceHolderID="HeadContent" runat="server">
  <script type="text/javascript">
    function findCustomer() {
      $.support.cors = true;
```

```
        var id = $('#customerId').val();
        $.getJSON("http://localhost:30218/api/customer/" + id,
          function (data) {
            var result = "Company: " + data.CompanyName +
              ', Contact: ' + data.ContactName;
            $('#foundCustomer').html(result);
          })
        .fail(
          function (jqXHR, textStatus, err) {
            $('#foundCustomer').html('Error: ' + err);
          });
      }
   </script>
  </asp:Content>
```

4. The final step is to run the code and view the results. Figure 21.6 shows an example. You can also download this code from the book's website.

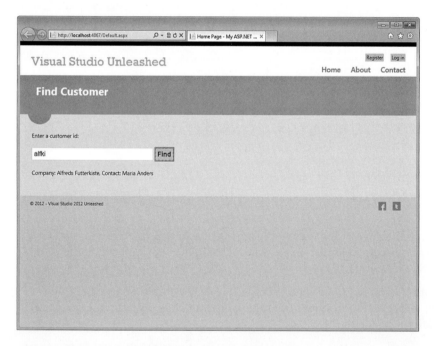

FIGURE 21.6   The ASP.NET Web Forms site using jQuery to call the ASP.NET Web API service.

> **NOTE**
>
> Notice the call to `$.support.cors = true` in the JavaScript example. This indicates to jQuery that you are allowing cross-domain scripting to run. This is not allowed by default as a security measure. Without this code, you can only use jQuery to call services from other web pages that are in the same domain as your website.

Consume a Service Using `HttpClient` in a Native Application

The .NET Framework allows you to consume HTTP services from native applications. In this example, you will look at consuming the `Customer` services created earlier from a Windows Forms application. The following walks you through this process:

1. Start by adding a Windows Forms application to your solution. You can do so by right-clicking the solution and choosing Add, New Project. Select Windows on the left and choose Windows Forms Application. Name your application **WinFormClient**.

2. Right-click the References folder in the new project and choose Add Reference. On the left of the dialog, select Assemblies, Framework. In the middle of the dialog, select System.Net.Http. This is the library that enables you to make HTTP requests to the service.

3. Open your form in the designer and add controls to look like Figure 21.7.

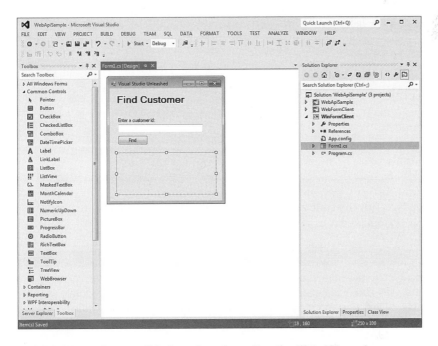

FIGURE 21.7   Create a Windows form for calling the Web API service.

4. Double-click the Find button to go to the code window. Here, add a `using` statement for `System.Net.Http.Headers`.

5. Next, add code to the button click event that calls the service. This code is very similar to the jQuery code in that it sets the URI, makes the call, and puts the results in a label on the form. Listing 21.2 shows an example.

LISTING 21.2   The Button Click Event That Calls the ASP.NET Web API Service

```
private void buttonFind_Click(object sender, EventArgs e)
{

  HttpClient client = new HttpClient();
  client.BaseAddress = new Uri("http://localhost:30218/");

  client.DefaultRequestHeaders.Accept.Add(
      new MediaTypeWithQualityHeaderValue("application/json"));

  HttpResponseMessage resp = client.GetAsync("api/customer/" +
➡ textBoxCustomerId.Text).Result;

  string result = "";
  if (resp.IsSuccessStatusCode)
  {
    result = resp.Content.ReadAsStringAsync().Result;
  }
  else
  {
    result = string.Format("{0} ({1})", (int)resp.StatusCode, resp.ReasonPhrase);
  }

  labelResults.Text = result;

}
```

6. The final step is to run the code and view the results. Figure 21.8 shows the code running in the Windows form.

> **NOTE**
>
> Microsoft is working on a new library for helping developers to consume ASP.NET Web API service results. This library is called the Microsoft ASP.NET Web API Client Library. It should be available by the time you read this but was not available as of this writing. It promises to have message parsing (formatting) for JSON, which would be a nice addition to the sample application.

{"CustomerID":"ALFKI","CompanyName":"Alfreds Futterkiste","PostalCode":"12209","ContactName":"Maria Anders","ContactTitle":"Sales Representative","Address":"Obere Str. 57","City":"Berlin","Country":"Germany","Phone":"030-0074321","Fax":"030-0076545"}

FIGURE 21.8   A native Windows application calling the ASP.NET Web API HTTP service.

WCF Service Applications

Like web services, Windows Communication Foundation (WCF) services have their own set of terms. It is important that you have a baseline understanding of these before trying to understand the key concepts related to WCF service applications:

▶ **WCF service**—A WCF service is a set of logic that you expose to multiple clients as a service. A service might have one or more service operations (think methods). A WCF service is exposed to clients through one or more endpoints that you define. Each endpoint has a binding and behaviors (see the "Endpoint" entry in this list). In this way, you can create a single service and configure it to work efficiently with multiple clients (such as HTTP, TCP, and named pipes).

▶ **WCF client**—A WCF client is an application generated by Visual Studio to call a WCF service. You can create a WCF client by adding a service reference to a client application. The client application is the actual application that consumes the results of the WCF service. Think of the WCF client as the go-between or proxy that helps connect your client code to the WCF service.

▶ **Host**—A host is a process that runs (or hosts) the WCF service. This process controls the lifetime of the service. This is similar to how ASP.NET provides a host for web services. You can write your own service host or allow a service to be self-hosted.

▶ **Contract**—Contracts define your WCF services. This is essentially the public contract you guarantee between your service and any clients. There is a service contract that defines the content of the service (such as its operations). There is also an operation contract for each service operation. This contract indicates the parameters and return type of the service operation. There are also message, data, and fault contracts.

▶ **Endpoint**—Endpoints are configured for each service operation. An endpoint is where messages for your service are sent and received. Each endpoint defines both an address and binding for communicating with a service. For example, you might have one endpoint that works with SOAP over HTTP. You might have another endpoint for the same service that enables the service to work with MSMQ. In this way, you can add and configure endpoints to your service independently of actually coding the service. This ensures that your service can be configured to work efficiently with both existing and new clients.

▶ **Address**—An address is a unique URI for a given service. The address is used by calling clients to locate the service. The URI also defines the protocol that is required to reach the address such as HTTP or TCP. Each endpoint you define for your service can have its own address.

▶ **Behaviors**—A behavior defines how an entire service, a specific endpoint, or a specific service operation behaves. You can define behaviors for such things as security credentials and service throttling.

▶ **Binding, binding element, and channel**—Endpoints have bindings that define how the endpoint communicates. A binding includes information about transport, encoding, and security. For example, you can configure an endpoint's binding to work with the HTTP transport encoded as text.

▶ A binding is made up of binding elements. Each element represents a single portion of the binding. You might, for example, have a binding element for the encoding and another for the transport. Binding elements and their configuration are implemented as channels. The binding elements are stacked together to create this channel. In this way, the channel represents the actual implementation of the binding.

Visual Studio provides various tools that make building WCF services easier. If you know that you intend to host your WCF service inside a website under IIS, you can actually add a WCF service to a website using the item templates. However, if you want to host outside of IIS or to decide on hosting at a different time, you can create a WCF project. In either case, you then define your service contract (as an interface). Next, you implement the service contract. Finally, you configure communication endpoints for the service. After your service is complete, you pick a hosting model and deploy it accordingly. Clients can then access the service. Let's take a look at each of these steps.

The WCF Project Template

You can use Visual Studio to create a WCF service project in much the same way as you define other projects (File, New, Project). From the Add New Project dialog box, you can select the WCF node under either C# or Visual Basic. This enables you to choose a WCF service project template. Figure 21.9 shows this dialog box.

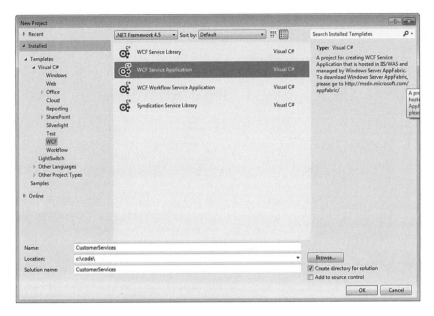

FIGURE 21.9   Use the WCF project templates to define your WCF service application.

Notice that there are a few WCF service templates from which to choose. These templates enable you to create WCF services based on your specific needs. There is a template for working with Windows workflow called WCF Workflow Service Application. The Syndication Service Library enables you to create a syndication service like an RSS feed. The template, WCF Service Library, enables you to create a basic WCF service and then deploy it to a host at a later time (see "Hosting and Deploying a WCF Service," later in this chapter). The final template, WCF Service Application, creates an ASP.NET website and a WCF service. This template provides a default host for the service (IIS). We use this template in the example.

> **NOTE**
>
> You can also create an ASP.NET website and add WCF services to it. In this case, the host for the service has been determined, and callers communicate with your service using IIS and ASP.NET.

WCF Service Application Files

The actual WCF Service Application project that is created through the Visual Studio template contains an interface for defining your service contract (IService1.cs), a file that represents the URI of your service (Service1.svc), and a related class file for implementing the service code (Service1.svc.cs). The project template also includes a Web.config file, for configuring the service, and the appropriate .NET references. Figure 21.10 shows a new project based on the template. Here the generated code for the start of the CustomerProfileService interface is depicted in the code window.

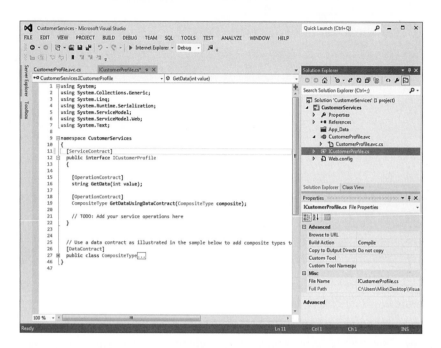

FIGURE 21.10   The WCF Service Application creates a service hosted in a website.

The service interface class (shown as ICustomerProfile.cs in the figure) is an interface you use to define your service contract. A contract includes the service operations and the data contract. Having the interface split into a separate file helps abstract all the WCF attributes and contract items away from your actual service logic.

The class is defined as a WCF service through the use of the ServiceContract attribute at the top of the class. In addition, the service operations (or service methods) are indicated as such through the OperationContract attribute applied to the method (GetData).

The actual service class (listed in the Solution Explorer as CustomerProfile.svc.cs) implements the service interface as follows:

```
namespace CustomerServices
{
  public class CustomerProfile : ICustomerProfile
  { ...
```

You place your service logic inside the class that implements the service interface. You might decide to actually put business code here or you might choose to call out to another library that contains the actual implementation code. Let's look at an example.

Creating a WCF Service

Now that you've seen the standard WCF service project template, it's time to walk through creating a WCF service with Visual Studio 2012. For this example, we develop a WCF customer profile service. Like previous examples, this service leverages the Entity Framework code-first model for getting data.

The following steps outline the process of exposing this functionality as a WCF service:

1. Start by creating a new WCF Service Application project. Name the project **CustomerServices**.

2. Use the Refactor, Rename option to rename the interface and service file to **ICustomerProfile.cs** and **CustomerProfile.svc**, respectively.

3. You will want to add the Northwind database and set up an EF code-first connection. You should be familiar with this process by now. However, if you're not, the following provides guidance:

   Add the Northwind database file to the App_Data folder for the project. You can get this file from the code for this book.

   Set a reference to System.Data.Entity for the project. To do so, right-click the References folder in Solution Explorer and choose Add Reference.

   Note that you might have to install EF 5.0 to the project. You can do that with NuGet. To do so, right-click the project in Solution Explorer and choose Manage NuGet Packages. From the resulting dialog, type **Entity Framework** into the Search box and click the Install button.

   Copy the Customer.cs and NwdContext.cs to the project. You can get these from earlier examples, re-create them, or download them from the book's code.

   Add a connection string to the Web.config file of the project to point to the Northwind database.

4. Open the ICustomerProfile.cs file. Remove the sample code in the file, and in its place, add method definitions for GetCustomer, GetCustomers, CreateCustomer, UpdateCustomer, and DeleteCustomer. Each method definition should be marked with the OperationContract attribute. Your code should look similar to that in Listing 21.3 (notice the using statement for the Models namespace in order to reference the Customer class).

LISTING 21.3   The ICustomerProfile Interface Definition

```
using System;
using System.Collections.Generic;
using System.Linq;
```

```
using System.Runtime.Serialization;
using System.ServiceModel;
using System.ServiceModel.Web;
using System.Text;
using Models;

namespace CustomerServices
{
  [ServiceContract]
  public interface ICustomerProfile
  {

    [OperationContract]
    IEnumerable<Customer> GetCustomers()

    [OperationContract]
    Customer GetCustomer(string id);
    [OperationContract]
    void DeleteCustomer(string customerId);

    [OperationContract]
    void CreateCustomer(Customer customer);

    [OperationContract]
    void UpdateCustomer(Customer customer);

  }
}
```

5. Next, open the CustomerProfileService.cs class file. Here you implement the code for the interface defined in the preceding step. To start, remove the code inside the class definition. Next, put your cursor inside the ICustomerProfile interface implementation on the class declaration line. You should see a small smart tag under ICustomerProfile. Click it and choose Implement Interface ICustomerProfile. Figure 21.11 shows an example. Clicking this option stubs out your service methods.

6. The next step is to write the code to connect your service methods to the EF code. Listing 21.4 shows what your code might look like. Note that error-handling code would still need to be added here.

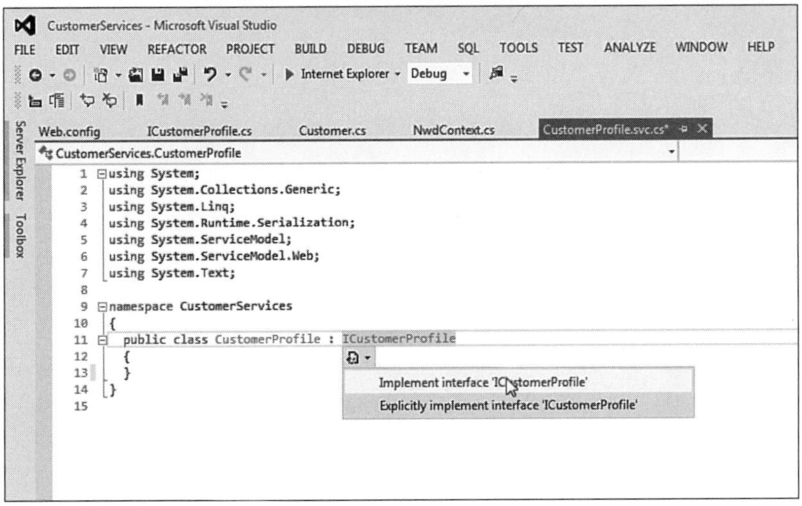

FIGURE 21.11   Use the smart tag in the code editor to implement the service interface.

LISTING 21.4   The CustomerProfile.svc.cs Implementation

```
using System;
using System.Collections.Generic;
using System.Linq;
using System.Runtime.Serialization;
using System.ServiceModel;
using System.ServiceModel.Web;
using System.Text;
using Models;
using System.Data.Entity;
using System.Data;

namespace CustomerServices
{
  public class CustomerProfile : ICustomerProfile
  {
    private NwdContext db = new NwdContext();

    public IEnumerable<Models.Customer> GetCustomers()
    {
      return db.Customers.AsEnumerable();
    }
```

```
    public Customer GetCustomer(string id)
    {
      return db.Customers.Find(id);
    }

    public void DeleteCustomer(string customerId)
    {
      Customer customer = db.Customers.Find(customerId);
      db.Customers.Remove(customer);
    }

    public void CreateCustomer(Models.Customer customer)
    {
      db.Customers.Add(customer);
      db.SaveChanges();
    }

    public void UpdateCustomer(Models.Customer customer)
    {
      db.Entry(customer).State = EntityState.Modified;
      db.SaveChanges();
    }
  }
}
```

7. You will now want to right-click your service, CustomerProfile.svc, in Solution Explorer and choose View Markup. Here you need to change the Service attribute to point to your actual service name. The following shows an example:

```
<%@ ServiceHost Language="C#" Debug="true"
Service="CustomerServices.CustomerProfile" CodeBehind="CustomerProfile.svc.cs" %>
```

That's it. You now have a simple WCF service hosted inside a web server. Next, we take a look at using Visual Studio to test the WCF service.

Running and Testing Your WCF Service

Whether you create a WCF Service Application (hosted in a website) or a WCF Service Library (hosted independently of the service definition), Visual Studio provides you a mechanism for running and debugging your services without having to deploy them first or write your own service client.

In this example, you used a WCF Service Application. Visual Studio leverage IIS Express to host this service. Visual Studio provides you a test client to run and debug the service. To use this test client, it is easiest to simply open the service in the IDE and click the Run button. Visual Studio will run the code in the current context by default and your service will launch in debug mode. Figure 21.12 shows the test client in action.

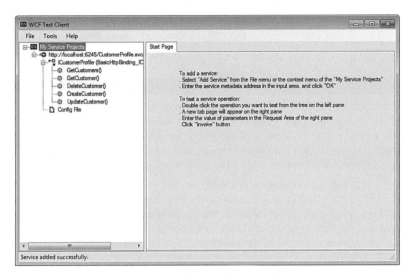

FIGURE 21.12   The WCF Test Client can help you test and debug your services.

Notice in Figure 21.12 that the WCF Test Client shows your service and all of its operations. If you double-click a given service, you get the test client on the right. Figure 21.13
shows a service execution in action. In this image, we have selected the service operation
GetCustomer, entered an ID value for the customer into the Test Client, and clicked the
Invoke button to view the results.

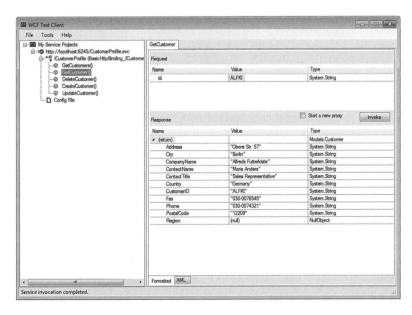

FIGURE 21.13   You can use the WCF Test Client to select a WCF Service Library, invoke it, and
view the results.

Notice that at the bottom of the form, you can toggle between the formatted results and XML. The XML view can be useful when debugging. To stop testing, select File, Exit in the WCF Test Client.

> **TIP**
>
> After your service exists, you can edit its configuration to support various clients. This means adding endpoints and related configuration information. Remember, the promise of WCF is that you can create a single service and then optimize it to work with multiple clients. One client might access via HTTP, another through TCP, and yet another with named pipes. You can support all of these clients (and more) through configuration.
>
> The WCF Service Library template contains an App.config file. The WCF Service Application contains the file Web.config. Both files define your service configuration. Typically, you edit the Web.config file using the XML editor in Visual Studio. However, when dealing with Service Library projects and multiple endpoints, it can be easier to edit this information using the Service Configuration Editor tool. To access this tool, right-click the config file and choose Edit WCF Configuration.
>
> If using Web.config, you want to click the Create a New Service link in this configuration editor. A wizard then walks you through the process to connect to configuration information about your service. From there, you can add additional endpoints and bindings as appropriate.

Consuming a WCF Service

You consume a WCF service from a .NET client by adding a service reference to your project. Visual Studio then generates a proxy class for calling your service. You use this proxy class to call your service from your .NET client application. Let's look at an example:

1. For this example, you leverage the clients created previously. If you did not create these, you can get them from the code for this book. There are two clients: a web form client project called WebFormClient and Windows Forms client called WinFormClient. Copy these projects from the previous example into the WcfCustomerServices solution directory.

2. In Solution Explorer, right-click the solution file and choose Add, Existing Project. Navigate to the WebFormClient project and select the WebFormClient.csproj file. Repeat this process for the WinFormClient project.

3. We will start with the WebFormClient. Right-click the project file in Solution Explorer and choose Add Service Reference to launch the Add Service Reference dialog box. You can use the Discover button on the right of the form to find the WCF services in the solution. Set the namespace for the reference to CustomerProfileService and click the OK button. Figure 21.14 shows an example of this step.

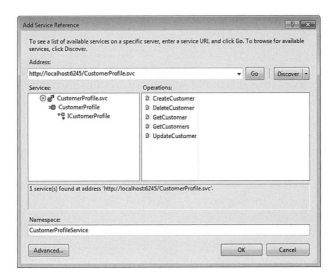

FIGURE 21.14   You can use the Add Service Reference dialog box to set a reference to a WCF service.

4. You should now see a service reference in your project and a new App.config file. In addition, if you open up the Web.config file, you will see a node called `<system.serviceModel>`; this represents your service configuration data. Right-click the Web.config file in Solution Explorer and choose Edit WCF Configuration to open the configuration (as shown in Figure 21.15). Select the Client folder. Note the client endpoint name and address (as you use them shortly) and close the editor.

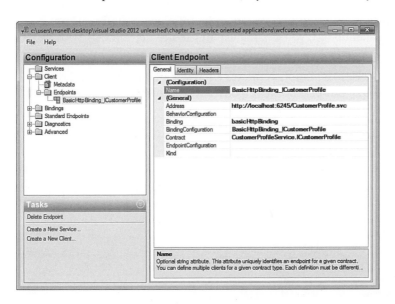

FIGURE 21.15   You can use the WCF service configuration editor to view and edit WCF client configurations.

5. The final step is to modify the code in Default.aspx page to call this new service reference. Recall that this page was originally written to use jQuery to call a Web API service. You could still use jQuery to call a WCF service, but in this case we want to examine the service reference code. Therefore, we call the service from the server in reaction to a button click event. Therefore, delete the JavaScript from the top of the page.

6. Swap the Input button, text box, and results label on the page to use ASP controls from the Toolbox. This will make the server-side coding easier. Your markup should look like this:

```
<asp:Content runat="server" ID="BodyContent" ContentPlaceHolderID="MainContent">
  <div>
    <p>Enter a customer id:</p>
    <asp:TextBox ID="TextBoxCutomerId" runat="server"></asp:TextBox>
    <asp:Button ID="Find" runat="server" Text="Find" OnClick="Find_Click" />
  </div>
  <div>
    <asp:Label ID="LabelResults" runat="server" Text=""></asp:Label>
  </div>
</asp:Content>
```

7. Double-click the button from the designer to create a click event. Here we will add code to call the customer profile service reference. Note that the service reference actually generates a proxy object with which to work. This includes creating a type to represent the Customer object. This makes programming with this service very straightforward.

First, you create the service proxy and pass an endpoint name to it. If you had configured additional endpoint, you could make the choice here.

Next, you simply use the proxy class reference to call GetCustomer and pass the text box value to this method. The results are returned as a Customer object and can be output to the web page as part of the response. The following code shows an example:

```
protected void Find_Click(object sender, EventArgs e)
{
  CustomerProfileService.CustomerProfileClient custSrv =
    new CustomerProfileService.CustomerProfileClient(
      "BasicHttpBinding_ICustomerProfile");

  CustomerProfileService.Customer cust =
    custSrv.GetCustomer(TextBoxCutomerId.Text);

  LabelResults.Text = string.Format("Company: {0}, Contact: {1}",
    cust.CompanyName, cust.ContactName);
}
```

8. The last step is to run the application. Figure 21.16 shows the results.

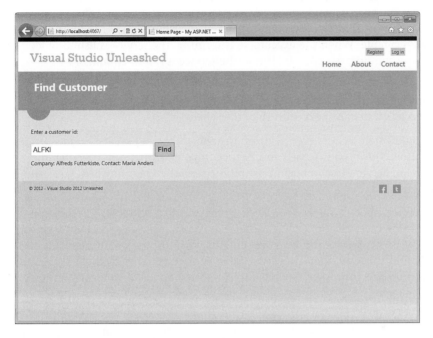

FIGURE 21.16   The web form application calling the WCF service.

> **NOTE**
>
> The Windows Forms client works the same way. You add a Service Reference to the WinForm project. You then call the service using the same code shown earlier in the web form example. The code for this book includes a complete example in the WcfCustomerServices solution.

Hosting and Deploying a WCF Service

For your services to accept requests, they have to be active and running, which means they need to be hosted in some runtime environment. Recall that when we covered web services, they were hosted for us by IIS. You can host your WCF services there, too. However, you do have other options.

You want to pick your host based on your needs. For example, if you have a peer-to-peer application, you might already know that each peer can host its own services. You also need to consider issues such as deployment, flexibility, monitoring, process lifetime management, security, and more. Here is a brief overview of the WCF host options available to you:

▶ **Self-hosted**—A self-hosted service contains the service within a running executable. The executable is managed code you write. You simply also embed one or more services within the executable. In this way, the service is self-hosted. It does not require an additional process to execute. Instead, its lifetime is managed by the lifetime of the executable. When the executable is running, the service is listening for requests and responding accordingly. If not, the service is out of commission.

Self-hosted services are great when your clients need to communicate with one another. This is the case with peer-to-peer applications like Microsoft's Groove. Each client has services that can speak with the other clients.

To create a self-hosted service, you create an instance of the `ServiceHost` class inside your application. This class is passed an instance of your service. You then call the Open method of ServiceHost to begin hosting the service. When finished, you call the Close method.

▶ **Windows service**—You can host your WCF service inside a Windows service application. A Windows service application is one that is installed as a service on a given machine. A Windows service can be configured to start, stop, and start up again on system reboot. In this way, they are very reliable and robust when you need services to simply stay up and running. They are also supported on all versions of Windows and Windows server.

To create a Windows service to host your WCF service, you create a class derived from ServiceBase. You then override the OnStart and OnStop methods to set up your service host. In the OnStart method, you create a global ServiceHost instance and then call the Open method to begin listening for requests. You then simply call the Close method in the OnStop method.

Finally, you create an Installer class for your service to install it in a machine's service directory. This class derives from the Installer class. You then compile the code and run installutil to get the service installed on a machine.

▶ **IIS**—IIS can host your WCF services. In this way, you can take advantage of the many features built in to this platform, including monitoring, high availability, high scalability, and more. You've seen how to create services hosted in a website in the preceding section.

▶ **WAS (Windows Process Activation Service)**—WAS was introduced with Windows Server 2008 (and available on Windows Vista/7). WAS gives you the benefits of IIS (health monitoring, process recycling, message-based activation, and so on) without the limitations of HTTP only. WAS works with HTTP, TCP, named pipes, and MSMQ. In addition, WAS does not require that you write hosting code (like the self-hosted and Windows Service options do). Instead, you simply configure WAS to be a host of your service (as you would IIS).

As you can see, you have many options for hosting your service. Each has its own plusses and minuses with respect to setup, coding, configuration, and deployment. Depending on your needs, spend some time learning more about your host options. You can find a how-to on each option inside the Microsoft Developer Network (MSDN). Simply search for "WCF hosting options" and you should find how-to's for each host just discussed.

Summary

This chapter presented both ASP.NET Web API services and those built on WCF. You saw how .NET abstracts the programming of services and provides tools to make your life easier. In this way, you can concentrate on building business functionality (and not writing plumbing code). Some key points in this chapter include the following:

▶ Web services are based on open standards. .NET adheres to these standards to ensure that heterogeneous applications can all work together with web services.

▶ An ASP.NET Web API service helps you write simple HTTP services that can be called from any application that speaks HTTP including web and native clients.

▶ The ASP.NET Web API is built on ASP.NET MVC and therefore includes a controller and routing engine for accessing your service methods. These service methods are written to leverage the HTTP verbs GET, POST, PUT, and DELETE.

▶ You can use jQuery to call a HTTP service asynchronously directly from a web browser on the client.

▶ A WCF service can be created with multiple endpoints to efficiently support multiple clients across different communication protocols. WCF services work across HTTP, TCP, named pipes, and more.

▶ You consume a service by adding a service reference. This generates a local proxy client for your code to call.

CHAPTER 22

Embedding Workflow in Your Applications

There are many types of applications you might encounter as a developer. You might build user interface controls, websites, rich clients, frameworks, services, data-driven reports, and more. There is a specific class of applications, however, that are created to manage a business process. A business process might involve many other applications, systems, and people. You may have even written an application like this. For example, you might have a library for processing an order. There may be a method on this library that knows how to identify the order, read some state out of the database, and respond accordingly to the current request. It is likely that this code works with other code libraries, services, and systems. This type of code can be referred to as a *workflow application*.

A workflow is simply a set of related activities that must be logically processed in order to realize a specific business goal or task. There are workflows everywhere. For example, processing documents such as expense reports, timesheets, purchase orders, invoices, and financial appropriations requests all represent possible workflows. In addition, tasks such as renting a movie, processing a loan, and reserving a hotel room are also workflows. You might have already written code like these examples (whether or not you called that code a workflow).

Visual Studio 2010 and the .NET Framework 4.0 rewrote much of Windows Workflow Foundation (WF), and Visual Studio 2012 with .NET Framework 4.5 bring incremental refinements to that effort. If you are familiar with earlier versions, you should note that some of the concepts are the same but most of the coding is new. Here we focus first on the fundamentals of the new model. We then cover the many activities that you use to create your workflow, including managing messages, handling errors, storing data, and controlling the flow within your business process. Finally, we walk through the core steps of building a workflow, including creating custom activities, defining sequences and flowcharts, hosting the workflow, running it, and working with persistence for long-running workflows. Let's get started.

> **NOTE**
>
> The WF tools and library were substantially revised with Visual Studio 2010. A lot of improvements have been made to creating and maintaining workflows. However, the SequentialWorkflowActivity and StateMachineActivity workflows from versions past are gone. In their place is a model based on activities that can host other activities. This new model is the focus of this chapter. Of course, you can still access the old model and its project templates by targeting the .NET Framework 3.5 for your given project.

Windows Workflow Fundamentals

You should think of a workflow as a series of activities that are interrelated to solve a specific business problem. These activities might call external code or services to accomplish their tasks. They typically also involve human intervention such as approval or some related form of processing. When an activity is complete, the next activity in the workflow gets executed until the specific workflow instance has completed. The workflow might have to pause during execution while waiting for a message or a user response. The workflow might be short lived or long running, spanning days or even months. In this way, a workflow mimics the needs of the actual business process.

Windows Workflow Foundation (WF) provides a set of activities for expressing workflows. You also write your own, custom activities that define steps in your business process. You then assemble both the base, WF activities and your custom activities using a graphical designer. Activities are assembled in some flow control mechanism such as another activity, a sequence, or a flowchart. Once complete, you then configure a host to handle the execution of your workflow and perhaps use the WF persistence service if your workflows are long running in nature. Let's take a look at how this works.

The Components of a Workflow

Before you begin developing workflows, it's important that you understand the components that work together to help you build and run them. The basic parts involved with creating, hosting, and running a workflow include the workflow itself, a host process, the workflow runtime, the workflow runtime services, and a client application that communicates with the workflow. We describe these components at a high level in this section, and you can get to know more about each component in coming sections.

- ▶ **A workflow**—A workflow is simply a collection of activity objects that work together to describe a process. The steps of a workflow are expressed as a hierarchy of activities. The top most, or outer, activity defines the workflow as a whole. It serves as an entry point and container for the workflow.

Most workflows are created from the base class activity and defined as Extensible Application Markup Language (XAML) using a graphical designer. You can also create custom activities that derive from CodeActivity or NativeActivity. An activity (and thus a workflow) can accept arguments and return values.

▶ **Workflow host process**—A workflow requires a host process in order to run. The host process can be any Windows process, including ASP.NET, a WPF application, a WCF host process, a Windows service, and more. The host process uses the workflow runtime to invoke a workflow and interact with it.

▶ **The workflow runtime engine**—Workflows execute inside the workflow runtime engine. The host application tells the workflow runtime engine how it wants to invoke the workflow. The runtime engine is responsible for executing, maintaining, persisting if necessary, and leveraging other workflow services such as tracking and tracing.

▶ **Workflow runtime services**—The workflow runtime may take advantage of the base services provided by the workflow environment including persisting long-running services and providing tracking information.

▶ **Client applications**—Workflows are typically executed by a host application in response to a client application request. For example, you might write a client application to submit a purchase request. This client application calls the host process and asks for a workflow instance to be created. It might then receive notifications or call back into the runtime (typically through the host) to query for information about a running workflow (such as status).

Figure 22.1 illustrates how these many components come together to form a solution.

Notice in the figure the workflow that is being executed by the workflow runtime. This workflow is typically created in Visual Studio as a separate project. You then use the graphical workflow designer to describe your process by connecting activities, defining arguments and variables, and creating dependencies among the activities. You can also define your workflow using code-only (C# or VB) or using markup (XAML).

Your workflow is compiled into an assembly and referenced by a host application that you create. Alternatively, you can invoke a workflow dynamically at runtime (using a XAML file (outside of a compiled assembly). The host application can be an ASP.NET site, a web service, a Windows Service, or any other .NET process. The host is responsible for managing client requests with respect to the workflow.

The host manages requests by working with the workflow runtime engine. It is the workflow runtime that creates instances of your workflow. It uses the workflow scheduler service to run the workflow based on how it was invoked. The runtime might also use the persistence service to save long-running workflows or to reactivate a saved workflow.

Clients communicate with a host through whatever mechanism you choose. In fact, you can combine the client and host as a single application. This can be useful for testing purposes and in applications in which workflows are relevant only when the client is running. A common scenario is to host a workflow inside a WCF service host or ASP.NET.

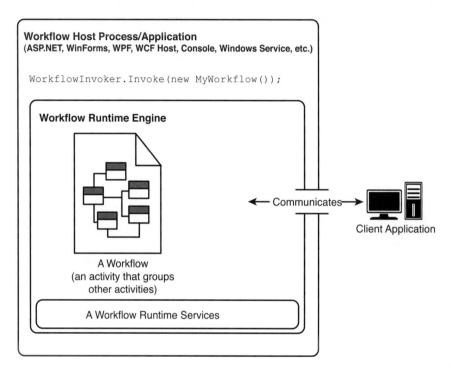

FIGURE 22.1   A Windows process is used to host a workflow. The host invokes the workflow. Client applications communicate with the workflow runtime via the host.

Now that you have a good foundation, let's look at the tools Visual Studio exposes for building workflows. We return to each of these concepts in the coming sections and demonstrate how they operate.

The Workflow Project Templates

You create a new workflow project like any other (File, New Project). Selecting the Workflow tab in the templates tree exposes four workflow project templates. You can create workflow projects in either Visual Basic or C#. Figure 22.2 shows an example of this dialog box for C#.

The Activity Library

The basic workflow template in this list is Activity Library. It is used to define a project that contains only workflow definitions. That means no host or client is in the project template; only the workflow itself is there. You are expected to create your own host and client applications to make use of the Activity Library workflow. This is the most common scenario after you learn to build workflow applications.

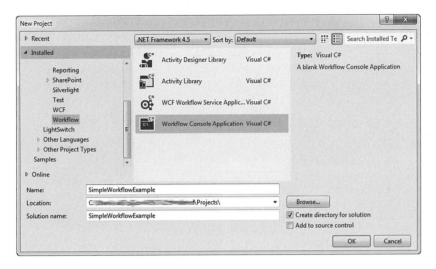

FIGURE 22.2   You select the Workflow node on the Installed Template tree to access the workflow project templates in Visual Studio.

WCF Workflow Service Application

The Workflow project templates also include two templates that combine a workflow host and the workflow library: WCF Workflow Service Application and Workflow Console Application. The WCF Workflow Service Application template creates a website to host a WCF service that exposes your workflow. The workflow has a ReceiveRequest for starting the workflow and a SendResponse for completing the service and returning a message to the caller.

Workflow Console Application

The Console application template creates a console application that serves as both host and client for working with your application. This is a great way to learn and test your workflows because you do not need to concern yourself with creating these items and can instead focus on the workflow itself. When you are ready to release, however, you will typically remove the Console application and switch this to a library (.dll) project.

Activity Designer Library

The final template, Activity Designer Library, is used to create a design-time experience for any custom activities you create. You use a version of the WPF XAML editor to define graphical representation of your custom activity. You can also create areas inside your activity where you expect other activities to be placed. Note that you can also create simplified workflow designers that you can expose to end users to enable them to configure portions of your workflow.

The Workflow Designer

When you create a new workflow project you typically interact with the designer to define your workflow (unless you are only creating CodeActivity types). This tool enables you to express your workflow in terms of a collection of connected activities. You also use the tools to work with each activity to configure its properties and set up relationships. Figure 22.3 shows an example of the workflow designer inside Visual Studio.

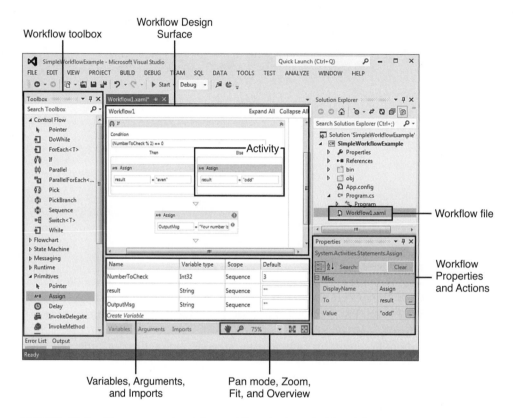

FIGURE 22.3   The many parts of the workflow designer in Visual Studio.

Notice first the center of the screen. This is the design surface for a workflow. This is a basic workflow activity in the process of being created. There is an outer Sequence activity that houses the steps within the workflow (If and Assign activities). Tools for zoom, fit to screen, and overview are in the lower right of the designer. These tools are useful because a workflow can become quite large and therefore you need to be able to find and focus on different areas.

You drag activities to the design surface from the workflow Toolbox shown on the left of the screen. Notice the many activities that can be used to express a workflow. We cover these in a moment.

The bottom right of Figure 22.3 shows the Properties window for the selected workflow activity. In this case, the Else branch of an If activity is selected. You can use the Properties window to set a display name for an activity, access the expression editor for defining a condition, connect an activity to code, and set many other configuration values depending on the selected activity.

The bottom center of the screen is used to define variables, arguments, and `imports` statements. The Imports area is where you set the namespaces your workflow is using or imports. Variables are used to store data in a workflow much like you would use them in your code. Arguments are used to pass data into and out of a workflow. More on these items in a moment.

The Workflow Item Templates

You add items to a workflow as you would any other project (right-click the project file, choose Add, and select New Item). This launches the Add New Item dialog box as shown in Figure 22.4. From this dialog box, you can add one of four item templates to your project: Activity, Activity Designer, Code Activity, and WCF Workflow Service.

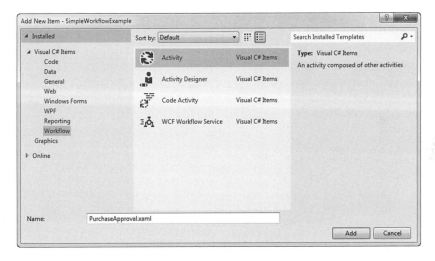

FIGURE 22.4   You can add new activities to your workflow projects using the Workflow item templates.

The following list describes each of the item templates shown in Figure 22.4:

▶ **Activity**—Use the Activity template to create a workflow using the designer or XAML markup. The Activity template defines an outer container that houses other activities that describe your business process.

▶ **Activity Designer**—Use the Activity Designer template to create a design-time appearance for the custom activities you create. This is useful if you intend to package an Activity and share it with other developers. You can provide a visual representation of your activity on the design surface and support drag and drop, configuration, and property settings. If you are simply creating workflows to use in your application, you do not need to use this template.

▶ **Code Activity**—Use the Code Activity if you want to express an activity (or entire workflow) as code inside the code editor (VB or C#). The Code Activity does not have a designer. Instead, you create your workflow as a collection of Activity objects using code.

▶ **WCF Workflow Service**—Use the WCF Workflow Service template to create a workflow that is exposed as a WCF service. (See Chapter 21, "Service-Oriented Applications," for details on WCF.) This template creates a .xamlx file. The template is based on the WorkflowService class (and not the Activity class). By default, the template creates a Sequence activity that contains a ReceiveRequest activity for getting a call from a service client. It also contains a SendResponse activity for sending results back to the service client.

The two most common item templates are Activity and CodeActivity. Let's explore using both templates to express a basic workflow.

The Basics of Creating a Workflow

To get started with WF, it is often easier to create a simple workflow to help better understand the core concepts. In this section, you create a workflow project that takes a number and determines if the number is odd or even and then returns an appropriate message. Of course, you could write this code in a couple lines and do not need a workflow to express something so simple. However, keeping this example simple helps illustrate how workflows are created, hosted, and executed. We cover a more real-world example later in this chapter.

Creating a Basic XAML-Based Workflow

In this example, you create a single project to serve as the workflow library, the host, and the client. Note that this example is available from the downloadable content for the book:

1. Open Visual Studio and create a new project (File, New Project).

2. Select the Workflow Console Application project template. Name this project **EvenOddWfHostAndClient**. It serves as the workflow library. We also use the Console application to host the workflow and interact with it.

3. Rename the workflow by changing both the filename and the class name. Open Workflow1.xaml in the designer.

4. To change the workflow's class name, select the workflow and view its Properties. Change the Name property to **EvenOddWfHostAndClient.EvenOddWf**.

5. To change the filename, right-click the file in Solution Explorer and choose Rename. Set the filename to EvenOddWf.xaml. Figure 22.5 shows an example of your workflow in Visual Studio. The renamed portions of the workflow are highlighted.

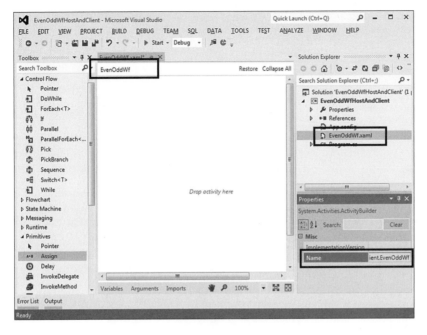

FIGURE 22.5 You use the Properties window of the workflow to rename the workflow class. Use Solution Explorer to rename the workflow file.

6. Define workflow arguments. The workflow should take a numeric value as an input. This argument serves as the number the workflow interrogates to determine if it is odd or even. It should also return a message to the user with the results of the workflow. To get started defining these arguments, double-click the EvenOddWf.xaml file in Solution Explorer to open the design surface.

7. Click the word *Arguments* at the bottom of the designer. This opens the Arguments editor. Click the empty row in the Name column. Enter the name **NumberToCheck**. Set the direction to In to indicate this is an inbound parameter only. Set the argument type to Int32 to define the data type.

8. Repeat the previous steps to define the output message parameter. Set Name to **OutputMsg**; set direction to Out to indicate this parameter can be read by the calling client as an output argument; set the argument type to String. Figure 22.6 shows an example of these arguments inside Visual Studio.

9. The next step is to design the workflow itself. To get started, be sure the workflow is open in the designer and the Toolbox is visible.

10. From the Control Flow section of the Toolbox, add a Sequence activity to the workflow. This activity acts as a container for other activities; it tells the workflow engine to execute these activities in a linked sequence. Click the sequence name in the designer and rename it (DisplayName property) to **Main Sequence**.

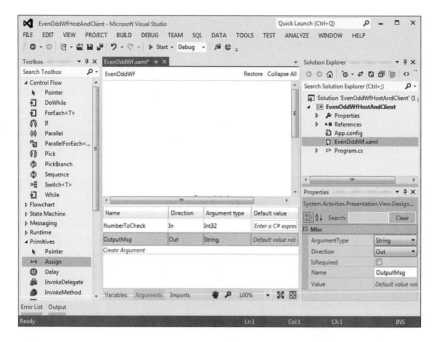

FIGURE 22.6   You can use the Arguments tab in the workflow designer to define inbound and outbound arguments for a given workflow.

11. Now is a good time to define the variable you will use to store the message before returning it to the client. Click the Variables tab at the bottom of the workflow designer; make sure you have the Sequence activity selected because variables in your workflow are scoped just like variables in code. Add a variable named result. Set its type to String and make sure the Scope is set to Main Sequence.

12. The next step is to define the If...Then condition logic. From inside the Control Flow section of the Toolbox, add an If activity to the Sequence activity. This activity defines the logic to determine if the input argument NumberToCheck is odd or even. Click the If activity and set the display name to If Number Is Odd / Even to help make the workflow more readable.

13. Inside the If activity, position your cursor in the Condition text box. From the Properties window, click the ellipsis button for the Condition property to bring up the Expression Editor for the condition. Note that our condition statement will be written using C# syntax because we created a C# workflow project. In this case, you need to write an expression that determines if the number passed to the workflow is odd or even. The following shows an example of such an expression:

```
NumberToCheck % 2 == 0
```

14. The next step is to define what happens when the If condition results to true or false. From the Primitives section of the Toolbox, drag an Assign activity to the Then (condition=true) section of the If activity. In the Assign activity, set the left box to the result variable and the right box to Even.

15. Repeat these steps for the Else (condition=false) side of the If condition. Set the result variable to Odd.

16. The final step in designing the workflow is to set the output message for the return argument from the workflow. To do so, add another Assign activity to the bottom of the sequence. Set the left side of this activity to the out argument, OutputMsg. Click the right side. From the Properties window, click the ellipsis button on the Value property. Use the condition editor to define the following string concatenation:

```
"Your number " + NumberToCheck.ToString() + " is " + result;
```

Your workflow should now look similar to that shown in Figure 22.7.

FIGURE 22.7   The final version of the EvenOddWf workflow in the designer.

17. Define a host program for the workflow and create a client to communicate with the workflow. In this example, both host and client are the Console application. Open the Program.cs file in the code editor.

18. The client code needs to enable a user to enter a numeric value to check. The code should validate this value before passing it to the workflow. (We could do this in the workflow, but we are trying to keep the workflow simple in this example.) The client code should call into the host and write out the results back to the user. The `Main` method in Listing 22.1 shows this client code.

19. The host code needs to invoke the workflow and pass in the `NumberToCheck` argument. This argument can be passed to the workflow when you instantiate it using property initializers. To get the return values from a workflow, you create an `IDictionary` generic collection and assign it to the results of the `WorkflowInvoker.Invoke` method. The `EvenOddWfHost` method shown in Listing 22.1 is an example.

Note that we separated this host code from the client just for clarity. We could have written this all in a single method.

LISTING 22.1   The EvenOdd Workflow Host and Client Code

```
using System;
using System.Linq;
using System.Activities;
using System.Activities.Statements;
using System.Collections.Generic;

namespace EvenOddWfHostAndClient
{
  class Program
  {
    static void Main(string[] args)
    {
      //client-code for user interaction
      Console.Write("Enter a number: ");
      string userInput = Console.ReadLine();

      //validate input and parse string to int (result)
      int result;
      while (!int.TryParse(userInput, out result))
      {
        Console.Write("Please enter a valid number: ");
        userInput = Console.ReadLine();
      }

      //call the workflow and write out results
      Console.WriteLine(EvenOddWfHost(result));

      //pause until user terminates
      Console.WriteLine("Press any key to close.");
      Console.ReadKey();
    }
```

```
    //separate host code from client code
    private static string EvenOddWfHost(int toCheck)
    {
      //create dictionary collection for out argument
      IDictionary<string, object> output;

      //invoke workflow, pass argument and get results (output)
      output = WorkflowInvoker.Invoke(
        new EvenOddWf() { NumberToCheck = toCheck });

      //return results
      return output["OutputMsg"].ToString();
    }
  }
}
```

20. Run the workflow and view the results. You can run the workflow like you would any other .NET program in Visual Studio. Figure 22.8 shows an example of the workflow running inside the console application.

FIGURE 22.8   The client running your workflow application.

Hosting and Invoking Workflows

In the preceding example, you used WorkflowInvoker to invoke the workflow. This class acts as your reference to the workflow through the runtime. In this way, it is said to "host" the workflow. Of course, you typically create your own host code to wrap this hosting. You can use two other classes to invoke and manage a workflow. The following provides a description of all three workflow host classes:

▶ **WorkflowInvoker**—This class enables you to invoke a workflow similar to calling a method on another class. The workflow is invoked synchronously on the calling thread. Arguments are passed into the workflow and a result is returned.

▶ **WorkflowApplication**—This class enables you explicit control over executing workflows. This class is used for writing your own host that needs granular control over the execution lifecycle of workflows. You can use this class to tell the WF runtime when to load, run, persist, terminate, cancel, unload, resume, and more. In most cases, you would not need this level of control over your workflows but should instead rely on the WF runtime engine.

▶ **WorkflowServiceHost**—The third way to invoke workflows is through the `WorkflowServiceHost` class. You use this class when you want to host and expose your workflow using WCF. This class is typically used when your application is running multiple instances of a workflow on different threads.

NOTE

Note that you do not need to explicitly use this class when you host your workflows inside of Internet Information Services (IIS) or Windows Activation Services (WAS). Instead, these hosts actually work with `WorkflowServiceHost` behind the scenes; you do not need to write code for it to work. See the example in the "Creating Activities and Workflow" section later in this chapter.

Express a Workflow as a Code Activity

In the earlier EvenOdd example, you created a XAML-based workflow. (You can actually right-click the file and choose View Code to view the XAML.) You can also express workflows directly using code (VB or C#) by adding a Code Activity item template to your project (refer to Figure 22.4).

A Code Activity is a class file that derives from the `CodeActivity` class. You can use this class to write code that represents your entire workflow or you can create an activity that includes code to be used as part of another workflow. For example, let's look at a couple ways we can replicate the EvenOdd workflow created previously using code.

To get started, let's assume you want to create the same functionality written previously but as a `CodeActivity` instance. Recall that the workflow returned an argument (`OutputMsg`). The good news is a Code Activity makes it easy to return a single value from a workflow. Instead of defining an out argument, we can simply have the workflow return a value.

To have the workflow return a value, you first indicate the workflow returns a type by passing the type name when you indicate inheritance. For example, the following line of code creates the new `EvenOddWfSimpleCode` class and indicates it inherits from `CodeActivity` and should return a string. Notice that you derive from `CodeActivity<TResult>`. This indicates that the workflow returns a value. If the workflow did not return a value, you simply derive from `CodeActivity`:

```
public sealed class EvenOddWfSimpleCode : CodeActivity<string>
{ ...
```

Remember that the EvenOdd workflow took an inbound parameter, too. You define this parameter at the class level as the type `InArgument`. The following code shows an example:

```
public sealed class EvenOddWfSimpleCode : CodeActivity<string>
{
  [RequiredArgument]
  public InArgument<int> NumberToCheck { get; set; }
...
```

To write the actual workflow code, you need to override the `Execute` method of the `CodeActivity` class. If you derived from `CodeActivity<TResult>`, the `Execute` method should return a value of the same type defined in `TResult` (in this case, string).

The `Execute` method takes a `CodeActivityContext` instance passed by the WF runtime engine. You use this context instance to access the actual properties (arguments) of the workflow instance. The following code shows the `Execute` method signature and the code to access the `NumberToCheck` argument:

```
protected override string Execute(CodeActivityContext context)
{
  //get the.input argument value
  int numToCheck = context.GetValue(this.NumberToCheck);
...
```

You can now express your workflow using standard code. In this case, an If...Else statement and some string concatenation for the result. This is the best use of the `CodeActivity` class (when you need to write code instead of using the workflow activities). Of course, you can still use the workflow activities to express the steps in your workflow when working with code. We look at that example next. Listing 22.2 shows the full code listing for this simple Code Activity workflow. You can run it and get the same results as before. Note that the code to call the workflow is similar to that provided back in Listing 22.1. You can download this example from the book's website.

LISTING 22.2   The Code Activity Version of the EvenOdd Workflow

```
using System;
using System.Collections.Generic;
using System.Collections;
using System.Linq;
using System.Text;
using System.Activities;
using System.Activities.Statements;

namespace EvenOddWfUsingActivity
{
  public sealed class EvenOddWfSimpleCode : CodeActivity<string>
  {
```

```
//define arguments
[RequiredArgument]
public InArgument<int> NumberToCheck { get; set; }

protected override string Execute(CodeActivityContext context)
{

  //get the input argument value
  int numToCheck = context.GetValue(this.NumberToCheck);

  string result = "";
  if (numToCheck % 2 == 0)
  {
    result = "Even";
  }
  else
  {
    result = "Odd";
  }

  return "Your number " + numToCheck.ToString() + " is " + result;
  }
 }
}
```

TIP

The `CodeActivity` class does have a drawback in that it does not support workflow Bookmarks. Bookmarks in WF enable a workflow to suspend (or wait) without holding on to a thread. You can then resume the workflow at a later time from the point of the bookmark. Again, those workflows derived from `CodeActivity` do not support this functionality.

Fortunately, there is the `NativeActivity` class. This, too, is a class used to create a workflow in code. You can change the inheritance structure of a `CodeActivity` to derive from `NativeActivity` and thus get the Bookmark capabilities. Of course, you might also have to make a few additional changes to support this new type.

Express a Workflow as an Activity Class

In the previous Code Activity example, we didn't so much create a workflow (a set of activities executed by the WF runtime engine) as we did write some code that got called by the WF runtime. To create an actual workflow, you need to express the same thing defined by the designer inside your code. This means using the WF Activities from code (instead of the designer). This type of programming takes some getting used to as something as simple as an If...Then statement in C# or VB now needs to be expressed with `Activity` objects in your code. Let's look at an example.

One of the most straightforward ways to define an actual workflow in code is by deriving from the `Activity` class. Remember, a workflow is simply a collection of `Activity` objects. You can still create arguments at the class-level scope (like you did with the Code Activity example).

However, instead of overriding the `Execute` method, you can create a default constructor for your workflow. Inside the default constructor, you set up the actual activities in the workflow. This includes defining variables for the workflow. You then use the base class property `Implementation` to indicate which activities should be added to your workflow.

For example, the following code shows the start of the default constructor for the class `EvenOddWfActivity` (another code-based workflow). Notice that a new `Variable` type called `result` is created. Next, `this.Implementation` is set to a new `Sequence` object and the `result` variable is scoped to the `Sequence`. This is just how you defined these items in the XAML-based version:

```
//create a constructor for the activity in order to define
//  the activity's implementation
public EvenOddWfActivity()
{
  //create an outbound variable in order to set the results of the activity
  Variable result = new Variable<string> { Name="OutputMsg", Default=null };

  //define the implementation as a new Sequence activity
  this.Implementation = () => new Sequence
  {
    //set the Sequence name and result variable
    DisplayName = "Main Sequence",
    Variables = { result },
```

Notice the use of property initializers for the `Sequence` object. This makes the code easier to read and understand. The next step is to add to the `Activities` property of the `Sequence` object to include the `If` and `Assign` activities. For the `If` activity, you need to define the `Condition` property, `Then`, and `Else`. In this case, you can set the `Condition` to a lambda expression to evaluate the `NumberToCheck` property. You use `Assign` activities to define both the `Then` and `Else` properties.

Finally, to define the result of the workflow to the result of the `Activity` execution, you create a new `Assign` activity and set the `To` to an `OutArgument` and make it reference `this.Result` for the workflow context. You set the `Value` to an `InArgument` and concatenate the message.

Listing 22.3 shows an example (with lots of comments) on how you would express the EvenOdd workflow using code and the WF activity classes. Again, this can take some getting used to, but after you do it a few times, it makes more sense (or you can always rely on the designer).

22

LISTING 22.3   The Activity Version of the EvenOdd Workflow

```
using System;
using System.Collections.Generic;
using System.Collections;
using System.Linq;
using System.Text;
using System.Activities;
using System.Activities.Statements;

namespace EvenOddWfUsingActivity
{
  //create a class that derives from Activity with a return type of string
  public class EvenOddWfActivity : Activity<string>
  {

    //define and inbound argument for the workflow
    [RequiredArgument]
    public InArgument<int> NumberToCheck { get; set; }

    //create a constructor for the activity in order to define
    //  the activitiy's implementation
    public EvenOddWfActivity()
    {
      //create an outbound variable in order to set the results of the activity
      Variable result = new Variable<string> { Name="OutputMsg", Default=null };

      //define the implementation as a new Sequence activity
      this.Implementation = () => new Sequence
      {
        //set the Sequence name and result variable
        DisplayName = "Main Sequence",
        Variables = { result },

        //add activities to the sequence (If, Assign)
        Activities =
        {
          //create the If Activity
          new If()
          {
            DisplayName = "If number is odd / even",

            //set the If Condition to a lambda expression that compares the
            //  inbound argument to Mod 2 = 0
            Condition = new InArgument<bool>((env) =>
              this.NumberToCheck.Get(env) % 2 == 0),
```

```
            //set the 'Then' parameter to a new Assign activity that sets the
            // variable, result, to "Even"
            Then = new Assign<string>
            {
              To = result,
              Value = new InArgument<string>("Even")
            },

            //set the 'Else' parameter to a new Assign activity that sets the
            // variable, result, to "Odd"
            Else = new Assign<string>
            {
              To = result,
              Value = new InArgument<string>("Odd")
            }
          },

          //add a final Assign activity to the Sequence for setting the
          // outbound, return parameter of the Activity<TResult> object (Result)
          new Assign<string>
          {
            DisplayName = "Assign result to output argument",
            To = new OutArgument<string>(env => this.Result.Get(env)),
            Value = new InArgument<string>(env =>
              "Your number " + this.NumberToCheck.Get(env).ToString() +
              " is " + result.Get(env))
          }
        }
      }
    };
  }
}
}
```

TIP

The Microsoft Developer Network (MSDN) contains a number of good (and download-able) examples of writing workflows in code. They may even already be installed on your machine. Look for the folder WF_WCF_Samples. If you cannot find it, or if just want to read the supporting documentation of these samples, search for "Windows Workflow Samples" on MSDN and you can navigate to a link that lets you download these exam-ples. Of course, you can get all the samples in this chapter from the downloadable content for this book.

Create a Dynamic Workflow

By default, your workflow definitions are compiled into the library in which they exist. This is fine if your workflows do not change often. However, you might sometimes need to tweak part of your workflow (set a threshold, change a condition) and not want to recompile and redeploy your entire application. In this case, you can create a dynamic workflow.

A dynamic workflow is one that is not compiled into a class library or application. Instead, it may exist on its own or be part of the project but be defined in such a way as to not get compiled with the project. You then invoke the workflow using `WorkflowInvoker.Invoke` but pass the workflow file in dynamically by calling `ActivityXamlServices.Load("fileName.xaml")`. You can then modify the XAML for your workflow without recompiling your application. The next call to invoke an instance of your modified workflow loads the newly modified workflow file.

To configure a dynamic workflow that exists as part of a project, you first indicate that your workflow should not be compiled with the project. You do so through the Properties window for the given workflow file. You need to set three properties here:

- ▶ **Build Action**—From XamlAppDef to Content
- ▶ **Copy to Output Directory**—From Do Not Copy to Copy Always
- ▶ **Custom Tool**—From MSBuild:Compile to Blank (Remove This Value)

Figure 22.9 shows an example of these property settings in the IDE.

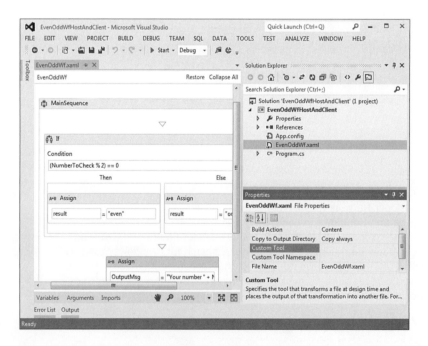

FIGURE 22.9   You use the Properties window to indicate your workflow class should not be included in the assembly but copied to the output directory along with the assembly.

The next step is to change the way you invoke the workflow. You first set a `using` statement for the namespace `using System.Activities.XamlIntegration`. You then change the `WorkflowInvoker.Invoke` call to pass the loaded workflow as the first parameter. Note that because this is not a strong type you cannot use property initialization to set the inbound argument `NumberToCheck`. To set this value, you define a type of `IDictionary` and add the named element there. You can then pass this `Dictionary` instance as another parameter to the `Invoke` method.

Listing 22.4 shows the `EvenOddWfHost` method revamped to load the workflow dynamically.

LISTING 22.4   The Activity Version of the EvenOdd Workflow

```
//separate host code from client code
private static string EvenOddWfHost(int toCheck)
{
  //create dictionary collection for out argument
  IDictionary<string, object> output;

  //create an input dictionary for input arguments to the workflow
  IDictionary<string, object> inputs = new Dictionary<string, object>();
  inputs.Add("NumberToCheck", toCheck);

  //invoke workflow, pass argument the loaded workflow, & inputs
  output = WorkflowInvoker.Invoke(
    ActivityXamlServices.Load("EvenOddWf.xaml"), inputs);

  //return results
  return output["OutputMsg"].ToString();
}
```

You can now build your project and change the workflow without recompiling by doing the following:

1. Open the project folder for your example. To do so, select the project in Solution Explorer and choose Project, Open Folder in Windows Explorer.

2. Navigate to the bin\Debug directory.

3. Open EvenOddWf.xaml in a text editor (such as Notepad).

4. Edit the final InArgument at the bottom of the file that does the concatenation of the results. Include the word *dynamic* in the concatenation.

5. Save and close the file.

6. Run the application (.exe) from the bin\Debug directory to see the modified workflow running without recompiling.

TIP

Workflows support full unit testing. You simply add a test project and set reference to the workflow namespaces. You can then call your workflow like you have seen in these examples. You then write assertions based on the results. For more information on writing unit tests, see Chapter 9, "Testing Code."

Working with the Built-In Workflow Activities

It's helpful to keep thinking of a workflow as mapping the steps of your business process to a set of activities in your workflow. You might have activities that call internal code for validating a purchase order, reach out to web services to look up a price, or call a member of a referenced assembly to calculate taxes. Your activities might branch based on dollar thresholds. You might use the activities to execute approval tasks in parallel.

The activities in Windows Workflow are a rich set of tools designed to make all these business activities (and more) possible. This section describes how each of the Activity controls in the Toolbox is meant to operate.

Controlling Flow

The Control Flow activities enable you to manage how activities are executed within your workflow. If you think of a workflow as a tree of activities, the Control Flow activities provide instruction on how this tree gets navigated. Figure 22.10 shows an example of the Activities for controlling activity flow of execution.

FIGURE 22.10   Use the Control Flow Toolbox items to handle how the activities in a workflow are executed, including sequencing, branching, and looping.

Notice that there are activities such as Sequence, While, DoWhile, and ForEach for managing order and branching. Control Flow also includes If, PickBranch, and Switch for handling branching logic. Table 22.1 lists each activity and a description.

TABLE 22.1   The Control Flow Activities

Activity	Description
DoWhile	You can put other activities inside the DoWhile activity. The contained activities execute once and then continue to execute repeatedly until a condition is satisfied.
ForEach	The ForEach activity contains other activities in the Body. These activities are executed once for every item in a collection. The collection might be a variable, an argument, or some other data picked up by the workflow.
If	The If condition enables you to execute other activities if a condition is true or false. You can, of course, nest If activities like you would in code.
Parallel	You use a Parallel activity to contain a set of activities that can be executed in parallel; they do not require a specific sequence. See the note after this table.
ParallelForEach	You use a ParallelForEach to execute a contained activity for each item in a given collection. The activity contained in the Body of the ParallelForEach are not executed in a sequence, one after another. Rather, they are scheduled asynchronously to be executed in parallel. See the note after this table.
Pick	The Pick activity provides an event-based model for controlling flow of your workflow. The Pick activity contains a group of triggers and related actions. After a trigger complete, its corresponding action is executed, and any other triggers executing or listening are canceled.
Sequence	You use a Sequence activity to execute a set of activities in a specific order (top to bottom).
Switch	A Switch activity works just like a Switch (Select...Case) statement in code. You define a type for the Switch statement, set an expression to be evaluated, and then define cases. You can add activities inside each case to be executed when the expression evaluates to that case value.
While	The While activity executes activities contained within it when a set condition is true. It repeats until the condition is false.

22

> **NOTE**
>
> The parallel activities (`Parallel` and `ParallelForEach`) enable you to define activities to be executed in parallel. However, like past versions of WF, only a single thread is used to execute a workflow. Therefore, these tasks actually execute sequentially in a round-robin fashion. If one of these activities blocks (waiting for input), however, it blocks other child activities of the parallel activity from executing until it finishes (unblocks).

Runtime and Primitives

The Runtime activities in the Toolbox enable you to communicate with the WF runtime engine to indicate persistence or termination of your workflow. The Primitives handle basics tasks such as variable assignment and writing text. Figure 22.11 shows these items in the Toolbox.

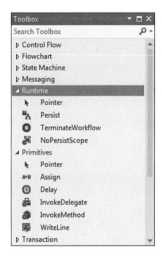

FIGURE 22.11   The Primitives activities enable you to do basic tasks in a workflow.

Notice the `Persist` activity in the Runtime group. This is used to persist the workflow's state to physical storage so memory can be freed; it can be retrieved at a later time. You can configure your workflows to persist as needed, or you can explicitly indicate persistence using this activity. Workflows are persisted to an instance store using the `WorkflowApplication` or `WorkflowServiceHost` classes. The .NET Framework includes the `SqlWorkflowInstanceStore` class to persist workflows to SQL server. Of course, you have to enable persistence on your workflow and your workflow host. (See "How to: Enable Persistence for Workflows and Workflow Services" in MSDN for details.)

Table 22.2 describes each activity in the Runtime and Primitive areas of the Toolbox.

TABLE 22.2   The Runtime and Primitive Activities

Activity	Description
Persist	Indicates that the workflow runtime engine should persist your workflow state when this activity is reached. Persisting a workflow releases it from memory and provides a point of recovery when it is reloaded. The workflow is persisted to an instance store such as SQL Server.
TerminateWorkflow	Use the `TerminateWorkflow` activity to indicate to the workflow runtime that the given workflow should end when this activity is reached.
NoPersistScope	Creates a container within your workflow that will prevent workflow state from being persisted. For instance, you may wish to prevent your workflow from being persisted if it is in the middle of processing a series of tightly bound, atomic activities.
Assign	Use the `Assign` activity to assign a value to a workflow variable.
Delay	Use the `Delay` activity to indicate a `TimeSpan` object that sets a pause in the workflow. You might use the `Delay` shape to pause inside a loop; after an elapsed time, you might check to see if what the workflow is waiting on has completed.
InvokeDelegate	Use the `InvokeDelegate` activity to invoke a specified `ActivityDelegate` object.
InvokeMethod	Use the `InvokeMethod` activity to execute a method on an referenced object. You set the `TargetObject` and `MethodName` properties to indicate both object and method.
WriteLine	Use the `WriteLine` activity to write a line of text to a specified `TextWriter` instance.

Error Handling

The Error Handling activities enable you to design the same Try...Catch error handling you would define for your code inside your workflow. Figure 22.12 shows these activities in the Toolbox. Table 22.3 describes the Error Handling activities shown in Figure 22.12.

TABLE 22.3   The Error Handling Activities

Activity	Description
Rethrow	Use the `Rethrow` activity to rethrow a caught exception after you are finished handling it (perhaps logging it).
Throw	Use the `Throw` activity to throw an exception from your workflow. You set the `Exception` property to "new up" an exception type to be thrown.
TryCatch	The `TryCatch` activity sets up three areas on your workflow: `Try`, `Catches`, and `Finally`. You can add activities to the `Try` section to be error-handled. You can define `Catches` to catch (and handle) specific error types.

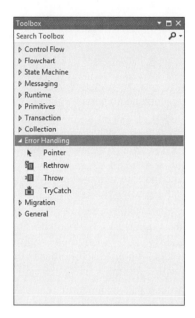

FIGURE 22.12   The Error Handling activities enable you to implement Try...Catch error handling in your workflow.

Collection Activities

The Collection activities provide the basic activities required to add, remove, and clear items in a collection of objects. You can also test to see if a specific item exists within your collection. A collection in this case might be a variable defined as a List type. You might pass a collection of values to the workflow or pick this collection up by calling some code. You can then combine a looping control flow activity such as for `ForEach` to iterate over the collection, interrogate it, and make decisions to remove or add items. Figure 22.13 shows the Collection activities in the Toolbox.

The `ExistsInCollection` activity enables you to return a Boolean indicating if a specific value exists in your collection. You define this activity by setting its `Type` property (it is a generic), a reference to the collection you are checking, and the `Item` property to indicate the item in the collection for which you are looking. You can use the `ExistsInCollection` as the condition to an `If` activity.

FIGURE 22.13   The Collection activities enable you to work with collections of data (an ICollection object) inside your workflow.

Table 22.4 provides a full list of the Collection activities and their usage.

TABLE 22.4   The Collection Activities

Activity	Description
AddToCollection<T>	Enables you to add an item to a collection by setting the Collection and Item properties.
ClearCollection<T>	Used to clear all items from a collection. You set the Collection property to indicate the collection to clear.
ExistsInCollection<T>	Use the ExistsInCollection activity to determine if a specific Item exists within the collection you assign to the activity. The result is a Boolean that can be used as part of a condition.
RemoveFromCollection<T>	Enables you to remove a specific Item from a collection you assign to the activity.

Supporting Transactions

The Transaction activities in the Toolbox enable you to group activities to be executed as a transaction. For sequential activities that execute without delay, you can use the TransactionScope activity. This is akin to using System.Transaction. For long-running transactions, you need to use the CompensableActivity (more on this in a moment). Figure 22.14 shows all the Transaction activities in the Toolbox.

FIGURE 22.14   You use the Transaction activities to indicate transaction processing for your workflow.

The `CompensableActivity` enables you to handle long-running transactions. In this case, you might have committed portions of a transaction to a data store and then paused part of the workflow. If an error condition happens days or weeks later or a user cancels the request, you have to undo any previous work. `CompensableActivity` enables you to set this scenario up in your workflow. You add the long-running workflow activities to the `Body` of the `CompensableActivity`. You then add activities to a `CompensationHandler` to indicate what should happen when your workflow needs to compensate. Figure 22.15 shows an example of this activity.

Table 22.5 describes the full set of Transaction activities you can use to define and manage transactions in your workflows.

TABLE 22.5   The Transaction Activities

Activity	Description
CancellationScope	Enables you to define a set of activities (a workflow) that can be canceled. You use the `Body` to define the cancelable scope. You then put activities inside the `CancellationHandler` to process what happens when the scope is canceled.
CompensableActivity	You use the `CompensableActivity` to define a set of activities that should be executed if your long-running transaction fails. You might add a `CompensableActivity` to a Catch block in your workflow to undo work based on an error condition.

Activity	Description
Compensate	Used to explicitly indicate that your workflow should compensate (call the `CompensationHandler`) based on some logic.
Confirm	Used to indicate that your workflow has completed and can be confirmed (calls the `ConfirmationHandler`).
TransactionScope	Enables you to define a set of activities that should executed together as a transaction. This is akin to participating in a `System.Transaction` transaction.

FIGURE 22.15   Use `CompensableActivity` to define transactions for long-running workflows.

Managing Messages

Windows workflow provides a set of messaging activities that enable you to expose your workflow as a WCF service as well as call out to other services. There are a number of message-based activities, each designed to enable you to configure various message exchange patterns, including Request-Response (or Send-Receive Reply). These activities also support correlation to make sure the right workflow instance gets the right message. Figure 22.16 shows the Messaging activities in the Toolbox.

The clearest way to learn the messaging activities is to create a message-based workflow, which you do in a moment. But first, take a minute to familiarize yourself with the Messaging activities described inside Table 22.6.

FIGURE 22.16   You use the Messaging activities to define send and receive message constructs for your workflow.

TABLE 22.6   The Messaging Activities

Activity	Description
CorrelationScope	Enables you to group a set of activities that participate in message correlation. Correlation defines how messages are related one another and the right workflow instance.
	For example, you might add a Send activity and a Receive activity to a CorrelationScope. The CorrelationScope activity is then responsible for correlating the received message with the right workflow instance that initiated the send message. Alternatively, you can set the individual activities' CorrelationHandle property to get the same behavior without a CorrelationScope object.
InitializeCorrelation	Used to initialize message correlation without actually sending or receiving a message. This is useful if you need to define a correlation handle prior to sending or receiving a message.
Receive	Enables you to receive a message as part of your workflow. This represents a WCF service that receives the messages. You configure the Receive and Send activities like you would a WCF service and client.
ReceiveAndSendReply	Creates a Sequence activity that contains a Receive and a SendReply activity. This provides support for the common pattern of receiving a messaging and replying that the message was received. You set the Request property of the SendReply activity to the name of the Receive activity to which it is replying.

Activity	Description
Send	Used to send a message from a workflow. You send the `Endpoint` property to indicate the binding (TCP, HTTP, and so on) and address to the destination. You can send a strongly typed message, an `XmlSerializable` type, or an untyped message.
SendAndReceiveReply	Creates a `Sequence` activity that contains a `Send` activity followed by a `ReceiveReply` activity. This provides support for sending messages and waiting for a correlated reply.
TransactedReceiveScope	Enables you to pass a transaction into a workflow as part of a message receive. You would typically add a `Receive` activity to the `Request` portion of the `TransactedReceiveScope` activity. You might then execute other activities in the `Body` and perhaps use a `Send` activity to send a response.

Creating a Message-Based Workflow

Recall the EvenOdd workflow from the earlier section. In this example, you create a version of the workflow that uses a message pattern to expose the workflow as a WCF service. The following outlines the steps to creating this workflow. (This code is available as downloadable content for this book.)

1. To get started, create a new workflow project as a WCF Workflow Service Application (File, New, Project). Name the project **EvenOddMessagingLib**.

2. Rename the workflow service to **EvenOddService** in both the filename and the Properties dialog box for the workflow (the class name).

3. Delete the activity Sequential Service that was defined by default on the workflow.

4. Open the Toolbox and navigate to Messaging. Add a `ReceiveAndSendReply` activity to the designer.

5. Click the Variables tab at the bottom of the designer. Define a variable to contain the number being sent to the service to check for odd or even; call this variable **numToCheck (Int32)**. Add a second variable to contain the response that will be sent back in the reply message; name this variable **result (string)**. Your workflow should now look similar to Figure 22.17.

6. Configure the `Receive` activity. First, set the `DisplayName` to `ReceiveNumToCheck`. Second, set the `OperationName` to `IsEvenOrOdd`. The `OperationName` indicates the name of the service method. Third, use the Properties window to set `CanCreateInstance` to `True` (check the box). Finally, click Define (or View Message) in the content section of the Receive shape. This launches the Content Definition window, which you can use to define the message and indicate parameters. In this case, create a new parameter called **NumberToCheck (Int32)**, which is passed to the service method (IsEvenOdd) of the workflow. Use the Assign To column to assign this parameter to the variable `numToCheck`. Figure 22.18 shows an example.

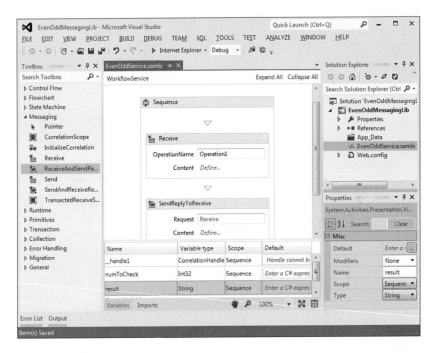

FIGURE 22.17   Define the variables to contain the receive and send data for the messages of your workflow.

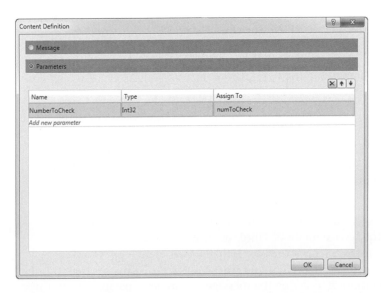

FIGURE 22.18   Map the variable `numToCheck` to the Receive message parameter `NumberToCheck`.

7. Now do a similar operation on the `SendReply` activity. Click the content area on the activity. Define a new parameter called **OutputMsg (string)**, which serves as the output of the workflow. Map this parameter to the result variable. Figure 22.19 shows this example.

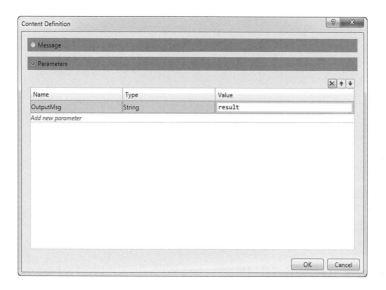

FIGURE 22.19 Map the internal variable `result` to the `OutputMsg` parameter of the `SendReply` activity.

8. Add the `If` activity between the `Receive` and `SendReply` activities. Configure this activity as you did previously to define a condition to check to see whether the number is divisible by two, and then assign the results. Figure 22.20 shows the final workflow in the designer.

9. Write a WCF client to pass the appropriate message and receive the result (refer to Chapter 21 for details). Recall, however, that WCF can generate a default and even host your service by default in ASP.NET. Therefore, to test the service, right-click the EvenOddService.xamlx file inside Solution Explorer and choose Set as Start Page.

10. Run the application. The WCF Test Client should launch as well as a local copy of the ASP.NET development server. Inside the WCF Test Client, navigate to your service method `IsEvenOrOdd`. Double-click the method and notice the test harness generates to the right of the dialog box.

Use the Request section to indicate a `NumberToCheck` and click the Invoke button.

Notice the results in the Response section. Figure 22.21 shows an example.

FIGURE 22.20   The message-based EvenOdd workflow inside the designer.

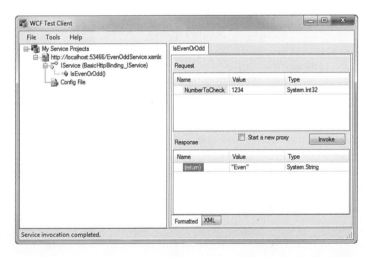

FIGURE 22.21   The message-based EvenOdd workflow running inside the default WCF Test Client application.

Note that you could also go back and connect the Console application from the earlier example to use this new message-based version.

Creating Flowchart Workflows

The Flowchart activities enable you to create a workflow using the well-understood flowchart paradigm. Processing starts at the top and works its way down. Along the way, different decisions are made, and the workflow branches accordingly. The workflow might loop back on itself, but it eventually ends. Flowchart workflows are much like what you would draw on a whiteboard when describing your business process (a lot of boxes and arrows). Figure 22.22 shows an example of the flowchart shapes in the Toolbox.

FIGURE 22.22   Use the Flowchart activities to create workflows based on the familiar model of a flowchart.

If you have created a basic workflow, a flowchart workflow is easy to understand. You simply connect activities using arrows going from the top of the flowchart to the bottom. Diamonds (FlowDecision) indicate branching conditions in the flowchart. Table 22.7 describes the Flowchart activities in the Toolbox.

TABLE 22.7   The Flowchart Activities

Activity	Description
Flowchart	Enables you to connect activities using the flowchart paradigm.
FlowDecision	Enables you to indicate a condition that changes the direction of the activity flow.
FlowSwitch<T>	Enables you to create a switch (Select...Case) feature in your code. You draw lines from the FlowSwitch to other workflow activities that should be executed based on a value of the Switch expression. You can use this feature to execute state-machine like behavior for your workflows.

Creating a flowchart is really just a different way of expressing the workflow concepts discussed thus far. In fact, Figure 22.23 shows the EvenOdd workflow expressed as a flowchart. Notice how similar this workflow looks to the original. In addition, the host and client code did not change at all. You can review this sample using the downloadable content for this book.

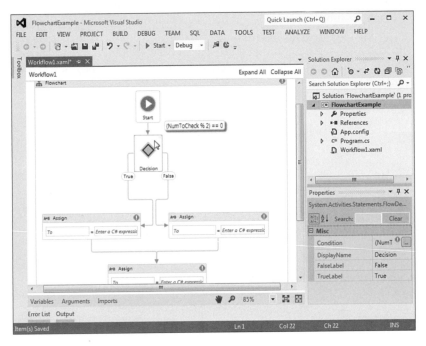

FIGURE 22.23   The EvenOdd example inside a flowchart-based workflow.

Creating a Workflow Application

You have now covered all the built-in workflow activities. You have also seen a number of basic examples. It's time to put the basics to work in a bigger example where you will learn more about things like hosting, messaging, persistence, and correlation with workflows. Let's get started.

> **TIP**
>
> This is a large application. We cover the highlights in the coming sections. If you are finding it difficult to follow along, you can open the solution from the downloadable content for this book. Please pay close attention to the ReadMe file for setting up the project to run correctly.

The Scenario: Travel Request

For this example, consider that you are working for the Contoso corporation and you need to automate and track the process of handling business travel requests. Here are the steps in this process:

1. A user initiates a travel request by filling out a travel request form. The actual form could be on a website, an InfoPath form, a rich client application, a mobile phone, or initiated via some other user interface application.

   Assume the form itself is connected to travel vendors for pricing and uses internal logic that calculates the total cost of the travel: airfare, rental car, per diem, parking, and mileage. The vendor provides a reservation id to keep track of the travel request before actually booking.

   Users are also asked to write a travel justification before submitting the request for approval.

2. The approval rules include a threshold. If the request is under $1,000 and the requestor is a manager or above, the request is automatically approved (and the workflow goes to step 5).

3. If the request is more than $1,000 or the requestor is not a manager, the request requires an approval from the requestor's direct manager. In this case, the user's direct manager is notified of the request by checking his request queue on a website. (We could send an email in addition to creating this log.)

4. The manager can sign into the travel request application where he or she can review the request and approve or reject it. Note that for this example, we keep the security and user management stuff out for now. (Check this book's blog for updates to this example.)

5. If approved, the travel reservations are booked using the reservation ID provided by the travel vendor. The vendor provides a service for booking this travel. The request is then marked approved and complete.

   Alternatively, if the request is rejected, the request is simply marked as complete.

The Application Project Templates

The first step with a scenario such as this should be to think it through and determine the general architecture of how this is created. This is where a simple diagram makes sense. Figure 22.24 shows the basic messaging structure, a few of the workflow decisions, and the projects that are used to build this solution.

Notice that Figure 22.24 alludes to a four specific projects inside the final solution. There are actually five in the final (a custom activity library). The following subsections outline each project, its type, and name.

Create the Projects

To get started, create a blank solution (File, New Project, Other Project Types, Visual Studio Solutions, Blank Solution). Name the solution **TravelRequestSystem**. Add the projects defined in Table 22.8 using the same names. Your Solution Explorer should look similar to Figure 22.25. (The figure shows an additional test project.)

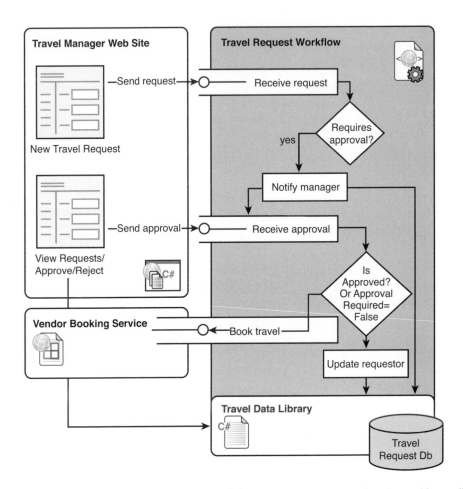

FIGURE 22.24   The Travel Request workflow has many connected parts, making a diagram essential.

TABLE 22.8   The Flowchart Activities

Project	Template	Description
TravelDataLib	Windows\Class Library	Travel Data Library
A class library used for communicating with the Travel Request database for storing requests and their state.		
TravelManagerWeb	Web\Web site	Travel Manager Website
The user interface for the application. It includes a home page (Default. aspx), a page for requesting travel (NewRequest.aspx), and a page for viewing pending requests and taking action (PendingRequests.aspx).		

Project	Template	Description
TravelRequestService The workflow that defines the travel request business process. It is exposed as a WCF service.	Workflow\WCF Workflow Service Application	Travel Request Workflow
UserLookupActivityLib A custom workflow activity to look up user information (such as the user's manager). This activity is used by the primary, travel request workflow.	Workflow\Activity Library	<Not shown>
VendorReservationService Simulates a vendor-based reservation system for handling a booking.	WCF\WCF Service Application	Vendor Booking Service

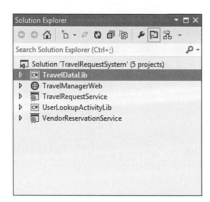

FIGURE 22.25   The projects as viewed from the Solution Explorer.

Creating the Database and Data Access Library

For this solution, you need to store the request details somewhere. You could implement an email-based system that send details in emails and allows someone to approve through an email client. In this case, however, you create a simple table to store the travel request in a queue for approval and tracking (different from the workflow tracking service).

Creating the Database

To create the database, just copy the TravelRequest.mdf file to your machine from the downloadable content for the book. However, if you want to create it from scratch, follow the outline shown in Figure 22.26.

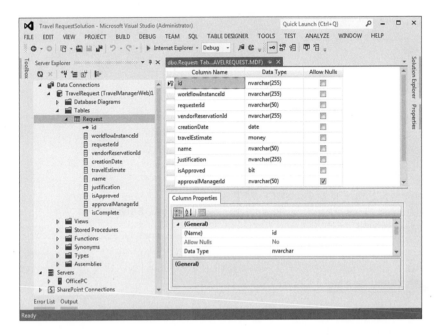

FIGURE 22.26   The TravelRequest.mdf acts as the queue of requests waiting approval from management.

The Request table contains a number of columns, as follows:

- ▶ **id**—The primary key of the workflow request. It is stored as a GUID. The request `id` is used for message correlation in the workflow (connecting messages with the right workflow instance).

- ▶ **workflowInstanceId**—The GUID of the actual workflow. We store it here in case we need it. However, in this example, it is not used.

- ▶ **requesterId**—The username of the person requesting the travel.

- ▶ **vendorReservationId**—The GUID the vendor system (simulated) provides so that the travel request can be booked after approval.

- ▶ **creationDate**—The date the request was made.

- ▶ **travelEstimate**—The estimated cost of the travel from the vendor system (simulated).

- ▶ **name**—The name or title of the request, such as Business travel to Seattle.

- ▶ **justification**—The reason the user is requesting the travel.

- ▶ **isApproved**—A flag indicating whether the travel has been approved. Note that if `isApproved` is false and `isComplete` is true, the workflow has been rejected (and is no longer pending approval).

▶ **approvalManagerId**—The username of the approving manager. You can use this to a greater extent in a later version after you wire up user logins to the site.

▶ **isComplete**—A flag indicating whether the workflow has completed (is no longer waiting on anything such as an approval). After complete, it is closed for good.

Creating the Data Access Library

The data access library is used in process by the travel request workflow to queue up approval requests and mark them approved or rejected. Because it is used in process, it leverages the connection strings defined in the applications that reference it. To create the classes in the TravelDataLib project, follow these steps:

1. Delete Class1.cs and add a new file to the solution called TravelRequestMsg.cs.

2. Add a reference to the System.Runtime.Serialization namespace. This is used to define the DataContract. Add a reference to System.Configuration. This will be used to pull connection string information from the config file of the application that runs this code.

3. Open the TravelRequestMsg class. Add a using statement for the referenced namespace.

4. Define a DataContract that is used for passing a travel request to the workflow. This contract should, in many ways, mimic the database structure created previously. Listing 22.5 shows an example.

LISTING 22.5   The `TravelRequestMsg DataContract` to Be Passed to the Workflow

```
using System;
using System.Collections.Generic;
using System.Linq;
using System.Text;
using System.Runtime.Serialization;

namespace TravelDataLib
{
  //defines a travel request
  [DataContract]
  public class TravelRequestMsg
  {
    [DataMember]
    public string Id { get; set; }

    [DataMember]
    public string WorkflowInstanceId { get; set; }

    [DataMember]
    public string VendorReservationId { get; set; }
```

```
        [DataMember]
        public string RequesterId { get; set; }

        [DataMember]
        public DateTime CreationDate { get; set; }

        [DataMember]
        public double TravelEstimate { get; set; }

        [DataMember]
        public string Name { get; set; }

        [DataMember]
        public string Justification { get; set; }

        [DataMember]
        public bool IsApproved { get; set; }

        [DataMember]
        public string ApprovalManagerId { get; set; }

    }
}
```

5. Define two methods (in a class called `TravelRequestDataAccess` class) for working with the Request table. The first, `Save`, adds a record to the `Request` table. It is called in the workflow to store the request for approval and completion. The second, `Complete`, is used to mark the workflow complete (and either approved or not). Both methods take an instance of the `TravelRequestMsg` written in the preceding step. Listing 22.6 shows an example of what this code should look like.

LISTING 22.6   The `Save` and `Complete` Methods Used for Working with the Request Data

```
using System;
using System;
using System.Collections.Generic;
using System.Linq;
using System.Text;
using System.Configuration;
using System.Data;
using System.Data.SqlClient;

namespace TravelDataLib
{
   public class TravelRequestDataAccess
```

```csharp
{
  //post a travel request to the queue (save to the db)
  public static void Save(TravelRequestMsg request)
  {
    string connectionString = ConfigurationManager.ConnectionStrings[
      "TravelRequest"].ConnectionString;

    StringBuilder sql = new StringBuilder("insert into request (id, ");
    sql.Append("workflowInstanceId, requesterId, ");
    sql.Append("vendorReservationId, creationDate, travelEstimate, name, ");
    sql.Append("justification, isApproved, approvalManagerId) ");
    sql.Append("values (@id, @workflowInstanceId, @requesterId, ");
    sql.Append("@vendorReservationId, @creationDate, @travelEstimate, ");
    sql.Append("@name, @justification, @isApproved, @approvalManagerId) ");

    using (SqlConnection connection = new SqlConnection(connectionString))
    {
      connection.Open();
      SqlCommand command = connection.CreateCommand();
      command.CommandType = CommandType.Text;
      command.CommandText = sql.ToString();

      command.Parameters.Add(new SqlParameter("@id", request.Id));
      command.Parameters.Add(new SqlParameter(
        "@workflowInstanceId", request.WorkflowInstanceId));
      command.Parameters.Add(new SqlParameter(
        "@requesterId", request.RequesterId));
      command.Parameters.Add(new SqlParameter(
        "@vendorReservationId", request.VendorReservationId));
      command.Parameters.Add(new SqlParameter(
        "@creationDate", request.CreationDate));
      command.Parameters.Add(new SqlParameter(
        "@travelEstimate", request.TravelEstimate));
      command.Parameters.Add(new SqlParameter(
        "@name", request.Name));
      command.Parameters.Add(new SqlParameter(
        "@justification", request.Justification));
      command.Parameters.Add(new SqlParameter("@isApproved", false));
      if (request.ApprovalManagerId == null)
      {
        request.ApprovalManagerId = "UNKNOWN";
      }
      command.Parameters.Add(new SqlParameter("@approvalManagerId",
        request.ApprovalManagerId));
```

```
        command.ExecuteNonQuery();
    }
}

public static void Complete(TravelRequestMsg request)
{
    string connectionString = ConfigurationManager.ConnectionStrings[
        "TravelRequest"].ConnectionString;

    StringBuilder sql = new StringBuilder("update request set ");
    sql.Append("isApproved=@isApproved, ");
    sql.Append("approvalManagerId=@approvalManagerId, isComplete=1 ");
    sql.Append("where id = @id ");

    using (SqlConnection connection = new SqlConnection(connectionString))
    {
        connection.Open();
        SqlCommand command = connection.CreateCommand();
        command.CommandType = CommandType.Text;
        command.CommandText = sql.ToString();

        command.Parameters.Add(new SqlParameter("@id", request.Id));
        command.Parameters.Add(new SqlParameter("@isApproved",
            request.IsApproved ? 1 : 0));
        command.Parameters.Add(new SqlParameter("@approvalManagerId",
            request.ApprovalManagerId));

        command.ExecuteNonQuery();
    }
}
}
}
```

Your data access library should now be complete. Notice the use of the `TravelRequest`
connection string. You set this inside the configuration files that use this library.

TIP

As an optional step, you might consider adding a test project to your solution and creating
unit tests for these methods. This type of application can make it difficult to debug things
such as a typo in your SQL. You need to create an app.config file to set the database
connection string in the test class.

Creating the Vendor Reservation Service

The vendor reservation service in this example is simply a simulated third-party service that the workflow might call. It is here to round out the business case and to demonstrate a useful feature of the workflow designer (more on this in the "Design the Workflow" section). Because it is simulated, we are not going to add too much to it. Follow these steps to define this simple mock object:

1. Start with the VendorReservationService WCF project. First, rename the service to **TravelBooking.svc** in Solution Explorer. You will need to open the class file and rename the class there, too. When you do so, use the smart tag to execute the rename refactor; otherwise, you will have to open the markup for the service (right-click TravelBooking.svc and choose View Markup) to rename the service in the markup.

2. Rename the service interface (IService1.cs) to **ITravelBooking** (both filename and interface name in the code). A rename in Solution Explorer should handle both. However, be sure to open the interface file and double check.

3. Inside ITravelBooking.cs, delete the `CompositeType` class. Then, remove the code inside the interface definition. Finally, add a method definition `BookTravel` that takes a string called `reservationId`. Your interface should look like this:

```
[ServiceContract]
public interface ITravelBooking
{
[OperationContract]
void BookTravel(string reservationId);
}
```

4. Open your service class (double-click TravelBooking.svc). Implement the new interface name at the class definition (public class `TravelBooking` : `ITravelBooking`).

5. Delete the code inside the `TravelBooking.svc` class (`GetData` and `GetDataUsingDataContract`).

6. Implement the ITravelBooking interface code inside the `TravelBooking` class. This code does not actually do anything; remember, this is for simulation and demo purposes. Listing 22.7 shows an example implementation.

LISTING 22.7   The `BookTravel` Service Method Is for Simulation Purposes

```
using System;
using System.Collections.Generic;
using System.Linq;
using System.Runtime.Serialization;
using System.ServiceModel;
using System.Text;
```

```
namespace VendorReservationService
{
  public class TravelBooking : ITravelBooking
  {
    public void BookTravel(string reservationId)
    {

      //TODO: write code to book the travel based on the reservation
      string rsvId = reservationId;

    }
  }
}
```

Creating the Custom Activity Library

In this step, you create two custom activities used for looking up a user to get her manager and to determine whether the user is a manager. The actual logic of these services is not material. In a production system, these activities would most likely call out to Active directory or an HR system. They might also be exposed as services. However, in this example, they serve the purpose of demonstrating how you can create custom activities in a separate project and then use them in your workflows.

Create the IsManager Custom Composite Activity

The first activity checks to see whether the user is a manager. To set this up, follow these steps:

1. Start with the UserLookupActivityLib project (an ActivityLibrary project). Rename the Activity1.xaml file to **IsManagerActivity.xaml**. You also have to open and then select the workflow in the designer and view its properties to change its class name to **UserLookupActivityLib.IsManagerActivity**.

2. As you can see, this custom activity is a XAML-based activity. Start by defining two arguments. (Click the Arguments tab at the bottom of the designer.) You should expect the UserId (string) as an inbound argument. You pass the IsManager (Boolean) as an output argument.

3. Drag an If activity from the Control Flow area of the Toolbox to the design surface.

4. Edit the Condition of the If activity with some logic to determine whether the user is a manager. In this case, the logic is secondary; you can use:
   UserId.EndsWith("mgr").

5. In the Then side of the If activity, use and Assign activity to set IsManager to True. Do the opposite for the Else condition.

Figure 22.27 shows what your IsManagerActivity should look like when complete.

FIGURE 22.27   You can use the workflow designer to quickly build custom composite activities.

Create the GetUsersManagerActivity Custom Code Activity

The second activity looks up a user's manager based on her username. To set this up, follow these steps:

1. Start with the UserLookupActivityLib project. Add a Code Activity to your project. Name this activity **GetUsersManagerActivity**.

2. Change the inheritance of this activity to inherit from CodeActivity<TResult> where TResult is a string. This is used to indicate the activity's return (Result) type.

3. Define an input parameter to enable users of the activity to pass a username. Define this parameter as an InArgument<string> public property of the activity.

4. Override the Execute method to get the user's manager. This method can return a string value that is set to the result of the activity execution. Listing 22.8 shows an example of what your code might look like. Notice that the "lookup" simply appends *mgr* to the username.

LISTING 22.8   Use `CodeActivity<TResult>` to Return a Single Value from Execute

```
using System;
using System.Collections.Generic;
using System.Linq;
using System.Text;
using System.Activities;

namespace UserLookupActivityLib
{

  public sealed class GetUsersManagerActivity : CodeActivity<string>
  {
    public InArgument<string> UserId { get; set; }

    protected override string Execute(CodeActivityContext context)
    {
      string userId = context.GetValue(this.UserId);

      //TODO: call code to lookup the user's manager

      return userId + "mgr";
    }
  }
}
```

You've now created both a XAML-based composite activity and a code-only activity. These activities are used in the workflow. In fact, you create a couple more code-only activities when you develop the workflow. We look at this work next.

TIP

You can actually define a designer for your custom activities. To do so, use the Activity Designer Library project template. You get a WPF-like designer for defining how your workflow activity should look and how users interact with it (such as setting sections that enable users to add other activities).

Designing the Workflow (Travel Request)

It's finally time to design the actual workflow. The following sections walk you through each step you need to complete to get the workflow up and running.

Project Housekeeping

The following takes you through a number of configuration and housekeeping steps for the workflow project (TravelRequestService):

1. Add project reference to both TravelDataLib and UserLookupActivityLib. Right-click the project file, choose Add Reference, select the Projects tab, and then select both these projects.

2. Define a WCF service reference to VendorReservationService. Right-click the project file and choose Add Service Reference. Click the Discover button on the Add Service Reference dialog box. Select the TravelBooking.svc service. Name your service reference **VendorReservationSrv**.

3. Define the database connection string. Open the Web.config file. Add a connection string to point to the TravelRequest.mdf file. Remember, this connection is used by the data access library so name the connection string TravelRequest. Your connection string should look similar to the following:

```
<connectionStrings>
  <add name="TravelRequest" connectionString=
    "Data Source=.\SQLEXPRESS;AttachDbFilename=C:\...\TravelRequest.mdf;
    Integrated Security=True;User Instance=True"
    providerName="System.Data.SqlClient" />
</connectionStrings>
```

Data Access Custom Activities

You need to create two more custom code activities. These activities wrap the calls to add an item to the travel request queue and to mark the activity complete (and possibly approved). The following steps walk you through this process:

1. Start with the TravelRequestService project. Queue a travel request to the database by adding a new Code Activity to your workflow project. Name this activity **TravelRequestQueueAddActivity.cs**.

2. Add two input parameters to the activity. The first, TravelRequest, should take the full travel request message. Recall this type was defined as the DataContract in the data access project. The second, ManagerId, should be a string used for passing the user's manager to the request.

3. The Execute method should call Save on the data access library after setting the appropriate parameters.

   Listing 22.9 shows an example of this code.

LISTING 22.9   The TravelRequestQueueAddActivity Custom Activity

```
using System;
using System.Collections.Generic;
using System.Linq;
using System.Text;
using System.Activities;
using TravelDataLib;
```

```
namespace TravelRequestService
{

    public sealed class TraveRequestQueueAddActivity : CodeActivity
    {
        //sends the travel request to the manager's queue (database)

        public InArgument<TravelRequestMsg> TravelRequest { get; set; }
        public InArgument<string> ManagerId { get; set; }

        protected override void Execute(CodeActivityContext context)
        {
            //get the travel request from the context
            TravelRequestMsg tRequest = context.GetValue(this.TravelRequest);

            //set workflow id for correlation
            tRequest.WorkflowInstanceId = context.WorkflowInstanceId.ToString();

            //set the approval manager to be notified
            tRequest.ApprovalManagerId = context.GetValue(this.ManagerId);

            //save the travel request
            TravelRequestDataAccess.Save(tRequest);


        }
    }
}
```

4. Indicate travel request is complete by adding a new Code Activity to your workflow project. Name this activity **CompleteTravelRequest.cs**.

5. Add three input parameters to the activity. The first, `TravelRequest`, should take the full travel request message. The second, `ManagerId`, should be a string used for passing the ID of the manager doing the approval. The third, `IsApproved`, is used to indicate whether the request has been approved.

6. The `Execute` method should call `Complete` on the data access library after setting the appropriate parameters.

Listing 22.10 shows an example of this code.

LISTING 22.10   The `CompleteTravelRequest` Custom Activity

```
using System;
using System.Collections.Generic;
using System.Linq;
```

```
using System.Text;
using System.Activities;
using TravelDataLib;

namespace TravelRequestService
{

  public sealed class CompleteTravelRequest : CodeActivity
  {

    //update the travel request with approval information

    public InArgument<TravelRequestMsg> TravelRequest { get; set; }
    public InArgument<string> ManagerId { get; set; }
    public InArgument<bool> IsApproved { get; set; }

    protected override void Execute(CodeActivityContext context)
    {
      //get the travel request from the context
      TravelRequestMsg tRequest = context.GetValue(this.TravelRequest);

      //set the approval manager doing the approval
      tRequest.ApprovalManagerId = context.GetValue(this.ManagerId);

      //set the approval status
      tRequest.IsApproved = context.GetValue(this.IsApproved);

      //save the travel request
      TravelRequestDataAccess.Complete(tRequest);
    }
  }
}
```

Design the Workflow

You are finally ready to create the actual workflow. The following steps walk you through this process:

1. Start by renaming your workflow inside the TravelRequestService project to **RequestTravel.xamlx**.

   Also, open the workflow and change the Name and Configuration name inside the Properties window to **RequestTravel**.

2. Delete the sequence that is shown by default.

3. Add a new sequence to the workflow. Set the Display name to **Travel Request Approval Sequence**.

4. Define variables by clicking the Variables tab at the bottom of the designer to define variables to be used by the workflow, including `requiresApproval` (Boolean), `isUserManager` (Boolean), `isApproved` (Boolean), and `managerUserId` (string). Make sure that your variables are all scoped at the sequence level.

You also need to add a variable to hold the inbound message (travel request). To do so, add a variable called `travelRequestMsg`. In the Variable type drop-down, select Browse for Types to launch the Browse and Select a .Net Type dialog box. In the Type Name box, enter **Travel**. This filters the list accordingly. Select the TravelRequestMsg type (from the referenced data access project).

Finally, add a variable called `processCorrelationHandle`, which is used for message correlation to make sure the approval message is correlated to the right workflow instance. Follow the steps from before to set this variable type to `System.ServiceModel.Activities.CorrelationHandle`.

Your variables should look similar to those shown in Figure 22.28.

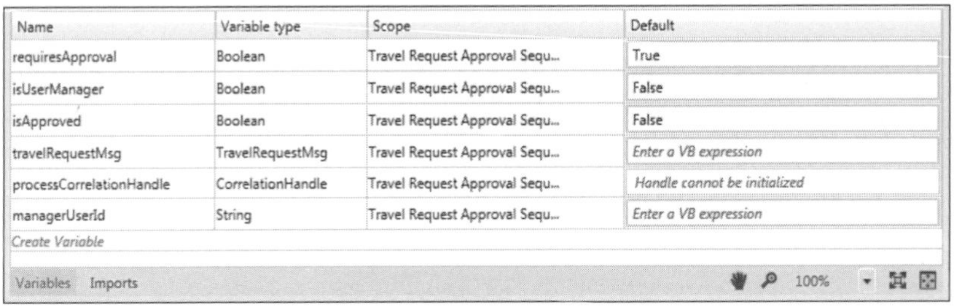

Name	Variable type	Scope	Default
requiresApproval	Boolean	Travel Request Approval Sequ...	True
isUserManager	Boolean	Travel Request Approval Sequ...	False
isApproved	Boolean	Travel Request Approval Sequ...	False
travelRequestMsg	TravelRequestMsg	Travel Request Approval Sequ...	Enter a VB expression
processCorrelationHandle	CorrelationHandle	Travel Request Approval Sequ...	Handle cannot be initialized
managerUserId	String	Travel Request Approval Sequ...	Enter a VB expression
Create Variable			

| Variables | Imports | | | | | 100% | ▾ |

FIGURE 22.28   The travel request workflow variables.

5. Define the message received by adding a `Receive` activity to the top of the `Sequence`. This activity serves to define the WCF service that your workflow exposes to the client (travel request user interface).

6. Set the OperationName to **ProcessTravelRequest**. This defines the actual service method name.

7. Click the Content link on the Receive activity to bring up the Content Definition window. Here you define the message that this service expects from clients. Click Message. In the Message data text box, type the variable name **travelRequestMsg** to indicate that the inbound message should be mapped to this variable. Under Message type, select the TravelDataLib.TravelRequestMsg type. Figure 22.29 shows an example.

8. *Important*: Select the Receive Request activity in the designer and view its properties. Set the `CanCreateInstance` to `true` (check the box). This indicates that this shape can create an instance of the workflow. If you miss this step, your workflow never processes.

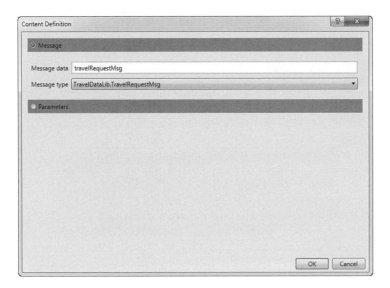

FIGURE 22.29   Configure the inbound message to the workflow.

9. The last step to configure the `Receive` activity is to initialize message correlation. You must complete this step; otherwise, when your workflow waits for an approval and then an approval is sent, the runtime engine does not know for which workflow the message is meant.

From the Properties dialog box, click the ellipsis button on the CorrelationInitializers property.

On the left side of the Add Correlation Initializers dialog box, click Add Initializer. Enter the variable name **processCorrelationHandle**. On the XPath side of the dialog box, select Query Correlation Initializer and set the key1 to Id:String using the drop-down that shows the message items from the travel request data contract. You use the ID because it is unique to each travel request; and, in this example, we are using content-based correlation (where ID is part of the message content).

Figure 22.30 shows an example of setting this correlation handler.

10. Take a look at the Toolbox. You should see a few new sections that contain the custom activities you have created thus far. If you don't see them, build the solution and take a look again. In the new section, UserLookupActivityLib, grab the `GetUsersManagerActivity` and drag it to the `Sequence` under the `Receive` activity. This is used to look up the user's manager information.

Use the Properties window to set the user to lookup (UserId) to `travelRequestMsg.RequesterId`. Set the Result property (the manager's ID) to the variable `managerUserId`.

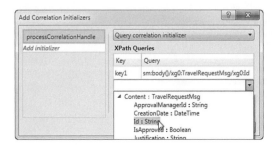

FIGURE 22.30   Initialize the content-based correlation to be used to correlate approval messages.

11. Again from the Toolbox, under the section TravelRequestService, select and drag the `TravelRequestQueueAddActivity` to the `Sequence` under the `GetUsersManagerActivity`. Recall this activity logs the request to the database.

Use the Properties window to set the `ManagerId` input parameter to the variable `managerUserId` and `TravelRequest` to the `travelRequestMsg` variable.

12. From the Toolbox, drag an `IsManagerActivity` from the `UserLookupActivityLib` area to the workflow. Place it under the `TravelRequestQueueAddActivity`.

Use the Properties pane to set `IsManager` to the `isUserManager` variable and `UserId` to travelRequestMsg.RequesterId.

Your workflow should now look similar to Figure 22.31.

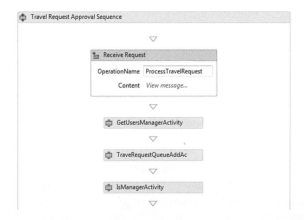

FIGURE 22.31   The first few steps in the travel request workflow.

13. The next step is to use the workflow activities to determine whether the given request requires an approval. For this logic, you use a Flowchart activity. Drag it onto the `Sequence` under the `IsManagerActivity`. You can set the `DisplayName` to **"Requires Approval?"**.

Notice that you can double-click this activity in its collapsed state to focus just on it. You use the navigation links at the top of the workflow to navigate back to the other layers of the workflow. Of course, you can expand all activities on the same window too.

The logic for the flowchart uses a `Decision` to check whether the request is more than a $1,000. If so, it uses an `Assign` to indicate `requiresApproval=True`. If not, you add another `Decision` to check `isUserManager`. If so, no approval is required (`requiresApproval=False`); otherwise, an approval is required.

Figure 22.32 shows this flowchart in the designer.

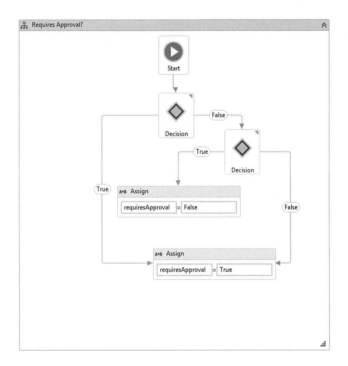

FIGURE 22.32   You can use a Flowchart activity to model the basic business logic of the workflow.

14. Add an `If` activity under the `Flowchart` in the `Sequence`. Set the `DisplayName` of this activity to `If Approval Is Required`.

15. Set the `If` `Condition` property to the `requiresApproval` variable.

16. Add a `Receive` activity to the `Then` side of the `If` condition. Set the `OperationName` to `ReceiveManagerApproval`. This will become the name of the service method your workflow exposes for handling manager approvals.

Use the Properties window to set the `ServiceContractName` property to `IRequestTravelService`.

17. Click the Define (or View parameter) link on the Receive activity (next to the Content option in the Receive designer). Inside the Content Definition window, set two parameters that you expect to receive from callers to this service: `travelRequestId`, String (for message correlation), and `isApproved`, Boolean. Be sure to assign the `isApproved` parameter to the `isApproved` variable on the workflow. Figure 22.33 shows an example.

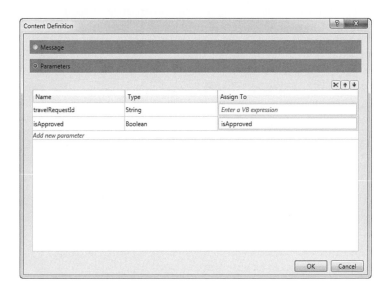

FIGURE 22.33   Set parameters for the `If Approval Is Required` Receive operation.

18. The `Receive` activity is exposed as a separate service method of your activity. Therefore, it requires message correlation. Use the Properties window to set `CorrelatesWith` to `processCorrelationHandle`. Then click the ellipsis button on CorrelatesOn. Make sure that you set key1 to the parameter `travelRequestId`. Figure 22.34 shows an example of setting this correlation query parameter. Notice that you select `travelRequestId` and the tool takes care of the rest.

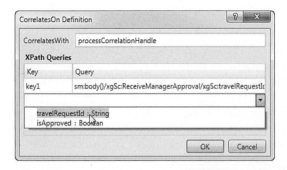

FIGURE 22.34   Set the `travelRequestId` parameter as the content-correlation query.

19. Inside the `Else` condition of `If Approval Is Required`, add an `Assign` activity. Set the variable `isApproved` to `True`. Recall that the else condition executes if the travel request does not require approval (under $1,000 and the user is a manager). Figure 22.35 shows the finished `If` activity.

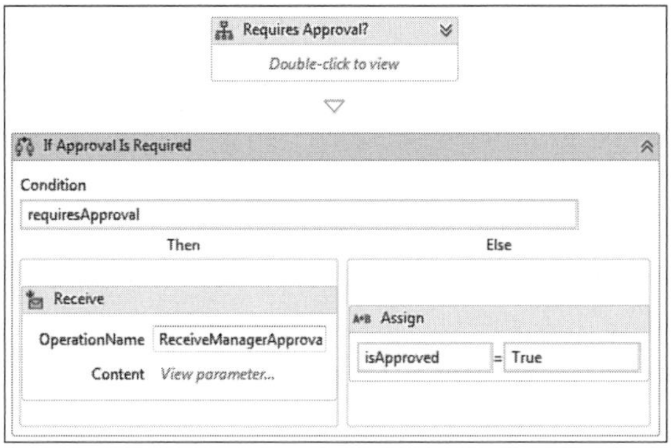

FIGURE 22.35   The completed `If Approval Is Required` If activity.

20. Add a final `If` activity to the bottom of the `Sequence`. This activity checks to see whether the request was approved or if approval is not required (`Condition: (isApproved) Or (requiresApproval = False)`). If you are good to book the travel, you need to send a message to the reservation system.

Recall that you set a reference earlier to the vendor reservation WCF service. When you did, Visual Studio was kind enough to generate a custom activity to call the `BookTravel` service method. It should be on the Toolbox (if not, rebuild your solution). Drag it to the `Then` area of the `If` condition. Use the Properties window to set the `reservationId` parameter to `travelRequestMsg.VendorReservationId`.

You can leave the `Else` section blank. Figure 22.36 shows an example of this `If` activity and the Properties window settings for `BookTravel`.

FIGURE 22.36   The If activity for booking travel (or not).

21. Indicate that the workflow has completed. Drag the custom `CompleteTravelRequest` code activity (you created this earlier) from the Toolbox to the last step in the `Sequence`. Configure the input parameters `IsApproved`, `ManagerId`, and `TravelRequest` accordingly.

Figure 22.37 shows the final workflow. (Most shapes are collapsed.)

FIGURE 22.37   The final workflow Sequence activity (with all activities collapsed).

Adding the Workflow Persistence Service

Workflows disappear if the memory is cleared (a process ends, the machine reboots). If you want them to persist, especially for long-running workflows, you must define a persistence store.

Create the Store   WF ships with a default SQL Server persistence store for you to use. It also defines how you can create and configure other persistence stores. In this example, we used the SQL Server persistence store.

To get started, you need a copy of SQL Server that you can use. We are using SQL Express in this example.

> **NOTE**
>
> To work with SQL Express, you might want to download the SQL Server Management Studio Express. It enables you to create SQL Express databases and run scripts. The fastest way we have found to install this locally is to use the Microsoft Web Platform installer and select it as an option. You can find this at http://www.microsoft.com/web/downloads/platform.aspx.

The first step is to make sure you have this store installed and running. To do so, you need to create the database. You can call the database InstanceStore (or similar). You typically use a form of SQL Server Management Studio to create your database. You then run scripts in your database to set up the schema and logic. These scripts can be found in the directory (Windows 7/Vista):

```
C:\Windows\Microsoft.NET\Framework\v4.0.30319\SQL\en
```

You need to use two scripts to install the schema for your persistence store: SqlWorkflowInstanceStoreSchema.sql and SqlWorkflowInstanceStoreLogic.sql. These set up the instance store for SQL server.

Communicate with the Store   You can communicate with the persistence store in multiple ways. You can create your own host application and use the workflow persistence services to communicate directly with a persistence store. This offers you a fine-grained approach to working with persistence.

For this example, however, the workflow is being hosted by WCF. This is great candidate to be hosted by WAS or IIS. In this case, you can simply configure the persistence store using the config file. When your workflow goes idle, it is automatically persisted for later use by the WF runtime engine. You can also use the Persist activity (and properties of other activities) to force a persist at key points in your workflow.

To configure persistence, open the Web.config file of the TravelRequestService. You then define a connection string as a service behavior called `sqlWorkflowInstanceStore`. The following shows an example. In this case, the instance store is installed on SQL Express:

```
<behaviors>
  <serviceBehaviors>
    <behavior>
      <sqlWorkflowInstanceStore connectionString=
        "Data Source=.\SQLExpress;Initial Catalog=InstanceStore;Integrated Security
        R=True;Asynchronous Processing=True"
        instanceEncodingOption="GZip" instanceCompletionAction="DeleteAll"
        instanceLockedExceptionAction="BasicRetry" hostLockRenewalPeriod="00:00:30"
runnableInstancesDetectionPeriod="00:00:10"></sqlWorkflowInstanceStore>
```

Creating the Client Application (Request and Approval Forms)

In this final step, you create a user interface for interacting with the workflow service.

Site Housekeeping

Use the following steps to complete the basic housekeeping tasks required to get things started:

1. Open the TravelManagerWeb website in Solution Explorer.

   Add a Service Reference to the TravelRequestService. (Right-click the project and select Add Service Reference.) Navigate to RequestTravel.xamlx or select Discover from the Add Service Reference dialog box. Name this reference **TravelRequestSvc**. This serves as the WCF proxy to your workflow.

2. Add a regular project reference to the TravelDataLib. You need this to define the message data contract to send to the travel request service.

3. Add new pages called NewRequest.aspx and PendingRequest.aspx. In the sample code, we use the default master page from the Web Site template. Therefore, make sure you select the Web Form Using Master Page Item template when creating these pages.

4. Open Site.Master. Change the menu items to include Home, New Request, and Pending Requests. The following shows this markup:

```
<div class="clear hideSkiplink">
    <asp:Menu ID="NavigationMenu" runat="server" CssClass="menu"
      EnableViewState="false" IncludeStyleBlock="false"
       ROrientation="Horizontal">
        <Items>
            <asp:MenuItem NavigateUrl="~/Default.aspx" Text="Home"/>
            <asp:MenuItem NavigateUrl="~/NewRequest.aspx" Text="New Request"/>
            <asp:MenuItem NavigateUrl="~/PendingRequests.aspx"
              Text="Pending Requests"/>
        </Items>
    </asp:Menu>
</div>
```

Create the New Travel Request Page

Follow these steps to create the new travel request page:

1. Open the NewRequest.aspx page.

2. Create the layout for the travel request. Figure 22.38 shows the layout for the new travel request web page. You can see this is pretty standard. There are two panels. The second panel (bottom) is hidden until after the request is sent. The top panel then is hidden and the bottom panel is shown.

3. The next step is to wire up the code-behind for the new travel request. In this case, you simulate working with the vendor service to get the reservation ID. You do so by setting the reservation ID inside the Page_Load event.

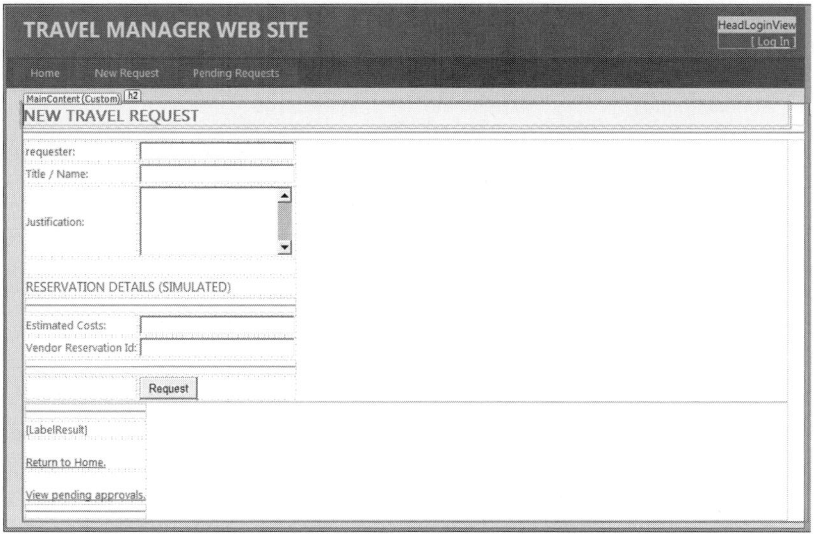

FIGURE 22.38   The new travel request web page.

4. Inside the click event for the request button, you create the data contract to be passed to the workflow. You then call the WCF proxy that was generated when you added a service reference. Finally, you call the `ProcessTravelRequest` method. (Remember, this was the `OperationName` set to the Receive activity of the workflow.)

Listing 22.11 shows an example of this code.

LISTING 22.11   The NewRequest.aspx.cs Code-Behind Class

```
using System;
using System.Collections.Generic;
using System.Linq;
using System.Web;
using System.Web.UI;
using System.Web.UI.WebControls;
using TravelDataLib;

namespace TravelManagerWeb
{
  public partial class NewRequest : System.Web.UI.Page
  {
    protected void Page_Load(object sender, EventArgs e)
    {
      if (!IsPostBack)
      {
        //init reservation
        TextBoxResId.Text = Guid.NewGuid().ToString();
```

```csharp
        }
    }

    protected void ButtonRequest_Click(object sender, EventArgs e)
    {
      //TODO: add validation to form and object

      //create a travel request object to be passed to the workflow
      TravelRequestMsg tRequest = new TravelRequestMsg()
      {
        CreationDate = DateTime.Now,
        Id = Guid.NewGuid().ToString(),
        Justification = TextBoxJust.Text,
        Name = TextBoxName.Text,
        RequesterId = TextBoxrequester.Text,
        TravelEstimate = double.Parse(TextBoxCost.Text),
        VendorReservationId = TextBoxResId.Text,
        ApprovalManagerId = "Unknown",
        IsApproved = false,
        WorkflowInstanceId = "TBD"
      };

      //create the workflow service client object
      TravelRequestSvc.RequestTravelClient client =
        new TravelRequestSvc.RequestTravelClient();

      //start the workflow (pass the request)
      client.ProcessTravelRequest(tRequest);
      client.Close();

      //return to home
      PanelRequest.Visible = false;
      LabelResult.Text = "Travel request sent!";
      PanelResult.Visible = true;

    }
  }
}
```

Create the Pending Requests Page

To create the pending requests page, complete the following steps:

1. Open the PendingRequests.aspx page.

2. Define two panels for the page. One shows the approvals pending queue. The other shows the result of a user action (and should thus be hidden to start).

3. Add a GridView control to the top panel.

4. Bind a GridView control to the Request table. You can do so walking through a wizard. You first select the Choose Data Source drop-down from the Grid View Tasks smart link. In the drop-down, select New Data Source. This walks you through a wizard that lets you create a SqlDataSource control linked to the Request table. It also adds a connection string to the Web.config file and ultimately binds the Request table to the GridView control.

Use the GridView smart tag to select, Enable Selection. In this case, users can select a single row in the GridView. When they click the Approve or Reject buttons, you determine their selection and process accordingly.

5. Add three buttons to the top of the form: Approve Selected Item, Reject Selected Item, and Refresh.

Your form should look similar to that shown in Figure 22.39.

Add event handlers to each button.

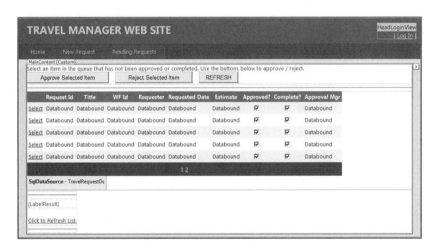

FIGURE 22.39   The new travel request web page.

6. Inside the code-behind, create a `ProcessApproval` method that takes an `isApproved` and `message` parameter. Add code to the Approve and Reject buttons to call this method.

7. Inside the `ProcessApproval` method, get the ID (GUID) of the selected travel request to use for message correlation. Then, call the service client to reach back out to your workflow with an approval. Remember, this is the call to `ReceiveManagerApproval`.

Listing 22.12 shows what your code-behind should look like.

LISTING 22.12   The PendingRequests.aspx.cs Code-Behind Class

```csharp
using System;
using System.Collections.Generic;
using System.Linq;
using System.Web;
using System.Web.UI;
using System.Web.UI.WebControls;

namespace TravelManagerWeb
{
  public partial class PendingRequests : System.Web.UI.Page
  {
    protected void Page_Load(object sender, EventArgs e)
    {
    }

    protected void ButtonApprove_Click(object sender, EventArgs e)
    {
      ProcessApproval(true, "Item approved!");
    }

    protected void ButtonReject_Click(object sender, EventArgs e)
    {
      ProcessApproval(true, "Item rejected!");
    }


    protected void ProcessApproval(bool isApproved, string message)
    {
      //get travel id fo the selected row
      string travelId = this.GridView1.SelectedRow.Cells[1].Text;

      //TODO: validate if already approved or completed

      //pass to the approval receive activity for correlation
      TravelRequestSvc.RequestTravelServiceClient client =
        new TravelRequestSvc.RequestTravelServiceClient();

      //start the workflow (pass the request)
      client.ReceiveManagerApproval(travelId, isApproved);
      client.Close();

      ShowResult(message);
    }
```

```
    private void ShowResult(string message)
    {
      PanelList.Visible = false;
      LabelResult.Text = message;
      PanelComplete.Visible = true;
    }

    protected void ButtonRefresh_Click(object sender, EventArgs e)
    {
      Response.Redirect("PendingRequests.aspx");
    }

  }
}
```

Running the Travel Request Workflow Application

You are nearly ready to run the application. First, however, you need to tell Visual Studio that you want to launch three projects when you click the Run button. This ensures that the services are available to call.

To do so, right-click the solution and select Properties to launch the property pages for the solution, as shown in Figure 22.40. Select the Multiple Startup Projects option. Indicate an Action of 'Start' for TravelRequestService, VendorReservationService, and TravelManagerWeb.

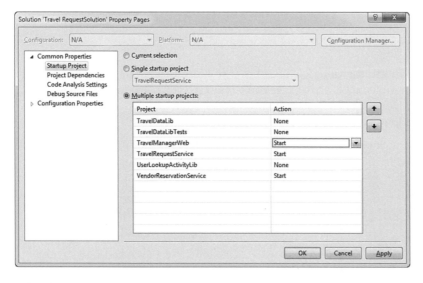

FIGURE 22.40   Set the solution to launch three projects at startup.

You are now ready to run the application! Click the Run button in Visual Studio. Give everything a minute to initialize.

Navigate to the NewRequest.aspx page from the Default.aspx page. Enter some basic travel request details, as shown in Figure 22.41, and click Request.

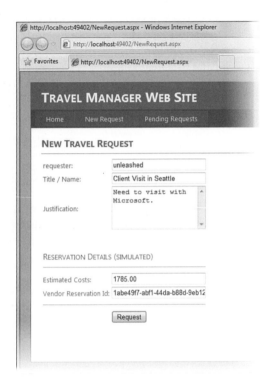

FIGURE 22.41   A request for travel is posted to the workflow.

This sends your request to the workflow and shows you a confirmation in the web page. Navigate to the PendingRequests.aspx page. You should see your new request listed. Remember, this was written to the database through a custom activity added to the workflow. Figure 22.42 shows an example.

Select your pending travel request (by clicking the Select link on the left of the grid). Click the Approve Selected Item button. On the confirmation page, select to refresh the grid. You should see your request as approved and completed. Note that you might have to click the Refresh button a couple of times, especially if you are pulling from persistence after letting the page site a minute or two. Figure 22.43 shows an example.

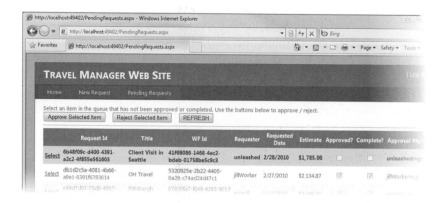

FIGURE 22.42   The request sits in the queue until being selected and approved.

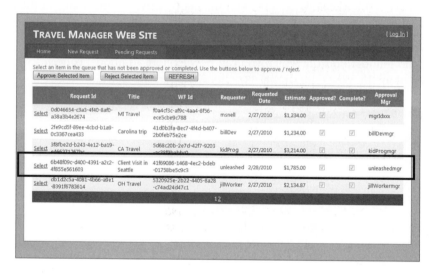

FIGURE 22.43   Request has been approved (and queue re-sorted).

Next Steps

This was a rather lengthy example. However, it should have answered the most pressing questions about building and hosting workflows. Of course, there are still a number of items left unfinished. We will do our best to tackle these issues and post blog entries and videos at http://visualstudiounleashed.com/workflow. These unfinished items include the following:

▶ Add support for the workflow tracking service

▶ Add the ability to cancel the request

▶ Add user input validation throughout

▶ Add error handling

▶ Add the concept of actua, logged-in users, and managers

▶ Make the vendor reservation process more robust

Summary

This chapter presented the fundamental concepts for building applications that work with Windows Workflow Foundation. These included the components of all workflow applications: client, host, and workflow. A client is any application that calls into a host to work with a workflow instance. A workflow is a set of steps that solve a business problem. Your workflow is compiled and hosted inside a host application. The host application manages calls between the client and the workflow runtime.

This chapter also covered the workflow designer and the many activities, including all the built-in activities used for creating workflows. (You also learned how to create your own custom activities.)

The chapter is a solid foundation from which you can now explore additional concepts and services provided by the WF.

CHAPTER 23

Developing Office Business Applications

Microsoft Office is the well-known, best-selling suite of information worker productivity applications. We are all familiar with the word processing, spreadsheet, email, and form features provided by Microsoft Word, Microsoft Excel, Microsoft Outlook, and Microsoft InfoPath. But these applications are capable of more than just their stock features: They are a development platform unto themselves, a platform that can be extended and customized to build out line-of-business applications that leverage and build on the best-of-breed features offered by each application.

For instance, a purchase-order application could leverage the end user's familiarity with Microsoft Word to allow for data entry using a Word form, and reports and charts can be generated against purchase-order history using Excel.

In the past, the primary tool for extending Microsoft Office applications has been Visual Basic for Applications (VBA). With VBA, developers and even end users could create a broad range of solutions from simple macros to more complicated features that implement business logic and access data stored in a database. VBA offers a simple "on ramp" for accessing the object models exposed by every application in the extended suite of Microsoft Office: Project, Word, Outlook, InfoPath, PowerPoint, Publisher, and so on.

But starting with the first release of the Visual Studio Tools for Office (VSTO), developers now have a robust way to create Office solutions in managed code (Visual Basic and Visual C#) from directly within Visual Studio.

Visual Studio 2010 was released with the fourth generation of VSTO, and it enabled you to target both Microsoft

Office 2007 and Microsoft Office 2010 applications. And finally, Visual Studio 2012 has continued its support for Office 2010 application development. The topic of using VSTO for Office development is a large topic that has entire books devoted to it; in this chapter, we hope to simply introduce the concepts involved with VSTO and show how the Visual Studio Office project types can be used to quickly create powerful applications that leverage the existing power of Word, Excel, and Outlook. Subjects we cover include these:

▶ Creating custom actions panes

▶ Creating custom task panes

▶ Customizing the Office ribbon

We specifically do not attempt to cover the object automation models for any of the Office applications, beyond the minimum necessary to understand the preceding concepts. For a more complete treatment of Office as a development platform, we recommend the VSTO team blog at http://blogs.msdn.com/b/vsto/, the book *Visual Studio Tools for Office 2007: VSTO for Excel, Word and Outlook,* by Eric Carter and Eric Lippert (Addison-Wesley Professional, 2009), and, of course, the various MSDN sections that cover VSTO.

Let's start with a quick run-through of the various Office features that are available for customization.

An Overview of Office Extension Features

Because each Office application has a unique and specialized function, it should come as no surprise that the ways in which you can customize an Office application depend on which Office application we are specifically talking about. Although they all share a common, general layout for their user interface, there are intricacies involved with each of them that dictate different capabilities from within VSTO.

For instance, both Excel and Word deal with files as their central work piece, whereas Outlook deals with emails (which might be stored locally or on a server or both). So, we can apply document-level extensions to Excel and Word, but this is not possible in Outlook. Conversely, the Outlook object model supports the concept of form regions, a concept absent in Excel and Word.

Office Features

Table 23.1 provides a matrix of the various features available for customization or extension within each Office application. We discuss each of these in the next section.

TABLE 23.1   Microsoft Office Extension Points

Application	Feature
Microsoft Excel 2010	Actions pane
	Task pane
	Data cache
	Ribbon
	Smart tags
Microsoft InfoPath 2010	Task pane
Microsoft Outlook 2010	Task pane
	Outlook form regions
Microsoft PowerPoint 2010	Task pane
Microsoft Word 2010	Actions pane
	Task pane
	Data cache
	Ribbon
	Smart tags

Some of these features are document-level features, and others are application-level features. The difference between the two is largely one of scope. Document-level customizations are attached to, and live with, a specific document, whether a Word .doc/.docx file or an Excel spreadsheet file. In contrast, application-level features are more global in reach and are implemented as add-ins to a specific Office application in exactly the same way that add-ins are created and implemented for Visual Studio itself (see Chapter 14, "Writing Add-Ins and Wizards").

We look at the mechanics of how document-level and application-level solutions are differentiated in just a bit when we overview the VSTO project types. First, let's examine the features mentioned in Table 23.1. Understanding these features is key to determining how you might leverage Office using VSTO in your solutions.

Task Panes and Actions Panes

Task panes in Office are used to expose commands and features that are central to the task at hand without disrupting the user from focusing on the currently loaded document. See Figure 23.1 for a screenshot of a Microsoft Word 2010 task pane for merging form letters. This task pane is able to guide the user through a series of steps while still allowing the loaded letter document to be visible. Task panes exist at the application level. Actions panes, in contrast, are a type of task pane implemented at the document level.

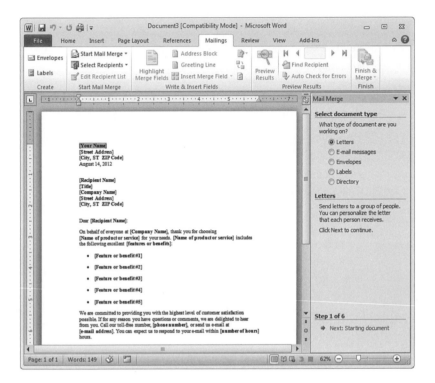

FIGURE 23.1 A Microsoft Word 2010 actions pane.

Data Cache

A data cache refers to the capability of VSTO to store data locally within a document. This cache is also sometimes referred to as a data island. Because VSTO can read and write to the data cache, it is a useful tool for storing information needed by your Office add-in or for shadowing data that resides in a database but is needed in certain disconnected scenarios.

Ribbon

The ribbon is a user interface element that premiered with Microsoft Office 2007. It represents a new way to present features to users without using the traditional toolbars and menus. Commands in the ribbon are grouped by task category, and within each task category commands are visually grouped with other similar commands. So with Word, for instance, we have a Review tab that consolidates all the commands related to document review. Because the ribbon makes the most-used commands immediately visible and available, the ribbon attempts to avoid the problems caused by the menu bar paradigm in which items could be grouped and nested several layers deep (and thus, out of sight) within the menu system.

The tabs of the ribbon and the command groupings within a tab are free to change from application to application depending on the context. Figure 23.2 compares the ribbon home tab for Word and PowerPoint.

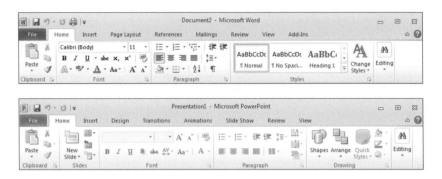

FIGURE 23.2   The Microsoft PowerPoint 2010 and Word 2010 ribbons.

Smart Tags

Smart tags in Office function in a similar way to the smart tags present in the Visual Studio IDE. (See Chapter 8, "Working with Visual Studio's Productivity Aids," to refresh your memory.) Word can recognize various pieces of content as it is typed into a document, such as names, dates, financial symbols, and telephone numbers. When one of these items is recognized, one or more commands may be added to a context menu that then enables you to interact with that data. For example, you might want to add someone's telephone number to your contact list. This action is easily executed from the Additional Actions context menu. You first highlight the phone number with the document, and then right-click the selection. From there, under the Additional Actions menu, you can choose to add the number to your contact list (see Figure 23.3).

With VSTO, you can create your own smart tag recognizers and commands associated with them.

> **NOTE**
>
> With Office 2007, data that was recognized by a smart tag was visually highlighted for you with a dotted, purple underline. This functionality has been deprecated starting with Office 2010. Now, you must manually select the text, and check for a smart tag action under the context menu's Additional Actions.

Visual Studio Office Project Types

In general, each Office application has a project type or family of project types available. Figure 23.4 shows the various project types available by expanding first your chosen language node and then the Office node within the New Project dialog box.

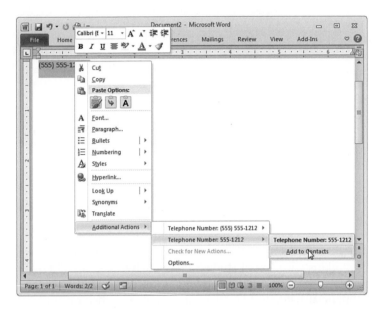

FIGURE 23.3   The Additional Actions menu in Microsoft Word 2010.

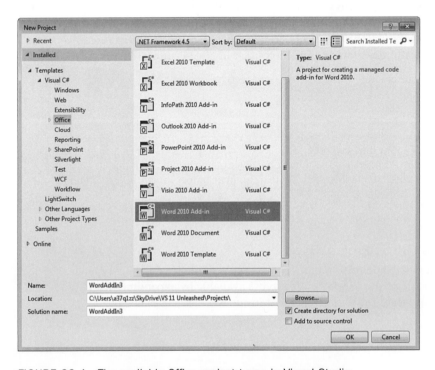

FIGURE 23.4   The available Office project types in Visual Studio.

NOTE

Visual Studio 2012 does not include project templates that enable you to target Office 2007; only Office 2010 templates are provided out of the box.

For Word and Excel, you see three project types each: an add-in template and two document-level templates. The document-level templates enable you to target either document files (for Word, this is referred to as the Word 2010 Document project template, and for Excel, this is referred to as the Excel 2010 Workbook project template) or Office template files (for example, you can customize a Word template).

As previously discussed, the difference between an application-level add-in and a document extension is one of scope: When you compile a VSTO project, just as with every other project type in Visual Studio, a managed code assembly is generated. That assembly can be attached or linked to an Office application (for example, Word or Excel), or to an Office document (for example, a .doc/.docx file or a .xls/.xlsx file). Document-level assemblies are loaded only when the document is loaded and are limited in scope to the document. Application-level add-ins are loaded during application startup (although this can be controlled by the user) and are more global in their reach.

NOTE

Although Visual Studio fully supports Microsoft Office projects right out of the box (at least with the Visual Studio Professional version), you also obviously need to have a copy of Microsoft Office and potentially various other components installed on your computer. See the MSDN article "How to: Install Visual Studio Tools for Office" for an in-depth look at VSTO requirements.

Creating an Office Add-In

To start creating your own Office add-in, create a new project in Visual Studio by selecting any of the Office add-in project types. Figure 23.5 shows the basic project structure created with a Word add-in project. We have a single code-file that establishes the startup entry point for the add-in, and provides us with the namespaces we need in order to access the Word automation object model.

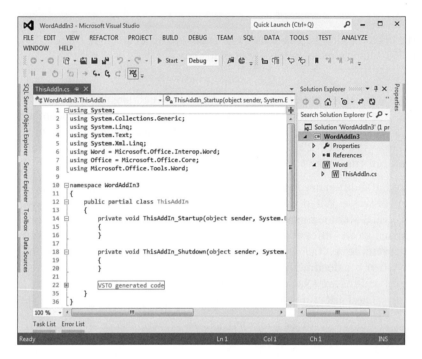

FIGURE 23.5   A Microsoft Word 2010 add-in project.

There isn't anything terribly compelling about the developer experience so far. But VSTO
provides a powerful set of visual designers you can use to craft your Office solution just
as you would any other project in Visual Studio. To access these, we need to add a project
item that has an associated designer. To start, let's see how to create a customized ribbon.

Customizing the Ribbon

Ribbon support within a VSTO project is enabled by adding a ribbon project item to the
project. Right-click the project within Solution Explorer and select Add New Item. In the
Add New Item dialog box (see Figure 23.6), you see two different ribbon templates available for selection: Ribbon (Visual Designer) and Ribbon (XML). As their names suggest, the
Visual Designer template provides you with a WYSIWYG design surface for creating your
ribbon customizations. Because this design surface can't be used to build certain types of
more advanced ribbon features, the Ribbon (XML) item template is provided to enable
you to handcraft ribbon features in XML. You need to use the Ribbon (XML) item if you
want to do any of the following:

▶ Add a built-in (as opposed to custom) group to a custom tab

▶ Add a built-in control to a custom group

▶ Customize the event handlers for any of the built-in controls

▶ Add or remove items from the Quick Access toolbar

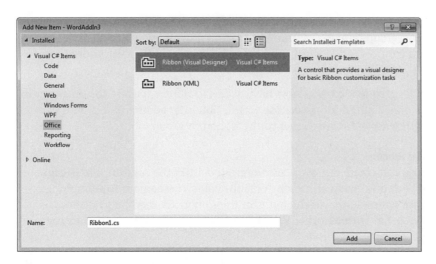

FIGURE 23.6   Office project item templates.

For our purposes, let's select the Ribbon (Visual Designer) item and add it to our project. This adds the Ribbon1.cs file to our project. In a fashion similar to Windows Forms, this file has a designer and a code-behind file attached to it.

The design surface you are presented with is an exact replica of an empty ribbon (see Figure 23.7).

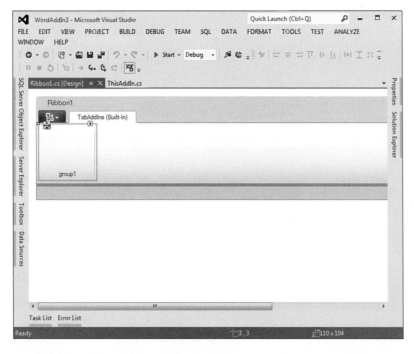

FIGURE 23.7   The ribbon design surface.

Ribbons are composed of several elements: Tabs are used to provide the high-level task grouping of features, groups are used within each tab to provide more granular sectioning of the features, and controls reside within the groups to build out the custom user interface for the add-in.

With the Ribbon Designer loaded, you now have access to ribbon-specific controls over in the Toolbox (see Figure 23.8). Adding controls to the ribbon or adding new groups is as simple as dragging the desired control over to the ribbon or group tab.

Adding Items to the Ribbon

To demonstrate, you can create our own custom group within the Add-Ins tab. Because you are presented with one group already by default, you can rename it to something more appropriate for your add-in. All the items in the ribbon are modified via the Properties window, just as with all other Visual Studio project types. We just click the group, and then set its label property.

Groups act as containers on the design surface, enabling us to now drag and drop a button into the group. Figure 23.9 shows the beginnings of a custom ribbon for a purchasing system integration add-in. To duplicate this, drag three buttons into the existing group on the ribbon, change their ControlSize property to RibbonControlSizeLarge, set their label properties to the appropriate text you want displayed on the button, and add some images of your choosing to the buttons by setting the Image property.

FIGURE 23.8   Office ribbon controls in the IDE toolbox.

FIGURE 23.9   Creating a custom Office ribbon.

TIP

The images used in this example were taken from the Visual Studio 2012 Image Library, but there is actually a cool way to reuse any of the icons that you see within Office. First, download the Icons Gallery add-in from the Microsoft Download Center (search for "Office 2010: Icons Gallery"). This download places a Word document file on your drive. Open the file, and then click the File tab at the top of the ribbon. Down the column on the left, you should see two entries labeled ImageMso 0 and ImageMso 1. Click either of these to see the gallery of icons.

Each icon has an accompanying label, a string that you can plug directly into a ribbon button's OfficeImageId property. As long as an image isn't already set for the button, this causes the identified Office icon to be used. This is a real boon for UI design, given the hundreds and hundreds of high-quality icons already available within Office. The image doesn't show in design time, but does display correctly at runtime.

Adding more groups to your ribbon involves more of the same drag-and-drop action from the Toolbox. You can change the order of the groups in the ribbon by selecting and then dragging a group to the left or right of any other existing groups.

NOTE

Notice that there is already a default tab implemented in the ribbon called TabAddIns (Built-In). When you're creating a ribbon for your add-in, its groups are automatically displayed under the Add-Ins tab within the target Office application. If you want to add items to one of the other default tabs in the Office application, or create your own tab, you have to use the Ribbon (XML) project item, and not the Ribbon Designer, to achieve that level of customization.

Handling Ribbon Control Events

Handling the events for our buttons is easy. Again, the idea behind VSTO is to provide Office customization capabilities using the same development paradigms already present in Visual Studio. This means that you can double-click a button to have the IDE automatically create and wire up an event-handler routine, ready to accept whatever code we need to write to implement the button's behavior.

To test this out, let's add the following to the Replace PO button:

```
private void buttonReplacePO_Click(object sender,
   RibbonControlEventArgs e)
{
   MessageBox.Show("buttonReplacePO_Click fired!");
}
```

If you run the project now by pressing F5, Word automatically launches; you can see your ribbon customizations by clicking the Add-Ins tab. Clicking the Replace PO button yields the results shown in Figure 23.10.

Customizing the Task Pane

Task panes don't have a dedicated visual designer because they are implemented through the creation of a user control, which already has a design surface. To add a custom task pane to your Word add-in, right-click the project, select Add New Item, and then select the Windows Forms User Control item.

FIGURE 23.10   Testing a ribbon button in Microsoft Word 2010.

Because actions panes are document-level concepts, you'll read about those separately in the section "Creating an Office Document Extension," later in this chapter. You follow the same general development process.

After the user control is added and the designer is loaded, you can set about creating the UI and code-behind for the task pane. The only VSTO-specific action item here is wiring the task pane user control into Word's object model. All of that work is accomplished in code within the add-in class. First, to make life a bit easier, you add a `using` statement to your add-in class (in this case, the `ThisAddIn` class):

```
using Microsoft.Office.Tools;
```

Then, you declare two local objects, one for the task pane and one for the user control:

```
private PurchaseOrderTaskControl poUserControl;
private CustomTaskPane poTaskPane;
```

And finally, you need the code to add the custom task pane to the application instance. You put this in the `Startup` event (for this example, `ThisAddIn_Startup`) so that the task pane is immediately available and visible when you run the add-in:

```
poUserControl = new PurchaseOrderTaskControl();
poTaskPane = this.CustomTaskPanes.Add(poUserControl, "Purchase Orders");
poTaskPane.Visible = true;
```

If you build and run the project now, you should see your task pane within the Word environment (see Figure 23.11).

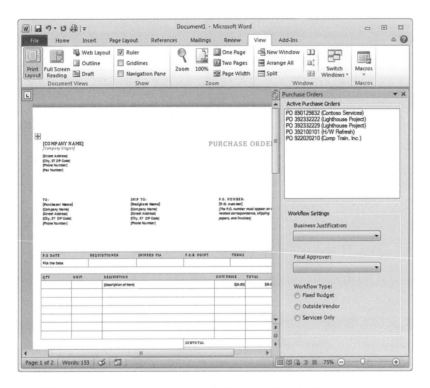

FIGURE 23.11   A custom task pane in Microsoft Word 2010.

TIP

The preceding example uses a Windows Forms user control. If you want to create your task pane using Windows Presentation Foundation (WPF) instead, you simply add a WPF user control to the project. Everything from a design and coding experience would work the same. Behind the scenes, Visual Studio will automatically create a `System.Windows.Forms.Integration.ElementHost` object and use that to parent/host your WPF controls within the targeted Office application.

Creating Outlook Form Regions

Let's turn our attention now to Outlook. As previously mentioned, Outlook has a unique extension point that is not available or relevant in Word or Excel; Outlook add-ins are capable of implementing form regions to any message class within Outlook. A message class is best thought of as the various entities that Outlook defines. These include notes, tasks, email, and so on. Put simply, a form region is the principal mechanism for developers to implement custom form fields within an existing form (for example, email, contact, or other custom forms not included in Outlook by default). To continue with the purchase order example from Word, perhaps a purchase order sent by email should have a set of editable fields and another user interface (UI) associated with it. You can implement those fields and UI in Outlook as a form region. The best way to really understand form regions is to jump right into the task of creating one.

Form regions are implemented by first creating an Outlook add-in project and then adding an Outlook Form Region item. This triggers the Form Region Wizard, which captures the information necessary to autogenerate a region class file. The first screen in the wizard is used to indicate whether you want to create a brand-new form region or use an existing one that was designed in Outlook itself. For this example, select the Design a New Form option.

The second page in the wizard, shown in Figure 23.12, specifies where the region presents itself. There are four options here, with a graphic that illustrates the positioning behavior of the region. Select Adjoining to create the purchase order UI at the bottom of the Outlook email form.

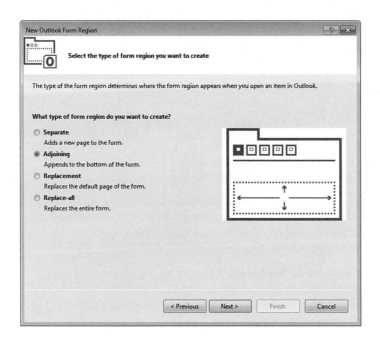

FIGURE 23.12   Selecting the Outlook form region type.

The third page of the wizard (see Figure 23.13) queries for the name of the region and which inspector display modes the region should support. Inspector is the Outlook term for the window used to view and edit a specific message class. For instance, when you compose a new email message in Outlook, you are actually seeing the email inspector in action.

FIGURE 23.13   Naming the form region and specifying the display mode.

The fourth and final page of the wizard (see Figure 23.14) associates the form region with any of the built-in Outlook message classes or with a custom message class implemented by a third party. For the purposes of this example, select only the Mail Message entry.

When finished, Visual Studio generates the code to match the form region properties provided in the wizard. You are now ready to construct the UI for your region.

The visual designer for an Outlook form region looks identical to the Windows Forms Designer: It is essentially a blank canvas onto which you drag controls. So at this point, the typical Windows Forms development process kicks in, enabling you to create the behavior and the look and feel as you need.

No other code is necessary for Outlook to display the form region when the associated message class is invoked. For this example, because we selected the mail message class earlier when we executed the Form Region Wizard, the region automatically shows up anytime we create a new email item (as shown in Figure 23.15).

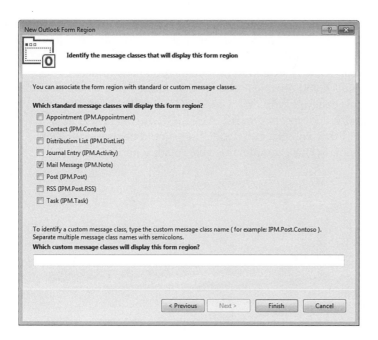

FIGURE 23.14   Associating the form region with a message class.

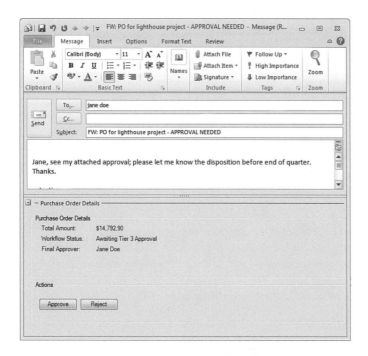

FIGURE 23.15   An Outlook form region in action.

Runtime Events

Outlook form regions are physically created using a factory pattern. This means that they aren't "newed up" via simple instantiation as we did in the earlier Word task pane example. The form region factory code is located in its code-behind class (called, by default, FormRegion1.cs, but this would obviously change depending on how you have named the project item). In this code file, you find a code region labeled Form Region Factory. And that region contains an important event, `FormRegionInitializing`. It is within the context of this event that you place any code that should be executed when the form region first loads. Again, in this example, this takes place whenever an email item is displayed:

```
#region Form Region Factory
    [Microsoft.Office.Tools.Outlook.
    FormRegionMessageClass
    (Microsoft.Office.Tools.Outlook.
    FormRegionMessageClassAttribute.Note)]
    [Microsoft.Office.Tools.Outlook.FormRegionName
    ("OutlookAddIn2.FormRegion1")]
    public partial class FormRegion1Factory
        {
            // Occurs before the form region is initialized.
            // To prevent the form region from appearing, set e.Cancel to true.
            // Use e.OutlookItem to get a reference to the current Outlook item.
            private void FormRegion1Factory_FormRegionInitializing
            (object sender,
             Microsoft.Office.Tools.Outlook.
             FormRegionInitializingEventArgs e)
            {
                // code to fetch purchase order details could go here
            }
        }
#endregion
```

The other important event is `FormRegionShowing`. As its name suggests, code within this event executes after the form region is initialized but before it is actually displayed:

```
// Occurs before the form region is displayed.
// Use this.OutlookItem to get a reference to the current Outlook item.
// Use this.OutlookFormRegion to get a reference to the form region.
private void FormRegion1_FormRegionShowing(object sender, System.EventArgs e)
    {
        // code to format purchase order details could go here
    }
```

Creating an Office Document Extension

You can customize Office documents themselves in various ways. You can host controls in a document, create actions panes specific to a document, implement your own smart tags, and store data within a document.

A document-level project is created using the same process we used for add-ins. This time, however, you select an Excel 2010 Workbook or Word 2010 Document project type. These project types use designers that represent the look and feel of an Excel workbook or a Word document.

Hosting Controls

Both Word and Excel have host items that function as containers for controls and code. A host item is essentially a proxy object that represents a physical document within either application. These are key to document-level customizations. For Word, we have the `Microsoft.Office.Tools.Word.Document` object, and for Excel, we have the `Microsoft.Office.Tools.Excel.Worksheet` object. Within Visual Studio, we build functionality using these host items through the use of designers. Each host item can host both Windows Forms controls and native Office controls.

> **NOTE**
>
> There is actually a third host item that represents an Excel workbook: `Microsoft.Office.Tools.Excel.Workbook` is a host item for enabling workbook-level customization, but is not an actual controls container. Instead, `Workbook` functions as a component tray and can accept components such as a `DataSet`.

Windows Forms Controls

You can add Windows Forms controls onto the document design surface just as if you were designing a Windows Forms application. In this example, we use an Excel workbook. The Excel 2010 Workbook project template automatically adds an .xslx file to our project, which includes three worksheets, each represented by its own class. (These are the host items we discussed previously.) These sheets have defined events for startup and shutdown, enabling us to perform work as the worksheet is first opened or closed.

The design surface for the worksheet looks identical to how the worksheet looks in Excel. From here, we can add Windows Forms controls to the worksheet by using the Visual Studio Toolbox, and implement code in the code-behind file to customize the action of those controls. Figure 23.16 shows a workbook designer in the IDE with a few controls added.

> **NOTE**
>
> Creating an Office document project requires that your system allow access to the Microsoft Office Visual Basic for Applications project system. Normally, this type of access is disabled for security reasons. If access is disabled, Visual Studio prompts you to enable it before creating your Office project.

Host Controls

Host controls is the term applied to native Office controls. These controls actually extend objects found in the Word or Excel object models to provide additional capabilities such as event handling and data binding. Building out a document using host controls follows the same process as with Windows Forms controls. With a document-level project loaded, you see a tab in the Visual Studio Toolbox that stores the host controls for the specific application that is targeted. For Excel, there is an Excel Controls tab, and for Word, there is a Word Controls tab.

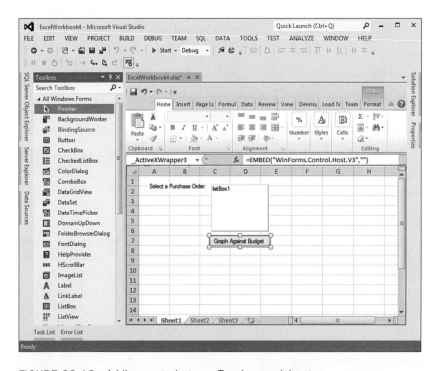

FIGURE 23.16   Adding controls to an Excel spreadsheet.

Table 23.2 itemizes the available host controls for both Excel and Word.

TABLE 23.2   Microsoft Office Extension Points

Project Type	Host Control	Function
Excel 2010 Workbook	`ListObject`	Displays data in rows and columns.
Excel 2010 Workbook	`NamedRange`	Represents an Excel range; can be bound to data and expose events.
Word 2010 Document	`Bookmark`	Represents a Word bookmark.
Word 2010 Document	`BuildingBlockGalleryContentControl`	Document building blocks are pieces of a document meant to be reused (a cover page, header, and so on). This control displays a list of building blocks that users can insert into a document.
Word 2010 Document	`ComboBoxContentControl`	A standard combo box.
Word 2010 Document	`DatePickerContentControl`	A standard date picker control.
Word 2010 Document	`DropDownListContentControl`	A drop-down list of items.
Word 2010 Document	`PictureContentControl`	Represents a document region that displays an image.
Word 2010 Document	`PlainTextContentControl`	Represents a block of text.
Word 2010 Document	`RichTextContentControl`	Represents a block of text; can contain rich content.

23

Creating an Actions Pane

In addition to customizing the interaction with users within a document, Windows Forms controls are used to craft custom actions panes. Actions panes should be used to provide contextual data and command options to users as they are editing/viewing a document (either a Word document or an Excel workbook file).

There are several reasons why you would elect to implement your document interface using an actions pane. One reason is that the actions pane is "linked" to the document but is not an actual part of the document; the contents of the actions pane won't be printed when the document is printed. Another reason to implement an actions pane is to preserve the application's document-centric focus: You can read and page through an entire document while keeping the information and commands in the actions pane in full view at all times.

Physically, actions panes are created with user controls and are represented by an Actions Pane Control item. Adding this item to your document project creates a user control class; you simply build out the UI of the control as normal. In general, though, you likely want to dynamically add or remove controls from the actions pane depending on what the user is doing within the document that is open in Word or Excel. Providing this level of contextual relevance is the strong point and target of the actions pane in the first place.

Controlling Stacking Behavior

Because the actions pane functions as a toolbar container that can be docked and moved around by the user, there is a complete control layout engine for dictating how the controls within the actions pane should be displayed. The `ActionsPane.StackOrder` property works with a `StackStyle` enum to control layout behavior. The various `StackStyle` values are documented for you in Table 23.3.

TABLE 23.3   `StackStyle` Values

Value	Description
FromBottom	Controls are stacked starting from the bottom of the actions pane.
FromLeft	Controls are stacked starting from the left of the actions pane.
FromRight	Controls are stacked starting from the right of the actions pane.
FromTop	Controls are stacked starting from the top of the actions pane.
None	No stacking is performed. (Order and layout are manually controlled.)

As we did with the custom task pane, after you have assembled a user control that you want to surface within the actions pane, you need to create a field variable to hold an instance of the control, and then add the control to the actions pane.

So in the `ThisWorkbook` class, we add the following declaration:

```
private ActionsPaneControl1 approvalPane = new ActionsPaneControl1();
```

And the following line of code, inserted into the `ThisWorkbook_Startup` event, adds our user control to the workbook's actions pane:

```
this.ActionsPane.Controls.Add(approvalPane);
```

Figure 23.17 shows a custom actions pane alongside its worksheet.

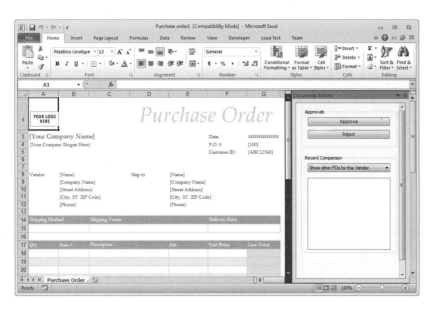

FIGURE 23.17   A custom actions pane in Excel.

Storing Data in the Data Cache

The data cache is a read/write location within an Office Word document or Excel workbook that can be leveraged by your Office application to store needed data. One common scenario is to bind host controls or Windows Forms controls in an actions pane or on a document surface to a data set stored in the document's data island.

Physically, this data island is implemented as an XML document that is embedded within the Office document. This XML container can host any data type that meets the following two requirements:

▶ It has to be implemented as a read/write public field on the host item (for example, the Word `ThisDocument` or Excel `ThisWorkbook` class).

▶ It must be serializable (the runtime uses the `XmlSerializer` to verbalize the object within the data island).

Most of the built-in .NET types meet these requirements. If you have written a custom type that also adheres to these requirements, it too can be stored within the data island.

Adding data to the data cache is easy. You mark the data type you want to store with the `CachedAttribute` attribute; assuming that the type meets the data cache requirements, and that you have created an instance of the type within your document-level VSTO project, it is automatically added to the data island.

`DataSet` objects turn out to be useful for conveyance within a data island. To declare a `DataSet` as cached, we write the following:

```
[Microsoft.VisualStudio.Tools.Applications.Runtime.Cached()]
public DataSet poDataSet;
```

This declaratively instructs the VSTO runtime to serialize the object and add it to the current document's data cache. The `DataSet` itself can be populated however you see fit.

There is also a way to imperatively cache an object in a document. Each host item exposes an `IsCached` method and a `StartCaching` method. By combining the two, you can check to see whether an object is already in the cache, and, if it isn't, add it to the cache. Using these two methods, we might end up with the following code to store our `poDataSet` object in a document:

```
if (!this.IsCached("poDataSet"))
{
    this.StartCaching("poDataSet ");
}
```

If you use the `StartCaching()` method, there is no need for the class to be decorated with the Cached attribute, but the object does still need to adhere to the other requirements for Office data island serialization. You can also use the `StopCaching` method on the host item to tell the VSTO runtime to remove the object from the document's data cache.

TIP

There is yet a third way to place an object into the data cache: the Properties window. If you use the Data Sources window to add a data set to your project, you can create an instance of the data set and then select it in the designer. In the Properties window for the data set instance, set the Cache in Document property to True. You also need to change the access type of the data set instance to Public.

Accessing the Data Cache

Many times, an Office business application relies on a server to function as a central repository for documents. This introduces a dilemma: The Office applications such as Word and Excel are not designed to be run in a server environment where many instances might need to be spooled up to serve multiple requests for document-level extensions. So far, we have been using objects within the Office object model to extend Office. And this implies that Office is installed on the machine running your assembly (something that is certainly not the case for typical server installations). Thankfully, one of the primary goals for document-level Office architecture is to enable the clean separation of data from the view of the data. Or, put another way, the VSTO architecture defines a way to access a document without actually using the Office client application. Instead, the VSTO runtime itself is used.

The key to accessing a document server side is the `ServerDocument` class. This class, which is part of the VSTO runtime and lives in the `Microsoft.VisualStudio.Tools.Applications` namespace, allows programmatic access to a document's data cache on machines that do not have Office installed. The process running on the server passes the path for the needed document into the `ServerDocument`'s constructor, and then uses the `CachedDataHostItem` class and the `CachedDataItem` class to obtain either the schema or the XML or both from the document's data island.

As long as the target computer has the VSTO runtime installed, the following code could be used to access the purchase order data from a server-side purchase order spreadsheet:

```
string poFile = @"C:\ServerData\po39233202.xls";
ServerDocument poDoc = null;
poDoc = new ServerDocument(poFile);
CachedDataHostItem dataHostItem =
    sd1.CachedData.HostItems["ExcelWorkbook1.DataSheet1"];
CachedDataItem dataCache = dataHostItem.CachedData["CachedPO"];
//The dataCache.Xml property will contain the XML
//from the specified data island
```

Using the `dataCache.Xml` property, you can now deserialize back into the source data type, view the data, and so on.

Summary

This chapter covered the capabilities present in Visual Studio 2012 for building on top of Microsoft Office 2010 applications and customizing their behavior at both the application level and the document level. The discussion about Office add-ins covered the capability to add your own items, tabs, and groupings to the ribbon; the construction of Outlook forms regions; and the development of custom task panes. The discussion about Office document-level extensions illustrated the concepts behind hosting Windows Forms controls and native Office controls on a document's surface, building custom actions panes to provide context-aware actions and information to users, and using the data cache architecture to both read and write data to Office documents on the client and server side.

Although this chapter focused on only a few of the Office applications that can be customized using VSTO, you should now have enough information about VSTO's projects and designers to get you started on your own investigation into Visual Studio and Office as a development platform.

CHAPTER 24

Developing Applications in the Cloud with Windows Azure

Microsoft continues to evolve Azure as a full-service, easy-to-scale, cloud-hosting platform. Azure offers website hosting, virtual machines, cloud services, storage, and media services. The following describes the core Azure offerings from Microsoft:

▶ **Websites**—The Azure platform allows fast and easy deployment and management of websites built on .NET, PHP, Node.js, and other technologies. These websites can take advantage of SQL databases, table storage, blog storage, caching, a content delivery network (CDN), and more.

▶ **Virtual machines**—This service allows you to deploy and run VMs based on Windows Server or Linux. You can then use the machines to custom configure and host your applications. This allows you to deploy existing code without changes and take advantage of custom hosting configurations.

▶ **Cloud services**—Cloud services is the platform as a service offering from Microsoft. You can use it to build cloud applications and services with elastic scalability.

▶ **Data**—The data services from Microsoft allow you to get insight from all your data using Hadoop, Business Analytics, Storage, and SQL.

▶ **Media**—The media services in Azure enable you to store, manage, and deliver media with the cloud. This includes encoding, content protection, and streaming.

This chapter focuses on the developer experience with Azure and Visual Studio 2012. We first cover how to get started with the Azure management portal. Then you learn how easy it is to use Visual Studio to deploy your websites to the cloud. The chapter closes using the Visual Studio Azure software development kit (SDK) to create scalable cloud services.

The Azure Management Portal

The first step is to set up your Azure account. Microsoft has a lot of deals for you to get started. This includes free trials, Microsoft Developer Network (MSDN) credits, spending limits, pay-as-you-go options, prepackaged deals, and more. You will want to visit http://www.windowsazure.com for details. This section assumes you have created a basic account and are ready to get started.

> **NOTE**
>
> At the time of this writing, Microsoft had just released a preview of their new Azure management portal. This was used for the screenshots and content here. Don't be surprised if things have changed a bit by the time you read this.

The Azure management portal is used to manage all the Azure services to which you subscribe. This chapter focuses on the developer services of websites, cloud services, and storage (and not things like VMs and business intelligence [BI] analytic tools). Figure 24.1 shows an empty management portal. The left side of the screen is where you manage the various services you use. (Notice that this portal has zero services under each item.) The bottom right is where you add a new service.

Creating a New Azure Service

You create a new item in the Azure management portal by first clicking the New button (bottom of Figure 24.1). This brings up options for selecting the type of service you want to create. Figure 24.2 shows selecting a new website. We will use this as an example and leverage this site in the next section, "Deploying a Website to the Cloud."

When you create a new website, Azure gives you a few suboptions, as shown in Figure 24.3. You can use Quick Create to quickly create a website with very few additional items to configure at this time. The Create with Database option enables you to define both a website and a related database. The From Gallery option allows you to start your site with a number of predefined templates, including blogs, content management sites, and e-commerce tools. In the example, you select the middle option, Create with Database.

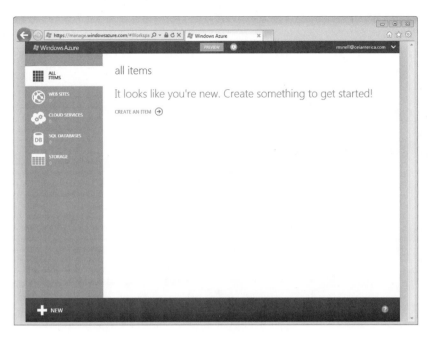

FIGURE 24.1   The Azure management portal Is where you manage and create sites, services, and storage Items.

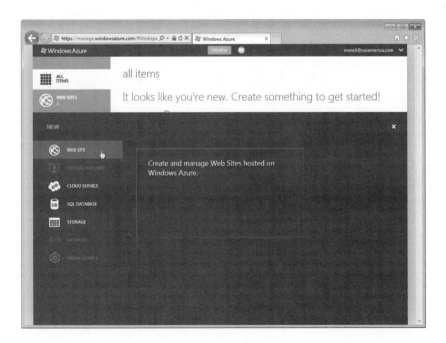

FIGURE 24.2   Use the New button to create a new Azure service, including websites.

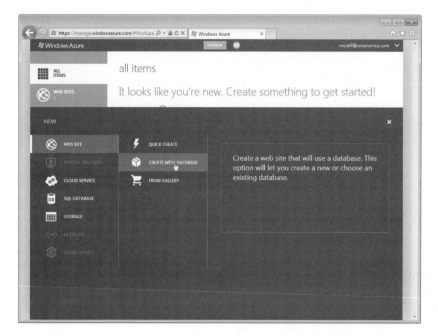

FIGURE 24.3   You have options when creating a new website, including creating a website that uses a database.

Azure asks you for a uniform resource locator (URL), database type, and hosting region as the first step in creating a website with a database. Figure 24.4 shows this in action. Your URL is, by default, accessible from http://domain.azurewebsites.net. This is a test URL. You can configure your domain name system (DNS) later to use your actual domain name. Given this is a test site, your domain must be unique across other Azure test sites. The tool verifies this and gives you a green check mark if all is well. You have two options when creating a database: SQL Server and MySQL. In this case, we select SQL Server. Finally, you select a hosting region. This gives your site a basic affinity to a region where most of your users might exist. You can change this or even scale across regions as your needs change.

The next step in the Website Setup Wizard is to provide additional details about your database. Here you define the name of your database, the edition of SQL you want to use, the database maximum size, language character support (collation), and the SQL database server you intend to use. Figure 24.5 shows an example.

The last step of this wizard is to set up a database server. Once set up, you can reuse this across sites and other databases. Figure 24.6 shows the options. Here you simply set basic credentials for authenticating to the database server. Be sure to indicate that Azure services can access the server.

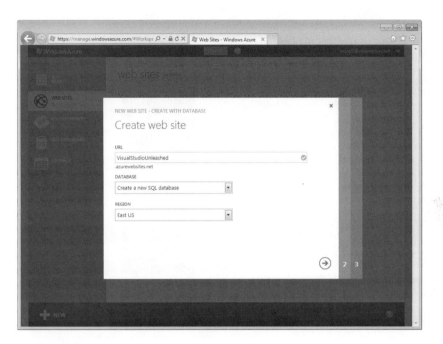

FIGURE 24.4   You set your site's URL, database technology, and hosting affinity region when creating your website.

FIGURE 24.5   The Azure Website Setup Wizard gives you common options when defining your database.

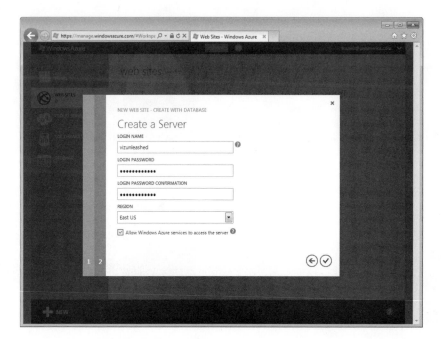

FIGURE 24.6   You must set up credentials when creating a new Azure SQL database.

When you finish the wizard, Azure goes about creating your website, SQL Server, and database. This does not take long. Upon completion, Azure starts your site and the database running.

Managing Your Azure Services

You manage your Azure services in the same management portal shown earlier. Here you can monitor, start, and stop running services. You can also add new services and delete existing ones. This is also where Azure provides detailed information about things happening in your hosted items.

Figure 24.7 shows an example of the website created earlier inside the management portal. Notice the site's status is Running and that it is hosted in the East US region. The bottom of the portal now has additional management buttons, as follows:

▶ **Browse**—Allows you to go directly to the site in your web browser. (The site returns a base Hypertext Markup Language [HTML] message by default.)

▶ **Stop**—Stops the website from running; you can always restart it.

▶ **Upload**—Uploads a package to the site. A package is a deployment unit for the site. More on this in a bit.

▶ **Delete**—Deletes the site from the Azure management portal (cannot be undone).

▶ **Web Matrix**—Launches the Web Platform Installer from Microsoft to install WebMatrix. WebMatrix is the free, lightweight development tool available from Microsoft for creating all things Web. It, too, works with Azure. See http://www.microsoft.com/web/webmatrix/ for more details.

FIGURE 24.7   You manage and monitor Azure items from the Azure control portal.

There are also the two icons to the right of this bottom toolbar. The first is where you receive notifications about things happening with your site; this includes information, warnings, and errors. Figure 24.8 shows an example. The second icon (?) launches Azure management portal help.

Manage a Website

Managing your website includes monitoring activity, changing configuration, scaling it, linking other Azure resources, and more. To access website management, you select your site's name from the portal page shown back in Figure 24.7. This takes you to features specific to just this site. Figure 24.9 shows an example.

The website management dashboard shows site statistics in the graph at the top of the page. This includes page requests, CPU time, and data volumes. You can use the check marks next to each of these items to turn them on and off from the grid. You can use the drop-down in the upper-right of the graph to change the data and time range of the data.

FIGURE 24.8   The management portal provides you details on things happening in your site, including information messages, warnings, and errors.

FIGURE 24.9   The website management dashboard allows you to monitor and configure your Azure website.

TIP

To work even closer with site statistic data, select the monitor link at the top of the web site management page. This brings up additional details about your data as well as an Add Metrics option in the bottom toolbar. The Add Metrics option allows you to configure which metrics you want to monitor on the graph.

Notice that the dashboard page also shows a number of activities you can perform with your site. The quick glance area to the right of the page provides links to each of these. This includes using TFS or Git to publish your sites from these source control systems. We look at a few of these other options in coming sections.

Scrolling down the page shows more usage data. Figure 24.10 shows an example. You want to keep an eye on this usage relative to what you have purchased (the gray available line).

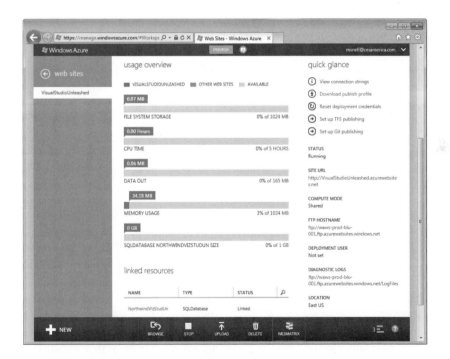

FIGURE 24.10   You can see additional details for your site by scrolling down the website dashboard page.

You click the Configure option at the top of the website management page to launch configuration options for your site. Here you set the version of the .NET Framework your site uses, change your site URL, turn on and off logging, configure application settings, view connection strings, and set default documents for your site. Figure 24.11 shows an example.

FIGURE 24.11   Use the configure page to configure core settings for your website.

You manage the elastic scale of your site by clicking the Scale option on the website management page. Here you can set if your site is on shared hosting hardware or gets hosted inside a reserved capacity VM. If using shared hosting, you can indicate the instances of the site that get scaled across shared servers. This will get you additional scale. Figure 24.12 shows changing this option from a single instance to two.

If you need reserved capacity, you need to switch to a running VM. To do so, click the Reserved option shown at the top of Figure 24.12. You then select your VM size; Figure 24.13 shows your options. Notice, too, you can indicate the number of instances you want to use here. Note that this has the capacity to dramatically increase your scale and the price you pay to host your site.

You save changes you make by clicking the Save button that appears on the bottom toolbar when you make configuration changes.

FIGURE 24.12   You can scale your shared web sites with a quick slide of a control (hosting charges apply of course).

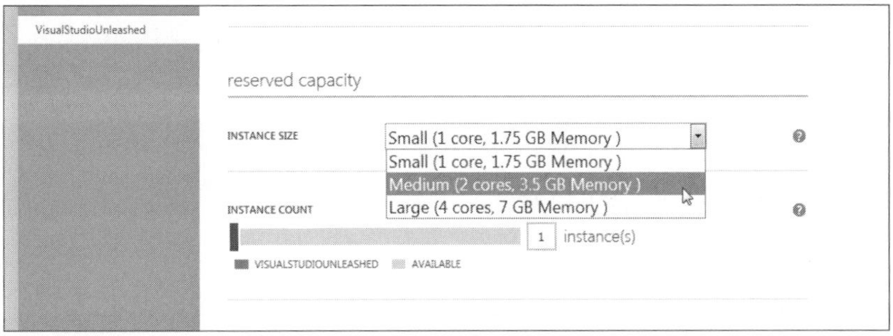

FIGURE 24.13   You can reserve your scale by changing to hosting instances.

Manage a SQL Database

You manage your SQL databases in a similar manner as your websites. You can access the management pages from the management portal home page. You start by clicking the SQL Databases option on the left of the page and then clicking your database name, as shown in Figure 24.14.

> **TIP**
>
> Clicking the server name in Figure 24.14 launches the database server configuration management page. Here you can configure allowed IP addresses, allowed services, and more.

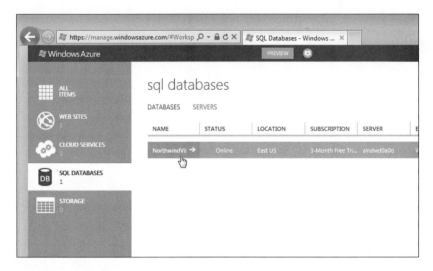

FIGURE 24.14   You click your database name to launch its management page.

The database management pages include a dashboard and scale page that are similar to the website pages shown previously. The dashboard page shows size usage. The scale page allows you to switch between web and business editions of the service. The web addition allows database scale size of 1GB or 5GB. If your needs are higher (10GB to 150GB), you need to switch to the Business Edition.

You can do more with database management through a separate management URL. You access this URL from either the Quick Start page, Design your Database link, or from the SQL Dashboard page, Manage URL link. Clicking either of these links takes you to the Windows Azure SQL Database management login screen. When you log in to the site (using your SQL credential set up earlier), you are taken to the home screen shown in Figure 24.15.

This site allows you to execute queries and create new tables, views, and stored procedures. For example, to create a new table, you click the Design link on the bottom left of Figure 24.15. Next, click the New Table link in the middle of the page. This brings up the table editor shown in Figure 24.16.

An easier way to manage the schema of your SQL Server is through the SQL management console or Visual Studio 2012. To do so in Visual Studio 2012, you use the database connection information from the Azure management portal to set up a new data connection in Server Explorer. Figure 24.17 shows an example.

You can then use the full database tools built in to Visual Studio 2012 (see Chapter 20, "Working with Databases"). Figure 24.18 shows an example. Here the Northwind database script is run inside a query window. Notice that Server Explorer shows the full Northwind database actually deployed to the Azure shared database server. Of course, you can flip between the Azure web management tool and Visual Studio management as required.

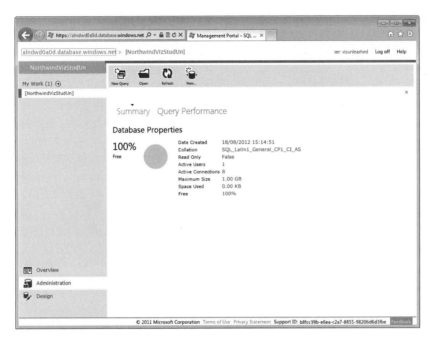

FIGURE 24.15   Use the Azure SQL management tools to configure your database.

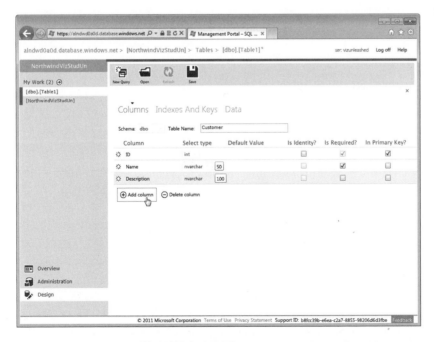

FIGURE 24.16   You can create new tables using the SQL database management tools.

FIGURE 24.17   You can set up a connection in Server Explorer to manage your database schema directly from Visual Studio 2012.

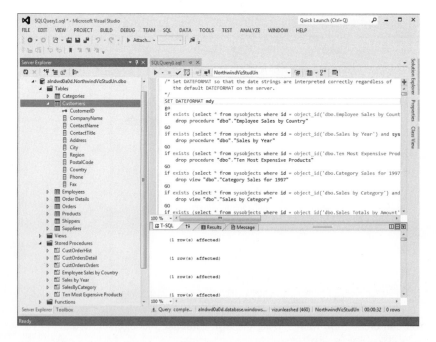

FIGURE 24.18   The Northwind database deployed to an Azure-hosted SQL Server instance.

Deploying a Website to the Cloud

You can deploy any ASP.NET web application to Azure. This includes ASP.NET Web Forms, MVC sites, and Web API services. In this way, Azure represents a scalable hosting option for your websites. Visual Studio 2012 does include publishing capabilities that makes deploying easier. Let's take a look at an example.

In this example, you leverage code created back in Chapter 17, "Building Websites with Razor and ASP.NET," to work with the Azure SQL Server database. You then use Visual Studio to deploy this application to your Azure website. To do so, follow these steps:

1. Use Visual Studio 2012 to create a new project (File, New Project). Select the ASP. NET MVC 4 template. Name your project **AzureWebSite**.

2. Open the site's Web.config file to edit the data connection. Here you point the site to the Azure database deployed in the previous section. Recall that you can pull connection information from the Azure management portal. Figure 24.19 shows an example. Grab the ADO.NET data connection string and add an entry to your Web.config file. You want to comment out the other connection string that is there.

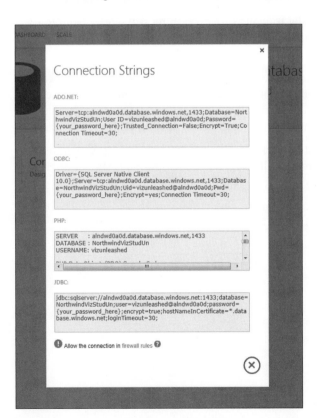

FIGURE 24.19   Use the connection information from the Azure management portal to configure your site's database connection in Web.config.

3. Right-click your project in Solution Explorer and Choose Add New Item. From the Add New Item dialog, select the Data node. Here, choose ADO.NET Entity Data Model. Name your model **NwdModel.edmx** and click the Add button. This will launch the ADO.NET Entity Data Model wizard.

On the first screen of the Entity Data Model Wizard, choose "Generate from database" and click the Next button.

On the next screen, select the connection string you added to the Web.config file and click the Next button.

Finally, select the Customers table in the "Choose Your Database Objects and Settings" option of the wizard. Click the Finish button to close.

4. Compile (build) your solution to ensure all worked correctly.

5. Next, right-click the Controllers folder and choose Add, Controller. In the Add Controller dialog, set the controller name to **CustomerController**. Set the Model class to Customer (AzureWebSite). Set the Data context class to NorthwindVizStudUnEntities (AzureWebSite). Click the Add button to complete.

6. You can run the application locally to make sure everything still works. Note that you are now connected to the cloud database (not your local database). Navigate to the Customer page to verify all is working.

7. To start deployment, you need to return to the Azure management portal to get a publish profile for your site. From the home page of the management portal, select Web Sites. Click your website name to get to the dashboard for your site. Under the Quick Glance section (see Figure 24.20), click the Download Publish Profile link.

This will allow you to download a file that includes settings that help Visual Studio deploy your application to Azure. IE will give you a Save option, as shown in Figure 24.21. Save this file on your machine (as you will use it momentarily).

8. Return to Visual Studio. Right-click your website in Solution Explorer and choose the Publish option. This brings up the Publish Web dialog shown in Figure 24.22.

FIGURE 24.20   Click Download Publish Profile to get the publishing profile file for your site.

FIGURE 24.21   Save the .publishsettings file to your machine for use in Visual Studio.

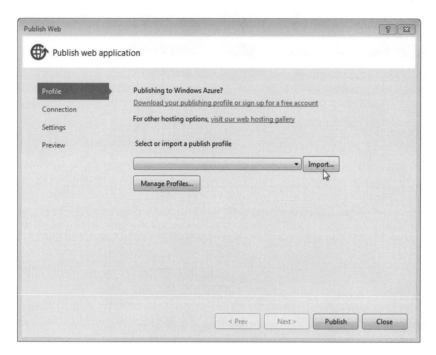

FIGURE 24.22   Use the Publish Web dialog to publish your website to Azure.

9. Click the Import button on the Publish Web dialog. Navigate to your .publishsettings file you downloaded from the Azure portal and click the Open button. This configures the Connections area of the Publish Web dialog as shown in Figure 24.23. Use the Publish method, Web Deploy. Click the Validate Connection button to validate the connection to your site. Click the Next button to continue.

10. You should now be on the Settings page (see Figure 24.24). Here you set your configuration (Release build). Notice that if you had files there, you could have Publish remove them first. The Databases area allows you to configure database connections. Notice that it is picking up connection settings from your Web.config file. The DefaultConnection is used to set connection information for ASP.NET Membership features. The NwdContext connection is set to connect to the SQL Azure database. Click Next to continue.

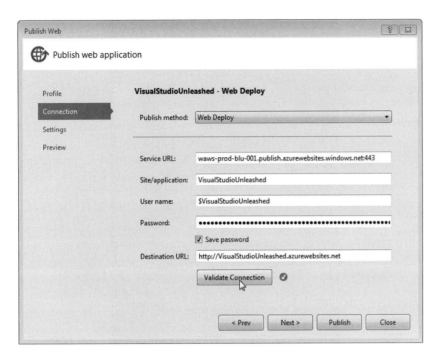

FIGURE 24.23   Verify the Connection settings for your site; use Validate Connection to do so.

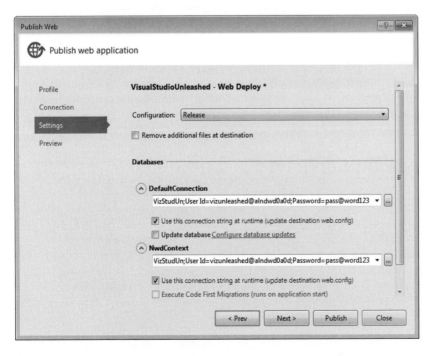

FIGURE 24.24   Configure the settings for your site before publishing.

11. The Preview page allows you to preview file changes that will be made before committing them. Figure 24.25 shows an example. You can click Start Preview to verify these files.

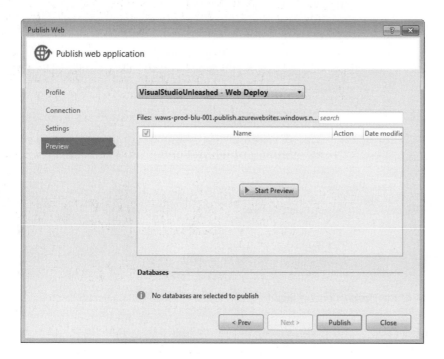

FIGURE 24.25   Preview files to be published before doing your final publish.

12. Click the Publish button. You can monitor the output window to monitor progress and know when deployment has completed. Your site should automatically open in the browser, as shown in Figure 24.26.

Creating a Cloud Service in Visual Studio

The application you deployed previously is essentially a website running in a shared hosting environment that offers ease of scale. However, Microsoft launched Azure with what they call cloud services. These are applications that run on the Microsoft AppFabric. This is much different from shared hosting. It offers developers provisioning across a huge array of servers in many locations. The service does health monitoring and provides continuous (99.95%) availability and near-infinite scale. You applications are automatically replicated and managed. The cloud service platform handles everything from networks, patches, upgrades, hardware outages, and more.

The cloud service is built to handle typical .NET applications you would write. This includes websites, services, background processing applications, and more. You just write code the way you would normally and deploy to this service.

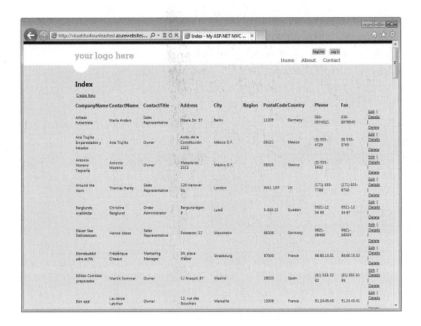

FIGURE 24.26   Your site running in the cloud.

Installing the Azure SDK for .NET

Visual Studio 2012 does not ship with the Azure SDK. Instead, it provides a link to download and install the SDK. To get started, create a new project (File, Add, Project). Select the Cloud option on the left of the New Project dialog. Figure 24.27 shows an example. Give your project a name and click the OK button to get started.

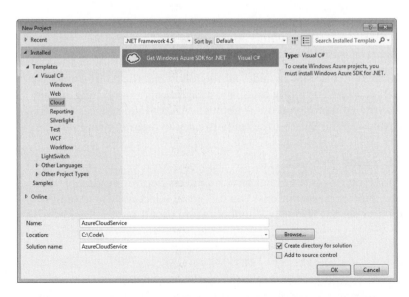

FIGURE 24.27   You must install the SDK before creating cloud projects for Azure.

This will create a near-empty project with an .html page. This page will launch in your IDE and give you a button to install the SDK. Figure 24.28 shows an example. Clicking this button takes you to an actual web page on the WindowsAzure .NET Developer Center. Here you will see a big Install button that will actually download the SDK.

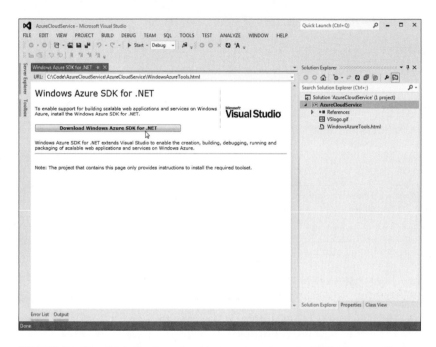

FIGURE 24.28   Click the Download button to get started with the installation.

The SDK gets installed from the Web Platform Installer. When you run the SDK installer you downloaded, you will see something similar to Figure 24.29. Use this tool to complete the installation. (You want to close Visual Studio first.)

The SDK installs a number of items. This includes all the following: the Azure Emulator, Azure tools, Azure libraries, Azure authoring tools, and a LightSwitch publishing add-on. Some of these tools, like the Emulator, you use to simulate Azure cloud services for debugging. The other tools extend Visual Studio to simplify the deployment of Azure services.

Creating a Cloud Service Project

Once the SDK is installed, you can create cloud service projects right from Visual Studio. You start with File, New, Project menu options. You can again select the Cloud option on the left; you should now see the template Windows Azure Cloud Service. Figure 24.30 shows an example.

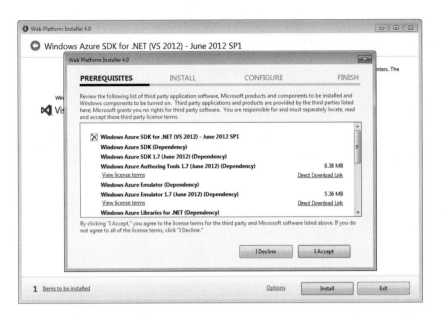

FIGURE 24.29   The Web Platform Installer walks you through adding these new templates and tools.

NOTE

Notice in Figure 24.30 that the target framework is set to .NET Framework 4.0. As of this book's completion, Azure did not yet support greater versions of the .NET Framework.

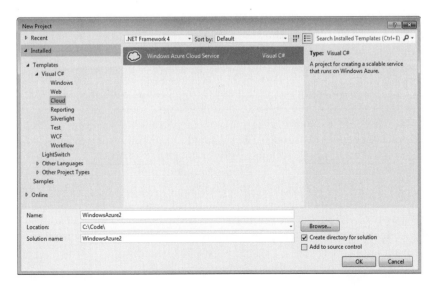

FIGURE 24.30   The SDK includes a number of Azure templates with which to work.

When you select the Cloud Service template, you are presented with some suboptions, as shown in Figure 24.31. You use this dialog to select the type of project you want to create. You might want to define a website, WCF service, cache service, service bus, or the like. In this case, we have selected the MVC 4 website template.

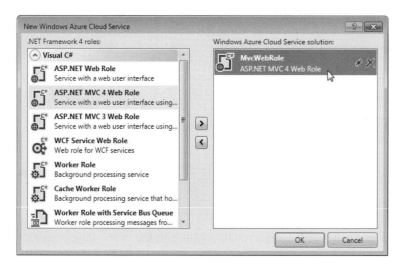

FIGURE 24.31   Choose a role for your new Azure service project.

In this case, Visual Studio actually creates two projects and adds them to a solution. The MVC Web role is simply an ASP.NET MVC website. The other project is an Azure configuration definition project for your service. Figure 24.32 shows an example inside Solution Explorer.

TIP

You can create your website as its own project and then add an Azure project for configuration. This proves to be especially useful if your website project already exists. To make this happen, right-click your project and choose the Add Windows Azure Cloud Service Project option, as shown in Figure 24.33.

You can run your application in debug mode inside Visual Studio. To do so, you must be running Visual Studio in elevated privileges mode. (Right-click the shortcut and choose Run as Administrator.) When debugging, Visual Studio launches the Azure emulator to host and run your service as it would be run on the Azure application platform. You likely will also be asked to set firewall rules for the emulator. If needed, you can access the emulator from the system tray. You will also note that your site runs on a local IP address and port number used by the emulator (and not localhost). Figure 24.34 shows the UI for the Azure Compute Emulator.

FIGURE 24.32   Visual Studio creates both a website and an Azure configuration project.

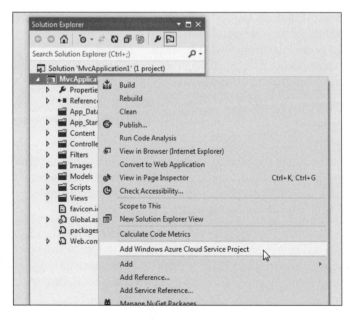

FIGURE 24.33   You can add a Windows Azure Cloud Service project to an existing site.

FIGURE 24.34   The Windows Azure emulator is used host your cloud service locally for debugging.

Deploying the Cloud Service Project

You have a couple options for deploying your Azure cloud service. The first option is to use the Azure management portal to create your cloud service and deploy your site as a package. In this case, you create the package from Visual Studio and upload it to your cloud service using the management portal. As a second option, Visual Studio lets you deploy directly from the IDE. Let's walk through this second option:

1. To get started, right-click your Azure project in Solution Explorer and choose the Publish option. This brings up the Publish Windows Azure Application dialog shown in Figure 24.35.

2. You must sign in to get started. Click the Sign In to Download Credentials link. This launches a browser window and takes you to the Azure site for sign in. Once signed in, you can download your Azure site credentials. Figure 24.36 shows an example. Click the Save button and store the credential file locally.

3. Next, you return to Visual Studio and click the Import button on the Publish Windows Azure Application dialog (see Figure 24.35). Navigate to the .publishsettings file created in the preceding step and select it to open it. Your subscription should now show in the drop-down (Figure 24.35 again). Click the Next button to continue.

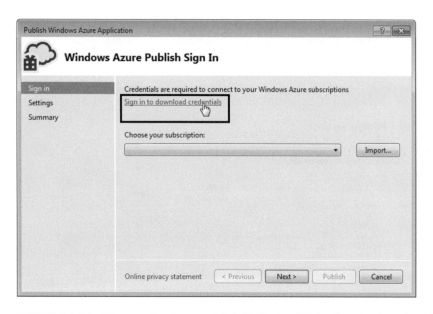

FIGURE 24.35   You use the Azure publish dialog to sign in, download credentials, and import those credentials to Visual Studio for publishing to Azure.

FIGURE 24.36   You must save your credential file (.publishsettings) for import back into Visual Studio.

4. If you had configured a cloud service in the Azure management portal, it would not be available for selection. If you have not, you will have to create one. Figure 24.37 shows an example. You give the service a name and select an affinity region.

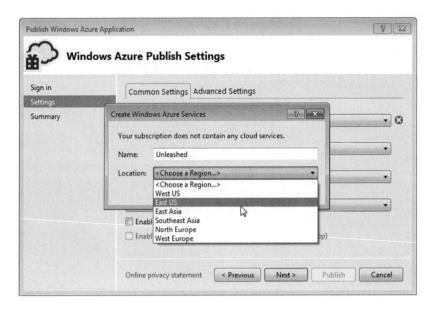

FIGURE 24.37   You must set up a cloud service in which to deploy.

5. You now need to configure some basic settings for your cloud service. This deployment could target a staging environment or production; you would configure that here. Figure 24.38 shows an example. Click the Next button to continue.

6. The publishing profile details should now be displayed for your review. Figure 24.39 shows an example. You can use the Save button on the right of the Target profile drop-down to save these details to your Azure cloud project in Visual Studio. When ready, click the Publish button to complete this wizard.

Visual Studio should now go through the process of publishing your site to Azure. Details will be provided to you through the Windows Azure activity log (see Figure 24.40). When complete, Visual Studio launches your application in a web browser. Figure 24.41 shows an example.

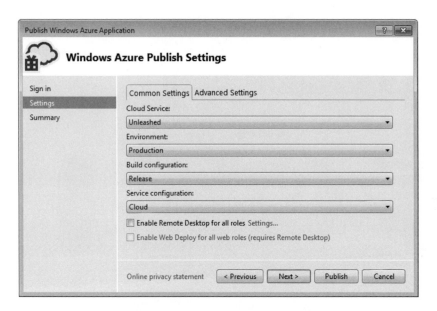

FIGURE 24.38   You need to configure cloud service settings as part of deployment.

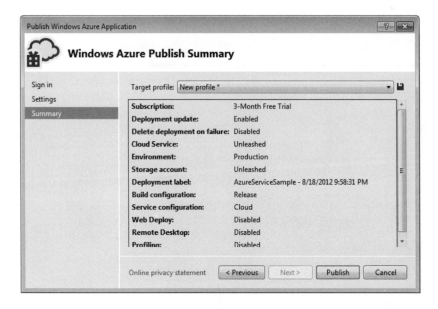

FIGURE 24.39   You can review your final publishing profile before executing the actual publish.

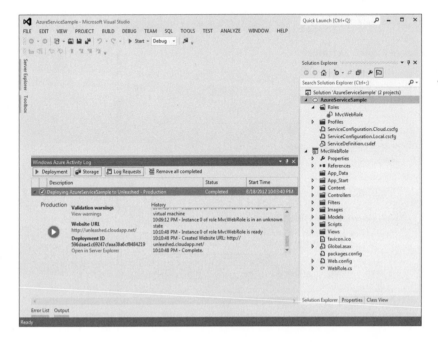

FIGURE 24.40   Monitor the publishing process through the Azure activity log.

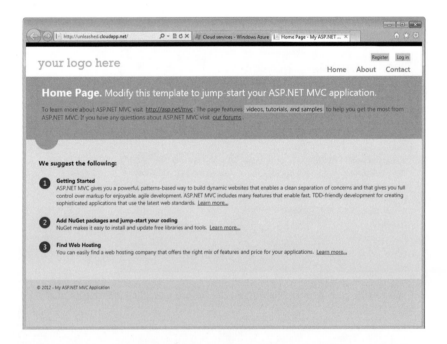

FIGURE 24.41   The fully functioning web site deployed to Azure as a cloud service.

> **NOTE**
>
> You get a similar set of features in the Azure management for cloud services. Don't forget to go back to the portal and review your monitoring, configuration, and scaling options for your cloud service.

This example deployed a simple ASP.NET MVC site. You could have just as easily deployed the site created previously that connected to the SQL Server database hosted in Azure. In that case, you would simply deploy the connection string as you did in that example. The site would then just connect to the SQL Azure database from the cloud service application.

> **NOTE**
>
> This chapter looked primarily at using SQL databases hosted in Azure. However, Azure also has nonrelational storage called blobs and tables. These are highly scalable, fault-tolerant data solutions that offer near-unlimited storage. You will want to do further exploration to understand whether they are right for your next application. For details, check out http://www.windowsazure.com/en-us/home/features/data-management/.

Summary

This chapter presented the building blocks for moving forward with Azure applications and Visual Studio 2012. You must create a Windows Azure account to use the service. Thankfully, Microsoft has created an easy to use management portal for configure all Azure items. You can use it to create websites, manage storage, monitor activity, and even design databases.

To work with Azure in Visual Studio 2012, you must download and install the Azure SDK. With it, you can emulate the Azure application platform and debug your apps before deploying them. These tools also simplify deploying services to Azure.

CHAPTER 25

Writing Windows Store Applications Using the Windows Runtime Library

Windows 8 represents a significant departure from Windows releases of the past. For the first time in many, many years, the core development model, application design approach, and operating system fundamentals have all undergone a major shift. With touch-enabled devices abounding, Microsoft needed an operating system that could cater equally well to mainstream desktop and to tablet and mobile form factors, and everything in between.

Therefore, Windows 8 ships with two distinct personalities: a desktop personality that looks and behaves somewhat similar to Windows 7; and a new touch-focused and mobile device-targeted personality. This new personality (which has been variously referred to as Immersive, Modern UI, Metro, or simply Windows 8 Applications) is backed by a Windows Store: an app store that serves as the single install source for all such applications.

This chapter introduces you to the Visual Studio tools that enable you to write applications that can be published into that Windows Store, applications that leverage the technical capabilities of Windows 8 while conforming to the new look and feel and behavior expectations that users will have on that platform. We examine the new Windows Runtime library, and do a deep dive into the Visual Studio project types and project item templates that await the Windows 8 developer. And finally, we put these concepts into action by writing a Windows 8 Modern UI application.

> **NOTE**
>
> Before getting into the material here, please know that to develop Modern UI applications targeted at Windows 8 and the Windows app store, you must be running Windows 8 on your development machine. Of course, you also need a copy of Visual Studio 2012 (any paid SKU or the free Visual Studio Express for Windows).

Introducing Windows 8 and the Modern UI

To start to understand the differences between the two Windows 8 UI personalities, and the change in design approach from Windows 7 to Windows 8, one needs look no further than the Windows 8 start screen (see Figure 25.1). As you can see, this looks nothing like the Windows of old. It has more in common, in fact, with Windows Phone. We see that applications are now surfaced as tiles. The tiles themselves are not simple, static icons: They are alive, and animated, providing up-to-date information surfaced from the prospective application. Thus, at a glance, we have information about our email, our calendar, the weather, current sports scores, and anything else we care to pin to our start screen.

FIGURE 25.1   The new Windows 8 start screen.

The work surface can be panned, scrolled, and flicked using touch interactions. In fact, everything on the new start screen works without the need for a keyboard or mouse if you have a touch-enabled screen/device. This Windows personality has been referred to as Metro style or, more recently, Modern UI style.

System-level and application-level settings are controlled via charms. Charms show to the right side of the screen as a sort of toolbar that slides into view when the mouse or touch input is directed to the top-right corner of the screen (see Figure 25.2).

Within each application, commands may also be accessed via an app bar that appears on right-click or via the swipe-up gesture on the screen. Figure 25.3 shows the app bar for the Windows 8 Messaging application. Note the Status, Invite, and Delete command buttons.

FIGURE 25.2   The Windows 8 charms bar.

FIGURE 25.3   An app bar at the bottom of the Messaging app.

You can likely infer many of the design characteristics of Modern UI applications by simply looking at these figures. But let's examine in some detail the principles to which every Modern UI application is expected to adhere.

Modern UI Attributes

A Windows 8 Modern UI application is built on a core set of principles:

▶ **Pride in craftsmanship**—Modern UI applications should be ruthless in their attention to detail and the level of fit and polish presented to the end user.

▶ **Fast and fluid**—Applications should be responsive, should fully embrace touch and gesture-driven interactions, and should be visually engaging for users.

▶ **Authentically digital**—Skeuomorphism is eschewed in favor of simple colors, typography, and connections to the digital world

▶ **Do more with less**—Content is king; more content, less chrome is the mantra here. Don't let applications get between users and their content.

▶ **Win as one**—Your applications should be subtly woven into the overall user experience. This implies sharing data with other applications, conforming to the overall UI model, and innovating within a common framework to provide consistency.

Compare and contrast Figures 25.4 and 25.5, which show a common Windows application, the Media Player, in both its standard and Modern UI variants. Note how the Modern UI version (see Figure 25.5) very clearly places an emphasis on content (songs and artists) over the presence of chrome and application-level UI elements. The desktop Media Player (see Figure 25.4) looks positively cluttered by comparison.

FIGURE 25.4   The desktop version of the Media Player in Windows 8.

FIGURE 25.5   The Modern UI version of the Media Player in Windows 8.

Controls

It is important to note that a Modern UI application doesn't just look different; it also behaves very differently from a traditional desktop application. As a developer, this means that there are a different set of expectations and requirements placed on any Modern UI application you may write. For instance, standard desktop applications usually make liberal use of dialog boxes, pop-up windows, and even multiple windows within the same application. This is not true of the Modern UI app, where everything UI-wise will take place within the same chunk of screen real estate. Therefore, we have app bars, and panels, and other constructs that overlay the application but that aren't separate windows entirely. There are four of these constructs that are pressed into play regularly:

- ▶ **App bar**—Overlays the bottom of the screen and hosts a small set of commands that are context sensitive to what is happening in your application at a given point in time.

- ▶ **Message dialog**—These are the Modern UI equivalents of the modal dialog box. Even though it is called a dialog, these are not actual window dialog boxes. Think of them as panels that will overlay your primary UI and prevent interaction "behind" them until the dialog is dismissed.

- ▶ **Context menu**—These UI elements follow the typical context menu approach by popping up to allow interaction with a specific object on the screen.

- ▶ **Fly-out**—Similar to a message dialog, these panels aren't modal. The user may elect to interact with them, or they can be dismissed by clicking/touching someplace else within the application.

25

These, and others, make up a standard control set that you can use in your applications. Figure 25.6 shows some of the many new Extensible Application Markup Language (XAML) controls loaded into the Visual Studio Toolbox.

FIGURE 25.6   The WinRT controls for XAML projects.

Along with the Modern UI design paradigm, Windows 8 also brings a completely new programming model and API: the Windows Runtime library (WinRT).

The Windows Runtime Library

WinRT, distilled to its simplest definition, is a Windows API that sits directly on top of the core Windows 8 services. As such, it is actually a direct peer of the previous Win32 API. Microsoft invested in a brand-new runtime library for a few different reasons. For one, Win32 APIs weren't the easiest to access and develop against from a .NET perspective. The impedance mismatch between the .NET Framework surface and the Win32 API/COM surface made for sometimes confusing, and sometimes impossible, development tasks.

And because the .NET Framework resides on top of the Win32 API, there has always been a level of performance sacrificed. When you call a WinRT method, no abstraction layer is involved; you are calling directly to an OS level service.

Figure 25.7 shows the traditional "layer cake" architecture diagram, clearly showing where the WinRT sits in relationship to the other parts of the OS and the development platform.

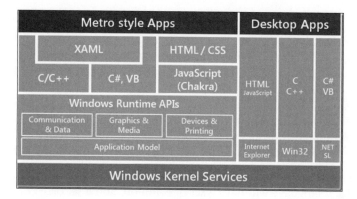

FIGURE 25.7   The WinRT architecture.

With WinRT, Microsoft has gone to great lengths to wrap all the underlying Windows behavior and surface functionality in a way that is a) straightforward for .NET developers to understand, and b) in many cases directly mimics or replicates the existing .NET Framework objects. This means no more p/invoke or COM attributes in your code.

Here is a simple example. The following line of XAML code performs identical things when compiled against WinRT and the .NET Framework:

```
<Button Click="Button_Click_1" Content="OK" />
```

Conversely, if we were to set out to write a Hello, World! application in WinRT, we might be tempted to write this:

```
MessageBox.Show("Hello, World!");
```

That line of C# would work great in either a standard WPF application or a Windows Forms application. If you were to try to implement this using WinRT, however, you would quickly discover that WinRT doesn't have a MessageBox class. It does, however, have a MessageDialog class:

```
MessageDialog dialog = new MessageDialog("Hello, World!");
Dialog.ShowAsync;
```

So, while the approach and syntax is familiar for .NET Framework developers, there is not a 100% match between .NET Framework classes and WinRT classes.

NOTE

WinRT, as shorthand for the Windows Runtime library, should not be confused with Windows RT. Windows RT is Microsoft's product name for the version of Windows 8 designed to run on ARM-based devices (as opposed to Intel- or AMD-based machines). Windows RT exposes only the Metro-themed personality.

Language Choices

As you can see from the earlier WinRT diagram (see Figure 25.7), another benefit of having WinRT in the picture is that you are no longer limited to your typical stable of managed code languages. So although you could develop your application C# or Visual Basic, all the WinRT objects are also available to JavaScript/HTML and C++ code. This widens the playing field quite a bit. There are no second-class citizens in the equation: WinRT is an equal-opportunity API. As a developer, you are free to concentrate on the toolset that you feel most comfortable with from a skill set and background perspective. The tooling and the API are there to support you.

With WinRT, you can develop a Modern UI application using DirectX, HTML/JavaScript/ CSS, C#, Visual Basic, or C++. Each language will have a set of common, and a set of unique, project types.

HTML and JavaScript and CSS

For developers coming from the web side of the business, Hypertext Markup Language (HTML), JavaScript, and Cascading Style Sheets (CSS) are familiar and capable technologies. Building a WinRT application using these languages results in a structure that is similar, if not identical, to a website/application:

▶ CSS is used for the presentation (that is, the layout and styling of the user interface).

▶ JavaScript is used to code the behavior (how the app handles interactions, events, business rules, and so on).

▶ HTML is used for the structure of the content within the UI.

To create a JavaScript application, click File, New Project, and then locate the JavaScript language selection to the left (see Figure 25.8).

Note that there are five selections to choose from, as described in Table 25.1.

TABLE 25.1   The JavaScript Project Choices

Project Type	Description
Blank App	This is the expected empty project. There are a handful of default files added for you, including a default.html file and a default.js file.
Grid App	The Grid App template will create a project containing three separate pages: a grid-based selection page containing groups of items, and then two details pages meant to display details of an item selected on the grid page.

Project Type	Description
Split App	The Split App template creates projects with two pages: a group selection page to display a list of grouped items, and then a details page that will show details of the selected item along with an item list of other items.
Fixed Layout App	As its name implies, Fixed Layout Apps are those that do not dynamically scale for different views, screen sizes, or positions on the screen. In general, these types of apps should not be created because they violate one of the fundamental principles of Modern UI; but there could be unique circumstances where they are necessary.
Navigation App	The Navigation App template creates a project with a home page, and basic forward back navigation structures.

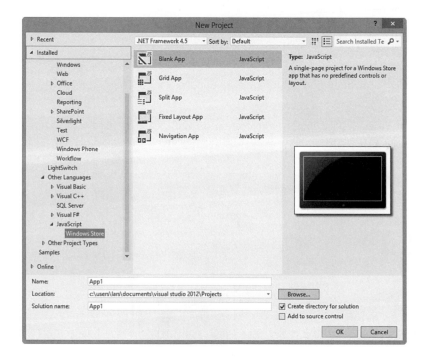

FIGURE 25.8   Creating a JavaScript application.

Figure 25.9 shows the default project structure for an HTML/JavaScript application.

C#/Visual Basic/XAML

Developers more familiar with WPF or Silverlight will benefit from using the XAML with C# or Visual Basic project templates, with this choice:

▶ XAML styles are used for the presentation.

▶ C# or Visual Basic is used to code the behavior.

▶ XAML is used for the structure of the content within the UI.

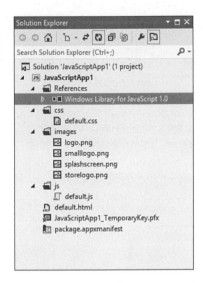

FIGURE 25.9   The project structure of an HTML/JavaScript application.

To create a XAML application, click File, New Project, and then locate the C# or Visual Basic language selection to the left (see Figure 25.10); then select Windows Store.

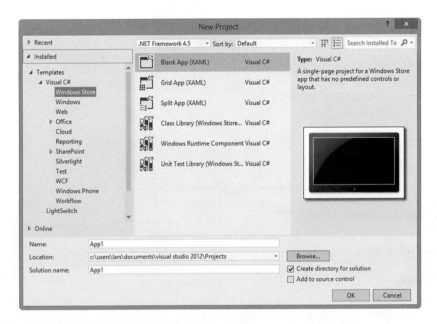

FIGURE 25.10   Creating a C# XAML application.

With C# XAML projects, note that there are only three primary selections to choose from, as described in Table 25.2.

TABLE 25.2   The XAML Project Choices

Project Type	Description
Blank App	An essentially empty project; represents a blank slate for development. There are a handful of default files added for you, including a MainPage.xaml file.
Grid App	The Grid App template will create a project containing three separate pages: a grid-based selection page containing groups of items, and then two details pages meant to display details of an item selected on the grid page.
Split App	The Split App template creates projects with two pages: a group selection page to display a list of grouped items, and then a details page that will show details of the selected item along with an item list of other items.

The Application Model

As discussed earlier in the chapter, Windows 8 Modern UI applications come with a different set of expectations and responsibilities when compared to their desktop brethren. And this means that an entirely new application model is implemented. A quick example here: Traditional desktop applications are used to doing anything that the logged-in user could do. In other words, if I write a Windows Forms application, I could write code to very easily read a document from the user's document library or to access the Internet. Because the application was running under the security context of a specific user, application developers (and, therefore, the applications themselves) did very little to police or report on their actions. In the WinRT/Modern UI world, this is no longer the case. Applications must now ask for permission by requesting specific capabilities. By default, a Metro application will have access to its own local file folder but cannot randomly access data anywhere else in the OS file system. The same is true for accessing the network connection, interacting with the camera or microphone, and so forth. These are referred to in the Windows 8/WinRT world as capabilities, and applications must be given explicit permission at install time to use the capabilities they are requesting.

Another difference involves the concept of application lifecycles. Desktop applications would generally be launched and, barring an application crash, would stay there, chewing up UI real estate, memory, and CPU cycles until the user explicitly closed them. Again, there is a big change with Modern UI applications. To provide an application model that would work effectively under adverse memory or processing conditions (as you might find on low-powered tablets, for instance), Windows 8 Modern UI applications are carefully managed by the OS. If an application isn't in the foreground (that is, has focus and is receiving user interaction), the application will be suspended.

A suspended application is no longer running, although it is kept loaded into memory. Once suspended, the OS may elect to actually kill the application at any point in time. This frees the OS to do what it needs to do to optimize system resources and frees the user from ever having to even worry about physically closing an application.

Implied in this lifecycle is the concept of implicit data storage. With desktop applications, data is typically stored when the user issues the Save command, and not before. But if the OS could suspend or kill an application at any time, that would lead to severe data loss potential (or at the very least, an intrusive message to the user along the lines of "this app is about to be killed, do you want to save your data?"). And so, Modern UI applications must embrace the concept of implicit saves. That is, the application will take full responsibility for always persisting whatever data has been entered.

Lifecycle States

Figure 25.11 shows the various lifecycle states that a WinRT Modern UI application can progress through. Note that although the OS could kill an application at any time and for any reason, the intent is to keep apps in suspended mode for as long as possible.

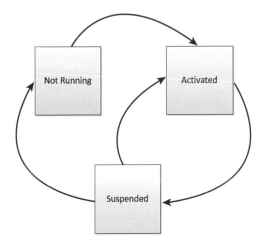

FIGURE 25.11   The application lifecycle.

Building a Windows Store Application

As with most concepts in the IDE, the best way to truly understand how the Visual Studio tools work is go through the process of creating an application using those tools. Our inspiration will be the WPF image viewer application that we build in Chapter 19, "Building Richer, Smarter User Interfaces." But instead of just constructing the same image editor, we'll create an application that enables you to rate pictures. We'll try to reuse as many of the concepts and actual code as we can from our earlier WPF effort, but we'll have some unique constructs to deal with as well in the WinRT world.

As a base set of requirements, here is what we will try to deliver:

▶ Displaying a list of pictures from the user's Pictures library.

▶ Clicking a photo will provide details about the photo

► You can edit the picture's rating value and save it back to disk

► Everything will be inherently usable on touch-enabled devices (that is, will work equally as well for touch only, as it will for keyboard and mouse setups).

The application will make use of the GridView, the app bar, and will use capabilities to tie into the Pictures library. With the end goal now in sight, let's get started.

NOTE

It is worthwhile to reinforce the fact that WinRT, although powerful in many different ways, is not a complete replacement either for Win32 or for the .NET Framework. In other words, there will still be some things that are extremely difficult or impossible to do with WinRT. For example, our WPF sample application from Chapter 19 was able to do some very simple image manipulations (such as blurring an image) in just a few lines of code. WinRT, however, doesn't have the required pixel shader classes to do this. And so trying to implement that same functionality using C#, XAML, and WinRT is nearly impossible (or at best, prohibitively difficult).

Keep in mind that WinRT was first and foremost designed to equip a certain class of applications with what they need to implement their feature set. Writing a full-fledged image-editing application like Adobe Photoshop is an exercise still best left in the desktop, and not Modern UI, world.

Selecting the Project Type

The language selection for us is easy: Because we are starting with an existing XAML-based C# WPF application, we should select an XAML-based C# WinRT project. Click File, New Project, Visual C# (as the language), and then under the Windows Store template, select the Blank App template. We'll call this **XamlImageViewer** (see Figure 25.12). Click OK to create the project structure.

As mentioned previously, the only way to install Windows 8 Modern UI applications is via the Windows Store. Each application published to the Windows Store is actually validated, verified, and then certified by Microsoft before it is made available. This has some ramifications. For one, you need a developer license to even deploy things to your own Windows 8 device as part of the normal code and debug process.

During the new project operation, if you don't have an existing and valid developer license, you are prompted to get one (see Figure 25.13). The process itself is automated; you merely need to click through a series of dialogs before your project will be created. These culminate in a notification dialog (see Figure 25.14) that indicates if your request for a license was successful or not and what the expiration date is for that license.

With the license out of the way, and the project structure in place, let's worry now about the design and layout.

FIGURE 25.12   Creating the new project.

FIGURE 25.13   Obtaining a developer license.

FIGURE 25.14   Developer licenses will have an expiration date.

Designing the Layout

Our prior WPF image viewer application relied on a relatively simple layout. Images from a selected folder were presented in a vertically scrolled list box to the left of the screen, and the right, main portion of the screen showed the selected image and allowed the user to alter the image in four basic ways: You could make the image a grayscale image, you could apply a blur effect to the image, you could rotate the image, and you could flip the image vertically.

Instead of using a single-page approach as we did with the original application, we now use two pages: a grid page that shows all the available images in the targeted folder (grouped by their rating value), and an edit/details page that shows the image selected from the grid and allows us to apply a new rating.

Figure 25.15 shows a sketch of the new application starting page, and Figure 25.16 shows the editing page.

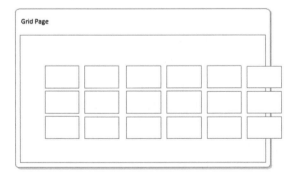

FIGURE 25.15   The grid of images.

FIGURE 25.16   The image-editing page.

Implementing the Grid Page UI

Because we chose the Blank App template, we have only a single page added to our project at this stage: MainPage.xaml. It's currently empty, so we have some work to do to implement our initial grid display (see Figure 25.17). Note that in the page designer, we have a graphical representation of a landscape-oriented tablet. This is nonfunctional chrome added to the window to enable developers to clearly visualize their application on the intended device. To the left of the designer window is a new tool window (the Device window) that is used to change how the designer displays its content. You can remove the device border chrome, change the screen size or resolution of the emulated device screen, or even put the display into different orientation modes.

With MainPage.xaml open, look at the XAML code. We need to modify the existing `Grid` element so that it has two rows. The top row will contain our app name, and the bottom will contain the `GridView` of images:

```
<Grid.RowDefinitions>
    <RowDefinition Height="140" />
    <RowDefinition Height="*" />
</Grid.RowDefinitions>
```

Next, comes the implementation of the `GridView`. There will be three basic attributes of the `GridView` that will require XAML: We need to create an event handler for the `GridView`'s `SelectionChanged` event, we need an `ItemTemplate` which will display our images, and we need to set the GridView's `ItemsSource` to our list of images. Let's defer that very last one for a bit and instead concentrate on the event handler and the item template.

Create a `GridView` element inside of the existing `Grid` and name it **ImagesGridView**; now, let Visual Studio do the work for you on the event handler side by adding the `SelectionChanged` event and selecting <New Event Handler> (see Figure 25.18). Visual Studio will stub out the code for us in the code behind file.

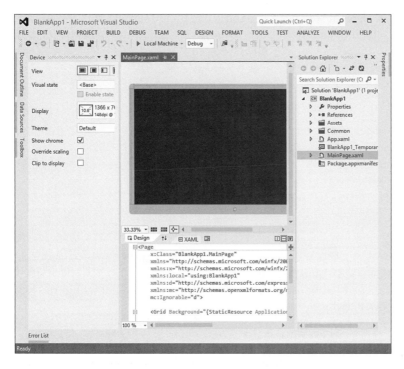

FIGURE 25.17   Getting started with the Blank App template.

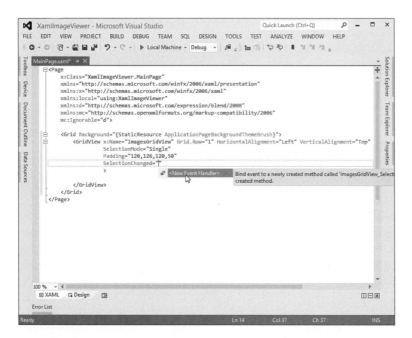

FIGURE 25.18   Creating the `SelectionChanged` event handler.

Also within the `GridView` element we need to establish the link to our data model. Set the `ItemsSource` property to bind to an object called `Images`. (This object doesn't exist yet, but we will get around to creating it in a short while.)

```
ItemsSource="{Binding Images}"
```

Your `GridView` declaration should now look like this:

```
<GridView x:Name="ImagesGridView" Grid.Row="1"
    HorizontalAlignment="Left" VerticalAlignment="Top"
    SelectionMode="Single"
    Padding="120,126,120,50"
    SelectionChanged="ImagesGridView_SelectionChanged"
    ItemsSource="{Binding Images}"
    />
```

An item template is now needed. Templates provide the structure around how data is displayed within the `GridView`. In our case, we are simply showing an image, and XAML has an `Image` element designed to do just that. To embed an `Image` element within the `GridView`, the syntax looks like this:

```
<GridView.ItemTemplate>
    <DataTemplate>
        <Grid HorizontalAlignment="Stretch">
            <Grid.RowDefinitions>
                <RowDefinition Height="175"/>
            </Grid.RowDefinitions>
            <Image Grid.Row="0" Height="175" Width="275"
                Source="{Binding Image}" Stretch="UniformToFill"/>
        </Grid>
    </DataTemplate>
</GridView.ItemTemplate>
```

One last minor piece of housekeeping: Open the App.xaml file and add a static string with the key `AppName` for storing the name of our application. This will be used across pages within the header area:

```
<Application
    x:Class="XamlImageViewer.App"
    xmlns="http://schemas.microsoft.com/winfx/2006/xaml/presentation"
    xmlns:x="http://schemas.microsoft.com/winfx/2006/xaml"
    xmlns:local="using:XamlImageViewer">

    <Application.Resources>
        <ResourceDictionary>
            <ResourceDictionary.MergedDictionaries>
```

```
    <!--
        Styles that define common aspects of the platform look and feel
        Required by Visual Studio project and item templates
    -->
    <ResourceDictionary Source="Common/StandardStyles.xaml"/>
</ResourceDictionary.MergedDictionaries>

<x:String x:Key="AppName">Xaml Image Viewer</x:String>
        </ResourceDictionary>
    </Application.Resources>
</Application>
```

We will reference the application name within the header area of the page (in other words, the top row of our outermost Grid) by using a simple TextBlock bound to that static string:

```
<TextBlock x:Name="pageTitle" Grid.Row="0"
    IsHitTestVisible="false"
    Style="{StaticResource PageHeaderTextStyle}"
    Text="{StaticResource AppName}"
    Margin="50,0,0,50"
    />
```

And with that, the structure of our main page's UI is in place.

Creating the Data Model

With our base UI in place, we turn our attention now to the classes that will hold our image information. We need two: one to store the list of images (obtained from the Pictures library folder), and a second to wrap each individual image file.

Add a new class to the project and call it **ImageFile**. To this class, add three properties: a string property called FileName, an ImageSource property called Image, and an integer property called Rating. All of these should be backed by private fields (called _fileName, _image, and _rating, respectively) and should implement getters and setters:

```
string _fileName;
private ImageSource _image = null;
private int _rating = 0;

public string FileName
{
    get { return _fileName; }
    set { _fileName = value; }
}

public int Rating
{
```

```
    get { return _rating; }
    set {_rating = value; }
}


public ImageSource Image
{
    get { return this._image; }
    set { this._image = value; }
}
```

Because this object will be contained within a collection, and we will want to know if properties change so that they can be signaled back to the parent collection, we will use the INotifyPropertyChanged pattern here.

First, inherit the ImageFile class from INotifyPropertyChanged. Then declare an event handler called PropertyChanged:

```
public event PropertyChangedEventHandler PropertyChanged;
```

Next, implement an OnPropertyChanged routine:

```
private void OnPropertyChanged(string propertyName)
{
    if (PropertyChanged != null)
        PropertyChanged(this, new PropertyChangedEventArgs(propertyName));
}
```

In each of the property sets, include a call to OnPropertyChanged, passing in the name of the property:

```
public string FileName
{
    get { return _fileName; }
    set { _fileName = value; OnPropertyChanged("FileName"); }
}


public int Rating
{
    get { return _rating; }
    set {_rating = value; OnPropertyChanged("Rating"); }
}


public ImageSource Image
{
    get { return this._image; }
    set { this._image = value; OnPropertyChanged("Image"); }
}
```

The actual bitmap that is the image file is assigned via the `Image` property. Let's write a `SetImage` routine that will take in the file, create a bitmap object from that file, and then assign it to our `Image` property:

```
public async void SetImage(StorageFile file)
{
    IRandomAccessStream fileStream =
        await file.OpenAsync(Windows.Storage.FileAccessMode.Read);
    BitmapImage bitmap = new BitmapImage();
    bitmap.SetSource(fileStream);
    Image = bitmap;
}
```

Before moving on, there is one last piece of functionality to add: a method that will examine the file's `Rating` property, transform it from its `0-100` value into a `0-5` value, and then assign that to our `ImageFile`'s `Rating` property. `Image` properties are held in the WinRT class `ImageProperties`, which we populate directly from the `StorageFile` instance via its `GetImagePropertiesAsync` method:

```
public async void SetRating(StorageFile file)
{
    // get the image properties for the file
    ImageProperties imageProps =
        await file.Properties.GetImagePropertiesAsync();

    // we are looking for the Rating property
    uint rating = imageProps.Rating;

    // rating is a number 0-100
    // we need to factor this down to a 0-5 rating

    // 0 == 0
    // 1-24 = 1
    // 25-49 = 2
    // 50-74 = 3
    // 75-98 = 4
    // 99 = 5
    if (rating == 0)
    {
        Rating = 0;
    }
    else if (rating > 98)
    {
        Rating = 5;
    }
    else if (rating >= 75)
    {
```

25

```
        Rating = 4;
    }
    else if (rating >= 50)
    {
        Rating = 3;
    }
    else if (rating >= 25)
    {
        Rating = 2;
    }
    else
    {
        Rating = 1;
    }

}
```

NOTE

We are making liberal use of the new async and await C# keywords in our code to reinforce app responsiveness via async processing. We touch on these keywords a bit in Chapter 3, "The .NET Languages," but it will be well worth your while to understand these patterns in detail to support your WinRT development efforts. Here is the best place to start: http://msdn.microsoft.com/en-us/library/hh191443(v=VS.110).aspx.

Creating the Collection Class

Now on to the class that will hold our collection of images. Add a new class to the project, and call this class **ImageList**. This class is simple in structure: It will hold an internal ObservableCollection of type ImageFile, and expose this collection via a property called Images. Just as with the ImageFile class, we want to implement the INotifyPropertyChanged pattern here:

```
private ObservableCollection<ImageFile> _imageList =
    new ObservableCollection<ImageFile>();

public ObservableCollection<ImageFile> Images
{
    get { return _imageList; }
    set
    {
        _imageList = value;
        OnPropertyChanged("ImageList");
    }
}
```

We also need a method to actually load the collection up with `ImageFile` instances. File and folder access in WinRT is accomplished via the `StorageFile` and `StorageFolder` classes. There is also a handy helper class, `KnownFolders`, that can be used to get a reference to specific libraries like the Music library or the Pictures library. We will first get a reference to the Pictures library folder, and then iterate through its collection of `StorageFile` instances. For each, we create a new `ImageFile` instance and populate its properties accordingly:

```
public async void LoadImages()
{
    // Folder and file objects
    StorageFolder folder;
    ImageFile imageFile;
    IReadOnlyList<IStorageFile> files;

    // Get reference to pictures library
    folder = KnownFolders.PicturesLibrary;

    // get the files within the pictures library
    files = (IReadOnlyList<IStorageFile>)await folder.GetFilesAsync();

    // iterate each file, create a new ImageFile to wrap it
    foreach (StorageFile file in files)
    {
        imageFile = new ImageFile();
        var stream = await file.OpenAsync(FileAccessMode.Read);

        imageFile.FileName = file.Name;
        imageFile.SetImage(file);
        imageFile.SetRating(file);
        this.Images.Add(imageFile);
    }
}
```

Binding the Data

We should have a fully functioning set of data objects at this stage. But we have to bind those images to our UI. First, create an instance of our data model within the MainPage.xaml.cs file. Open up the code-behind and add a private field to the page class for our `ImageList` object:

```
private ImageList _imageList;
```

In the page constructor, we need to set the data context for our page to the `ImageList` and make the call to load the image list:

```
public MainPage()
{
    this._imageList = new ImageList();
    this.DataContext = this._imageList;
    this.InitializeComponent();
}
```

At this stage, our data model should be functionally complete. However, if you try and run the application now, you will get the error message shown in Figure 25.19.

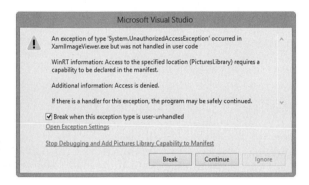

FIGURE 25.19   An un-authorized access exception.

If you recall from our earlier discussion around the concept of capabilities, Windows Store applications do not, by default, have permission to access file directories. We need to request that permission. And that is done via *capabilities*.

Requesting Capabilities

Capabilities, put simply, are access categories that an application must first be granted permission to. This includes things such as file system access, network access, and access to hardware devices like cameras and microphones. Capabilities are requested via the applications package manifest file. Find this file in Solution Explorer, and double-click it to open up the manifest editor (see Figure 25.20). For our application to work, we need to place a check mark next to the Pictures Library entry on the Capabilities tab.

In a normal situation where a user is downloading your application from the Windows Store, these special permission requests are clearly identified within the store and again when the application is installed. The user has the option, at that point, of disallowing the access or not installing the app at all. The user is in the driver's seat here, not the application. When you are debugging applications under Visual Studio, the access is automatically granted at runtime provided you have checked the appropriate box and saved the manifest file.

With that done, run the application. Assuming you have images in the root of your Pictures library, the application should look like Figure 25.21.

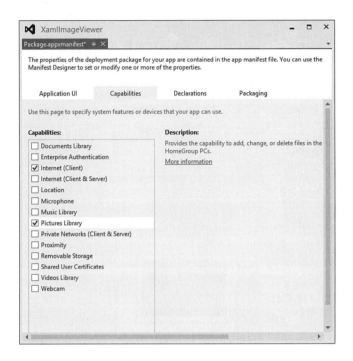

FIGURE 25.20   Gaining access to the Pictures library.

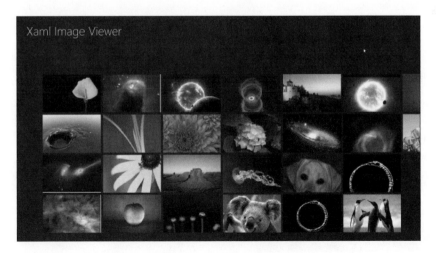

FIGURE 25.21   The main page with images loaded.

Now we can focus on the second page, which will allow us to view and change the rating for the selected image.

Implementing the Image Editor Page

Right-click the project in the Solution Explorer window and select Add, New Item. From the Templates list, we want to add an Items Detail page, as shown in Figure 25.22. Name the page **ImagePage**.

FIGURE 25.22   Adding the image detail page.

When you add this page to your project, you will see a warning dialog (see Figure 25.23). The template for this page is preplumbed to do a variety of things for you, the developer, and to do those things it relies on a bunch of standard helper classes and XAML constructs. These are normally placed within the Common folder of your project and in the project root. Because we haven't added these yet (remember, we started with a basic blank project), Visual Studio has detected that they are missing and offers to add them for you. Click Yes.

FIGURE 25.23   Automatically adding *common* dependencies.

The first thing we do in this page is fix up the app name header (find the `TextBlock` with the name `pageTitle` and bind its `Text` to `"{StaticResource AppName}"` just as we did on `MainPage`). Then, clear out everything sitting within the outermost `Grid` element except for the `VisualStateManager` markup you will see; we won't be using any of those default UI elements, although we will keep some of the code structure that was created as part of the items detail template.

So, with an empty `Grid` consisting of two columns, we can get to work on our layout. We want a large `Image` element to the left of the screen in the left column (to hold the selected image from `MainPage`) and a form area to the right (in the right column) that will display the image's rating value and its filename. For now, we are going to use a standard slider control to display and edit the image's rating value.

Here is the XAML for the image area within the root `Grid`. This contains both the display of the image itself and its filename and rating values. Note that we are binding the controls to properties off of our `ImageFile` class:

```
<Grid x:Name="ImageGrid" Grid.Row="1">
    <Grid.ColumnDefinitions>
        <ColumnDefinition Width=".65*" />
        <ColumnDefinition Width=".35*" />
    </Grid.ColumnDefinitions>

    <Image x:Name="SelectedImage" Grid.Column="0"
            Margin="50,0,25,25"
            Source="{Binding Image}"/>

    <Grid Grid.Column="1">

        <Grid.ColumnDefinitions>
            <ColumnDefinition Width="100" />
            <ColumnDefinition Width="*"/>
        </Grid.ColumnDefinitions>
        <Grid.RowDefinitions>
            <RowDefinition Height="auto" />
            <RowDefinition Height="auto" />

        </Grid.RowDefinitions>

        <!-- Image rating and filename display -->
        <Slider Grid.Row="0" Grid.Column="1" Grid.ColumnSpan="2"
                x:Name= "RatingSlider"
                Style="{StaticResource RatingSliderStyle}"
                TickPlacement="Inline" TickFrequency="1" Minimum="0" Maximum="5"
                HorizontalAlignment="Left" Orientation="Horizontal" Width="300"
                Margin="15,0,0,0"
                Value="{Binding Rating}"
                SnapsTo="Ticks"/>
```

```
    <TextBlock Grid.Column="0" Grid.Row="1" Margin="5,5,0,5"
               Style="{StaticResource BasicTextStyle}"
               HorizontalAlignment="Left" VerticalAlignment="Center"
               Height="20">File name:</TextBlock>

    <TextBlock Grid.Column="1" Grid.Row="1" x:Name="FileNameTextBlock"
               Style="{StaticResource BasicTextStyle}" Margin="5,5,0,5"
               HorizontalAlignment="Left" Text="{Binding FileName}"
               Width="auto"/>

    </Grid>
</Grid>
```

This page isn't done yet. We have two major areas to work on: passing the selected image into the page, and then saving the rating information back to the image file. Let's tackle these in that order.

Page Navigation and Passing State

If you examine the code in ImagePage.xaml.cs, you will notice a routine called LoadState. This was stubbed out for us as part of this page's template; this routine is called when the page is navigated to and provides something crucial: a navigation parameter that enables us to pass objects around between pages. To make this work, we have to take a quick trip back to MainPage.xaml.cs and write some code in our SelectionChanged event handler to navigate to the details page and pass along the ImageFile object we need:

```
private void ImagesGridView_SelectionChanged(object sender,
    SelectionChangedEventArgs e)
{
    //navigate to the next page, passing the selected image along

    // cast selected item to ImageFile
    ImageFile image = (ImageFile)ImagesGridView.SelectedItem;
    this.Frame.Navigate(typeof(ImagePage), image);
}
```

With that code in place, we are now ready to fill out the LoadState routine in ImagePage.xaml.cs. Add a private field and property in the page to hold the passed-in ImageFile:

```
private ImageFile _imageFile;

public ImageFile ImageFileInstance
{
    get { return _imageFile; }
    set { _imageFile = value; }
}
```

Now, assign `ImageFileInstance` within the `LoadState` routine. Because we have bound our UI controls to the `ImageFile` properties, we also need to update our page's data context to point to the `ImageFileInstance` property:

```
protected override void LoadState(Object navigationParameter,
    Dictionary<String, Object> pageState)
{
    ImageFileInstance = navigationParameter as ImageFile;
    this.DataContext = ImageFileInstance;
}
```

As a quick check, let's run the app. With the navigation state passing and data binding working, we have a page that does everything but save rating information back to the file (see Figure 25.24).

FIGURE 25.24   The image detail page.

Creating an App Bar

Even though we have discussed the fact that Windows Store applications will generally save data implicitly and not explicitly, in this case we want our users to actively tell the application that they want a changed rating value to be saved back to the file. So, we start by implement a simple app bar with a single Save button to execute that process.

App bars can appear at either the top of the page or at the bottom. The convention is that navigation-related commands go on top and application commands go on the bottom. Our app bar with its solitary Save button will live at the bottom.

In the ImagePage.xaml, create a `Page.BottomAppBar` element outside of the outermost layout grid but within the page itself. Within that element, we want to nest an actual `AppBar` element. `AppBar` objects are typically structured using a simple `StackPanel` containing your app bar buttons. Remember that our UI should work well with touch devices, including tablets. For that reason, we want to actually avoid centering our button in the middle of the bar. With a tablet device, a user will want to be able to press the button using only the thumbs of the hands gripping the tablet. And that means that buttons should be placed to the far right or far left of the app bar. We'll go to the right with ours:

```
<Page.BottomAppBar>
    <AppBar x:Name="BottomAppBar1" Padding="10,0,10,0"
        AutomationProperties.Name="Bottom App Bar">
        <Grid>
            <StackPanel x:Name="AppBarStackPanel"
                Orientation="Horizontal"
                Grid.Column="0" HorizontalAlignment="Right">
                <Button x:Name="SaveButton"
                    Style="{StaticResource SaveAppBarButtonStyle}"
                    Tag="Edit"
                    Click="SaveButton_Click"/>
            </StackPanel>
        </Grid>
    </AppBar>
</Page.BottomAppBar>
```

If you carefully examine the `Button` that we have defined, you will notice a style reference to `SaveAppBarButtonStyle`. With WinRT XAML projects, a StandardStyles.xaml resource dictionary is included for you by default. And within that XAML file are many, many style resources for a wide spectrum of app bar buttons for commands ranging from save to search to rename to volume. They are all commented out to start; simply pick the ones you need and copy them into your page or uncomment them.

That's all the XAML we need. The app bar is now fully functioning. We are now just missing the save routine itself.

TIP

The app bar button styles use a unique approach to their embedded icons: these buttons are intrinsically aware of the Segoe UI Symbol character set. By setting their `Content` property to an offset value, WinRT will automatically grab the appropriate glyph/icon from that character set and use it. Because that font has hundreds of basic Metro-style icons, it is a perfect match and simple to implement. The best way for you to find icons this way is to fire up the charmap.exe program on Windows 8. Select Segoe UI Symbol in the top drop-down, and then click the icon you want. Its offset will display in the status bar. For instance, a "star" icon is located at offset E113. Therefore, we would have a content tag set to "".

We'll call the save routine from the `SaveButton_Click` event; the routine itself will retrieve the file property information, change the `Rating` property to whatever the current value of the rating slider is, and then will save the properties back out using the `SavePropertiesAsync()` method call:

```
private void SaveButton_Click(object sender, RoutedEventArgs e)
{
    SaveRating();
}

private async void SaveRating()
{
    var file =
        await KnownFolders.PicturesLibrary.GetFileAsync(_imageFile.FileName);

    var fileProperties = await file.Properties.GetImagePropertiesAsync();

    fileProperties.Rating = (uint)this.RatingSlider.Value;

    await fileProperties.SavePropertiesAsync();
}
```

Reacting to Lifecycle Events

We have already discussed the application model and its attendant lifecycle. Refer back to
Figure 25.11. We have three possible application states:

▶ Activated

▶ Suspended

▶ Not Running

At the application level, you are notified of app changes via a series of events that correspond to the arrows you see in Figure 25.11. To handle these events and react appropriately means you need to write some event handlers; your project's App class is your vehicle
for hooking these events. In fact, the standard App.xaml.cs file created for you already
contains code to wire up the Suspending event:

```
public App()
{
    this.InitializeComponent();
    this.Suspending += OnSuspending;
}

private void OnSuspending(object sender, SuspendingEventArgs e)
{
    var deferral = e.SuspendingOperation.GetDeferral();
    //TODO: Save application state and stop any background activity
    deferral.Complete();
}
```

25

The use of the `deferral` object may seem confusing at first, but its job is fairly simple. While running your program, when the end of the `OnSuspending` routine is reached, the runtime will assume that you have taken care of everything that need to be taken care of and will promptly suspend the application. But if your application has followed good practice, your state saving activity will be executed asynchronously. And that means that the `OnSuspending` routine could conclude before your async activity has actually completed.

The `SuspendingDeferral` object, which is returned from the call shown above to `e.SuspendingOperation.GetDeferral`, is used to signal to Windows that you want to explicitly tell the runtime when you are done with your state housekeeping. There is a caveat here: Windows will suspend your application regardless of your deferral object if you take longer than approximately 5 seconds to complete your work. So in essence, having the deferral object created means "don't suspend the application until I tell you to, or until my 5 seconds are up, whichever comes first."

The flip side of the `Suspending` event, when an application is being resumed, is the `Resuming` event, which looks very similar. (You need to add this yourself; it isn't included automatically.)

```
this.Resuming += OnResuming;
```

Finally, the `OnLaunched` routine is called when your application is launched. This could be by a user clicking/tapping the app tile, or it could be because a user is going back to your app after it has been suspended and then terminated:

```
protected override void OnLaunched(LaunchActivatedEventArgs args)
{
    Frame rootFrame = Window.Current.Content as Frame;

    // Do not repeat app initialization when the Window already has content,
    // just ensure that the window is active
    if (rootFrame == null)
    {
        // Create a frame to act as the navigation context and
        // navigate to the first page
        rootFrame = new Frame();

        if (args.PreviousExecutionState == ApplicationExecutionState.Terminated)
        {
            //TODO: Load state from previously suspended application
        }

        // Place the frame in the current Window
        Window.Current.Content = rootFrame;
    }
```

```
if (rootFrame.Content == null)
{
    // When the navigation stack isn't restored navigate to the first page,
    // configuring the new page by passing required information as a navigation
    // parameter
    if (!rootFrame.Navigate(typeof(MainPage), args.Arguments))
    {
        throw new Exception("Failed to create initial page");
    }
}
// Ensure the current window is active
Window.Current.Activate();
}
```

Storing State

Once your application is aware of these events, you can react to them appropriately. There is no stock answer here in terms of how you should read and write your applications state. But the simple high-level pattern is this: When your application is suspending, do a final save of its state, and when it is resuming, restore the state. One attractive option is the use of local storage. Each application has default permissions to access the local storage area. (In other words, it isn't a capability that needs to be explicitly declared.) For our image viewing app, if we wanted to store the page name of the current page, along with the file name of any currently loaded image, we could do that quite easily by a) creating a general object to store those items and b) serializing that object into local storage.

Saving into the application storage area can be accomplished via the familiar StorageFile class and serializer (commonly, DataContractSerializer). A great way to bootstrap your application state storage development is to take a look at a helper class delivered by Microsoft, called SuspensionManager. This class maintains a Dictionary object that in turn contains the objects making up your application's state. If you add your state information to its dictionary, you can then call a SaveAsync method on the class, which will take care of serializing everything to disk:

```
// Save the current session state
static async public Task SaveAsync()
{
    // Get the output stream for the SessionState file.
    StorageFile file = await
        ApplicationData.Current.LocalFolder.CreateFileAsync(filename,
        CreationCollisionOption.ReplaceExisting);

    using (StorageStreamTransaction transaction = await
        file.OpenTransactedWriteAsync())
    {
        // Serialize the Session State.
```

```
        DataContractSerializer serializer = new
            DataContractSerializer(typeof(Dictionary<string, object>), knownTypes_);

        serializer.WriteObject(transaction.Stream.AsStreamForWrite(),
            sessionState_);

        await transaction.CommitAsync();
    }
}
```

Similarly, you can rehydrate your state information via its `RestoreAsync` method:

```
// Restore the saved session state
static async public Task RestoreAsync()
{
    // Get the input stream for the SessionState file.
    try
    {
        StorageFile file = await
            ApplicationData.Current.LocalFolder.GetFileAsync(filename);

        if (file == null) return;

        using (IInputStream inStream = await file.OpenSequentialReadAsync())
        {
            // Deserialize the Session State.
            DataContractSerializer serializer = new
                DataContractSerializer(typeof(Dictionary<string, object>),
                    knownTypes_);

            sessionState_ = (Dictionary<string,
                object>)serializer.ReadObject(inStream.AsStreamForRead());
        }
    }
    catch (Exception)
    {
        // Restoring state is best-effort.  If it fails, the app will
        // just come up with a new session.
    }
}
```

As mentioned previously in this chapter, remember that if you are dealing with anything more than a moderate amount of data in your application, you should consider saving that data regardless of whether any of the lifecycle events have been triggered. You don't want to get into a scenario where the time it takes to save your data is longer than the allotted window for either application startup or suspension. In the case of the former, Windows will assume that the app is hung and will kill it. And in the case of the latter, you might not get all of your data committed before the application process disappears. If the application is then subsequently terminated, you have now permanently lost data.

Publishing to the Windows Store

When your application is complete and you want to share it with the rest of the world (for profit or not), it is time to publish it into the Windows Store. That means you will need a developer's account. At the time of this writing, the Windows Store was not yet completely open for business. But the process itself is straightforward: Using your Microsoft Account, you register for access to the store as a developer. After your registration has been approved, you can reserve your application's name, establish a price, and upload your packaged application into the store.

Once again, Visual Studio makes this process seamless with development: From within the IDE, you can select Store under the Project menu and execute all the activities needed to go from no account to published application (see Figure 25.25).

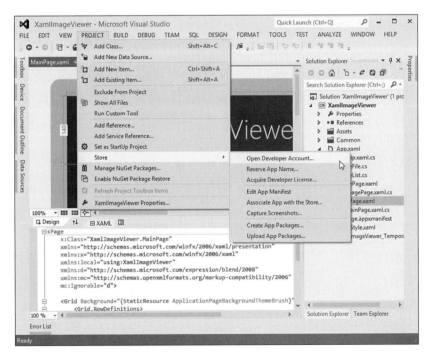

FIGURE 25.25   Using the Store menu.

When your application is finally published, you can expect its landing page to look something like Figure 25.26.

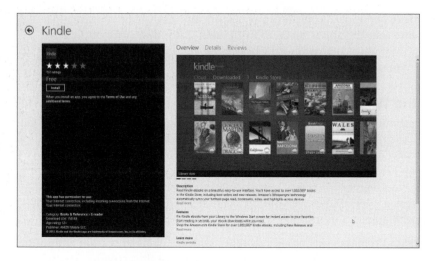

FIGURE 25.26   The Kindle app in the Windows Store.

As a final word: Please visit this book's download site (just search for the book title on InformIt.com) to get the complete source code for the XAML image viewer application. The final application adds some fit and finish to the walkthrough presented here, including a splash screen, app tile, and other things like a restyled rating slider control. Listings 25.1 and 25.2 provide the XAML and C# code for the MainWindow page, and Listings 25.3 and 25.4 provide the XAML and C# code for the ImageDetails page.

LISTING 25.1   The Image Viewer XAML Code: MainPage.xaml

```
<Page
    x:Class="XamlImageViewer.MainPage"
    xmlns="http://schemas.microsoft.com/winfx/2006/xaml/presentation"
    xmlns:x="http://schemas.microsoft.com/winfx/2006/xaml"
    xmlns:local="using:XamlImageViewer"
    xmlns:d="http://schemas.microsoft.com/expression/blend/2008"
    xmlns:mc="http://schemas.openxmlformats.org/markup-compatibility/2006"
    mc:Ignorable="d">

    <Grid Background="{StaticResource ApplicationPageBackgroundThemeBrush}">
        <Grid.RowDefinitions>
            <RowDefinition Height="140" />
            <RowDefinition Height="*" />
        </Grid.RowDefinitions>

        <TextBlock x:Name="pageTitle" Grid.Row="0" IsHitTestVisible="false"
                   Style="{StaticResource PageHeaderTextStyle}"
                   Text="{StaticResource AppName}"
                   Margin="50,0,0,50"/>
```

```xml
        <GridView x:Name="ImagesGridView" Grid.Row="1"
                HorizontalAlignment="Left" VerticalAlignment="Top"
                                    SelectionMode="Single"
                Padding="120,126,120,50"
                SelectionChanged="ImagesGridView_SelectionChanged"
                ItemsSource="{Binding Images}"
                >
            <GridView.ItemContainerStyle>
                <Style TargetType="GridViewItem">
                    <Setter Property="HorizontalContentAlignment" Value="Stretch"/>
                    <Setter Property="VerticalContentAlignment" Value="Top"/>
                    <Setter Property="HorizontalAlignment" Value="Stretch"/>
                    <Setter Property="VerticalAlignment" Value="Top"/>
                </Style>
            </GridView.ItemContainerStyle>
            <GridView.ItemTemplate>
                <DataTemplate>
                    <Grid HorizontalAlignment="Stretch">
                        <Grid.RowDefinitions>
                            <RowDefinition Height="175"/>
                        </Grid.RowDefinitions>
                        <Image Grid.Row="0" Height="175" Width="275"
                                Source="{Binding Image}"
                                Stretch="UniformToFill"/>
                    </Grid>
                </DataTemplate>
            </GridView.ItemTemplate>

        </GridView>

    </Grid>
</Page>
```

LISTING 25.2   The Image Viewer XAML Code: MainPage.xaml.cs

```csharp
using System;
using System.Collections.Generic;
using System.IO;
using System.Linq;
using Windows.Foundation;
using Windows.Foundation.Collections;
using Windows.UI.Xaml;
using Windows.UI.Xaml.Controls;
using Windows.UI.Xaml.Controls.Primitives;
using Windows.UI.Xaml.Data;
```

```csharp
using Windows.UI.Xaml.Input;
using Windows.UI.Xaml.Media;
using Windows.UI.Xaml.Navigation;



namespace XamlImageViewer
{
    /// <summary>
    /// An empty page that can be used on its own or navigated to within a frame.
    /// </summary>
    public sealed partial class MainPage : Page
    {
        private ImageList _imageList;

        public MainPage()
        {
            this._imageList = new ImageList();
            this.DataContext = this._imageList;
            this._imageList.LoadImages();

            this.InitializeComponent();
        }


        /// <summary>
        /// Invoked when this page is about to be displayed in a frame.
        /// </summary>
        /// <param name="e">Event data that describes how this page was reached.
        /// The Parameter property is typically used to configure the page.</param>
        protected override void OnNavigatedTo(NavigationEventArgs e)
        {
        }

        private void ImagesGridView_SelectionChanged(object sender,
            SelectionChangedEventArgs e)
        {
            //navigate to the next page, passing the selected image along

            // cast selected item to ImageFile
            ImageFile image = (ImageFile)ImagesGridView.SelectedItem;
            this.Frame.Navigate(typeof(ImagePage), image);


        }
    }
}
```

LISTING 25.3   The Image Viewer XAML Code: ImagePage.xaml

```
<common:LayoutAwarePage
    x:Name="pageRoot"
    x:Class="XamlImageViewer.ImagePage"
    DataContext="{Binding DefaultViewModel, RelativeSource={RelativeSource Self}}"
    xmlns="http://schemas.microsoft.com/winfx/2006/xaml/presentation"
    xmlns:x="http://schemas.microsoft.com/winfx/2006/xaml"
    xmlns:local="using:XamlImageViewer"
    xmlns:common="using:XamlImageViewer.Common"
    xmlns:d="http://schemas.microsoft.com/expression/blend/2008"
    xmlns:mc="http://schemas.openxmlformats.org/markup-compatibility/2006"
    mc:Ignorable="d">

    <Page.Resources>
        <ResourceDictionary Source="SliderStyle.xaml"/>
    </Page.Resources>

<Page.BottomAppBar>
    <AppBar x:Name="BottomAppBar1" Padding="10,0,10,0"
➥AutomationProperties.Name="Bottom App Bar">
        <Grid>
            <StackPanel x:Name="AppBarStackPanel" Orientation="Horizontal"
                    Grid.Column="0" HorizontalAlignment="Right">
                <Button x:Name="SaveButton"
                        Style="{StaticResource SaveAppBarButtonStyle}"
                        Tag="Save"
                    Click="SaveButton_Click" />
            </StackPanel>
        </Grid>
    </AppBar>
</Page.BottomAppBar>
    <!--
        This grid acts as a root panel for the page that defines two rows:
        * Row 0 contains the back button and page title
        * Row 1 contains the rest of the page layout
    -->
    <Grid Style="{StaticResource LayoutRootStyle}">
        <Grid.RowDefinitions>
            <RowDefinition Height="140"/>
            <RowDefinition Height="*"/>
        </Grid.RowDefinitions>

        <!-- Back button and page title -->
        <Grid>
            <Grid.ColumnDefinitions>
```

```
        <ColumnDefinition Width="Auto"/>
        <ColumnDefinition Width="*"/>
    </Grid.ColumnDefinitions>
    <Button x:Name="backButton" Click="GoBack"
            IsEnabled="{Binding Frame.CanGoBack, ElementName=pageRoot}"
            Style="{StaticResource BackButtonStyle}"/>

    <TextBlock x:Name="pageTitle" Grid.Column="1"
            Text="{StaticResource AppName}"
            Style="{StaticResource PageHeaderTextStyle}"/>

</Grid>

<Grid x:Name="ImageGrid" Grid.Row="1">
    <Grid.ColumnDefinitions>
        <ColumnDefinition Width=".65*" />
        <ColumnDefinition Width=".35*" />
    </Grid.ColumnDefinitions>

    <Image x:Name="SelectedImage" Grid.Column="0"
            Margin="50,0,25,25"
            Source="{Binding Image}"/>

    <Grid Grid.Column="1">

        <Grid.ColumnDefinitions>
            <ColumnDefinition Width="100" />
            <ColumnDefinition Width="*"/>
        </Grid.ColumnDefinitions>
        <Grid.RowDefinitions>
            <RowDefinition Height="auto" />
            <RowDefinition Height="auto" />

        </Grid.RowDefinitions>

        <!-- Image rating and filename display -->
        <Slider Grid.Row="0" Grid.Column="1" Grid.ColumnSpan="2"
                x:Name="RatingSlider"
                TickPlacement="Inline" TickFrequency="1"
                Minimum="0" Maximum="5"
                HorizontalAlignment="Left"
                Orientation="Horizontal" Width="300"
                Style="{StaticResource RatingSliderStyle}"
                Margin="15,0,0,0"
                Value="{Binding Rating}"
                SnapsTo="Ticks"/>
```

```
            <TextBlock Grid.Column="0" Grid.Row="1" Margin="5,5,0,5"
                    Style="{StaticResource BasicTextStyle}"
                    HorizontalAlignment="Left" VerticalAlignment="Center"
                    Height="20">File name:</TextBlock>

            <TextBlock Grid.Column="1" Grid.Row="1"
                    x:Name="FileNameTextBlock"
                    Style="{StaticResource BasicTextStyle}"
                    Margin="5,5,0,5"
                    HorizontalAlignment="Left" Text="{Binding FileName}"
                    Width="auto"/>

        </Grid>
    </Grid>


<VisualStateManager.VisualStateGroups>

    <!-- Visual states reflect the application's view state -->
    <VisualStateGroup x:Name="ApplicationViewStates">
        <VisualState x:Name="FullScreenLandscape"/>
        <VisualState x:Name="Filled"/>

        <!-- The entire page respects the narrower 100-pixel margin
convention for portrait -->
        <VisualState x:Name="FullScreenPortrait">
            <Storyboard>
                <ObjectAnimationUsingKeyFrames
                 Storyboard.TargetName="backButton"
                 Storyboard.TargetProperty="Style">
                    <DiscreteObjectKeyFrame KeyTime="0"
                        Value="{StaticResource PortraitBackButtonStyle}"/>
                </ObjectAnimationUsingKeyFrames>
            </Storyboard>
        </VisualState>

        <VisualState x:Name="Snapped">
            <Storyboard>
                <ObjectAnimationUsingKeyFrames
                    Storyboard.TargetName="backButton"
                    Storyboard.TargetProperty="Style">
                    <DiscreteObjectKeyFrame
                        KeyTime="0"
                        Value="{StaticResource SnappedBackButtonStyle}"/>
                </ObjectAnimationUsingKeyFrames>
                <ObjectAnimationUsingKeyFrames
```

```
                              Storyboard.TargetName="pageTitle"
                              Storyboard.TargetProperty="Style">
                              <DiscreteObjectKeyFrame
                                  KeyTime="0"
                                  Value="{StaticResource
                                  SnappedPageHeaderTextStyle}"/>
                         </ObjectAnimationUsingKeyFrames>
                      </Storyboard>
                  </VisualState>
              </VisualStateGroup>
          </VisualStateManager.VisualStateGroups>
      </Grid>
</common:LayoutAwarePage>
```

LISTING 25.4   The Image Viewer C# Code: ImagePage.xaml.cs

```csharp
using System;
using System.Collections.Generic;
using System.IO;
using System.Linq;
using Windows.Foundation;
using Windows.Foundation.Collections;
using Windows.Storage;
using Windows.UI.Xaml;
using Windows.UI.Xaml.Controls;
using Windows.UI.Xaml.Controls.Primitives;
using Windows.UI.Xaml.Data;
using Windows.UI.Xaml.Input;
using Windows.UI.Xaml.Media;
using Windows.UI.Xaml.Navigation;




namespace XamlImageViewer
{
    /// <summary>
    /// A page that displays details for a single item within a group while
    /// allowing gestures to flip through other items belonging to the
    /// same group.
    /// </summary>
    public sealed partial class ImagePage :
        XamlImageViewer.Common.LayoutAwarePage
    {
        private ImageFile _imageFile;
```

```
public ImageFile ImageFileInstance
{
    get { return _imageFile; }
    set { _imageFile = value; }
}

public ImagePage()
{
    this.DataContext = ImageFileInstance;
    this.InitializeComponent();
}

/// <summary>
/// Populates the page with content passed during navigation.
/// Any saved state is also provided when recreating a
/// page from a prior session.
/// </summary>
/// <param name="navigationParameter">The parameter value
/// passed to
/// <see cref="Frame.Navigate(Type, Object)"/> when this page was
/// initially requested.
/// </param>
/// <param name="pageState">A dictionary of state preserved
/// by this page during an earlier session.  This will be null
/// the first time a page is visited.</param>
protected override void LoadState(Object navigationParameter,
    Dictionary<String, Object> pageState)
{
    ImageFileInstance = navigationParameter as ImageFile;
    this.DataContext = ImageFileInstance;
}

/// <summary>
/// Preserves state associated with this page in case the
/// application is suspended or the page is discarded
/// from the navigation cache.  Values must conform to
/// the serialization
/// requirements of <see cref="SuspensionManager.SessionState"/>.
/// </summary>
/// <param name="pageState">An empty dictionary to be
/// populated with serializable state.</param>
protected override void SaveState(Dictionary<String, Object> pageState)
{
    // TODO: Derive a serializable navigation parameter
    // and assign it to pageState["SelectedItem"]
}
```

25

```
private void SaveButton_Click(object sender, RoutedEventArgs e)
{
    SaveRating();
}

private async void SaveRating()
{
    var file = await
        KnownFolders.PicturesLibrary.GetFileAsync(_imageFile.FileName);
    var fileProperties = await
        file.Properties.GetImagePropertiesAsync();

    fileProperties.Rating =
        (uint)this.RatingSlider.Value;

    await fileProperties.SavePropertiesAsync();
}
```

Summary

This chapter introduced you to the new Windows Runtime library (WinRT) and the new Visual Studio project and item templates for creating Windows Store applications for Windows 8. We discussed the fundamentals of WinRT, including its goals, its high-level architecture, its programming model, and the Application Lifecycle Model for WinRT applications.

We visited the primary design principles that underlie Modern UI applications and discussed how those principles are enabling a new class of applications to run on the Windows 8 operating system.

The various language choices for doing WinRT development were explored, and the basics of control layout were bridged from the existing WPF world to the XAML/WinRT world.

And finally, we explored in depth the construction of a WinRT/Windows Store application from the ground up, expanding on concepts first touched on in Chapter 19.

Although WinRT will look familiar, and be comfortable, for .NET developers at large, the devil is in the details. Before you embark on any serious WinRT development projects, we highly recommend that you start here first: http://msdn.microsoft.com/en-us/windows/apps/br229512.aspx.

Index

Symbols

@Html helper (Razor), 733

A

absolute positioning, forms, 652-656
AbsoluteCharOffset property (EditPoint
 object), 530
AccessDataSource control, 699, 893
Accessibility Validation options (Build
 page), 638
Accordion control, 717
Action method, 741-755
ActionResult objects (ASP.NET MVC), 753-754
Actions panes (Office), 1015
 creating, 1032
Activate method
 Documents object, 525
 OutputWindowPane object, 516
 Window object, 503
ActiveWindow property (Document object), 525
activities, workflow, 966-980
Activity Designer template, 951
activity libraries, creating, 990-992
Activity template, 951
AdaptiveMenu property (CommandBar
 object), 523
Add Controller dialog box, 750-751
Add New Item - Solution Items dialog box, 159
Add New Item Wizard, creating, 591-597
Add New Line on Enter at End of Fully Typed Word
 option (IntelliSense), 345
Add Style Rule dialog box, 239
AddControl method (Command object), 539
AddIn automation type, 492
Add-In Wizard, 588
 creating add-ins, 546-554

add-ins, 292, 545, 597
 automation objects, 563
 color palette, creating, 563-588
 commands, reacting to, 560-562
 creating, 546-554
 exposing settings, 571-588
 lifecycle, 554-560
 managing, 562-563
 Office, creating, 1019-1030
 projects, 588
 structure, 554-560
AddToCollection<T> activity (Collection), 971
adornments (code editor), 604
AJAX (Asynchronous JavaScript and XML),
 26, 30-31
 ASP.NET AJAX
 building UIs (user interfaces), 703-721
 Control Toolkit, 713-721
 extensions, 704-705
 library toolkit, 713-716
 partial-page updates, 706-710
AjaxFileUpload control, 717
ALM (Application Lifecycle Management), 10
AlwaysVisibleControlExtender control, 717
Analyze menu, 61
anchoring controls, forms, 768-769
API (application programming interface), 489
app bar (Modern UI), 1075
app bars, creating, 1099-1101
App_Browsers directory (ASP.NET), 632
App_Code directory (ASP.NET), 632
App_Data directory (ASP.NET), 632
App_GlobalResources directory (ASP.NET), 632
App_LocalResources directory (ASP.NET), 632
App_Themes directory (ASP.NET), 632
App_WebReferences directory (ASP.NET), 632
appearance, forms, customizing, 240-241
Application class, 796
Application Files screen (InstallShield), 476-477
application hosts, add-ins, choosing, 547-548
Application Lifecycle Management (ALM), 10

C

D

G

H

J

K-L

M

O

P

Q

R

S

T

U

V

W

X-Z

UNLEASHED

Microsoft Visual Studio LightSwitch Unleashed
ISBN-13: 9780672335532

OTHER UNLEASHED TITLES

Windows Phone 7.5 Unleashed
ISBN-13: 9780672333484

ASP.NET Dynamic Data Unleashed
ISBN-13: 9780672335655

Microsoft System Center 2012 Unleashed
ISBN-13: 9780672336126

System Center 2012 Configuration Manager (SCCM) Unleashed
ISBN-13: 9780672334375

Windows Server 2012 Unleashed
ISBN-13: 9780672336225

Microsoft Exchange Server 2013 Unleashed
ISBN-13: 9780672336119

MVVM Unleashed
ISBN-13: 9780672334382

System Center 2012 Operations Manager Unleashed
ISBN-13: 9780672335914

Microsoft Dynamics CRM 2011 Unleashed
ISBN-13: 9780672335389

SharePoint Designer 2010 Unleashed
ISBN-13: 9780672331053

ASP.NET 4.0 Unleashed
ISBN-13: 9780672331121

Silverlight 4 Unleashed
ISBN-13: 9780672333361

Windows 8 Apps with XAML and C# Unleashed
ISBN-13: 9780672336010

Windows 8 Apps with HTML5 and JavaScript Unleashed
ISBN-13: 9780672336058

SAMS

informit.com/sams

Mike Snell
Lars Powers

Microsoft
Visual Studio
2012
UNLEASHED

SAMS

FREE
Online Edition

Safari
Books Online

Your purchase of **Microsoft® Visual Studio® 2012 Unleashed** includes access to a free online edition for 45 days through the **Safari Books Online** subscription service. Nearly every Sams book is available online through **Safari Books Online**, along with thousands of books and videos from publishers such as Addison-Wesley Professional, Cisco Press, Exam Cram, IBM Press, O'Reilly Media, Prentice Hall, Que, and VMware Press.

Safari Books Online is a digital library providing searchable, on-demand access to thousands of technology, digital media, and professional development books and videos from leading publishers. With one monthly or yearly subscription price, you get unlimited access to learning tools and information on topics including mobile app and software development, tips and tricks on using your favorite gadgets, networking, project management, graphic design, and much more.

Activate your FREE Online Edition at
informit.com/safarifree

STEP 1: Enter the coupon code: EWYWDDB.

STEP 2: New Safari users, complete the brief registration form.
Safari subscribers, just log in.

If you have difficulty registering on Safari or accessing the online edition,
please e-mail customer-service@safaribooksonline.com

  Addison Wesley · AdobePress · ALPHA · Cisco Press ·  Press FINANCIAL TIMES · IBM Press · Microsoft Press · New Riders · O'REILLY

Peachpit Press · PRENTICE HALL · que · Redbooks · SAMS · SAS Publishing · vmware PRESS · WILEY · wrox